JEWISH PHILOSOPHY
in the Middle Ages

EMUNOT: Jewish Philosophy and Kabbalah

ACADEMIC
STUDIES
PRESS

JEWISH PHILOSOPHY
in the Middle Ages

Raphael Jospe
רפאל ישפה

Boston
2009

Library of Congress Cataloging-in-Publication Data

Jospe, Raphael.
Jewish philosophy in the Middle Ages / Raphael Jospe.
    p. cm. — (EMUNOT: Jewish philosophy and Kabbalah)
Includes bibliographical references.
ISBN 978-1-934843-09-3 (hardcover) — ISBN 978-1-934843-27-7 (pbk.)
1. Philosophy, Jewish—History. 2. Philosophy, Medieval—History. I. Title.
B755.J675 2009
181'.06—dc22
        2009024458

Foreground:
Statue of Maimonides by Amadeo Ruiz Olmos (1964) in the Plaza de Tiberiades in
"la Judería" (the Jewish Quarter) of Cordoba, Spain, near the medieval synagogue.
Photograph kindly provided by Israel Ronen of the Open University of Israel.

Background:
A bifolio, dismembered from a manuscript (14th-century, Spain), containing the first page of
Perush Ha-Millot Ha-Zarot (1213), a glossary by Samuel ibn Tibbon, appended to his Hebrew
translation of Maimonides' *Guide of the Perplexed*. The bifolio was reused in 1713 as a cover
of a register of the series "Giusdicenze." Hebrew Fragment 520.1 in the State Archive of
Modena, Italy, kindly provided by Prof. Mauro Perani of the University of Bologna.

Book design by Ivan Grave

ISBN 978-1-934843-09-3 (hardcover)
ISBN 978-1-934843-27-7 (pbk.)

Published by Academic Studies Press in 2009
28 Montfern Avenue
Brighton, MA 02135, USA
press@academicstudiespress.com
www.academicstudiespress.com

To my sisters
Susanne and Naomi

אמור לחכמה אחותי את
(משלי ז:ד)

Say to wisdom, you are my sister
(*Proverbs 7:4*)

and to

Elihu Davison

קנה לך חבר
(אבות א:ו)

Acquire for yourself a friend
(*Sayings of the Fathers 1:6*)

Contents

Section II
TRANSITIONS

Section III
RAMBAM

Section IV
THE CONTROVERSY OVER PHILOSOPHY AND RAMBAM

Appendices

PREFACE

This book is a condensation of a three-volume series in Hebrew, *Jewish Philosophy in the Middle Ages: From Sa'adiah Ga'on to Rambam*, published by the Open University of Israel. My sincere thanks to the Open University for its support and for permission to use that material as the basis for this English volume.

Besides the obvious difference of language, the three volumes in Hebrew (totaling some 1650 pages) include extensive text analysis important for the Hebrew reader, since one of the explicit goals of the books was to familiarize the reader with medieval Hebrew philosophical terminology and expression. This important aspect of the original books is not relevant to the reader in other languages. Nevertheless, I have attempted to include in the discussion, at least parenthetically, Hebrew and Arabic terms, which may prove useful or interesting to the reader.

On the other hand, this book has a new concluding chapter (Chapter Eleven) on "The Controversy over Philosophy and Rambam" that was outside the scope of the original Hebrew books.

I wish to express my heartfelt thanks to my friend and colleague (and occasional co-author), Professor Dov Schwartz of Bar Ilan University, editor of the series in which this book is being published, for his constant friendship, encouragement and support over the years. I also wish to express my thanks to Dr. Igor Nemirovsky of Academic Studies Press for supporting this project.

Above all, I wish to express my loving gratitude to my wife Darlene; to our children Deena, Ilan, Calanitte, Tamar, Yaron, Uri and Keren; and to our happily growing family of grandchildren.

INTRODUCTION

Jewish Philosophy in the Middle Ages presents an overview of the formative period of medieval Jewish philosophy, from its beginnings with Sa'adiah Ga'on to its apex in Rambam (Maimonides). This period constitutes a discrete and unique cultural phenomenon, in which Jews living in Islamic countries and writing in Arabic were the first to develop a conscious and continuous tradition of Jewish philosophy.

In ancient Alexandria, Egypt, Philo was probably the first pioneer (at least the first whose works have survived) in Jewish philosophy, but his works, written in Greek, were unknown to Jews in the Middle Ages, and there was a gap of some eight centuries between Philo and the first medieval Jewish philosophers. Jewish philosophy as a discrete cultural tradition thus begins in the Middle Ages with the period covered by this book. Subsequent Jewish philosophy generally was developed in a Christian-European cultural context, and was written in Hebrew or (in more recent centuries) in European languages. In the later Middle Ages and Renaissance, and even in modern times, much of Jewish philosophy was shaped by or in reaction to the thought of Rambam, and was also reflected specific issues arising in the Jewish-Christian encounter, and was affected by European historical developments. An introduction to Jewish philosophy culminating in Rambam, therefore, sets the stage for these later developments, and is justified historically, thematically, and pedagogically.[1]

Why is yet another introduction to medieval Jewish philosophy necessary in the English language? Isaac Husik's *History of Medieval Jewish Philosophy* (1916) gives the student a convenient outline of the thought of diverse thinkers, and is accessible to undergraduate students, but it does so with little discussion of the cultural frameworks and ideological schools of thought in which these philosophies evolved and to which they are responding, nor does it engage

---

[1] For this reason, Colette Sirat's latest, French version of her history of medieval Jewish philosophy is divided into two separate volumes, *La Philosophie Juive Medievale en Terre d'Islam* and *La Philosophie Juive Medievale en Pays de Chretiente* (1988), although her earlier English *History of Jewish Philosophy in the Middle Ages* (1985) presents both periods in one larger volume.

in extensive analysis of the thought itself. Julius Guttmann's *Philosophies of Judaism* (German, 1933; revised and expanded in Hebrew, 1951; English translation of the Hebrew version, 1964) engages in analysis and in discussion of Greek and/or Arabic sources, but does so without introducing the student systematically to these sources, background and schools of thought. Guttmann's sophisticated analysis (in many respects still unrivalled, certainly in terms of scope), is a valuable and essential reference for scholars and advanced graduate students, but frequently is not helpful to undergraduates and to the general reader. Colette Sirat's *History of Jewish Philosophy in the Middle Ages* (1985) contains a great deal of valuable information, especially on many previously ignored secondary thinkers and works (in some cases, works that still only exist in manuscript), but the book is encyclopedic in character, and as such invaluable for reference purposes, but it does not always present overviews and comparative analyses of the thought of the various thinkers, nor of the schools of thought influencing them. The comprehensive *History of Jewish Philosophy* (Routledge History of World Philosophies, Vol. 2) (1997) includes many important discussions of the historical, social and cultural contexts of Jewish philosophy, and areas and issues previously unexplored. However, as an anthology of presentations by some thirty-five authors, it cannot have overall consistency, including comparisons among the thinkers and ideas, and accordingly it often also lacks systematic overviews of the philosophy of a given thinker.

None of this is meant as criticism of these important books, which I constantly use in my own research, and recommend to my students. It simply means that different books are written for different purposes, which complement each other, and do not compete with each other.

My **Jewish Philosophy in the Middle Ages** does not deal with all the thinkers and issues covered by the other books, and is not intended to be a comprehensive history. Instead, I have attempted to do something different (although of course there is inevitable overlap with the others), by focusing on selected thinkers, representing important philosophical schools of thought and literary genres, including comparative cross-references.

Among the book's distinctive features are a general introductory survey, "What is Jewish Philosophy?" in which a wide range of opinions is presented and analyzed. The book includes didactic charts and tables, for example, presenting schemes of cosmology, emanation and comparative terminology for the categories and for the faculties of the soul, which become clarified by such graphic presentation. The various chapters of the book also present the Greek and/or Arabic schools of thought, such as the Kalam, Neoplatonism and Aristotelianism, including surveys of the major thinkers and themes representative of these schools of thought, prior to the discussion of the Jewish philosophers who were influenced by these ideas and how they responded to them. Whenever feasible and pertinent, the discussion also includes surveys of major scholarly opinions on various questions of interpretation of the medieval thinkers.

It is my hope that these features of the book will render it useful as an introduction to major themes and thinkers in the history of the formative period of Jewish philosophy in the Middle Ages, the period which continues not only to interest but to shape Jewish thought in our day.

Isaac Husik concluded his pioneering history, nearly a century ago, with the pessimistic observation that "there are Jews now, and there are philosophers, but there are no Jewish philosophers and there is no Jewish philosophy."

The exponentially increasing publications of books in Jewish philosophy, in Israel and abroad, in Hebrew and in other languages, of original thought and of scholarly analysis, prove that Husik's conclusion was exaggerated, premature, and ultimately far off the mark. His own work helped start the revival of a field for which he—like nineteenth century scholars of *Wissenschaft des Judentums*—mistakenly thought he was writing an epitaph.

In recent years we have been witness to expanding study of Jewish philosophy, not only among Jews, but also among non-Jews; not only in Israel and in other countries with large Jewish communities, but also in countries with few Jews (or few surviving Jews). For many of these students of Jewish philosophy, it is not only of academic interest, but also of existential importance. It is my hope that this book, like my others, will also contribute, however modestly, to these welcome developments, and will constitute yet another link in the ongoing and ever growing chain of Jewish philosophy.

Raphael Jospe רפאל ישפה
Jerusalem
Adar 5769 / February 2009

Section I

FOUNDATIONS

Chapter One

WHAT IS JEWISH PHILOSOPHY?

[1.1]   WHAT IS JEWISH PHILOSOPHY?

It may appear obvious to some what is meant by the term "Jewish philosophy," but any attempt to construct a curriculum, course, textbook or history in "Jewish philosophy" forces us at the outset to deal with this seemingly elementary point, both for theoretical and practical reasons. On the practical level, which philosophers should be included in the discussion? The only philosopher produced by the Jewish people who is routinely included in histories of western philosophy is Baruch (Benedict) Spinoza, but many treatments of Jewish philosophy exclude Spinoza, and paradoxically, in the Jewish National and Hebrew University Library in Jerusalem, his books are to be found on the shelves of the general reading room, and not in the Judaica reading room together with those of other Jewish philosophers. What place, if any, should be assigned to Jews in the Middle Ages who converted to Islam, like Abu'l Barakat (Netanel) Al-Baghdadi, or to Christianity, like Abner of Burgos (Alfonso of Valladolid)? Should we treat these thinkers and their works as Jewish until the time of their apostasy, or in light of their subsequent conversion, retroactively as non-Jewish? In the modern period, shall we include under the rubric of "Jewish philosophy" the work of such figures as Henri Bergson, Herbert Marcuse, Paul Weiss or Karl Marx?

Reversing the question, we face the same problem. When a philosopher, such as Levi ben Gershom (Ralbag; Gersonides) whose philosophy is generally recognized to be "Jewish" also engages (sometimes in the same book) in such "general" sciences as astronomy and mathematics, is that philosophy (or book, or even chapter) an appropriate subject for presenting as "Jewish?"

As we shall see, these questions force us to deal with our conceptions not only of Jewish philosophy, but our very conceptions of Judaism and philosophy.

[I.1.a]   WHAT IS PHILOSOPHY?

Our frame of reference for discussion "what is philosophy" is the world of medieval Jewish philosophy, and the Islamic philosophy which served as the context for the formative period of Jewish philosophy until Rambam (Maimonides; Rabbi Moses ben Maimon, d. 1204). For our purposes, what Plato and Aristotle may have actually said may often be less significant than what Muslim and Jewish philosophers in the Middle Ages thought they said, sometimes on the basis of pseudepigraphical works like the Neoplatonic *Theology of Aristotle* (which, in fact, has nothing to do with Aristotle, but is an Arabic abridgement and paraphrase of Plotinus' *Enneads*).

We diverge today from the classical and medieval understanding of philosophy when we distinguish it from the natural sciences and routinely assign philosophy a place among the Humanities in universities. In the Middle Ages, however, philosophy was understood by Muslim, Christian and Jewish philosophers to be a scientific method of inquiry, indeed as the "mother of the sciences," and our dichotomy between philosophy and science would have been totally alien to them. It is, however, precisely this categorization of philosophy as one of the humanities, and not as an empirical, natural science, that renders philosophy subject to particular cultural influences and forms of expression, as are history, literature and the arts, and thus makes possible our historical and cultural question, "What is Jewish philosophy?" The classical and medieval view, however, was different, because in their own mind, they were not engaging in historical or cultural questions, but in the universal quest for truth, transcending particular national cultures and religions.

The first Arab philosopher, Abu Yusuf Ya'qub ibn Isḥaq Al-Kindi (Iraq, 9th century), defined philosophy in his pioneering work *On First Philosophy* ("first philosophy" = metaphysics), as "the most noble" art, aiming at knowledge of "the true nature of things." The philosopher seeks, therefore, on a theoretical level, to know the truth, and on a practical level, to act truthfully.[1] Since philosophy aims at "the true nature of things," and the truth cannot be limited to one particular nation or religious community, Al-Kindi teaches us that we should accept the truth from anyone, regardless of nation, race or religion. "For the seeker of truth, nothing takes precedence over the truth."[2]

A generation after Al-Kindi, Abu Naṣr Al-Farabi (870–950) described philosophy as reaching the Greeks from Semitic sources in Iraq, via Egypt. The Greeks called "the scientific state of mind philosophy, by which they meant the quest and love for the highest wisdom...The called it the science of sciences, the mother of sciences, the wisdom of wisdoms, and the art of

---

1   *Al-Kindi's Metaphysics*, translated by Alfred Ivry (Albany: S.U.N.Y. Press, 1974), p. 55.
2   *Al-Kindi's Metaphysics*, pp. 57–58.

arts."[3] For Al-Farabi, as for Al-Kindi, philosophy has a practical as well as theoretical, scientific component, because it involves moral and religious responsibility. Religion is, in effect, an "imitation of philosophy," because what philosophy studies by scientific demonstration, religion teaches to the masses by persuasive methods; what philosophy knows intellectually, religion imitates through imagined images.

Rambam's contemporary, Abu'l Walid Muḥammad Ibn Rushd (Averroes; 1126–1198) took these arguments further. The study of philosophy, including that of the non-Muslim ancients, is not merely permitted, it is a religious obligation, "regardless of whether this other one shares our religion or not." Philosophy is "the door by which the law summons them to knowledge of God." To forbid the study of philosophy because of its foreign source is like denying a person water, so that he dies of thirst, just because some people have choked on water.[4]

These views were echoed receptively by Jewish authors. Rambam, whose *Guide of the Perplexed* cites by name various Greek and Arab authors, but not any of the earlier Jewish philosophers,[5] prefaces his *Eight Chapters on Ethics* by stating explicitly that he borrowed "from the words of the philosophers, ancient and recent, and also from the works of various authors, as one should accept the truth from whoever says it."[6]

Similar sentiments were expressed in the late 13ᵗʰ century by the philosopher, Hebrew translator of Arabic philosophy, and defender of Rambam in the controversy over philosophy, Shem Tov ben Joseph ibn Falaquera. In his Hebrew encyclopedia of the sciences, *The Opinions of the Philosophers* (*De 'ot Ha-Pilosofim*), Falaquera equates the philosopher with the Hebrew *ḥasid*,

---

[3]   Al-Farabi, *The Attainment of Happiness* #53–55, translated by Muhsin Mahdi, in *Al-Farabi's Philosophy of Plato and Aristotle* (Ithaca: Cornell University Press, 1969), pp. 43–44. The passage may also be found in Arthur Hyman and James Walsh (eds.), *Philosophy in the Middle Ages* (2ⁿᵈ edition, Indianapolis, 1983), p. 227, and in Ralph Lerner and Muhsin Mahdi (eds.), *Medieval Political Philosophy: A Sourcebook* (Ithaca: Cornell University Press, 1978), p. 76.

[4]   Ibn Rushd's "Decisive Treatise Determining What the Connection Is Between Religion and Philosophy" was published as *Averroes on the Harmony of Religion and Philosophy*, translated by George Hourani (London: Luzac, 1961), pp. 46–49. Abridged versions may be found in Arthur Hyman and James Walsh (eds.), *Philosophy in the Middle Ages*, and in Ralph Lerner and Muhsin Mahdi (eds.), *Medieval Political Philosophy: A Sourcebook*.

[5]   See the discussion of this in Shlomo Pines' Introduction, "The Philosophic Sources of the *Guide of the Perplexed*," to his English translation of Maimonides' *Guide of the Perplexed* (Chicago: University of Chicago Press, 1963).

[6]   My translation. The *Eight Chapters* are the introduction to Maimonides' commentary to the Mishnah Avot. Cf. *The Eight Chapters of Maimonides on Ethics*, translated by Joseph Gorfinkle (New York: Columbia University Press, 1912), pp. 35–36. An abridgement may be found in *A Maimonides Reader*, edited by Isadore Twersky (New York: Berhman House, 1972).

emphasizing the view he shared with other Jewish and Muslim philosophers, that philosophy is a moral and religious, and not merely an intellectual, undertaking:

> Therefore, according to them, the true philosopher is one whose intention is to attain knowledge of the truth and to do the righteous and true act, one who intends that all his actions attain for him these two types of perfection, and whose entire effort in life is to attain them as perfectly as is humanly possible. The term "philosopher" refers to this notion, according to them, and the term *ḥasid* ("righteous") refers to this notion in our language; he is one who has acquired the moral and rational virtues. But since a common person (*'am ha-arez*) lacks the rational virtues, even thought he has acquired the ethical ones, the rabbis said, "A common person cannot be righteous." (Mishnah Avot 2:6)[7]

The ultimate object of philosophic knowledge being God, the philosopher is thus also a religious personality:

> The ethically perfect person is one who studies all existing things, and tries to know them. He is distinguished from the rest of humanity in order to attain and cleave to his Creator. In Greek, he is called "philosopher," i.e., the lover of wisdom.[8]

Therefore,

> a person should learn whatever he is capable [of learning] from those who speak the truth, even if they are non-believers, just as one takes honey from a bee...For a person cannot know by himself everything he needs of these things, as the ancients said. It makes no difference whether these ancients were of our faith or not. When the speculation is correct and perfect, [free] from any defect, we do not notice whether these people are of our faith."[9]
>
> Many of the common folk who are empty and devoid of wisdom [find it] very difficult when an author brings a proof from the words of non-Jewish philosophers, and they regard their words as worthless. They say that it is not proper to accept them. These ignorant fools never remember, nor understand, nor do they ever consider, that it is appropriate to accept the truth from any person, even if he is on a lower level than oneself or from another nation...It is not proper to look at the speaker, but rather at what is said."[10]

---

7   Falaquera, *De 'ot Ha-Pilosofim*, ms. Parma f. 4a, ms. Leyden f. 106b, cited in my *Torah and Sophia: The Life and Thought of Shem Tov ibn Falaquera* (Cincinnati: Hebrew Union College Press, 1988), p. 127.

8   Falaquera, *The Book of the Seeker*, p. 102.

9   Falaquera, *Epistle of the Debate*, p. 13. Cf. Steven Harvey, *Falaquera's Epistle of the Debate: An Introduction to Jewish Philosophy* (Cambridge: Harvard University Press, 1987), p. 19.

10   Falaquera, *The Book of Degrees*, pp. 11–12.

Finally, in the Introduction to his encyclopedic *Opinions of the Philosophers*, Falaquera states:

> It is not proper for an intelligent person who seeks to know the truth to reject many things which were revealed to the philosophers, which they explained by a true proof, and which are indubitable, as they said, just because they are not of our people. Rather, he should listen to the truth from the one who says it, and he should not look at the speaker but rather at the truth of what he says."[11]

[I.1.b] WHAT IS JEWISH PHILOSOPHY: A MODERN QUESTION

Our interest is to define Jewish philosophy. And yet, the passages cited above from medieval Muslim and Jewish sources are noteworthy for the fact that they all deal exclusively with the general question, "what is philosophy?" and none of them deals with the question of what is Jewish philosophy (or Islamic philosophy, as the case may be). So far as I know, the question we are asking, what is Jewish philosophy, is never discussed by the medieval Jewish philosophers (nor the parallel question of Islamic philosophy among the medieval Arabs).[12]

Since, evidently, our question did not interest philosophers in the Middle Ages, who are the subject of this book, why should it interest us?

By their own self-definition, the philosophers were "lovers of wisdom" in the sense that they sought to attain whatever rational truths humans are capable of attaining. The medieval philosophers recognized and insisted, despite their loyalty to a particular religious doctrine (Jewish, Christian or Muslim), that one can and should learn the truth from any person, and not only from members of one's own community. Jewish philosophers, therefore, did not, and could not, restrict their philosophizing to Jewish sources, by the very universal nature of philosophy. To the contrary, their task was to defend their right, indeed their duty, to learn the philosophic truth from any source, since the truth respects no national or religious borders.

We, however, face an entirely different challenge, as much as we may admire and identify with the universalistic and humanistic spirit that motivated these medieval philosophers. We are not dealing with philosophy itself, in the pure sense of the term, but rather with the history of Jewish philosophy. Jewish

---

11 Falaquera, *De 'ot Ha-Pilosofim*, ms. Parma, f. 3b, ms. Leyden, f. 106a.

12 On the other hand, given Al-Farabi's idea, which is reflected in medieval Jewish thought, that the Greeks learned philosophy from Semitic sources, one could argue that medieval Jewish thinkers, by engaging in universal philosophy, without regard to national origin, in a sense saw themselves as engaging in something that is ultimately Jewish.

philosophy did not develop in a vacuum, but was influenced, directly and indirectly, by different thinkers, representing a wide spectrum of philosophical and religious schools of thought in the Greek, Latin-Christian, and Arabic-Islamic cultures. Rambam, for example, cannot be understood without reference to such Greek philosophers as Aristotle and Muslim philosophers like Al-Farabi.

Nevertheless, philosophers like Aristotle and Al-Farabi, for all that they influenced the development of Jewish philosophy, do not belong to, nor do they share in, Jewish philosophy, for the simple reason that they were not Jews. Of course their influence was great — but it was an external, not internal influence. To reiterate: we are not here engaging in the pure philosophic quest for the abstract truth, whatever that may be. We are engaging in a historical quest for an understanding of how philosophy developed among the Jews. We must, therefore, ask the very question which is, from a philosophical perspective, invalid and illegitimate, but which is necessary and justified from a historical perspective: Who is the speaker? We must, despite what the medievals said so eloquently, look at the speaker, and not just at what he said.

At a certain point, we may wish to challenge and question the positions taken by various Jewish philosophers, to determine whether they were correct or incorrect, and whether from our perspective their philosophy was true or false. But we shall not have completed our task until we ask the additional and more fundamental question: were their philosophies Jewish? We may, for example, conclude that on a given point, a Jewish philosopher was wrong and a non-Jewish philosopher was correct. But, at least for the moment, we are not asking whether one was correct, but only an entirely different question, which was the Jewish philosopher? And what are our criteria for making this judgment?

Our question is modern, in two respects: philosophic and Jewish. From a philosophic perspective, we have already noted that the dichotomy between philosophy and the natural sciences is a modern one. In the Middle Ages, so long as philosophers were considered, and considered themselves to be, true scientists, it was impossible to distinguish the scientific truth of one nation from that of another, just as today we would not be prepared to categorize the truths of physics as "German" (even if many of the great physicists were products of German education). It is only in modern times, when philosophy came to be regarded as one of the Humanities, that one could speak of philosophy within the context of a particular culture, as philosophy flourished in, or was influenced by, different cultures. (We thus speak of continental rationalism versus British empiricism). Our historical-cultural approach to philosophy, therefore, is an approach that only became possible in modern times.

From a Jewish perspective, we again find that the problem is a modern one. For it is only in modern times that we no longer have a clear, uniform and unequivocal answer to the question: "Who is a Jew?" (even, and especially, in the State of Israel). For with the obvious exception of the situation in modern totalitarian regimes, most clearly with the Nazi racial definition of the Jew, modern Jewish identity differs from that of previous eras precisely in its individualistic and voluntaristic quality, without reference to a binding community, system of law, or other historic norms. The Jew was now free to change, reform or totally negate his Jewish identity, and could effectively assimilate and opt out of Jewish identity without converting to Christianity or Islam.

As we asked before, how, shall we regard the apostates Abu'l Barakat (Neganel) Al-Baghdadi and Abner of Burgos? More significantly, how shall we regard Spinoza, who was excommunicated by his Amsterdam community, but who, like many Jews after him, never converted to another religion?

There is no clear consensus among Jewish philosophers and scholars of Jewish philosophy regarding the proper definition of the field. The approaches to our question are not all mutually exclusive, and, therefore, we find thinkers and scholars who may support more than one approach. The responses to "what is Jewish philosophy" include a denial of "Jewish philosophy" as an oxymoron; purely biographical or linguistic criteria; religious "philosophy of Judaism;" harmonizing Judaism and philosophy; essentialist message vs. method; and contextual criteria, including Jewish sources, motives, audience and impact. All of these approaches, in turn, raise further questions.

[I.1.c]   JEWISH PHILOSOPHY: AN OXYMORON?

For some philosophers, including Leo Strauss and Emmanuel Levinas, and for some scholars, like Joseph Sermoneta and Zev Levy, philosophy (at least when it deals with purely philosophical questions of logic, ethics, esthetics, epistemology and the like) is essentially a universal discipline, like physics, and therefore they regard "Jewish philosophy" as an oxymoron, a contradiction in terms. Like other scientific methods of inquiry, they argue that philosophy must be universal, transcending particular cultures, and thus cannot be "Jewish," just as a Bulgarian who studies biology is not engaging in "Bulgarian biology." If, as the medievals thought, and some believe today, philosophy is a true science, how can it be defined in national or religious terms? Levinas, for example, accordingly regarded his philosophical and his Jewish writings to be different and basically unrelated genres (although many of his interpreters and readers, Levy included, question that dichotomy in Levinas' self-evaluation).

Historically, it is immediately evident that philosophy is not a Jewish invention or discovery (despite the view that the Greeks learned their wisdom from Semitic sources). In the passages cited above, we saw an open and honest awareness, among Arabs and Jews alike, of the Greek origins of philosophy, and not merely an etymological understanding of the Greek term "philosophy." The medieval Jewish philosophers freely acknowledged their own indebtedness to their Greek and Islamic sources, and their use of Arabic translations and original works. How, then, can such a foreign transplant be called "Jewish?"

However universal philosophy may be, it nevertheless seems that the expression "Jewish philosophy" is not a contradiction in terms the way "Jewish physics" would be, because there is no connection between physics and a particular culture. Some areas of philosophy, like logic, also have an affinity to such universal and precise sciences as mathematics. On the other hand, many other areas of philosophical inquiry do have some connection to their cultural and linguistic context, so at least in those areas philosophy resembles other Humanities, such as literature and art, which are not universal in their content or expression. So "Jewish philosophy" need not be a contradiction in terms the way "Jewish physics" would be. Even in the case of physics, there need not necessarily be a contradiction in terms. For example, when we say "Greek physics," we are not describing the scientific content but the historical context of the discipline: the science of physics was first developed within the context of ancient Greek philosophy and science, and Aristotle's *Physics* served as one of the foundations of western science, as well as philosophy, for centuries. (Indeed, to this day, Aristotle is called the "Father of Biology). By "Greek physics" we do not mean that physics belongs to Greek culture, but only the historical fact that the Greeks first discovered or invented a scientific system (physics), which is essentially universal, and which over the centuries became universal not merely in theory but in practice. So we can speak of "Greek physics" two thousand years ago, but not today.

[I.1.d] EXTREME FORMALISM IN DEFINING JEWISH PHILOSOPHY: BIOGRAPHIC AND LINGUISTIC CRITERIA

One way of resolving the issue is to resort to extreme formalism in defining Jewish philosophy, not in terms of the essence or content of the philosophy, but in formal terms of the Jewish identity of the philosopher, or the Jewish language in which the philosophy was written, regardless of its content. The criteria of Jewishness, in other words, have nothing to do with the content of the philosophy, but are a function of external, formal criteria, biographical and/or linguistic. It should be readily clear that a mere biographic fact—a philosopher's Jewish identity—is not sufficient to determine that his philosophy is a Jewish philosophy, i.e., of a Jewish character, just as we would not deduce that a Jew playing football is playing Jewish football. Again, without getting involved in the controversial question of "who is a Jew," we can simply agree that a given philosopher, by all accounts, is a Jew. For most scholars of Jewish philosophy, the philosopher's Jewish identity is a necessary, but not sufficient, condition for determining that his philosophy is Jewish. Reversing the formula, they would agree that Jewish philosophy cannot be developed by a non-Jew. So a non-Jew cannot write Jewish philosophy — but is the philosophy written by a Jew necessarily Jewish?

Similarly, is the fact that philosophy is written in Hebrew or another Jewish language a sufficient criterion for determining the Jewishness of the philosophy, a criterion proposed by no less of a scholar than Jacob Klatzkin, whose *Ozar Ha-Munahim Ha-Filosofiyim* (*Thesaurus Philosophicus Linguae Hebraicae*, 1928–1933) remains a classic reference book for students of medieval Jewish philosophy? Does translating the works of non-Jewish philosophers into Hebrew "convert" their philosophy and make it Jewish? Are the Greek works of Philo, and the Arabic works of all the early medieval Jewish philosophers from Sa'adiah Ga'on to Rambam, and the modern works of Jewish thought in European languages, not to be considered "Jewish" on these linguistic grounds?

An additional biographical factor has been suggested by such thinkers as Zev Levy, namely Jewish motivation, namely that the Jewish motives of the philosopher endow his philosophy with a Jewish character. This approach also proves problematical. Levy argues that Albert Einstein did not engage in physics out of Jewish motives, and he is presumably correct. But let us take another example: perhaps there is a disease which afflicts primarily the Jewish population, such as Tay-Sachs. One can easily conceive of a Jewish researcher studying that particular disease out of a Jewish motivation — to help his own people, community or perhaps even his own family to overcome that particularly Jewish disease. The researcher's motives are Jewish, but they do not thereby endow his medical research with the character of "Jewish medicine." The medicine remains universal, despite the fact that in this instance the patients are Jews, the researcher is a Jew, and his motives are Jewish.

Conversely, we can also conceive of a philosopher, who happens to be a Jew, and who engages in, and regards himself as engaging in, general philosophy, without any conscious connection to the Jews and Judaism. Philosophy interests him, not Judaism, and he seems to lack any Jewish motives. Yet, his philosophy succeeded in having a great influence on other Jewish philosophers (or, to be more careful in our phrasing, other Jews who were philosophers or philosophers who were Jews). These other philosophers discovered connections, of which our philosopher was not aware (and which he would have denied), between his philosophy and Jewish sources. It makes no difference whether the connections these philosophers discovered existing connections, of which our philosophers was unaware, or whether they invented connections that did not previously exist. Either way, the connections now exist and exert influence on these Jewish philosophers, and his philosophy, despite the lack of Jewish motivations, is now seen as "Jewish."

Baruch (Benedict) Spinoza is an outstanding example of such a development. It is difficult to determine if Spinoza had any "Jewish motives" (whatever they might be) in writing his *Ethics*, despite the clear influence of Jewish philosophers like Rambam on his thought, as amply documented by Harry Austryn Wolfson. The book, which is still routinely studied within the context of general philosophy, in turn influenced later Jewish philosophers, from Mendelssohn to our own day. So on the basis of Jewish influences on Spinoza, and of his influence on later Jewish thought, can the book be considered to be "Jewish philosophy?" Influence, moreover, can go in different directions. Such twentieth-centuries thinkers as Martin Buber and Abraham Joshua Heschel, although their thought is overtly Jewish in content, have frequently had significant impact on certain trends in Christian thought.

In short, biographic criteria, which are a necessary condition for Jewish philosophy, seem insufficient for determining the Jewishness of a philosophy.

[I.1.e]   THE ESSENTIALIST APPROACH: JEWISH PHILOSOPHY AS THE RELIGIOUS PHILOSOPHY OF JUDAISM

Some scholars, as we have seen, reject a national-cultural approach to defining Jewish philosophy, on the grounds that philosophy, as a universal science, cannot also be particular, i.e., unique to one nation or culture. Other thinkers and scholars, including some of the great names in the field, also rejected a national-cultural approach on different grounds. In their view, Jewish philosophy is analogous to Christian or Islamic philosophy, and not to a national-cultural school of philosophy, such as German or American philosophy. According to them, Judaism is a religion based on prophetic revelation, and, therefore, Jewish philosophy must be religious, not national, in its essential character.

The late twentieth-century thinker Emil Fackenheim was among those who suggested that Jewish philosophy refers to the combination of the essential Jewish message with the general philosophical method. The message is the ethical teaching of the classical prophets of ancient Israel, and the method is that of Socrates, Plato and Aristotle. While undoubtedly accurate when applied to such philosophers as Fackenheim himself, such a definition has a less obvious application when the subject of the philosophizing is something other than ethics, and deals with such questions as cosmology or creation vs. eternity, which may be hinted at in various books of the Bible but are by no means central to the concerns of the prophets.

The idea that Judaism has some identifiable and definable religious essence, presumed by Fackenheim, becomes much more pronounced in the essentialist approach of such scholars as Julius Guttmann and Alexander Altmann, for whom Jewish philosophy is the religious philosophy of Judaism. Guttmann's classical book, which is still unrivaled in its scope as the work of a single author surveying Jewish philosophy in all its periods, is deliberately called *Philosophies of Judaism* (although in the German original, and in the expanded Hebrew translation from which the English version was prepared, the title appears in the singular: *Die Philosophie des Judentums*), and not a "history of Jewish philosophy." Guttmann denied that "the philosophy of Judaism" was analogous to Greek, Roman, French or German philosophy. Rather, it formally resembles the philosophy of Christianity or Islam in its religious orientation, and in its philosophizing about Jewish religion, i.e., where the religion is the subject of the philosophy, just as the philosophy of law philosophizes about the law.[13]

Similarly, Altmann, whose scholarly interest encompassed Kabbalah as well as Jewish philosophy, maintained that one cannot speak of Jewish philosophy as a philosophic system, like American, English, French or German philosophy. It is, rather, analogous to Christian and Islamic philosophy in being religious in character.[14] "Judaism is a religion, and the truths it teaches are religious truths. They spring from the source of religious experience, not from pure reason."[15]

In the essentialist view of scholars like Guttmann and Altmann, Jewish religion is clearly prior in time to the development of Jewish philosophy, and took its classical shape long before Jews, responding to foreign influences, began philosophizing. Jewish philosophy thus arises in reaction to religious problems, not in reaction to rationalist-philosophical problems, and is, therefore, a religious philosophy. Moreover, since Jewish philosophy cannot be characterized as a single school of philosophical thought, it is not analogous to national philosophical schools of thought, such as continental rationalism or British empiricism.

Is the analogy of Jewish philosophy as a religious philosophy of Judaism, comparable to Christian and Islamic philosophy, useful in our search for a definition of our field?

---

[13] Julius Guttmann, *Philosophies of Judaism*, English translation by D. Silverman (New York: Holt, Rinehart, Winston, 1964), p. 4; cf. R.J.Z. Werblowsky's Introduction to the volume, pp. viii–ix.

[14] Alexander Altmann, ""Jewish Philosophy," in *History of Philosophy Eastern and Western*, ed. S. Radhakrishnan (London, 1953), vol. 2, p. 76.

[15] Alexander Altmann, "Judaism and World Philosophy," in Louis Finkelstein (ed.), *The Jews: Their History, Culture and Religion* (Philadelphia: Jewish Publication Society, 1949), vol. 2, p. 954.

[I.1.f] A COMPARISON: CHRISTIAN PHILOSOPHY ACCORDING TO ETIENNE GILSON

Etienne Gilson, one of the great scholars of medieval Latin philosophy, wrote an essay, "What is Christian Philosophy?" As a faithful Christian and loyal Roman Catholic, Gilson accepted the truth of Christianity as divinely revealed. In his view, the doctrine of the Incarnation is a rational truth, more certain and "rational" than the truths of philosophy. The truths of revelation—a single God, who created the world and guides it providentially, and who revealed his will to all humans—are clearer and more satisfying rationally than the truths of reason.[16]

Gilson concluded that "Christian philosophy" is the union of the study of philosophy with obedience to the Christian faith; this union preserves what Gilson called the "ever present truth" of Christianity, a truth discovered by the true Christian philosopher, Thomas Aquinas. Being Christian, such philosophy will protect us from error; being true philosophy, it will not limit our freedom and philosophical opinions.

If, for the sake of the comparison suggested by Guttmann and Altmann, we accept Gilson's definition of Christian philosophy, we now return to the question of the usefulness of the analogy. Many Jewish philosophers also believed, like Gilson, in the superiority of revelation to unassisted reason, and the problem of "faith and reason" was certainly a central theme, as Altmann pointed out, in much of their work. Nevertheless, it is interesting to note that all of the religious doctrines cited by Gilson as examples of religious truth which is more rational than philosophic truth, are Jewish (and therefore shared by Christianity and Islam as well), not specifically Christian, i.e., truths held only by Christians (such as the Incarnation and Trinity). In this respect, Gilson's position resembles somewhat the position taken by the fictional Christian spokesman with the King of the Khazars in Judah Ha-Levi's *Kuzari* 1:4–5, where the Christian says:

> I believe that all existing things were created, and that only the Creator is eternal... I similarly believe that all humans are descended from Adam...I believe that God exercises providence over his creatures, and relates to humans...I believe in everything taught in the Torah and the historical books of the Israelites.

Only then does the Christian spokesman continue to describe those beliefs which are specifically Christian. However, the King of the Khazars is willing to accept only those teachings common to Christianity and Islam, namely those doctrines derived from Jewish Scripture, which are inherently

---

[16]   Etienne Gilson, "What is Christian Philosophy?" in *A Gilson Reader*, ed. Anton Pegis (Garden City, N.Y., 957), pp. 178–179.

reasonable, and he rejects as incompatible with reason those doctrines which are uniquely Christian, saying:

> There is no rational basis for what yhou say; indeed, logic refutes most of these things...As for me, I cannot accept these tings from a rational point of view, because they are new to me, and I was not raised in them.[17]

From a non-Christian perspective, in short, Gilson's view that the specifically Christian truth is clearer and rationally more satisfying than the conclusions of reason itself is not persuasive, and in any event, was not shared by those medieval Jewish philosophers who dealt with Christianity.[18]

Second, Gilson's equation of Christian philosophy with true philosophy is obviously not acceptable to a non-Christian, who does not believe in the truth of the Christian religion. But it is also difficult to understand from a philosophic perspective. Despite Gilson's assurances that being true philosophy, Christian philosophy will not limit our freedom and philosophical opinions, the moment one demands that the conclusions of philosophy be in accord with certain pre-determined positions (in this case, religious), and thereby precludes from the outset the possibility of arriving at different conclusions, has he not, in fact, essentially violated the philosophic method itself, by attempting to close an open system? What *a priori* limitations does the philosophic method of inquiry place on itself before even beginning the inquiry? In short, if we accept Gilson's definition, what is the difference between philosophy and theology?

On a different level, perhaps in a Christian context Gilson may demand such accord at the outset between philosophy and religion, because classical Christianity (and certainly the Roman Catholic church) has official beliefs, dogmas and creeds which are obligatory upon all adherents. But Judaism has no equivalent central authority to determine practice, let alone belief, such as the papacy or synods of bishops. Therefore, despite various individual Jewish attempts to formulate Jewish dogma or creeds (most notably, Rambam's famous "Thirteen Principles"), Jewish thinkers never succeeded in transforming the creeds or dogmas they formulated individually and on their own initiative, into official creeds, formally and actually binding upon all Jews, or even accepted by all Jews.[19]

---

17   Judah Ha-Levi, *Kuzari* 1:4–5.

18   See, for example, the discussion in Daniel J. Lasker, *Jewish Philosophical Polemics Against Christianity in the Middle Ages* (New York, 1977; second edition, 2007).

19   On this problem, see Menachem Kellner, *Dogma in Medieval Jewish Thought* (Oxford: Littman Library, 1986), and *Must a Jew Believe Anything?* (London: Littman Library, 1999; second edition, 2006); Marc B. Shapiro, *The Limits of Orthodox Theology: Maimonides' Thirteen Principles Reappraised* (Oxford: Littman Library, 2004).

Jewish law clearly established that "a Jew, though he sin, remains a Jew,"[20] regardless of whether or not he affirms a particular set of dogmatic principles. While Gilson, therefore, may be able to define Christian philosophy in the light of its compatibility with official truth, in a Jewish context, without such a uniform let alone official truth, how can one demand that Jewish philosophy accord with that truth?

Moreover, let us return to the question of "Jewish" philosophy versus "true" philosophy. Gilson, as we saw, equates Christian philosophy with the truth. A comparable Jewish equation (Jewish philosophy = true philosophy) is impossible, and not merely because there is no single Jewish "truth." Philosophers who, according to all opinions, were "Jewish philosophers," differed radically from each other on many issues. Let us take, for example, the question of creation. According to Rambam (in the *Guide of the Perplexed* 2:13) there are three views on creation: (1) Creation *ex nihilo*; (2) Creation from prime matter; (3) Eternity. Now at most one of these views may be assumed to be true, to the exclusion of the others. (There may be another view, to the exclusion of these three, which is correct). Among those thinkers universally acknowledged to be "Jewish philosophers," we find a variety of points of view on creation, more or less among the views outlined by Rambam. These views, of course, are mutually exclusive (at most one can be correct)—but they are all Jewish, despite the fact that they cannot all be true. "Jewish" and "true" are not synonymous or correlative categories. (Let us also recall that at the outset we differentiated our question, what is Jewish philosophy, from the question guiding the medievals we cited, namely what is philosophy).

Moreover, even if we somehow should become convinced that a certain point of view is demonstrably true, it is quite conceivable that we should find not only Jews, but also Christians and Muslims, or other philosophers, who affirm that particular position. The conclusion we are forced to reach is therefore clear: there are true philosophical positions held in common by Jewish and non-Jewish philosophers, and there are false philosophical positions held by Jewish (as well as by non-Jewish) philosophers. Once again, we cannot honestly equate Jewish philosophy with the truth. There are Jewish philosophies which are not true, and there are true philosophies which are not Jewish. We are not attempting to define "true philosophy" but "Jewish philosophy." The comparison with Christian philosophy suggested by Guttmann and Altmann, has, therefore, not helped us to understand what is Jewish philosophy.

---

20   Babylonian Talmud Sanhedrin 44a. Commenting on Joshua 7:11, "Israel sinned," "Rabbi Abba bar Zavdai said, 'Although he has sinned, he is [still] Israel'." Rashi comments: "Since it does not say, 'The people have sinned,' they still have their holy name [Israel]."

[I.1.g] ANOTHER COMPARISON: ISLAMIC-ARABIC PHILOSOPHY

What about the second analogy suggested by Guttmann and Altmann, namely Islamic or Arabic philosophy, which Jewish philosophy is also supposed to resemble? In the case of Islam, we encounter a different set of problems. Shall we properly speak of Islamic philosophy or of Arabic philosophy?

One of the great scholars of Islamic-Arabic philosophy, Henri Corbin, strongly rejected the view that "Islamic" and "Arabic" are interchangeable or equivalent terms. In his *Histoire de la Philosophie Islamique*, Corbin wrote that "Arab" is a national-political identity. The overwhelming majority of Muslims are not Arabs; and Islam is a universal religion. Even from a purely linguistic perspective, we cannot really speak of "Arabic" philosophy. Although most books of Islamic philosophy were written in Arabic, many important works of Islamic philosophy were written in other languages, such as Persian (including some of the books of one of the great Islamic philosophers, Ibn Sina [Avicenna]). Islamic philosophy is, therefore, not necessarily Arabic philosophy.

We may, moreover, add to Corbin, that Arabic philosophy is not necessarily Islamic. Christian Arabs also wrote in Arabic. Indeed, the important early translations of Greek philosophical works into Arabic, which paved the way for Islamic philosophy to flourish, were made in ninth-century Baghdad by such Nestorian Christians as Ḥunayn ibn Isḥaq (whose original *Adab Al-Falasifah* ["Aphorisms of the Philosophers"] has survived in the Hebrew translation, *Musarei Ha-Pilosofim*). In addition, of course, for several centuries Arabic (or Judeo-Arabic) was the language in which many Jews wrote philosophical and scientific works.

According to Corbin, then, Islamic philosophy is philosophy tied to the religious or spiritual reality of Islam,[21] and thus resembles Guttmann's and Altmann's approach to Jewish philosophy as the religious philosophy of Judaism. Corbin's approach, however, is challenged by Majid Fakhry, in his *History of Islamic Philosophy* (note the identical names of Corbin's French book and Fakhry's English book). Fakhry points out that Islamic philosophy is a product of Syrian, Arab, Persian, Turkish, Berber and other thinkers. The Arab component, however, is so dominant that Islamic philosophy basically is Arabic philosophy, and the Arabic language was used by Muslims from widely separated geographic regions. The Arabs, Fakhry insists, were the ones who contributed the one universal, common denominator to this broad culture, namely the religion of Islam.[22]

---

[21]   Henri Corbin, *Histoire de la Philosophie Islamique* (Paris, 1964), p. 6.
[22]   Majid Fakhry, *History of Islamic Philosophy* (2nd edition, New York, 1983), p. xv.

It is not our task to decide whether to call the phenomenon Islamic or Arabic philosophy, and we shall use the terms interchangeably. Nevertheless, the debate can be instructive for us in our quest, in terms both of similarities and differences.

In terms of similarities, there is also a Hebrew linguistic component to medieval Jewish philosophy. The later philosophic literature (generally, in the period following Rambam) was mostly written in Hebrew. As for the earlier period, from the time of Sa'adiah Ga'on and Isaac Israeli, much of it was translated rapidly into Hebrew. In the case of Rambam's *Guide of the Perplexed*, it was translated into Hebrew for the first time during Rambam's life. In addition, many of the Arabic works of Jewish philosophy were written in Judeo-Arabic (i.e., Arabic written in Hebrew letters, with an admixture of Hebrew words and expressions), and not in pure Arabic.

Also in terms of similarity, Corbin and Fakhry speak of Islamic philosophy in terms of harmonizing foreign philosophy with Islamic needs, without prejudging or determining the truth of those philosophic positions from a religious perspective; as such their approach is more flexible than is Gilson's more dogmatic approach to Christian philosophy. Many scholars of Jewish philosophy also speak of harmonization as a feature of Jewish philosophy.

In terms of differences, on the linguistic level even Fakhry, who more or less equated Islamic and Arabic philosophy, nevertheless decided to call his book "Islamic" and not "Arabic" philosophy, presumably since not all Islamic philosophers wrote in Arabic, and non-Muslim philosophers (Christians and Jews) wrote in Arabic. However, even if there is a linguistic component to Jewish philosophy in the Middle Ages, in the modern period, most works of Jewish philosophy have been written in European languages and not in Hebrew or other Jewish languages.

The differences are at least as pronounced on the religious-cultural level. Corbin and others strenuously rejected any attempt to identify Islam, which they saw as a universalistic religion transcending nationality and race (including the Arabs), with any particular people, namely the Arabs. They clearly distinguish universal and religious Muslim identity from the particular national-linguistic Arab identity. By contrast, in a Jewish context, there is no such dichotomy between religious and national identity. Jews differ sharply with each other to the extent to which they affirm traditional Jewish practice and law, i.e. to what extent Jewish religious law applies to the Jewish people, but none of them suggests that non-Jews are bound by the commandments addressed in the Torah to "the children of Israel." To the contrary, the Torah itself refers to its being "the heritage of the community of Jacob" (Deuteronomy 33:4).

Therefore, although scholars like Guttmann and Altmann may well be correct that Jewish philosophy is not analogous to a national philosophic school of thought (French, German, American, etc.), because it often lacks linguistic uniformity as well as a uniformity of ideas of approach (i.e., an identifiable school of thought), their attempt to define Jewish philosophy in religious terms, analogous to the philosophies of universalistic, trans-national religions like Christianity and Islam, proves no less problematical.

[I.1.h]   THE ESSENTIALIST APPROACH
AND THE ESSENCE OF JUDAISM

If the essentialist approach to defining Jewish philosophy were to succeed, it would first have to establish what is the essence of Judaism, in light of which one could then determine that the content of a given philosophy is in accord with that essence, or that Judaism is the subject of the philosophical inquiry, which accordingly qualifies as Jewish philosophy. This approach, as we saw, was implicit in Fackenheim's reference to the essential Jewish "message" vs. the philosophical "method" of inquiry, and was explicit in Guttmann's and Altmann's religious philosophy of Judaism. Another historian of Jewish philosophy, S. B. Urbach, also explicitly adopted such essentialist criteria:

> Jewish philosophy, from its very beginning and in all its periods, has been a religious philosophy, a philosophy of Judaism, whose essential purpose was to establish a basis for Judaism and verify the Torah of Israel. Its innovations are primarily methodological: a systematic presentation, determining foundations and sometimes principles, logical strengthening of basic beliefs.[23]

We have to ask ourselves whether such a rigid and restrictive definition, as clear as it may be, really solves our problem. Actually, it would appear that Urbach's approach to Jewish philosophy in many respects parallel's Gilson's approach to Christian philosophy, and, therefore, is subject to the same criticisms. As in the case of Gilson, we have not a description of what the philosophy is, but a prescription of what it should be. Like Gilson, has not Urbach effectively erased the distinction between philosophy and theology, by suggesting that its function is to "verify the Torah of Israel," and come close to reducing it to a graduate-level catechism?

The title of Guttmann's book, *Die Philosophy des Judentums*, similarly led Leon Roth explicitly to equate "Jewish philosophy" with "an inquiry into Judaism," i.e., "a philosophy of Judaism." Jewish philosophy, according to Roth,

---

[23]   S.B. Urbach, *'Amudei Ha-Maḥshavah Ha-Yisra'elit* ("Foundations of Jewish Thought") (Jerusalem, 1971), Part 1, p. 41. My translation.

> Is not philosophy in the authentic historical sense of a universal curiosity and a universal questioning into the widest aspects of human experience...The philosophy of Judaism is the thinking and rethinking of the fundamentals of Judaism...The object of the discussion was not the nature of the world at large but the nature of Judaism.[24]

Such essentialism requires that Jewish philosophy, as the philosophy of Judaism, verify, or in the very least accord itself with, Judaism. To the essentialist way of thinking, Judaism is a fact, preceding philosophy, something defined and given, possessing its own unique essence. Nevertheless, despite their "essentialism," and for whatever reasons, the essentialists generally did not see fit to define that "essence of Judaism."

[I.1.i]   THE ESSENCE OF JUDAISM ACCORDING TO BERKOVITS

We find such an attempt to define the essence of Judaism in an article entitled "What is Jewish Philosophy?" by the scholar and philosopher, Eliezer Berkovits. According to Berkovits, philosophy is a variable human phenomenon, influenced by changing circumstances, but Judaism is a constant, unchanging historic fact, based on God's revelation to Israel at Sinai. That invariable and constant "given fact" of the revelation at Sinai is prior to any philosopher's inquiry, and such inquiry is limited to variable interpretations of the invariable fact:

> The philosophy, the theology, are the variables. Judaism contains the element of constancy, because it is founded not on ideas but on certain facts and events...[which] do have their philosophical, theological, metaphysical relevance. But such relevance is always a matter of interpretation, and as such, subject to change...The facts having entered into history are...unalterable, irrevocable...The conceptual interpretation of these facts is Jewish philosophy. The concepts may change with the times, the events remain forever.[25]

If, indeed, Judaism is based on incontrovertible historical facts, and if, indeed, Judaism never changes, because it is a divinely "given fact," and whatever happened has actually happened, then any philosophy developed by a Jew which denies these facts, and which substitutes the metaphysical idea for the historic event, is not Jewish philosophy. The function of philosophy and science is to understand the facts:

---

[24]   Leon Roth, "Is There a Jewish Philosophy?" in Raymond Goldwater (ed.), *Jewish Philosophy and Philosophers* (London, 1962), pp. 10–11.

[25]   Eliezer Berkovits, "What is Jewish Philosophy?" in *Tradition*, vol. 3, no. 2 (Spring, 1961), pp. 120–121.

Modern science began when the human intellect finally realized that it could not ignore what Galileo called "irreducible and stubborn facts"...The Jew who does not acknowledge the "irreducible and stubborn facts" of Judaism remains a Jew, and...he may even be a thinking Jew, but he is not a Jewish thinker.[26]

Now it is interesting that Berkovits should cite Galileo's "irreducible and stubborn facts," and equate them with what he considers to be the "factual givenness of Judaism itself," the divinely given facts which "having entered into history are, as such, unalterable and irrevocable," "events [which] remain forever."

The centrality of the public revelation at Sinai to much of Jewish philosophy is clear, from Sa'adiah Ga'on at the outset of medieval Jewish philosophy, to Moses Mendelssohn at the outset of modern Jewish thought in the eighteenth century, and to the nineteenth century Neo-Orthodoxy of Samson Raphael Hirsch, as well as to twentieth-century Orthodox thinkers like Joseph Soloveitchik. In that sense, Berkovits stands in good company. But is the analogy to Galileo correct?

Is the belief in the facticity of the revelation at Sinai, which Berkovits mandates for authentic Jewish philosophy, subject to scientific verification, by microscope, telescope, or other empirical means? Galileo's claim was radical (both in the sense of fundamental and in the sense of revolutionary), because he claimed, and could demonstrate, that the religiously sanctioned beliefs of his day, which were considered to be scientific truth, were in fact neither scientific nor true, because they did not accord with the facts, namely what he saw through his telescope. But are alleged historic events, however hallowed and venerated by ancient tradition, subject to empirical observation and verification in the same way that natural phenomena are?

Without entering the debate as to whether scientific methods of studying the past like archeology have, to date, succeeded in providing empirical evidence to prove or disprove particular historical passages in the Bible, what scientific and philosophic (as opposed to religious and theological) assurance does Berkovits have that, at least hypothetically, the "facts" uncovered scientifically will always accord with the traditional, biblical account?

Now, of course, as Berkovits states, whatever happened, happened. His view that Jews may follow any interpretation of the facts, so long as they acknowledge those facts, permits a wide range of freedom and pluralistic interpretations. But does it suffice? Are the facts as they "they entered into history" (i.e., as we know them, as opposed to what actually happened) really "unalterable and irrevocable?" Did Galileo merely challenge an interpretation of what he agreed to be the facts, or did he not challenge what was alleged

---

[26]   Berkovits, ibid, pp. 126–127.

to be the facts themselves? Are Berkovits' "facts" irreducible and stubborn, because they are empirically demonstrable?

Do Jews and Christians, for example, merely differ over the interpretation of alleged historical facts? Or is not the issue far more fundamental: did something happen or did it not? In his Letter to the Corinthians, Paul put it succinctly:

> Now if Christ is preached as raised from the dead, how can some of you say that there is no resurrection of the dead? But if there is no resurrection of the dead, then Christ has not been raised; if Christ has not been raised, then our preaching is in vain and your faith is in vain. We are even found to be misrepresenting God, because we testified of God that he raised Christ, whom he did not raise...If Christ has not been raised, your faith is futile, and you are still in your sins...But in fact Christ has been raised from the dead.[27]

Jews can presumably accept Paul's conditional these, "if Christ has not been raised, then our preaching is in vain," because as non-Christians they differ from Christians not only on the level of interpreting the "fact" of the resurrection, but on the level of the facticity of the alleged resurrection itself.

Berkovits, although he leaves broad latitude for interpretation, limits Jewish philosophy to the interpretation of religious facts. Unless these facts can be subjected to scientific verification, however, it is not clear how we can know for sure that they are "irreducible and stubborn," "unalterable and irrevocable," and not subject to further question. Without such scientific and empirically verifiable certainty, how can we then, like Berkovits, require *a priori* that all Jewish philosophy be limited to the interpretation of these facts, and not to questioning the facts themselves?

What was implicit in the essentialist criteria of Guttmann became more pronounced in Urbach, and explicit in Berkovits:

1) Jewish philosophy is a philosophy of Judaism, i.e., a philosophy whose subject of inquiry is Judaism; or

2) Jewish philosophy is a philosophy which verifies, or in the very least accords with, Judaism.

In both cases, Judaism is understood to be an invariable "given," prior to and transcending changing philosophies. Above and beyond transient philosophy, which changes according to the *Zeitgeist*, stands the "essence of Judaism," namely that eternal and unchanging truth which the philosophers interpret as they may over the generations.

---

27   I Corinthians 15:12–20 (Revised Standard Version).

[I.1.j]   HARMONIZING PHILOSOPHY
WITH JEWISH TRADITION: COLETTE SIRAT

A more flexible version of the essentialist approach was adopted by Colette
Sirat, whose own position has manifested a moderating evolution of sorts
over the years. In the Introduction to the first, Hebrew edition of her book
on Jewish philosophy in the Middle Ages (*Hagut Pilosofit Bi-Yemei Ha-
Beinayim*, 1975), Sirat wrote:

> To the extent that philosophy would relate to the Bible and would draw its
> justification from it... it is Jewish philosophy... Medieval Jewish philosophy
> is philosophy which was adapted to the Jewish tradition by finding agreement
> or similarity of expression between it and Jewish religious tradition... Only the
> combination of philosophy and Jewish tradition forms Jewish philosophy... The
> essence of Jewish philosophy is the harmonizing of a particular system of thought
> with the Jewish sources.[28]

In other words, not only must Jewish philosophy be a philosophy of
Judaism, i.e. a philosophy whose subject of inquiry is Judaism, as Guttmann
maintained, but it must be a philosophy in agreement with "the Jewish
tradition," harmonizing that system with "the Jewish sources." Some ten
years later, in the Introduction to her revised and expanded English book,
A History of Jewish Philosophy in the Middle Ages (1985), Sirat adopted
a more flexible formulation, recognizing the excessive restrictiveness of her
earlier essentialism, in its implication that there is one, uniform and monolithic
essence of Judaism referred to as "the Jewish tradition." Now Sirat recognized
the manifold spectrum of Jewish opinions, and broadened the scope of what
she called "Jewish tradition" to include Jewish philosophy as well:

> A given philosophy... was brought into connection with the Jewish tradition...
> The Jewish tradition referred to by the Jewish philosophers may be one specific
> part of what we now call "Jewish tradition"... The history of Jewish philosophy
> in the Middle Ages is the history of efforts of Jews to reconcile philosophy (or
> a system of rationalist thought) and Scripture... The harmonizing of these two
> systems of thought in one unique verity was the theme of almost all Jewish
> medieval philosophy.[29]

Jewish tradition is no longer seen here as being characterized by some
kind of monolithic "essence," and Jewish philosophy is philosophy "brought

---

[28]   Colette Sirat, *Hagut Pilosofit Bi-Yemei Ha-Beinayim* (Jerusalem: Keter, 1975), pp. 7–8.
      My translation.
[29]   Colette Sirat, *A History of Jewish Philosophy in the Middle Ages* (Cambridge: Cambridge
      University Press, 1985), pp. 4–5.

into connection with the Jewish tradition." Nevertheless, the approach is still essentialist, because it requires that the philosophy be "harmonized" with the traditional sources. Spinoza was a Jew but his philosophy was not Jewish, because although rooted in Jewish tradition, it rejected that tradition.

[I.1.k] PROBLEMS WITH THE ESSENTIALIST APPROACH

However unsatisfactory the first, extreme formalist approach to defining Jewish philososphy may have proven, because it relied exclusively on biographical or linguistic criteria, or on motives, the essentialist approach also has proven problematical. We saw, for example, that scholars like Guttmann and Altmann presupposed that Judaism has an essence, without defining it. But without some kind of objective definition of that essence, how can one determine, from an essentialist perspective, which philosophy accords with the essence of Judaism, and accordingly may be considered "Jewish philosophy?" Without a definition of the essence of Judaism, such determinations remain subjective and without objective reference.

The essentialists seem, however, to follow Rambam's *via negativa*. Rambam maintained that we cannot define God positively, only negatively (not what God is, but what God is not). So it seems that the essentialists find it easier to define Judaism negatively (for example, Judaism is not Christianity or Islam) than to state positively what the essence of Judaism is.

Conversely, attempts to define the essence of Judaism positively, such as Berkovits endeavored, proved equally unsuccessful. In the very least, their definition is not universally accepted. Moreover, such attempts, which accept the factual givenness of Judaism and limit Jewish philosophy to its interpretation, verification or justification, tend to destroy in a Jewish context, as Gilson did in a Christian context, the distinction between philosophy, a free, open and rational method of investigation, and theology, a closed method of justifying or verifying what has already been accepted as true and given.

In short, either the essentialists refrain from defining the essence of Judaism, in which case they lack essentialist criteria for defining Jewish philosophy; or they attempt to define the essence of Judaism, in which case they run into a different problem: no Jewish philosopher (even Rambam, with his "Thirteen Principles"),[30] and no Jewish scholar have ever succeeded in dogmatically defining the essence of Judaism to the satisfaction of all, or even most, other philosophers and scholars. And the moment they do define the

---

[30]   On the misunderstanding and distortions of Rambam's "Thirteen Principles" in contemporary Orthodoxy, and on the disagreement with and opposition to Rambam's dogmas in medieval and early modern Jewish thought, see the important studies by Menachem Kellner and Marc Shapiro (above, note 19).

essence of Judaism, at least to their own satisfaction, they run into the danger of converting Jewish philosophy into theology. In which case, what have they accomplished?

Here we come to a fundamental problem with the essentialist approach, despite its clarity: it is prescriptive rather than descriptive, and mandates what Jewish philosophy should be, rather than understanding what it is and has been. It thereby limits us to a predefined or preconceived notion of what is legitimate within the context of Judaism, and fails to take into account the varied, and often opposing, points of view that we find throughout Jewish literature, a richness of perspectives that is manifested even in the Bible and Talmud. Shall we, for example, define the belief in creation *ex nihilo* as an essential Jewish doctrine, to the exclusion of those Jewish philosophers, major and minor alike (including Ralbag [Gersonides], Moses Narboni, Samuel ibn Tibbon, Shem Tov ibn Falaquera, and quite possible Rambam himself) who held a different view? Most medieval Jewish philosophers affirmed the freedom of the human will—but does that entitle us to exclude from the ranks of Jewish philosophy the minority view of Ḥasdai Crescas, surely an important figure, because he affirmed a deterministic view?

[I.1.I] A JEWISH CAKE WITH NON-JEWISH INGREDIENTS

Another problem with the essentialist approach is its creating artificial dichotomies between the "Jewish" and the "non-Jewish" aspects of the thought of a Jewish philosopher, sometimes in a single book or chapter. When that philosopher's thought, or book, or part of a book, deals with an overtly Jewish subject, or accords with the "essence of Judaism," or "the Jewish tradition," it qualifies as Jewish philosophy according to the two essentialist criteria summarized above. But when that same philosopher's thought, book, or chapter deals with a theme that is not overtly Jewish, or does not accord with the "essence of Judaism" or "the Jewish tradition," it is not called Jewish philosophy. The same person, it seems, may therefore be a Jewish philosopher and a non-Jewish (i.e., general) philosopher; the same book can be both Jewish and non-Jewish (or general), and so forth.

The problem exists not only in the case of marginal Jewish philosophers (marginal either Jewishly or philosophically), but in many other cases as well (including such mainstream figures as Rambam himself, who is certainly universally considered to be a Jewish philosopher, indeed is often regarded as the greatest Jewish philosopher). Let us take, for example, Rambam's four arguments for the existence, incorporeality and unity of God (in Part II of the *Guide of the Perplexed*). Such arguments or proofs presumably meet the two conditions the essentialists posed for Jewish philosophy: (1) the subject (the existence of God) is a Jewish religious subject; and (2) the conclusion (that

God exists) is in accord with Jewish tradition, however its essence might be defined. In light of these criteria, surely Rambam's arguments are "essentially" Jewish philosophy.

Conversely, Aristotelian physics and metaphysics presumably fail to meet the test of Jewish philosophy, by these same criteria: (1) the subject of physics (the motion of physical bodies) is not a Jewish-religious subject, but rather a general, scientific topic; and (2) the conclusions of physics, and certainly metaphysics (even more so, Aristotelian metaphysics) are not necessarily in accord with at least some of Jewish tradition, as it is usually understood, Rambam notwithstanding. An Aristotelian impersonal unmoved mover and first cause of an eternal and unchanging world, which sublimely knows only itself and is not involved in the world it caused, might not necessarily prove to be identical, or even reconcilable, with the personal creator of Genesis — in Judah Ha-Levi's terms, the difference between "the God of Aristotle" and "the God of Abraham."[31]

If what we have said here is correct, then we are left with the following paradox: a supposedly "Jewish" proof consists entirely of non-Jewish elements! In his proofs, Rambam explicitly relies entirely on propositions derived from Aristotelian physics and metaphysics, which he regarded as having been sufficiently demonstrated by Aristotle and therefore not warranting further demonstration. From an essentialist perspective, how can we bake such a kosher-Jewish cake from non-kosher, non-Jewish ingredients?

[I.1.m]   JEWISH DISAGREEMENT WITH JEWS AND AGREEMENT WITH NON-JEWS

If, again, we take for our example Rambam's arguments or proofs for the existence, incorporeality and unity of God in Part II of the *Guide of the Perplexed*, we are faced with another paradox: we can find similar or identical proofs in the Islamic philosophical literature Rambam read, as well as in the Christian philosophical authors (e.g., Thomas Aquinas) who read Rambam. The "Jewish" proof is thus equally a Muslim and a Christian one. On the other hand, there are other Jewish philosophers, such as Sa'adiah Ga'on, whose positions and method of proving the existence of God Rambam strenuously rejected and attacked. Sa'adiah Ga'on, for example, based his proofs for the existence of God on creation, an approach Rambam considered methodologically unsound and pedagogically unacceptable. Rambam's "Jewish" proof is thus not accepted by many other Jewish philosophers (beginning with Sa'adiah Ga'on centuries earlier); nevertheless, they are all Jews, and their philosophies are generally considered "Jewish" philosophies. And the "Jewish" proof, not

---

31   Judah Ha-Levi, *Kuzari* 4:16.

accepted by many other Jews, was accepted by some Muslim and Christian philosophers, who do not, thereby, lose their respective identities. How can the content (the "essence") of the proof, therefore, constitute its Jewishness, when it is not upheld by many Jews, and when non-Jews do affirm it?

[I.1.n]   A SINGLE, UNIFORM JEWISH TRADITION?

The essentialist approach requires, as we have seen, that Jewish philosophy constitute a "philosophy of Judaism" (according to Guttmann and others), or "philosophy which was adapted to the Jewish tradition by finding agreement or similarity of expression between it and Jewish religious tradition" (according to Sirat's earlier formulation), or acknowledges and then interprets the "irreducible and stubborn facts" of Judaism (according to Berkovits). Here, too, we face a historical paradox.

Is there a continuous and uniform tradition we can call "Judaism" or "the Jewish tradition?" Of course, from a chronological perspective, it is correct that Judaism evolved for centuries, and that much of classical rabbinic Judaism had taken shape, before the encounter with philosophy. But that same "Judaism" was shaped, at least in part, by encounters with foreign cultures in each generation or period, especially in the Middle Ages. All these encounters involved adoptions of at least certain foreign influences, which were then adapted to Jewish needs, and which in turn then contributed to what later generations regarded as "Judaism" and "Jewish tradition." These adoptions of and adaptations to foreign influences, tendencies which became accelerated in the modern era, were not always conscious. Indeed, the open acknowledgement of such borrowing of foreign materials in Jewish philosophy was unusual, not because similar tendencies could not be documented in other areas of life, but because in other areas they were not necessarily so obvious or explicit, or because they were not consciously undertaken. In short, the philosophers were aware of, and candidly acknowledged, the foreign sources of their wisdom, and this in turn opened them up to the charge that philosophy is foreign, and not authentically or legitimately Jewish. Their opponents, on the other hand, did not understand that the tradition they sought to insulate and isolate from foreign philosophical contamination had itself been shaped in part by ideas and trends not originally Jewish, ideas and trends they accepted as traditionally Jewish without being aware of their origin.

The innovations of one generation became the orthodoxy of the next, especially for those whose Jewish fervor was unchallenged by historically accurate knowledge. Rambam is today everyone's hero, regardless of whether he is actually understood, and whether his philosophic as well as his popular or halakhic works are studied; but he was scarcely a heroic figure to those who sought to have his books burned in the thirteenth century.

These innovations, regardless of their source, are not, and never were, limited to philosophy. The introduction by the mystics of sixteenth century Tsefat of the *Kabbalat Shabbat* ("welcoming the Sabbath") psalms before the Friday evening service, and especially the "Lekha Dodi" poem by Shelomo Alkabetz, greeting the Sabbath as bride and queen, which came to be accepted by almost all Jewish communities, became a lovely feature of Jewish "tradition" for later generations, which is no less lovely or meaningful for its being a relatively recent addition to "traditional" Jewish liturgy.

Or to take, for example, another innovation in traditional Jewish liturgy, the hymn "Yigdal Elohim Ḥai," often sung at the conclusion of the service, is based on Rambam's "Thirteen Principles." How many Jews understand the innovative and controversial philosophical principles underlying what is now a "traditional" song? In his great legal code, the *Mishneh Torah*,[32] Rambam categorized as a heretic (*min*) anyone "who says that there is one God, but that He is a body or has shape." To which Rambam's opponent, Ravad (Rabbi Abraham ben David of Posquières, France), objected:

> Why should he call such a person a heretic? Greater and better than he (Rambam) have followed this way of thinking, based upon what they saw in biblical passages, or even more in the words of *aggadot* (legends) which corrupt one's thought.[33]

Now I doubt that we will find many Jews in our generation who affirm a corporeal God; most are likely to acknowledge that the God in whom they do (or alternatively, do not) believe "has neither body nor shape" (in the words of the "Yigdal" hymn). Over hundreds of years, the idea of the incorporeality of God has become fundamental to what is called "Judaism" or "Jewish tradition." Yet, in the twelfth century, Rambam had to argue for this radical idea, which was innovative in both philosophic and halakhic terms, and which aroused the opposition of Ravad and so many others.

In short, "the Jewish tradition" with which Jewish philosophy is supposed to be in accord, is itself a tradition that has evolved and undergone many changes, innovations, adoptions and adaptations of foreign materials. Among those innovations and changes are philosophical influences as well. So with which pure and unchanging Jewish tradition need philosophy be harmonized? Jewish philosophy, from its very beginning, became an integral part of the evolving Jewish tradition.

---

32 *Misnheh Torah, Sefer Mada'* ("Book of Knowledge"), Hilkhot Teshuvah (Laws of Repentance) 3:7.

33 Note that Ravad himself did not affirm corporeality, which he regarded as corrupt thinking, but he rejected Rambam's right to categorize such erroneous belief as heresy. On the issue of rabbinic belief in corporeality, see Jacob Neusner, "Conversation in Nauvoo about the Corporeality of God," in *B.Y.U. Studies* 36/1 (1996–7), pp. 7–30.

[I.1.o]   THE TALMUDIC RABBIS AND PHILOSOPHY

Regarding Jewish borrowing of philosophic culture, since the works, or at least the ideas, of the Greek philosophers were available by the time the rabbis of the Talmud formulated their teachings, we may ask whether rabbinic literature manifests any Greek philosophical influence. While the rabbis had some acquaintance with Greek philosophical ideas, particularly with those of the Stoics (in popular versions), Saul Lieberman has shown that they were not familiar with formal philosophy.[34] Harry A. Wolfson (1887–1974) stated that he was unable to discover a single Greek philosophic term in rabbinic literature.[35] To which Lieberman replied: "I want to state more positively: Greek philosophic terms are absent from the entire ancient rabbinic literature."[36] Lieberman also wrote that while the rabbis knew certain elements of Greek science, their knowledge was probably derived from secondary sources.[37]

This conventional view has been challenged by Jacob Neusner in a series of studies. Neusner acknowledges that there are no overtly philosophical terms in rabbinic literature, that the rabbis never cited any Greek philosophical texts, and that it is unlikely that they had any direct personal or literary contact with philosophy. Nevertheless, Neusner argues that much of the Mishnah is "philosophical in method, manner of formulating results, and . . . in specific philosophical program," and that when read philosophically, the Mishnah's arguments coincide with Aristotle's rules of classification, and its issues and positions are congruent with those of Greek philosophy.[38] Neusner basically argues that Wolfson and Lieberman, by looking only at the trees, failed to see the forest. In his view, the Mishnah is philosophy and not theology, because it doesn't merely cite Scripture, but analyzes its principles rationally. In the Mishnah, as in Aristotle, God serves as a principle, but is not involved in the system of classification of natural reality. Neusner later extended this argument to the Gemara as well, because of its dialectical analysis. However, Neusner is careful to argue that his claim is "congruity," i.e., similarity, and not direct continuity or contact between the rabbis and

---

[34]   See Saul Lieberman, "How Much Greek in Jewish Palestine," in Alexander Altmann (ed.), *Biblical and Other Studies* (Cambridge: Harvard University Press, 1963), pp. 123–141.

[35]   Harry Wolfson, *Philo: Foundations of Religious Philosophy in Judaism, Christianity and Islam* (Cambridge: Harvard University Press, 1947), vol. 1, p. 92.

[36]   Lieberman, "How Much Greek in Jewish Palestine," p. 130.

[37]   Lieberman, *Greek in Jewish Palestine* (New York, 1942), pp. 1–2.

[38]   Jacob Neusner, *Judaism as a Philosophy: The Method and Message of the Mishnah* (Columbia: University of South Carolina Press, 1991); reissued as *The Method and Message of the Mishnah* (1997).

Greek philosophy.[39] Neusner there suggests that the concrete cases of law, at least sometimes, reflect a "philosophical template," in which diverse subjects yield an orderly system of abstract thought.[40]

It would seem, then, that rabbinic tradition includes or reflects, even if only by congruity (as suggested by Neusner), or by indirect contact by secondary sources (as suggested by Lieberman) some aspects of philosophic thought, despite the absence of philosophic terminology. The challenge for Philo of Alexandria, and then for the Jewish philosophers in the Middle Ages, was to convert what was covert and implicit in rabbinic tradition, into an overt and explicit encounter between Jewish tradition (however understood) and philosophy.

[I.1.p] PHILOSOPHY IN A JEWISH CONTEXT

We have surveyed extreme formalist and essentialist scholarly approaches to defining Jewish philosophy. Other contemporary scholars take a different approach to the problem. This approach shares with the essentialists a rejection of extreme formalism, which is satisfied with mere biographic criteria (the philosopher's Jewish identity), linguistic criteria (Hebrew or other Jewish languages), or motivation, without any consideration for the content of the what is being discussed. The contextual approach they adopt tends more toward formalism in its rejection of the essentialist criteria of content, because one cannot limit Jewish philosophy to philosophy of Judaism, nor demand essential agreement with predefined positions. The criteria of the contextual approach resemble those of the formalists inasmuch as they also determine the Jewishness of the philosophy by external criteria, namely the Jewish context, rather than by the Jewish content, of the philosophy.

Zev Levy, for example, has suggested that it is not whether a philosophical book was written by a Jew, nor by the author's identifying with the Jewish people and its destiny, "but whether the book provides an expression for creativity within the field of the religious and national culture of Judaism over the generations, that determines Jewish philosophy."[41]

Similarly, Isaac Franck, in discussing whether Spinoza can be considered a "Jewish" philosopher (i.e., that Spinoza's philosophy is a Jewish philosophy), suggested three contextual criteria for determining Jewish philosophy:

---

[39]   Jacob Neusner, *The Transformation of Judaism: From Philosophy to Religion* (Champaign: University of Illinois Press, 1992) and *Jerusalem and Athens: The Congruity of Talmudic and Classical Philosophy* (Leiden: Brill, Supplements to the Journal for the Study of Judaism, 1997).

[40]   Jacob Neusner, *Intellectual Templates of the Halakhah* (Lanham: University Press of America, 2006).

[41]   Zev Levy, "Hagut Yehudit — Mah Hi?" in *Kivunim* (20, Fall, 1986), pp. 52–53.

That the philosopher's ideas grew out of the collective experience of the Jewish people;
That the philosopher aimed at a Jewish audience, and sought to advance Jewish thought;
That the philosopher did, in fact, contribute to the advance of Jewish thought.[42]

Franck's first contextual criterion may also be seen as the past dimension of Jewish philosophy—the sources and culture underlying the philosopher's thinking. The second contextual criterion may be called the present dimension of Jewish philosophy—the philosopher's community of dialogue. And the third contextual criterion may be regarded as the future dimension of Jewish philosophy—what impact did a given philosopher have upon subsequent generations of Jews and Jewish philosophers?

The second criterion, the dimension of the present, is the most difficult to determine, because it deals with a philosopher's motives and intentions, which may not be fully known to himself, let alone to us. Moreover, as we saw above in our discussion of motives, a Jewish scientists "Jewish" motive for studying a disease like Tay-Sachs does not necessarily render his biology Jewish.

The first criterion, the dimension of the past, is less problematical and less subjective, and far easier to document. In the case of Spinoza, many (like Guttmann and Sirat) who deny that Spinoza's philosophy qualifies as Jewish philosophy, fully recognize the impact of Jewish philosophy on him, as amply documented in Harry Austryn Wolfson's important study, *The Philosophy of Spinoza*. Guttmann's chapter on Spinoza is accordingly carefully titled, "The influence of Jewish philosophy on the system of Spinoza."

The third criterion, the dimension of the future, is also less problematical and less subjective than the second, because we are once again studying impact and influence (in this case, the philosopher's impact on Jewish philosophy, not the impact of Jewish philosophy on him). This criterion, however, requires the perspective of time, and therefore may not necessarily be immediately applicable to contemporary or very recent thinkers whose impact cannot yet be gauged.

When we take Spinoza as a test case for these contextual criteria, we do not arrive at a clear and unequivocal answer. As already mentioned, the requirements of the first criterion—Jewish sources and influences—are clearly met by Spinoza, who is influenced by philosophers like Rambam even as he rebels against them. Did Spinoza intend to address a Jewish audience and advance Jewish thought (the second criterion)? Many, including Guttmann and Franck, think not, and prefer to place him in the development of European, rather than Jewish philosophy.

---

42   Isaac Franck, "Spinoza's Onslaught on Judaism" in *Judaism*, vol. 28, no. 2 (Spring, 1979), and "Was Spinoza a 'Jewish' Philosopher?" in *Judaism*, vol. 28, no. 3 (Summer, 1979).

According to Guttmann, Spinoza's philosophy was opposed to the Jewish religion, and he did not attempt a harmonization of philosophy and Judaism.

> Separated from any connection to the Jewish religion, his philosophy is no longer directed to believers in Judaism, but to the community of European thinkers... His influence was exclusively beyond the boundaries of the world of Judaism... The historic roots of Spinoza's philosophy... extended far beyond the Jewish sphere.[43]

Guttmann's last statement that Spinoza's roots "extended far beyond the Jewish sphere" is undoubtedly correct. But what Jewish philosopher read, or cited, only Jewish sources? As Shlomo Pines has pointed out in his essay, "The Philosophic Sources of the *Guide of the Perplexed*," what is noteworthy is the fact that Rambam cites by name many Greek and Arabic sources (as Pines clearly documents), but not any of the earlier Jewish philosophers.

As for Guttmann's comment that Spinoza's "influence was exclusively beyond the boundaries of the world of Judaism," that statement is directly contradicted by Guttmann's own important essay, "Mendelssohn's *Jerusalem* and Spinoza's *Theological-Political Treatise*."[44] Spinoza thus clearly fulfills the first criterion (the dimension of the past); he did not, or did not overtly, fulfill the second criterion (the dimension of the present); and he did, at least in some respects, fulfill the third criterion (the dimension of the future).

Was Spinoza, then, a Jewish philosopher in our sense of the term? The essentialist would presumably respond negatively, as did Guttmann. The extreme formalist, who is satisfied with the mere biographical fact of Jewish identity (unless we accept the validity of the Amsterdam community's excommunication of Spinoza), would presumably respond affirmatively. The contextualist could not answer the question as unequivocally as the formalist or essentialist, but probably would respond with a qualified yes, in light of the first and third contextual criteria.

[I.1.q] BROAD AND NARROW SENSES OF JEWISH PHILOSOPHY

Because of the uncertainty of some of the contextual criteria, especially the second and to some extent the third, some scholars, such as Jacob Levinger, distinguish between Jewish philosophy in the narrow sense of the term (what Guttmann and others called "philosophy of Judaism") and

---

43   Guttmann, *Philosophies of Judaism*, pp. 265–266.

44   The English translation of the essay may be found in *Studies in Jewish Thought: An Anthology of German-Jewish Scholarship*, edited by Alfred Jospe (Detroit: Wayne State University Press, 1981), pp. 361–386.

Jewish philosophy in the broad sense of the term (philosophy which has Jewish sources). Citations from Jewish sources endow the philosophy with "an overtly Jewish character."[45] Nevertheless, there are books whose Jewish philosophical character is not overt or obvious. In fact, the more a book is purely philosophical, the less likely it is to cite such non-philosophical Jewish sources as the Bible or Talmud, and therefore the less overt and obvious its Jewish character will be. Yet, we can determine, occasionally after the fact, that a philosophical book is Jewish, despite its lack of overt Jewish character. The outstanding example of this in the Middle Ages is the *Fons Vitae* (*Meqor Hayyim*) by Solomon ibn Gabirol, which lacks any blatant Jewish character or citations. Nevertheless, since it was rediscovered as a Jewish book in the nineteenth century by Solomon Munk (on the basis of Shem Tov ibn Falaquera's Hebrew translation of "Selections" [*Liqqutim*] of the book), the book has been regarded as an outstanding example of Jewish Neoplatonism.

[I.1.r]   JEWISH PHILOSOPHY AS ENCOUNTER

Given the inadequacy of both the formalist and essentialist approaches to defining Jewish philosophy, other scholars have sought to resolve the problem in terms of encounter. Shalom Rosenberg, for example, has written:

> After all the ways in which people have attempted somehow to define Jewish philosophy, there remains one possibility, one which does not regard the Jewishness of a philosophy either in terms of content or in terms of form, but in terms of their encounter. "Jewish philosophy" is nothing other than these encounters of Judaism with philosophy... The result of this encounter... is Jewish philosophy... Any reference to a school of thought is entirely secondary... The very fact that a Jew is confronted by and relates to all the different systems, problems and periods, is what makes the essence of Jewish philosophy. The principal subject of this philosophy is the encounter of Judaism, in the sense of the Torah in all its respects and as it appears to the thinker, with his autonomous philosophic position.[46]

From a historical perspective, we can also describe Jewish philosophy as an encounter, since frequently the philosophizing arose in response to encounters with foreign cultures, whose ideological claims contradicted the traditional claims of Judaism. These challenges often led Jewish thinkers to formulate Jewish-philosophic positions, with the explicit intention of

---

45   Jacob Levinger, in "Pilosofiah Yehudit—Mah Hi? Symposion" in *Hitgalut, Emunah, Tevunah*, edited by Moshe Hallamish and Moshe Schwartz (Ramat Gan, 1976), p. 149.
46   Shalom Rosenberg, in "Pilosofiah Yehudit—Mah Hi? Symposion" in *Hitgalut, Emunah, Tevunah*, edited by Moshe Hallamish and Moshe Schwartz (Ramat Gan, 1976), p. 160.

defending the Torah and representing it rationally. This was the express aim of different Jewish philosophers, going back to Philo of Alexandria, and to the first of the major medieval Jewish philosophers, Sa'adiah Ga'on. Sa'adiah stated that the purpose of his *Kitab Al-Amanat W'al-I'tiqadat* (*Sefer Ha-Emunot Veha-De'ot*; "The Book of Beliefs and Opinions") is twofold: "One, to verify for us in actuality what we know from the prophets of God; second, to respond to whoever challenges us regarding our belief."[47]

Eliezer Schweid accordingly comments about the external stimuli or catalysts of Jewish philosophy:

> We see before us a body of thought which did not grow from within, but is the product of encounters with external cultures, and therefore can be seen as one of the branches of a philosophical tradition, whose relation to any particular religion is merely episodic.[48]

Aviezer Ravitzky has also approached our question in terms of such encounter, and suggests that what is common is the question, not the answer. Jewish philosophy, he concludes,

> is a philosophy which deals with a certain problem (or more precisely, a certain type of problem, namely the confrontation or encounter of the non-philosophic Jewish sources and the non-Jewish philosophic sources...That is, it deals with the problem of the existence of the Jew as a Jew confronted by his universal philosophic knowledge and consciousness...The problem which motivates the rise of Jewish philosophy is the encounter of two traditions, the Jewish tradition and the philosophic tradition.[49]

What we have here is not a return to essentialism, which from the outset limits Jewish philosophy to a philosophy of Judaism or a theology which verifies Judaism (although that was Sa'adiah Ga'on's explicit intention, and was, therefore, one of the reasons that his Jewish version of *Kalam*-theology was philosophically unacceptable to Rambam). Here we are only speaking of the historical stimuli in a given period and set of circumstances which led Jews to study philosophy and to philosophize.

It is the Jewish context which determines what is uniquely Jewish about Jewish philosophy, a context of encounter between philosophy and Judaism, dealing with Jewish and philosophic sources which together formed the existing Jewish tradition. Such encounters continually formed a new Jewish

---

47   *Emunot Ve-De'ot*, Introduction, #6.
48   Eliezer Schweid, *Toledot Ha-Pilosofiah Ha-Yehudit Mi-Rasag 'ad Rambam* (Jerusalem: Academon, 1971), p. 3.
49   Aviezer Ravitzky, "On the Study of Medieval Jewish Philosophy," in *History and Faith: Studies in Jewish Philosophy* (Amsterdam: Gieben, 1996), pp. 4, 7.

synthesis, which in turn became "Jewish tradition" for later generations, who themselves then had to deal with the renewed encounters of their Judaism with philosophy.

What those philosophers shared, therefore, was not one specific challenge, nor one specific response, but the historic context of Jewish philosophy arising to meet ideological challenge—not content, but context; not a shared response, but a shared question; not a common position, but a common quest.

[I.2]   PHILO JUDAEUS OF ALEXANDRIA

From the time it was founded by Alexander the Great in 332 B.C.E., Jews lived in Green city of Alexandria on the northern coast of Egypt. The Jewish community's successful integration in the cultural, political and economic life of the city aroused the resentment of the local Greeks, which occasionally erupted into violence and even warfare. Despite these difficulties, the Jews of Alexandria for many years enjoyed rights similar to those of the city's citizens and also a certain degree of autonomy. Thousands of Jews were killed in the riots of 66 C.E. (when the Great Revolt against Rome broke out in Judea). During the revolt of Jews throughout the Roman empire in 115–117 C.E. many more Jews were killed, and the Alexandrian Jewish community declined. Nevertheless, for many years, the Alexandrian Jewish community developed a Greek-Jewish culture that would have an impact on western civilization last for centuries after the decline of the community, when Jews no longer continued to write in Greek. This impact was notable in two areas: the Bible and philosophy. However, in both cases, since Jews no longer wrote in Greek, it was the Christian Church which preserved their achievements, because the Alexandrian Jewish attempt to bridge the Bible and Greek culture proved vital for the development of Christianity as a Gentile religion, outside of and separate from Judaism.

[I.2.a]   THE SEPTUAGINT

The first translation of the Hebrew Bible was the Greek translation of the Jews of Alexandria, beginning in the third century B.C.E., known as the "Septuagint" ("the seventy"),[50] based on a legend in the "Letter of Aristeas". According

---

50   The Septuagint includes books referred to as the Apocrypha ("hidden" books), also called "the external books." These Jewish books were included in the Septuagint (and later in the Latin "Vulgate," which became the official Bible of the Roman Catholic Church), but were not ultimately regarded as canonical by the Jews and were not included in the Hebrew Bible, nor did most of the original Hebrew books survive.

to that source, the Egyptian ruler Ptolemy II Philadelphus wanted a Greek translation of Jewish sacred writings for the great library in Alexandria, and asked Eleazar, the high priest in Jerusalem, to send him expert translators. Eleazar sent a team of 72 scholars, fluent in both Hebrew and Greek, who then translated the Scriptures into Greek. The Greek translation, in turn, was accepted by the Alexandrian Jewish community, who prohibited making any changes in it. The Babylonian Talmud (Megillah 9a) also records the story; in the talmudic version, the 72 scholars, although isolated from each other, all produced an identical translation. The passage in the Talmud then lists verses where the Septuagint differs from the Hebrew Bible, to avoid anthropomorphisms which might offend Greek intellectual sensibilities, or to avoid political offense to Ptolemy and the Egyptians. Although the Letter of Aristeas and the Talmud refer only to the translation of the Pentateuch, the translation project continued, and the term "Septuagint" is generally applied to the entire project, and not just the five books of the Torah. The Septuagint serves to this day as the "Old Testament" of the Greek Orthodox Church. The Alexandrian-Jewish attempt to bridge the Bible and Greek culture proved of vital importance to the Church, as Christianity grew, outside the confines of the Jewish people, as a Gentile religion. The historic significance of the Septuagint may, therefore, be summarized as follows:

1) For the first time, Jewish Scripture was translated, specifically into the language of intellectuals in the Roman empire. The Bible, which had previously been exclusively Jewish literature, thus became accessible to gentiles.

2) The Greco-Roman intelligentsia now became exposed, directly or indirectly, via the Septuagint, to the ethical monotheism of the Jews. The spread of Christianity among Gentiles was thereby facilitated.

3) Since the Septuagint includes Jewish books, some originally written in Greek, others translated from Hebrew, which did not survive among the Jews, these books would have been lost to history had not the Septuagint been adopted by the Church. It was also the Church that preserved the works of Philo.

4) The Septuagint is based on a Hebrew text which differs in some respects from the Masoretic text that became standard among Jews, and is thus an important link in the history of the biblical text. Moreover, with the exception of the Dead Sea Scrolls, some manuscripts of the Septuagint are older than the earliest surviving Hebrew manuscripts.

5) The Septuagint was the product of Alexandrian-Jewish culture, and in turn, shaped that culture, and paved the way for the attempts of Jews like Philo to bridge Jewish and Greek culture, the Bible and philosophy.

[I.2.b] PHILO: THE ARCHETYPE OF WESTERN RELIGIOUS PHILOSOPHY

Philo Judaeus was born in Alexandria in 20 B.C.E., and died in approximately 50 C.E. Although not much is known about his life, we do know that he participated in the Jewish mission to the emperor Caligula in 40 C.E., to request the removal of statues of the emperor that had been placed in the synagogues of Alexandria. He also made the pilgrimage to the Temple in Jerusalem.

Since following the decline of the Alexandrian community Jews by and large no longer read and wrote their works in Greek, Philo's books (which, as noted above, were preserved by the Church) were not known to later generations of Jews, and the first subsequent Jewish reference to Philo is that of Azariah di Rossi in the sixteenth century, who calls him "Yedidiah" ("yedid" = "philon" = "friend"). In one sense, then, Philo was an exceptional and lone figure, and there is a break in Jewish philosophical literature from the first century until the tenth century C.E., when Jews in a different cultural milieu, Arabic-Islamic culture, resumed philosophical activity. Why, then, is Philo important to subsequent developments in the Middle Ages, some nine centuries after his death?

Philo's innovation was to attempt to discover philosophical truth in Scripture, and thereby to bridge philosophy and revelation. Harry Austryn Wolfson, in his two-volume study, *Philo: Foundations of Religious Philosophy in Judaism, Christianity and Islam* (1942) developed the thesis that Philo was the archetypal religious philosopher for all of western philosophy, whether in Hebrew, Latin or Arabic "garb," because all three cultures faced the same problem that Philo did, how to relate the truths of philosophy and the truths of revelation.[51] In Wolfson's view, Philo is the most important western philosopher after Plato and Aristotle. The Greek philosophers, as pagans, had no concept of revealed truth and authoritative Scripture, and the Bible has no concept of independent rational truth. Philo was the first "synthetic philosopher," because of his attempt to synthesize religious and rational truth. Prior to Philo, there was only the "single belief," either in the divinely revealed truth of Scripture or in the human, rational truth of philosophy. Philo pioneered what Wolfson called the "double belief" in both revelation and reason as true, and therefore as necessitating synthesis.[52]

---

[51]   It is ironic that the Hebrew translation of Wolfson's book, although otherwise complete, misrepresents his thesis by changing the title to "Philo: Foundations of Religious Jewish Philosophy."

[52]   The "double belief" is not to be confused with the "double truth" theory (for example, of the Latin Averroists at the University of Paris in the thirteenth century), that reason and revelation are two entirely autonomous and separate realms of truth, and that something can be true in the one system, while not being true in the other system.

The Philonic "double belief" in revelation and reason, and the attempt to form a "synthetic philosophy" bridging revelation and reason, are common to philosophy in Judaism, Christianity and Islam, and therefore all western religious philosophy in the Middle Ages was "Philonic," despite the fact that Philo was unknown to the Jews and Muslims for most of that period. That Philonic structure, Wolfson maintains, lasted for some seventeen centuries, until it was destroyed by Spinoza, who freed philosophy from its relation (often subservient) to revelation, and thereby paved the way for modern philosophy. In Wolfson's thesis, it was thus a Jew, Philo of Alexandria, who founded the medieval tradition of western religious philosophy by synthesizing reason and revelation, and it was a Jew, Spinoza, who founded modern philosophy by separating reason from revelation.

[I.2.c] PHILOSOPHY AS THE HANDMAIDEN OF REVELATION (SCRIPTURE)

Although both revelation and reason are sources of truth and must be synthesized, for Philo they are not equal. Revelation is superior, and philosophy is revelation's "handmaiden." Philosophy is subservient to revelation, because reason, although divinely implanted in the human being, is limited and fallible. The disagreements among philosophers (as Judah Ha-Levi would also argue forcefully eleven hundred years later) are evidence of reason's fallibility, on such matters as the creation of the world and whether it would last forever; this is why God revealed in Scripture the truth in these questions. The errors of philosophy must, therefore, be corrected in light of revealed Scripture's truths.

Ultimately, however, philosophy and revelation need each other. Philosophy needs revelation to correct its errors. Revealed Scripture, however, needs philosophy to discover and uncover the esoteric truths it teaches, truths which are ultimately identical with the truths of philosophy.

[I.2.d] THE ALLEGORICAL METHOD OF INTERPRETING SCRIPTURE

For Philo, Scripture addresses people in language they are capable of understanding. As a constitution for all Israel, given to the people who had just been liberated from slavery, it could not express the truths in language only the intelligentsia, the philosophers, can understand. Its true intention, accordingly, is often hidden, and cannot always be understood by the simple person who only understands the surface meaning of Scripture. What is required, therefore, is for the intelligent person to know how to read Scripture esoterically, to understand its true meaning, by allegorical interpretation.[53] Philo's works are, therefore, largely written as allegorical commentaries on the Bible or on biblical themes.

Philo was by no means the first to employ the allegorical method. The Greek philosophers had interpreted the traditional Greek myths allegorically, and the rabbis used allegorical interpretation to understand such biblical books as the Song of Songs. According to Rabbi Akiva, "all Scripture is holy, and the Song of Songs is the holy of holies."[54] Therefore, rather than reading it literally as a dialogue between human lovers, the Midrash Rabba[55] understands the male lover as symbolizing God, the female lover as symbolizing the people of Israel, and the "kisses of his mouth" (Song of Songs 1:2) as the commandments God gave to Israel. (In Christian interpretation the book was similarly interpreted as an allegory of the love of Christ for the Church). Philo's innovation, then, was not philosophical allegorization, nor allegorization of Scripture, but the application of philosophic allegorization to Scripture, a method of reading their respective Scriptures that was adopted by later philosophers (without knowing of its origin in Philo) in Judaism, Christianity and Islam.

Philo was prescient in realizing the inherent danger of the allegorical method. Although he sincerely believed that the allegorical method would uncover the true, esoteric meaning of Scripture, which is identical with philosophic truth, he was emphatic that the esoteric meaning cannot replace the literal, surface meaning (*peshat*), because the observance of the Torah's commandments (*mizvot*) depends on the *peshat*. However we may interpret those commandments' spiritual meaning figuratively, we are still obligated to observe them literally. He explains, for example, that although the Sabbath teaches us about the power of the uncreated God, and that creatures are entitled to rest, it does not follow that we may simply focus on the spiritual truth and neglect the actual observance of the Sabbath laws, such as the laws prohibiting lighting fire, carrying, or conducting business.[56]

As such, Philo anticipated two major controversies which became pronounced in the Middle Ages. Within Judaism, in the controversy over philosophy, in the century after Rambam, the anti-rationalists frequently accused the philosophers of allegorizing the Torah, and therefore of ignoring the commandments or being lax in their observance, a charge rigorously denied by the philosophers. Externally, allegorization also played a role in the Jewish-Christian debate in the Middle Ages, as Christians accused the Jews

---

53   "Allegory" comes from the Greek "allos" (other) and "agorein" (to speak publicly), namely to speak in another way from the way it sounds, to convey a different meaning.
54   Mishnah Yadayim 3:5.
55   Midrash Rabba on Song of Songs, also called "Midrash Ḥazita".
56   Philo, *On the Migration of Abraham* 16:89–90, cited in Nahum Glatzer (ed.), *The Essential Philo* (New York: Schocken Books, 1971), pp. 158–160.

of understanding only the "carnal," i.e., physical, literal level of Scripture, and failing to appreciate its true "spiritual" meaning (for example, the true meaning of circumcision is the spiritual "circumcision of the heart" and not the physical operation), and as Jews (like Abraham ibn Ezra, in his Introduction to the Torah) accused the Christians of taking liberties with the text and misunderstanding it by consistently reading it allegorically, even when there was no rational need to do so. Philo, in short, anticipated these controversies by insisting that the allegorical meaning must supplement, but not supplant, the *peshat*; that the spiritual reading enhances, but does not replace, the literal observance of the *mizvot*. In these ways Philo proved again to be an archetype, albeit an unknown one, for those who came after him.

[I.3] THE RISE OF JEWISH PHILOSOPHY IN THE MIDDLE AGES

Jewish philosophy, as we have seen, often arose in response to encounters with surrounding majority cultures. This phenomenon can be discerned in three different periods, when Jewish intellectuals engaged in dialogue with their non-Jewish peers. The first of these periods was towards the end of the Second Temple period, in Philo's Alexandria. That pioneering encounter, although it provided an unconscious and unknown archetype for subsequent developments in Judaism, Christianity and Islam, did not give rise to a continuous and conscious tradition of Jewish philosophizing, such as we find in the second and third periods, because of the disappearance of Greek-Jewish culture following the decline of the Alexandrian Jewish community in the second century C.E. The second period of Jewish philosophy was in the early and late Middle Ages, initially in Islamic countries (the subject of this book), when the works of ancient Greek philosophy became available in Arabic translation, and then later in Christian Europe. The third period, beginning in the seventeenth, and especially eighteenth century, was the still ongoing encounter of Jews with modern philosophy in Europe.

In all three periods, Jewish philosophers attempted to create new syntheses of philosophy as they knew it and their Jewish culture. Philo identified the truth of the Torah with Platonic philosophy. In the Middle Ages, Jews created syntheses with the diverse Arabic schools of thought, such as the Kalam, Neoplatonism and Aristotelianism, which were prevalent in intellectual circles in Islamic countries. In modern times, Jews attempted (and continue to attempt) to bridge Judaism in various forms with diverse modern philosophies, including political, social and economic thought (such as socialism).

Our focus is on the formative period of medieval Jewish philosophy, from its beginnings with Sa'adiah Ga'on to its apex in Maimonides. This period constitutes a discrete and unique cultural phenomenon, in which Jews living in Islamic countries and writing in Arabic were the first to develop a conscious and continuous tradition of Jewish philosophy. Subsequent Jewish philosophy generally was developed in a Christian-European cultural context, and was written in Hebrew or (in more recent centuries) in European languages. In the later Middle Ages and Renaissance, and even in modern times, much of Jewish philosophy was shaped by or in reaction to the thought of Maimonides, and also reflected specific issues arising in the Jewish-Christian encounter.

[I.3.a]   THE INTERNAL CHALLENGE: KARAISM

The rapid rise and spread of Islam in the seventh century C.E. also gave rise to ideological and intellectual developments among the Jews exposed to the new religious civilization. Many of those developments were passing phenomena, which did not leave a lasting impression on Jewish history and culture. Karaism, however, had a great impact for much of the Middle Ages, and is still an active, although small minority movement, in Judaism.[57] The Karaite movement, which arose in Babylonia in the middle of the eighth century C.E., rapidly spread throughout the Jewish world, and proved particularly appealing in intellectual circles. It posed a serious ideological challenge to rabbinic Judaism, based on the Talmud, because it undermined the traditional rabbinic belief that there are two Torahs of equally divine authority, the written Torah and the oral Torah (which came to be written down as the Talmud and Midrash). Rabbinic Judaism relates to Scripture (the written Torah) through the lenses of the talmudic traditions of the oral Torah, and many common rabbinic practices—such as lighting candles on the eve of the Sabbath and festivals, and such festivals as Ḥanukkah—are rabbinic, not biblical, in origin and authority. The Karaites (or "Benei Miqra," children of the Bible) opposed this rabbinic belief in the oral Torah, as the equal of the written Torah and through which the written Torah was filtered. The Karaites, by contrast, followed the motto attributed to 'Anan ben David, the founder of Karaism, "Search well in the Torah, and do not rely on my opinion." In other words, each Jew should search for the truth in the Torah, and should not rely upon fixed, traditional interpretations of others (even those of 'Anan himself).[58]

Karaite intellectuals found the anthropomorphisms of the Talmud offensive. Rejecting the Talmud, however, didn't really solve the problem of the

---

[57]   For a clear survey, see Daniel J. Lasker, "Rabbanism and Karaism: The Contest for Supremacy" in *Great Schisms in Jewish History*, edited by Raphael Jospe and Stanley Wagner (New York/Hoboken: Ktav, 1981), pp. 47–72.

[58]   There is a clear parallel between this Jewish view and the Protestant Christian notion of "sola Scriptura" in the sixteenth century Reformation.

Bible, in which the Karaites believed, and which contains many anthropo-morphic passages which are not less problematical. The differences of approach often focused on specific practices based on diverse understandings of the biblical text. Unlike the rejection of the Talmud's authority in some radical Reform ideology in nineteenth century Germany and America, Karaite practice was often stricter and more rigorous than rabbinic practice. For example, the Torah's commandment "do not to kindle fire in your habitations on the Sabbath day" (Exodus 35:3) was interpreted strictly by the Karaites as a prohibition of having any burning fire in the Jewish home on the Sabbath (and, accordingly, the prohibition of having light or eating hot food), whereas the rabbinic interpretation was more liberal and flexible: one may not kindle or extinguish fire on the Sabbath, but a pre-lit fire, kindled before the Sabbath, may continue to provide light and heat, and to keep pre-cooked food warm on the Sabbath. Another example is the differing interpretation of the "lex talionis," the law of retaliation in Exodus 21:23–25, "an eye for an eye," which the Karaites, like the ancient Sadducees, interpreted literally as physical retaliation, and which rabbinic Jews, like the ancient Pharisees, understood to mean financial compensation for the injury, i.e., the worth of the eye. Given the diametrically opposed concepts of halakhic authority, the only neutral, common language for discussion was that of philosophy. So when Abraham ibn Ezra's commentary on the law of retaliation cites a dispute between Sa'adiah Ga'on and a Karaite named Ben Zuta (as we shall see), the rabbinic argument culminates with the idea that the literalist Karaite interpretation is rationally impossible: "reason cannot tolerate it (*ein ha-da'at sovelet*)."

[I.3.b]   EXTERNAL CHALLENGES: PHILOSOPHY, ISLAM AND CHRISTIANITY

Religion was a paramount force in the Middle Ages. Christianity, and especially Islam, were relatively new religions, controlling huge territories and competing for the hearts of believers. The Jews were a barely tolerated minority in both areas, and often faced critical challenges from both majority religions. Under these conditions, philosophy proved to be a double-edged sword. On the one hand, philosophical, or at least rationalist, arguments were employed to buttress these inter-religious challenges, but on the other hand, all the religions were challenged by general philosophical arguments undermining their respective beliefs in a personal God, revelation and prophecy. Nevertheless, the mutually exclusive claims of the religions forced them to resort to a neutral, common language of discourse, and that language was philosophical, since philosophical arguments could be used to reinforce one's own beliefs, or to undermine the beliefs of others.

Jews, then, as an oppressed minority, needed to resort to philosophy to deal with these internal and external intellectual challenges. They now also had the opportunity to resort to philosophy, as they became exposed to the rise of Arabic philosophy in Islamic countries.

[I.3.c]   THE RISE OF PHILOSOPHY IN THE WORLD OF ISLAM

Greek philosophy declined after the closure of the Academy in Athens (which had been founded by Plato, circa 287 B.C.E.) by the emperor Justinian in 529 C.E. In Justinian's view, pagan philosophy had no place in the Christian Roman empire. But at about the same time, Syrian Christians of the Nestorian Church began translating into Syriac (a dialect of Aramaic) the Greek New Testament and other Greek literature, including medical, scientific and philosophical works. Following the Muslim conquest of much of the Middle East and Mediterranean basin, Arabic replaced many of the indigenous languages. The Syrian Christian translators were then requested by the Muslim rulers to translate these Greek works into Arabic (sometimes indirectly via the Syriac versions, and at other times directly). The Syrian Christians thus served as the initial cultural bridge between ancient Greece and Islamic civilization. One of the most important Syrian Christian translators was Ḥunayn ibn Isḥaq (810–873 C.E.) in Baghdad, who also was the author of a collection of ethical sayings, *Adab Al-Falasifa* ("The Aphorisms of the Philosophers"), which has survived in the Hebrew translation, *Musarei Ha-Pilosofim* by Judah Al-Ḥarizi. Ḥunayn ibn Isḥaq's translations shaped an Arabic philosophical, scientific and medical vocabulary and technical terminology. Ḥunayn's son, Isḥaq ibn Ḥunayn, (d. 910 C.E. in Baghdad), who was a physician, also engaged in extensive translations into Arabic, including works of Aristotle.

These Arabic translations were supported and encouraged by a center for scientific research and translation, *Beit Al-Ḥikmah* ("The House of Wisdom"), which was established in Baghdad by the Abbasid Caliph Al-Ma'mun in 830 C.E., and housed a major scientific library. The new availability in Arabic of the wisdom of ancient Greece facilitated the rapid rise and spread of philosophical culture in the Islamic world, which in turn made possible the rise of medieval Jewish philosophy, some nine centuries after the death of Philo.

Under Islam, Jews (and Christians), were recognized legally as *ahl al-kitab*, "people of the book," and had an inferior but tolerated and "protected" (*dhimmi*) status, which required them to pay the *jizya* tax but also enabled them to participate to a fair degree in the cultural as well as economic life of the countries in which they lived. The Jews spoke, read and wrote Arabic, and were thus able to benefit from the development of Arabic philosophical, scientific and medical literature. All this is in sharp contrast with the Jews of Christian Europe. The Jews were the only non-Christians remaining in Europe, and their continued life as Jews directly contradicted the Christian claim to have replaced the Jewish people as "verus Israel" ("the true Israel). Jews generally did not know Latin, and were excluded from the universities, as well as from the monastic centers of learning. The Jews of Christian Europe were, therefore, not exposed to the Arabic philosophical and scientific culture in which the Jews of Islamic countries participated, and had no access to the Arabic or Judeo-Arabic works of Jewish philosophy until Hebrew translations reached them. In the century after Rambam (as we shall see in Chapter Eleven), this led to a controversy over philosophy and to anti-Maimonidean agitation, when these Jews, who had no prior exposure to philosophy, first came into contact with translations and original works of philosophy in Hebrew.

For the Jews in Islamic countries, however, the intervening centuries led to a consolidation of Jewish philosophy as an integral and vital part of Jewish culture. At the beginning of the period we are studying, Sa'adiah Ga'on's *Book of Beliefs and Opinions* had to show Jews who were loyal to religious tradition why philosophy is important and accords with the religious truth in which they believed. By the end of the period we are studying, Rambam's *Guide of the Perplexed* had the opposite problem — to show Jews thoroughly imbued with philosophy why the Torah accords with the philosophy in which they believed. In other words, whereas Sa'adiah Ga'on had to justify philosophy in terms of the Torah, Rambam had to justify the Torah in terms of philosophy.

Chapter Two

SA'ADIAH GA'ON
AND THE KALAM

[II.1] SA'ADIAH GA'ON AND THE KALAM

The new availability of philosophical, scientific and medical works in Arabic served as a catalyst for the development of the Kalam, Islamic theology. The name Kalam means "word" or "speech," and those who engaged in Kalam were called Mutakallimun ("speakers"). The notion of speech or words plays a special role in theology, since for believers, the sacred books of revelation record the word of God. Moreover, in the first chapter of Genesis, God created the world by means of the word: "And God said, 'Let there be light' and there was light" (Genesis 1:3).

The Greek term *logos* (literally: word) also took on special meaning in philosophical and religious discourse. In Plato, the *logos* is the form of forms, the highest truth and reality. For Philo, the *logos* (plural: *logoi*) did not merely denote God's revealed word and his creative power, but also a being intermediating between God as the creator and the created, material world. Philo also identifies the *logoi* with the angels. In the New Testament, the term *logos* becomes identified with Jesus, who essentially replaces the Torah as the pre-existing "word of God" and thus ultimately is with God: "In the beginning was the word (*logos*), and the word was with God, and the word was God" (John 1:1).

Speech also became, in medieval Arabic and Hebrew philosophical literature, a synonym for reason, and the term "speakers," which can signify the Mutallimun-theologians, can also simply denote human beings. Homo sapiens is differentiated from the animals by virtue of reason, of which speech (also a uniquely human faculty, at least in classical and medieval thought) is the external expression. So the Arabic term *natiq*, and the Hebrew term *devari*, can refer to speech or to reason, and the Arabic *'ilm al-natiq* means the science of logic (also derived from *logos*), i.e., the correct way of thinking.

The origin of the Kalam is described in a book about diverse religious and philosophical schools, *Kitab Al-Milal W'al-Nihal* ("The Book of Religious Communities and Sects") by the Muslim historian Muḥammad Al-Shahrastani (circa 1076–1153 C.E.). According to Al-Shahrastani, the name "Kalam" comes either from "the word of God" or from "logic," since "word" and "logic" are synonymous. He further notes that the Mu'tazilah[1] Mutakallimun who had studied the works of the Greek philosophers translated into Arabic in the time of Al-Ma'mun (the founder of *Beit Al-Ḥikmah* in Baghdad), combined the methods of theology with the methods of philosophy.[2]

According to the *Muqaddimah* ("Introduction" to history) by the Arab historian 'Abd Al-Raḥman Ibn Khaldun (Tunis, 1332–1406), in the gene-rations following the death of the prophet Muḥammad, controversies arose regarding the correct interpretation of the Qur'an, both on practical and theoretical matters. In order to resolve differences of interpretation and questions of *fiqh* (Islamic jurisprudence), scholars had to rely not only on the plain, surface meaning of the Qur'an, but also on a new principle, *qiyas* (logical analogy or deduction), by which a text or situation could be understood by analogy to another text or situation, with which it had something in common. Like Al-Shahrastani, Ibn Khaldun regarded philosophy as loaning its rational methods of deduction to the religious disciplines.[3] *Qiyas* was then adopted not only in the practical areas of jurisprudence (*fiqh*) but also in the theoretical areas of theology (*kalam*).

[II.1.a]   KALAM: PHILOSOPHY OR THEOLOGY?

There is no absolute and clear boundary between philosophy and theology. In principle, philosophy was understood in the Middle Ages to be an open system of scientific inquiry, unlimited by religious presuppositions. As such, it is the integrity of the method which validates the conclusion. The philosophical method could, therefore, lead to conclusions contrary to conventional religious belief. Conversely, the Kalam, as theology, was regarded by various Muslim and Jewish philosophers as a closed system, commited to and bound by previously accepted religious beliefs. Reason could explain, clarify, justify and verify those beliefs, but it was subordinate to them and could not contradict them. The Kalam could, therefore, adopt philosophic arguments and methods,

---

[1]   On the Mu'tazilah, see below.

[2]   Al-Shahrastani, *Kitab Al-Milal W'al-Niḥal*, fourth introduction.

[3]   Ibn Khaldun's *The Muqaddimah: An Introduction to History* was translated into English by Franz Rosenthal (Princeton: Bollingen Series, 1958); abridged edition edited by N.J. Dawood (Princeton: Bollingen Series, 1969). The discussion may be found in the abridged edition, Chapter 6, on "The Various Kinds of Sciences—The Methods of Instruction." For example, Ibn Khaldun states there: "In time, the science of logic spread in Islam...(Scholars) studied the basic premises the earlier theologians had established. They refuted most of them with the help of arguments leading them to (a different opinion). Many of these were derived from philosophical discussions of physics and metaphysics" (p. 352).

but only within the framework of the religious truths regarded as given or divinely revealed, and therefore accepted *a priori.*

Whereas Al-Shahrastani and Ibn Khaldun attributed the rise of Kalam to internal Islamic needs, namely the need for *qiyas* to resolve practical problems of jurisprudence and theoretical problems of theology, the philosopher Abu Naṣr Al-Farabi[4] attributed its rise to the external stimulus of inter-religious polemic. In his *Iḥsa Al-'Ulum* ("The Enumeration of the Sciences"), Al-Farabi described the Kalam as rationally justifying and verifying religious beliefs and practices, and as nullifying conflicting claims, thereby strengthening religious belief and endowing it with rational certainty. Al-Shahrastani and Ibn Khaldun regarded jurisprudence and theology as sharing a common rational method, which was applied respectively to law and to belief. For Al-Farabi, however, they do not share a common method. Jurisprudence accepts beliefs and practices prescribed in Scripture, and develops their details, without questioning why they are true or given. The question "why," to justify and verify beliefs and practices, belongs to theology — Kalam.

In the Hebrew paraphrase of Al-Farabi's *Iḥsa Al-'Ulum* in *Reshit Ḥokhmah,*"The Beginning of Wisdom") by the thirteenth-century Spanish Jewish philosopher Shem Tov ibn Falaquera,[5] each nation has its distinctive religious beliefs and practices, and the science of jurisprudence (*fiqh*) enables the person to develop specific and detailed measures for what Scripture commands generally. The science of theology (*kalam*) enables a person

> to defend the beliefs and defined actions established by the founder of that religion, and to refute those who oppose it. This science is divided into two sections: one section concerning beliefs and the other section concerning actions, but differently from the sciences of jurisprudence. A judge takes these accepted beliefs and actions as they were established by the founder of the religion, and makes them roots to develop whatever is derivative from them. The theologian defends those things which the judge makes into roots, without making them roots for other things.[6]

The judge, then, relies on tradition, which is given and not questioned, whereas the theologian examines and verifies religious belief based on his understanding of reality.[7] The method of the theologians is not, however, truly scientific. For Ibn Khaldun, although the Kalam borrows methods from philosophy, theology cannot be confused with true philosophy, because philosophy examines something unknown in order to arrive at knowledge,

---

4   On Al-Farabi, see Chapter One (I.1.a), above.
5   On Falaquera, see Chapter One (I.1.a), above.
6   Falaquera, *Reshit Ḥokhmah*, p. 59.
7   Falaquera, *Moreh Ha-Moreh*, p. 152.

whereas the Kalam reverses the order, by beginning with something known—the religious law as revealed to the prophet by God—which transcends reason and cannot be analyzed rationally. The original or pure Kalam used rational arguments based on *qiyas* to counter the claims of the heretics, using the only common language possible. That original Kalam, in Ibn Khaldun's view, should not be confused with more recent Kalam, which adopted philosophical physics and metaphysics. Such a mixture of theology and philosophy is illegitimate, because it is neither true theology (based on known revelation) nor true philosophy (based on rational analysis of the unknown).[8]

Nevertheless, it is precisely such philosophical Kalam (which Ibn Khaldun opposed) that is of importance to our study of the influence, or to use Wolfson's term, the "repercussions," of the Kalam in Jewish philosophy, especially in the thought of Sa'adiah Ga'on. First, however, we need to survey some of the basic principles of the Kalam, as described by Judah Ha-Levi (both positively and negatively) and by Rambam (who opposed the Kalam in principle, but adopted some of their arguments).

[II.1.b] THE PRINCIPLES OF THE KALAM ACCORDING TO JUDAH HA-LEVI

Judah Ha-Levi's description of the Kalam (in *Kuzari* 5:15–18) is somewhat ambivalent. On the one had, the Kalam may be necessary to combat heretical ideas, as the rabbis said, "Know what to respond to a heretic."[9] On the other hand, the truly religious individual, secure in his belief, does not need the Kalam. An insecure person may be helped by the Kalam's arguments, but he may also be harmed by them, since the same rational arguments which may persuade one person of religious truth may lead another person to doubt the truth.

Ha-Levi then summarized in ten brief "chapters" the principles of the Kalam, many of which are similar to points made by Sa'adiah Ga'on. The first three principles concern the world, and the remaining seven concern God. They may be epitomized as follows:
1) Time has a beginning, because infinite time is impossible.
2) Therefore, the world has a beginning, i.e., is created.
3) The creation of the world requires an agent.
4) Whereas the world is created, God is eternal, meaning that there is no agent prior to him in time which caused his existence.

---

8   These arguments may be found in Ibn Khaldun's *Muqaddimah*, Part 6, ch. 21.
9   Avot 2:19. The word used there is "Apiqoros" (from Epicurus), a term used by the rabbis in a generic sense to refer to a person who denies Jewish belief and religious practice.

5) Just as God has no beginning, he has no end, because just as there is no cause of his existence, so there is no cause which would end his existence.

6) God is not a body, because there are no bodies without changing accidents. God's existence is not accidental, i.e., dependent upon some external cause.

7) God is omniscient.

8) God is alive; that is to say, something which is not alive cannot be conceived of as possessing knowledge and power.

9) God has will.

10) However, God's will functions in accordance with his wisdom. God's attributes—life, knowledge and power—are inseparable in his being.

[II.1.c]　THE PRINCIPLES OF THE KALAM ACCORDING TO RAMBAM

In the final chapters of Part I of his *Guide of the Perplexed* (I:71–76), Rambam surveyed in some detail the principles of the Kalam. Despite his general opposition in principle to the Kalam on methodological grounds, Rambam did not hesitate to adopt specific points and arguments made by the Mutakallimun. For example, in the *Guide of the Perplexed* II:1, Rambam cites a proof of the unity of God which he calls "demonstrative" (i.e., scientifically and philosophically valid) which is identical with the second Kalam proof of unity in the *Guide of the Perplexed* I:75, which he also calls "a demonstrative, philosophical" proof despite its being a Kalam proof.

Rambam's presentation of the Kalam as a whole need not concern us, but of particular importance is his discussion in *Guide of the Perplexed* I:73 of twelve "general propositions" (or "principles" or "premises") of the Mutakallimun required to prove the creation of the world, and God's existence, unity and incorporeality. These may be summarized as follows:

1) Atoms. The world consists of atoms, all of which are identical, and do not possess quantity.

2) The vacuum. The atoms are separated by a vacuum, which enables them to move.

3) Instants. Time, like space, is divided into indivisible units.

4) Substance. Substance cannot exist without accidents.

5) Accidents. Atoms cannot exist without accidents, which subsist in the atoms.

6) Accidents by themselves cannot endure in time, i.e., from moment to moment. Their endurance thus requires continual creation. Therefore there is no causality.

7) Privations. Privations, such as rest (which is the privation of motion), are accidental or "acquired" properties. As such privations are not necessary, and require an agent (namely, God's will).

8) All that exists is either substance or accidents; the natural form is an accident.

9) Accidents cannot be borne by other accidents, but only by substance.

10) Whatever can be imagined can be, for everything is possible, regardless of whether it actually exists.

11) Infinity. The infinite is impossible, whether actual, potential or accidental.

12) The senses. The senses are unreliable and often err.

The atomic theory of the Kalam follows from the Islamic emphasis on God's omnipotence. If God is omnipotent, that is to say, not only that God is all-powerful but that all power belongs to God, then there is no power other than God's. Accordingly, there can be no laws of nature, nor any natural causality (all of which imply power independent of God). Created reality, down to the atomic level, thus cannot have any independent power of its own, including the power to endure from moment to moment. Rather, its continued existence from moment to moment depends, at every instant, upon the intervention of the divine will to sustain it. This notion, that God must continually and directly intervene at every instant, or every "occasion," is known as "occasionalism." For example, there is no causal connection between an archer shooting an arrow and the arrow hitting the target, between the position of the arrow at one moment and its position in another moment. Without God's direct intervention, the arrow would not exist from one moment to the next; it would not exist in one location or another; it would not be in motion; and it would not hit the target. In short, the occasionalism of the Kalam derives from the Islamic emphasis on the absolute and exclusive omnipotence of God.

Rambam, who was convinced that Aristotle's terrestrial physics had been conclusively demonstrated (although our knowledge of the heavens is extremely limited, so what Aristotle maintained concerning the heavens lacks such certainty),[10] could not possibly agree with the Kalam's atomism, nor, more importantly, with its occasionalist denial of natural causality. As Rambam summarized it: "The general principle is that one cannot ever say that this is the cause of that."[11]

In Rambam's view, what led the Mutakallimun astray, however, was their flawed method: they accepted false premises, which have no scientific validity and have been disproven, because those premises accord with their preconceived religious beliefs. Instead of adjusting their opinions to reality, they attempted

---

[10]   *Guide of the Perplexed* II:24.
[11]   *Guide of the Perplexed* I:73.

to force reality to adjust to their preconceptions.[12] There method is, therefore, unscientific and closed, even if their specific conclusions or arguments were sometimes correct, eg., their arguments for the unity of God.

[II.1.d] THE MU'TAZILAH AND THE ASH'ARIYYA

In Rambam's view, the Kalam arose because of the need to support the principles of Islam against the contrary views of the Greek philosophers and the Syrian Christians, views to which the Muslim community became exposed with the victorious Arab conquest of the Middle East.

> Since the opinions of the philosophers were widespread among those communities in which philosophy had arisen, and there arose kings who defended religion, the sages of those generations among the Greeks and Syrians saw that these arguments would clearly and greatly contradict those philosophic opinions. Thus the Kalam arose among them. They began to establish premises useful for them in [supporting] their belief and in refuting those opinions contradicting the foundations of their law ... They selected from the opinions of the first philosophers whatever suited the one who chose it, although the later philosophers had already demonstrated that it is false, such as [the existence of] atoms and the vacuum ... The first Mutakallimun among the Greek converts to Christianity and among the Muslims did not conform their premises to what can be seen to exist, but rather how existence should be in order to provide a proof for the correctness of [their] opinion, or at least should not contradict it.[13]

Rambam then suggests that Jewish thinkers adopted many of the views of the Mu'tazilah school of Kalam, rather than of the Ash'ariyya school, because the Mu'tazilah developed first and these Jews regarded the Mu'tazilah opinions as having been conclusively demonstrated. The Mu'tazilah school of Kalam was founded in Abassid Baghdad in the early eighth century C.E. by Waṣil bin 'Ata (d. 748 C.E.). The name Mu'tazilah means "separatists," presumably reflecting the view among their opponents that these rationalist theologians were not truly orthodox Muslims. In the early Islamic controversy regarding the status of sinners, Waṣil bin 'Ata disagreed with both prevailing views, namely that a believer may sin, but that the sin does not disqualify his true belief, versus the view a person who sins is *ipso facto* a heretic. In his compromise view, which "separated" him from both conventional views, the sinner has an intermediate status, between that of a believer or a heretic. The Mu'tazilah Mutakallimun referred to themselves as *aṣhab al-'adl w'al-tawḥid*, "the men of justice and unity," because of their rationalist emphasis on the absolute justice and unity of God.

---

12 *Guide of the Perplexed* I:71.
13 *Guide of the Perplexed* I:71.

The Muʻtazilah Kalam remained the official theology of the Abassids for approximately a century and a half (c. 750–900 C.E.), until it was replaced by the Ashʻariyya Kalam, which became dominant for a millennium (10th — 19th centuries C.E.). This school of Kalam took its name from its founder, Abu Al-Ḥasan ʻAli Al-Ashʻari (Iraq, 873–935 C.E.), and rejected Muʻtazilah rationalism in favor of orthodox Islamic doctrine. Nevertheless, both movements employed rationalist arguments to support traditional belief, unlike other Islamic movements which rejected reason out of hand. Among the points of disagreement between the Muʻtazilah and Ashʻariyya schools of Kalam were the eternity of God and the status of the Qurʼan; God's absolute unity and the divine attributes; and human free will.

Regarding the eternity of God and the status of the Qurʼan, the Muʻtazilah insisted that only God is eternal; nothing else can be eternal, not even the Qurʼan, and to attribute eternity to anything else is to undermine not only God's absolute eternity but also his absolute unity (since there would then be more than one eternal being). The Qurʼan pre-existed the world (a view similar to the rabbinic notion that the Torah pre-existed the world and was the divine blueprint for creating the world), but it was created and is not eternal. The Ashʻariyya, on the other hand, insisted that the Qurʼan, as the word of God, must be eternal, because to affirm that the word of God came into being is to imply change in God's word and thus in God himself.

Regarding God's unity and the divine attributes, the Muʻtazilah maintained that the absolute unity of God precludes affirming the divine attributes as actual and eternal, in other words as real beings added to the divine essence. The Ashʻariyya affirmed the divine attributes as real and as identical with the divine essence, and thus as eternal.

Regarding human free will, in the Muʻtazilah view, the absolute justice of God necessitates human free will and the ability (or power) to act in accordance with the will. The belief that everything is predetermined by divine decree, and that humans have no free will nor any independent power to act in accordance with their will, impugns God's absolute justice. God endowed humans with the rational faculty to discern good and evil, and the ability to act accordingly. That is why God gave people commandments and prohibitions, which they are free to choose to obey or disobey, and for which they, therefore, justly deserve to be rewarded and punished. Conversely, the Ashʻariyya regarded human free will and ability to act as they will to be a violation of divine omnipotence and omniscience, and therefore affirmed predetermination.

The two schools of Kalam thus were in basic agreement in their atomism and occasionalism, in other words, in their cosmology. As presented by Rambam, where they differed was in the religious implications of those theories for their understanding of the human situation. The occasionalist determinism of the Ashʻariyya derives from the notion that there can be no power outside of God;

humans, therefore, have no free will nor the ability to act independently. In the absence of any causality, there can also be no causal connection between what a person does and the consequences of his or her actions, and any such connection must be attributable only to direct divine intervention. For the Mu'tazilah, such determinism is incompatible with an equally important theological principle, God's justice. God is also ultimately responsible, therefore, but in a different way, because it was God who endowed humans with at least a degree of free will and the power to act in accordance with their will. Both schools, then, shared a common method—they resorted to rationalist proofs of core theological doctrines, such as creation and the existence, unity and incorporeality of God. They differed regarding religious doctrines, and the relative emphasis they placed respectively on divine unity or attributes; divine justice or omnipotence; eternity only of God or also of the Qur'an.

Rambam, as we saw, attributed the greater influence among Jews of the Mu'tazilah school of Kalam to the fact that it developed first. Without denying the chronological factor, the fact is that Jews (including Rambam himself) were familiar with the Ash'ariyya, and could easily have adopted Ash'ariyya doctrines had they been so inclined. The greater Jewish responsiveness to Mu'tazilah ideas may also reflect its more pronounced rationalist character, and the fact that there is a far greater emphasis in Jewish literature on free will and human responsibility than there is on the kind of Islamic determinism underlying much of Ash'ariyya doctrine. Harry Austryn Wolfson (whose theories regarding Philo we discussed in Chapter 1) carefully spoke, therefore, not of Kalam "influence" on Jews, but on "repercussions of the Kalam in Jewish philosophy."[14] By this distinction Wolfson meant to emphasize that cultural and ideological influence cannot be entirely one-way, and that there could be no such influence if there were not an already existing tendency and receptivity to such ideas in the borrowing culture.

[II.2]   SA'ADIAH GA'ON: LIFE AND WORKS

Sa'adiah Ga'on was not the first medieval Jewish philosopher. He corresponded with an older colleague, Isaac Israeli, a physician and Neoplatonic philosopher, whom we shall discuss in Chapter 3. Although considerably younger than Israeli, Sa'adiah is often considered the pioneer of Jewish philosophy in the Middle Ages for two reasons. First, his approach was similar to that of the

---

14   Wolfson's two great studies of the Kalam were published posthumously: *The Philosophy of the Kalam* (Cambridge: Harvard University Press, 1976) and *Repercussions of the Kalam in Jewish Philosophy* (Cambridge: Harvard University Press, 1979).

Mu'tazilah Kalam, and so he represents the beginning of Jewish rationalism. Second, Sa'adiah exerted a tremendous influence, whether direct or indirect, on subsequent Jewish thought. Even Rambam, who as we have seen strongly opposed the Kalam, had a high personal regard for Sa'adiah. In his "Letter to Yemen" Rambam wrote that

> we evaluate Rabbi Sa'adiah positively... because in his generation there were many corrupt opinions, and the divine Torah would have been lost without him. He revealed what is hidden in the Torah, and strengthened what had become weakened... Everything he did was for the sake of heaven.

Sa'adiah was born in Fayum, Egypt in 882 C.E. Later he moved to the Land of Israel, and then to Syria. In 922 C.E. a controversy broke out between Aharon ben Me'ir, the head of the *yeshivah* (talmudic academy) in Jerusalem, and the Babylonian rabbis, concerning conflicting claims to the authority to determine the calendar. Sa'adiah, who was in Aleppo, Syria at the time, successfully supported the claims of the Babylonian rabbis and the Exilarch,[15] David ben Zakkai. That same year Sa'adiah migrated to Babylonia, and in 928 C.E. David ben Zakkai appointed him "Ga'on," namely the head of the *yeshivah* and spiritual leader of the Jewish community in Sura. Following disputes with the Exilarch, Sa'adiah was deposed as Ga'on, but in 937 C.E. he was reinstated and served as Ga'on until his death in 942 C.E. He was particularly renowned for his active opposition to Karaism, based in part on rationalist grounds: "Reason cannot tolerate this."[16]

A prolific writer, Sa'adiah produced books dealing with *halakhah* and liturgy. He published one of the first complete prayer books in Jewish history, including not only the Hebrew text of the prayers but an Arabic commentary and *piyyutim*, liturgical poems he composed himself. He also published a Hebrew dictionary for poetry (*Sefer Ha-Agron*) and a dictionary of seventy (later expanded to ninety) *hapax legomena*, terms which appear only once in the Bible (and whose meaning is accordingly often obscure). One of his major works was the *Tafsir*, an Arabic translation and commentary to the Torah.

In 931 C.E. Sa'adiah also wrote an Arabic commentary to the *Sefer Yeẓirah* ("The Book of Creation" or "The Book of Formation"), a mystical text attributed to Abraham, but which Sa'adiah attributed to the tanaitic (early rabbinic) period (a view shared by many modern scholars). Some of Sa'adiah's interpretations proved to be decisive in the way the book, which is

---

15   Exilarch = *resh galuta*, "the head of the exile," the political governor of the Babylonian Jews, who was appointed by the ruler.

16   See Chapter 1 (I.3.a) on Sa'adiah's dispute with the Karaite Ben Zuta regarding the meaning of "an eye for an eye," and Sa'adiah's point that "reason cannot tolerate this" (i.e., the Karaite literalist interpretation of the verse).

often obscure, was read and understood by subsequent generations, by mystics and rationalists alike. In Sa'adiah's view, the book, containing ancient Jewish wisdom, is particularly important because it deals with how the universe came into being, a question Sa'adiah refers to as "the most important attained by the reason of those who contemplate it, and the most difficult considered by the researchers who dealt with it."[17] The question of creation leads directly, in turn, to the question of the prophetic experience of revelation, because in addition to the formation of the four elements—earth, water, air and fire—a "second air," finer than the regular air, was formed. It is this air, according to Sa'adiah, that the Bible refers to as the divine *kavod* (glory), and that the rabbis refer to as the *shekhinah* (divine presence). It was this second, fine air that the prophets saw as visions or heard as voices, and thereby ensured that their experience was objective, of something real, and not subjective and imaginary.

[II.3] SA'ADIAH GA'ON: *THE BOOK OF BELIEFS AND OPINIONS*

[II.3.a] THE NAME AND PURPOSE OF THE BOOK

In 933 C.E., roughly three years after writing his commentary to the *Sefer Yezirah*, Sa'adiah published his major philosophic work, *Kitab Al-Amanat W'al-I'tiqadat* (Hebrew: *Sefer Ha-Emunot Veha-De'ot*; "The Book of Beliefs and Opinions"). The book was translated from Arabic into Hebrew by Judah ibn Tibbon in the twelfth century, and in its Hebrew version became a classic, the first major book of Jewish philosophy widely known to later generations, and read and studied down to our own day. (A different, early Hebrew version of the book exerted a great influence on the mystical *Hasidut Ashkenaz* [German hasidic or pietistic movement] in the 12th–13th centuries). Two English translations of the book exist. Alexander Altmann published an abridged translation, *Book of Doctrines and Beliefs*,[18]; and a few years later Samuel Rosenblatt published a complete translation, *The Book of Beliefs and Opinions*.[19]

Although it largely reflects Mu'tazilah Kalam thought, the book also reflects some Platonic and Aristotelian ideas, and was written in response to the

---

17 Sa'adiah Ga'on, Introduction to the Commentary to *Sefer Yezirah*.

18 Published in *Three Jewish Philosophers* (Philadelphia: Jewish Publication Society, 1945; republished New York: Harper Torchbooks, 1965).

19 Saadia Gaon, *The Book of Beliefs and Opinions* (New Haven: Yale University Press, 1948). Rosenblatt's translation includes as an appendix the variant version of Ch. 7, on resurrection, based on the Hebrew translation by Judah ibn Tibbon, who had a different Arabic version of this chapter.

clash of conflicting religious and philosophic ideas. In typical Kalam fashion, Sa'adiah explicitly states that the purpose of the book is "twofold, first to verify for us in actuality what we know from the prophets of God, and second, to respond to everyone who argues with us about our religion."[20] Unlike Rambam's *Guide of the Perplexed*, which was intended only for the intelligentsia and was written in such a way as to conceal its meaning from the unqualified masses, Sa'adiah's *Book of Beliefs and Opinions* was deliberately written in such a way as to facilitate its being understood by the community at large, surely a factor in its subsequent popularity. In his biography of Sa'adiah,[21] Henry Malter suggests that Sa'adiah's importance lies not in philosophic originality, but in his ability to communicate clearly a large body of foreign ideas, and thereby to shape and help foster subsequent Jewish thought.

The name of the book, *Beliefs and Opinions*, is indicative of its aim. What is the difference between beliefs and opinions? Malter suggests that "belief" refers to philosophic ideas, whereas "opinion" refers to religious ideas, but this suggestion is inconsistent with Sa'adiah's own expressed statement. In the Introduction to the book (section #4), Sa'adiah states that the term *i'tiqad* (plural: *i'tiqadat*; Hebrew: *de'ah, de'ot*), usually translated as "opinion," does not refer to anything a person happens to believe, but to something a person affirms with a higher degree of certainty, following study and rational understanding. In other words, "opinion" corresponds to objective reality, and does not merely reflect our subjective view. Conversely, *amanah* (plural: *amanat*; Hebrew: *emunah, emunot*), usually translated as "belief," is prior to "opinion," and refers to what a person affirms without study or rational understanding. In a sense, therefore, we must reverse Malter's suggestion: "belief" refers to religious ideas, accepted on the basis of tradition, and "opinion" refers to philosophic ideas, affirmed on the basis of research and rational understanding. The name of the book, therefore, is indicative of an pedagogic direction, namely the intellectual and spiritual transition from simple religious "belief" based on tradition, to rationally supported "opinion."[22] Thereby, Sa'adiah states in the Introduction,[23] the reader who seeks truth will reach the truth, and his doubts (resulting from the conflicting ideas to which he was exposed) will be resolved. Instead of merely believing what he was told by others, the reader will have progressed to true opinions, based on a reasoned affirmation based on research and understanding.

---

20   Sa'adiah Ga'on, *Beliefs and Opinions*, Introduction, Section #6.

21   Henry Malter, *Saadia Gaon: His Life and Works* (Philadelphia: Jewish Publication Society, 1920. Reprinted: New York: Hermon Press, 1969).

22   This is the position taken by Alexander Altmann in the Introduction to his abridged English translation of the book (p. 20).

23   Sa'adiah Ga'on, *Beliefs and Opinions*, Introduction, Section #2.

[II.3.b] THE SOURCES OF KNOWLEDGE

How, then, can a person be assured that his or her opinions, however researched, will actually be true, i.e., conforming, as Saʿadiah puts it, to "the thing as it is…that something black is black, and something white is white?" In other words, what is the basis for affirming that we know something to be true?

There are three sources of or paths to knowledge (*ʿilm*), which all humans possess.[24] The first is empirical knowledge by direct observation (*ʿilm al-shahid*; Hebrew: *yediʿat ha-nir'eh*). Such knowledge is contingent, because it depends on how things actually are, and they could be different. For example, under different circumstances (such as a change in the production line of a clothing factory), a red shirt could be blue, and a shirt which exists might not exist. So the existence of the red shirt is possible, not necessary, and our knowledge of it is contingent upon its existence and being red. The only way to verify this is empirically, to see if the shirt exists, and if so, if it is red. The second source is rational knowledge (*ʿilm al-ʿaql*; Hebrew: *madaʿ ha-sekhel*) implanted in the intellect, the "primary intelligibles" like "a circle is not square." Such knowledge is necessary, and could never be different, for under no circumstances could a circle ever be square, and the very notion of a square circle is absurd in the technical sense of being a contradiction in terms; we understand this by the very meaning of the words, and do not need any empirical verification of its truth. The third source of knowledge is deductive, what we infer by logical necessity (*ʿilm ma dafaʿat al-darura 'ilahu*; Hebrew: *yediʿat mah sheha-hekhrah mevi elav*). This deductive type of knowledge combines elements of the first two, so that the truth of the premises, as well as the logical structure of the deduction, necessitate the conclusion. For example, if A=B and B=C, then necessarily A=C. The truth of the proposition, however, is not necessary in and of itself (as in the second type of knowledge), but is dependant on the truth of its premises and the validity of the deduction.

In addition to these three universal sources of knowledge, there is a fourth type:

> But we, the community of monotheists (*jamaʿat al-muwahadin*; Hebrew: *qehal ha-meyahadim*), verify these three sources of knowledge, but add to them a fourth source, which we derive from those three and which has become another foundation. It is the validity of authentic tradition (*al-khabr al-ṣadiq*; Hebrew: *ha-hagadah ha-ne'emenet* or *ha-masoret ha-amitit*), which is based on empirical knowledge and rational knowledge…and verifies for us the three sources which are true knowledge.[25]

---

24   Saʿadiah Gaʾon, *Beliefs and Opinions*, Introduction, Section #5.
25   Saʿadiah Gaʾon, *Beliefs and Opinions*, Introduction, Section #5.

This fourth type of knowledge, which can be translated as "authentic tradition," "true tradition," "reliable tradition," or as "reliable report" or "true report," is not universal. Unlike the first three types, it is not shared by all human beings, but is common to "the community of monotheists." Some scholars, such as Shlomo Pines, understand "the community of monotheists" to refer to the Jewish people, but it is more likely that it is not limited to Jews. In other places Sa'adiah uses the plural "communities," and his proofs of the unity of God are borrowed directly from Islamic Kalam literature. Even his arguments against the Christian concept of the Trinity are included in the section of the book dealing with the unity of God. Moreover, the examples Sa'adiah gives of this type of knowledge are by no means limited to the Jewish people. He states, for example, that without reliable reports a person would not heed warnings about dangers on a given road, nor would know that certain acts are prohibited. If people would rely only on what they directly saw or heard, there would be no law and order, and chaos would ensue. They would not even be able to determine paternity, if they were unwilling to accept the reliability of the mother's report, since they did not witness the child's conception.

By "authentic tradition" Sa'adiah is referring in particular to what we would call historical knowledge. How do we verify a historical report? We cannot verify empirically what happened centuries ago, which we ourselves do not witness directly. Nor are historical facts subject to rational verification — a circle can never be square, but it is possible that our historical information is wrong, and someone else, not George Washington, was the first president of the U.S.A. A historical proposition cannot be verified empirically or rationally, and also is not subject to deductive verification, since deduction combines empirical and rational elements. Sa'adiah argues that verification of historical propositions is a function of two factors: the reliability of the report of the original witnesses to the event; and the reliability of the process of transmission of that original testimony in subsequent generations. In both cases, i.e., the original witnesses and those subsequently transmitting the testimony, the more there are people involved, the more reliable is the report, because with more people, there is less chance of error, deceit, delusion or collusion. The reliability of the historical reports in the Bible of the exodus, the revelation at Sinai, and other miracles, such as the manna people ate during the forty years of Israel's wandering in the wilderness, is certain and irrefutable, because of the public nature of what is claimed — the events were experienced by thousands of people, and the reports have ever since been transmitted publicly, by thousands of people in each generation. Sa'adiah's argument, that the public nature of these events proves their facticity and lends credence to the reports, was shared by Judah Ha-Levi (who, as we shall see in Ch. 6, made it the starting point of his philosophy), and in the modern period by Moses Mendelssohn, and is still cited by many contemporary Orthodox thinkers.

[II.3.c] THE NEED FOR REVELATION

In light of our having four certain sources of knowledge, why do we need divine revelation of the truth that we should, in principle, be able to discover on our own? Saʿadiah's answer is that revelation is, in effect, a short cut to the rational or scientific truth. For instance, a teacher may give his students a complex problem to solve in geometry or physics, and may then give them the answer, and tell them to prove it. In their lack of understanding of geometry or physics, without such direction and assistance, the students would not on their own know where to look, and in which direction to work out the problem. Similarly, Saʿadiah explains that rational investigation is a lengthy process. In revelation, we are given the conclusions at the outset, before we could arrive at them rationally on our own. Therefore, in the interim, we are enabled by revelation to know both the theoretical truth and, on a practical level, correct behavior. Moreover, some people are never capable of arriving at the truth by themselves, and such people are given the truth through revelation, so they might obey God's commandments and thus merit reward.[26]

What is known in revelation is thus rational, and in principle is identical to the truth arrived at by rational investigation. The difference is not in content, but in the method of arriving at the truth. Revelation permits immediate knowledge of truth we could arrive at rationally only after a lengthy process of investigation.

[II.3.d] PROOFS OF CREATION
AND OF THE EXISTENCE OF GOD

Having discussed in the Introduction to the *Book of Beliefs and Opinions* his theory of knowledge, Saʿadiah now moves to the main themes of the book, beginning, as it were, with the beginning, namely the creation of the world in the first section of the book.[27] The Torah, of course, opens in the first chapters of Genesis with the account of creation, a topic Saʿadiah had already described (in the Introduction to his commentary to the *Sefer Yeẓirah*, cited above) as "the most important attained by the reason of those who contemplate it, and the most difficult considered by the researchers who dealt with it." He thus adopts the Kalam method of proving the existence of God by proving that the world was created, but with a critical difference. Saʿadiah did not accept the Kalam's atomism — its division of matter into atoms and of time into indivisible moments. His four proofs of creation, therefore, although adopted from the Kalam, had to be adapted accordingly, to avoid the Kalam's atomism.

---

26   Saʿadiah Gaʾon, *Beliefs and Opinions*, Introduction, Section #6.
27   Saʿadiah Gaʾon, *Beliefs and Opinions* I:1.

[II.3.d.i] *The argument from finitude*

The first proof of creation argues from the fact that the world is finite in size that it must also be finite in time, i.e., have a beginning. We need to keep in mind that classical and medieval cosmology was geocentric, with the earth surrounded by concentric heavenly spheres which rotate around it.[28] The universe must be finite in size, Sa'adiah maintains, because the spheres complete a rotation around the earth every 24 hours. A finite body cannot contain an infinite force. The force sustaining the finite universe, accordingly, cannot itself be infinite. Since the force sustaining the universe must be finite, at some point that force did not exist, and at that point, without the force to sustain it, the universe could not have existed. In other words, the universe must have had a beginning.

Sa'adiah's proof must not be confused with the Aristotelian concept of a first mover or prime cause, which we will discuss in Chapter 10. Sa'adiah has in mind a force which must be finite in time because it is contained by a spatially finite world. The Aristotelian notion is not of a force contained in a body, as it is in Sa'adiah, but of an external and eternal mover or cause of an eternal world. As such, the Aristotelian concept is not of a first mover or cause in the sense of the first link in a series, but of a mover or cause that is "first" in the sense of being above and outside of the series. Rambam and other Jewish philosophers who were Aristotelian in their orientation could not, therefore, accept the premises of Sa'adiah's proof. Moreover, as we shall see, Rambam rejected Sa'adiah's Kalam approach on both methodological and pedagogic grounds, in favor of proofs of God's existence, incorporeality and unity based on an eternal universe.

[II.3.d.ii] *The argument from the combination of parts*

The second argument infers "from the combination of parts and the composition of connections" between things—in other words, from the formation of compound bodies, both individual bodies and the cosmos as a whole—that these compounds cannot have come into being accidentally. Their compound design is evidence of a creator who formed them.

Sa'adiah's second proof is largely the same as the third Kalam proof of creation outlined by Rambam in the *Guide of the Perplexed* I:74. Sa'adiah's rejection of Kalam atomism and occasionalism, however, undermined the logic of the Kalam proof. In an occasionalist framework, the atoms themselves require divine intervention to endure from moment to moment, and that logic applies all the more so to compound beings. In the absence of such atomism and occasionalism, Sa'adiah's second proof at best constitutes what is known as

---

28   At this point, refer to the cosmology chart in the Appendix.

the "teleological argument,"[29] namely that the order of the cosmos is evidence of some kind of design and plan, but it does not prove that the elements (from which those compound beings were composed) were themselves created. A piece of furniture, for example, is evidence of the existence of a carpenter who built it according to some plan, but the carpenter did not create the wood and other components from which he built the furniture.

[II.3.d.iii] *The argument from changing accidents*

This proof, which is similar to the fourth Kalam proof of creation outlined by Rambam in the *Guide of the Perplexed* I:74, and to the second principle of the Kalam discussed by Judah Ha-Levi in the *Kuzari* 5:18, concludes from the notion that accidents cannot be eternal, that the world cannot be eternal. Accidents have no independent existence of their own, but subsist in substances. The substance exists, but it cannot exist without accidents, such as quantity, quality, relation, place or time.

For example, a shirt cannot exist without its being a certain size and color, and without existing in a certain time and place. Although the substance must have some accidents, they are not necessary (if they were, they would not be accidents!), and the substance could have had other accidents. The shirt, for example, could have been cut larger or smaller; the cloth could have been dyed a different color; and the shirt could have been sewn at a different time and in a different place. So the shirt necessarily has some size and some color, but not necessarily this particular size and color; it must exist in a particular time and place, but not necessarily in this time and place. Similarly, accidents cannot be eternal, because if it's possible for something to be different, that change need not occur in any given time (a day, year, or millennium), but if it never changed over eternity, then that change was never possible to begin with. And if it is never possible over eternity for it to be different, then, by definition, it isn't an accident.

The third proof, then, argues that bodies, terrestrial and heavenly, cannot exist without accidents.

Since accidents cannot be eternal, and are always changing, at such time as there were no accidents, the substance, i.e. the bodies sustaining them, cannot have existed. Thus the world must have had a beginning.

This proof, however, also entails difficulties. Granted that a substance cannot exist without accidents and that accidents cannot be eternal, all that argument proves is that a body (or the world) cannot exist prior to and free of accidents. It does not prove what it claims, namely that the body (in this case, the world) must have a beginning, because it does not take into account the

---

29 "Teleological," from "telos" (Greek: end, purpose), referring to the theory that natural phenomena manifest purpose and intention.

possibility of an eternal succession of changing accidents. Its conclusion, that a body cannot exist without accidents, is thus identical with its premise, that a body cannot exist without accidents.

[II.3.d.iv] *The argument from time*

The fourth proof of creation is based on our conception of time, and is similar to the second principle of the Kalam in Judah Ha-Levi's *Kuzari* 5:18, and to the seventh Kalam proof of creation in Rambam's *Guide of the Perplexed* I:74. Underlying this proof is the idea that an actual infinity is impossible and a contradiction in terms. We frequently and erroneously treat the infinite as a large number or quantity, when it really is neither, because at any given point, what we have, however large, is not infinite, and we can always continue to add to it.

For example, a passenger sitting at the rear of a bus traveling at 100 km/hour who walks to the front of the bus at 5 km/hour, is moving at 105 km/hour relative to the earth, and when he returns to his seat at 5 km/hour, his motion relative to the earth is 95 km/hour. But if, hypothetically, the bus were traveling at an infinite speed (which is not only physically impossible, of course, but also theoretically impossible according to Einstein's theory of relativity), the passenger walking to the front would not be moving relative to the earth at infinite +5 km/hour, and the passenger returning to his seat would not be moving at infinite −5 km/hour. In both cases, he would be moving at a rate of infinite km/hour, because the infinite is not a number or quantity, and infinite −5 is still infinite, and infinite +5 is still infinite.

Although the infinite can exist potentially—I can potentially always continue to add to or multiply my quantity—it cannot exist in actuality, because that would mean that at a given moment I already have attained an infinite quantity. But that is a contradiction in terms, because infinity is not a fixed quantity, since by definition I can always add to or multiply it. Applying this principle to time, if the world is eternal, it has already existed in actuality for an infinite number of moments (days, years, millennia). That would mean that at any given moment, the world has already completed an actual infinite quantity of moments, which is impossible.

Sa'adiah's proof, then, proceeds as follows. Time can be divided into past, present and future. The present is immediately transient, because as soon as we experience a moment from the future, it becomes past. The present thus resembles the geometric point which has no quantity. If one were to imagine the present as a point on a line of time, one could never traverse (Sa'adiah says: climb) the line from that point (i.e., the present) to infinite past time. In other words, we could never reach an actually infinitely distant past point in time. However, time does not proceed from present to past, but from past to present, and from present to future. Therefore, if the world is eternal, i.e., past time is infinite, we could never actually traverse (Sa'adiah says: descend) the line from the infinitely distant past all the way to the present. But if we cannot actually reach the present, we and the world do not exist (since we exist in the present, however transient). Since, however, it is evident that we do exist, we cannot have traversed an infinitely distant past, and therefore the past (i.e., the world) must have a beginning.

To illustrate Sa'adiah's argument, let time be represented as a line, with the present as a point on the line:

Time line: **PAST**   **PRESENT**   **FUTURE**

Imagine that one could traverse the time line backwards towards the infinite past ("climbing" in Sa'adiah's example). One can never actually reach an infinitely distant point in the past.

             INFINITE PAST   **PRESENT**   **FUTURE**

∞ ←

Time, of course, progresses forward towards the future, and not backwards towards the past. Just as we could not traverse the time line backwards and reach the infinitely distant past (Sa'adiah's "climbing"), so, reversing the direction, we can never completely traverse the time line forwards ("descending" in Sa'adiah's example) and reach the present point on the line.

             INFINITE PAST   **PRESENT**   **FUTURE**

∞ ─────────────→

But if we can never actually reach the present point on the line, i.e., the present in which we live, then we and the world do not exist. The choice, then, is simple: an eternal world, i.e., an infinite past, means that we do not exist. Since it is evident that we do exist, the past cannot be infinite, and the world cannot be eternal, but must have a beginning.

Having proven (at least to his own way of thinking) that the world must have been created, Sa'adiah moves to the next question, namely the existence of the creator. Inanimate bodies (a table, for example) do not have the power to create themselves, to make themselves exist; something else (the carpenter, for example) must be the agent of their existence. If an existing object lacks the power to create itself, then all the more so would something which does not yet exist (the world, before its creation) have the power to create itself. The creation of the world thus implies the existence of the creator. Rambam, who was critical of and rejected Sa'adiah's proofs of creation, agrees on this last point, and in the *Guide of the Perplexed* II:2 stated that if something came into existence after not existing, it must have something which generated it (caused it to come into being), and it could not have caused, before it existed, its own existence.

Sa'adiah further argues that the creation of the world must have been creation *ex nihilo* (from nothing), in contrast with the way a carpenter forms furniture out of existing components. Plato's conception of creation was such a formation of the world out of pre-existing, i.e., eternal, prime matter. Sa'adiah, however, agreed with the Mu'tazilah rejection of anything co-eternal with God (in the case of the Mu'tazilah, even the Qur'an). Why, argued the Mu'tazilah, and now Sa'adiah, should something that had eternally co-existed with God suddenly become subject to and dependant upon God's creative power?[30]

Had the world been created out of something already existing, then presumably that pre-existing thing came from something which existed before it, which in turn came to something which existed before it. In short, the notion of creation out of something leads us to an infinite regress, which is impossible. Just as we saw in the fourth proof of creation that our inability to traverse an infinite past would mean that we never reach the present, and thus do not exist, so, Sa'adiah argues, our inability to complete an infinite series of things from which the world was created would mean that the world does not exist. Since it is evident that the world does exist, at some point whatever the world is made of must have been created from nothing.

To emphasize that the world was created *ex nihilo* (so far as we know, the Hebrew phrase *yesh me-ayin*, "something out of nothing," had not yet been coined in Sa'adiah's time), Sa'adiah, writing in Arabic, carefully used the phrase *la min shay* ("not from something"). He thus made a stronger and clearer statement, and avoided the ambiguity of *min la shay* ("from no-thing"), because, as Harry Wolfson suggested,[31] "from no-thing" could be construed as something. For instance, if we say that the carpenter formed the table out of "no-wood" it does not mean that he made it from nothing, but simply not from wood, but from some other material.

[II.3.e]   TWO DIFFERENT LISTS OF THEORIES OF CREATION

Having established the correct view, namely that the world is created, that it was created by a creator, and that it was created "not from something," Sa'adiah proceeds to describe twelve erroneous theories concerning creation. This list,

---

30   Sa'adiah Ga'on, *Beliefs and Opinions* I:2.
31   Wolfson, *The Philosophy of the Kalam*, p. 371.

however, differs from his description of nine theories in his commentary to the *Sefer Yeẓirah*.

Although there is overlap between the twelve theories in the *Book of Beliefs and Opinions* and the nine theories in the commentary to *Sefer Yeẓirah*, there are differences both of content and of order. Henry Malter suggested that the nine theories in the *Sefer Yeẓirah* commentary are presented in an ascending order of reasonableness, beginning with the least likely theory, that of the materialist and atheist "Dahriya," which denied creation, and culminating in the true (i.e., Sa'adiah's own) theory of creation. In contrast, Malter points out that the twelve theories in the *Book of Beliefs and Opinions* are listed in a descending order of accuracy, beginning with Sa'adiah's three principles (creation; creation by a creator; and creation "not from something"), and ending with the most problematical theory. Malter has no explanation (nor do we) for the discrepancies between the two lists, nor for Sa'adiah's failure to discuss in his commentary on the *Sefer Yeẓirah* the book's theory that the world was formed out of the ten cardinal numbers and the twenty-two letters of the Hebrew alphabet.

[II.3.f]   RAMBAM'S CRITIQUE OF THE KALAM APPROACH

Rambam devotes a section of his *Guide of the Perplexed* I:71 to a critique of the Kalam approach, followed by Sa'adiah, to proving the existence of God based on proofs of creation *ex nihilo*. In Rambam's view, the Mutakallimun erred in basing their proofs on false premises. Moreover, creation cannot be demonstrated conclusively, and the Mutakallimun should rather have developed arguments against the Aristotelian arguments for eternity. In any event, there is a more fundamental methodological consideration: it is preferable to base proofs of God's existence, incorporeality and unity on eternity, not creation. Proofs based on creation will at best be valid if, in the final analysis, it turns out that the world is created; if it turns out that the world is eternal, the proofs will collapse. Conversely, if the proofs are based on eternity, both eventualities—eternity and creation—are covered and the proofs will be valid. Thus, if it turns out that the world is actually eternal, then the existence, incorporeality and unity of God will be conclusively demonstrated; and if it turns out that the world is created, the existence of the creator is all the more evident.

[II.3.g]   THE UNITY AND INCORPOREALITY OF GOD

Having established that the world is created and has a creator, Sa'adiah, again in typical Mu'tazilah fashion, proceeds to discuss the unity and incorporeality of God in the second section of the *Book of Beliefs and Opinions*. The concept of the unity of God can be understood in two different respects, external and internal. In its external sense, unity is a quantitative or numerical concept, and refers to there being only one of something. The numerical sense of unity is external, because it actually doesn't tell us anything about the object itself, but only that there aren't any others. In its internal sense, unity means absolute simplicity, that something is indivisible, not compound, and has no parts or components. Internal, simple unity was often understood to transcend human understanding, and to necessitate the negation of attributes from God. Such "negative theology" permeated much of medieval thought, especially Neoplatonic, but was also fundamental to such thinkers as Rambam.

According to Wolfson,[32] the biblical concept of the unity of God is external and numerical—there is only one God. "You were shown, that you might know, that the Lord is God, there is none other beside him" (Deuteronomy 4:35). The Mu'tazilah emphasis on the absolute unity of God in the internal sense of simplicity led Jewish philosophers to apply this understanding of unity to the biblical concept as well, so that "Listen, Israel, the Lord our God, the Lord is one" (Deuteronomy 6:4) was taken to mean both senses of unity. Wolfson suggests, however, that the philosophical notion of absolute simplicity and rejection of real attributes cannot be traced back to the Greek philosophers, but to Philo, who synthesized it with the biblical notion of the uniqueness or unlikeness of God (that God is unique, and unlike creatures). Philo's innovation then permeated later Greek and early Christian thought. The Mu'tazilah, in turn, adopted it from the Christians, and the Jews from the Mu'tazilah. As we shall see, for Sa'adiah, the external and internal senses of unity are correlative—each implies and necessitates the other (just as mountain and valley, or "heads and tails" of a coin, are correlative concepts).

Sa'adiah lists three brief proofs of unity:
  (i) Number and multiplicity are features of created beings, and the conditions applying to creatures do not apply to the creator.
  (ii) The arguments for the existence of God prove at least one God—but any additional gods are superfluous.
  (iii) The existence of one God can only be proven by creation.

Any proof that there cannot be two (or more) gods, suffices to prove that there is only one God. If there were two gods, and both were needed for something to exist, neither would be omnipotent. If both of them were omnipotent, they could coerce or interfere with each other. Two gods could will opposites; for instance, one god could will X to exist, and the other could will X not to exist.

Moreover, if there are two gods, and they are identical, then they would be one, not two. If they are two, that means that there is a third factor differentiating between them. This last argument, which is based, at least implicitly, on the

---

[32]　Wolfson, *Repercussions of the Kalam in Jewish Philosophy*, pp. 3–4.

correlative internal and external respects of unity, is what Rambam listed in the *Guide of the Perplexed* I:75 as the second Kalam method of proving unity, which Rambam calls "a conclusive philosophic demonstration." As Rambam formulates it: If there are two gods, they both would necessarily have something (divine) in common; they would also have something differentiating and dividing them.

The external, numerical unity of God thus necessitates his internal, simple unity. If we assume that there are two gods, god A and god B, then each must have common divine denominator C. God A thus has two components: the common divine denominator C, and the particular differentiation A, so god A is a composite AC. God B also has two components: the common denominator C, and the particular differentiation B, and thus is composite BC. The two gods thus must have three components: A, B, C.

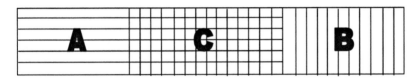

In other words, if there are two (or more) gods, than each god is composite, compounded of two (or more) elements. In that case, as compounds, they would be material, not gods. Conversely, the internal, simple unity of God necessitates external, numerical unity, because if God is simple, there cannot be components A+C or B+C, and, therefore, there cannot be two gods. The external and internal senses of unity are thus correlative and necessitate each other. God's unity is also correlative with incorporeality, since everything material is compound and divisible, so that something simple cannot be material. By proving unity, we thereby also prove incorporeality.

[II.3.h]   THE DIVINE ATTRIBUTES

As we saw, the Mu'tazilah emphasis on absolute unity of God led them to deny the reality of the divine attributes, in contrast with the Ash'ariyya affirmation of real attributes. What can one say, then, of God and attribute to him? Sa'adiah replies that we learn from Scripture five attributes of God: unity; uniqueness (that nothing resembles him); life (Arabic: *hay*; Hebrew: *hai*); omnipotence (Arabic: *qadir*; Hebrew: *yakhol*); and omniscience (Arabic: *'alim*; Hebrew: *hakham*).[33] Unity and uniqueness are basically negative concepts, telling us

---

33   Sa'adiah, *Book of Beliefs and Opinions* 2:1. The Arabic *'alim*, knowing, could also be translated in Hebrew as *yode'a*, but Judah ibn Tibbon translated it as *hakham* (wise), and that has become the standard usage.

what God is not, and were proven above. The three remaining attributes—life, omnipotence and omniscience—are positive—they tell us something about God—but if we wish to preserve God's absolute unity, they cannot be three separate notions. They are, Sa'adiah suggests, implied by the notion of God as creator, because only something possessing power (omnipotence) is capable of acting, and only something alive has power, and only something possessing knowledge can act deliberately.[34] But this brings us back to the problem of absolute unity: how can three attributes, which are not identical, be reconciled with God's absolute unity? Sa'adiah's answer is that the multiplicity is merely linguistic, not real. We lack a single term to express these different ideas simultaneously, all of which are simultaneously conceived intellectually as implicit in the idea of the creator, and are, therefore, essential attributes of God. Many of the later thinkers that we shall discuss rejected Sa'adiah's solution to the problem, and rejected essential attributes as inconsistent with the unity of God, since in their view the linguistic distinction reflects a real distinction, and thus introduces multiplicity into the divine essence.

[II.3.i] THE LANGUAGE AND MEANING OF SCRIPTURE

In light of philosophical conceptions of the incorporeality of God, how should we understand biblical anthropomorphisms and anthropopathisms?[35] Sa'adiah clearly regards all such expressions as metaphorical, and not meant literally. Why, then, does not Scripture restrict itself to true terms, and why does it employ terms that are not literally true, thereby causing confusion and perplexity? Sa'adiah's response is that if we were to restrict our usage to what is literally true, we would lose much of our language and ability to express ourselves, and in the case of God, we would not be able to affirm anything other than his bare existence.[36]

Anthropomorphisms and anthropopathisms, while not literally true, establish in the mind of the believer that God is personal. By "personal," of course, we do not mean that God is a person in a physical sense, but rather than we attribute personality to God, that God knows us, cares about us, reveals his will and hears our prayer, as if he were a person, not that he is a person. Conversely, although we could not exist without gravity, we do not attribute personality to gravity; we do not imagine that gravity knows us or cares about us, that gravity possesses consciousness or will, or that gravity hears prayers. We would not think

---

[34]   Sa'adiah, *Book of Beliefs and Opinions* 2:4.

[35]   Anthropomorphism—attributing human bodily characteristics to God (such as hand, face, ears, eyes). Anthropopathism—attributing human feelings or emotions to God (such as happiness, anger, sympathy, compassion).

[36]   Sa'adiah, *Book of Beliefs and Opinions* 2:10.

of praying to gravity. In all these ways, we conceive of gravity impersonally, and God personally. Metaphorical language, then, helps us to relate to God personally, although we know it is not literally true. God's "head" symbolizes greatness, Sa'adiah suggests; his "eye" symbolizes divine providence; his "face" symbolizes will and anger; God's "ear" represents accepting human prayer; the "hand" is a symbol of power; the "heart" represents wisdom.[37]

Given our philosophical understanding of Scripture as frequently metaphorical, how can we know when it is to be taken literally, and when non-literally?

[II.3.j] WHEN IS SCRIPTURE TO BE TAKEN LITERALLY, AND WHEN METAPHORICALLY?

In order to avoid utter subjectivism (one of the charges leveled by rabbinic Jews against the Karaites' lack of authoritative tradition), Sa'adiah formulates four criteria for metaphorical interpretation of Scripture. Since he deals with this issue in three different places in the *Book of Beliefs and Opinions*, each time in greater detail, he obviously regarded this question as of great practical as well as theoretical importance.

In the first passage, Sa'adiah states that the literal or surface sense (*peshat*) of Scripture is to be retained as a general rule, except when the *peshat* "differs from what true speculation requires." In such a case, "it is undoubtedly metaphorical language."[38]

In the second passage, Sa'adiah explicates the four criteria for metaphorical interpretation. We are to interpret the Bible metaphorically when the verse contradicts what we know "empirically, or rationally, or another Scriptural verse, or tradition."[39] By "tradition," of course, he means the tradition of the talmudic rabbis.

In the third passage,[40] Sa'adiah raises the question of metaphorical interpretation in the context of his discussion of the resurrection of the dead, a doctrine he regarded as even more reasonable than creation *ex nihilo* (since, unlike creation, resurrection is not *ex nihilo*). That being the case, references or allusions to resurrection in the Bible should be taken at face value, literally, and not interpreted metaphorically. He then reiterates the four criteria for metaphorical interpretation, but adds examples. We are to maintain the literal meaning of Scripture's words unless they "deny [what we know] empirically." For example, the Torah says that the first woman was called Eve

---

[37]   Sa'adiah, *Book of Beliefs and Opinions* 2:10.
[38]   Sa'adiah, *Book of Beliefs and Opinions* 2:3.
[39]   Sa'adiah, *Book of Beliefs and Opinions* 5:8.
[40]   Sa'adiah, *Book of Beliefs and Opinions* 7:2 (in the original version).

(*ḥavah* = living) "because she was the mother of everything living" (Genesis 3:20), and of course Eve was not literally the mother of every living being. The second criterion is "Or when it is inconsistent with reason." For example, the Torah says "that the Lord your God is a consuming fire" (Deuteronomy 4:24). The third criterion is "or to contradict something in another Scriptural verse." For example, Malachi 3:10 has God telling Israel to "test" or "try" him, when in Deuteronomy 6:16 there is an explicit prohibition on testing God. The fourth criterion is "Or when [a verse] contradicts what we have received from our ancestors (i.e., the talmudic rabbis)." For example, Deuteronomy 25:3 specifies the punishment of forty lashes for certain crimes, which the rabbis then reduced to thirty-nine. When, however, none of these four criteria applies, and there is no such need, "one should not seek metaphor...nor interpret non-literally."

As we shall see in chapter 5, Sa'adiah's relatively conservative approach was shared by Abraham ibn Ezra (who cites Sa'adiah at various points in his Bible commentaries), and who criticized Christian exegetes for widescale and unwarranted allegorical interpretation. "If reason does not tolerate [the literal meaning], or [the literal meaning] destroys what is empirically clear, then one should seek esoteric meaning (*sod*), for reason is the foundation."[41]

[II.3.k] THE PROPHET AND MIRACLES

As we saw above, Sa'adiah regarded resurrection as possible, and as more "reasonable" than creation *ex nihilo*. Verses alluding to resurrection are, accordingly, to be taken literally, since they do not contradict reason or empirical knowledge. This raises, however, the broader question of Sa'adiah's understanding of miracles and why, in his view, they were necessary. Keeping in mind Sa'adiah's position that revelation is a short-cut in attaining rational truth, miracles play an important role in revelation. Miracles reinforce the mission of the prophet receiving divine revelation, by proving to the people, and sometimes even to the prophet himself, that his mission is, in fact, from God.[42] The people, when they see the miracles, are led to obey the prophet immediately. Only afterwards do they reflect on the commandments, and begin to understand the rationale for the commandments.[43]

Although supranatural miracles persuade the people, and the prophet himself, if necessary, that the prophet is a genuine prophet and that his mission is actually from God, they cannot actually verify the prophet's message. In other words, miracles can reinforce the credibility of the prophet, but cannot

---

41   Abraham ibn Ezra, Introduction to the Torah, "the third way."
42   Sa'adiah, *Book of Beliefs and Opinions*, Introduction, Section #6).
43   Sa'adiah, *Book of Beliefs and Opinions* 3:1.

verify the content of the prophecy. A false prophet, for example, may also be able to perform wonders, but these wonders cannot verify untruth or ideas contrary to the Torah. The truth must be inherently true; it cannot be verified by miracles.

> The reason we believe Moses was not just the signs and miracles. The reason we believed him and any prophet is first that he calls us to what is permitted. When we hear his word and see that it is permitted, we ask him for miracles, and when he performs them, we believe him. But if we first hear his claim and see that it is not permitted, we do not ask him for miracles, because there can be no miraculous [proof] of something impossible.[44]

Sa'adiah's position here, that miracles cannot verify a message that is intrinsically false or the message of a false prophet, i.e., a prophet who makes a claim against the Torah, is consistent with the test of miracles provided in the Torah itself. A prophet who performs successful miracles, but then calls the people to worship other gods is a false prophet who is to be put to death.[45]

In short, for Sa'adiah, it is ultimately only the content of the message, and not miracles performed by the messenger, which determine the truth of the prophecy. Miracles only lend credibility to the messenger, that he is, in fact, a messenger of God, so that people will listen to him, but they cannot verify the message.

[II.3.1]   RATIONAL VERSUS TRADITIONAL COMMANDMENTS

The rational veracity of the prophet's message comes into further question regarding the commandments. The rationale for some commandments, such as not to murder or to steal, is obvious. Many other commandments, however, lack such obvious rationale, such as the dietary laws (*kashrut*). Why, then, were they revealed? Are such laws in the same category as anthropomorphisms, which must be understood metaphorically and not literally? The difference is that anthropomorphisms, understood literally, are irrational, meaning that they contradict reason and are, therefore, absurd and impossible (like a "square circle"), whereas the commandments in question, are not irrational but non-rational—they are not impossible from a rational perspective, but they are also not necessary from a rational perspective. They are, rather, possible and non-rational (like preference for one flavor of ice cream over another). In Sa'adiah's terms, "reason neither precludes them nor necessitates them." Since reason does not preclude or reject them, and they are optional

---

44   Sa'adiah, *Book of Beliefs and Opinions* 3:8. Rosenblatt (p. 163) translates the Arabic term *ja'iz* here as "proper. It can also be translated as "possible."
45   Deuteronomy 13:2–6.

("possible") from a rational perspective, these commandments are to be taken literally and observed.

Sa'adiah accordingly divides the Torah's commandments into two categories: rational commandments (Arabic: *al-shara'ia al-'aqliyah*; Hebrew: *mizvot sikhliyot*) and traditional commandments (Arabic: *al-shara'ia al-sam'iah*; Hebrew: *mizvot shim'iyot*).[46] The first category, whose rationale is evident, we would legislate on rational grounds even if they had not been revealed in the Torah. The second group derives its authority exclusively from their having been revealed (literally: "heard") in the Torah, and had they not been revealed, we would not deduce them rationally.

There are four reasons, Sa'adiah suggests, for observing the commandments. First, reason requires a person to reciprocate the benefits he received to his benefactor, and if the benefactor himself has no need of such benefit, he should at least thank him. Second, reason requires that we not insult a benefactor. Third, reason requires that we prevent people from harming each other. Fourth, reason requires that we enable a person to earn the reward for his actions. The first three reasons fall under the category of rational commandments. The fourth falls under the category of traditional commandments. Reason requires that a person be given the opportunity to merit reward by his actions, but does not specify how; these specific commandments, therefore, are traditional.[47]

The traditional commandments, although not rationally necessary, do not lack utility and purpose, and Sa'adiah goes into some detail to explain their social benefit, although we may not always understand the divine wisdom behind them. For example, sanctifying certain times, such as the Sabbath and festivals, enables people to rest, to study, to pray and to socialize. The dietary laws, which categorize certain animals as pure and other animals as impure, prevent us from worshipping these animals as gods: one does not regard as divine a pure animal which one eats, nor an animal which is impure.[48]

Scholars have questioned the meaning of Sa'adiah's categorization of the commandments, and its implication for the relation between what is divinely commanded and what is good. The Ash'ariya maintained that whatever God commands is, by definition, good, whereas the Mu'tazilah, to the contrary, maintained that the good is inherently good, and therefore God commands it. According to the Ash'ariya conception, that whatever God commands is, by definition, good, had God commanded something else, it would have been good, and not what we think of as good. The Ash'ariya approach is characterized by "voluntarism"—whatever God wills. Good and evil are not independent and

---

46   Sa'adiah, *Book of Beliefs and Opinions* 3:2.
47   Sa'adiah, *Book of Beliefs and Opinions* 3:1.
48   Sa'adiah, *Book of Beliefs and Opinions* 3:1–2.

inherent categories (which would, therefore, limit God's omnipotence), but depend upon what God decrees. The opposing Mu'tazilah view, according to which God commands what is good, maintains that the inherent categories of good and evil do not limit God's omnipotence, because God acts not only in accordance with his will but also in accordance with his wisdom; what he wills conforms to wisdom, and therefore God only wills and commands what is good. In his article, "Saadya's Conception of the Law,"[49] Alexander Altmann suggests that Sa'adiah's position is a compromise between the two Kalam approaches. The rational commandments were commanded because they are good (the Mu'tazilah position), and the traditional commandments are good because they were commanded (the Ash'ariya position).

However, as we have seen, Sa'adiah does attempt, in Mu'tazilah fashion, to find at least utilitarian rationale behind the traditional commandments, so they are not justified purely on the basis of Ash'ariya voluntarism. But what of the rational commandments — in what regard are they really "rational?" Rambam, as we shall see in Chapter Ten, insisted that we not confuse the theoretical distinction of true and false, with the practical distinction of good (or: proper) and evil (or: improper). A person who makes an error in a mathematical equation has arrived at a false conclusion, but has not done something evil, and a person who murders has done something evil, not false. Now if Rambam's differentiation between theoretical and moral judgments is correct, we need to ask in what respect Sa'adiah could have understood the cognitive status of the rational commandments.

According to both Altmann[50] and Marvin Fox,[51] Sa'adiah's "rational commandments" are not rational in the narrow and pure sense of theoretical intellect and logic, but in a broader social utilitarian sense of practical reason and natural morality. Now of course Altmann and Fox are correct in pointing out the utilitarian benefits of the rational commandments, however, as we saw, Sa'adiah also attempted to find utility and social benefit in the traditional commandments. The difference between the rational and traditional commandments is not, therefore, in the utility and social benefits of the rational commandments, because the traditional commandments are also seen as serving beneficial, utilitarian purposes (although we may not always understand all of them). The difference is relative. Both categories are beneficial and utilitarian, but the rational ones are to a greater degree, and the traditional

---

[49]   Alexander Altmann, "Saadya's Conception of the Law," in *Bulletin of the John Rylands Library* 28 (1944), pp. 3–24.

[50]   Altmann, ibid.

[51]   Marvin Fox, "Maimonides and Aquinas on Natural Law," in *Interpreting Maimonides: Studies in Methodology, Metaphysics and Moral Philosophy* (Chicago: University of Chicago Press, 1990), and "On the Rational commandments in Saadia's Philosophy: A Reexamination," in *Modern Jewish Ethics* (Ohio State University Press, 1975), pp. 174–187.

ones are to a lesser degree.[52] To the extent that social benefit and utility can be categorized as "rational," even the "traditional" commandments are, to some lesser extent, also "rational commandments." The "rational" commandments are thus not purely rational, and the "traditional" commandments are not purely traditional.

We thus return to Sa'adiah's conception of revelation as a short-cut in the rational process, insofar as that applies to the commandments. Both rational and traditional commandments, of course, are revealed in the Torah. The need to reveal the traditional commandments is clear—they have no rationale which is obvious *a priori*, although we can, *a posteriori*, attempt to discover their utilitarian rationale and social benefit. Moreover, by performing them a person can merit reward.

Regarding the rational commandments, their revelation makes it possible for people to know how to behave, long before they would arrive at these conclusions by their unaided reason, if ever. Moreover, even if reason could deduce general principles, it could not deduce the specific manner in which to implement those principles. We therefore need revelation of both the traditional and the rational commandments.[53] In Abraham Joshua Heschel's analysis, this conception does not render reason inferior, but emphasizes the need for revelation transcending reason.[54]

[II.3.m]   FREE WILL

Commandments imply both human ability to act and free will to choose to act. In the absence of both factors—the power and the choice to act—commandments make no sense. Moreover, if a person's actions are determined, reward and punishment are meaningless and inconsistent with divine justice. Sa'adiah accordingly attempts to prove in four different ways that humans possess free will; his proofs are based on empirical experience, reason, Scripture, and rabbinic tradition.[55]

Our empirical experience is that of freedom; we do not feel any coercion when we make our choices. On the basis of reason, we know that one act cannot be caused by two separate causes, and if God determines our behavior, then both God and the person cause the same act, which is impossible. Moreover, it is absurd and inconsistent with divine justice to argue that God determines our behavior, but at the same time rewards and punishes us for behavior for

---

52   Sa'adiah, *Book of Beliefs and Opinions* 3:1–2.

53   Sa'adiah, *Book of Beliefs and Opinions* 3:3.

54   Abraham Joshua Heschel, "Reason and Revelation in Saadya's Philosophy," in *The Jewish Quarterly Review* (n.s.) 34, 4 (1943–1944), pp. 391–408.

55   Sa'adiah, *Book of Beliefs and Opinions* 4:4.

which we are not responsible, since both righteous and wicked, believer and heretic, are equally coerced, and therefore should all be rewarded for doing what God forces them to do. There are various biblical verses alluding to free will, including Deuteronomy 30:19, "choose life." Rabbinic tradition also supports free will, for example, "Everything is in the hands of heaven except for the fear of heaven, as it says (Deuteronomy 10:12), 'And now, Israel, what does the Lord your God ask of you, except to fear the Lord your God'."[56]

How, then, can human free will be reconciled with God's omniscience? Saʻadiah answers that god's knowledge of something does not cause its existence. Since God is eternal, if God always knew something, and his knowledge caused its existence, then that thing would also be eternal. Since, however, we have proven that the world is created, not eternal, God's eternal knowledge cannot be the cause of the existence of whatever he knows.[57]

[II.3.n]　REWARD AND PUNISHMENT, AND THE WORLD TO COME

Humans deserve reward and punishment for their behavior. Nevertheless, we see that injustice often prevails in this world. Why is there such injustice, so that the righteous suffer and the wicked prosper? Saʻadiah's response is that no person is absolutely righteous or wicked. The righteous person may be punished in this world for his sins, and then rewarded in the world to come, whereas the wicked may be rewarded in this world for whatever good he has done, and then be punished in the world to come. The suffering of the righteous may also be a test, to increase their reward in the world to come. Nevertheless, there is injustice in this world, and God's absolute justice, therefore, requires that there be another realm, the world to come, in which appropriate reward and punishment will be meted out.[58]

Just as body and soul are united in this world and act in conjunction with each other, so it is appropriate that in the world to come the reward and punishment affect both body and soul. Divine justice, which necessitated there being the world to come, also necessitates resurrection, namely that after death, a person's body and soul are reunited. Resurrection, as we have already seen, is a supranatural miracle, but it is not rationally impossible. Unlike creation *ex nihilo*, resurrection is the recombination of the person out of existing elements, although not in his original, former form. As such, resurrection is more rationally likely than creation *ex nihilo*.[59]

56　Babylonian Talmud, Berakhot 33b.
57　Saʻadiah, *Book of Beliefs and Opinions* 4:4.
58　Saʻadiah, *Book of Beliefs and Opinions* 9:1.
59　Saʻadiah, *Book of Beliefs and Opinions*, Section 7 (in the alternate Ibn Tibbon version).

For Sa'adiah, the world to come follows the messianic era, and has a physical as well as spiritual dimension. As such, Sa'adiah's concept differs sharply from Rambam's purely intellectual and impersonal concept of the world to come, which we will discuss in Chapter 8, and which is totally different from his concept of the messianic era, which is an ideal future state in this world.

[II.3.o]   PSYCHOLOGY

Sa'adiah's *Book of Beliefs and Opinions* concludes with a discussion of proper conduct in this world (on the basis of which a person is rewarded or punished in the world to come), and his conception of the human soul and proper conduct reflects the tri-partite psychology of Plato's *Republic*, which Sa'adiah then equates with three biblical terms for the soul. The following chart shows this tri-partite psychology as it is found in two different places in Sa'adiah's *Book of Beliefs and Opinions*, and compares it with a similar scheme in Judah Ha-Levi's *Kuzari*.

The biblical name of the soul's faculty, according to Sa'adiah, *Book of Beliefs and Opinions* 6:3	The name of the soul's faculty in Sa'adiah, *Book of Beliefs and Opinions* 6:3	The name of the soul's faculty in Sa'adiah, *Book of Beliefs and Opinions* 10:2	The name of the soul's faculty in Judah Ha-Levi's *Kuzari* 2:50
Nefesh (= Appetite)	Arabic: *Mushtahiyah* Hebrew: *Mit'aveh*	Arabic: *Al-Shahwah* Hebrew: *Ta'avah*	Arabic: *Al-Shahwah* Hebrew: *Ta'avah*
Ru'aḥ (= Anger, Passion, Emotion)	Arabic: *Ghaḍibah* Hebrew: *Ko'es*	Arabic: *Al-Ghaḍab* Hebrew: *Ka'as*	Arabic: *Al-Ghalabah* Hebrew: *Niẓaḥon*
Neshamah (= Knowledge, Cognition, Thought)	Arabic: *'Alimah* Hebrew: *Mada'i*	Arabic: *Al-Tamyiz* Hebrew: *Ha-Hakarah*	Arabic: *Al-Fikr* Hebrew: *Maḥshavah*

The wise person exercises self-control and discipline, because correct behavior is characterized by balance. Each of the soul's faculties should receive in proportion to its needs, so that it may function properly and proportionately.[60]

---

60   Sa'adiah, *Book of Beliefs and Opinions* 10:2. We will discuss this Platonic conception in greater detail in Chapter 6, on Judah Ha-Levi. Plato's *Republic* draws the parallel between the three faculties of the soul and the three classes of the state—the philosophers, the soldiers, and the workers—and defines justice in both cases in terms of balance: each should receive in accordance with its needs, and give in accordance with its ability. It was this Platonic formula which Karl Marx took over.

Sa'adiah then proceeds to describe thirteen ways of life: asceticism, eating and drinking, sexual intercourse, eroticism, accumulating money, having children, inhabiting the world, longevity, dominion and power, revenge, wisdom, worship, and rest.[61] He then summarizes by saying that the reader of his book should combine all these ways of life, for the correct way to behave is a balanced combination of all of them together. He should enjoy the life of this world, not for its own sake, but for the sake of the world to come, since this world is a corridor leading to the next.[62]

In the Introduction to the *Book of Beliefs and Opinions*, Sa'adiah expressed the hope that it would benefit the reader in helping him attain justice and truth. Now, at the end of the book, we see that the book's benefit is less dependant upon the author than upon the efforts of the reader sincerely seeking to improve himself.

[II.3.p] CONCLUSION

In conclusion, Sa'adiah Ga'on's importance is not a function of great originality (given his receptivity to Mu'tazilah methods of argumentation) nor of exceptional profundity. Nor is his immense significance merely a reflection of his having been one of the very first Jewish philosophers. What establishes Sa'adiah's reputation is that he is the founder of an ongoing tradition of Jewish philosophy throughout the Middle Ages and beyond. His *Book of Beliefs and Opinions* continues to be read and studied widely today. To some extent, of course, his philosophic fame, like that of Rambam and some other medieval thinkers, reflects their leadership positions in the Jewish community and in the world of rabbinic scholarship. But even that does not explain fully his signal significance. Let us recall what Wolfson emphasized about the influence of ideas: they can only exert meaningful influence if there is already a predisposition, a receptivity, for those ideas. Therefore "influence" is less descriptive of the ways ideas affect other cultures and generations than "repercussions." The same may be said of Sa'adiah. Had there not been among Jews of his day, and even more, among subsequent generations of Jews, a receptivity, an intellectual and spiritual need for what Sa'adiah strove to attain, he might have been a passing phenomenon, like Philo, or an interesting but not terribly significant, let alone influential, side-line in Jewish intellectual history, like his older contemporary Isaac Israeli.

What matters, therefore, is less whether his conclusions on various specific points are correct, or even whether his method of proving them—combining empirical, rational, biblical and rabbinic sources of argumentation—is

---

61   Sa'adiah, *Book of Beliefs and Opinions*, Section 10.
62   Sa'adiah, *Book of Beliefs and Opinions* 10:17.

philosophically valid and intellectually compelling. Of far greater significance, ultimately, is what later generations could identify with in his thought. Here we come, then, to his intellectual legacy. First, later generations could share, and therefore follow, his genuine commitment, in the Philonic tradition, to the "double faith" in revelation and reason as true and as in ultimate harmony. Second, the underlying affirmation in both revelation and reason, that the Torah, even the "traditional commandments," must make rational sense—if not in the purely rational sense of logic, then in a broader sense of utility and social benefit. Third, Sa'adiah's honest recognition that mere tradition alone cannot satisfy a thinking person, who is exposed to contrasting and conflicting ideological claims, but that the tradition one affirms, and to which one makes an existential as well as intellectual commitment, must be a reasoned as well as a reasonable tradition. Finally, that people committed to a particular tradition have nothing to fear from the wisdom of other cultures and religions if, like Sa'adiah, they learn how to adopt that foreign wisdom and to adapt it to their own cultural and religious context, thereby strengthening and enriching their own tradition, and thereby facilitating the transition—on both the individual and collective levels—from blind belief to reasoned opinion.

Chapter Three

JEWISH NEOPLATONISM:
ISAAC ISRAELI
AND SOLOMON IBN GABIROL

[III.1] INTRODUCTION:
THE BACKGROUND OF NEOPLATONISM

As mentioned in the previous chapter, Sa'adiah Ga'on was a younger contemporary of Isaac Israeli. Their approaches, however, differed fundamentally, because Sa'adiah's frame of reference was the Mu'tazilah Kalam, whereas Isaac Israeli was the first Jew whose philosophy was shaped by Neoplatonism.

Neoplatonism was the last stage of ancient Greek philosophy. Founded by Plotinus in the 3rd century C.E., it became the dominant philosophical school of thought from the 3rd to the 6th centuries C.E. Although by its very name Neoplatonism refers to a renewal of Platonic thought, in fact it combines various approaches, including that of Aristotle (especially in the field of psychology). Although earlier philosophers, including Philo, renewed Platonic ideas, it was Plotinus who developed the new school of thought we call Neoplatonism. His philosophy, in turn, was developed into a comprehensive system by his disciples, especially Proclus in the 5th century C.E. In their Arabic translations, the works of Plotinus and Proclus had a great impact on Muslim and Jewish thought, and in their Latin translations, on Christian thought.

The Neoplatonic cosmology begins with the "One," from which everything else was emanated in successive stages: "universal intellect," "universal soul," "nature" and the material world. Since the One, however, transcends intellect, it is above knowledge.[1] Emanation, as we shall see, is a process, not a deliberate and conscious act of will, and one of the challenges faced by such Jewish Neoplatonists as Isaac Israeli and Solomon ibn Gabirol (like their colleagues in Christianity and Islam) was to attempt to bridge the impersonal, emanationist scheme of Neoplatonic philosophy with the biblical doctrine of creation by a personal God who knows and relates to his creatures in love. A similar challenge was to bridge the difference between monism and monotheism. Monism ("monos" = "one," "alone," "only" in Greek) refers to the philosophic

---

[1] Refer here to the chart of Emanation in the Appendix.

notion that all reality is ultimately one and derives from the same source, as opposed to religious monotheism, which affirms one God, but in its classical forms regards God as transcending the world. In monotheism, God and the world exist, but are usually understood to exist but in different senses, whereas in monism, there cannot be different senses of being, and all being is one.

Before dealing with these Jewish Neoplatonic philosophers, we first need to review some of the differences between Plato and Aristotle, as these affected classical Neoplatonic thought, which in turn served as the background for Isaac Israeli and Solomon Ibn Gabirol.

[III.1.a] PLATO AND ARISTOTLE

The Academy in Athens, founded in 387/8 B.C.E. by Plato (428/9—347/8 B.C.E.), lasted for some nine centuries. Although Plato's works, written in dialogical form, deal with a vast array of questions, his influence on Neoplatonism was primarily in the area of metaphysics. In Plato's understanding, there is a fundamental opposition between the changing sensible objects that we know empirically through our senses, and the eternal essences, the "ideas" or "forms" that we know intellectually. These forms are true reality, and they are the source and cause of the phenomena of the sensible world. The supreme idea is the idea of "the good," which is the cause of all causes.

Plato's metaphysics is based on the conception that it is the perfect ideal, the universal form or idea, that is real, whereas the particular, material sensible object in this world is merely an imitation or shadow of the universal idea. For Plato, the particular material object is less "real," and its existence is less perfect, than the immaterial and perfect idea. To demonstrate Plato's approach, let us imagine a triangle. In its ideal essence, in other words its definition, the triangle is a two-dimensional geometric figure comprised of three intersecting straight lines, which by their intersections form internal angles totaling 180 degrees.

Let us then draw a triangle:

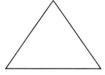

If we were in a class, and Plato were our teacher, he would ask us: "What do you see?" When someone would reply, "A triangle," Plato would question him. "How can you say that you see a triangle? A triangle is a form comprised of three straight lines which intersect and form inner angles totaling 180 degrees. But if you look carefully (perhaps with a magnifying glass or microscope), you will see that the lines we have drawn are not perfectly straight, and the angles do not total exactly 180 degrees, no matter how carefully we have drawn it and measured it. Therefore, what you see is not a true triangle, but only an imperfect imitation of a triangle, and thus not really a triangle at all. Indeed, nobody has ever actually seen a true triangle!"

The true triangle, therefore, is the perfect ideal triangle which we can only know intellectually. That universal "idea" or "form" is never known empirically through the senses, but only as we conceive it in our mind. We tend to think, erroneously, that the ideal form is "only" mental, and that it is, therefore, less "real" than the particular and sensible concrete triangle which we think of as "real." Plato, however, forces us to acknowledge that it is the abstract and universal "idea" of the triangle which is real, and that the particular, concrete triangle is a less real and less perfect imitation and shadow of the ideal one, from which it derives whatever imperfect and incomplete reality it possesses. The existence of the eternal ideal and universal form is thus prior to and more perfect than, the existence of the transient particular sensible object, and our intellectual knowledge of ideal is prior to, and more perfect than, our empirical knowledge of the concrete material object.

For Plato, then, everything that exists in the material world is imperfect, and ultimately derives whatever reality it has from the ideal world. This is also the case with the human being. The sensible human body is transient, and the soul, which governs it and is the formal cause of its life, is imprisoned in it. The ultimate purpose of life is to know the truth. A person can do this by engaging in contemplation (the Greek word "theoria" means contemplation), which is to say by freeing his soul from its bonds to the body and the sense, and thereby enabling it to approach its ideal form. These Platonic themes, as we shall see, resound in the metaphysics[2] or ontology[3]—"the downward way"—and in the ethics—"the upward way"—of Neoplatonism.

[III.1.b] ARISTOTLE AND ARISTOTELIANISM

Aristotle (384–322 B.C.E.) was born in Macedonia, and as a youth studied in Plato's Academy. He served for some time as the tutor of Alexander the Great, but in 334 B.C.E. returned to Athens and founded a school for the sciences called the Lykeion (known in Latin as "Lyceum," from which the French *lycée* is derived.) because of its proximity to the temple of Apollo Lykeios. The Lykeion had a covered walkway called *peripatos* (from the

---

2   "Metaphysics" literally means that which is after or beyond physics; Aristotle's *Metaphysics* is the book following his *Physics*. In thematic terms, it also means after or beyond physics, in the sense of studying the underlying principles (such as causation) of physical reality.

3   "Ontology," from the Greek *onta* = being, and *logos* = theory, in other words, the theory of being or existence.

verb *peripatein*, to walk around something), where Aristotle would teach his students while walking around. This led to the Aristotelian philosophers being called "Peripatetics," namely those who walk about.[4] In opposition to his teacher Plato, Aristotle emphasized the study of empirical facts, and his epistemology is based on sensible experience.

According to Aristotle, our sensible apprehension of concrete phenomena precedes our intellectual comprehension of their causes. Therefore, we must first study the phenomena and then proceed to investigate their causes. Every particular substance consists of two components—essence or form, and accidental qualities.[5] Changes occur on the level of the accidents, but the essence is unchanging, and is known through a process of abstraction and generalization.

Form and matter, which together constitute particular substances, do not exist independently of each other. It is the combination which is real, and it is only in our minds that we can abstract the formal and the material aspects of substance from each other. A particular dog is real; its form does not exist independently of its body. The universal canine form, i.e., its definition by genus and species, is an intellectual abstraction, and has no real existence outside our mind. Therefore, according to Aristotle, and again in opposition to Plato, the existence of particular substances is prior to the abstract universals, and our sensible apprehension of concrete particulars is prior to our intellection comprehension of the universals.

Aristotle, accordingly, was a master of classification (which is why he is known as the "father of biology"). He classified all existing things into ten "categories."[6] Substance is the first category, and is the substratum bearing the other nine categories, as we shall see below. Aristotle also classified the sciences into theoretical, practical and productive. The "first philosophy," however, is the "divine science," i.e., theology, because it deals with the unchanging and insensible substances (such as the heavenly spheres), and because its specific subject is God, the active and final cause of all being.

Aristotle's approach to the concrete individual, consisting of form and matter, as real applies also to humans. The human being also consists of two components. The body is his matter, and the soul is the form giving life to the body. The soul is the person's "form" not in the sense of shape, but in these sense of his or her essential definition as a human.

---

[4]   In medieval Arabic texts the Peripatetics were therefore called *al-masha'iyin*, and in medieval Hebrew texts or translations they were accordingly called *ha-masa'iyim* (cf. Rambam, *Guide of the Perplexed* II:Introduction), or *ha-holekhim* ("the walkers"), as in Judah Ha-Levi's *Kuzari* 5:14.

[5]   Refer back at this point to the discussion in Chapter Two, II:3:d:iii.

[6]   Refer back at this point to "categories" in the Appendix: Dictionary of Selected Philosophic Terms.

In conclusion, we need to note that not all the works of Plato and Aristotle known to us were known to medieval Islamic and Jewish thinkers. Conversely, there were later works erroneously attributed to them, especially to Aristotle, such as the Neoplatonic *Theology of Aristotle* and *Liber de Causis* (which we will discuss below). Moreover, the early and influential Muslim philosopher Muḥammad Abu-Naṣr Al-Farabi (870–950)[7] wrote a book attempting to harmonize Plato and Aristotle's philosophies, *The Agreement Between the Opinions of the Divine Plato and Aristotle*,[8] in three parts: "The Attainment of Happiness;" "The Philosophy of Plato;" and "The Philosophy of Aristotle." Therefore, when medieval philosophers, even philosophers with a fine critical sense like Rambam, attributed certain opinions to Plato or especially to Aristotle, these opinions are not necessarily actually those of the ancient Greek masters. For our purposes, however, since we are not dealing with Greek philosophy, the actual views of Plato and Aristotle as understood by scholars today, are less important than how they were understood in the Middle Ages.

[III.1.c] PLOTINUS AND "THE THEOLOGY OF ARISTOTLE"

Plotinus was born in Egypt in 205 C.E., but at the age of 40 settled in Rome, where a group of disciples studied with him. When he was 50 years old he began writing essays for his students, usually based on a text of Plato or Aristotle or one of their commentators. His student Porphyry edited his writings, and arranged them artificially, ostensibly thematically, in six books, each consisting of nine essays. The collection was, therefore, called the *Enneads* (from the Greek "ennea" = 9). An Arabic paraphrase of the *Enneads*, Books IV, V and VI, including material not found in the original, was falsely attributed to Aristotle and was called the *Theology of Aristotle*. It opens with the words: "The first chapter of the book of Aristotle the philosopher, called in Greek *Theologia*, being the discourse on the divine sovereignty."[9]

Through this Arabic paraphrase, which was prepared at the request of Al-Kindi,[10] Plotinus exerted a great influence on Islamic thought (and thereby, indirectly, on Jewish thought), although without the Neoplatonists being

---

7   See Chapter One (I.1.a) and Chapter Two (2.1.a).

8   Muhsin Mahdi published an English translation, *Alfarabi's Philosophy of Plato and Aristotle* (Ithaca: Cornell University Press, 1962). Selections may be found in *Philosophy in the Middle Ages*, edited by Arthur Hyman and James Walsh (Indianapolis: Hacket, 1973) and *Medieval Political Philosophy*, edited by Ralph Lerner and Muhsin Mahdi (Ithaca: Cornell University Press, 1963).

9   *Theology of Aristotle*, translated by Geoffrey Lewis, in *Plotini Opera*, vol. 2, edited by Paul Henry and Hans-Rudolf Schwyzer (Paris and Brussels, 1959), p. 486.

10 The opening paragraph of the *Theology of Aristotle* (p. 486) refers to the translation having been requested by Al-Kindi. On Al-Kindi, see Chapter One (I.1.a).

aware of Plotinus' true identity. Two versions of the *Theology of Aristotle* have survived, a long version and a short version. Both contain material not derived from Plotinus' *Enneads*, and the long version in particular contains new ideas which have no basis in Plotinus. Other fragmentary Neoplatonic texts attributed to "Al-Shaykh Al-Yunani" ("The Greek Sheikh," i.e., the Greek elder or teacher) also reflect Plotinus' *Enneads*. It was only in modern times, however, that the connection to Plotinus of the *Theology of Aristotle* and the "Shaykh Yunani" texts was identified by scholars.

Another Neoplatonic book in Arabic translation, *Fi'l Khair al-Maḥḍ* ("On the Absolute Good") was later known to Latin scholastics in the 13th century as the *Liber de Causis* ("The Book of the Cause"), and was also mistakenly attributed to Aristotle, but is actually based on the *Stoicheiosis Thelogike* ("Elements of Theology") by Proclus.

[III.1.d]   TERMS FOR EMANATION

One of the most prominent features of Plotinus' monistic philosophy was the theory of emanation (Arabic: *faiḍ*; Hebrew: *azilut* or *ha'azalah*; Latin: *emanatio*), which attempts to explain how many can come from one, and how the material can come from the spiritual.[11] The Latin and Arabic terms mean to flow or overflow. The Hebrew root *azal* is found in the Torah, describing how Moses'spirit flowed over to the seventy elders. God says to Moses: "I will come down and speak with you there, and I will make the spirit which is on you flow over, and will place it on them...The Lord descended in the cloud and spoke with him, and made the spirit which was on him flow over, and gave it to the seventy elders. When the spirit rested on them they prophesied..." (Numbers 11:17–25). The verb *azal* here (which we translated as "flow over") was understood in different ways. The Aramaic "Targum Onqelos" translated it as *arbei*, "increased." Other ancient translations, however, understood it as meaning to reduce or diminish. The Septuagint rendered it *aphelo*, and the Latin Vulgate similarly translated it as *aufere*, meaning to take; both thus imply a diminishing of Moses' spirit by taking from it and giving to others. The Syriac Peshitta translated by the root *bzr*, meaning to diminish.

In the twelfth century, Abraham ibn Ezra (whose thought has a Neoplatonic orientation, as we shall see in Chapter 5) interpreted *azal* in the sense of *ezel* (with, next to), and says in his commentary to this passage:

> It means I took what was with (*ezel*) you. Know that the spirit is like wisdom, and if you give of one person's wisdom to another person, the first person's [wisdom] is not decreased, but remains as it was, like the example of a candle.

---

[11]   Refer again to the charts of emanation and spheres in the Appendix.

In other words, just as one can use one candle to light others, without reducing the light of the first, *azal* means to give to another without any diminishing or reduction of the first one.

In the thirteenth century, Ramban (Rabbi Moses ben Naḥman, or Naḥmanides)[12] commented on our passage:

> The meaning of *azal* is that I will leave with (*ezel*) myself some of the spirit which I am putting on you and that I put on them (i.e., the elders)...*Azilut* (emanation) always refers to leaving something with (*ezel*) him.

The source of the emanation, in other words, suffers no diminishing or reduction, because the spirit stays with it. Ramban continues:

> For *azilut* (emanation) means drawing out or leaving and separating [something] with (*ezel*) the giver...Moreover, the giver draws out the given thing that is with (*ezel*) him and that remains with him.

When referring to emanation, medieval Hebrew texts frequently also use such terms as *nava'* (flow), *mashakh* (pull, attract), and *maqor* (source, fountain) for the Arabic *faiḍ*, meaning flow or overflow, and *faiḍ* is the term by which Sa'adiah's *Tafsir* (Arabic translation and commentary to the Torah) translates *azal* in our passage. All of these terms, then, employ the imagery of flowing water and/or light to symbolize the process by which a primary source emanates, in successive stages, all spiritual and material reality. Each stage emanates the stage below it, without thereby being affected or reduced in any way. The image of light again applies: just as light is progressively weakened the farther away one is from its source, so the successive stages, as they are emanated from the stage above them, are marked by a lessening of the perfection, unity, spirituality and purity of the higher stage.

[III.1.e] PLOTINUS, THE DOWNWARD WAY OF EMANATION AND THE ASCENT OF THE SOUL

Plotinus' monistic and eternal system of emanation posits an ideal world transcending the material world, consisting of three stages: the One, the universal intellect, and the universal soul. The One, which is the equivalent of God, thus transcends thought or consciousness, since the very act of thinking

---

12   Ramban was a major figure in *halakhah* as well as *kabbalah*, and represented the Jewish cause in the Barcelona disputation of 1263; in 1267 he immigrated to the Land of Israel, and played an important role in the revival of Jewish life in Jerusalem. His synagogue still stands beneath the "Ḥurvah" synagogue in the Jewish Quarter of the Old City of Jerusalem. In Chapter 11 we will refer to Ramban's role in the Maimonidean controversy.

is inconsistent with absolute unity, beginning with the duality of subject and object of thought. Even if one were to argue along Aristotelian lines for the unity of the subject, act and object of thought (a theme that will recur among some of the Jewish philosophers, as we shall see in later chapters), the mere fact that the intellect can intelligize multiple ideas is inconsistent with absolute unity. The universal intellect is the perfect image of the One, but is emanated from the One and is thus not identical with the One. When we come to the Neoplatonic "upward way," i.e., the ethical path of the soul seeking to purify itself and return to its spiritual source, the universal intellect is the highest stage attainable by the pure soul; the One is utterly transcendent and unattainable. Continuing in the Neoplatonic metaphysical or ontological "downward way," the universal intellect emanates the universal soul, which is its image, and intermediates between the universal intellect above it and then nature and then the material world below it. It is capable of uniting with the material world, but essentially it belongs to the spiritual world and can reunite with the universal intellect and enjoy its enlightenment.

The *Theology of Aristotle* states at the outset that its purpose is to examine and explain the divine sovereignty, which is the first cause, the cause of causes, transcending eternity and time, which emanates successively the universal intellect, the universal soul, nature, and the world of generation and corruption (i.e., what comes into being and what passes away). "This action arises from it without motion; the motion of all things comes from it and is caused by it, and things move towards it by a kind of longing and desire."[13] In other words, motion is characteristic of the lower stages, in their desire to assimilate to the stages above them, but the emanation by the higher stage of the lower stage is without motion or action; it is an overflowing of its own essence.

[III.1.e.i] *The One*

All reality begins with the One. In Plotinus' scheme, and in sharp contrast with the biblical conception of a personal creator God, the One does not act or create with volition. No quantity or multiplicity can be conceived without the prior concept of the One, as the basis of all subsequent quantity and multiplicity. Quantity and multiplicity are not created by the One, but are emanated indirectly from its essence. The only entity directly emanating from the One is the universal intellect. The absolute and unique simplicity of the One is thereby maintained, because it is only on the subsequent level of universal intellect that quantity and multiplicity can first be discerned. Plotinus' One is thus God, the cause of all causes and the source of being of all existing things.

---

[13]   *Theology of Aristotle*, translated by Geoffrey Lewis, Proemium, p. 487.

All things are in it, and it is not in any of the things, for all things gush forth from it…How is it possible for the things to be from the simple One, in which there is no duality or plurality in an respect?…Because it is One, absolute and simple, containing none of these things, and it being pujre One, all things gush forth from it.[14]

The One is the source of quantity, but has no quantity, because all quantity is compounded from unities. The number two contains two ones, but the one is not thereby destroyed or split. Unity thus exists in every number, but transcends and differs from every number.[15] The One is thus the source of number, but is not itself a number. As the source of all being, the One transcends being, and as the source of universal intellect, it transcends thought and consciousness.[16]

Thought cannot be attributed to the One, not only because it is the source of thought, but because of the inherent duality in thought of subject and object of the thought, a duality impermissible in the One. Divine foreknowledge of events is thus also precluded, not only because of the duality inherent in all knowledge, but also because foreknowledge implies that the knower knows now what will happen in the future, a distinction inapplicable to the One transcending time, in which all things exist simultaneously, in the present.[17]

Plotinus asks, how can the One emanate something—quantity or multiplicity—which it itself lacks? His answer is that what comes from it is not identical with it.[18] The individuation of things into separate entities occurs only after they were emanated from the One, just as the rays of light are not identical with their source, and the multiplicity of rays in no way implies multiplicity in their source.

The One is thus no-thing, but at the same time everything. It is no-thing, because it is the cause of things. It is everything, because it is the source of everything, and as the source of everything, it is their supreme good.[19] Nevertheless, it is only "good" in the sense of causing their being. In itself, it transcends all attributes, including "good." As the source of all, including goodness, it transcends all, including goodness. If the One were itself good, it could not be the source of goodness, nor would it truly be the One.

As the eternal source of all being, the One is like a source of light radiating its rays in all directions. While the subsequent stages can be envisaged as

---

[14] *Theology of Aristotle*, ch. 10, p. 291 (based on *Enneads* V:2).
[15] *Enneads* V:5.
[16] *Enneads* V:4.
[17] *Enneads* VI:7.
[18] *Enneads* V:3.
[19] *Enneads* V:5.

lower steps in the ladder of being, they can also be envisaged as surrounding the One as the center of a circle, radiating in all directions, and not merely in one linear direction.[20]

Again, this process of emanation cannot be conceived as an activity, because activity is a type of motion or change, and motion (or change) implies imperfection: something moves or changes to attain perfection. Will also implies imperfection, because one desires that which one lacks. The One thus has no volition or activity. It can, however, in the inactive and passive sense be the object of desire in the universal intellect, just as the universal intellect can be the object of desire of universal soul. Each stage is conscious of the stage above it and of its greater perfection; this arouses in each stage love and the desire to resemble the higher stage. Love and desire being forms of motion, the One can thus, as the object of love and desire, cause their motion without in any way moving or being in motion itself. It is, therefore, the unmoved mover, the motionless source of motion.[21] However, the universal intellect and universal soul, although they are also spiritual entities, are active, unlike the One, because they desire what is above them.[22]

To reiterate, the process of emanation is not volitional. A standard teleological argument for the existence of a personal creator is the intention manifested in the order of nature. Plotinus explicitly rejects this religious line of thinking. The order of nature is a function, not of volition and intentional creation, but of necessity. The One, as we saw, transcends thought, and thus intention or volition, and the world is emanated from the One by necessity, and could not have been other than it is.[23]

Although, as we shall see, medieval Jewish philosophers (like their Muslim and Christian counterparts) could not agree with the impersonal and monistic aspects of Plotinus' thought, his emphasis on the One's absolute unity, transcending all quantity and the source of all quantity, would resonate in their thought. For example, in words of the hymn "Yigdal Elohim Ḥai" (a poetic Hebrew rendition of Rambam's thirteen principles),[24] "One, whose unity is unique, hidden and infinite in his unity."

---

20   *Enneads* V:1.
21   *Enneads* V:1.
22   *Enneads* V:3.
23   *Enneads* VI:7.
24   The hymn, which dates to the 13th—14th centuries, has been attributed both to Daniel ben Judah (a rabbi in Rome in the early 14th century) and to Emmanuel ben Solomon of Rome (1261–1336), whose poetic collection *Maḥbarot* includes a poem of which "Yigdal" is an abridged adaptation. The hymn is recited in many communities at the conclusion of Sabbath and festival evening services.

[III.1.e.ii] *Universal intellect*

Universal intellect knows both itself and the source from which it was emanated, the One. Its unity is, therefore, not absolute. Its unity is further undermined by its knowledge of what it emanates, i.e., what is below it. This does not mean that the universal intellect knows tangible reality external to itself; it does not. Rather, by knowing itself, the universal intellect knows the forms of what is below it—universal soul and nature—as they first exist perfectly in the universal intellect itself (just as in Platonic thought the ideal form of the triangle is prior to and more perfect and real than concrete, particular triangles). Plotinus' universal soul thus corresponds to Plato's realm of intelligible forms. Universal intellect thus manifests both the duality of knower and known, and the unity of combining in itself as their cause all the ideal forms in their perfection.[25]

[III.1.e.iii] *Universal soul*

The universal intellect knows the One above it and desires it, but it also knows the universal soul below it, which it emanates. Just as the human soul participates in and links the human intellect with bodily functions, so the universal soul has upper and lower aspects. The first aspect is its upward orientation, by which it participates in the intellectual realm above it. The second aspect is its downward orientation, towards the sensible world of nature, which is the basis of life, motion and order in the material world. As such, the universal soul forms the link between the higher, spiritual world of universal intellect and the lower, material world of nature. How is the universal soul emanated from the universal intellect? As the universal intellect desires to resemble and unite with the One above it, it also desires to cause something else to exist, much as a pregnant woman desires to give birth to a child.[26] This desire causes the emanation of the universal soul. However, the existence of the universal intellect is not dependent upon the existence of the universal soul, but the universal soul, of course, is dependent upon the universal intellect (just as the child's existence is dependent upon the mother's, but the mother's existence is not dependent upon the child's).

[III.1.e.iv] *The human soul*

As for the individual human soul, the lower functions of the soul (the vegetative and animal faculties) die with the body, but the rational faculty is not directly dependent upon the body, and therefore, does not die with it. The immortality of the rational human soul leads Plotinus to affirm reincarnation (Hebrew: *gilgul nefashot*), namely the belief that after the soul leaves a person's body,

---

[25]   *Enneads* VI:7.
[26]   *Enneads* IV:7.

it is reincarnated in another body, whether human or animal. The more a soul
is pure and free from bodily appetites, it has the power to ascend and return
to its spiritual source; the more a soul is defiled by bodily appetites, the more
it returns to other bodies, even those of animals.[27] However, the immortal
rational soul cannot recall in a later existence what happened to it in a previous
existence, because memory is a function of knowledge acquired by the bodily
senses, not of the intellect.[28]

[III.1.e.v] *The upward way: the ascent of the soul*

The "upward way" refers to the soul's ascent and return to its spiritual source.
By purifying itself through abandoning bodily appetites, the soul becomes
freed from its physical imprisonment. If the soul is sufficiently pure, it can
free itself from the cycle of reincarnation and unite with the intellect after the
body's death. In some cases, if the soul is exceptionally pure, it can achieve
such unification while still alive and attached to the body. Plotinus claimed to
have experienced personally such a "mystical union" (*unio mystica*), consisting
of seeing an inexpressible brilliant light. The "mystical union" passage in the
Theology of Aristotle,[29] (based on *Enneads* IV:8) was paraphrased in Hebrew
by Shem Tov ibn Falaquera (Spain, 13th century) in his *Sefer Ha-Ma'alot*
("Book of Degrees"):[30]

> Aristotle said: Sometimes I was alone with myself and, as it were, I discarded my
> body, and became a simple substance without body. I saw in myself such beauty
> and splendor that I was wondering and astonished. I knew that I was one of the
> parts of the perfect and excellent supernal world and that I possessed active life.
> When this became verified for me, I ascended in my thought from this world
> to the divine cause, as if I were placed in it and cleaving to it. I was above the
> entire world of the intellect, and I saw myself as if I were standing in the divine
> intellectual realm. I became, as it were, joined to it, as if I were standing in the
> divine world of intellect. I saw there light and radiance that tongues cannot
> describe and hearts cannot comprehend. When that radiance and light were too
> great for me to bear, I descended from the [world of the] intellect to thought and
> contemplation. When I am in the world of thought, the thought hid from me that
> light and radiance, and I was left wondering how I descended from the supernal
> divine place and came to be in the place of thought, after my soul had been able
> to leave her body and to ascend to the world of the intellect, and after that to the
> divine [realm], until she was in the place of light and radiance which is the cause
> of all light and of all radiance. I wondered how I saw my soul filled with light.
> But after I considered this and thought deeply about it, I became upset, and I

---

27   *Enneads* IV:7.
28   *Enneads* IV:3.
29   *Theology of Aristotle*, ch. 1, pp. 225–227.
30   Falaquera, *Sefer Ha-Ma'a lot*, pp. 22–23.

remembered Heraclitus,[31] for he commanded one to seek and inquire about the substance of the sublime soul and the haste of the ascent to the supernal, sublime realm. He said that whoever hastens to do this and ascends to the supernal realm will necessarily receive a good reward. Therefore a person should not hesitate to seek that hasty ascent to that supernal realm, despite the fatigue and toil, because he has ahead of him the rest, after which there is no fatigue or toil. By this statement he meant to warn us to seek intellectual things, which can be found as he found them, and which we can attain as he attained them.

The true life, then, is for Plotinus not the mortal life of the body in this material world, but the immortal life of the soul as it seeks to free itself from its physical constraints and return to its source in the intellectual realm, and even to transcend that human intellectual level to the divine realm of universal intellect.

[III.1.f] NEOPLATONISM AFTER PLOTINUS

Let us briefly review some major figures in the history of Neoplatonism after Plotinus.

[III.1.f.i] *Porphyry*

Porphyry, as mentioned above, was the student of Plotinus who edited his teacher's writings as the *Enneads*. He was born to a Syrian family in Tyre in 232 C.E., and the name Porphyry (the Greek *porphyra* means purple) alludes to his Phoenician background (since the Phoenecians were known for their purple dye, in Greek *phoinikeos*). After studying in Athens, he studied with Plotinus in Rome in the years 263–268 C.E. He lived for years in Sicily, and in his old age returned to Athens, where he may have served as head of the Academy, and where he edited the *Enneads*, to which he added a biography of his teacher and a chronological chart indicating which sections of the *Enneads* were written before, during and after his years studying with Plotinus.

Porphyry wrote more than seventy books, including commentaries on Aristotle, but most of these books have been lost. One of his books which has survived is the *Isagoge* ("Introduction"), an introduction to Aristotle's logic, which was subsequently translated into Latin by Boethius (see below), and into Syriac and Arabic. His interest and proficiency in Aristotle resulted in his introducing Aristotelian ideas into Neoplatonic thought. Porphyry died c. 305 C.E.

---

31   Heraclitus (535–475 B.C.E.) was a pre-Socratic philosopher who maintained that the cosmos is characterized by change and motion. The reference to Heraclitus in the *Theology of Aristotle* is presumably to some pseudepigraphical Neoplatonic work.

[III.1.f.ii] *Iamblichus*

Iamblichus (d. 330 C.E.), a Syrian, was Porphyry's student. He played a major role in shaping late Neoplatonism, and transforming it from a philosophic school of thought into a spiritualist and esoteric religious doctrine. His students attempted unsuccessfully to revive paganism in Rome during the reign of the emperor Julian "the Apostate" in the fourth century. Iamblichus' thought emphasized the "triads," namely the Plotinian idea that the spiritual reality transcending the material world consists of three stages, the One, universal intellect, and universal soul.

[III.1.f.iii] *Plutarch*

Plutarch (350–433 C.E.) was the first Neoplatonic head of the Academy in Athens. His commentaries on Plato and Aristotle have been lost, and we know of them only by citations in later works. He seems to have been especially interested in Aristotle's theory of the soul.

[III.1.f.iv] *Proclus*

Proclus (410–485 C.E.) was a student of Plutarch, and was the last important pagan Greek philosopher. His *Stoicheiosis Theologike* ("Elements of Theology") was translated into Latin under the name *Liber de Causis* ("Book of the Cause") and into Arabic as *Fi 'l-Khair Al-Maḥḍ* ("On the Pure [or: Absolute] Good"). Proclus was responsible for systematizing Neoplatonism into the school of thought known in medieval Christianity and Islam.

Proclus added a fourth stage, being, to Plotinus' spiritual triad, thus forming a "tetrad" (a group of four): the One, being, universal intellect, and universal soul. The One transcends being, but being must be prior to universal intellect and soul. Another innovation was his broadening of Plotinus' theory of emanation to include not only vertical but horizontal components. In Plotinus, as we have seen, the downward way of emanation is essentially linear and vertical: each stage emanates the stage below it. Proclus expanded this scheme to include a horizontal dimension: besides emanating subsequent inferior stages, a stage can exert horizontal influence on similar spiritual entities on its own level. For example, the One emanates not only the stage of being below it, but also emanates "henads" ("ones," from the Greek *hen* = one), which Proclus identifies with the Greek gods. Similarly, universal intellect emanates not only universal soul below it, but also other intellects.

The horizontal dimension of the downward way (if it can still be called that) of emanation led Proclus to another insight, that "all things are in all things." In other words, every reality or consciousness reflects, and is reflected in, every other reality. The human mind knows the One, but its knowledge differs from the One, and the One contains ideal knowledge of the human.

As for the upward way, the moral task of humans is to repress bodily appetites and to avoid, so far as possible, involvement in social and political life, so that the soul might return to its spiritual source, a source which reflects, and is reflected in, the human intellect. The moral goal, i.e., the upward way of the ascent of the soul, thus again is a reversal of the downward direction of metaphysical, ontological emanation. As Laurence Rosán has aptly put it, "Proclus' ethics is almost nothing but his metaphysics in reverse—a retracing from the lowest human level to the highest Reality of the stages through which the highest originally declined into the lowest."[32]

[III.1.f.v] *Boethius*

Boethius (480–525 C.E.), a member of an aristocratic Roman family, received both classical and Christian education. From a young age he held public office, and in 510 became Consul, but was later executed by the Gothic ruler of Rome, Theodoric. The author of many books in diverse fields including mathematics, geometry, music, philosophy and theology, Boethius reflects Platonic, Aristotelian and Stoic thought. Although Boethius is not generally regarded as an original thinker, his clear formulations exerted great influence on Catholic Europe until the 12th century. His best-known work, written while Boethius was in prison, is *De Consolatione Philosophiae* ("The Consolation of Philosophy").

[III.1.f.vi] *John Philoponus*

John Philoponus lived in 6th century Alexandria. A Christian Neoplatonist, he was known to medieval Jews as "John the grammarian" (*Yoḥanan Ha-Medaqdeq*) because of his famous grammatical works. Rambam refers to him as one of the early philosophic sources of the Kalam.[33] Philoponus was familiar with theology, linguistics, mathematics and the natural sciences, and was a sharp critic of Aristotle's physics and cosmology. His works, written in Greek and later translated in Arabic, include commentaries on Aristotle and original works, *On the Eternity of the Cosmos Against Proclus*, and *On the Creation of the World*.

As a Christian monotheist, he believed in creation *ex nihilo*, and argued against Aristotle's and Proclus' affirmation of eternity. God created the heavens and the earth, and therefore there cannot be any difference in their physical

---

32 Laurence Rosán, "Proclus," in *Encyclopedia of Philosophy* (New York: Macmillan and Free Press, 1967), vol. 6, p. 482.

33 *Guide of the Perplexed* I:71. As Shlomo Pines has shown (in his essay, "The Philosophic Sources of the *Guide of the Perplexed*," the translator's introduction to Pine's English translation of the *Guide of the Perplexed* (Chicago: University of Chicago Press, 1963), Rambam's claim that John Philoponus was a source of the Kalam is chronologically untenable, because Philoponus' works, which were quite influential in Rambam's day (the 12th century) had not yet been translated into Arabic when the early Kalam developed.

structure. The heavenly bodies are not divine, nor are they composed of eternal matter. The stars consist of fire—one of the four earthly elements—and are, therefore, subject to the same laws of change as are the other earthly elements. Philoponus also rejected Aristotle's law of motion, according to which a body in motion constantly requires a mover. Instead, he developed the concept of impetus, a forerunner of the modern physical notion that a constant force produces acceleration and not constant motion.

Because of his rejection of Aristotelian and classical Neoplatonic eternity in favor of the religious (in his case, Christian) belief in creation, Philoponus exerted a great influence on Islamic thought. He is, therefore, an important link in the transmission of classical Greek philosophy to Arabic philosophy, and thereby to Jewish philosophy.

[III.1.f.vii] *The Pure Brethren (Ikhwan Al-Ṣafa)*

Another major source of Neoplatonic influence on Jewish thought was an Arabic collection known as *Rasa'il Ikhwan Al-Ṣafa* ("The Letters of the Pure [or: Sincere] Brethren"). This collection of 51 or 52 letters[34] was the product of a secret fraternity of intellectuals in Baṣra, Iraq. Many scholars have suggested that the Brethren reflect doctrines within Shi'ite Islam of the Isma'ili sect, which was founded in the eighth century and was influenced by Neoplatonic and other philosophic and theological schools, but other scholars reject the Isma'ili connection. In any event, we do not know for certain who the Pure Brethren were.

The "Letters of the Pure Brethren" form a sort of philosophical and religious encyclopedia. The first group of letters (letters #1–14) deals with mathematics and logic. The second group (letters #15–31) deals with physics and the body. The third group (letters #32–41) deals with theories of the soul and intellect. The fourth group (letters #42–52) deals with religious law, religion and God. Y. Marquet[35] has suggested that the literary structure of the letters (which is not followed consistently, perhaps to give each one of the four sections roughly equal weight) progresses gradually, from the concrete to the abstract, and reflects a four-fold categorization in letter #27: mathematics (the foundation of all other sciences), logic, physics and metaphysics.

As Lenn Goodman has shown,[36] although all the persons named in the "Letters" lived in Baṣra, the "Letters" are imbued with a cosmopolitan spirit

---

34   There is confusion regarding the correct number. We have 52 letters, but the letters themselves refer to the number 51. Letter #51, according to our count, may have been added later, because it reviews and repeats material in earlier letters. The letters also allude to an additional, secret "general" letter, summarizing the Brethren's theories, but it was kept secret and may not have survived.

35   Y. Marquet, "Ikhwan al-Safa," in *New Encyclopedia of Islam*, vol. III, cols. 1071–1076.

36   Lenn Goodman, *The Case of Animals versus Man Before the King of the Jinn* (Boston: Twayne Publishers, 1978).

of fellowship with similarly minded people everywhere. The Brethren rejected and mocked partisan and sectarian differences, which they attributed to ignorance and the desire for power and domination. The mixture of religion and politics is the main cause of the failure of religion to fulfill its true purpose.

With their tolerant, cosmopolitan outlook, the Brethren sought to learn the truth from a wide variety of sources. People of different cultures and personal temperament need all the diverse approaches and different schools of thought, just as different medicines are required for various diseases. The Brethren, therefore, compiled an encyclopedic collection of all the known sciences. The collection reflects significant Neoplatonic influences, but also some Pythagorean ideas,[37] according to which "all is number," i.e. numbers are not merely quantitative concepts, but are the building blocks of reality.

[III.2]   ISAAC ISRAELI

Isaac ben Solomon Israeli was the first Jewish Neoplatonist. According to a late tenth-century Arabic source, Ibn Juljul's *Generations of the Physicians*, Israeli was born in Egypt in 855 C.E. and died after 955 C.E. at the age of over 100.[38] A physician, he never married or had children. According to Ibn Juljul, when Israeli was asked if he would have liked to have had a child, he replied that he would be better remembered for his *Book of Fevers*. He was indeed known to later generations primarily as a physician, and his medical works, written in Arabic, were translated into Hebrew.

Israeli's philosophical works include *Kitab Al-Ḥudud w'al-Rusum* ("The Book of Definitions"), which in Hebrew was known as *Sefer Ha-Gevulim* and as *Sefer Ha-Gedarim*, and which survived in a 14th-century Hebrew translation by Nissim ben Solomon and in two Latin translations. On the other hand, Israeli's *Kitab Al-Jawahir* ("The Book of Substances") has survived only in Arabic fragments. Another work, *Sefer Ha-Ru'aḥ Veha-Nefesh* ("The Book of the Spirit and the Soul") has survived only in Hebrew translation, and may be part of a larger work. Israeli's most comprehensive work was his *Kitab Al-Usṭuquṣat* ("The Book of the Elements"), known in Hebrew as *Sefer Ha-Yesodot*, which survived in two Hebrew translations and in a Latin translation. An important commentary to the *Sefer Yeẓirah* (to which, it will

---

37   Pythagoras of Samos (572–497 B.C.E.) developed what is still known as the Pythagorean theorem, that the square of the length of the hypotenuse of a right triangle is equal to the squares of the lengths of both of the other two sides: $A^2 + B^2 = C^2$.

38   Ibn Juljul, *Generations of the Physicians*, cited by Alexander Altmann and M.S. Stern, *Isaac Israeli: A Neoplatonic Philosopher of the Early Tenth Century* (London: Oxford University Press, 1958), p. xvii.

be recalled, Israeli's younger contemporary Sa'adiah Ga'on also wrote a commentary) was written by Israeli's student Dunash ben Tamim, and reflects Israeli's views.

In their important study of Isaac Israeli,[39] Alexander Altmann and S.M. Stern showed that Israeli, Abraham ibn Ḥasday, the first Arab philosopher Al-Kindi,[40] and the long version of the *Theology of Aristotle* share a common but unidentified Neoplatonic source. Israeli's philosophic influence on later Neoplatonists like Solomon ibn Gabirol was noticeable, as it was on the first kabbalists in Gerona,[41] and his works were cited by later Jewish philosophers. Not all of the later Jewish philosophers regarded Israeli's philosophy positively. Rambam, for example, in his letter to Samuel ibn Tibbon (whose translation of the *Guide of the Perplexed* into Hebrew was approved by Rambam late in his life), refers disparagingly to *The Book of Definitions* and *The Book of the Elements* and says that Israeli was only a physician. Rambam's opinion of Isaac Israeli was shared by Shem Tov ibn Falaquera in the 13th century, who wrote that "Isaac Israeli's [medical] books are very beneficial."[42] Other philosophers, however, had a high regard for Israeli as a philosopher, such as David Kimḥi (Radak), who cites Israeli favorably in his Bible commentary,[43] and Abraham ibn Ḥasday (who translated Israeli's *Book of the Elements* into Hebrew at the request of Kimḥi).

[III.2.a] THE "DESCRIPTION" OF PHILOSOPHY

In Chapter 1, we saw that the modern classification of philosophy among the humanities differs sharply from the classical and medieval view of philosophy as the mother of all sciences. We tend to regard the "hard" natural sciences as having an objective quality of certainty lacking in the humanities, because science is either based on empirical observation, or subjects its hypotheses to empirical verification, whereas the humanities may reflect cultural differences and subjective values and opinion. Judah Ha-Levi, as we shall see in Chapter 6, was exceptional in regarding philosophy (or at least the dominant Aristotelian philosophy of the day) as unscientific and lacking objective validity, *inter alia*, because of disagreements among the philosophers (who would not disagree if their views were truly scientifically demonstrated):

---

[39]   *Isaac Israeli: A Neoplatonic Philosopher of the Early Tenth Century* (London: Oxford University Press, 1958), cited in the previous note.

[40]   On Al-Kindi, see ch. 1 (I.1.a).

[41]   For example, 'Azri'el of Gerona's *Perush Ha-Aggadot* (13th century) has sections resembling Isaac Israeli's "Chapter on the Elements." According to 'Azri'el, the differences between the philosophers and the kabbalists are merely terminological.

[42]   Shem Tov ibn Falaquera, *Sefer Ha-Mevaqesh* ("The Book of the Seeker"), p. 36.

[43]   See Radak on Genesis 1:2 and Genesis 1:10.

If you ask the philosophers, you do not find them agreeing about any action or any opinion, because they only have arguments, some of which they can prove, some of which are satisfactory, and some of which are unsatisfactory, and are certainly not proven.[44]

When the philosophers agree, Ha-Levi concludes, they do so not because their opinion has been proven scientifically, but because they accept on faith and as authoritative the conclusion of whichever master they happen to follow, such as Plato or Aristotle or Pythagoras, who disagree with each other.[45]

Similar challenges to the scientific and objective character of philosophy, as evidenced by the disagreements among the philosophers, may have existed some two centuries before Judah Ha-Levi, judging from Isaac Israeli's vigorous rejection of this criticism. Disagreements do not disqualify philosophy as such, nor are they evidence that the philosophic method is defective. Philosophers reach different conclusions not because they are merely expressing personal opinion (as Ha-Levi charged), but because their different conclusions are based on differing assumptions or definitions. Israeli's *Book of Definitions* begins, accordingly, by defining "definition."

How does one define something? According to Israeli, there are four ways of inquiry which enable one to define something, and each type of definition answers a different question. The first question is whether something exists, to which the answer is yes or no. The second question is what something is, to which the response is to define its essence, its "quiddity" (its "whatness"). The third question is how something is, namely its quality, to which the answer is to affirm or deny that it has properties X, Y, or Z. The fourth question is why something is as it is, to which the response is the ultimate purpose for which it exists.

Israeli's example is to define the human being. (1) Does the human exist? Yes. (2) What is the human being? A rational and mortal living being. (3) What kind of qualities does he have? When the question of qualities is clarified and specified, we can answer that a man has or does not have these specific qualities. (4) Why is the human being rational? To know the truth and to do what is right, so as ultimately to be rewarded by God.[46]

Thus far, Israeli's four inquiries of definition are based on similar ideas in Al-Kindi's *Fi Al-Falasifah al-Ula* ("On First Philosophy"),[47] and ultimately on Aristotle's four causes (material, formal, efficient, and final). Nevertheless,

---

44   Judah Ha-Levi, *Kuzari* 1:13.

45   Judah Ha-Levi, *Kuzari* 4:25. Cf. *Kuzari* 5:14.

46   *Book of Definitions* #1, English translation in Altman and Stern, *Isaac Israeli*, pp. 11–12.

47   On Al-Kindi, see Ch. 1 (I.1.a). See Alfred Ivry, *Al-Kindi's Metaphysics* (Albany: State University of New York Press, 1974), p. 56.

when it comes to defining philosophy, Israeli and Al-Kindi part ways. For Al-Kindi, the "first philosophy" (i.e., metaphysics) encompasses all other branches of philosophy and science, and to know philosophy is to have a complete knowledge of its definition. For Israeli, however, philosophy is unique and therefore cannot be defined, but only described. A scientific definition consists of two components: the element common to all members of that species, and that which specifies the particular individual. Since philosophy is *sui generis*, it is not a member of a class with any other discipline, and therefore cannot be defined. Nevertheless, in terms of its content, Israeli's "description" resembles Al-Kindi's "definition.

The second definition in the *Book of Definitions*, accordingly, is a "description," rather than a definition, of philosophy. Philosophy can be described in three ways: (1) by its name, (2) by its properties, (3) and by its traces and actions. When described by its name, philosophy means the love of wisdom. When described by its properties, philosophy means resembling God by knowing the truth of things (by knowing, in turn, their four Aristotelian causes) and by right action. When described by its effects, philosophy is a person's knowledge of himself. Here Israeli (like Al-Kindi) introduces the macrocosm-microcosm theme: by knowing himself as both spiritual and material, the human being, as a microcosm, has knowledge of all reality, and is worthy of being called a philosopher.[48] Philosophy thus understood has both theoretical and practical dimensions—knowing the truth and acting morally—and thereby constitutes a way for a person to resemble God. These two dimensions, theoretical and practical, respectively reflect the downward and upward way. Knowing the truth of things means knowing their causes—in other words, how they come to be. Acting morally means the ascent of the soul, as it frees itself from bodily appetites. Israeli cites a saying, attributed to Plato, that philosophy is striving for death, in the sense of killing the appetites.[49] In the Platonic way of thinking, as we will recall, the ideal is more real than the concrete, which is a mere imitation or shadow of the ideal. Similarly, true life is that of the spiritual realm, not of the body in the material world. By seeking "death" one thus seeks true life.

What, then, of the bulk of humanity who are not philosophers? How are they to know the truth and how to behave? Like Al-Kindi, Isaac Israeli introduces at this point the prophets, who are messengers of God to meet this need. But again, Israeli differs from Al-Kindi, because unlike his Arab colleague, Israeli treats prophecy within a larger Neoplatonic scheme, namely the upward way, and

---

[48]   *Book of Definitions* #2, English translation in Altman and Stern, *Isaac Israeli*, pp. 24–27.

[49]   Neoplatonic literature is replete with such statements attributed to Plato. Their source is in *Phaedon* 62c, 64a, 68b, where Plato says that the philosopher seeks death, namely to be freed from enslavement from bodily appetites and defilement.

adds to that the notion (similar to Sa'adiah Ga'on's) of rational commandments. God reveals to the prophets rational commandments by which to guide people to knowledge of the truth and to right action. Those who refuse to obey these rational commandments will be defiled by their impurities, which will weigh them down and prevent them "from ascending to the world of truth."[50] Those who follow the rational commandments transmitted by messengers of God will, like the philosophers (although not necessarily on the same level as the philosophers), learn to "kill" their bodily appetites and thereby to ascend to the world of truth.

Israeli thus introduces new Jewish elements into his Neoplatonic world view. In the upward way, as we have seen, he introduces the idea of "rational commandments" revealed to the prophet. The prophet does not merely seek his own personal upward way and spiritual fulfillment, but has a social obligation to guide others to the upward way through the Torah's rational commandments. In this way Israeli moderates the Neoplatonic tendency towards individual fulfillment and asceticism. In the downward way, as we shall see, he also introduces a Jewish element, that of creation, to counter and moderate the impersonal monism of Neoplatonism.

[III.2.b] THE DOWNWARD WAY: GOD AND CREATION

In his description of philosophy by its properties, i.e., by knowing it according to the four Aristotelian causes, Israeli discusses the final cause—the ultimate purpose—of human beings:

> A case of a spiritual final cause is the union of soul and body to the end that the truths of the subject of science may become clear to man; that he may distinguish between good and evil...that he may do what corresponds to truth...in order thereby to obtain the reward of his Creator...which is the union with the upper soul, and the illumination by the light of intellect and by the beauty and splendour of wisdom. When attaining this rank, he becomes spiritual, and will be joined in union to the light which is created, without mediator, by the power of God.[51]

These lines, which of course describe the upward way, refer ambiguously to the downward way of "the light which is created, without mediator, by the power of God." What does Israeli mean by this reference to unmediated creation by the power of God? His ideas become clearer later in the book, in definitions #42–44, when he differentiates (42) God's unique *'ibda'*, causing things to exist from non-existence, i.e., creation *ex nihilo*, from (43) the creative power of nature, which produces things out of already existing things, and similarly

---

50   *Book of Definitions* #2, English translation in Altman and Stern, *Isaac Israeli*, pp. 26–27.
51   *Book of Definitions* #2, English translation in Altman and Stern, *Isaac Israeli*, pp. 25–26.

from (44) natural generation by the power of the spheres. Only God creates *ex nihilo* and is, therefore, worthy of being worshipped.[52] We thus have in Isaac Israeli's cosmology a combination of the religious doctrine of creation with the Neoplatonic scheme of emanation: the first stage, God (called *bari*, creator) is not part of the emanatory process (as in Plotinus) but transcends it.

Israeli's cosmology may be represented by the following chart.

ISAAC ISRAELI—COSMOLOGY

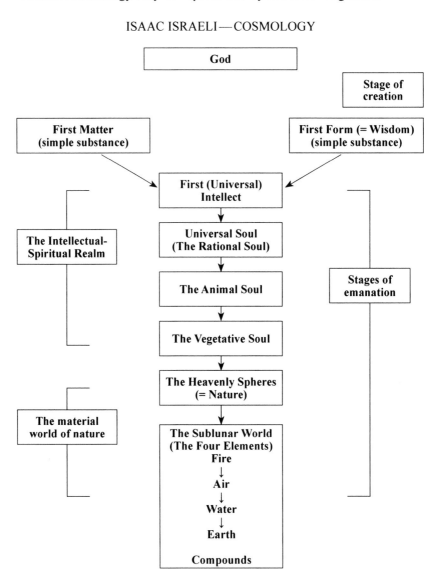

---

52 *Book of Definitions* #42–43, English translation in Altman and Stern, *Isaac Israeli*, pp. 66 ff.

Further emphasis of the importance of creation may be found in Isaac Israeli's *Book of Substances*, where he argues against the opponents of the theory of creation. Israeli does not identify these opponents, but judging from his arguments, their claims are similar to Rambam's description (in the *Guide of the Perplexed* II:14) of two arguments of the followers of Aristotle in favor of eternity: (1) If the world is created, then prior to the creation God was first a potential agent, and then after his creation of the world, an actual agent of the world. Such change in God, from potential to actual agent, is impossible. (2) If the world is created, that means that at one time God acted creatively and not at another time, which in turn means that some cause external to God prevented the action at one time and necessitated the action at the other time. This is also impossible, because God cannot be subject to other causes.

According to Israeli, the fundamental error of the opponents of creation is to attribute change to the agent, God, rather than to that which is affected (acted upon), namely the world. Change in that which is affected — its transition from potentiality to actuality — does not imply change in the activity of the agent, namely that first it was a potential agent and then it became an actual agent. Moreover, if the change from potential to actual is impossible, it is impossible for that which is affected, and not for the agent. For example, Israeli suggests, there were many generations between Adam and Moses. Could not Moses have been made to exist in the time of Adam? The impossibility of Moses' living in the time of Adam does not reflect on God's inability to cause it, but on the impossibility from the perspective of the people thus affected. Thousands of years passed between Adam and Moses, and to place Moses in Adam's generation would be to nullify all the generations between them. The obstacle is thus not in the creator but in the creatures. Since nature is generated by divine wisdom, to suggest that God acts contrary to natural order is to imply that God acts contrary to his wisdom, which is absurd.[53]

Despite his clear affirmation of creation *ex nihilo*, Israeli continues to employ Neoplatonic language, and to construct a clear hierarchical structure, for the emanation of subsequent spiritual and material reality from first form and first matter, beginning with the emanation from them of the first intellect, using such key terms as radiance, brilliance and splendor. Each stage is characterized by progressively diminished light, radiance, brilliance and splendor. In the *Book of the Spirit and the Soul* he describes the progressive emanation from the first intellect:

A radiance and brilliance went forth from [the first intellect's] shade like the radiance which goes forth from the shade of the glass balls and the mirrors

---

53   Isaac Israeli, *The Book of Substances*, fragment 2, English translation in Altmann and Stern, *Isaac Israeli*, p. 82.

which are set in windows of baths and houses, when the ray of the sun falls on them; from this the nature of the rational soul comes into being. Its splendour and brilliance are less than the splendour and brilliance of the intellect; the reason being that the degree of intellect is intermediate between the soul and its Creator.[54]

The universal or rational soul, in like manner, emanates the animal soul, which emanates the vegetative soul, which emanates the heavenly spheres (or nature); their motions produce fire, which emanates air, which emanates water, which emanates earth, and from these four elements all animals and plants are compounded. Compounds all perish by returning to their component elements; the soul, however, is not compounded from any sensible elements, and therefore is imperishable.

In Isaac Israeli's cosmology, we thus have a combination of creation *ex nihilo* with emanation. The first stage is creation *ex nihilo* by God's will and power of the first matter and of the first form (which Israeli equates with wisdom). The first matter and first form combine to form the first intellect. Thus far we have creation. Henceforth we have the degrees of emanation, beginning with emanation by the first intellect of the rational soul described in the text of the *Book of the Spirit and the Soul* cited above. Why, then, does creation *ex nihilo* not extend throughout all of reality? Israeli differentiates, as we have seen, between creation, as an act of will, bringing something into existence after its non-existence (i.e., from nothing), and emanation, which is not a conscious act at all, let alone an act of conscious will, but a necessary overflow from the essence of the higher to the essence of the lower, and thus causes something to exist from something else. As we have seen, Israeli thus modifies the impersonal monism of Plotinus' cosmology to introduce a personal monotheistic dimension necessary for religious life. At the same time, Israeli modifies the traditional religious scheme for philosophic reasons: God is no longer directly responsible for the creation of all the cosmos, but only of its highest stage, the universal or first intellect, combining first matter and first form.

[III.2.b.i] *First matter and first form*

Perhaps also in order to emphasize God's transcendence as creator,[55] Isaac Israeli inserts an extra stage, that of "simple substances"—first matter and first form (or "wisdom")—between God and universal, first intellect. These simple substances are not emanated but created by God. They are "substances"

---

54   Isaac Israeli, *The Book of the Spirit and the Soul* #9, English translation in Altmann and Stern, *Isaac Israeli*, pp. 110–11.

55   Alexander Altmann (*Isaac Israeli*, p. 163) suggests this possibility, "to facilitate the adoption of the concept of creation within the framework of Neoplatonic metaphysics."

because they exist in and of themselves, and are not dependant on anything else, since they were not created from anything else. They are "simple" because they are spiritual and indivisible, unlike terrestrial matter and form. Therefore, they are also "the beginning of all roots" (*reshit ha-shorashim*)—they were created by God from nothing, but the existence of everything else, beginning with the first intellect (which is compounded of these two roots), is based on their existence.

> First matter is the root of roots... It subsists in itself and is the substratum of diversity... Substantial form... is perfect wisdom, pure radiance, and clear splendour, by the conjunction of which with first matter the nature and form of intellect came into being.[56]

First matter is thus not "material" in our three-dimensional bodily sense, but is a simple, spiritual substance. It is called "matter" because it is the unchanging "substratum of diversity," just as terrestrial matter is the unchanging substratum sustaining diverse, changing forms.

[III.2.b.ii] *Universal first intellect*

As we have seen, universal first intellect is no longer emanated directly from God (as in Plotinus), but is a combination of the two simple substances, first matter and first form, created by God out of nothing. Israeli argues that the first intellect cannot consist only of first matter or only of first form. If it consisted only of first matter, without form, it would be empty and devoid of content, i.e., it would know nothing. Its form is its "wisdom," giving it the content of knowledge. At the same time, first intellect cannot consist only of first form, without matter, because without matter, it would have no substratum on which to subsist. Its substratum also cannot be the rational soul below it, because if the rational soul were first intellect's "matter," the rational soul could not exist without the intellect's knowledge, whereas in fact souls are able to exist without intellectual knowledge. The rational soul cannot, therefore, be the intellect's "matter," nor the intellect the "form" of the rational soul. The first intellect, accordingly, must consist of both simple substances, first matter and first soul, which are, therefore, prior to it in creation.[57] However, they are prior to first intellect not in time but in nature and rank: the higher and lower stages of emanation exist together, simultaneously.

---

[56]   Isaac Israeli, "The Chapter on the Elements," English translation in Altmann and Stern, *Isaac Israeli*, p. 119.

[57]   Isaac Israeli, *Book of the Substances*, fragment 4, English translation in Altmann and Stern, *Isaac Israeli*, pp. 85–88.

[III.2.b.iii] *The soul*

In the previous chapter (II.3.o) we saw that Isaac Israeli's younger contemporary Sa'adiah Ga'on, and later Judah Ha-Levi, adopt the Platonic tri-partite division of the soul (rational, anger, appetites). Israeli's theory of the soul is also tri-partite, although with different names (rational, animal, vegetative). However, for Israeli, this tri-partite structure of the human soul is a microcosm of a parallel structure in the universal soul. As the radiant light emanates down through successive stages, as we recall, it becomes weaker and dimmer. Only the first intellect receives the light without intermediation, directly from the divine will and power. The light reaching the universal rational soul, being intermediated by the first intellect, is according weaker, and each successive stage of the soul receives less and less of the light, because of the interfering shadows of the intermediating stages above it.

Since the universal rational soul receives a dimmer and weaker light, it is unable to know the truth directly and independently, by its own power, and it requires the aid of instruction. The light reaching the animal soul is even weaker, and so it cannot know the truth without the aid of the external senses and the imagination. The vegetative soul, which receives even less light, has no such cognition, and its functions are limited to growth and procreation. The power of nature is even more deficient, and natural bodies (both celestial and terrestrial) lack any independent power of action or motion, and can only be affected by external forces.

The structure Isaac Israeli's psychology thus reflects the structure of his cosmology, reinforcing the theme of the microcosm-macrocosm in his theory.

[III.2.b.iv] *The Material Realm—Nature*

The celestial sphere, which is the first material stage in Isaac Israeli's cosmology, is also, in a sense, the final spiritual stage, which is why it is equated with "Nature." Its intermediate status, between material and spiritual, reflects its matter, which does not resemble the coarse matter of the terrestrial world, consisting of the four elements. Rather, celestial matter consists of a "fifth element," even finer and purer than fire (the finest and purest terrestrial element). This fifth element of the sphere, as Israeli explains in the *Book of Definitions*, is emanated directed and without intermediary from the shadow of the vegetative soul, and in turn affects the motions and events in the terrestrial world, including events in human history.[58]

---

[58]   Isaac Israeli, *Book of Definitions* #6, English translation in Altman and Stern, *Isaac Israeli*, pp. 45–47.

[III.2.c] THE UPWARD WAY: THE ASCENT OF THE SOUL

Thus far we have discussed the metaphysical or ontological "downward way." Turning now to the "upward way" of the ascent of the soul, Isaac Israeli differentiates among three stages:

    i.   Purification of the soul (Al-Kindi's *taṭ-hir*; Proclus' *via purgativa*).

    ii.   Enlightenment of the soul (Al-Kindi's *'inara*; Proclus' *via illuminativa*) by the intellect.

    iii. Union or conjunction of the soul with the light of the intellect (Al-Kind's *'ilham*, inspiration; Proclus' *via unitiva*).

First the soul must abandon the bodily appetites and reject material defilement; it can then receive enlightenment from the intellect; and then it can "return" to its divine source and unite with the divine light. Let us return to a passage (reminiscent of Plotinus' description of his *unio mystica*) previously cited about the final purpose of life:

> To obtain the reward of his Creator... which is the union with the upper soul, and the illumination by the light of intellect and by the beauty and splendour of wisdom. When attaining this rank, he becomes spiritual, and will be joined in union to the light which is created, without mediator, by the power of God.[59]

[III.2.d] PROPHECY

As has already been mentioned, most people are not philosophers, and either do not understand the demands of the upward way, or are unable to meet those difficult demands. Prophets, who are messengers of God, can convey to the people God's rational commandments, and thereby guide them to knowledge of the truth and to right action. Thanks to the prophets, people who follow the rational commandments, though not themselves philosophers, can learn, like the philosophers, to repress their bodily appetites and become spiritual.

In his Commentary to the *Sefer Yeẓirah*, Isaac Israeli's student Dunash ben Tamim, whose ideas often reflect those of his teacher, describes three grades of prophets: (1) The lowest rank of prophecy is when a person hears a voice, called *bat qol*, created in the air.[60] (2) A higher grade of prophecy is vision seen by the prophet, called *ru'aḥ* (spirit). (3) The highest rank of

---

[59]   Isaac Israeli, *Book of Definitions* #2, English translation in Altman and Stern, *Isaac Israeli*, pp. 25–26.

[60]   There is a similarity between this view and Sa'adiah Ga'on's notion of the prophet hearing a "second air" called *kavod* or *shekhinah*. See the discussion in ch. 2 (II.2).

prophecy was experienced by Moses, who spoke "face to face" with God. This prophetic "speech" is, according to Dunash, the stage of union or conjunction with the divine light.

How does the prophet differ from the philosopher? Both attain intellectual perfection and conjunction with the divine light. The prophet, however, in addition to his intellectual perfection, also has perfected his imaginative faculty, and prophecy involves the activity of both intellect and imagination.[61] The vision seen by the prophet is not a result of external sensation, but of intellectual stimulation of the imagination.

The imagination ordinarily receives the forms its sees from the external senses. In addition to the five external senses (sight, hearing, taste, smell and touch) a person has a "common sense" (Latin: *sensus communis*). This does not refer to what in English is called common sense (meaning a basic prudence and sound judgment, not based on intellectual reasoning), but to an internal faculty of the soul organizing, coordinating and synchronizing the various external sense impressions, which it then passes on to the imagination. The forms of the common sense are, according to this understanding, "intermediate" between the material and sensible forms perceived by the external senses, and the spiritual forms of the intellect.

In the case of the prophet, his imaginative faculty receives not only these "intermediate" forms from the common sense below it, but also "spiritual" forms from the intellect above it. Why, then, does the prophet's intellect pass these spiritual forms on to the imagination? Here we have the critical difference between the philosopher, whose perfection is individual, and the prophet, who also has individual perfection, but also has a social function—that of instructing other people how to attain perfection.

By receiving spiritual forms from the intellect, the prophet's imagination thus enables him to instruct and lead other people to spiritual perfection. The prophet would not be able to do this by means of intellect alone, due to the limited understanding of the people. His message must, therefore, be expressed by images which are "intermediate" between spiritual and material, in other words, forms derived from the intellect and then processed by the imagination into terms the people can comprehend and which will motivate them. The philosopher and the prophet, in short, both apprehend the theoretical intellectual truth, but the prophet has the additional ability—due to his developed imagination—to communicate that truth effectively to people in terms they can understand.

---

[61]   The idea that the prophet has perfect imagination as well as perfect intellect plays an important role in Rambam's understanding of the political role of the philosopher, based on Al-Farabi, as we shall see in ch. 10.

In conclusion, we have seen how Isaac Israeli combines and modifies general Neoplatonic themes of the downward and upward ways, with specific Jewish religious concerns. In the downward way, he accomplished this modification by introducing an additional stage—the simple spiritual substances—between God and the first intellect, to emphasize God's transcendence as creator, a personal God who creates *ex nihilo* by an act of will, in contrast with the impersonal and necessary process of emanation commencing only thereafter, with the first intellect's emanation of the rational soul. In the upward way, he modifies the philosophic ideal by broadening it to include non-philosophers. He does so by introducing the prophet, who has the ability, due to his developed imagination, to convey to the people the rational commandments they need for right behavior, and to translate the abstract intellectual truth into language they can comprehend, so that the people, and not just the philosophers, can share in human perfection and enlightenment.

[III.3] SOLOMON IBN GABIROL

Solomon ben Judah ibn Gabirol, called Avicebron in Latin, was born in Malaga, Spain c. 1020 C.E. and was educated in Saragossa. Orphaned at an early age, he seems to have been sickly and of short stature. He began writing poetry in his youth, but resented his financial dependence on wealthy patrons. When his long-time and influential patron Yekutiel ibn Ḥassan was murdered, Ibn Gabirol no longer was able to support himself in Saragossa, and left the city, and we have little information about him thereafter. He seems to have died c. 1057 C.E. at the age of 37. Mainly famous for his extensive poetry, Ibn Gabirol also wrote ethical and philosophical works.

[III.3.a] ETHICAL WORKS

[III.3.a.i] *Mivḥar Peninim ("Choice of Pearls")*

This short work, which is a collection of 652 moral aphorisms divided into 64 sections (such as wisdom, friendship and love) was written in Arabic, and translated into Hebrew by Judah ibn Tibbon in the 12th century.[62] It resembles other ethical literature of the period, such as *Adab Al-Falasifa* ("The Aphorisms of the Philosophers") by the Syrian-Christian translator, Ḥunayn

---

[62]   An English translation by A. Cohen, *Solomon ibn Gabirol's Choice of Pearls* was published in 1925 (New York: Bloch Publishing Co.).

ibn Isḥaq (810–873 C.E.) in Baghdad,[63] which survived in the Hebrew translation, *Musarei Ha-Pilosofim* by Judah Al-Ḥarizi. However, Ibn Gabirol's
authorship of the book has been seriously questioned by modern scholars,
and was already questioned in the 13th century by the Spanish philosopher
and translator Shem Tov ibn Falaquera (to whom we shall return below), who
explicitly stated that it was written by a non-Jew.[64]

[III.3.a.ii] *Tiqqun Midot Ha-Nefesh*
("The Improvement of Moral Qualities")

The *Improvement of Moral Qualities*[65] was also written in Arabic and translated into Hebrew by Judah ibn Tibbon, and is the first Jewish book presenting
ethics in a systematic, philosophical manner. Strangely, although Ibn Gabirol
cites Biblical verses to support various points, he never cites any rabbinic
ethical statements. Despite the citations of Scripture, the book is not religious
in tone, but attempts to provide an objective basis for ethics by connecting
moral qualities of the soul to physical traits of the body.

The human being is the choice or apex of all creation, and resembles the
angels in his intellect and speech. The ultimate purpose of life, therefore, is
to repress the bodily senses to the minimum necessary for life, and to focus
on "the realm of the intellect which is the world to come (*'olam ha-ba*).[66]
The Neoplatonic upper way resonates clearly here. Nevertheless, there is
an innovation—the connection Ibn Gabirol makes between the bodily senses
and moral qualities.

The faculty is sight is the most noble of the external senses, because it
perceives instantaneously and from a distance, and leads a person to approach
or to draw away from something; it is related to the qualities of pride and
humility. The sense of hearing is less noble, and functions through the medium
of air. People are less inclined to believe what they hear than to believe what
they see. It enables a person to avoid things we should fear, and to incline
towards worthy things to which we should listen. The faculty of smell, like
hearing, functions through the medium of air. However, unlike sight and
hearing, which we control voluntarily, smell does not function voluntarily,
and therefore is unrelated to good or bad qualities. The sense of taste, although
inferior to the others, is essential in differentiating beneficial from harmful
food, and to a certain extent functions voluntarily, thereby enabling us to

---

63   On Ḥunayn ibn Isḥaq see chapter 1 (I.3.c).
64   Shem Tov ibn Falaquera, *Sefer Ha-Mevaqesh* ("Book of the Seeker"), p. 48.
65   The Arabic original, *Kitab Iṣlah al-Akhlaq*, was published together with an English
      translation by S. Wise (New York, 1902).
66   *Tiqqun Midot Ha-Nefesh*, p. 3.

avoid forbidden foods. The fifth faculty is the sense of touch, which (like taste) is essential in avoiding bodily harm, but does not play a role in the needs of the soul.

Each of the five senses has four qualities, related to the four "mixtures" or "temperaments" (Hebrew: *mezeg*): wet, dry, hot and cold. Each bodily temperament, in turn, is related to a quality of the soul, resulting in a total of twenty main qualities (four for each of the five senses).

Depending on the mixture, the sense of sight is related to pride, humility, shame and arrogance. Hearing is related to hate, love, compassion and cruelty. Smell is related to anger, favor, envy and diligence. Taste is related to joy, worry, regret and calm. Touch is related to generosity, stinginess, courage and cowardice.

The following chart shows the connections Ibn Gabirol draws between moral qualities, the four temperaments or mixtures (Hot, Cold, Wet, Dry), the four elements (Fire, Air, Water, Earth) and the four natures (Red bile, Blood, White bile, Black bile).

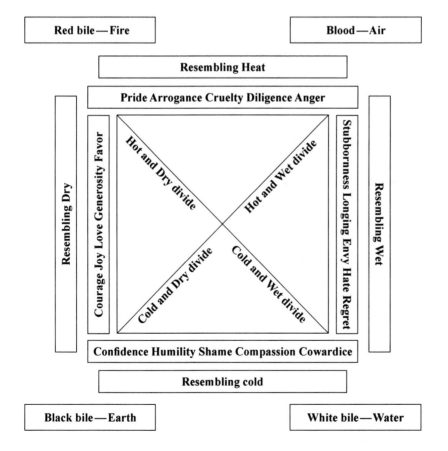

As the name of the book indicates, Ibn Gabirol's purpose in writing the *Improvement of Moral Qualities* was moral improvement, not merely academic, i.e., to explain the physical foundations of moral qualities. The structure of the book accordingly follows the twenty qualities in five sections, each for one of the senses.

[III.3.b]   POETRY

Ibn Gabirol was primarily famous as a Hebrew poet.[67] His poems are both secular—dealing with friendship, wine, love and morals—and sacred, and some of his sacred poems were adopted by various Jewish communities as part of the liturgy for the New Year and Day of Atonement. For example, his poem "He who dwells forever" (*Shokhen 'Ad Me-Az*) was included in the New Year's Eve liturgy of the Sephardic Jews, and is, in effect, a sort of running commentary on the *Sefer Yeẓirah*.[68] Line 12 of this poem includes the phrase *qanah me-ayin yesh* ("he acquired something from nothing"), i.e., God created *ex nihilo*. The concept of creation *ex nihilo* is, of course, not new, and played an important role in Sa'adiah Ga'on's thought and also in Isaac Israeli's definitions. Nevertheless, according to Yehudah Liebes, Ibn Gabirol's poem may well be the first use of the Hebrew phrase *yesh me-ayin* ("something from nothing"), which became the standard Hebrew expression for creation *ex nihilo*.[69] Ibn Gabirol's greatest poem is his *Keter Malkhut* ("The Royal Crown"), which forms a précis of his philosophy. The poem is divided into three sections of forty stanzas of rhymed prose. The first section (stanzas 1–9) deals with God. The second section (stanzas 10–32) deals with creation, and the third section (standzas 33–40) deals with the human being. The poem, which Ibn Gabirol himself referred to as a prayer, was included in many communities' liturgy for the New Year and Day of Atonement.

---

67   A bilingual edition, *Selected Religious Poems of Solomon ibn Gabirol*, Hebrew text edited by Israel Davidson, English translation by Israel Zangwill, was published by the Jewish Publication Society (Philadelphia, 1923). Fifteen poems by Ibn Gabirol may also be found in *The Jewish Poets of Spain 900–1250*, translated by David Goldstein (London: Penguin Books, 1965).

68   On the *Sefer Yeẓirah* and Sa'adiah Ga'on's commentary on it, see the discussion in Ch. 2 (II.2).

69   The phrase may also be found in the poem *Keter Malkhut* ("The Royal Crown") #29: *ve-yaẓa me-ayin la-yesh* ("it went from nothing to something").

[III.3.c] THE *MEQOR ḤAYYIM* ("FOUNTAIN OF LIFE")

[III.3.c.i] *The name Meqor Ḥayyim*

Solomon ibn Gabirol's *Meqor Ḥayyim* was written in Arabic, but the original was lost. The Hebrew phrase *meqor ḥayyim* ("fountain of life"), which is found six times in the Hebrew Bible,[70] appears in Ibn Gabirol's *Keter Malkhut* ("Royal Crown," 9, verse 74): "You are wise, and wisdom flows from you as a fountain of life." The book itself concludes with the hope for "liberation from death and cleaving to the fountain of life."[71]

A translation of the book from Arabic into Latin, *Fons Vitae*, was made in the twelfth century by the apostate Jew Johannes Hispalensus and the Dominican friar Dominicus Gundissalinus, and the author was referred to as Avicebron or Avicebrol; the author's identity, however, was not known, and the assumption was that he was a Muslim or Christian Arab. In its Latin translation, the book was cited by Thomas Aquinas, who generally rejected its approach, and by Franciscans, who were more sympathetic to it.

The *Fons Vitae* deals with general philosophical questions, and lacks any overtly Jewish character, such as citations from the Bible or other Jewish literature. There is only one possible allusion in the book to a Jewish source, namely that God compounded the world from numbers and letters in the air, which may refer to the beginning of the *Sefer Yeẓirah*, where God created the world out of thirty-two mysterious ways, namely the twenty-two letters of the Hebrew alphabet and the ten cardinal numbers.[72]

Avicebron's identity as Ibn Gabirol was only determined in the early nineteenth century, when the French-Jewish scholar Solomon Munk (1803–1867) discovered in Paris a manuscript of a book by the 13th-century Spanish-Jewish philosopher Shem Tov ibn Falaquera, called *Liqqutim Mi-Sefer Meqor Ḥayyim* ("Selections from the Book *Meqor Ḥayyim* [Fountain of Life]"), in which Falaquera wrote: "I studied the book composed by the sage Rabbi Solomon ibn Gabirol called *Meqor Ḥayyim*…I selected selections from its words; these selections contain his complete opinion."[73] On the basis of Falaquera's *Liqqutim* ("Selections") Munk was able to identify Avicebron as Ibn Gabirol, and the *Fons Vitae* as *Meqor Ḥayyim*.[74]

---

[70]   Jeremiah 2:13; Psalm 36:10, Proverbs 10:11, 13:14, 14:27, 16:22.

[71]   *Fons Vitae* 5:43 = *Liqqutim* 5:73.

[72]   *Fons Vitae* 2:21 = *Liqqutim* 2:27.

[73]   Falaquera, *Liqqutim*, Introduction.

[74]   The modern Hebrew translation by Jacob Blubstein (1926) is based on the Latin *Fons Vitae*, as are the abridged English translation of Part III of the book by H.E. Wedeck (London: Peter Owen, 1962), and the complete English translation of the book by Alfred Jacob (Stanwood, Washington: Sabian Publishing Society, 1987).

[III.3.c.ii] *Shem Tov ibn Falaquera's Liqqutim ("Selections")*

The *Fountain of Life* is written in the form of a dialogue between a student and his teacher. However, unlike Plato's dialogues or the dialogue between the king of the Khazars and a Jew in Judah Ha-Levi's *Kuzari*, the dialogue does not prepare the student, step by step, to grasp the truth. Rather, the student's questions merely create a platform for the teacher to expound his theory. Falaquera decided not to translate the Arabic book in its entirety, but as he did with other books, he translated only "Selections" (*liqqutim*), which do not preserve the dialogical format of the original. In many cases, as might be expected from "Selections," the selections abridge the original argument, but in some cases, the selections are actually longer than the original, and include additional examples. Furthermore, Falaquera sometimes changed the order of the selections, so they do not simply follow the original order. Falaquera may have felt free to add to the original argument and to change its order, because in the original the teacher says to the student:

> I shall provide for you a variety of proofs...But I do not undertake to arrange the proofs in proper order because this would serve little purpose; and also so that you may drill yourself in classifying them and grouping each with any corresponding one.[75]

[III.3.c.ii] *Abraham ibn Da'ud's Critique:* *Problems with the book*

The philosopher Abraham ibn Da'ud (1110–1180), who represents the Jewish transition to Aristotelian philosophy,[76] sharply criticized Solomon ibn Gabirol for his excessive verbosity, for citing several invalid proofs rather than one true proof, for faulty reasoning, and observed that Ibn Gabirol could have made his points more effectively in a book of less than 10% of the length of the *Meqor Ḥayyim*. Ibn Da'ud's criticism is not far off the mark. For example, in Part III of the book, Ibn Gabirol lists no less than 56 proofs of the existence of the simple substance intermediating between the first agent and corporeal substance, and no less than 61 proofs that the sensible forms flow from spiritual substance. Ibn Da'ud's criticism of Ibn Gabirol may have persuaded Falaquera to translate only selections, rather than the whole book.

   Ibn Gabirol's comment (in the name of the teacher) that "I do not undertake to arrange the proofs in proper order because this would serve little purpose" may indicate that he himself perhaps recognized that his book was

---

[75]   *Fountain of Life* 3:1, Jacob translation p. 74.
[76]   Abraham ibn Da'ud will be discussed below, in chapter 7.

problematical. Elsewhere, discussing various names for substance, the teacher also says:

> There is no need to worry about assigning a name, because we shall call this underlying reality that supports the structure of the universe, sometimes material and sometimes hyle. In fact, we are not concerned over the correctness of such names.[77]

The *Fountain of Life* is also frequently contradictory. In one place Ibn Gabirol states that both matter and form flow from the divine will,[78] whereas elsewhere matter emanates from God's essence while form emanates from the divine will.[79] Sometimes Ibn Gabirol posits matter as common to all existents, while form differentiates and individuates them,[80] and in other places he reverses it, and posits form as the common denominator, with matter differentiating and individuating them.[81]

[III.3.c.iv] *Solomon ibn Gabirol's cosmology*

Despite these problems of order, imprecise formulation and inconsistencies or contradictions, certain basic features of Ibn Gabirol's philosophy are clear. Like Isaac Israeli before him, Ibn Gabirol posits universal matter and universal form as preceding universal intellect. All being, from the universal level down, is thus characterized by the duality of matter and form. We find, therefore, that there are both spiritual form and material form, and spiritual matter and material matter.

Ibn Gabirol's innovation, therefore, is not in positing such duality throughout reality, which we already found in Isaac Israeli, but in his inserting a new spiritual stage into the top of his cosmology, namely, the divine will. For Ibn Gabirol, the divine will intermediates between God, namely the One and the first agent, and the stage of universal matter and universal form. He also inserts another stage, Nature, near the bottom of his cosmology (between soul and the spheres), a stage not explicit in Israeli's cosmology.

---

[77] *Fountain of Life* 2:11, Jacob translation p. 46.
[78] *Fountain of Life* 5:38.
[79] *Fountain of Life* 5:42.
[80] *Fountain of Life* 1:10–12, 4:1, 4:9
[81] *Fountain of Life* 2:20, 4:14.

SOLOMON IBN GABIROL — COSMOLOGY

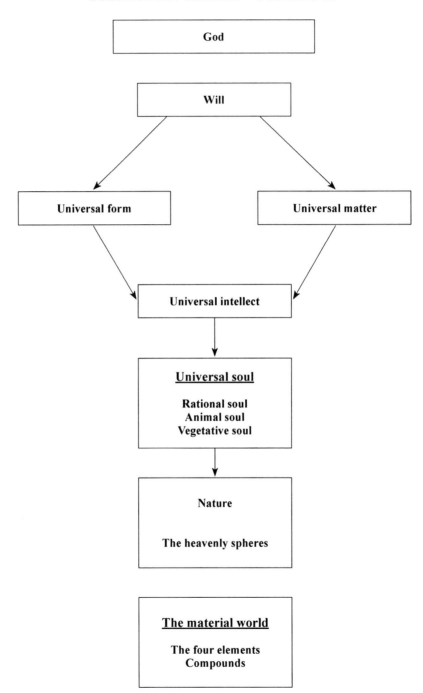

[III.3.d] THEORY OF KNOWLEDGE

The *Fountain of Life* opens with the question, for what purpose was the human being created?[82] Ibn Gabirol immediately answers that the human being was created to acquire knowledge. By knowing himself, he knows everything, and this knowledge constitutes his ultimate happiness and immortality. Although he does not mention the term explicitly, Ibn Gabirol is referring here to the notion that the human, being both material and spiritual, is a microcosm (*'olam qatan*), a theme we already found in Isaac Israeli and Al-Kindi.[83]

The same themes are reflected in "The Royal Crown" (stanzas 29–30):[84]

O Lord, who can comprehend Thy power?
For Thou hast created for the splendour of Thy glory a pure radiance...
Thou hast imparted it to the spirit of wisdom
And called it the Soul.
And of flames of intellectual fire has Thou wrought its form...
And sent it to the body to serve and guard it,
And it is as fire in the midst thereof yet doth not consume it,
For it is from the fire of the soul that the body hath been created,
And goes from Nothingness to Being[85]...

O Lord, who can reach Thy wisdom?
For Thou gavest the soul the faculty of knowledge that is fixed therein,
And knowledge is the fount of her glory.
Therefore hath destruction no power over her...
The soul with her wisdom shall not see death...

Knowledge, which endows the rational soul with immortality, may be divided into three sections: knowledge of matter and form, knowledge of the divine will (*razon*), and knowledge of the first existent.[86] Ibn Gabirol returns to this theme towards the end of the book: the three parts of knowledge are knowledge of matter and form, knowledge of the divine will's command, and knowledge of the first substance.[87] In "The Royal Crown" we find a similar three-fold division of knowledge, but in the poem instead of the divine will Ibn Gabirol refers to "the throne of glory" (*kisé ha-kavod*),[88] which God "raised higher than the sphere of the intellect.

---

82   *Fountain of Life* 1:2, Jacob translation pp. 4–5 = Falaquera, *Liqqutim* 1:1.
83   See the discussion above, in III.2.a.
84   "The Royal Crown," in *Selected Religious Poems of Solomon ibn Gabirol*, Hebrew text ed. Israel Davidson, English translation by Israel Zangwill, pp. 104–105.
85   On this phrase, *ve-yaza me-ayin la-yesh*, see note 69 above.
86   *Fountain of Life* 1:7.
87   *Fountain of Life* 5:36 = Falaquera, *Liqqutim* 5:56.
88   "The Royal Crown" stanza #26, in *Selected Religious Poems of Solomon ibn Gabirol*, p. 102.

Knowledge of the divine will or the throne of glory is impossible to attain, let alone knowledge of God himself, "the first substance" or "the first existent." So of the three parts of knowledge, only the lowest level—knowledge of matter and form—is attainable at all, and even that is very difficult to attain, and Ibn Gabirol accordingly refers to matter and form as "two closed gates."[89]

As described in Falaquera's "Selections," the rare person who attains such knowledge "has reached the final purpose (*takhlit*) (of life), and has become almost divinely spiritual, taking pleasure in the perfect good. His motion ceases and his pleasure continues."[90] His soul is at rest ("his motion ceases") because it no longer has to strive for the perfection it has already attained.

Why, however, is knowledge of matter and form so difficult to attain? Ibn Gabirol's answer is that matter and form cannot be defined but only described. Isaac Israeli, it will be recalled, regarded philosophy as unique; since philosophy is *sui generis*, it is not a member of a class with any other discipline, and therefore cannot be defined but only described.[91] Similarly, Ibn Gabirol maintained that matter and form cannot be defined but only described, because they are unique, since they derive directly from the divine will, and do not belong to any common "genus above them." They can only described, therefore, by their qualities. Matter is described as a substance which is self-subsisting and which is the substratum for changing forms. Universal form is described as the "substance" of all the forms, and as "perfect wisdom and pure light."[92]

While it is thus possible to describe, although not to define, matter and form, the divine will cannot even be described precisely, but only approximately, and not in terms of what it is, but only in terms of its actions. The divine will unites matter and form in universal intellect, and thereby moves and governs all other existents as the universal intellect emanates them.[93]

The purpose of human life is thus knowledge, but that knowledge is highly restricted. Matter and form can be known with difficulty, but only by description, not by definition. The divine will itself cannot be known, even by description, and only its actions can be described. The first substance or being, namely God, cannot be known at all; all that can be discerned is God's actions in the upper, spiritual realm and in the lower, terrestrial realm. The cosmos, as God's "action," (or "work") is thus testimony to God. As Ibn Gabirol wrote in the first stanza of "The Royal Crown:"

---

89   *Fountain of Life* 5:35 = Falaquera, *Liqqutim* 5:55.
90   Falaquera, *Liqqutim* 5:55 = *Fountain of Life* 5:35.
91   See the discussion above, III.2.a.
92   Falaquera, *Liqqutim* 5:29 = *Fountain of Life* 5:22.
93   Falaquera, *Liqqqutim* 5:60 = *Fountain of Life* 5:38.

Wonderful are thy works, as my soul overwhelmingly knoweth...

Thine [are] the creatures of the heights and depths.

They bear witness that they perish, while Thou endurest.

Thine is the might in whose mystery our thoughts can find no stay, so far art Thou beyond us.

In Thee is the veiled retreat of power, the secret (*sod*) and the foundation (*yesod*).[94]

Ultimately, then, all one can know is that God exists. We cannot even understand God's unity. Unlike the Kalam approach to proving God's unity, adopted by Sa'adiah Ga'on, Ibn Gabirol's approach is Neoplatonic: the One is neither number nor quantity, but the source or foundation (*yesod*) of all number and quantity:

Thou art One, the first of every number, and the foundation of every structure,

Thou art One, and at the mystery (*sod*) of Thy Oneness the wise of heart are struck dumb,

For they know not what it is...

Thou art One, but not like a unit to be grasped or counted,

For number and change cannot reach Thee.[95]

The One transcends the categories of time and space: "Thou existest, and before Time began Thou wast / And without place Thou does abide. Thou existest, and Thy secret is hidden and who shall attain to it?"[96]

Since our knowledge is thus highly limited, Ibn Gabirol informs us towards the end of the *Fountain of Life* that the book dealt only with the lowest of the three types of knowledge — i.e., knowledge of matter and form — and not with knowledge of the divine will, let alone with knowledge of God. Therefore, when the student asks the teacher to explain the creator and creation, the teacher replies that the topics they have studied do not prepare him for knowledge of the divine will or of creation.[97] The teacher adds that he has planned a book dealing with the divine will, *The Source of Plenty* or *The Cause of Being*. We do not know, however, whether Ibn Gabirol ever wrote such a book; if he did, we do not have it.

---

[94] "The Royal Crown," stanza #1, in *Selected Religious Poems of Solomon ibn Gabirol*, p. 82.

[95] "The Royal Crown," stanza #2, in *Selected Religious Poems of Solomon ibn Gabirol*, pp. 83–84.

[96] "The Royal Crown," stanza #3, in *Selected Religious Poems of Solomon ibn Gabirol*, p. 84.

[97] *Fountain of Life* 5:40.

[III.3.e] COEXISTENCE OF MATTER AND FORM

The *Fountain of Life*, as Ibn Gabirol stated, deals only with the first level of knowledge, that of universal or "spiritual" matter and form, from which universal intellect is emanated. Plotinus, it will be recalled, conceived of universal intellect as a simple spiritual substance, whereas both Isaac Israeli and Ibn Gabirol posited the duality of matter and form as prior to any of the spiritual substances and as characteristic of all of them, including universal intellect. The divine will emanates first or universal matter and form.

This first matter, however, is spiritual, not material. Unlike terrestrial matter, the first matter has no tangible qualities or physical dimensions, and we know it intelligibly, not sensibly. The first or universal matter, which Ibn Gabirol frequently calls *yesod* ("foundation") is a principle, namely the unchanging foundation or substratum bearing the spiritual forms, and these changing forms are what is born by matter.[98] In other words, Ibn Gabirol posits these two spiritual principles, matter and form, to explain change. In order to explain how things are subject to change, we must first assume an unchanging principle underlying them and common to them all. Change does not just happen—it happens to something. We must, therefore, posit the existence of something unchanging and constant to be the substratum bearing change. We cannot conceive of forms without something to sustain them, just as we cannot conceive of a formless "matter" or substratum.

These two principles, then, first or spiritual matter and form, are not contrary concepts, but complementary and correlative concepts: they cannot be conceived or defined without reference to each other, and each implies the other. Their true existence, accordingly, is a compound co-existence, and it is only for the purpose of our understanding that we differentiate between them and regard them separately.

The downward way of Neoplatonism, as we have repeatedly seen, is an attempt to explain how the multiple can derive from the one, and the material from the spiritual. Ibn Gabirol's theory is an overt attempt to resolve this problem. All existence, beginning with universal intellect, is characterized by duality, because of the necessary co-existence of matter and form. Neither of these principles exists completely or perfectly by itself. It is only their correlative co-existence which is perfect.[99]

Another feature of the Neoplatonic downward way is that the lower principle constitutes a reflection of the higher principle. All terrestrial existence is characterized by the correlation of matter and form. This correlative co-existence, therefore, must be a reflection of a similar duality

---

98   *Fountain of Life* 5:2.
99   *Fountain of Life* 5:25.

in the higher, simple spiritual substances, namely universal intellect, soul and nature.[100]

Ibn Gabirol's "matter" (*homer*) or "foundation" (*yesod*) are thus ambivalent terms, capable of diverse meanings. They may denote "spiritual matter," when referring to the principle of the substratum of the spiritual forms. At other times, they may denote "bodily" or "physical" matter, when referring to the substance bearing the nine other categories, such as quality and quantity. Ibn Gabirol sometimes refers to matter as existing, because it makes possible the existence of the forms. At other times, matter is the absence or "privation" of existence, because matter itself has only potential existence, and it exists actually only in combination with a form.

Although Ibn Gabirol often uses the terms "matter" (*homer*) and "substance" (*'ezem*) interchangeably, there is a difference between them, and he explains that matter is the substratum prepared or disposed to receive the form, before it has received it, whereas substance is the substratum which actually bears the form. In this regard, matter can be understood to be potential substance, and substance is actualized matter.[101]

As we have seen, Ibn Gabirol's use of the term "matter" is ambivalent, but what is common to the diverse usages is the idea of a substratum, whether material or spiritual, bearing material or spiritual forms. Another term used interchangeably with "matter" is "place" (*maqom*), which similarly can be spiritual or material.

> The foundation (*yesod*) is the place (*maqom*) of the form, that is to say, that it bears [the form] which is borne by it. It is similarly said that the will is the place (*maqom*) of both of them together.[102]

How, then, does material or physical matter derive from spiritual matter? Universal form and matter (which, as we have seen, are spiritual principles) together emanate the universal soul, which in turn emanates nature, which emanates the heavenly spheres. The spheres consist of a fifth element, finer and purer than the finest and purest of the four terrestrial elements, namely fire, which is why fire ascends towards the finer heavenly element above it. This fifth element is also material and is the first being characterized by spatial extension, and should, therefore, not be confused with the first or universal "spiritual matter" previously discussed. Nature (the lowest spiritual stage) and the material spheres (the highest physical stage) thus intermediate between the fully spiritual realm and the fully material realm.

---

100   Falaquera, *Liqqutim* 4:11 = *Fountain of Life* 4:6. Cf. *Fountain of Life* 2:24.
101   Falaquera, *Liqqutim* 2:15 = *Fountain of Life* 2:11.
102   Falaquera, *Liqqutim* 5:42 = *Fountain of Life* 5:31.

[III.3.f] THE CATEGORIES

In the previous section, we saw that the function of matter, foundation, or place is to serve as an unchanging substratum for the changing forms. More precisely, this is the function of substance, which is the substratum actually bearing the form (whereas matter is the substratum prepared or disposed to bear the form, before it has received it).

Both heavenly and terrestrial matter are substance when they bear their respective forms, and Ibn Gabirol devotes major sections of the *Fountain of Life* to discussion of the concept of substance, which is the first of Aristotle's ten "categories." Ibn Gabirol's innovation lies not in his presentation of the categories themselves, but in his combining them with the Neoplatonic doctrine that the lower stage is emanated from, and is a reflection or imitation of, the higher stage.[103]

The Greek term "categoria" refers to a sentence (either in a linguistic sense, or in the legal context of a sentence charging someone in a trial). This was translated into Arabic as *maqul* (plural: *maqulat*), and in Hebrew as *ma'amar* (plual: *ma'amarot*) or *ne'emar* (plural: *ne'emarot*), i.e., a statement.

Samuel ibn Tibbon, the translator of Rambam's *Guide of the Perplexed* from Arabic into Hebrew, added to his translation an appendix, *Perush Ha-Milim Ha-Zarot* ("Explanation of Unusual Terms"), in which he states:

> The ten categories in one of which every existent must be: one of them is substance, and nine of them are accidents, which Aristotle already explained in his Categories.

In an early logical work usually attributed to Rambam (although his authorship of it has been questioned), *Milot Ha-Higayon* ("Logical Terms"), the ten categories are described as "the supreme genera of all existents."

Aristotle posited the ten categories as ways of thoroughly describing existence, with substance as the subject of a sentence and the other nine categories as its predicates. These categories answer different questions. For example: Substance answers the question, "what is this?" To which the answer is: a person or a horse. Quantity answers the question, "how much or many is it?" To which the answer is, two or three cubits. Quality asks the question, how is it? To which the answer is: it is white. Relation asks the question, what is its relation? To which the answer is, it is larger than X. Place asks the question, where is it? To which the answer is, it is in the market. Time asks the question, when is it? To which the answer is, yesterday. Possession asks the question, what does he possess? To which the answer is, he possesses an item

---

[103]   Falaquera, *Liqqutim* 2:11–12 = *Fountain of Life* 2:6–7.

of clothing. State asks the question, what is his state? To which the answer is, he is lying down or standing. Action asks the question, what is he doing? To which the answer is, he is stabbing. Affection (passion) asks the question, what is affecting (acting on) him? To which the answer is, he is being stabbed.[104]

What follows is a list of the categories, with their medieval Hebrew and Arabic names:[105]

ENGLISH	HEBREW	ARABIC
1. Substance	*'Eẓem*	*Jawhar*
2. Quantity	*Kamut, Kamah*	*Kamm*
3. Quality	*Eikhut, Ha-Eikh*	*Kayf*
4. Relation	*Ha-Miẓtaref (Ha-Nispaḥ)*	*Muḍaf*
5. Place	*Maqom, Ha-Anah*	*Makan*
6. Time	*Zeman, Ha-Matai*	*Zaman*
7. Possession	*Qinyan, Lo*	*Milk*
8. State	*Maẓav (Qimah)*	*Nuṣbah*
9. Action	*Po'el, She-yif'al*	*Fa'il*
10. Affection, passion	*Nif'al, She-yitpa'el*	*Munfa'il*

In the grammatical terms of a sentence, substance is the subject of the sentence, and the other categories are its predicates. In ontological terms, substance is what exists by itself and is the substratum of the other categories, which are accidents describing it and dependent upon its existence; they have no independent existence of their own.

Despite the overtly Aristotelian source of Ibn Gabirol's discussion of the categories, Ibn Gabirol's innovation, as mentioned above, was to insert the categories into his Neoplatonic cosmology, in two respects: (1) the duality of matter (substance) and form (the other nine categories) is characteristic of both spiritual and material reality; and (2) that duality on a lower level is emanated from, and in turn reflects, the duality on a higher level.

[III.3.g] EMANATION

Despite the similarity between lower stages and the upper stages from which they are emanated, the lower stages of matter and form differ in an important respect from the upper ones. Higher reality is finer and purer, and more characterized by unity and simplicity, whereas lower reality is coarser and grosser, and more multiple and compound. "Whatever is lowered and comes

---

[104]   Aristotle, *Categories*, ch. 3–4.
[105]   Hebrew terms in parentheses are those of Yosef Kafiḥ.

down from the simple ones to the compound ones is thicker and grosser, and whatever ascends becomes purer and finer."[106] The higher unity is eternal and unchanging, whereas the lower unity is created (it has both beginning and end) and changes, because it is divisible.

God, "the first and true unity," creates the will, which also is a "unity." Thereafter, as we have seen, all reality is marked by duality. Describing the downward way of matter, Ibn Gabirol says (in Falaquera's paraphrase):

> Since the first unity is a unity unto itself, it is the agent of the unity below it (i.e., the will). Since this unity (of the will) is created by the true, first unity (i.e., God), this unity (of the will) cannot have any beginning or end, nor any change or differentiation. Any unity emanating from it, in other words created, must have beginning and end, and must suffer change and differentiation. Therefore, it does not truly resemble the perfect unity, and is subject to plurality, differentiation and change, and must be divided and possessing different stages. The closer the unity is to the first, true unity, the stronger and simpler will be the unity of the matter represented in it. And to the contrary, the farther it is from the first unity, the stronger and more compound is its plurality.[107]

Similarly, describing the downward way of form, Ibn Gabirol emphasizes that lower forms are increasingly mixed with materiality and plurality, because matter is what causes multiplicity and change:

> Every one of the forms of the simple substances is one, and is indivisible, for how can it be divisible and yet [one]? Unity is divisible by quantity because of the substance which is its substratum. Do you not see that all unities differ according to their substratum? The proof of this is that unity sustains the matter in which it is borne. When matter is fine and simple and remote from division, unity is equated with it, and [the matter and unity] are one thing, indivisible in actuality. But when matter is grosser and weaker, unity is not equated with it, and is too weak to unify it and join it together. Then the matter becomes separated from unity, and the unity is multiplied or divided.[108]

Material beings are emanated in nine stages (perhaps paralleling the nine accidental categories attaching to substance).

1) The first stage is the emanation of universal matter and form from the divine will.
2) The existence of universal form in universal matter.
3) The existence of several simple substances.
4) The existence of "simple accidents in the simple substances."

---

106   Falaquera, *Liqqutim* 2:23 = *Fountain of Life* 2:14.
107   Falaquera, *Liqqutim* 2:26 = *Fountain of Life* 2:20.
108   Falaquera, *Liqqutim* 2:28 = *Fountain of Life* 2:23.

5) The existence of quantity in substance.
6) The existence of planes in bodies, lines in the planes, and dots in the lines.
7) The existence of colors and shapes in the planes.
8) The existence of some parts of bodies resembling some other parts.
9) The existence of some bodies in other bodies in a specific place.

Ibn Gabirol then concludes (in Falaquera's paraphrase, cited above): "Whatever is lowered and comes down from the simple ones to the compound ones is thicker and grosser, and whatever ascends becomes purer and finer."[109]

In the downward way of emanation, the weakening of the light in each stage is not a function of that stage's form but of its increasingly gross, thick and compound matter.[110] In other words, in the higher stages, form (which is identified with light) is more dominant, whereas in the lower stages, matter is increasingly dominant. As a result, only the higher stages, marked by greater light and spirituality, possess knowledge:

> For knowledge and cognition belong to form, not matter, and the form is absolute light, and matter is the opposite. The finer the matter is as it ascends higher because of the light shining on it, the more that substance knows and the more perfect it is, like the intellect and soul. And the opposite: the lower the matter is, the grosser it is, because of the distance it progressed from the light extending over it.[111]

The same principle applies to divine providence, which attaches to genera in accordance with the light extending over matter. The higher the genus or species, the finer it is, and the more it receives this light and providence:

> Regarding light extending over matter, the more something is pure and cleansed of matter, the more perfect and stronger it is. Similarly, the more it participates in the pure part of matter than in the gross part of matter, the more its species is protected and the stronger it is and the more it endures.[112]

To summarize, although all the stages of reality below the divine will are characterized by the duality of form and matter, in the downward way of emanation the relationship of form (identified with light) and matter gradually changes: in each stage the spirituality of form decreases, and materiality increasingly dominates the spirituality of the form, resulting in a weakening of the original light.

---

109 Falaquera, *Liqqutim* 2:23 = *Fountain of Life* 2:14.
110 Falaquera, *Liqqutim* 4:22 = *Fountain of Life* 4:14.
111 Falaquera, *Liqqutim* 4:22 = *Fountain of Life* 4:14.
112 Falaquera, *Liqqutim* 4:22 = *Fountain of Life* 4:14.

[III.3.h] CREATION *EX NIHILO*

As mentioned above,[113] although Ibn Gabirol was by no means the first to affirm the doctrine of creation *ex nihilo* (which played in important role in the thought of Sa'adiah Ga'on and Isaac Israeli), he may have been the first to use in his poem "The Royal Crown" what would become the standard Hebrew expression, *yesh me-ayin* ("something from nothing"). Sa'adiah Ga'on and Isaac Israeli, after all, wrote in Arabic, not Hebrew. A similar Hebrew phrase may be found in the *Sefer Yeẓirah*—*ve-'asah et eino yeshno* ("He made his nothing his something")—but Ibn Gabirol transformed *ein* (the adjective "no" or "none" or adverb "not") into a noun *ayin* ("nothing"). The innovation is thus terminological, not conceptual.

There is also no conceptual innovation in Ibn Gabirol's combination of creation *ex nihilo* within the structure of Neoplatonic emanation, a combination pioneered by Isaac Israeli before him. What is new, again, is terminological: how that combination is expressed in Hebrew in his poem,

"The Royal Crown," where he first used the expression *yesh me-ayin* in one form or another. One of the Hebrew terms for emanation is the noun *meshekh*, from the verb *mashakh*, meaning to draw, pull, attract or extend. In the poem, we find the following rhyme of *ayin* (nothing) with *'ayin* (eye), playing with the emanationist theme of light:

> *Li-meshokh meshekh ha-yesh min ha-ayin /*
> *ke-himashekh ha-or ha-yoẓé min ha-'ayin.*

> To draw the extent of being from nothing /
> Like the drawing of light coming out from the eye.[114]

The *Fountain of Life* also combines the language of creation with the language of emanation. In the first paragraphs of the third section of the book, Ibn Gabirol argues that there must be an intermediate stage between the first agent and the first material substance which is the substratum of the other nine categories. This intermediary must be a simple substance, from which compound, material bodies are emanated. Although Ibn Gabirol adds a stage (the divine will), the first stage, as in Isaac Israeli, is created *ex nihilo*, and from that stage on subsequent reality is emanated. Emanation is thus creation from something else—albeit something purer and more refined and spiritual—as opposed to creation *ex nihilo* at the highest stage.

---

113   See the discussion in III.3.b.
114   "The Royal Crown," stanza #9, line 79.

The act of the primary Creator is to create something from nothing. Now the substance that sustains the categories derives from its constituents.[115] It was therefore not created from nothing.[116]

Universal matter and form, as we have seen, cannot exist separately, but must co-exist. Neither could precede the other. They were, therefore, created simultaneously.[117] This creation must have been *ex nihilo*, because if something is created from something else, there would be no end to the process, and "creation would endure infinitely."[118] But even this creation *ex nihilo* of universal matter and form by the divine will is manifests an aspect of emanationist theory, namely that whatever is characteristic of a lower stage reflects something similarly characteristic of a higher stage. The union of universal matter and form in universal intellect is effected by, and must also reflect, a higher unity, and that higher unity is found in the divine will which created them. The product of the divine will's unification of matter and form is the universal intellect, which then begins the process by which all subsequent stages are emanated.

[III.3.i]   THE WILL

As we saw above,[119] matter and form can be known with difficulty, but only by description, not by definition. The divine will itself cannot be known, even by description, and only its actions can be described "approximately." Therefore, when the student asks the teacher to explain the creator and creation, the teacher replies that the topics they have studied do not prepare him for knowledge of the divine will or of creation.[120] Nevertheless, Ibn Gabirol did discuss at least a few aspects of the will's actions. In the beginning of the *Fountain of Life*, he states that "the will is a divine force creating and moving everything, and nothing is empty of it."[121] And towards the end of the book he states that the divine will creates *ex nihilo* universal matter and form, and is their substratum (*maqom*, "place").[122]

As the "place" (i.e., substratum), creator and mover of matter and form, the divine will contains all subsequently emanated reality, both spiritual and

---

115   Its constituents—i.e., universal matter and form.
116   *Fountain of Life* III:3, proof #16, Jacob translation, p. 78.
117   Falaquera, *Liqqutim* 5:42–43 = *Fountain of Life* 5:31.
118   *Fountain of Life* 5:31.
119   See the discussion in III:3:d.
120   *Fountain of Life* 5:40. In this passage, the teacher adds that he has planned a book dealing with the divine will, *The Source of Plenty* or *The Cause of Being* (a book, which if Ibn Gabirol ever wrote it, was lost).
121   Falaquera, *Liqqutim* 1:2 = *Fountain of Life* 1:2.
122   Falaquera, *Liqqutim* 5:42 = *Fountain of Life* 5:31.

material.[123] Why, then, did Ibn Gabirol insert this additional stage—the divine will—between the creator and universal matter and form? Why could God not create matter and form directly, without this intermediary? Ibn Gabirol's answer, as we saw in the previous section, is that there must be an "intermediary" between two opposite "extremes," because the intermediary in some respects resembles each of the opposite extremes.

God is the infinite and absolute unity, whereas all subsequent existents (including the spiritual substances, beginning with universal intellect) are finite and characterized by duality or other multiplicity. The necessary intermediary between the infinity and unity of God, and the finitude and duality of matter and form, is the divine will, which reflects the active infinity of God above it (because it is the agent of all lower reality), but, like lower reality, is limited because it itself is acted upon, since God is its agent. The will is thus simultaneously infinite, in its essence, and finite, in its activity. Its activity is finite because its products, universal matter and form, are themselves finite in nature.[124] The will is also infinite insofar as it has no beginning, and finite insofar as it has an end: it ends with matter and form. Conversely, universal intellect has a beginning—it begins with matter and form—but no end, because continually emanates everything below it.[125] The finitude of the will is thus not a function of its infinite essence, but is imposed by the finitude of the matter and form it produces.

Nevertheless, despite its finitude, the activity of the divine will is unique, and is called the divine "command" or "statement," and differs from all subsequent activity. The will acts on matter and form, but is not affected by them; it moves them but is not moved by them. The simple substances, and all the more, the material substances, act but are also affected; they move, but are also moved. They act on and move what is below them, and they are affected and moved by what is above them.[126]

The divine will's action on universal form and matter, uniting them in coexistence, is timeless and motionless, whereas matter moves in time. Ibn Gabirol compares this creative activity of the will to writing: the will is "the writer;" the form created or emanated by the will is "the writing;" and the matter bearing the form is the "tablet" or "page" bearing the writing. He also compares the activity of the will to sunlight: the will is the sun radiating the light; form is the rays of light; and matter is the air bearing the light.[127]

---

123 Falaquera, *Liqqutim* 2:18 = *Fountain of Life* 2:13.
124 *Fountain of Life* 4:19.
125 Falaquera, *Liqqutim* 3:39 = *Fountain of Life* 3:57.
126 Falaquera, *Liqqutim* 5:57–58 = *Fountain of Life* 5:36.
127 Falaquera, *Liqqutim* 5:62–64 = *Fountain of Life* 5:38–41.

To summarize, Isaac Israeli introduced into Plotinus' scheme of the downward way a new stage, first form and first matter, in order to harmonize the biblical notion of creation with the Neoplatonic notion of eternal emanation. For similar reasons, Solomon ibn Gabirol adds yet another stage, that of the divine will, between the infinity and unity of God and the finitude and duality of universal matter and form. Since an intermediary must resemble in some ways what is above it and what is below it, the divine will is infinite in its essence, but finite in its activity, and that finitude is imposed by the matter and form the will acts on.

Since the *Fountain of Life* does not have a fully developed theory of the divine will (supposedly discussed in a different book that is no longer extant, if it ever existed), there are various ambiguities and inconsistencies in Ibn Gabirol's limited "description" of the will's actions. Is the will itself created by God? Sometimes he refers to the will's unity as "a unity created by the first, true unity,"[128] and at other times he describes it as emanated from God.[129] Is the will's activity creation *ex nihilo*, in other words a "command" or "word,"[130] or does it emanate the spiritual substances, beginning with universal matter and form, like flowing water or like the impression of a form on a mirror?,[131] resembling the emanation of light?[132]

None of these points is clear, nor are the limited references entirely consistent, in the absence of a more extensive discussion. What is clear is the general hierarchical structure of the downward way, and the will's function as an intermediary between God and universal matter and form.

[III.3.j]   THE ULTIMATE HUMAN END: THE SOUL'S ASCENT TO KNOWLEDGE

The end of the *Fountain of Life* brings us back to the beginning of the book. Knowledge of the downward way, discussed until now, is what makes possible the ultimate human end, namely the upward way, the soul's ascent to knowledge. The human being, it will be recalled, was created to acquire knowledge, and it is knowledge—specifically knowledge of himself as a microcosm—that endows the rational soul with immortality.

> Since the knowing part of the human is the most glorious of all his parts, what he should seek is knowledge. The knowledge that he should seek is knowledge of himself, by which he can know all other things which are not himself, because

---

128   Falaquera, *Liqqutim* 2:26 = *Fountain of Life* 2:20.
129   "The Royal Crown," stanza 9, line 76.
130   Falaquera, *Liqqutim* 5:57 = *Fountain of Life* 5:36.
131   Falaquera, *Liqqutim* 5:64 = *Fountain of Life* 5:41.
132   Falaquera, *Liqqutim* 5:62–64 = *Fountain of Life* 5:38–41.

he comprises and covers all things...He should seek to know the final cause for which he exists, by which to attain his felicity (*haẓlaḥah*), because the generation of the human being has a final cause for which he exists, for everything comes under the will of the One.[133]

This ultimate perfection and happiness, the knowledge of the human being's spiritual source through knowledge of oneself as the spiritual and physical microcosm, is described in "The Royal Crown:"[134]

> Who can approach Thy seat?
> For beyond the sphere of Intelligence hast Thou established the throne of Thy glory;
> There standeth the splendour of Thy veiled habitation,
> And the mystery (*sod*) and the foundation (*yesod*).
> Thus far reacheth Intelligence, but cometh here to a standstill,
> For higher still hast Thou mounted, and ascended Thy mighty throne,
> "And no man may go up with Thee."
>
> O Lord, who shall do deeds like unto Thine?
> For Thou hast established under the throne of Thy glory
> A standing place for the souls of Thy saints,
> And there is the abode of the pure souls
> That are bound up in the bundle of life...
> And here is delight without end or limit,
> For it is The World to Come (*ha-'olam ha-ba*).

The soul's ascent to knowledge requires that it be liberated from the body's limits, appetites and impurities. Ibn Gabirol describes the upward way to union with the spiritual world in terms borrowed from Plotinus' *unio mystica* in the *Theology of Aristotle,* where, as we saw above,[135] the *unio mystica* was described as follows:

> Aristotle said: Sometimes I was alone with myself and, as it were, I discarded my body, and became a simple substance without body...I knew that I was one of the parts of the perfect and excellent supernal world and that I possessed active life... as if I were placed in it and cleaving to it. I was above the entire world of the intellect, and I saw myself as if I were standing in the divine intellectual realm. I became, as it were, joined to it, as if I were standing in the divine world of intellect.[136]

---

133   Falaquera, *Liqqutim* 1:1 = *Fountain of Life* 1:2.

134   "The Royal Crown," stanzas #26–27, in *Selected Religious Poems of Solomon ibn Gabirol*, pp. 102–103.

135   See the discussion above, III:1:e:v.

136   Translation of the Hebrew paraphrase by Shem Tov ibn Falaquera (Spain, 13th century) in his *Sefer Ha-Ma'alot* ("Book of Degrees"), pp. 22–23 of the *Theology of Aristotle*, ch. 1, pp. 225–227, (based on *Enneads* IV:8).

This is how Ibn Gabirol describes the upward way, the microcosm theme, and the *unio mystica*:

Master:...In general, when you want to imagine these substances, the manner in which your essence spreads therein and comprehends them, you must raise your intelligence to the supreme intelligible, strip it and purify it of every stain of the sensible, deliver it from the prison of nature, and attain by the virtue of the intelligence to the highest knowledge that you can achieve of the truth of the intelligible substances, until you are, as it were, divested of the sensible substance, and are in this respect, so to speak, in a state of ignorance. Then you will enclose in some fashion the entire corporeal world in your essence, and you will set it as if in a niche of your soul. When you have done this, you will understand the pettiness of the sensible in relation to the grandeur of the intelligible. And the spiritual substances will stand ready within your reach: set before you, you will see them envelop and dominate you, and it will seem to you that your own essence becomes one with these substances. And presently you will think that you are some part of these substances, on account of your connection with the corporeal substance. Then again you will think that you are the entirety of these substances and that there is no difference between them and yourself, on account of the union of your essence with their essences, and the conjunction of your form with their forms.

Pupil:...I rise according to the degrees of the intelligible substances, and I stroll in their pleasant gardens. I find the sensible bodies in comparison with the intelligible substances extremely low and extremely imperfect, and I see the corporeal world entirely swimming in them like a boat in the sea and a fledgling in the air.

Master: You have observed well and understood well. But if you rise to the universal primal matter and if you are illuminated by its shadow, you will then see that which surpasses all admiration: apply yourself therefore zealously to this, for it is in sight of this that the human soul exists, and there is a great joy therein and perfect happiness.[137]

The purified soul, which ascends to this knowledge and union with the spiritual substances, is immortal. As Ibn Gabirol described it in "The Royal Crown:"[138]

O Lord, who can reach Thy wisdom?
For Thou gavest the soul the faculty of knowledge that is fixed therein,
And knowledge is the fount of her glory.
Therefore hath destruction no power over her...
The soul with her wisdom shall not see death...

---

[137] *Fountain of Life* 3:56–57 (= Falaquera, *Liqqutim* 3:37–38), English translation by H.E. Wedeck, *The Fountain of Life* (London: Peter Owen, 1962), pp. 126–128.

[138] "The Royal Crown," stanza 30, in *Selected Religious Poems of Solomon ibn Gabirol*, pp. 104–105. See the complete passage cited above, III:3:d.

The way to attain this ultimate felicity and immortality is to "separate yourself from the sensibles, and immerse yourself in the intelligibles. Depend on the beneficent one, because when you do this, he will look at you and benefit you, because he is the source of all beneficence."[139] The *Fountain of Life* thus leads the student, and the reader, to the ascent of the soul to knowledge, the theme which, at the beginning of the book, was defined as the ultimate human purpose.

> Always strive to know the substance of universal matter and universal form ... Know how matter [derives] from form, and form from the will, and ... all of them from the One ... When you know this with a correct knowledge, your soul will be pure, and your intellect will be clear and penetrate the intelligible world. You will then look over the totality of matter and form ... The intention of all this is to know the divine world ... The ascent of this faculty progresses gradually, until one reaches its beginning and source. The result of this striving is the happiness of immortality and union with the Fountain of Life.[140]

The *Fountain of Life* thus concludes by returning to its beginning, just as the ultimate purpose of the perfect life is to return to its source.

[III.4]   CONCLUSION

Neoplatonic philosophy exerted a great influence on much of medieval Jewish thought, especially in its early period. Even such later Aristotelian thinkers as Abraham ibn Da'ud and Rambam incorporated some Neoplatonic elements, such as emanation, into their cosmology, epistemology and theories of prophecy.

Neoplatonists like Isaac Israeli and Solomon ibn Gabirol attempted to broaden and modify the monism of emanation, to harmonize it with the monotheistic religious concept of creation, by adding new stages to Plotinus' cosmology. Ibn Gabirol's introduction of the divine will into the scheme of emanation was a clear attempt in this direction.

Interestingly enough, despite this clearly religious adaptation of Neoplatonic doctrine, the philosophical works of Isaac Israeli and especially Ibn Gabirol, are notable for their lack of overtly Jewish elements, such as citations from or references to the Bible or Talmud, a feature of the *Fountain of Life* which resulted, for centuries, in ignorance of the Jewish identity of its author. Nevertheless, if we resort to the three criteria for determining Jewish philosophy discussed in the first chapter, there is little question of the

---

[139]   Falaquera, *Liqqutim* 5:74 = *Fountain of Life* 5:43.
[140]   Falaquera, *Liqqutim* 5:73 = *Fountain of Life* 5:43.

place of these works in the tradition of Jewish philosophy. In terms of the dimension of the past, there is reliance on Jewish sources, even if they are not cited explicitly, for example, in Isaac Israeli's discussion of prophecy and of the rational and traditional commandments, and in Solomon ibn Gabirol's innovation in his poetry of the Hebrew phrase *yesh me-ayin* for the earlier concept of creation *ex nihilo*, and similarities (if not actual citations) in his poetry and *Fountain of Life* with ideas and expressions in the *Sefer Yezirah*. In terms of the dimension of the present, they responded as Jews to Neoplatonic philosophy, by incorporating creation into the structure of emanation. In terms of the dimension of the future, they were known to, and cited by, later Jewish philosophers (as evidenced most clearly by Falaquera's *Liqqutim* of the *Fountain of Life*). The thought of Isaac Israeli and Solomon ibn Gabirol, especially in their adaptation of Neoplatonic monist emanation to incorporate monotheistic creation *ex nihilo*, thus exemplifies — even without overt Jewish references — philosophy in a Jewish context.

Chapter Four

BAḤYA IBN PAQUDA:
THE DUTIES OF THE HEART

[IV.1] BAḤYA IBN PAQUDA'S IDEOLOGICAL BACKGROUND

Baḥya ben Joseph ibn Paquda's thought is eclectic, and reflects diverse ideological backgrounds. For instance, his proofs of creation and of the existence and unity of God are borrowed from the Kalam; his emphasis on the absolute unity and simplicity of God, and on the purification of the soul and its ascent to its spiritual source and enlightenment reflects Neoplatonic themes. Baḥya also seems to have been influenced by Sufism and by the "Pure Brethren" (*Ikhwan Al-Safa*). Despite the diversity of influences, Baḥya's thought is consistent and original, and came in later generations to have a great impact on Jewish religious and moral thought, including in circles which generally avoided philosophy.

[IV.1.a] SUFISM

The mystical movement in Islam is known as Sufism, from the term *ṣuf* (wool), denoting the simple woolen garment worn by the mystics, often in protest against the materialism and conspicuous consumption of the ruling classes in the Islamic state. In their desire for communion with God, the mystics developed steps by which a person could become purified and progress spiritually, and to struggle with himself in order to attain spiritual "states" which are gifts of God. One of these steps is asceticism, to which we shall return.

[IV.1.a.i] *Sufism According to Ibn Khaldun*

The Arab historian 'Abd Al-Raḥman ibn Khaldun (1332–1406) describes "the science of Sufism" in Part VI of his book *Al-Muqaddimah* ("An Introduction [to History]").[1]

---

[1]   Citations here are from the abridged edition, English translation by Franz Rosenthal, abridged and edited by N.J. Dawood (Bollingen Series: Princeton University Press, 1967), based on the three-volume edition translated with introduction by Franz Rosenthal (New York, 1958).

Sufism belongs to the sciences of the religious law that originated in Islam ... The Sufi approach is based upon constant application to divine worship, complete devotion to God, aversion to the false splendour of the world, abstinence from pleasure, property, and position to which the great mass aspire, and retirement from the world into solitude for divine worship. These things were general among the men around Muḥammad and the early Muslims.

... The Sufis came to represent asceticism. They developed a particular kind of perception which comes about through ecstatic experience ... Man is distinguished from all the other animals by his ability to perceive ... He can perceive sciences and matters of knowledge ... Also, he can perceive "states" persisting in himself, such as joy and grief, anxiety and relaxation ... The exertion and worship of the Sufi novice must lead to a "state" that is the result of his exertion. That state may be a kind of divine worship ... The Sufi novice progresses from station to station, until he reaches the (recognition of the) oneness of God and the gnosis (*ma'rifah*) which is the desired goal of happiness ... The science of Sufism became a systematically treated discipline in Islam.[2]

Ibn Khaldun describes Sufism as a process of internalization: the Sufi is isolated, and this permits him to devote all his energies to God in a process called *dhikr* (recollection, remembrance), i.e., incessant repetition of the name Allah and of praises of God, often accompanied by beating of drums, music and dance. These techniques gradually bring the Sufi to a state of ecstasy in which, as it were, he loses his external senses, so that he is not distracted by hearing or seeing external objects. In such a state of ecstasy, the Sufi

beholds divine worlds which a person subject to the senses cannot perceive at all. The spirit belongs to those worlds ... It had been knowledge. Now, it becomes vision. [The spirit] is now ready for the holy gifts, for the sciences of the divine presence, and for the outpourings of the Deity. Its essence realizes its own true character and draws close to the highest sphere, the sphere of the angels.[3]

Bahya's thought reflects some of these ideas and terminology, including such Sufi notions as applying oneself exclusively to the worship of God; devotion to God alone; avoiding worldly temptations; the gradual, step by step ascent; self-examination. Nevertheless, none of this makes Bahya a Jewish Sufi. He rejects the extreme asceticism of the Sufis as opposed to the way of the Torah. Most important, as emphasized by such scholars as Julius Guttmann,[4] Georges Vajda,[5] and Menahem Mansoor,[6] Bahya is no mystic, because his

---

2   Ibn Khaldun, *The Muqaddimah*, pp. 358–360.

3   Ibn Khaldun, *The Muqaddimah*, p. 360.

4   Julius Guttmann, *Philosophies of Judaism*, pp. 109–110.

5   Georges Vajda, "Bahya ben Joseph ibn Paquda," in *Encyclopaedia Judaica* IV:105–108.

6   Menahem Mansoor, "Arabic Sources of Ibn Pakuda's *Duties of the Heart*," in *Proceedings of the Sixth World Congress of Jewish Studies* (1973), III, Division C, pp. 81–90.

more moderate asceticism leads not to mystical union with God, but ultimately to the true love of God.

[IV.1.a.ii] *Al-Ghazali*

Ibn Khaldun's description of the Sufis includes a reference to Abu Ḥamid Muḥammad Al-Ghazali (1058–1111), a Persian, who was a major figure in the history of Islamic thought. Originally an orthodox Muslim, Al-Ghazali became disillusioned with the dominant Islamic rationalism and legalism, and found solace in the life of a wandering Sufi. His many works include *Maqaṣid Al-Falasifa* ("Intentions of the Philosophers"), which summarizes the philosophies of Al-Farabi and Ibn Sina, and his later *Tahafut Al-Falasifa* ("Incoherence of the Philosophers"), containing twenty chapters, which systematically criticizes and directly attacks their philosophies, leading to the conclusion that the philosophers are heretics because of their denial of creation, of God's omniscience, and of bodily resurrection. (Ibn Rushd [Averroes], a contemporary of Rambam, subsequently composed a counter-attack in defense of philosophy, *Tahafut Al-Tahafut* ["The Incoherence of the Incoherence"]). Al-Ghazali's "Intentions" and "Incoherence" were translated into Hebrew in the Middle Ages, and exerted considerable influence among Jewish thinkers. His *Iḥya 'Ulum Al-Din* ("Revival of the Religious Sciences") claims that Sufism cannot be considered heretical from an orthodox Islamic perspective, and that orthodoxy and mysticism are compatible.

Al-Ghazali's quasi-autobiographical *Al-Munqidh Min Al-Ḍalal* ("The Deliverer From Error") describes the spiritual crisis he underwent in his progression from skepticism to Kalam, from Kalam to philosophy, and finally to Sufism. In the sixth chapter of this book, Al-Ghazali describes the theory and practice of Sufism, aiming at purifying the heart from all its defilements, to permit exclusive devotion to God. Merely learning Sufi theory is insufficient; the practice is much more important. One must "taste," i.e. directly experience internally, the reality of God,[7] just as objective knowledge of the definition of health cannot be compared to actually being healthy. Al-Ghazali accordingly differentiates three grades of knowledge: (1) "faith," based on what one hears from others; (2) "knowledge," based on demonstrative proofs; (3) "taste," based on direct, internal experience.

This emphasis on internal, existential experience, rather than mere cognitive, intellectual understanding would resonate in Baḥya ibn Paquda's *Duties of the Heart* and in Judah Ha-Levi's *Kuzari*. However, as we have

---

7　　As we shall see in Ch. 6, Judah Ha-Levi similarly differentiated *dhauq* ("taste," i.e. direct experience) of the God of Abraham from *qiyas* (deductive knowledge) of the God of Aristotle.

already mentioned, the internalization of religious experience in Baḥya (and in Judah Ha-Levi) does not lead to Al-Ghazali's explicit abnegation of the self in mystical union with God. The ultimate goal is not mystical union but love of God, in which the duality of lover and the object of love is preserved.

As Hava Lazarus-Yafeh has shown, there is also a remarkable similarity between the second chapter of Baḥya's *Duties of the Heart*, "Examination of Creation," and Al-Ghazali's *Al-Ḥikmah Fi Makhluqat Allah* ("God's Wisdom on His Creations").[8] This similarity led scholars to assume that Baḥya borrowed or copied from Al-Ghazali. Since Baḥya was a contemporary of Al-Ghazali and did not know his work, Lazarus-Yafeh concludes that this assumption is incorrect, but that both thinkers were influenced by common sources, which they adapted, respectively, to their own needs.

[IV.1.a.iii] *Al-Muḥasibi*

According to Amos Goldreich,[9] the common source used by both Al-Ghazali and Baḥya ibn Paquda was Abu 'Abd-Allah Al-Muḥasibi (781–857), one of the first Sufi writers, who, like Al-Ghazali, moved from Kalam to Sufism. Al-Muḥasibi and later Sufis make the distinction, so fundamental to Baḥya's thought, between "duties of the limbs" and "duties of the heart." These similarities, once again, point to the Sufi background of important aspects in Baḥya's thought, but do not mean that Baḥya was ultimately a mystic.

[IV.1.b]   *IKHWAN AL-ṢAFA*
          ("THE PURE BRETHREN")

When Baḥya cites "the philosophers," he is often actually citing an Arabic collection known as *Rasa'il Ikhwan Al-Ṣafa* ("The Letters of the Pure [or: Sincere] Brethren") which form a sort of philosophical and religious encyclopedia.[10] As will be recalled, this collection of 51 or 52 letters[11] of a Neoplatonic outlook was the product of a secret fraternity of intellectuals in Baṣra, Iraq. As David Kaufmann has shown, both the literary style and

---

8   Hava Lazarus-Yafeh, "On the Character of Judeo-Arabic Culture" (Hebrew), published by the Israel Historical Society (Jerusalem, 1973), pp. 265–285.

9   Amos Goldreich, "Possible Arabic Sources of the Distinction Between 'Duties of the Limbs' and 'Duties of the Heart'" (Hebrew), in *Te'udah 6: Studies in Hebrew and Arabic*, ed. A. Dothan (Tel Aviv, 1988), pp. 179–208.

10   See the discussion of the Pure Brethren in Ch. 3 (III.1.f.vii).

11   There is confusion regarding the correct number. We have 52 letters, but the letters themselves refer to the number 51. Letter #51, according to our count, may have been added later, because it reviews and repeats material in earlier letters. The letters also allude to an additional, secret "general" letter, summarizing the Brethren's theories, but it was kept secret and may not have survived.

specific ideas in Baḥya's *Duties of the Heart* reflect the Letters.[12] In addition, Baḥya shares with the Pure Brethren a marked tendency towards asceticism (at least a moderate asceticism), and a strong emphasis on the inner life of the spirit over the external and formal practices of institutional religion, as well as recognition of the need to elevate the moral and spiritual level of the community at large through education.

[IV.1.c] BAḤYA IBN PAQUDA'S ECLECTICISM

Baḥya's use of material derived from Kalam, Neoplatonism, Sufism, and the Pure Brethren is eclectic. He adopted material selectively, adapting it to his needs, and combining it with Jewish sources, such as citations from biblical and rabbinic sources, thereby creating a consistent and rich ideological tapestry, while avoiding elements he found objectionable or incompatible with his thought, such as the frequent references to demons, evil spirits, angels and astrology in the Pure Brethren's "Letters." According to Kaufmann, the influence of Kalam ideas, which are particularly pronounced in the first two sections of the *Duties of the Heart*, the most overtly philosophical parts of the book, is probably derived from Sa'adiah Ga'on and not from Arab Mutakallimun, whereas his other sources would have to have been directly Islamic.[13]

Nevertheless, as Eliezer Schweid has suggested,[14] even his use of material based on Sa'adiah Ga'on's *Book of Beliefs and Opinions* was selective, not blind, and it often takes on new meaning, because of the different context into which the ideas (such as the sources of knowledge, the relationship of revelation and reason, proofs of God and creation, and the distinction between rational and traditional commandments) were absorbed. Sa'adiah, for example, discusses the sources of knowledge and the relationship of revelation and reason in the context of his polemic with ideological rivals to rabbinic Judaism (philosophy, Christianity, Islam, and Karaite Judaism), whereas for Baḥya the true challenge is not external but internal: the tension between the formal practices of institutional religion on the one hand, and on the other hand, inner spiritual life and pure intention. Yes, Baḥya adopts Sa'adiah's distinction between rational and traditional commandments, but this leads him to his innovation with Jewish literature: the duties of the heart vs. the duties of the limbs. Rational knowledge is no longer desired for its own sake, but as a necessary stage in the long spiritual journey to the love of God.

---

12 David Kaufmann, "Baḥya ibn Paquda's Theology," in *Studies in the Hebrew Literature of the Middle Ages* (Hebrew), trans. I. Eldad (Jerusalem, 1965), pp. 21–22, note 36.
13 David Kaufmann, "Baḥya ibn Paquda's Theology," in *Studies in the Hebrew Literature of the Middle Ages*, pp. 26–28.
14 Eliezer Schweid, *Toledot Ha-Pilosofiyah He-Yehudit Mi-Rasag 'Ad Rambam* (Jerusalem: Academon, 1968).

[IV.1.d]   BAḤYA IBN PAQUDA'S SOCIAL BACKGROUND

We know little about Baḥya's life; even his dates of birth and death are unknown. All we know is that he lived in Muslim Spain in the second half of the eleventh century, when Jews enjoyed economic, social and cultural prosperity. Bezalel Safran has suggested that the Jewish courtier class adopted the mores of the ruling Muslims, including their materialism and their enjoyment of elegant manners and poetry, and that Baḥya's educational program in the *Duties of the Heart* represents a criticism of the mores and values of the courtier class.[15] Baḥya's criticism is both philosophic and religious. It is philosophic, because the courtiers' superficial education aimed at social status and professional advancement, rather than with true, internal wisdom. It is religious, because their education is shallow, and relies on what is traditional and customary, without requiring the student to immerse himself in Torah. As such, the courtier curriculum cannot fulfill its obligation to teach a person to serve God out of love: its emphasis on subjects leading to personal and professional advancement encourages a person to love himself, not God.

[IV.2]   THE *DUTIES OF THE HEART*

[IV.2.a]   THE NAME AND PURPOSE OF THE BOOK

Baḥya's *Duties of the Heart* (Arabic: *Kitab Al-Hidaya 'Ila Fara'iḍ Al-Qulub*; Hebrew: *Sefer Torat Ḥovot Ha-Levavot*)[16] was written in Arabic circa 1080, and was translated into Hebrew by Judah ibn Tibbon circa 1160–1161 at the request of Rabbi Meshullam ben Jacob of Lunel, and later by Joseph Kimḥi. In our generation it was translated into Hebrew by Yosef Kafiḥ. In the Ibn Tibbon translation, the book became one of the most popular works of Jewish thought and ethics.

Baḥya's distinction between "duties of the limbs" (Arabic: *fara'iḍ al-jawariḥ*; Hebrew: *ḥovot ha-evarim*) and "duties of the heart" (Arabic: *fara'iḍ al-*

---

15   Bezalel Safran, "Bahya ibn Paquda's Attitude Toward the Courtier Class," in Isadore Twersky, ed., *Studies in Medieval Jewish History and Literature* (Cambridge: Harvard University Press, 1979), pp. 154–196.

16   The full title means "The Book of Instruction (or: Guidance) to the Duties of the Heart." There are two English translations: *Duties of the Heart*, Hebrew text of Ibn Tibbon with English translation (based on the Ibn Tibbon version) by Moses Hyamson (2 volumes, 1925–1947, reprint: Jerusalem, 1965), and *The Book of Direction to the Duties of the Heart*, by Menahem Mansoor (Oxford: Littman Library, 1973). Citations are from the Hyamson translation, with my modifications.

qulub; Hebrew: *hovot ha-levavot*) is innovative in Jewish literature, although it has precedents in Sufi writings. The book's educational program and direction are manifested in its Arabic title: it is a book of instruction *towards* ("to") the duties of the heart, and is intended to guide the reader in his gradual transition from his current situation to a new spiritual state.[17]

That transition "to the duties of the heart," as Bahya explains in the Introduction, is required by reason, the Torah, and tradition. It is a gradual transition of internalization, away from a person's external physical and material concerns to internal, spiritual experience, and from a mechanical observance of "the duties of the limbs" to a deliberate and intentional observance of "the duties of the heart." The "duties of the limbs," as important as they are for the welfare of the body, do not suffice for a person's ultimate, spiritual welfare. Therefore, Bahya states,

> I said to myself that I would compose a book on this subject that would deal systematically with the principles and precepts of the Duties of the Heart...point out the good and right way; serve as a guide to the customs of the ancient sages and the discipline of the pious; awaken men from the senseless sleep; explore the minutiae of this science, recall to men the knowledge of God and of His Law, promote the salvation of the soul.[18]

The process of internalization thus answers two questions: why and how to observe the precepts ("duties"). As for the first question, why to observe the precepts, the traditional Jewish religious response is that a person's obligations are heteronomous—their authority rests not autonomously in the person himself, but in God who commanded them. Without denying the heteronomous, divine source of the commandments, Bahya attempted to promote their observance not merely out of obedience to their external authority, but out of inner, personal conviction, meaning and sincere intention.

As for the second question, how to observe the precepts, Bahya points out that a person can observe them with his "limbs" alone. In other words, the precepts can be performed as mechanical actions of the body, without internal thought or intention, a danger inherent in any fixed ritual of institutionalized religion, where repeated actions become merely habitual. The true worship of God, however, lies in the "duties of the heart," which do not replace the "duties of the limbs" but give them enhanced meaning. The action is the same; what differs is the intention or meaning of the act, when the external act expresses inner conviction and spiritual experience.

---

17   In the Hebrew title of Ibn Tibbon's translation, the preposition "to" was dropped.
18   Bahya ibn Paquda, *Duties of the Heart*, Introduction, English translation by Moses Hyamson, vol. 1, p. 39.

This is how Bahya describes the process of spiritual internalization:

> When these arguments from Reason, Scripture and Tradition—all pointing to the indispensability of the Duties of the Heart—had come home to me, I began to train myself in them and imposed on myself the task of studying and practicing them. The discovery of one principle revealed another related to it...I resolved, therefore, to write down my reflections and put them together in a work that would comprehend the general principles of the subject and include its subdivisions as well as many of the detailed applications; and so I would always be able to exhort myself to learn these duties and oblige myself to fulfil them. Where my practice would accord with my doctrine, I would thank God for having helped me thereto, and shown me His ways. Where it was inconsistent with it, or fell short of it, I should chide my soul, reprove it, argue with it; so that from the standard of righteousness set forth in the work, my soul might realize its own iniquity; ... from the perfection there taught, realize its own shortcomings.
>
> I aimed to make the book one of permanent value, a treasury of things hitherto not known, a lamp to illuminate men's paths and show them the way in which they should go. I hoped that the book would be of still greater use to others than to myself; that, besides answering my own needs, it would to a still larger degree be a source of general instruction.[19]

Bahya's challenge is thus internal, in contradistinction from the external challenges motivating Sa'adiah Ga'on to write his *Book of Beliefs and Opinions*. The *Duties of the Heart* is needed because of the internal challenge, to convert the routine observance of fixed commandments into an internal process of spiritual purification. The external act should thus lead to, and at the same time express, the internal intention. Sa'adiah Ga'on needed to provide rational proofs justifying the Torah and enabling a Jew to respond effectively to external challenges to rabbinic Judaism. The dangers Bahya ibn Paquda faced are not from without, but from within, rabbinic Judaism itself, namely that the Torah can become a system of fixed, mechanical actions, lacking any corresponding inner spiritual meaning. Focusing on the technicalities of the actions can lead us to forget their inherent meaning. This book is necessary to "awaken" us from our "senseless sleep," and to recall "the knowledge of God and of His Law." We need, in other words, to reveal the knowledge already latent in our souls.

> After I had arrived as the principles by Reasoning, I searched our Scriptures and Traditions, and found them indicated in several passages...To the entire book I have given a title that accords with my aim in writing it. It is called "A System of the Duties of the Heart."

---

[19]   Bahya ibn Paquda, *Duties of the Heart*, Introduction, vol. 1, p. 39. This passage immediately precedes the passage cited above.

My object in this work is to obtain wisdom for myself, and at the same time to stimulate the simple and negligent among those who hold our faith and have inherited the precepts of our religion, by adducing proofs satisfactory to them, and the clearness and truth of which will be confirmed by Reason...My purpose in this work was not to refute those who dispute the fundamentals of our faith. My aim is rather to bring to light the root principles of our Religion that are deeply fixed in the unsophisticated intellect—those pivot principles of our Torah which are latent in our souls. Once we rouse our minds to meditate on them, their truth becomes clear to us inwardly and their bright rays will even be manifest in us externally...I wish to do the same with the hidden treasures of the heart; namely, to bring them to light and exhibit their shining excellence, so that anyone who desires to draw near to God and cling to Him may do likewise.[20]

Baḥya's intention, according to what he says here and elsewhere, is not to develop a systematic philosophy. Philosophy serves as a means to an ultimately religious purpose, because knowledge of the truth is necessary for the love of God (and the book is structured accordingly, as we shall see). Baḥya's *Duties of the Hearts*, therefore, is aimed at the religious community at large, and thus differs in this respect from Rambam's *Guide of the Perplexed*, which was explicitly intended only for the elite intelligentsia. With the exception of Judah Ha-Levi's *Kuzari*, the *Duties of the Heart* was probably the most popular and most widely read Jewish philosophical book in the Middle Ages, including in circles uninterested in, or even hostile to, philosophy.

As Julius Guttmann has noted, it is paradoxical that this book, which has an overtly Jewish character (such as citations of the Bible and Talmud) as was intended for, and received by, the Jewish community, freely assimilated so many non-Jewish concepts and terms (as discussed in the previous section).

Its warm and simple piety made it a favorite of devotional reading, widely appreciated as the truest and purest expression of Jewish piety. No doubt the book would have been influential...even if it had not been written in a profoundly and originally Jewish spirit. It is, therefore, all the more instructive to note the extent to which the book bears the marks of the influence of alien religions...Baḥya mentions many more exemplars of piety than he does philosophic authorities, and the Jewish sage does not hesitate to appeal for the confirmation of his teachings to the great ascetics of Islam, who, though he does not mention them by name, seem so close to him in spirit.[21]

A further historic irony is that in the controversy over philosophy after the death of Rambam, many of the opponents of philosophy as a foreign wisdom

---

20   Baḥya ibn Paquda, *Duties of the Heart*, Introduction, vol. 1, pp. 47–49.
21   Julius Guttmann, *Philosophies of Judaism*, pp. 104–105.

inappropriate for Jews, were deeply influenced by Baḥya, who himself did not hesitate to cite or paraphrase non-Jewish thinkers, whom he refers to as the "ancients" (Arabic: *salaf*; Hebrew: *qadmonim*) and as the "pious" (Arabic: *ṣaliḥin*; Ibn Tibbon: *ḥasidim*; Kafiḥ: *ẓadiqim*). Baḥya thus respected non-Jewish wisdom; at the same time he felt free to criticize the failure of his fellow Jews to understand the truth of the Torah and the duties of the heart, Jews who observed only the duties of the limbs. Once again, the true challenge is internal. Non-Jewish wisdom can, therefore, be used to correct Jewish error. As Isaac Husik has observed on Baḥya:

> It is not the rationalization of Jewish dogma that he is interested in, nor the reconciliation of religion and philosophy. It is the purification of religion itself from within which he seeks to accomplish. Sincerity and consistency in our words and our thoughts, so far as the service of God is concerned, is the fundamental requirement and essential value of the duties of the heart. To be sure, this cannot be attained without intelligence. The knowledge of God and of his unity is a prerequisite for a proper understanding and an adequate appreciation of our religious duties. Philosophy therefore becomes a necessity in the interest of a purer and truer religion, without reference to the dangers threatening it from without.[22]

[IV.2.b] THE LITERARY STRUCTURE OF THE *DUTIES OF THE HEART*

As previously mentioned, the full title of Baḥya's work, "The Book of Instruction (or: Guidance) to the Duties of the Heart," indicates a program and transition to a new spiritual state, a direction implied by the preposition "to." This direction is also reflected in the literary structure of the book, as Baḥya explains towards the end of the Introduction. The first duty of the heart, the "root and foundation" of all the other duties, is to know the unity of God, which is, accordingly, the subject of the first chapter of the book. However, the only way to know God is by examining his creations, the subject of the second chapter. God alone is the supreme ruler of the world, and thus alone worthy of worship, the subject of the third chapter. The following chapters deal with (4) trust in God, (5) wholehearted devotion to God, (6) humility, (7) repentance, (8) spiritual accounting (self-examination), and (9) asceticism (*zuhd*). In this way the subjects and chapters of the book are arranged in linear progression, leading to the tenth and final chapter, which deals with the ultimate purpose and perfection of human existence, the love of God.

---

22   Isaac Husik, *A History of Mediaeval Jewish Philosophy* (New York: Atheneum, 1916/1973), p. 85.

Eliezer Schweid has suggested that the structure of Baḥya's *Duties of the Heart* is "dramatic," as opposed to the "epic" structure of Sa'adiah Ga'on's *Book of Beliefs and Opinions*. By this Schweid means that Sa'adiah's book is aimed at the community observing the normative and institutional *halakhah* (Jewish religious law), whereas Baḥya's book is aimed at the spiritual progress of an individual seeking to transcend the collective norm, and to go beyond the measure of the law (*lifnim mi-shurat ha-din*) to reach a higher, supererogatory level.[23]

The linear structure of the book is even more evident in a Hebrew poem which Baḥya wrote at the very end of the tenth chapter. The poem is an acrostic spelling out his name "Baḥya bar Joseph," consisting of ten verses which summarize the themes of the ten chapters of the book. Baḥya introduces the poem by saying:

> I conclude my book with these strophes, that they may serve you as a reminder, so that you can repeat them without a book and turn them over in your heart and mind at night and by day, when you are reposing and when you are active. Thus you will never cease to think of the topics of this book of mine and keep in mind its fundamental precepts.[24]

Amos Goldreich has pointed out the similarity between Baḥya's language here and some of the phrases of the "Shema'" (Deuteronomy 6:6–7: "These words which I command you this day should be in your heart. Teach them to your children and speak of them, when you are sitting in your home, when you are walking on the way, when you lie down and when you rise up.").

Goldreich then also suggests that the structure of the book in ten chapters may not be a mere literary device, but may be an attempt to associate the ten chapters with the Decalogue, which according to midrashic interpretation, contains all 613 commandments of the Torah, a "daring and far reaching" attempt in which "the duties of the heart" thus parallel the 613 "duties of the limbs" of the Torah.[25]

A final literary observation: Baḥya also freely acknowledges in the Introduction that he intermixes philosophical arguments (what he calls *al-qiyas*, i.e., logical deduction) with arguments based on citations of Scripture (*al-maktub*) and rabbinic tradition (*al-manqul*). These three sources—reason, Scripture and tradition—constitute the three "gates which the creator opened to know his Torah and religion."

---

23 Schweid, *Toledot Ha-Pilosofiyah Ha-Yehudit Mi-Rasag 'Ad Rambam*, pp. 75–76.
24 Baḥya ibn Paquda, *Duties of the Heart*, vol. 2, p. 381.
25 Amos Goldreich, "Possible Arabic Sources of the Distinction Between 'Duties of the Limbs' and 'Duties of the Heart,'" pp. 182–183.

[IV.3]   THE DUTIES OF THE LIMBS AND THE DUTIES OF THE HEART

In his Introduction, Baḥya states that the "science of the Torah" encompasses knowledge of the external duties of the limbs and the internal duties of the heart.

> As the science of the religion deals with two parts, external and inward religion, I studied the books of the ancient writers who flourished after the Talmud, and who composed many works dealing with the precepts, in the expectation of learning from them the science of inward religion...I examined these writings but failed to find among them a treatise specially devoted in inward duties. This department of knowledge, the science of the duties of the heart, had, I saw, been entirely neglected...I was so greatly surprised that I said to myself, "Possibly this class of duties is not enjoined by the Torah, but is only an ethical obligation, the aim of which is to teach us the right and proper way. Possibly is belongs to the class of supererogatory practices that are optional, for which we will not be called to account nor be punished if we disregard them. And therefore our predecessors omitted to treat of it in a special work." A careful examination, however, by the light of reason, scripture and tradition, of the question whether the duties of the heart are obligatory or not, convinced me that they indeed form the foundation of all the precepts, and that if there is any shortcoming in their observance, no external duties whatever can be properly fulfilled.[26]

The study of "the science of inward religion" is thus obligatory from a religious perspective, and this in turn involves the study of philosophy, since all the duties of the heart are rational, and as already mentioned, the first duty of the heart, the "root and foundation" of all the other duties, is to know the unity of God, which is, accordingly, the subject of the first chapter of the book. However, the only way to know God is by examining his creations, the subject of the second chapter. In short, one cannot fulfill one's external religious obligations, the duties of the limbs, without the internal duties of the heart, and one cannot fulfill the rational duties of the heart, beginning with knowing the unity of God, without knowledge of philosophy. At the end of the

---

[26] Baḥya ibn Paquda, *Duties of the Heart*, Introduction, vol. 1, pp. 19–21. Approximately a century after Baḥya thus concluded that "the science of the duties of the heart" is obligatory, Rambam's contemporary, the Arab philosopher Abu Al-Walid Ibn Rushd (Averroes, 1126–1198), asked a similar question about philosophy in general: is the study of philosophy forbidden, permitted, or obligatory from a religious perspective? His conclusion, in his *Decisive Treatise Determining the Nature of the Connection Between Religion and Philosophy* (*Faṣl Al-Maqal*), is that the study of philosophy is obligatory. Ibn Rushd's treatise is available in an English translation by G.F. Hourani, *Averroes on the Harmony of Religion and Philosophy* (London: Luzac, 1961).

Introduction, Baḥya accordingly recommends reading "the works of Sa'adiah Ga'on, which brighten the mind, sharpen the understanding, instruct the simple, and stimulate the indolent."[27]

However, since Sa'adiah did not deal with the duties of the hearts, Baḥya took that challenge upon himself.

Sa'adiah, as we recall,[28] had divided the Torah's commandments into two categories: rational commandments (Arabic: *al-sharai'a al-'aqliyah*; Hebrew: *miẓvot sikhliyot*) and traditional commandments (Arabic: *al-sharai'a al-sam'iah*; Hebrew: *miẓvot shim'iyot*).[29] Baḥya's differentiation between duties of the heart and duties of the limbs builds on this distinction, and takes it a step further. The duties of the limbs may be either rational or traditional (in Sa'adiah's categories), but the duties of the heart are exclusively rational.

What does Baḥya mean by his distinction between duties of the heart and duties of the limbs, and why did he make it? Eliezer Schweid[30] suggests that Baḥya here is reflecting, but also extending, the tension between institutional religion and true religiosity. In other words, normative Jewish religious life within the framework of the *halakhah* needs to be refined, to avoid emphasizing only external ritual actions—the duties of the limbs—in order to strengthen its internal, spiritual dimension—the duties of the heart. The ritual actions commanded by the Torah, as important as they are in shaping communal life, are incomplete if they fail to bring the individual to his inner, spiritual purpose of worshiping God in understanding and love.

Joseph Dan[31] proposes a different explanation for the distinction between the duties of the limbs and the duties of the heart. In his view, the distinction reflects the Neoplatonic dualism of matter and spirit. A person must worship God on both levels, body and soul, and he has duties on both levels, duties of the limbs and duties of the heart. These two levels, in Dan's view, are not integrated, but always remain separate.

But the distinction is not that simple. When we examine Baḥya's examples of the two different kinds of duties, we find unexpected categorizations of the commandments. Baḥya gives us the following description of the duties of the limbs and of the heart:[32]

> First, the arguments from reason. Man, we know, consists of body and of soul; both of them are marks of the Creator's goodness to us. One of these elements of our being is seen; the other, unseen. We are, accordingly, bound to render the

---

27   Baḥya ibn Paquda, *Duties of the Heart*, Introduction, vol. 1, p. 53.
28   See chapter 2 (II.3.1).
29   Sa'adiah, *Book of Beliefs and Opinions* 3:2.
30   Schweid, *Toledot Ha-Pilosofiyah Ha-Yehudit Mi-Rasag 'Ad Rambam*, p. 70.
31   Joseph Dan, *Sifrut Ha-Musar Veha-Derush* (Jerusalem: Keter, 1975), p. 49.
32   Baḥya ibn Paquda, *Duties of the Heart*, Introduction, vol. 1, p. 21.

Creator visible and invisible service. The outward service is the observance of practical precepts [i.e., duties of the limbs]; e.g., praying, fasting, almsgiving, learning the Torah and teaching it; erecting a booth (*sukkah*) for the feast of Tabernacles (*Sukkot*) and waving palm branches (*lulav*) on the festival;[33] wearing fringes (*ẓiẓit*);[34] attaching the *mezuzah* to the doorposts;[35] erecting a parapet on the roof;[36] fulfillment of other precepts which call for the exercise of the physical organs. Inward service, on the other hand, consists of the fulfillment of the duties of the heart; e.g., that we should acknowledge the unity of God in our hearts; believe in Him and in His laws and accept His service; revere Him; be humble and abashed before Him; love Him; trust in Him; and surrender our very lives to Him; abstain from what He hates; dedicate our activities to His name; meditate on the benefits He bestows; and similar duties that are fulfilled in thought and by the exercise of inward faculties, but do not call for the activity of the bodily organs.

Joseph Dan, noting that Baḥya lists the study of Torah and prayer as duties of the limbs, and not (as we might expect) as "spiritual" commandments, suggests that Baḥya's category of "duties of the heart" is essentially negative: commandments which do not involve a physical organ are "duties of the heart," whereas anything involving a bodily organ are "duties of the limbs." Since, Dan observes, prayer is recited by the mouth, and the Torah, when read publicly, is heard, these commandments involve bodily organs and must, accordingly, be categorized as "duties of the limbs."

The distinction may, however, be subtler than the mere involvement of a bodily organ. Baḥya lists prayer as a duty of the limbs, but then explicitly states that we "acknowledge the unity of God in our hearts ... and accept his service," as duties of the heart. What is the difference between the first worship (prayer) which is "seen" and the second worship which is "hidden" or "unseen"? Prayer is a fixed, public, communal act, which must be performed at fixed times, three times daily. The study of Torah, although it has no fixed times as prayer does, is still a fixed, definite commandment in the Torah, a commandment which applies not only to the individual, but also to the community, which must hold public, official reading of the Torah at fixed times. Prayer and study of Torah are, therefore, "duties of the limbs" because of their fixed and public character.

Conversely, besides, and in addition to the mandatory, institutional prayers and study (i.e., reading) of the Torah, there is also "the worship of the heart" (*'avodah sheba-lev*), including prayer and study of Torah, which can be

---

[33]   Cf. Leviticus 23:39–43.
[34]   Cf. Numbers 15:37–41.
[35]   Cf. Deuteronomy 6:9, 11:20.
[36]   Cf. Deuteronomy 22:8.

categorized as "duties of the heart," because it is neither fixed nor public, but is performed spontaneously by the individual, whether in his heart (i.e., silently) or out loud. In other words, if the prayer or Torah study is performed publicly, according to the times fixed for it, it comes under the category of "duties of the limbs." But if it is "the service of the heart," in the sense of an individual performing it spontaneously, out of free intention, rather than in conformity to an institutional framework, is falls under the category of "duties of the heart," without regard for the involvement of a bodily limb (such as the mouth expressing a spontaneous prayer of the heart). In other words, the distinction applies not only to what one does, but to how one does it.

There is also a formal, halakhic dimension to the distinction between duties of the heart and duties of the limbs. Bahya explains that the duties of the limbs have a fixed, known number, "like the 613 commandments," whereas the duties of the hearts "and their derivatives" are so many that they have no number.[37] Nevertheless, the 613 commandments of the Torah include commandments which, by any definition, would be categorized as duties of the heart. Perhaps that is why Bahya does not explicitly equate the duties of the limbs with the 613 commandments, but merely says that they have a fixed number "like the 613 commandments." Whatever Bahya actually meant by this phrase, Amos Goldreich suggests that the duties of the limbs are what the Jew is obliged to perform according to the *halakhah*, whereas the duties of the heart are the supererogatory obligations the Jew takes upon himself voluntarily.[38] The distinction, if Goldreich is correct, is thus of obligations according to the letter of the law (*din*) and additional, voluntary obligations beyond the measure of the law (*lifnim mi-shurat ha-din*).

In other words, although there is a quantitative aspect to the distinction— the duties of the limbs = the 613 commandments, as opposed to the innu-merable duties of the heart—the real distinction is qualitative and essential, and follows from the different character of the two kinds of duties. The duties of the limbs are fixed in the Torah; their character is primarily public, legal and formal. Therefore, as formal and public laws, their number is fixed, since people can only be obligated, in public behavior, to what has been formally legislated. People can, however, act spontaneously and individually in various areas which, by their very nature, are not legislated formally, and cannot in principle, be governed by such legislation. These possible spontaneous and individual actions have no fixed, finite number, because the possibilities are as limitless as life and the human imagination and spirit permit. They derive not from the finite number of external laws imposed heteronomously, but

---

37   Bahya ibn Paquda, *Duties of the Heart*, Introduction, vol. 1, p. 27.
38   Amos Goldreich, "Possible Arabic Sources of the Distinction Between 'Duties of the Limbs' and 'Duties of the Heart,'" p. 181.

internally, from the free and autonomous heart of every person. Their free, spontaneous and autonomous nature, therefore, precludes their having a fixed number.

Another dimension of the distinction between duties of the limbs and duties of the heart rests in the intention underlying the action. When fulfilling an obligation, what is the person's intention? Any fair system of law must differentiate clearly between two actions, which have a similar or identical outcome, but which derive from different intentions. An intentional or premeditated act cannot be compared to an unintentional or unpremeditated act, even if they lead to the same external result. We cannot compare, in moral terms, a person who drives his car slowly and carefully, and nevertheless accidentally kills a child who runs into the street after his ball, with a terrorist who plants a bomb on a school bus and kills a child. On the level of the external action, the result is the same—in both cases, a child has been killed. However, in moral and legal terms, the two cases are incomparable, because of their differing internal intention.

Intention is thus critical to the distinction between the duties of the limbs and the duties of the heart. Bahya states explicitly:

> I also saw an argument from the Scriptures in the rule that when homicide is accidental, no capital punishment is inflicted. So, too, if a precept was un-wittingly violated, the willful infringement of which would have entailed either the penalty of one of the four modes of execution or the penalty of excision (karet), the violator had only to bring a sin-offering or trespass-offering. All this proves that the essential condition of liability to punishment is the association of mind and body in a forbidden act—the mind by its intention, the body by its movement...And since every act hinges and rests on the intention and hidden sentiment of the heart, a system of the duties of the heart should naturally take precedence over a system of practical precepts [i.e., duties of the limbs].[39]

Bahya is addressing here a fundamental religious question: from a religious perspective, can a person be compelled to obey the law? There are opinions in *halakhah* which affirm coercion: "One coerces him until he says, 'I want [to do it]'."[40] "A person should always engage in Torah and commandments, even if not for its own sake, for out of doing it not for its own sake, he comes to do it for its own sake."[41] Bahya presumably maintained the opposite view, that the religious value or quality of an act is a function of the free will and intention of a person performing the act out of love of God. Worship (i.e., service of God) which is not "for the sake of heaven" is not worship at all. Therefore, as

---

39   Bahya ibn Paquda, *Duties of the Heart*, Introduction, vol. 1, pp. 23–25.

40   Babylonian Talmud, Rosh Ha-Shanah 6a, Yevamot 106a).

41   Babylonian Talmud, Pesahim 50b and other passages.

he stated, "every act hinges and rests on the intention and hidden sentiment of the heart." If that is true of the duties of the limbs, it is certainly all the truer of the duties of the heart.

A similar position, emphasizing the necessity of free choice and proper intention, was taken, in a completely different historical, social and political context, by Moses Mendelssohn (Germany, 1729–1786). Baḥya, as we have seen, was dealing with the spiritual internalization of religious duty. Mendelssohn applied those insights to a new political situation, in which the question was the proper relationship of religion and state in general, and specifically, whether traditional Jewish loyalty to the Torah is compatible with religious freedom and a repudiation of religious coercion. In Mendelssohn's words:

> The state will thus be content with mere deeds — with conduct without conviction, with conformity of action without concurrence in thought...Not so with religion. It knows no act not founded on conviction, no work without spirit, no deed without inner concurrence, no consensus regarding action without agreement upon its meaning. Religious deeds without religious motivation are empty mechanical motions, not service of God. Religious deeds must spring from conviction; they can neither be purchased by the promise of a reward nor enforced by the threat of punishment.[42]

The requisite free intentionality of the duties of the heart may also shed light on another distinction that Baḥya makes between duties of the heart and duties of the limbs. As we have already seen, the duties of the limbs may include both rational commandments (*miẓvot sikhliyot*) and traditional or revealed commandments (*miẓvot shim'iyot*), in Sa'adiah Gaon's categories, which Baḥya adopted, whereas the duties of the heart are always rational. We may now have a better understanding of this distinction. Duties of the limbs may be rational, i.e., their rationale may be obvious; or they may be traditional, possessing some social utility (such as the dietary laws of *kashrut*), even if that utility is not overtly rationally evident. The duties of the heart, however, must be rational, because a person accepts and performs them intentionally, by free and deliberate choice. The duties of the heart always have a rational basis, because a condition for their free acceptance and deliberate performance is that they be understood, in other words, that their inner meaning be known. Rational understanding is thus always a necessary condition and foundation of the duties of the heart, but not (or at least not always) of the duties of the limbs.

---

42   Moses Mendelssohn, *Jerusalem and Other Jewish Writings*, translated and edited by Alfred Jospe (New York: Schocken, 1969), p. 22. Cf. *Jerusalem, or On Religious Power and Judaism*, translated by Allan Arkush, Introduction and Commentary by Alexander Altmann (Hanover: University Press of New England, 1983), p. 44.

[IV.4] THE EXISTENCE OF GOD
AND THE CREATION OF THE WORLD

The first duty of the heart is to know the unity of God. However, before one can affirm God's unity, one must first prove God's existence. Bahya's discussion of these questions in the first section of the *Duties of the Heart*—the most overtly philosophical section of the book—clearly exemplifies his eclecticism, by adopting a Kalam approach—in which the existence and unity of God are discussed together—and at the same time beginning with the Neoplatonic four definitions answering four questions (whether, what, how and why?), and concluding with the Neoplatonic unity of God transcending numerical unity.

Like Al-Kindi and Isaac Israeli before him, Bahya maintained that in the case of God, however, only the first of the four questions can be asked, namely whether God exists, but not what he is, how he is, or why he is,[43] because God's essence cannot be defined, one cannot attribute any qualities to him, nor can one posit a reason for which God exists (which would then, in effect, be the cause of God's existence). Ultimately, then, all that can be known and demonstrated is that God exists.

In order to prove that God exists, Bahya posits three premises; once proven, these premises can be employed to demonstrate that the world has a creator who created it *ex nihilo*. The first premise is "that a thing does not make itself."[44] Sa'adiah Ga'on, it will be recalled, discussed four proofs of creation,[45] and thereafter added three arguments that things cannot make themselves.[46] Bahya reverses Sa'adiah's order: first he proves that things cannot make themselves, and then he proves that they are created and must have a creator.

Why cannot something make itself? There are two possibilities regarding existing things: either they made themselves or something else made them. If something made itself, once again, there are two possibilities: either it made itself prior to its generation, or it made itself after its generation. Both of these possibilities are absurd. If it made itself after its generation, it didn't do anything, because it already existed. If it made itself prior to its generation, it was nothing, and it's absurd to suggest that nothing can do something. It is impossible, therefore, for something to have made itself; something else must have made it. Applied to the world as a whole, this principle means that there must be a creator.

The second premise is "that causes are limited in number; and since their number is limited, they must have a first cause unpreceded by a previous

---

43   Bahya ibn Paquda, *Duties of the Heart* 1:4, vol. 1, p. 69.
44   Bahya ibn Paquda, *Duties of the Heart* 1:5, vol. 1, p. 71.
45   Sa'adiah Ga'on, *Book of Beliefs and Opinions* 1:1. See the discussion in Ch. 2 (2.3.d).
46   Sa'adiah Ga'on, *Book of Beliefs and Opinions* 1:2.

cause."[47] Baḥya's argument here resembles Saʿadiah Gaʾon's fourth argument, the argument from time.[48] Whatever has an end must have a beginning, and whatever has no beginning has no end. "Where a thing has no beginning, there is no point where one could stop."[49] In other words, Baḥya is arguing here (like Saʿadiah) that in an eternal world, past time is infinite. But that means that at any given point, "where one could stop," one would have actually traversed an infinite number of moments, but that contradicts the very nature of the infinite, which can never be completed. In which case, one can never reach a given point, such as the present, and if we cannot reach the present, then we do not exist. Our existence and the existence of the world thus prove that an infinite time cannot have been traversed, in which case the world must have a beginning. Time must also have a beginning, since time, being the measure of a body in motion, cannot exist without the world.[50]

The second premise is based on the notion that there cannot be an actual infinity. If there were an actual infinity, and we removed a part of it, the remainder would still be infinite, but would be a smaller infinity than we had before the part was removed, in which case we would have two infinities, one larger than the other, which is absurd. Conversely, if by removing a part the infinity would be reduced to a finite magnitude, in which case we would have two finite magnitudes: the part we removed and the remainder. We would then face an equally absurd situation, in which two finite magnitudes together constitute an infinite magnitude. An actual infinity thus cannot exist, and all actual series must be finite and begin with a first cause; the world, too, must thus have a beginning and a first cause. (This proof is not based on Saʿadiah Gaʾon, but resembles the seventh Kalam proof of creation in Rambam's *Guide of the Perplexed* I:74).

The third premise is "that every thing that is a compound must have been brought into existence,"[51] and is based on Saʿadiah's second proof of creation in the *Book of Beliefs and Opinions* 1:1. Even if we were to assume that the elements are eternal, we could not conclude that compounds are eternal, since their constituent elements must exist before the compounds. But if the world is eternal, the elements could not precede the existence of the compounds. Since the elements must exist before their compounds, the world cannot be eternal.

It is not clear, however, whether this argument establishes that the precedence of the elements must be in time or in nature. For example, a "star of David"

---

47   Baḥya ibn Paquda, *Duties of the Heart* 1:5, vol. 1, p. 71.
48   Saʿadiah Gaʾon, *Book of Beliefs and Opinions* 1:1. See the discussion in Ch. 2 (2.3.d.iv).
49   Baḥya ibn Paquda, *Duties of the Heart* 1:5, vol. 1, p. 71.
50   Velocity ("V") is defined as distance ("D") divided by time ("T"); by the same token, time ("T") equals distance ("D") divided by velocity ("V"). Without the material world, there is no distance, no motion, and thus no time.
51   Baḥya ibn Paquda, *Duties of the Heart* 1:5, vol. 1, p. 71.

(*magen david*) is compounded from two equilateral triangles, which in turn, are compounded of straight lines. But is it true that the lines precede the triangles, and the triangles precede the "star of David" in time? Or is it the case that the priority here is logical and not necessarily physical, in time? If the priority is only logical, then the argument fails to prove that the world has a beginning.

In any event, in this chapter (*Duties of the Heart* 1:5), Bahya employed cosmological arguments to prove creation, and thus the existence of God as creator. The three premises are all based on observed patterns of causality in nature, leading to the conclusion that there must be a first cause of the cosmos. In other words, the argument starts with observed reality, and deduces something about how that reality came to be. In the next chapter, however (*Duties of the Heart* 1:6), discussing the creator, Bahya shifts to a teleological argument,[52] namely an argument based on the order and purpose of the universe, which are understood to be evidence of divine ordering and governance.[53] The teleological argument, however, at most proves that the universe manifests order, intention and purpose, not that it was created, let alone created *ex nihilo*.

The natural order of compound beings cannot have occurred by chance, in Bahya's presentation of the teleological argument:

> There are men who say that the world came into existence by chance, without a creator who caused and formed it. I wonder how any rational person in a normal state of mind can entertain such a notion. If one holding such an opinion would hear a person expressing a similar view in regard to a water-wheel that revolves, in order to irrigate a portion of a field or garden, and were to say that he thinks it had been set up without any intention on the part of the mechanic who labored to put it together...the hearer would wonder, be exceedingly astonished, and think the man who made such a statement extremely foolish...Now if such a statement is rejected in regard to a small and insignificant wheel...how can anyone permit himself to harbor such a thought concerning the immense sphere that encompasses the whole earth with all the creatures on it...How can one say that it all came into existence without a wise and mighty designer purposing and conceiving it?...What we have adduced from his works to demonstrate the existence of a creator will suffice to convince anyone intelligent and candid enough to admit the truth, and will serve to refute those who maintain that the universe is eternal, and to disprove their contentions.[54]

Bahya thus claims that we have here proofs of two different principles, namely the existence of God and the creation of the universe, and that these two principles are "adduced from his works."

---

[52]   "Teleological," from the Greek *telos*, end or purpose.

[53]   In contemporary discourse, the teleological argument is often adopted by "creationists," who reject the idea that evolution proceeds by random selection or chance mutation.

[54]   Bahya ibn Paquda, *Duties of the Heart* 1:6, vol. 1, pp. 77–79.

[IV.5]   THE UNITY OF GOD

The stage is thus set for his discussion of the unity of God, which Baḥya calls the "root and foundation of our religion" and "the first of the gates of the Torah."[55] Although Baḥya's proofs of unity are based on the Kalam approach of Saʿadiah Ga'on, his concept of unity itself is Neoplatonic. Baḥya's purpose in the discussion of unity also differs from Saʿadiah's. Saʿadiah's discussion was a polemic against religious and philosophical views which denied the unity of God, such as the dualistic belief in two divine powers, and even Christian Trinitarianism. In short, Saʿadiah's polemic was aimed at external ideologies. Baḥya, on the other hand, was concerned with an internal Jewish problem, to purify Jewish belief, since correct belief is the foundation, both theoretical and practical, of the Torah: "By the acceptance of the unity of God, the believer is distinguished from the infidel. It is the head...of religious truth. Whoever has deviated from it will neither practice any duty properly nor retain any creed permanently."[56]

However, people have different conceptions of God's unity, and mere verbal affirmation of God's unity does not mean a true understanding of its meaning, and without such understanding, one's worship is not true worship. Therefore, it will only be possible to have a true understanding of the unity of God "after one is able to demonstrate the doctrine and has knowledge of the connotation of his absolute unity, obtained by the rational method of investigation."[57]

Accordingly, Baḥya differentiates four different degrees of belief in the unity of God.[58] The first three degrees represent imperfect belief:

(1) An inferior belief in God's unity, namely mere verbal affirmation, without understanding what one is affirming.

(2) Belief in the heart, as well as "in the mouth" (i.e., verbal affirmation), based only on the authority of tradition, without rational understanding its meaning.

(3) Belief in the heart, as well as "in the mouth" (i.e., verbal affirmation), based on rational understanding of proofs of God's unity, but without understanding true unity as opposed to metaphorical unity.

(4) True and perfect belief, based on rational understanding of proofs of God's unity, with understanding of the true meaning of unity.

Baḥya then discusses seven different proofs of God's unity. The first proof resembles the Neoplatonic idea that multiplicity is derived from unity, and the

---

55   Baḥya ibn Paquda, *Duties of the Heart* 1:Introduction, vol. 1, p. 55.
56   Baḥya ibn Paquda, *Duties of the Heart* 1:Introduction, vol. 1, p. 55.
57   Baḥya ibn Paquda, *Duties of the Heart* 1:1, vol. 1, p. 61.
58   Baḥya ibn Paquda, *Duties of the Heart* 1:2.

farther one is removed from the source of unity, the more multiplicity there is. Causes are, therefore, less numerous than their effects, and the more remote the causes, the less there are. The regression of causes thus ultimately leads us to a single "cause of causes."

The second proof of God's unity is teleological. The unity of creation (i.e., the unified order evident in the cosmos) reflects the unity of the creator.

The third proof resembles Sa'adiah Ga'on's first proof of God's unity, and the fifth Kalam proof of unity cited in Rambam's *Guide of the Perplexed* I:75. According to this argument, one creator is sufficient to explain the creation of the world, and additional creators would, therefore, be superfluous.

The fourth proof resembles Sa'adiah Ga'on's second proof of unity, and the second Kalam proof cited in the *Guide of the Perplexed* I:75. According to this argument, God's external (i.e., numerical, quantitative) unity necessitates his internal unity (i.e., indivisible simplicity). As we saw in Ch. 2,[59] the external, numerical unity of God necessitates his internal, simple unity. If we assume that there are two gods, god A and god B, then each must have common divine denominator C. God A thus has two components: the common divine denominator C, and the particular differentiation A, so god A is a composite AC. God B also has two components: the common denominator C, and the particular differentiation B, and thus is composite BC. The two gods thus must have three components: A, B, C.

In other words, if there are two (or more) gods, than each god is composite, compounded of two (or more) elements. In that case, as compounds, they would not be eternal, but would be preceded by their constituent elements, which are their causes. But things which are caused are not gods. Conversely, the internal, simple unity of God necessitates external, numerical unity, because if God is simple, there cannot be components A+C or B+C, and, therefore, there cannot be two gods. The external and internal senses of unity are thus correlative and necessitate each other.

The fifth proof is based on Euclid's definition of unity.[60] According to this argument, unity must be prior to units. In other words, before there can be various units, there must be unity. Multiplicity is a collection of units. In other words, before multiplicity, there had to be units, and before there were units, there had to be unity.

According to the sixth proof, multiplicity and quantity are accidents attaching to something's essence. If we are asked to define a chair, that essential

---

59   See the discussion in Ch. 2 (II.3.g).

60   Euclid, the famous Greek mathematician, lived in the fourth century B.C.E. in Alexandria, Egypt. His *Stoicheia* ("Elements") in 13 books was well known in the Middle Ages in Arabic translation. Hebrew translations from the Arabic were prepared by Moses ben Samuel ben Judah ibn Tibbon in 1270 and by Jacob ben Makhir.

definition has nothing to do with the extraneous question of how many chairs there may be. As an accident, quantity cannot be attributed to God as the creator of both substance and accidents.

Bahya's seventh proof resembles Sa'adiah Ga'on's second proof in the *Book of Beliefs and Opinions* and the first Kalam proof of unity in Rambam's *Guide of the Perplexed* 1:75, namely that two (or more gods) would suffer reciprocal hindering. If we assume that there are two creators, and one of them is capable of creating, then the other one (as suggested above, in Bahya's third proof) would be superfluous. Conversely, if neither were capable of creating alone, then both of them are imperfect and impotent. On the other hand, if both were fully capable of creating alone, then they would hinder each other.

All seven arguments lead to the unity of God, in both its external and internal senses. However, they lead only to the third level of belief in unity, based on rational understanding of proofs of God's unity, but without understanding true unity as opposed to metaphorical unity. We have the proofs of unity, but still do not understand what unity really means, because unity can be understood in two different senses: true, i.e., absolute unity, and metaphorical, i.e., relative unity.

Metaphorical or relative unity is accidental, because it refers to a unity produced by combining individuals or compounding single elements. The total is thus not truly one, but consists of multiple components; it unites the many, but is not essentially one, like the unity of a species uniting many individuals. Such relative unity is metaphorical

> because the things included under one name are homogeneous; and everyone of them may be called plural, since it includes many things, which, separated and isolated, will each be called one... Each of them is a unit from one point of view, and plural from another aspect.[61]

Accidental unity also refers to "a single individual, who, though seemingly not plural and not an aggregate of several things, yet is essentially plural, being composed of matter and form, substance and accident."[62]

Conversely, there are two kinds of true, absolute unity: mental and actual. Mental unity refers to the mathematical one, which is the root and source of all number. It is mental, because it is a concept which does not exist in actuality, outside the mind. So if we refer to "one chair," it is the chair which actually exists, and "one" is an accidental quantity of the chair, and has no actual existence of its own.

Bahya's concept of actual absolute unity is Neoplatonic, and refers to

---

61   Bahya ibn Paquda, *Duties of the Heart* 1:8, vol. 1, p. 91.
62   Bahya ibn Paquda, *Duties of the Heart* 1:8, vol 1, p. 91.

a real being. Therefore, although the only way to define it is negatively, it is a positive concept of the source of all unity and quantity, and not (as in Saʻadiah and the Kalam) merely a negation of multiplicity. In Baḥya's words:

> The second kind of true (absolute) unity exists actually. It is that which is neither plural, nor susceptible of change or transformation; it is not described by any one of the corporeal attributes; is not subject to creation, destruction or limitation; does not move or waver; resembles naught, has naught resembling it and is not associated with aught. It is in all respects true unity and the root of everything plural. For...unity is the cause of plurality.
>
> The true unity has neither beginning nor end...and change is inconsistent with unity...Absolute unity, in its essence, is not subject in any respect to accidental properties...The ascription of unity to the absolutely one is intended to express the exclusion of multitude and plurality...The absolute One is not to be described by any attribute that would imply in his glorious essence multiplicity, change or variation.[63]

The One is thus the direct source of unity and the indirect source of multiplicity (since multiplicity consists of combinations of units and thus derives from unity). As such, the One is the first cause of all being and the creator.

> As the first cause is neither a plurality nor a combination of unity and plurality, it must necessarily be an absolute unity. We have already, in the course of our arguments, observed that the higher the causes, the fewer they become, till at last, the root of all numbers is reached, the true unity. And this true unity is the creator...It has thus been expounded and demonstrated that the creator of the universe is the true unity and that there is no true unity beside him. For anything else, other than the creator, to which the designation "one" applies, if it is a unit from one point of view, is plural from another. But the creator, as has been explained, is one in every respect.[64]

Baḥya's concept of absolute and actual unity obviously precludes any corporeality, since corporeality would, by definition, involve the duality of matter and form, and also quantitative extension. Therefore, whereas Saʻadiah Gaʼon had to follow his discussion of unity with a discussion of incorporeality, for Baḥya, unity precludes corporeality to begin with, and there is, accordingly, no need for a separate discussion of incorporeality. Baḥya could proceed, accordingly, directly to a discussion of the divine attributes.

---

63   Baḥya ibn Paquda, *Duties of the Heart* 1:8, vol. 1, p. 93.
64   Baḥya ibn Paquda, *Duties of the Heart* 1:9, vol. 1, pp. 95–97.

[IV.6]   THE DIVINE ATTRIBUTES

In Chapter Two,[65] we saw that the absolute unity of God was understood to be incompatible with multiple attributes, or at least with certain types of attributes. Aware of this problem, Baḥya differentiated between essential and active attributes. Essential attributes are those which

> belonged to God before the existence of any creatures; and after all creatures shall have ceased to exist, these attributes will continue to apply to him and to his glorious essence. These attributes are three: that He is; that He is one; and that He is eternal without beginning.[66]

We must attribute existence to God, because something non-existent could not have acted and produced the universe. Similarly, we must attribute eternity to God, because, as we have seen, the world must have a beginning, and the creator, as "the beginning without the beginning," must be eternal. We must also attribute unity to God.

> This unity implies the absence implies of plurality in his being, the absence of change, transformation, accident, origin or extinction, combination or any other properties of objects that are plural.[67]

But do not these three essential attributes themselves imply multiplicity in God's essence? Baḥya's answer is that these essential attributes are negative in their meaning, denying their contraries. "What the attribution of them should convey to our minds is that the creator of the world is neither plural, nor non-existent, nor created."[68]

Sa'adiah Ga'on, as we may recall, had also posited three essential attributes—omnipotence, life, and omniscience—and regarded all three as implicit in the concept of creator, so that they were only plural in their verbal expression, not in their actual meaning. For Baḥya, with his even stronger Neoplatonic orientation, the absolute unity of God was incompatible with this kind of multiple expression. Therefore, whereas Sa'adiah could admit at least verbal multiplicity, Baḥya had to reject even that limited multiplicity, and define the essential attributes negatively. The Neoplatonic "negative way" (*via negativa*), therefore, led Baḥya and such later figures as Judah Ha-Levi

---

65   See the discussion in Ch. 2 (II.3.h).
66   Baḥya ibn Paquda, *Duties of the Heart* 1:10, vol. 1, p. 99. Moses Hyamson translates this as "without predecessor" but the Arabic *awal* and Hebrew *reshit* are better translated as "beginning."
67   Baḥya ibn Paquda, *Duties of the Heart* 1:10, vol. 1, p. 99.
68   Baḥya ibn Paquda, *Duties of the Heart* 1:10, vol. 1, p. 101.

and Rambam to reject Sa'adiah's approach: the distinction between his three essential attributes is not merely verbal, as he claimed, because life is not identical in meaning with omnipotence, nor omnipotence with omniscience. These three (and any other) essential attributes, accordingly, are incompatible with God's unity.

Like Sa'adiah, Baḥya also argues that the apparent multiplicity is merely verbal:

> As we do not find in any of the spoken languages a word that would designate the true conception of God, we express it in more than one word. This plurality in the creator's attributes does not, however, exist in his glorious essence, but is due to inadequacy of language on the part of the speaker to express the conception in one term.[69]

Nevertheless, despite this seeming agreement with Sa'adiah Ga'on, Baḥya immediately explains that despite their positive formulation, the meaning of these attributes is actually negative:

> Whatever attributes you ascribe to the creator, you are to infer from them the denial of their contraries... The creator of substance and accident has not the qualities of his creatures. The denial of such qualities to him is undoubtedly true and appropriate to him. For He is above all quality and form, similarity or comparison. These attributes are, accordingly, to be understood as the negation of their opposites.[70]

In addition to the essential, but actually negative, attributes, Baḥya posits active attributes. "The active attributes of the Deity are those ascribed to the creator, with reference to his works."[71] These can have a positive content, because they describe God's actions, and not God himself, and a single agent can have multiple actions without implying any multiplicity in the agent itself. For example, for thousands of years people knew how to use fire (i.e., its "actions") without understanding its essence as a chemical process of oxidation with heat. Similarly, a single flame can heat, cook, give light, and ignite other flames, without any implication that each of these "actions" is a result of a different essence. Attributes of action, accordingly, can be ascribed positively to God, and (as we shall see in Chapter Nine) even Rambam, who took the *via negativa* to a logical extreme, affirmed, like Baḥya, these attributes.

According to Baḥya, Scripture ascribes active attributes to God in two manners, either as anthropomorphisms, which "indicate forms and bodily likeness," (such as biblical references to God's image, mouth, hands, eyes) or

---

69   Baḥya ibn Paquda, *Duties of the Heart* 1:10, vol. 1, p. 103.
70   Baḥya ibn Paquda, *Duties of the Heart* 1:10, vol. 1, p. 103.
71   Baḥya ibn Paquda, *Duties of the Heart* 1:10, vol. l, p. 103.

as "bodily movements and actions" (such as God seeing, hearing, smelling, remembering).[72] Citing by name Sa'adiah Ga'on's treatment of the subject, Baḥya maintained that

> necessity forced us to ascribe corporeal attributes to God, and to describe him by attributes properly belonging to his creatures, so as to obtain some conception by which the thought of God's existence should be fixed in the minds of men. The books of the prophets expressed this in corporeal terms which were more easily understood by their contemporaries. Had they limited themselves to abstract terms and concepts appropriate to God, we would have understood neither the terms nor the concepts; and it would have been impossible for us to worship a being whom we did not know, since that worship of that which is unknown is impossible. The words and ideas had, accordingly, to be such as were adapted to the hearer's mental capacity, so that the subject would first sink into his mind in the corporeal sense in which the concrete terms are understood.[73]

The Torah was revealed to the generation of slaves who came out of Egypt, not to the intelligentsia, and needed, therefore, to address them in terms they could understand. For such people, like children, what is real is physical. Borrowing (like Rambam after him) Rabbi Yishma'el's statement, "The Torah speaks according to human language,"[74] Baḥya understands this to mean that the Torah had to adapt its manner of expression to the limited understanding of the people to whom it was given. Nevertheless, the prophets only ascribed to God corporeal attributes that in human terms are indicative of perfection, not deficiency. Technically, of course, no corporealism is true, but in pedagogical terms, attributes which are perceived to indicate perfection in a human being lead the simple believer to affirm God's perfection.

Subsequently, as people gain wisdom and understanding, they can appreciate the metaphorical nature and true esoteric meaning of such anthropomorphic language.

> The wise thinker will endeavor to strip the husk of the terms—their materialist meaning—from the kernel, and will raise his conception, step by step, till he will at last attain to as much knowledge of the truth as his intellect is capable of apprehending.[75]

---

72 Baḥya ibn Paquda, *Duties of the Heart* 1:10, vol. 1, p. 103.

73 Baḥya ibn Paquda, *Duties of the Heart* 1:10, vol. 1, p. 105.

74 See the discussion of this in Ch. 9. The talmudic expression does not have the philosophical meaning given it by Baḥya and later by Rambam, but reflects Rabbi Yishma'el's naturalistic and rationalist hermeneutic, in contrast with the hermeneutical approach of Rabbi Akiva who sought homiletical and esoteric meaning in the repetition of words and other features of the biblical text.

75 Baḥya ibn Paquda, *Duties of the Heart* 1:10, vol. 1, p. 105.

[IV.7] EXAMINING THE CREATED WORLD

As has already been mentioned, the first section of the *Duties of the Heart*, dealing with the unity of God, is the most philosophical part of the book, because of the basic requirement to know God in order to serve and love him, since, as Baḥya insists, one cannot serve or love what one does not know. The following nine sections of the book deal with more practical, and less theoretical, questions, and contributed to the popularity of the book over the centuries as an ethical guide. Nevertheless, these sections of the book do contain theoretical material of philosophical, and not merely moral and religious, significance.

The second section of the *Duties of the Heart* deals with the examination of the created world. This section, as noted above,[76] bears a striking similarity to Al-Ghazali's *Al-Ḥikmah Fi Makhluqat Allah* ("God's Wisdom on His Creations").

People are obligated to examine the created world in order to discern in creation the wisdom of the creator.

> The wise and intelligent man will choose from the world for study its fine and spiritual elements; use them as a ladder by which to obtain proofs of the existence of the creator, to whose service he will then devote himself with zeal according to his heartfelt recognition of the goodness of the creator.[77]

By examining the material world a person can choose for himself only those things necessary for his existence, and avoid superfluous luxuries he should avoid. The examination thus serves both spiritual and physical needs. On the spiritual level, the examination leads him to appreciate God's wisdom in creation. On the physical level, the examination permits him to discover the seven "pillars of wisdom" (in the phrase of Proverbs 9:1) necessary for proper conduct. These seven pillars are:
— Knowledge of the structure of the world.
— Knowledge of the human species.
— Knowledge of the physical constitution of the human being, how body and soul are joined together, the light of the intellect, and how the human being is a microcosm resembling the cosmos.
— Knowledge of the animal kingdom.
— Knowledge of the vegetable kingdom.
— Knowledge of the moral rules of human conduct.

---

[76] See IV.1.a.ii above, and the reference there to Hava Lazarus-Yafeh, "On the Character of Judeo-Arabic Culture" (Hebrew), published by the Israel Historical Society (Jerusalem, 1973), pp. 265–285.

[77] Baḥya ibn Paquda, *Duties of the Heart* 2:3, vol. 1, p. 141.

— Knowledge of the religious service of God as established in the Torah, leading to happiness in this world and to later reward in the world to come. In addition to knowledge of the true service of God in the Torah, one is obligated to study the customs of other nations, which are important and useful in the affairs of this world.[78]

Examining the created world thus leads to both theoretical benefit—knowledge of the wisdom of God in the world—and practical benefit—knowledge of moral conduct—and thereby makes possible the true worship of God.

[IV.8]   SERVICE OF GOD
AND AROUSAL OF THE SOUL

A basic human obligation is to thank a benefactor. In the case of human benefactors, their generosity to others is mixed with an element of self-interest. In the case of God, the benefaction is not limited by any such self-interest, and the duty to thank and serve him is, therefore, all the greater. Many people, however, because of their intellectual and moral immaturity, fail to recognize their obligation to be grateful and to serve God, and need to be "aroused" to perform their duty.

Such "arousal" or "awakening" (Arabic: *tanbih*; Hebrew: *he'arah*) can have its source in reason or in the Torah. In principle, reason should provide this arousal.

> But between the time when the benefits that man receives and the time when he has sufficient intelligence to realize the services he should render in return for them, a long period intervenes. Hence, calling attention to the external acts and inward faith which make the service of God complete, is a duty, so that a human being should not be without religion up to the time when his mental powers have become fully developed.[79]

Bahya's differentiation between arousal by reason and arousal by the Torah reflects, both terminologically and conceptually, Sa'adiah Ga'on's parallel categories of rational and traditional commandments, and as we saw above, Bahya overtly adopts Sa'adiah's categories and applies them to the duties of the limbs (which may be rational or traditional) and the duties of the heart (which are exclusively rational). Nevertheless, once again, there is a difference. For Sa'adiah, the focus is external. Revelation, and the revealed commandments, were historically necessary as a short-cut in the rational

---

[78]   Bahya ibn Paquda, *Duties of the Heart* 2:4, vol. 1, p. 147.
[79]   Bahya ibn Paquda, *Duties of the Heart* 3:1, vol. 1, p. 193.

process of understanding, to provide people in general, and the Jewish people in particular, with an understanding of the truth and of proper behavior at a point in history when they lacked the capacity to arrive at the truth with their unaided reason.

For Baḥya, those historical considerations are legitimate, but there is also an internal dimension to the need. The spiritual and moral immaturity that necessitate arousal by the Torah are not merely a historical stage in human development in general, but also an existential condition of all people at all times. The problem is within each person, and derives from the person being compounded from two separate elements, body and soul, which are in dialectical tension with each other.

That continual tension between a person's physical and spiritual nature creates a situation in which intellectual arousal is frequently insufficient, especially in light of the strength of the bodily appetites. Intellectual arousal, therefore, needs to be reinforced by the arousal of the divinely revealed Torah. The Torah's arousal thus serves three purposes. It strengthens the intellectual arousal in the face of the bodily appetites; it provides a cure for the diseases of the world caused by the appetites; it reinforces the intellect, which does not function constantly, to enable it to overcome the bodily appetites which function constantly.[80]

What is the relation of these two types of arousal? Arousal by the Torah is a "preparation" and "introduction" to rational arousal.

> The stimulus [i.e., arousal] of the Torah is a preparation for, and introduction to, that of the intellect, the reason being that a man in his youth needs training and guidance, and restraint from yielding to his passions, till the time comes when his understanding has become strong and firm. So, too, some women and frivolous men do not follow the intellectual lead because its control over them is weak and loose. This condition made it necessary to provide guidance of a medium character which they can endure, and which will not be impossible for them to stand. Hence, the instructions of the Torah turn about hope and fear — the poles of its axis. Whoever does not fall short in fulfilling the obligations of this service belongs to the class of the truly pious and is worthy of reward in this world and in the next. But one who rises from this stage to the service of God, induced by reason, reaches the degree of the prophets and the elect of the Supreme — the saints. His recompense here on earth is joy in the sweetness of the service of the Lord.[81]

This passage brings out, once again, the internalization characteristic of Baḥya's approach. Each individual needs the Torah's arousal (the level of

---

80   Baḥya ibn Paquda, *Duties of the Heart* 3:2.
81   Baḥya ibn Paquda, *Duties of the Heart* 3:3, vol. 1, p. 207.

the pious) as a "preparation" and "introduction" as the basis for progressing to the higher stage of rational arousal (the level of the prophets and the elect of God). Baḥya then describes ten degrees or stages in understanding the Torah and serving God—a sort of Neoplatonic "upward way" of spiritual progress. Each individual has the obligation to attempt to progress from lower to higher degrees.

> It is possible that there may be other degrees among men of understanding in the Torah, gradations other than those that we have set forth. But we only mentioned those degrees that are found among the large majority of the people. Still, the list of degrees that we have given will obviously be of use to one who seeks the right way, for if he finds in this list a degree to which he is sufficiently near, knows what is the next higher degree and strives to rise to it, then notes the distance between the degree that he has attained and the highest of the degrees, and strives to ascend to it gradually, one degree after the other—he will find the ascent easier to accomplish.[82]

The tenth and highest degree for which a person should strive is that of

> those who have a reasoned conviction of the truth of the Torah and of all the duties...They do not fix their attention on reward or punishment, but hasten to fulfill the service of God for his name's sake, to magnify and exalt him with longing and wholehearted devotion, because they know him and have realized what is due to his infinite majesty. This is the high degree to be attained by those who profess allegiance to the Torah. This is the degree that was attained by the prophets and saints who were devoted to God.[83]

The tenth degree is the culmination of arousal based on the Torah, and provides the transition to rational arousal, because the prophets and saints have attained rational understanding; they "know him and have realized what is due" to God.

People on a lower level of spiritual development are motivated to do what is right and to fulfill their obligations out of the hope for reward and the fear of punishment. Those who have progressed to the highest level of spiritual development "do not fix their attention on reward or punishment." Rather, they serve God out of love.

What, then, is the higher rational arousal which a person should strive to attain?

> To be urged by the intellect means that God reminds a human being through his intellect of his duty to know him, and to become cognizant of the marks

---

[82] Baḥya ibn Paquda, *Duties of the Heart* 3:4, vol. 1, p. 231.
[83] Baḥya ibn Paquda, *Duties of the Heart* 3:4, vol. 1, p. 229.

of divine wisdom. This call of God comes to one who has taken the Torah as the light of his path, attained intellectual maturity and capacity for clear apprehension, yearns to gain the Almighty's favor and rise to the spiritual heights of the saints, and turns his heart away from worldly cares and anxieties. To reach the stage where one experiences this intellectual urge, the requisites are that a person should clearly realize what the creator has implanted in the human mind, namely: to esteem truth, detest falsehood, choose righteousness, avoid injustice, requite benefactors with good deeds and express gratitude to them, punish the wicked and condemn them, keep at peace with all human beings and act beneficently towards them...and forgiveness of transgressors when they truly repent.[84]

In summary, rational arousal is implanted in the human heart and leads him to the knowledge of God and to recognize "the marks of divine wisdom" in the world. The source of this arousal is rational, but not its ultimate purpose, because the goal is not merely intellectual knowledge of God but spiritual conduct—serving God out of love. Knowledge of God and examining the evidence of divine wisdom in the created world lead a person to the stage in which he "yearns to gain the Almighty's favor and rise to the spiritual heights of the saints."

[IV.9]   THE DIALOGUE OF THE INTELLECT AND THE SOUL

The intellect arouses the soul from its bodily involvement by engaging it in a dialogue, in order to attract it to the service of God. The dialogue of the intellect and the soul was a literary form Bahya may well have encountered in the *Rasa'il Ikhwan Al-Safa* ("The Letters of the Pure Brethren") or in Arabic translations of Hermetic texts.[85] For example, the soul asks what forces to avoid, and the intellect replies that it should avoid superfluous eating, drinking, dress, sleep, rest, and tranquility, and excess speech, love of praise and honor, and envy. The soul then says:

> To renounce these faults would be very hard for me, on account of the long time that I have been habituated to them; therefore, be kind enough to show me in what way I can do so more easily.

---

84   Bahya ibn Paquda, *Duties of the Heart* 3:5, vol 1, p. 233.

85   The Hermetic texts were Greek works produced in Egypt c. 100–300 C.E., of a philosophic, scientific and magical character. They were attributed to Hermes, the god of writing, science and magic, identified with the Egyptian god Thoth, and known as Hermes Trismegistus (i.e., Hermes the three-times great [sage]), in Arabic "Al-Hirmis Al-Muthalath."

The intellect replies:

> Surely you know that a sensible man will consent to the amputation of one of his limbs and to its loss, if it is attacked by some disease which he fears will spread and affect the remaining limbs...So, too, if you wish that the separation which is so hard should seem easy to you, concentrate your mind and employ your intelligence in weighing the good you will derive from the separation and the evil which will befall you if you continue your association with it; and then separation from your reprehensible disposition, which seems so hard, will be easy.

The soul then asks:

> What is the good that separation from it will bring me?

And the intellect replies:

> The good will consist in your spiritual tranquility and relief from the darkness of this gloomy world, the pleasures of which are mingled with griefs, while its lusts soon cease; also, that your strengthened power of perception will finally lead you to realize your destiny in the place of your repose [the life hereafter], and that therefore you should busy yourself and be concerned about it. This is one of the portals on which depend your salvation and your life. The evil...is recurrence of your anxiety, reduplication of your grief, continuance of your mourning at the non-fulfillment of your desires in this world, which, if they were satisfied, would only bring you something that is vain, without permanence or continuance.[86]

[IV.9.a]   THE TRUE SPIRITUAL BENEFIT

As the dialogue continues, Baḥya describes four degrees of benefit the soul enjoys when it avoids bodily and social evils, and turns to the true service of God recommended by the intellect. The first degree includes those universal benefits all people are granted by God; therefore all humans should serve God. For this universal service, the entire human species was given the rational laws followed by Adam, Enoch, Noah and his children, and Job and his companions, until the time of Moses, in other words, what the rabbis called "the seven commandments of the children of Noah."[87]

The second degree includes the special benefits granted to the people of Israel, by taking them out of Egypt and bringing them to the promised land. The particular service of Israel, over and above the universal, rational service of all humans, consists of the ritual, i.e. "traditional" commandments of the Torah.

---

86   Baḥya ibn Paquda, *Duties of the Heart* 3:5, vol. 1, pp. 237–239.
87   Baḥya ibn Paquda, *Duties of the Heart* 3:6.

Within the Jewish people there is a special class, the third degree, of benefits granted to the Levites and priests (*kohanim*) descended from Aaron, and the royal family of David. They, in turn, were given special service unique to them. The final and fourth class includes the special benefits granted to unique individuals, the prophets and sages, who accordingly also had special obligations of service.

Bahya thus classifies all humanity by four hierarchical degrees, each of which has its appropriate service in response to its level of benefit. As we shall see in Ch. 6, Judah Ha-Levi has a similar hierarchical structure in his *Kuzari* 2:44, where he discusses three sections of the Additional (*Musaf*) service on the New Year and Day of Atonement, which refer respectively to "all that you created" (i.e., all humanity), to "your people" (i.e., the Jewish people), and to "the righteous". However, a more direct parallel to Bahya's four degrees may be found in Psalm 118, describing four degrees of acknowledgment of and gratitude to God:

	Bahya's four degrees of benefit	Psalm 118:1–4
1	Universal human benefit	Acknowledge that the Lord is good; his kindness endures forever.
2	Particular benefit of the Jewish people	Let Israel say, his kindness endures forever.
3	Particular benefit of the Levites, *kohanim* and royal dynasty of David	Let the household of Aaron say, his kindness endures forever.
4	Particular benefit of the prophets and sages	Let those who revere the Lord say, his kindness endures forever.

The duty of serving God thus applies to all human beings, in proportion to the benefits they receive from God.

Despite what it has learned in its dialogue with the intellect about benefits and the service of God, the soul remains troubled by the problem of determinism. Many ancient books indicate that God determines human destiny. The Torah, on the other hand, refers in various passages to human free will. What, then, is the correct view? And if a person's behavior is predetermined, what is the point of the soul's striving to avoid physical and social involvement in order to concentrate its powers on the service of God?

The intellect (representing, of course, Bahya) replies that we do not understand this, and cannot resolve the contradiction inherent in this divine "secret," but must operate simultaneous on two opposite working assumptions: to trust in God's necessary decree, but at the same time to act appropriately based on the freedom we do possess.[88]

---

[88]   Bahya ibn Paquda, *Duties of the Heart* 3:8.

[IV.10]　TRUST IN GOD, PREDETERMINATION AND FREE WILL

The third section of the *Duties of the Heart*, on the service of God, thus ends with the affirmation of trust in God, despite our inability to resolve the contradiction between predetermination and freedom. What does this "trust" mean, and how does it differ from faith in God? For Baḥya, trust is much more than mere faith; it is the emotional and behavioral consequence of faith and spiritual response to faith.

> What is trust? It is tranquility of the soul in the one who trusts; his hearty reliance on the one in whom he trusts, that the latter will do what is right and proper in the matter of the trust, to the extent of his ability and knowledge, for the benefit of the one who trusts... out of pure benevolence and kindness.[89]

Faith refers to affirmation of a truth. As we saw, Baḥya employs rational proofs at the beginning of the book to verify the existence and unity of God. Trust is based on faith, and as an emotional and behavioral response to the faith, is necessary for the service of God. It is only a person's trust in God that enables him to avoid other pursuits, however attractive and pleasurable, and devote himself to such service, however difficult.

As we have seen, Baḥya affirms predetermination by God's decree, and at the same time, human free will. It is, therefore, only the trust in God which enables a person to affirm that the divine decree is for the best, and that he still must use his freedom of will to choose and take responsibility for his life.

[IV.11]　REPENTANCE AND AROUSAL

In the fifth section of the *Duties of the Heart*, discussing wholehearted devotion to God, Baḥya explains that a person's actions, both public and private, should all be devoted to the service of God. Such wholehearted devotion requires that the person's convictions and actions be in complete harmony. In the sixth section of the *Duties of the Heart*, dealing with humility, i.e., a person's submission to God, Baḥya then explains that in order to devote oneself to the service of God, one must avoid pride and submit to God. The seventh section, in turn, deals with repentance (Hebrew: *teshuvah*): when a person truly submits to God, his submission leads him to repent, namely, to correct the failures that are inevitable in every person's life.

89　Baḥya ibn Paquda, *Duties of the Heart* 4:1, vol. 1, p. 295.

Like Sa'adiah Ga'on before him,[90] and Rambam after him,[91] Baḥya lists conditions or stages in the process of repentance.

(1) That the penitent should regret the iniquities already committed;
(2) That he should renounce and abandon them;
(3) That he should confess them and beseech forgiveness for having committed them;
(4) That he should firmly pledge himself with heart and soul not to repeat them.[92]

As was the case with the service of God, the process of repentance also requires "arousal" or "awakening" (Arabic: *tanbih*; Hebrew: *he'arah*). There are four ways in which a person can be "aroused" to repent truly: (a) when the person recognizes God's greatness and beneficence; (b) when the person is rebuked by God, either through a prophet or through the Torah; (c) when the person witnesses how other people are tested by God by means of suffering (like Job); (d) when sinners receive their deserved punishment.[93]

The role of arousal continues to be an important component of the process of self-examination or spiritual accounting (*ḥeshbon ha-nefesh*) in the eighth section of the *Duties of the Heart*. True self-examination is at the same time both a necessary condition for repentance and a way of arousing the soul to repent. In his introduction to this section, Baḥya states:

> As the previous treatise [i.e., section 7] dealt with the essentials of repentance and its conditions, and as spiritual accounting is one of these conditions, I have deemed it fit to follow with an exposition of taking spiritual account with one's soul, because of the subjects in which this stirs [i.e. arouses, awakes] the soul to what will further its well-being in both worlds [i.e., this world and the world to come].[94]

In subsequent passages, Baḥya continues to discuss the need for such arousal of the soul, however he no longer used the Arabic term *tanbih* (which Judah ibn Tibbon and Yosef Kafiḥ both translated as *he'arah*), but forms of the root *yaqiẓ*, which Ibn Tibbon translated by the cognate Hebrew *heqiẓ*.[95] Regardless of which term is used, the arousal of the soul remains a central feature of these three inter-related spiritual processes, self-examination, repentance and service of God. By these processes, the soul undergoes moral

---

[90]   Sa'adiah Ga'on, *Book of Beliefs and Opinions* 5:5.
[91]   Rambam, *Mishneh Torah* (Code of Law), Book of Knowledge, Laws of Repentance, ch. 2.
[92]   Baḥya ibn Paquda, *Duties of the Heart* 7:4, vol. 2, p. 141.
[93]   Baḥya ibn Paquda, *Duties of the Heart* 7:6.
[94]   Baḥya ibn Paquda, *Duties of the Heart* 8:Introduction, vol. 2, p. 185.
[95]   Kafiḥ, however, does not differentiate between the two terms, both of which mean to arouse or awake, and continues to translate it as *he'arah*.

improvement and spiritual progress, as it abandons and avoids preoccupation with physical activities and bodily appetites, and gradually removes the veil separating it from the light of the intellect.

[IV.12] ASCETICISM

The spiritual progress brought about by self-examination and repentance should lead the person to the true service of God, namely, the pure spiritual life, by avoidance and rejection of preoccupation with the pleasures of the body and its appetites, namely by asceticism or abstinence (Arabic: *zuhd*; Hebrew: *perishut*, literally "separation"), discussed in the ninth section of the book. Such asceticism removes a person not only from preoccupation with the body and its appetites, but also from excessive involvement in society. Asceticism thereby leads to a life of sanctity.

This connection between asceticism and sanctity may already be found in rabbinic readings of Scripture. "Be holy, for I, the Lord your God, am holy" (Leviticus 19:2) was understood in the Sifra[96] to mean: "You be separate because I am holy, in other words, if you sanctify yourselves upwards, I regard it as if you sanctified me." Rashi (basing himself on Midrash Leviticus Rabba on this verse) interprets it similarly: "You be holy—be separate from sexual immorality and transgression."

Although Baḥya rejected the extreme asceticism of the Sufis, as mentioned above, he did advocate a more moderate form of asceticism. Nevertheless, although his asceticism was moderate by Sufi standards, it was relatively extreme in a Jewish context. The Talmud records two opposite opinions regarding asceticism, based on differing readings of Numbers 6:11. The Torah is referring here to a Nazirite who became defiled by coming into contact with a human corpse and must undergo a process of purification, at the end of which he comes to the Temple to offer a sin-offering (*ḥatat*). The phrase the Torah uses is that the sacrificial atonement is necessary, literally "because he sinned against the soul" (*me-asher ḥata 'al ha-nefesh*). The plain meaning of the text is that he sinned by coming into contact with a corpse, but the rabbis asked which soul did he sin against? They conclude that he sinned against himself, i.e., his own soul. How did he sin against his own soul?

In one passage (Babylonian Talmud, Nedarim 10a), Abayé, Simon the Just, Rabbi Simon and Rabbi El'azar Ha-Kappar agree that the Nazirite is a sinner, who sinned against himself (his own soul), by denying himself wine. And if a person who denies himself wine is a sinner, someone who denies

---

96   The Sifra is a *midrash halakhah* on Leviticus from the school of Rabbi Akiva, also known as *Torat Kohanim*. The passage in question is found in Sifra, Qedoshim 1:1.

himself all pleasure is certainly a greater sinner. The opposite view of Rabbi El'azar is recorded in another passage (Babylonian Talmud, Ta'anit 11a), that the Nazirite way of life is holy, and that the Nazirite sins against himself by ending his period of Nazirite vows and returning to normal social life. According to this view, if a person who denies himself wine is holy, someone who denies himself all pleasures is certainly much holier. The same difference of interpretation may be found in the disagreement between Rambam (Maimonides),[97] who agrees with the anti-ascetic view of the first passage, and Ramban (Naḥmanides), who agrees with the ascetic interpretation of Rabbi El'azar,[98] and equates holiness (*qedushah*) with asceticism (*perishut*), for example, in his commentary to Numbers 21:6 (that the priests should be holy): "Holiness is asceticism... The priests should abstain [literally: separate themselves] even from what is permitted to Israel."

Baḥya's attitude towards asceticism is favorable, and typically, he differentiates between two types of asceticism: general, for the physical and social benefit of the entire human species in this world, and a special asceticism for the Jewish people, for their spiritual benefit in the world to come.

> The plain meaning of abstinence is bridling the inner lust, voluntarily refraining from something that is in our power and which we have the opportunity to do... An abstainer... is one who has the power and does not use it. The obligation which restrains the inner lust falls into two divisions. One of these applies to mankind... the other is specifically limited to rational beings who are adherents of the Torah.
>
> General abstinence is that which is practiced to improve our physical condition and keep our secular affairs in good order... Specific abstinence is the kind which the Torah and reason indicate for the welfare of our souls in the world to come.[99]

Asceticism is beneficial both physically and spiritually. On the physical level, it preserves the body and society. On the spiritual level, it is necessary "to discipline the soul and test it in this world, so that it might be purified and attain the character of the holy angels."[100] Asceticism is thus, for Baḥya, the method for implementing the Neoplatonic upward way, for the soul to purify itself from contamination by the body, in order to be liberated from its bodily involvement and return to its spiritual source. Asceticism, in this way, makes it possible for the human soul to "attain the character of the holy angels," i.e., to return to its true nature and purpose.

---

97   Cf. Rambam's *Shemonah Peraqim* ("Eight Chapters on Ethics"), ch. 4, and his *Mishneh Torah* (Code of Law), Book of Knowledge, Laws of Ethical Conduct (*De 'ot*) 3:1, and the discussion of this in Ch. 10.

98   Naḥmanides, commentary to Numbers 6:11.

99   Baḥya ibn Paquda, *Duties of the Heart* 9:1, vol. 2, p. 291.

100   Baḥya ibn Paquda, *Duties of the Heart* 9:1, vol. 2, p. 291.

At the same time, Baḥya acknowledges the danger inherent in asceticism, when taken too far. Not everyone should become an ascetic. "It would not, however, conduce to the improvement of the world that all human beings should practice asceticism, for this would lead to the abandonment of civilization, and the continuance of the human race would cease."[101] Nevertheless, there is a need for some people to adopt the ascetic way of life, "so that every class of human beings shall learn from them, each according to its needs and in harmony with its customs and dispositions."[102]

The Torah's intention, then, is to bring about a situation in which reason controls the bodily appetites. Asceticism is thus necessary both on the general, social plane (so that others can learn self-control and self-discipline from the ascetics) and on the inner, individual plane (purification and liberation of the soul from bodily appetites). The general asceticism necessary for the welfare of the human species is relatively moderate, but the special asceticism prescribed by the Torah can and should be more extreme, to cultivate the spiritual life. However, even within the Jewish people, extreme asceticism cannot become the norm, and is only appropriate for certain extraordinary individuals:

> It is necessary that among the followers of the Torah there should be individuals who dedicate themselves to special abstinence and undertake its conditions, and so be useful to their co-religionists, when their souls turn and their dispositions, together with their impulses, incline to bestial lusts. Thus these abstainers are physicians to the souls in matters of religion...Such men as these abstainers have made it their aim to heal anyone who is sick in his faith. If one suffers from the maladies of skepticism, they hasten to relieve him by their genuine wisdom.[103]

Asceticism thus functions on two parallel planes: general and individual. On the general plane, asceticism provides the human species as a whole, and the people of Israel, a social counter-balance. The welfare and improvement of society necessitate that people engage in self-restraint, and the ascetics counter-balance the many undisciplined people in society who follow and yield to their bestial impulses. On the individual plane, asceticism provides each person—especially those extraordinary individuals who seek to purify their souls—a counter-balance to their powerful bodily appetites which divert them from their true spiritual purpose.

Rambam also regarded asceticism as providing a necessary social and individual counter-balance. However, in Rambam's case, that counter-balance

---

101　Baḥya ibn Paquda, *Duties of the Heart* 9:1, vol. 2, p. 293.
102　Baḥya ibn Paquda, *Duties of the Heart* 9:1, vol. 2, p. 293.
103　Baḥya ibn Paquda, *Duties of the Heart* 9:2, vol. 2, p. 299.

is a temporary measure, depending on a given situation, and not a desired goal in itself. Bahya, on the other hand, transformed asceticism from a temporary remedy into a permanent life-style desirable in itself.

Once again, Bahya distinguishes three different degrees of true asceticism "in order to strengthen religion." The first degree of true ascetics are those who live in accordance with the highest definition of asceticism, who strive to live a purely spiritual life.

> They renounce everything that distracts them from the thought of God. They flee from inhabited places to the deserts or high mountains, where there is no company, no society. They eat whatever they find... They dress in worn garments and raw wool.[104] They take shelter in the rocks... The love of God delights them so much that they do not think of the love of human beings.[105]

These extreme ascetics are the farthest removed from the mean prescribed by the Torah, "because they renounce worldly interests completely, and our religion does not bid us to give up social life altogether."[106]

The second degree of true ascetics are more moderate and follow the median form of asceticism. They spurn the world's luxuries and bridle their desire for them. However, unlike the first group of true ascetics, they do not withdraw from society. "Instead of deserts and mountains, they chose solitude in their homes and isolation in their dwellings... They are nearer the right way that is in accord with the Torah."[107] In other words, they are not physically isolated from society, but spiritually insulated within it.

The third degree of true ascetics are even more moderate and closer to the Torah's mean.

> These separated themselves from the world in their hearts and minds, but joined their fellowmen in physical occupations for the material benefit of mankind... They also engaged actively in the service of the blessed creator, realizing that a human's being's position in this world is a state of trial and imprisonment, that of a stranger who had been taken from the world of spirits and brought hither. Hence their souls hold this world and its wealth in abhorrence, yearn for the world hereafter, wait for death, and yet are wary of it... From this world they take the minimum of what they need for their maintenance.[108]

Besides these three degrees of true ascetics, there are those who practice abstinence for utilitarian purposes, "whose abstinence is physical but not in

---

[104]   Note the reference here to the woolen garb of the Sufis.
[105]   Bahya ibn Paquda, *Duties of the Heart* 9:3, vol. 2, p. 303.
[106]   Bahya ibn Paquda, *Duties of the Heart* 9:3, vol. 2, p. 303.
[107]   Bahya ibn Paquda, *Duties of the Heart* 9:3, vol. 2, p. 303.
[108]   Bahya ibn Paquda, *Duties of the Heart* 9:3, vol. 2, p. 305.

their minds and hearts."[109] They may seek fame as ascetics, so that people will entrust them with their money. Others abstain because they have acquired some money and possessions but fear they will lose them. Still others abstain because of their poverty. Such asceticism is not genuine.

Returning to genuine asceticism, why does Baḥya consistently emphasize the need for asceticism, since the identifies the most moderate form of asceticism as closest to the ethical standard of the Torah, namely the mean? Should not our ethical standards be those of the Torah? Baḥya's response is that in the period of Abraham, Isaac and Jacob people possessed strong intellects, and had only a weak evil inclination (*yezer ha-ra'*). Therefore that generation did not require many commandments to govern their behavior, nor did they require the cure of radical asceticism in order to serve God. To the contrary, the ethical mean of the Torah sufficed for them. "They did not need asceticism, which departs from the middle of the road that the Torah prescribes."[110] Subsequently, however, as a result of the prolonged enslavement of the Israelites in Egypt, "their sensual lust became strong, their desire increased and their evil inclination prevailed over their reason."[111] Matters became worse with their conquest of the promised land, when they could enjoy its material bounty.

> The more the land was settled, the more did their understanding deteriorate…And the more their lusts increased and strengthened, the weaker became their understanding, and the more it delayed attaining the proper course. Hence they stood in need of a severe asceticism by means of which they might be able to resist their sensual feelings. Such was the way of the Nazirite…In subsequent generations, the understanding has become still weaker and the lust has become stronger; and when people occupy themselves with secular affairs, they are distracted from concentrating themselves with their interests in the hereafter. Hence, they need to free themselves from this world…The ancients, with their strong understanding and pure souls, could work for this world and also for the future life, and neither occupation was detrimental to the other.[112]

The discrepancy between the Torah's mean ethical standard and the later need for asceticism thus becomes clear: asceticism became increasingly necessary to counter progressive moral and spiritual decline. The Torah's standard was appropriate for conditions in its day, but later generations have required ever stricter and more extreme ascetic standards. And yet, despite Baḥya's explaining the discrepancy in terms of changing social-historical circumstances, his emphasis remains internal. As he states in the introduction

---

109   Baḥya ibn Paquda, *Duties of the Heart* 9:3, vol. 2, p. 305.
110   Baḥya ibn Paquda, *Duties of the Heart* 9:7, vol. 2, p. 333.
111   Baḥya ibn Paquda, *Duties of the Heart* 9:7, vol. 2, p. 333.
112   Baḥya ibn Paquda, *Duties of the Heart* 9:7, vol. 2, pp. 333–335.

to the tenth and final section of the *Duties of the Heart*, on the wholehearted love of God, the purpose of the lengthy discussion of asceticism in the ninth section of the book was to promote wholehearted love of God by freeing the person from material and physical concerns. The moderate asceticism closest to the Torah's standards permits its adherents to participate externally, with their bodies, in the necessary physical and material welfare of the world, while spiritually detached and insulated from materials concerns "in their hearts and minds." Even that moderate asceticism deviates from, and is thus extreme in relation to, the normative ethical mean of the Torah. Asceticism, in one degree or another, thus provides a moral antidote to external social decline, and an inner means of purifying and liberating the soul for wholehearted devotion to, and love of, God. Asceticism thus is needed for the welfare of society in this world and for the welfare of the soul in this world and its preparation for the world to come.

[IV.13]   THE LOVE OF GOD

The purpose of asceticism, as we have seen, is to free the soul from physical entanglement for the wholehearted service of God, and the true service of God is service out of love. The love of God is, therefore, the culmination of the linear literary structure of the *Duties of the Heart*, but it is also the culmination of the upward way, the process of refining and purifying the soul. The Neoplatonic upward way is thus maintained in an overtly Jewish context, for it ends not with Plotinus' *unio mystica* but with the fulfillment of the Torah's commandment, "Love the Lord your God with all your heart, with all your soul, and with all your might" (Deuteronomy 6:5), a commandment, as Baḥya points out, that is repeatedly emphasized in the Torah. Directly addressing his reader, Baḥya says in the introduction to the tenth section of the book, on the wholehearted love of God:

> It is proper, my brother, that you understand and know, that all that has been mentioned in this work on the duties of the heart, on morals and spiritual nobility, are rungs and steps leading to the supreme object which it is our purpose to expound in this treatise. It is also proper for you to know, that every duty and every good quality — whether it be rational, found in Scripture or based on tradition — are all forms and steps by which [human beings] ascend to this, their ultimate aim, and there is no degree above or beyond it.[113]

The human soul, being a simple spiritual substance, as opposed to the compound physical body, seeks to free itself from the physical world and draw

---

[113]   Baḥya ibn Paquda, *Duties of the Heart* 10:Introduction, vol. 2, p. 339.

near to the spiritual world. Just as we saw that the moderate ascetic who is closest to the Torah remains physically active in society but is insulated in his heart and mind, so now we see that those who love God remain physically in the world, but in their hearts turn inward, away from the external physical world, towards the object of their love, God.

> In their hearts and minds they are disinterested in their secular interests and care of their bodies; occupying themselves in these concerns, with their physical senses, only when it is necessary and urgent, because they regard this world cheaply and of little importance. They turn their souls and hearts to their religious interests and to the service of God, to honor and exalt him and keep his commandments. Their bodies are physical; their hearts, spiritual.[114]

Those who truly love God are thus the third and most moderate degree of ascetics described earlier, who are closest to the mean ethic of the Torah, and who externally participate in the affairs of this world, but internally serve God in love. In this way they are able to fulfill their external duties of the limbs and also the internal duties of the heart: "Their bodies are physical; their hearts, spiritual."

---

[114]   Baḥya ibn Paquda, *Duties of the Heart* 10:7, vol. 2, pp. 373–375.

Section II

TRANSITIONS

Chapter Five

PHILOSOPHICAL EXEGESIS OF
THE BIBLE: ABRAHAM IBN EZRA

[v.1]   BIBLE EXEGESIS AS A PHILOSOPHICAL
LITERARY GENRE

Jewish philosophical literature, like other philosophical literature, was written
in various literary genres. For example, both in the Middle Ages and in the
modern era, Jews wrote philosophical works in the form of Platonic dialogues
or novels. The medieval religious polemics among Jews, Christians and
Muslims frequently employed rationalist-philosophical arguments, and not
merely religious claims based on their respective scriptures or general moral
considerations. The common, neutral philosophical language could thus be
used to disprove the claims of the other religions and to prove one's own. As
Daniel Lasker has written:

> The purpose of the intellect in religious disputes is to distinguish between
> a possibly true religion and an obviously false religion. A true religion does not
> teach irrational beliefs. Intellect cannot prove that a religion is, indeed, true,
> because there are theological matters that are beyond the realm of the intellect;
> nevertheless, the intellect can establish that a particular religion is not divine if
> its beliefs contradict reason.[1]

Hebrew poetry was also a genre for philosophical expression by medieval
Jewish philosophers, and many of the greatest Hebrew poets, like Solomon ibn
Gabirol (whom we discussed in Chapter Three), Judah Ha-Levi (who will be
discussed in Chapter Six) and Abraham ibn Ezra, were also among the most
important Jewish philosophers of the period, and their poetry includes poems
of a philosophical nature.[2]

---

[1] Hasdai Crescas, *The Refutation of the Christian Principles*, translated with introduction
by Daniel J. Lasker (Albany: State University of New York Press, 1992), p. 6. Also see
Lasker's *Jewish Philosophical Polemics Against Christianity in the Middle Ages* (Oxford:
Littman Library of Jewish Civilization, 2007).
[2] In Ch. 3, for example, we frequently referred to Ibn Gabirol's "Royal Crown."

Another important medieval philosophical literary genre was philosophical exegesis of the Bible. This literary genre follows necessarily from the very nature of western religious philosophy. As we saw in Chapter One, in many respects, there is no difference between medieval Jewish, Christian or Islamic philosophy, all of which, in the famous thesis of Harry A. Wolfson, was "Philonic." Philosophers in all three western religious traditions, all of which are based on divine revelation recorded in holy scripture, struggled with the question of the relation between religion and reason. Such "synthetic philosophers," who maintained what Wolfson called "the double-faith theory" affirming the truth of both revelation and reason, were forced to deal with the question of the relation between these two sources of and paths to the truth. How can the apparent contradictions between religion and reason be resolved, and how can a person really affirm both? The harmonization of faith and reason, or at least some kind of mutual understanding between them, thus became necessary from the perspective of both religion and reason. Philo was, as Wolfson showed, the first to attempt such a synthesis, by adapting the method of Greek allegorical interpretation of classical mythology to Bible exegesis, and the medievals, most of whom never heard of Philo, adopted the Philonic structure, regardless of its Hebrew, Arabic or Latin linguistic and cultural "garb." In Wolfson's words:

> For those who have followed in [Philo's] footsteps...the interpretation of Scripture in terms of philosophy was not simply a matter of mechanically substituting one set of doctrines with another. To all of them it was a complicated study of similarities and differences. They all started with certain general conceptions as to what constituted true religious doctrines, conceptions which ultimately go back to the Hebrew Scripture and Jewish tradition. Corresponding to these they all had another set of conceptions derived from Greek philosophy. Between these two sets of conceptions they all tried to show that there could be no real contradiction.[3]

Philosophical exegesis of the Bible is, therefore, at the same time a way of understanding Scripture philosophically and a way of reconciling philo-sophic doctrines with the requirements of revealed religion. Furthermore, it provides an occasion both for teaching philosophy within the religious community, and for demonstrating the rational validity of religion within the philosophic community. Many medieval philosophers, such as Thomas Aquinas in Christianity and Ibn Rushd (Averroes) in Islam, cited and commented on scriptural passages in their philosophic works. Within Judaism, not only did philosophers similarly relate to biblical passages,

---

3   Harry A. Wolfson, *Philo: Foundations of Religious Philosophy in Judaism, Christianity, and Islam* (Cambridge: Harvard University Press, 1947/1962), vol. 1, pp. 103–104.

but they created a new Jewish literary genre, namely philosophical Bible exegesis, whether as full-fledged, independent works of exegesis, or as extensive passages within other kinds of works. Such exegetical works do not neglect other important areas of scriptural study, including linguistic analysis of the text, grammatical and literary analysis, and homiletical and halakhic lessons. Nevertheless, their exegetical works are, to a greater or lesser extent, philosophical in nature.

In this chapter, we shall study the philosophic ideas of Abraham ibn Ezra, in particular as they are expressed in his Bible commentaries. Unlike the other philosophers we are studying, from Sa'adiah Ga'on to Rambam, all of whom wrote their philosophical works in Arabic, Ibn Ezra (who knew and read Arabic) wrote his philosophic, scientific, mathematical, astronomical and astrological works in Hebrew. Although himself a poet graced with a fine Hebrew style, his works are often difficult to understand, for two reasons. First, it is often difficult to abstract his ideas from the specific exegetical context in which they were written, frequently including technical linguistic or grammatical analysis of the text. Second, as he states many times, he is only "hinting" or "alluding" to his point, and the subject discussed "has a secret (i.e., esoteric)" meaning. By his own admission, therefore, he did not always reveal his true intention.

Much of our attention will be devoted to two major features of Ibn Ezra's thought, which render his philosophical exegesis of Scripture unusual, even among other philosophical exegetes: Bible criticism and astrology. We shall devote particular attention to his astrological theory, because it impinges upon many other significant areas of his thought, including cosmology, free will, and the distinctiveness of the Jewish people.

[V.2]   ABRAHAM IBN EZRA:
LIFE AND WORKS

Abraham ben Meir ibn Ezra was born in Tudela, in northern Spain, probably c. 1089, although that date is questioned. He died at the age of 75, apparently in 1164. Ibn Ezra was a friend of Judah Ha-Levi's, and his commentaries cite Ha-Levi's views. According to one opinion, he was Judah Ha-Levi's son-in-law, but so far as we know it was Ibn Ezra's son Isaac who was married to Ha-Levi's daughter. He had other children, but only Isaac survived, and it was Isaac who accompanied Judah Ha-Levi on his journey to the Land of Israel. Isaac, by the way, at one point converted to Islam, but in one of his poems says that he always remained faithful to the Torah and had repented and returned to Judaism.

For the first fifty years of his life Abraham ibn Ezra lived in Spain and wrote hundreds of poems (both sacred and secular), but never was financially successful. In one of his poems ("Luckless") he writes:[4]

The planets and spheres in their stations
Changed their order when I first drew breath.
If I were to be a seller of lamps,
The sun would not set till after my death!

The stars in heaven have ruined my life.
I cannot succeed however I strive.
If I were to be a seller of shrouds,
No one would die while I was alive!

The latter years of his life were a period of wandering, to which made various references. When Judah Ha-Levi set out for Israel, Ibn Ezra was wandering throughout Europe, with stays in various countries including Italy, France and England. During this period he wrote dozens of works of grammar, philosophy, astronomy and astrology, mathematics, and calculations of the Hebrew calendar, as well as his works of Bible exegesis.[5] His love for poetic expression remained, however, and compositions like his Introduction to the Torah include rhymed prose and poetry.

Perhaps his wandering and lack of books led Ibn Ezra to write several commentaries to the same books. For example, the version of his commentary to Exodus printed in standard rabbinic Bibles (*Miqra'ot Gedolot*, i.e., the biblical text accompanied by major medieval commentaries) is his second and longer commentary, and not the first and shorter commentary,[6] he similarly wrote complete and partial commentaries to Genesis. Some of his works were lost over the years.

His independent philosophical books are *Sefer Ha-Shem* ("The Book of the Name"), on the names of God, and *Yesod Mora Ve-Sod Ha-Torah* ("The Foundation of Piety and the Secret of the Torah"), on the categories and

---

4   The poem, "Galgal U-Mazalot" may be found in Jefim Ḥayyim Schirmann, *Ha-Shirah Ha-'Ivrit Bi-Sefarad Uve-Provence* (Jerusalem, 1961), vol. 1, pp. 575–576. The translation cited here is by David Goldstein in his anthology *The Jewish Poets of Spain 900–1250* (Middlesex: Penguin Books, 1971), p. 155. A translation by Solomon Solis-Cohen may be found in Nathan and Marynn Ausubel, *A Treasury of Jewish Poetry* (New York: Crown, 1957), p. 179. The poem also reflects Ibn Ezra's interest in astrology.

5   For a bibliography of Ibn Ezra's works and works on Ibn Ezra, see "Ibn Ezra, Abraham" by Uriel Simon and Raphael Jospe, in *Encyclopaedia Judaica* (2nd) edition, vol. 9, pp. 665–672.

6   The rabbinic Bible called *Torat Ḥayyim* published by Mosad Ha-Rav Kook includes both versions, edited by Asher Weiser. The scientific edition *Miqra'ot Gedolot Ha-Keter*, edited by Menachem Cohen, being published by Bar Ilan University, also contains both versions.

rationale of the Torah's commandments. However it is his Bible commentaries for which Ibn Ezra is, rightfully, best known, and it is in these works that his multifaceted personality and interests find expression. It is also in these exegetical works that his unusual philosophic approach comes out, for instance, in his astrological explanations of various biblical phenomena, and in his Neoplatonic interpretation of the creation story. His scientific and critical mind led him to ask hard questions—generally not explicit, but allusions—which have led many, including Spinoza, to regard Ibn Ezra as the pioneer of what later came to be known as "higher" Bible criticism.

[V.3]   IBN EZRA AND BIBLE CRITICISM

[V.3.a]   IBN EZRA'S RATIONALIST EXIGETICAL APPROACH

Ibn Ezra's exegesis reflects, and is a direct product of, his rationalist philosophy, and he sought a scientific (at least in his terms) approach to understanding the Bible. Unlike many other medieval exegetes, Ibn Ezra's interest was primarily only in the *peshat*, the plain or surface meaning, often contextual, of the text, as opposed to *derash* (homiletical meaning for the purpose of deriving a lesson), *remez* (metaphorical or allegorical meaning), and *sod* (esoteric or mystical meaning).[7] Ibn Ezra's analysis of the text was, therefore, frequently linguistic, grammatical or literary. In this his analysis resembles

---

7   Together, the initials of these four levels of meaning spell PaRDeS, an orchard or paradise. For example of *remez*, the talmudic rabbis regarded the Song of Songs as an allegory of God's love for Israel; this allegorical understanding of the book led Rabbi Akiva to state that "all the scriptural books are holy, and the Song of Songs is the holy of holies" (Mishnah, Yadayim 3:5). In Christian exegesis, this allegory was transformed into Christ's love of the church. An example of *derash* would be the interpretation of Rashi (1040–1105), based on rabbinic *midrash*, of Exodus 33:23 as meaning that God "showed Moses the knot of his *tefillin*." *Sod* would include, for example, calculating the numerical value of words (*gematria*), since each letter of the Hebrew alphabet has a numerical equivalent, showing that two words with the same numerical value are, therefore, equivalent or related. The boundaries of these categories are not clear or fixed. Rashi, for instance, states that his purpose was "to resolve the *peshat*" (Rashi on Genesis 33:20; cf. on Genesis 3:8), although he frequently engages in *derash* (as on Exodus 33:23). The argument between the Pharisees and the Sadducees, and the parallel argument centuries later between rabbinic Jews and the Karaites, over the meaning of the law of retaliation ("an eye for an eye," Exodus 21:24), and whether it means physical punishment or monetary compensation, also comes down to whether, as the Pharisaic and later rabbinic view insists, the principle of compensation is the actual, original meaning of the Torah, i.e. the *peshat*, or whether, as the Sadducees and Karaites insisted, a literal reading of the passage as meaning physical punishment is correct and the original meaning of the Torah, and that the rabbinic interpretation is a much later innovation and *derash* inconsistent with the Torah's intention.

much of modern scientific exegesis. On the other hand, he differs from most of the other medievals, and of course from modern scholarship, in his applying astrological and Neoplatonic cosmological theories (which, again, he regarded as scientifically valid) to explain various biblical phenomena. But in both cases—his regard for *peshat* and his application of astrological and cosmological theories of the text—Ibn Ezra is consistently rationalist in his attempt to understand and explain Scripture in light of the science in which he believed.

[V.3.b] BIBLE CRITICISM

Ibn Ezra's approach differs from traditional Bible exegesis, and resembles modern academic or scientific research, in asking critical questions. Bible criticism is an approach to the text which does not necessarily accept traditional religious assumptions regarding the text itself or its presumed authorship or redaction; on the other hand, it admits historical influences of foreign cultures on the evolution of the Bible, and applies to the Bible literary analysis and the findings of archeology. "Lower criticism" refers to a critical approach to the actual words of the text, in an attempt to reconstruct, if necessary by emendation, the original version. "Higher criticism" refers to questions of the origin and authorship of the text: who composed it, when, were, and in which historical and cultural setting? For example, is the Book of Isaiah the work of one prophet (as traditionally affirmed) or two or more? A critical reading of the book suggests that whoever composed the last third of the book (from Ch. 40 on) could not have been the prophet Isaiah ben Amoz who lived in the eighth century B.C.E., but was someone else, who lived in the period of Babylonian exile following the destruction of the first Temple in the sixth century B.C.E. Some scholarly opinion also suggests that there was a third author of some of the later prophecies, by a person who lived in Israel after the return to Zion after 538 B.C.E.

The question of the authorship of the Pentateuch (the five books of the Torah) is more complex and problematical. In the traditional religious view, Moses authored all of the Torah, from the beginning of Genesis until the end of Deuteronomy, including descriptions of what happened before his time, and including a prophetic description (in the last chapter of Deuteronomy) of his death. The critical method, on the other hand, follows what is known as the "documentary hypothesis," that the Pentateuch is a collection of documents, written in different places and at different times, which were redacted hundreds of years later into their current form.[8]

---

8   According to the documentary hypothesis, these documents are characterized by different
     linguistic and stylistic features, and differ in their content and emphases. Among the

The questions raised by Bible criticism, in turn, raise other questions. If, for example, we assume along with the "documentary hypothesis" that the Torah was actually composed from different documents by different authors, who edited these diverse documents into their final form, and when and where did this final redaction take place, and by whose authority?[9] On a religious level, the question is asked as to the implications of Bible criticism — especially higher criticism — for traditional belief in the divine revelation of the Torah, known as *Torah min ha-shamayim* ("the Torah from heaven") and *Torah mi-sinai* ("the Torah from Sinai"). Is the divine authority of the Torah necessarily tantamount to and dependent upon the question of its authorship? Is a critical approach to these questions incompatible with a personal religious commitment to the text?

As Uriel Simon has suggested, some other medieval Jewish commentators engaged in questions of lower criticism of the text, but Abraham ibn Ezra, whose attitude towards the integrity of the traditional text was conservative and who avoided "lower criticism," asked questions, and made pointed allusions to problems, which have led many to conclude that he directly or indirectly dealt with issues of "higher criticism."[10] Since, however, he nowhere states explicitly any such critical conclusion, there is no way to prove conclusively that he, in fact, maintained such critical views, and various later commentators on his work, and some modern scholars, regard Ibn Ezra as having alluded to those opinions because he regarded them as false and wished to refute them. Others however, regard Ibn Ezra as raising these points within the limits imposed by discretion, in the hope that "the intelligent" (to whom he refers) would understand what he was hinting at by calling it *sod* ("secret" meaning), as suggested by Spinoza.

---

differences are the names by which God is called: "J" refers to passages in which the Tetragrammaton (the four-lettered name Y-H-V-H or Y-H-W-H) is featured, and "E" refers to passages referring to the generic name "Elohim" (God). "P" refers to passages dealing in detail with the priestly cult, the sacrifices and the construction of the portable tabernacle (*mishkan*) including the latter chapters of Exodus and much of Leviticus, and "D" refers to Deuteronomy and various passages in Numbers and Joshua.

9   The redaction is frequently attributed to Ezra or at least to his time.

10   Cf. Uriel Simon, "Tanakh: Parshanut" in *Encyclopaedia Biblica* (Jerusalem: Mosad Bialik, 1982) 8:677–680; "Ibn Ezra between Medievalism and Modernism: The Case of Isaiah XL-LXVI" in *Vetus Testamentum* 36, pp. 257–271; "Ibn Ezra ve-Radaq — Shetei Gishot Li-She'elat Mehemanut Nusaḥ Ha-Miqra" in *Bar Ilan Annual* 6 (1968), pp. 191–237; and Raphael Jospe, "Biblical Exegesis as a Philosophical Literary Genre: Abraham ibn Ezra and Moses Mendelssohn" in *Jewish Philosophy: Foundations and Extensions*, vol. 1, *General Questions and Considerations* (Lanham: University Press of America, 2008), pp. 115–153, originally published in *Jewish Philosophy and the Academy*, ed. Emil Fackenheim and Raphael Jospe (Madison and Teaneck: Fairleigh Dickinson University Press and Associated University Presses, 1996), pp. 48–92.

**[V.3.c]   IBN EZRA'S CRITICAL APPROACH
ACCORDING TO SPINOZA**

In 1670, Baruch (Benedict de) Spinoza wrote in his *Theologico-Political Treatise*, Ch. 8:

> Aben Ezra, a man of enlightened intelligence and no small learning...[who] was the first, so far as I know, to treat of this opinion, dared not express his meaning openly, but confined himself to dark hints which I shall not scruple to elucidate, thus throwing full light on the subject...In these few words he hints, and also shows, that it was not Moses who wrote the Pentateuch, but someone who lived long after him, and further, that the book which Moses wrote was something different from any now extant.[11]

Spinoza then lists the six verses mentioned by Ibn Ezra which could not possibly have been written by Moses. However, Spinoza concludes that Ibn Ezra could not openly state his opinion, and, therefore, could only allude to it by vague hints. Spinoza thus anticipated by centuries the approach of Leo Strauss, whose essay "Persecution and the Art of Writing"[12] suggests that the medieval philosophers could not explicitly and openly express their true, radical views in a society which did not recognize the right of dissent and free speech. Therefore, when their views contradicted the conventional and traditional view, such thinkers had to hide their true intention by writing esoterically, and the modern reader must learn to read between the lines, to discern not only what is said, but also what is not said.

[V.3.c.i]   *Modern Scholars on ibn Ezra and Bible Criticism*

Is Spinoza's reading of Ibn Ezra correct? Did Ibn Ezra question the Mosaic authorship of the Torah, but limit his radical views to "hints" to the intelligent reader? Many modern scholars of Ibn Ezra agree with Spinoza's reading. We have already referred to Uriel Simon. A similar view is that of Nahum Sarna, who wrote:

> Thoroughly intriguing are Ibn Ezra's own views. In the first place, one wonders why he so frequently cited the "heresies" of others when the effect was to give wide circulation to the very ideas he so vehemently denounced...The virulence of his attacks creates the impression that he protests too much...Not only does he frequently not refute the objectionable opinions, but even when he buttresses invective by reasoned argument the latter is usually far less satisfying than the

---

11   Translation from the Latin by R.H.M. Elwes (1883), reprinted in *The Chief Works of Benedict de Spinoza* (New York: Dover Publications, 1951), vol. 1, pp. 120–121.

12   Leo Strauss, *Persecution and the Art of Writing* (Glencoe: The Free Press, 1952). The title essay was first published in 1941.

original "heresy." Finally, Ibn Ezra himself listed six pentateuchal passages which seem to be post-Mosaic interpolations.[13]

However, as already mentioned, not all modern scholars conclude with Spinoza that Ibn Ezra pioneered a critical approach to Scripture in general and the Torah in particular. Michael Friedlaender, for example, in his major study, *Essays on the Writings of Abraham ibn Ezra*, rejects this view: "Ibn Ezra firmly believed that the Pentateuch, with the exception of the last few verses, was the same as written by Moses, without any alteration or addition."[14] More recently, Amos Funkenstein has also argued against construing Ibn Ezra as a Bible critic who believed that the Torah contains later interpolations.

> It is true that Ibn Ezra preserved many critical arguments...In general, we find that his position is totally conservative, that he does not wish to impugn the unity of the Torah or the authorship of Moses' Torah...It is only for the sake of argument that he preserved some of the arguments which bible criticism later employed.[15]

Our reading of Ibn Ezra agrees with that of Simon and Sarna, but for us the essential point is that his "higher criticism" is a logical development of his rationalist philosophy and reading of Scripture.

[V.3.c.ii] *Traditionalist Interpretations*

Ibn Ezra's attitude toward the Mosaic authorship of the entire Pentateuch concerned many of the commentators on his commentary. In the nineteenth century several important commentators vigorously affirmed Ibn Ezra's alleged traditionalism. Their attempts to defend him from what they regarded as heretical beliefs indicate two points of significance to us: that in their eyes Ibn Ezra was an important and authoritative religious thinker, and that they were aware of the claims that he held radical ideas.

Solomon Zalman Netter, author of the super-commentary on Ibn Ezra printed in many standard editions of the *Miqra'ot Gedolot* wrote in his commentary to Deuteronomy 1:2:

> Some say that the Sage's opinion is that Joshua wrote [the last twelve verses of the Torah describing the death of Moses]...However, in fact, Rabbi Abraham was not of this opinion, Rather, these [verses] were told to Moses prophetically and he wrote them.

---

13   Nahum Sarna, "Hebrew Bible Studies in Medieval Spain," in *The Sephardi Heritage* (London: Valentine, Mitchel, n.d.), pp. 349–350.
14   Michael Friedlaender, *Essays on the Writings of Abraham ibn Ezra* (London, 1877), p. 67.
15   Amos Funkenstein, *Signonot Be-Farshanut Ha-Miqra Bi-Yemei Ha-Beinayim* (Tel Aviv: Ministry of Defense, 1990), p. 33.

Netter's interpretation of Ibn Ezra is strange because it contradicts Ibn Ezra's explicit statement on Deuteronomy 34:1 that "in my opinion Joshua wrote from this verse to the end [of the Torah], for after Moses went up, he did not write anything." It is also peculiar that Netter and so many other medieval and traditionalist modern commentators sought to read Ibn Ezra as affirming the Mosaic authorship of the final verses describing his own death, when the Talmud itself (Bava Batra 15a) records in a totally non-controversial manner a dispute on the question, without any implication that the view attributing these verses to Joshua constitutes a problem. Netter's interpretation of Ibn Ezra is also problematical because it contradicts his own comment on Deuteronomy 34:1 that Moses did not write the passage.

Another important nineteenth century writer, Judah Leib Krinsky, author of the super-commentary *Meḥoqeqei Yehudah* also misreads Ibn Ezra here, and said: "Some who pretend to be wise (*mitḥakmim*) and who are free-thinkers (*poqerim*)... tried to make the Sage fall into the same pits into which they fell." Krinsky then refers to Shadal's defense of Ibn Ezra as a traditionalist.

Shadal (Samuel David Luzzatto, Italy, 1800–1865) did, in fact, argue for a traditionalist reading of Ibn Ezra, and many of his arguments were used later by Michael Friedlaender. Shadal, however, argues interestingly and more narrowly, that there is no basis for interpreting Ibn Ezra as denying the Mosaic authorship of the Torah as a whole. Ibn Ezra regarded only these last verses as later additions. If the Torah as a whole did not derive from the time of Moses, then these verses would not be anachronistic, in which case there would be no problem.[16] Shadal further suggests that Spinoza's erroneous reading of Ibn Ezra may have been based on the fourteenth-century super-commentary on Ibn Ezra by Samuel ben Sa'adiah ibn Motot.

Motot, who was active in Spain c. 1370, interpreted Ibn Ezra here as a traditionalist: "His opinion was that all this was said to Moses prophetically." The same view was held by his contemporary Samuel ibn Seneh Ẓarẓa in his super-commentary *Meqor Ḥayyim*, who suggested that all the verses which are problematical because of their alleged anachronism were written prophetically by Moses. In short, their defense of Ibn Ezra proves that Jewish exegetes and philosophers were aware of and troubled by the problem several centuries before Spinoza addressed it openly and publicly.

[V.3.c.iii] *Genesis 12:6 "The Canaanite was then in the Land"*

One of the main controversies concerns Ibn Ezra's interpretation of the word "then" (*az*) in Genesis 12:6, "the Canaanite was then in the land." Ibn Ezra wrote: "It is possible that Canaan seized the land of Canaan from someone

---

[16]   Shadal, *Commentary on the Pentateuch*, Deuteronomy 1:2, ed. Pinhas Schlesinger (Tel Aviv: Dvir,1965), pp. 507–509.

else. If it does not mean that, it has a secret meaning (*sod*), and the intelligent should keep silent."

The question, as correctly understood by Motot and Ẓarẓa, is whether in Ibn Ezra's understanding the term "then" means then but not before, or then but not later? Does the term refer back to an earlier time (i.e., at that time, namely the time of Abraham, the land was controlled by the Canaanites, but it had not previously been controlled by the Canaanites, who conquered it from others)? If that is the meaning of "then," the verse is innocuous but gives us essentially irrelevant information, because the history of the land before Abraham's immigration bears no importance to the story of Abraham and his descendants. Conversely, does the term "then" refer forward, to a later time (i.e., this passage was written in a later time, when the Canaanites no longer controlled the land, implying that it must have been written long after the time of Moses, in whose day the Canaanites did occupy the land)?

Ẓarẓa states the problem clearly and correctly:

"It has a secret meaning." According to some, the word "then" has two meanings. Then and not before, or then and not later. If we say that the word "then" means that [Canaan] was not there earlier, it has no secret meaning. If this is not the case, it has a secret meaning, and the secret is that the term "then" can also refer to "then and not now." If you understand this, you should keep silent.

In other words, Ẓarẓa candidly admits that Ibn Ezra is referring here to a possibility which is quite problematical: it is a secret, which if understood, should not be discussed (or at least not openly).

Let us look at it from the opposite perspective: if what Ibn Ezra is suggesting (and Ẓarẓa understood), at least as a logical possibility, is not at variance with the traditional belief in the unity and Mosaic authorship of the entire Torah, why should he call it a secret and advise the intelligent to keep silent about it? Conversely, if Ibn Ezra was a traditionalist who rejected these radical possibilities, why mention them at all, or why, if it is necessary to mention them, did he not see fit to explain why they are methodologically unacceptable and religiously dangerous?

There are other anachronistic passages that Ibn Ezra discusses that Spinoza did not mention. In all these cases, however, in our reading of Ibn Ezra we must be careful not to infer too little or too much. He seems not to have objected to the radical ideological implications of a critical attitude, but his arguments are essentially methodological, not ideological. However, just as he seems not to have had a problem with at least a degree of Bible criticism (keeping in mind Shadal's point that these passages are only anachronistic if, in general, the Torah is affirmed as having been written in the time of Moses), he also cannot have rejected all prophecies of the future as later interpolations. To do so would have been to deny the phenomenon of prophecy itself.

The issue for Ibn Ezra, therefore, cannot have been whether a prophet could, in principle, predict the future. What is questioned, rather, is the intelligibility and meaningfulness of such a prophecy to the prophet himself, and certainly to his audience. What Ibn Ezra rejects as impossible and incompatible with the very rationality of revelation is any revelation that is inherently unintelligible. If revelation is to be meaningful, it must be comprehensible to its recipients, even if it conveys new information about the as yet unknown future.

Ibn Ezra's openness to—if not explicit acceptance of—critical possibilities regarding the authorship and redaction of the Torah is thus a direct function of his rationalist understanding of revelation.[17]

[V.4]   THE BIBLE AND REASON

[V.4.a]   WHEN IS SCRIPTURE TO BE READ LITERALLY, AND WHEN NON-LITERALLY?

According to Philo's "double faith theory" the truth as revealed in Scripture and the truth as known in philosophy must ultimately be the same truth. The allegorical method employed by Philo was intended to uncover the esoteric rational truth present in the Scripture itself. This, however, raises a fundamental methodological question with which Ibn Ezra had to deal: when is Scripture to be read literally, and when non-literally? Philo, it will be recalled, explicitly stipulated that the allegorical meaning must supplement, but not supplant, the *peshat*; that the spiritual reading enhances, but does not replace, the literal observance of the *mizvot*.[18]

Ibn Ezra's commitment to the rationality of revelation led him, as we have seen, to be open to questions of "higher criticism," when it would be meaningless to attribute the verse to Moses, in whose day it would have been unintelligible. The rationality of revelation is also the ground for taking passages non-literally, when a literal reading contradicts scientific truth.

---

17   The eighth of Rambam's "Thirteen Principles" (which we shall discuss in Ch. 8) is often cited against higher criticism, because of its reference to the belief "that the whole of this Torah found in our hands today is the Torah that was handed down by Moses and that it is all of divine origin." However, higher criticism, i.e., the idea that the Torah is composed of post-Mosaic documents edited much later, is not the issue concerning Rambam here. What he rejects is the claim that the Torah has "a kernel and a shell" (i.e., important and unimportant parts) and that any of it was composed by Moses, but on his own authority and initiative, and not by divine instruction. For Rambam, the rabbinic traditions, i.e., the oral Torah, are equally divinely revealed ("Torah from heaven"). Rambam thus does not address Ibn Ezra's question of possible post-Mosaic authorship, but insists that all the Torah—the earlier written Torah and the later rabbinic oral Torah alike—is of divine authority.

18   See the discussion in Ch. 1 (I.2.d).

In general, Ibn Ezra affirms the rabbinic principle that "the Bible never leaves its literal meaning" (*ein miqra yoẓé mi-yedei peshuto*).[19] Indeed, his exegetical approach emphasizes scientific study of the *peshat*, and avoidance of rabbinic homiletical *derash*.[20] Nevertheless, like Sa'adiah Ga'on before him (whom he quotes in various places in his commentaries), Ibn Ezra formulated criteria for non-literal interpretation. Sa'adiah, it will be recalled,[21] had stated that in general we are to retain the *peshat*, but we are to interpret the Bible metaphorically when the verse contradicts what we know "empirically, or rationally, or another Scriptural verse, or tradition."[22] By "tradition," of course, he means the tradition of the talmudic rabbis. Ibn Ezra shared Sa'adiah's relatively conservative approach, and criticized Christian exegetes for widescale and unjustified allegorical interpretation. "If reason does not tolerate [the literal meaning], or [the literal meaning] destroys what is empirically clear, then one should seek esoteric meaning (*sod*), for reason is the foundation."[23] In other words, it is only when the *peshat* contradicts what we know rationally or empirically, that we should engage in non-literal interpretation. The key phrase, however, is "for reason is the foundation" (*ki shiqul ha-da'at hu ha-yesod*). As we shall see, for Ibn Ezra it is reason that guides us to a correct, scientific understanding of Scripture, and helps us to avoid not only the excessive Christian allegorization, but also absurd Karaite literalism, and unwarranted rabbinic *derash*, all at the expense of the true *peshat*. Paradoxically, Ibn Ezra therefore uses the same phrase, "reason cannot tolerate this" (*ein ha-da'at sovelet*) against both Karaite literalism and rabbinic *derash* when they offend reason.

For Ibn Ezra, as for Sa'adiah and Philo before him, a conservative attitude towards the *peshat* followed logically from the belief that Scripture is the record of divine revelation, and from the fact that Jewish religious practice rests on the observance of the biblical precepts and would be completely undermined by freely taking the commandments allegorically, as was frequently the

---

19   Babylonian Talmud, Shabbat 63a, Yevamot 24a.

20   Rashi (Rabbi Solomon ben Isaac, 1040–1105), the pre-eminent Bible and Talmud commentator of rabbinic Judaism, states: "I only came to resolve the *peshat*" (commentary on Genesis 33:20; cf. on Genesis 3:8). In the Introduction to his *Safah Berurah*, Ibn Ezra states that the talmudic rabbis knew the *peshat*, and that their *derash* supplemented the *peshat* but did not supplant it. He complains, however, that in recent generations, others, like Rashi, "made every *derash* the important point and root. He thinks that he [interprets] according to the *peshat*, but his books only contain no *peshat* except for 1/1000." Cf. the discussion of this in Abraham ibn Ezra, *Yesod Mora Ve-Sod Torah*, annotated critical edition (second edition) by Joseph Cohen and Uriel Simon (Ramat Gan: Bar Ilan University Press, 2007), p. 40.

21   See the discussion in Ch. 2 (II.3.j).

22   Sa'adiah, *Book of Beliefs and Opinions* 5:8.

23   Abraham ibn Ezra, Introduction to the Torah, "the third way."

case in Christian exegesis. It is reason, then, that is fundamental to revelation and must provide accurate criteria for when non-literal interpretation is warranted.

These considerations underlie Ibn Ezra's reaffirmation of *peshat* in his interpretation of Exodus 13:9, "Let it be a sign for you on your hand and a reminder between your eyes." Rashi, reflecting standard rabbinic reading of the passage, understands it to refer to the *tefillin* (phylacteries), and his grandson Rashbam, while not rejecting the traditional view, suggests that the literal meaning of the verse is simply that it serve as a reminder. Ibn Ezra rejects the non-literal association of the verse with the *tefillin*. Scripture may only be taken figuratively when, as in the book of Proverbs (*Mishlei*, from the word *mashal*, which in this context means a figurative or metaphorical meaning), the text itself explicitly states its figurative character (*mashal*), or when the literal sense contradicts reason:

> But there is no passage in the Torah which is, God forbid, meant figuratively; rather, it is mean literally (*ke-mashma'o*). Therefore, we never take it out of its literal context (*mi-yedei peshuto*). For its literal meaning does not contradict reason (*shiqul ha-da'at*), such as "Circumcise the foreskins of your heart" does, which we must correct in accordance with reason (*le-taqqeno le-fi ha-da'at*).[24]

Reason must guide us not only in reading Scripture—the written Torah—but also in reading rabbinic midrash. When the literal meaning of midrash—the oral Torah—contradicts reason, it also must be taken non-literally. This rule in interpreting Scripture, "the body," applies all the more to rabbinic midrash, "the clothing" covering the body.[25] These principles—a conservative approach to the *peshat*, with rationality as the criterion for determining when to take Scripture non-literally—consistently underlie Ibn Ezra's survey of different exegetical methodologies in his Introduction to the Torah.

[V.4.b]   INTRODUCTION TO THE TORAH

In his survey, Ibn Ezra compares the truth to the center of a circle, and then places each of the five exegetical methodologies somewhere in, on, or outside the circle.

[V.4.b.i]   *Ignorance of science: The Babylonian academies*

The first exegetical approach is that of the Babylonian academies, i.e., the Jews living in the Islamic east. Their approach is so faulty that it resembles the circumference of the circle, which never reaches the truth at the center. Their

---

24   Ibn Ezra, Long (i.e., standard) commentary to Exodus 13:9.
25   Ibn Ezra, Introduction to Lamentations.

method is faulty because they did not master "the external sciences," and are, therefore, unable to provide proofs (*re'ayot*) for their conclusions.

[V.4.b.ii] *Lack of authentic tradition: The Karaites*

The second deficient exegetical approach is that of the Karaites, who think that they are at the circle's center, but don't even know its location. Their exegesis is faulty because of its inherent subjective individualism (since they lack an authoritative tradition to guide them), even regarding the commandments. Moreover, they are ignorant of proper Hebrew and grammar. Without having recourse to authentic (i.e., rabbinic) tradition (*qabbalah u-masoret*), they have no way to understand many passages in Scripture, such as biblical laws concerning the calendar, upon which much of Jewish observance depends, but which are not explicated in the Bible.

[V.4.b.iii] *Indiscriminate allegorization: The Christians*

The third approach, which is characterized by darkness and is completely outside the circle, is that of Christian allegorists, who indiscriminately find secret meaning (*sodot*) everywhere in Scripture. One should, however, only seek such secret (i.e., esoteric) meaning when the literal meaning contradicts reason or empirical experience. These allegorists are only correct in that they subject everything, whether pertaining to a major or minor commandment, to the judgment of reason.

> For reason has been implanted in the [human] heart by divine wisdom. If reason cannot tolerate something, or if it destroys what is clearly [known] empirically (*ba-hargashot*), then one should seek its secret meaning, because the judgment of reason is the foundation (*ki shiqul ha-da'at hu ha-yesod*), and the Torah was not given to those who lack reason. The angel [intermediating] between man and his God is his intellect (*sekhel*). [However], we should interpret whatever reason does not deny literally (*ki-feshuto u-mishpato*). We should understand its measure (*matkonet*), and believe that this is its truth, and we should not grope along the wall like the blind. [Rather], we should take things in accordance with our needs. Why should we turn clear things (*nir'im*) into hidden (*nistarim*)?[26]

[V.4.b.iv] *Excessive derash: The academies of Rome*

The fourth approach is "close to the center" of the circle; it is the approach of the Jewish scholars living in the Christian west, in Greece and Rome (i.e., the eastern Byzantine and western Roman Christian empires). Their approach is faulty because they rely excessively on rabbinic homiletics (*derash*), and not on reason or scientific grammar. At least these scholars rely on the writings of

---

[26]   Ibn Ezra, Introduction to the Torah, in *Torat Ḥayyim*, p. 8.

the ancient rabbis. On the other hand, why bother repeating what the ancients have already said? Moreover, these scholars do not recognize that one rabbinic homily can often contradict another, and that rabbinic statements—no less than Scripture—may also have an implicit esoteric meaning and should be taken allegorically. By taking these statements literally, one ends up contradicting reason. In short, there is no end to rabbinic homiletical exegesis, and one should rather abide by the sound rabbinic principle, "the Bible never leaves its literal meaning" (*ein miqra yoẓé mi-yedei peshuto*).

[V.4.b.v] *The true, scientific approach: Abraham ibn Ezra*

The fifth and true approach followed by Ibn Ezra avoids such faulty methodology, because it is based on scientific philology. It seeks, first of all, to understand the proper grammar of the text. There may be occasional need to resort to rabbinic *derash*, but only to add to what the rabbis said, not merely to repeat it. In any event, "the literal meaning (*peshat*) is never replaced by the homiletical meaning (*derash*), for the Torah has seventy faces."[27]

To reiterate: for Ibn Ezra, reason is fundamental to the very notion of revelation, and therefore provides the primary basis for a proper exegetical methodology. All three Jewish approaches mentioned by Ibn Ezra (the first, second and fourth methods) ultimately fail for lack of solid, scientific methodology, although there are additional faults in their method (the Karaites lack authentic tradition, and the scholars of Greek and Rome rely excessively on rabbinic tradition). They are all guilty of ignorance of science in general, and specifically of philology, linguistics and grammar. The Babylonians don't know how to construct scientific proofs, the Karaites have no basis for avoiding subjectivity, the Christians don't know when to take the *peshat* literally, and the Greek and Roman scholars don't know when to take rabbinic *derash* figuratively. In all these cases, reason is the key to a correct understanding of Scripture and the basis of any scientific exegetical method.

The rationality of Scripture thus consistently recurs as a theme in Ibn Ezra's commentaries. Two passages will exemplify this. In the first case, rationality provides the basis for rejecting excessive and literalist reliance on rabbinic *derash* on the Decalogue, and in the second case, for rejecting the Karaites' literalist interpretation—untempered by reason or by rabbinic tradition—of the law of retaliation.

---

27   "The Torah has seventy faces" or "facets." Cf. (*inter alia*) Midrash Numbers Rabba 13:15.

[V.4.c] SCIENTIFIC-RATIONALIST EXEGESIS

[V.4.c.i] *Ibn Ezra on the Decalogue (Exodus 20:1)*

In his long (i.e., standard) commentary to Exodus 20:1, Ibn Ezra expounds at great length on the many differences between the two versions of the Decalogue in Exodus 20 (what he regarded as the actual revelation at Sinai) and in Deuteronomy 5 (which, in his view, was Moses' paraphrase forty years later). Many of these differences are minor and do not affect the meaning. Some, however, especially the two versions of the commandment to observe the Sabbath, differ sharply. For example, in the first version the verb is *zakhor* (remember, commemorate), and the rationale of the Sabbath is to commemorate the creation of the world, whereas in the second version the verb is *shamor* (guard, observe), and the rationale is to commemorate the exodus from Egyptian bondage. The Talmud records a rabbinic tradition that both versions were revealed together and simultaneously (*zakhor ve-shamor be-dibbur eḥad ne'emru*).[28] Ibn Ezra rejects this *derash* as impossible: "Reason cannot tolerate any of these things" (*ein ha-da'at sovelet*). However, since in Ibn Ezra's view the oral Torah of the rabbis is also divinely revealed and authoritative, he could not explicitly state that the rabbis were wrong. Instead, he argues that in this case, as in others, their statements are true on a different level, and cannot be taken literally, at face value. Once again, reason is the criterion for determining the truth.

> In the first [version] it is written, "God spoke all of these words, saying" (Exodus 20:1), and in the second [version], "These are the Lords which the Lord spoke to all of your assembly" (Deuteronomy 5:18). When we searched in the words of the Sages what they had to say about this, we found that they held that "'remember' (Exodus 20:8) and 'observe' (Deuteronomy 5:12) were said in one statement." This statement is the most difficult of all the problems we have, as I shall explain. God forbid that I should say that [the Sages] did not speak corectly, for our knowledge is insignificant compared to theirs. It is only that people in our generation think that what they said is meant literally (*ke-mashma'am*). This is not the case, as I shall explain at the end, after I have mentioned the problems. Finally, I shall explain the correct way (*ha-derekh ha-yesharah*)[29] in order to resolve all the problems and questions in this portion. It is impossible that "remember" and "observe" could have been said simultaneously, except by a miracle. But [in that case] we would still acknowledge that we should ask, why doesn't it say [both] "remember and observe" in both the first and the second [versions]? What shall we do with such verses as "remember" and

---

28   Babylonian Talmud, Rosh Ha-Shanah 27a *et al*, cited by Rashi and Ramban on Exodus 20:8.

29   *Ha-derekh ha-yesharah*, "the correct way" means, for Ibn Ezra, the literal meaning, understood by proper scientific methodology, and meeting the test of rationality. Cf. Uriel Simon, "Bible Exegesis" in *Encyclopaedia Biblica* 8:672.

"observe" if they were said simultaneously, and why didn't the Sages mention this? What is even more astonishing than two words, which mean identically the same thing, having been said simultaneously, is that many [different] verses, which do not mean the same thing, could have been said simultaneously in a miraculous manner... **Reason cannot tolerate (*ein ha-da'at sovelet*) any of these things.** The most difficult of what I mentioned is that all the wonders performed by Moses bear some resemblance to other things; and the intelligent will understand.[30] But this would be the most wondrous of all, that God would have spoken "remember" and "observe" simultaneously, [in which case] this should have been explicitly written down in the Torah, more than all of the [miraculous] signs and proofs which were written down. If we should say that God's speech is not like human speech, then how could the Israelites have understood God's speech? For if a person would hear "remember" and "observe" simultaneously, he would not understand either one. One could not understand what the speaker spoke, even one word like "remember" [*zakhor*], if one does not hear the [letter] *zayin* before the *kaf* and the *resh*. Now we know that the perception of the eye is more noble than the perception of the ear, for we know with absolute proofs that the moment we see the lightning is the same moment as that of the thunder, but the eye sees from a distance, whereas the air conveys the sound [of the thunder] to the ear, and [the sound] proceeds slowly and only reaches the ear after a moment has passed... So the sound of the letter *zayin* [of the word *zakhor*] enters the ear before the *kaf* and the *vav* and the *resh*. Now if we say that this was a wonder, that "observe" and "remember" were said simultaneously, how could the ear hear [them]? And if we say that it is a wonder that the ear heard two words simultaneously, when it is not habituated to hearing to letters [simultaneously], why did the Sages not mention this?...And what should we [then] do with the remaining problems of the differences between the verses [in the first and second versions], which do not mean the same thing?...Now I shall explain for you the aforementioned questions. Know that God said all the Decalogue as written in this portion; as it says, "God spoke all of these words, saying," beginning with "I am" (Exodus 20:2), and ending with "whatever belongs to your fellow" (Exodus 20:13). Moses, when he mentioned the Decalogue in the second [version], said "These are the words which the Lord spoke to all your assembly" (Deuteronomy 5:18), one right after the other.

Ibn Ezra's point is clear. Consistent with his criticism of the unscientific approach of the Jewish scholars of Greece and Rome (the fourth approach, in the Introduction to the Torah), Ibn Ezra rejects on rational grounds a literal reading of the rabbinic *derash* that both versions of the Decalogue were revealed simultaneously. The problem is not whether God could have created two different but simultaneous sounds, and more important, two simultaneous meanings. The problem is whether the human ear is capable of simultaneously

---

30   Asher Weiser suggests here that Ibn Ezra means that the intelligent will understand how to distinguish the miraculous from the natural.

hearing and intelligibly perceiving two different sounds, and whether the human mind is capable of simultaneously and intelligibly processing and understanding two different ideas. As we shall see later, in our discussion of Ibn Ezra's astrological theory, what is below is no less important in determining events than what is above. That same principle applies to revelation: the limits of intelligibility are imposed not by God above, but below, by the human recipient of the revelation, just as it would be meaningless to broadcast on radio frequencies for which there are no receivers. As a rational process, revelation must be subject to rational limitations, and those limitations reflect the human recipient, and not the divine giver, of the message.[31] Anything else would be absurd, and "reason cannot tolerate any of these things."

[V.4.c.ii] *Ibn Ezra on the Law of Retaliation (Exodus 21:24)*

The same principle, "reason cannot tolerate any of these things," that Ibn Ezra applied to rabbinic *derash* on the Decalogue, is also applied to Karaite literalist reading of the law of retaliation, "an eye for an eye," in Exodus 21:24. The rabbanite critique of Karaism, reflected in Ibn Ezra's second exegetical way in his Introduction to the Torah, centered on the argument that the Torah frequently gives no explicit or specific instructions regarding its precepts, and without recourse the reliable tradition one has no assurance that one's individual and subjective interpretation is correct. In the case of the law of retaliation, the challenge for the rabbanite position was to demonstrate that the principle of compensation is not merely a later rabbinic *derash* superimposed upon the original *peshat*, the apparent meaning of which is physical punishment, but that the principle of compensation was the original *peshat*, properly understood, in accordance with the dictates of reason.

The rabbanite interpretation was grounded both on reason and on a comparison of "an eye for an eye" with other similar passages, in which "X for X" was explicitly linked to financial compensation, as in Leviticus 24:18 ("Whoever takes the life of a beast shall pay for it, life for life"). In Judges 15:11, the expression "as they have done to me, so have I done to them" would appear to mean literal retaliation, but in fact clearly refers not to an identical action (kidnapping and raping women) but giving the offender his just deserts (killing him).

In his discussion of "an eye for an eye," Ibn Ezra repeats the standard rabbinic arguments for compensation (such as are also cited by Rashi and

---

31   As we have already seen, it is precisely this consideration — the intelligibility of revelation to the recipients — that guided Ibn Ezra on the problems of anachronistic passages in Scripture. The issue is not prophetic prediction of information about the future *per se*, but whether the information conveyed would be intelligible to the prophet and his audience. The limitations are, once again, imposed from below, by the capacity of understanding of the human recipient of the revelation.

Ramban), but adds to them the critical point that this position is the only possible one in rational terms, and that the Karaite position is absurd: "Reason cannot tolerate any of these things." Therefore, unless one wishes to impute irrationality to the revealed text, one must conclude that compensation is the correct meaning of the *peshat* itself, and not a later *derash*. Ibn Ezra's long (i.e., standard) commentary to Exodus 21:24 cites a dispute between Sa'adiah Ga'on and a Karaite, Ben Zuta, on this point:

> Rabbi Sa'adiah said: We cannot interpret this verse literally (*ke-mashma'o*). For if a person struck the eye of his fellow, and a third of his vision is lost, how can he be struck with the same injury, without any greater or lesser [injury]? Perhaps he will become completely blind, or the burn or the wound or the bruise would be more severe. If they were in a dangerous location, perhaps he will die. **Reason cannot tolerate (*ein ha-da'at sovelet*) any of these things.** Ben Zuta said to him: But is it not written elsewhere, "Whenever someone makes a blemish in a person, so should be done to him" (Leviticus 24:20)? Sa'adiah replied:... This means, so should he be given a punishment. But Ben Zuta replied: "As he did, so should be done to him" (Leviticus 24:19). The Ga'on replied: Samson said, "As they did to me, so have I done to them" (Judges 15:11), but Samson did not take the [Philistines'] wives and give them to other men; he only gave them what they deserved. Ben Zuta replied: But if the one who struck the other is poor, what should his punishment be [i.e., how can he pay compensation]? The Ga'on replied: If a blind person blinds a person who sees, what should be done to him? The poor man may perhaps become rich and [then] pay, but the blind man will never be able to pay [with his sight]. The general principles [*kelal*] is: we cannot properly interpret the commandments of the Torah if we do not rely on the words of the rabbis... For as we have received the Torah from our ancestors, so have we received the oral Torah, and there is no difference between them.

In his commentary to the other passage in question (Leviticus 24:19), Ibn Ezra summarizes these arguments, and states: "The Ga'on brought proofs based on reason" (*shiqul ha-da'at*). We should also note that Ibn Ezra's contemporary and friend, Judah Ha-Levi (whose views he cites, and sometimes argues with, in his commentaries) similarly cited the passage in Leviticus to prove that "an eye for an eye" in Exodus must mean compensation, not physical retaliation, and proves the need for tradition (*al-taqlid*; *qabbalah*), and that "reason contradicts" reading the text literally, as the Karaites do.[32] Philosophic exegetes like Sa'adiah Ga'on, Abraham Ibn Ezra, and (in his own way) Judah Ha-Levi, thus differ from non-philosophic exegetes in their insistence that it is the very rationality of Scripture that precludes taking the text literally here: "Reason cannot tolerate any of these things." For rationalist philosophers like Sa'adiah and Ibn Ezra, revelation is itself fundamentally a rational process. For Ha-Levi (as we shall

---

32   Judah Ha-Levi, *Kuzari* 3:46–47.

see in Ch. 6), revelation transcends reason but cannot contradict reason. In either case, reason is so fundamental to the truth of revealed Scripture that any text that, when taken at face value, contradicts reason, cannot in fact truly mean what it appears to say, and must then be taken figuratively. It is reason, then, that ensures the integrity of proper exegetical method, safeguarding against the errors of rabbanite and Karaite Jews, as well as of Christians, all of whom either took the text too literally or not literally enough.

[V.4.d] RATIONAL COMMANDMENTS AND THE COMMANDMENTS' RATIONALE

Ibn Ezra's belief in the rationality of revelation led him to interpret in rational terms *ta'am ha-miẓvot*, the purpose or rationale of the commandments. His approach essentially combines and builds on Sa'adiah Ga'on's distinction between rational (*sikhliyot*) and traditional (*shim'iyot*) commandments, and Baḥya ibn Paquda's categories of duties of the heart and duties of the limbs.

In his discussion of the Decalogue,[33] Ibn Ezra comments that there are "commandments implanted by God in the heart of all rational people" (i.e., rational commandments). Nine of the "ten commandments"[34] are rational — in other words, all of the Decalogue except for the commandment regarding the Sabbath. There are also "hidden commandments" (*miẓvot ne'elamot*), which are the equivalent of Sa'adiah's "traditional" commandments, namely commandments the rationale of which is not obvious, but which, nevertheless, do not contradict reason (*shiqul ha-da'at*) in any way. The Torah's commandments also fall into three categories, depending on the manner in which they are performed: commandments of the heart, commandments of the tongue (or mouth), and commandments of the limbs (i.e., action). Each of these three categories is further subdivided into positive commandments (what we are obliged to do) and negative commandments (what we are forbidden to do). Commandments of the heart are "the most important and noble" of the commandments, because they provide the belief structure underlying all commandments.

This three-fold division of the commandments according to their mode of performance — heart, mouth and limbs — permits Ibn Ezra to resolve a problem regarding the first or prefatory verse of the Decalogue: "I am the Lord your God" (Exodus 20:2). Is this verse one of the ten (and thus one of the

---

[33]   Ibn Ezra, Long (i.e., standard) commentary to Exodus 20:2.

[34]   The Hebrew term found three times in the Torah is *'aseret ha-devarim*; in later Hebrew, it is usually *'aseret ha-dibberot*. Both mean "ten statements" or "ten words" (thus, "Decalogue"), and not "ten commandments." There are different Jewish interpretations and divisions of the text, and in Rambam's count, the "ten statements" actually contain fourteen of the 613 commandments.

613 commandments) or is it a preface or introduction to ten others, and not one of the ten?

[V.4.d.i] *"I am the Lord your God"—One of the 613 Commandments?*

According to Rambam's *Book of the Commandments* (*Sefer Ha-Miẓvot*), which categorizes and lists the 613 commandments according to criteria elucidated in the introduction to the book, the affirmation of God as the cause and agent of everything is the first positive commandment, and Rambam cites "I am the Lord your God" as the source and proof-text of this commandment. In his critical notes (*hasagot*) to the *Book of the Commandments*, Ramban (Naḥmanides) agrees with Rambam, but also cites the opposing opinion that belief in God cannot be included as one of the commandments, because "it is the principle and root from which [the commandments] are derived, and it is not counted as one of them."

The disagreement rests, in part, on the linguistic point that the verse has no imperative verb, and differs in that respect from the rest of the Decalogue: not to have any other gods, not to make images, not to take God's name in vain, to observe the Sabbath, to honor parents, etc. The disagreement also reflects a problem with the content: can belief be commanded? Is belief something over which a person has voluntary control, which it then makes sense to command him to do?

Ibn Ezra takes the position that "I am the Lord your God" is, in fact, a positive commandment, but his reasoning differs from that of Rambam and others, and he equates the Decalogue with the ten Aristotelian categories. Accordingly, "I am the Lord your God" is the first category, substance, and the other nine are its accidents dependent on it. As such, it is the first of the ten (as substance is the first of the ten categories), and not a separate preface. The Decalogue is also comparable to the ten cardinal numbers, in which case "I am the Lord your God" is also the equivalent of the number one, which is the source and foundation of all number. Therefore, "the first statement which God said includes all the commandments of the heart and tongue and action, because anyone who does not believe in God in his heart Is not obligated by any commandment...I have already explained that the first statement is the foundation, on which all the structures of the commandments [are based]."[35] Ibn Ezra's innovative interpretation of "I am the Lord your God" thus reflects an Aristotelian doctrine (the ten categories), Neoplatonic theory (the One as the source of all number), and Baḥya ibn Paquda's *Duties of the Heart* (the commandments of the heart).

Such philosophical considerations, however, could not be understood or appreciated by the masses. Ibn Ezra differentiates, therefore, between the first

---

[35]   Ibn Ezra, Long (i.e. standard) commentary to Exodus 20:1.

part of the verse, "I am the Lord your God," and its continuation, "who brought you out of the land of Egypt, the house of bondage." The first part of the verse is aimed at the intelligentsia, and the second part at the masses. In his commentary on this verse, Ibn Ezra cites a disagreement with Judah Ha-Levi, for whom the verse is a statement of indisputable historical truth that is far more certain than unreliable metaphysical speculation (as we shall see in Ch. 6).

> Judah Ha-Levi asked me why the Torah says, "I am the Lord your God, who brought you out of the land of Egypt," and did not say, "who created the heaven and the earth, and I made you." This was my response to him. Know, that the degrees of people are not equal regarding the belief in their heart, i.e., that they believe in God. Many believe in what they hear, when their masters tell them something. Above them are those who saw something written in the Torah that God gave to Moses. But if a heretic were to claim that there is no God, they would cover their mouths with their hand, and not know how to respond. But one who is motivated to study the sciences…recognizes the action of God in the minerals, plants and animals, and in the human body itself…And his heart will rise afterwards to know the heavenly spheres, which are God's action in the enduring middle world…He will know all these things with indubitable and absolute proofs. By knowing God's ways the intelligent comes to know God…God mentioned in the first statement, "I am the Lord your God," which can only be understood by a great sage…that only God endures without change…Therefore, "I am the Lord your God" suffices for the intelligent of every nation…However, only Israel acknowledge this, and the sages of the nations do not deny, that only God made heaven and earth. The [gentiles sages], however, say that God eternally makes [the world], without beginning or end. But God performed signs and wonders in Egypt…God did for Israel what he did not do for any other nation…Everyone saw this — sages and those who are not sages, great and small…He mentioned "I am the Lord your God" for the intelligent, and added "who brought you out," for the intelligent and for those who are not intelligent.[36]

In other words, for the intelligent, who recognize in the structure of the world, including the human body, the work of God's wisdom, it would have been sufficient to state merely "I am the Lord your God." God's existence is recognized by all intelligent people, Jews and gentiles alike, although the gentile intelligentsia affirm God as the agent of an eternal, rather than created, world. Since, however, the Torah was given to the entire people, it could not base the commandments upon an abstract metaphysical principle the masses are incapable of comprehending, so God added "who brought you out of the land of Egypt," which all the Israelites — intelligentsia and masses alike — had personally experienced and could comprehend.

---

36   Ibn Ezra, long (standard) commentary to Exodus 20:2.

[V.4.e]   THE TORAH'S HISTORICAL CONTEXT

In Ibn Ezra's understanding, the rationale for the commandments often reflects the historical context in which the Torah was given. The reference to the exodus, as we saw, is a concession to the masses who cannot comprehend the abstract metaphysical principle of God's existence ("am the Lord your God"). In another instance of reference to historical circumstances, Ibn Ezra observed that the Egyptians "to this day" refrained from eating certain animals, and the Torah, accordingly, prescribes those animals for sacrifices and food, as an effective social mechanism for differentiating Israel from surrounding cultures, and preventing the Israelites from worshiping those animals as gods.[37]

[V.5]   COSMOGONY AND COSMOLOGY

In the *Guide of the Perplexed* II:13, Rambam divides classical cosmogonies[38] into three "opinions." The first is "the opinion of the Torah," which he equates with creation *ex nihilo*. According to this view, God created the world by a deliberate act of will. The second is "the opinion of Plato," namely creation from eternal, prime matter, in other words, that God gave form and order to the world, but that formless matter always existed. The third view is the "opinion of Aristotle," according to whom the world as a whole—the heavenly spheres and the terrestrial species—are all eternal; only individuals are subject to generation and corruption.

[V.5.a]   IBN EZRA'S PLATONIC COSMOGONY

[V.5.a.i]   *"In the Beginning God Created" (Genesis 1:1)*

Ibn Ezra's interpretation of the Genesis story falls into what Rambam later categorized as the Platonic view. In Ibn Ezra's analysis of the language of Genesis 1:1, the term *bereishit* ("in the beginning") is in construct form, and thus really means "in the beginning of." Although many other commentators understand the verb *bara* ("created") to mean creation *ex nihilo*, it is also used in the Hebrew Bible for making something out of something else, as in Genesis 1:21, that God "created the great sea-monsters" and Genesis 1:27, that "God created the human" (i.e., God created them out of the already created

---

37   Ibn Ezra, commentary to Exodus 8:22.

38   Theories of the origin of the universe. See the discussion of Rambam on this point in Ch. 10.

elements). The term *bara*, Ibn Ezra concludes, actually means "to cut, and to establish a differentiated boundary. The intelligent will understand."[39]

Thus, according to Ibn Ezra's analysis, instead of understanding the verse to mean that "in the beginning God created the heaven and earth; and the earth was formless and chaotic (*tohu va-vohu*)," we should understand it as reading "in the beginning of God's creating the heaven and earth, the earth was formless and chaotic." In other words, there was already formless matter when God began to create by ordering and organizing the universe, by differentiating or "cutting" (i.e., establishing boundaries and limits) among the various formless elements, by giving each element its specific, differentiated form. Since the common, traditional religious reading of Genesis is that it means creation *ex nihilo*, Ibn Ezra may have recognized the need for discretion here (as he did with anachronistic passages), and therefore avoided going into further detail, simply adding "the intelligent will understand."

[V.5.a.ii] *Creation ex nihilo or from something?*

In his introduction to Kohelet (Ecclesiastes), Ibn Ezra emphasizes that when humans make something, they can never create substance, but can only change its accidental qualities. But what about the creation of substance itself? Is it, in Ibn Ezra's understanding, creation *ex nihilo* or creation from something?

Scholarly opinion differs on how to interpret Ibn Ezra on this point. Michael Friedlaender understands Ibn Ezra as affirming God's creation *ex nihilo* of substance:

> The chaos, the *tohu va-vohu* of the Bible, consisted of the four elements, fire, air, water and earth. These elements are, to a certain degree, indestructible, but not eternal. The indestructibility is not a property inherent in such elements, but is a consequence of the non-existence of any power in nature by which they could be destroyed. No created thing, Ibn Ezra says, can utterly annihilate another created thing; but the Creator himself, we may infer from this proposition, can undo his own work. In the same way, he states that a created thing cannot produce anything out of nothing; created beings can only transform. From this we again infer, that the Creator has the power of producing things from nothing.[40]

Friedlaender is certainly correct that Ibn Ezra limits human creativity to transforming (i.e., changing the accidental qualities) and not creating

---

[39] The term *gazar* literally means to "cut," and also means to limit, differentiate, establish boundaries, and to decide (as in a judge's verdict). Ibn Ezra cites other passages to support his understanding of *bara* as *gazar*. In his alternate commentary (*Shitah Aheret*) to Genesis 1:1, Ibn Ezra understands *bara* both as *gazar* and as *hitukh* (the common term for cutting).

[40] Michael Friedlaender, *Essays on the Writings of Abraham ibn Ezra* (London, 1877), pp. 7–8.

substance itself. However, does this human limitation necessarily imply that God is not limited in this way and can create substance *ex nihilo*? A more recent scholar, Joseph Cohen, concludes that Ibn Ezra's understanding of *bara* as *gazar* can only mean Platonic creation from something.[41] In that sense God can create substance, but humans can only transform substance's accidents. Material substance already exists "when God began to create," but only in an imperfect and unordered manner. All matter is limited when it is "cut" and given form — it exists as X and not as Y. To the extent that it exists, it is good, and whatever God creates is good. To the extent that it is limited and does not exist beyond X, its non-existence is the source of evil. "God only makes something good... The root of evil is the deficiency of the receiver."[42] Since God only creates the good, and matter, being limited, is thus at least indirectly the source of evil, we may infer that in Ibn Ezra's Platonic view God does not create matter itself *ex nihilo*, but rather "cuts" already existing formless matter by giving it form.

[V.5.a.iii] *Creation of the Terrestrial World*

Ibn Ezra's cosmology, as we shall see, is not limited to the terrestrial world, but he explains that the Torah deals only with the creation of the terrestrial world, and not to the celestial and angelic realms above it.[43] Humans, who are part of the physical world but whose intellects are of the same "species" as the angels, are the apex of terrestrial creation. The celestial realms, however, being superior, cannot be said to be created for the sake of humans. Indeed, they cannot be said to be created at all in the same sense as the terrestrial world.

Ibn Ezra's lack of systematic presentation (which in any event would not be possible in exegetical works) and his discreet reluctance to explicate his theories fully, have led scholars to radically different conclusions about his true views. Asher Weiser inferred from Ibn Ezra's concept of creation as "cutting" that he maintained a Platonic belief in prime matter.[44] Joseph Cohen rejected this reading, arguing that Ibn Ezra had no such concept of prime matter, and concluded, therefore, that at least regarding the celestial realms, Ibn Ezra tended to the Aristotelian concept of eternity.[45] Julius Guttmann, on the other hand, interpreted Ibn Ezra's view in terms of Neoplatonic emanation and pantheism.

---

41   Joseph Cohen, *The Religious-Philosophical Thought of Abraham ibn Ezra* (Hebrew) (Ph.D. dissertation, Bar Ilan University, 1983), p. 140; cf. Cohen, *The Philosophical Thought of Abraham ibn Ezra* (Hebrew) (Rishon Le-Zion: Shai Press, 1996), p. 175.

42   Ibn Ezra, Introduction to Kohelet (Ecclesiastes).

43   Ibn Ezra, alternate commentary (*Shitah Aḥeret*) to Genesis 1:1.

44   Asher Weiser, Ibn Ezra's commentary to Genesis 1:1, note 17.

45   Joseph Cohen, *The Philosophical Thought of Abraham ibn Ezra*, p. 167.

Ibn Ezra was moved more profoundly than most of his Jewish predecessors by the mysterious depths of Neoplatonism, approaching its metaphysical content more closely than any of the others except Gabirol. This is especially true of his doctrine of God...Ibn Ezra's theology is filled with a genuinely pantheistic spirit...As in Neoplatonism generally, this pantheism must be understood in an emanationist fashion; God is one with the totality of the world, because he is the primeval force from which all separate powers flow, and whose effects penetrate all things. This relationship is explicitly stated in regard to the super-mundane world, which neither came into being nor will pass away, but which exists through God alone...The biblical account of creation relates only to the terrestrial world, which has a temporal beginning, though even here Ibn Ezra combines the idea of creation with that of emanation by saying that it came into being through the mediation of the eternal intelligible substances.[46]

Although, as Cohen has pointed out, Ibn Ezra has no clear concept of prime matter, his repeated references to *bara* as creation from something would seem to imply a Platonic view of creation, at least of the terrestrial realm. The fact that this description of creation does not apply to the celestial and angelic realms does not warrant the inference that they are eternal in the Aristotelian sense, since Aristotelian eternity applies to the entire cosmos and does not permit any type of "creation" of any of its parts. Ibn Ezra's cosmogony, therefore, seems to be Platonic, mixed with Neoplatonic cosmological elements.

[V.5.b]   IBN EZRA'S THREE-FOLD COSMOLOGY

Above the terrestrial world in which we live are two higher realms, the celestial and the angelic. Ibn Ezra describes this three-fold cosmology in two passages, but they differ from each other.

[V.5.b.i]   *The First Cosmology: Commentary to Exodus*
Ibn Ezra's first three-fold cosmology is to be found in his long (i.e., standard) commentary to Exodus 3:15, and then again (in less detail) on Exodus 2:2–3. In the first passage, he states that the "lowest world" (*'olam shafel*) in which we live consists of minerals, plants, animals and humans. "Only the human is of the highest degree in the lowest world," but only the human body is subject to change, not his intellect. Above it is the "middle world" (*'olam tikhon*) which has "many degrees," and contains the five planets (the rotations of which are subject to change) and the fixed stars and constellations (the rotations of which are not subject to change). Above that is the "upper world (*'olam 'elyon*),

---

[46]   Julius Guttmann, *Philosophies of Judaism* (New York: Holt, Rinehart, Winston, 1964), p. 119.

which is the world of the holy angels, which are not bodies nor in bodies like the human rational soul (*neshamah*)." This upper, angelic world is not subject to any motion or change, and is eternal; however, it exists not because of its own power, but because of God.

Ibn Ezra then inserts an astrological note into his cosmology (points we shall examine later): since the human rational soul is of the same species as the angels, "if the rational soul is wise," it can receive a "higher power" from the angelic world, transcending and greater than the "higher power" of the stars, and ultimately can "cleave" (*daveq*) to God.

The second passage adds another emphasis: by knowing the three realms, a person "knows God's actions...and by knowing God's actions, the intelligent knows God." Thus, although people are subject to astral decrees resulting from the motions of the stars in the middle world, the human rational soul is of the same species as the angels in the upper world. When the rational soul attains knowledge of God's ways, it becomes itself angelic and capable of transcending astral decrees, exercising free will, and cleaving directly to God.

[V.5.b.ii] *The Second Cosmology: Commentary to Daniel*

Ibn Ezra's second three-fold cosmology is found in his commentary to Daniel 10:21 (which refers to "Michael your prince"). In this passage he begins by discussing "the One who is prior to any number; in one respect he is the cause of all number, and in another sense he is all number...This One is the first world (*'olam rishon*), opposite all the other worlds which are after it." The "second world" (*'olam sheni*) is the "middle" (*tikhon*) realm containing the multiplicity of the bodiless angels and the imperishable stars, where the angels Michael and Gabriel may be found. The third world (*'olam shelishi*) is the terrestrial, material world, including humans. "The human alone is the secret (*sod*) of this lowest world, which was created for him. But his rational soul is linked to the higher rational souls (i.e., the angels)."

[V.5.b.iii] *The Two Cosmologies: The Upward and Downward Ways*

When we compare the two cosmologies, we see significant differences, especially regarding (a) the direction of the cosmology (an ascending order in Exodus, and a descending order in Daniel); (b) the intermediate stage of the cosmology, which in the commentary to Exodus includes only the stars, but in the commentary to Daniel includes both the stars and the angels; and (c) the inclusion of God ("the One") in the second cosmology, but not in the first. The following chart will facilitate our comparison.

IBN EZRA'S THREE-FOLD COSMOLOGY	
Ascending Order **(Commentary to Exodus)**	**Descending Order** **(Commentary to Daniel)**
The lowest world (*'olam shafel*) Minerals Plants Animals Humans	**The first world (*'olam rishon*)** The One (= God)
The middle world (*'olam tikhon*) Planets Stars and constellations	**The second world (*'olam sheni*)** Bodiless angels Stars (imperishable matter)
The upper world (*'olam 'elyon*) Angels	**The third world (*'olam shelishi*)** Terrestrial, material world (including humans)
COMMENTS	
1. God transcends the cosmology and is not included in it. 2. The angels are the upper world; they have no bodies nor any motion. 3. The stars are the middle world; they have bodies and motions.	1. God is the first world. 2. The bodiless and motionless angels are in the second world, together with the material stars. 3. The second world thus consists of both bodiless, motionless angels and of stars which are material and are in motion.

Joseph Cohen suggests two possible ways of resolving the inconsistencies and contradictions between the two cosmologies.[47] The first possibility is that Ibn Ezra changed his mind between writing the first and second cosmologies. Since, however, both commentaries in question were written within a few years of each other, towards the end of his life, it is unlikely that he changed his mind on such fundamental questions. The other possibility is based on the different directions of the cosmologies, and suggests that Ibn Ezra had a different purpose in mind in each case. The ascending order of the version in his commentary to Exodus is intended to explain the ascent of the rational soul and its ability to by-pass and transcend the astral effects of the middle world by connecting directly with the angelic upper world. The upward way does not include God, who is above the structure, because the highest perfection attainable by the human soul is the angelic realm. The descending order of the version in the commentary to Daniel is intended to explain how

---

[47]   Joseph Cohen, *The Religious-Philosophical Thought of Abraham ibn Ezra*, pp. 77–78; cf. Cohen, *The Philosophical Thought of Abraham ibn Ezra*, pp. 91–93.

the angelic realm, deriving its power from God, ultimately affects everything below it. Therefore the downward way begins with God, on whom everything else — even the eternal angels and celestial spheres — depends.

When Ibn Ezra describes the ontological descending order (in the commentary to Daniel), i.e., the Neoplatonic downward way, he must begin with the One, the source of all being, from whom the second world emanates, consisting of the angels and the heavenly bodies. The bodiless angels and the heavenly bodies are related, because the angels are the separate intelligences of the imperishable, but material, moving spheres of the stars. The second realm is thus the heavenly realm, which includes both the celestial spheres and their angelic separate intelligences, above the terrestrial realm, and intermediating between the One and the lowest realm. Conversely, when Ibn Ezra describes the spiritual ascending order (the Neoplatonic upward way), he is describing the soul's progressive purification from corporeality, and its ascent to its sources. That ascent begins with material existence, and the highest degree of perfection attainable is wisdom, namely the rank of the angels (who are of the same species as the human rational soul). Since that is the highest level a human being can hope to attain, the ascending order does not mention God, the One, transcending all other reality, and beyond wisdom.

The two cosmologies are thus different, but not contradictory, because, as their respective directions imply, they are describing different processes: the downward way of the emanation of the lower from the higher, starting with the One, and the upward way of the rational soul seeking to transcend astral effects by connecting directly with the angels, who are of the same species as the rational soul and are the apex of its spiritual ascent.

[V.6]   THE NAMES OF GOD

[V.6.a]   THE NAME "ELOHIM" AND THE ANGELS

Ibn Ezra's cosmology accorded the angels important functions, both as intermediaries in the downward way from the One to the terrestrial realm, and as the apex of the upward way of the rational soul, which is of the same species as the angels. The name of God, "Elohim," used in the creation story in Genesis Ch. 1, is a generic term for divinity, is in the plural form, and often refers to the angels (as the Neoplatonic intermediaries between the One and the lower levels of reality), because "all of the actions of the Lord are by means of the angels who do his will."[48] The Hebrew term *mal'akh*, like the Greek *angelos*, means a messenger. As Joseph Cohen puts it, "the angels are thus

---

[48]   Ibn Ezra, commentary to Genesis 1:1.

the spiritual forces operating material existence."[49] As the spiritual forces and intermediaries by which God operates in the world, the angels may also be called *elohim*.

The name "Elohim" is thus not unique to the One, but, as Ibn Ezra explains, indicates any divinity, or an angel, or those human judges who execute divine justice on earth. That is why, in Exodus 4:16, God can say to Moses that his brother Aaron will be his spokesman and that "you will be as God to him." Because "Elohim" is a generic term for divinity, the Torah differentiates between a person who is merely guilty of cursing "Elohim" and a person who incurs the death penalty for cursing "the name of the Lord."[50] As Ibn Ezra comments, since the term *elohim* is equivocal, applying not only to God but to any divinity, and to angels and human judges,[51] there is not way for us to know what the person who is cursing had in mind, and he is only liable to the death penalty if he explicitly pronounces the specific name of God.

The name "Elohim" thus is equivocal, and refers to a creative divine force in the world, whether that means God himself or an angelic or even human agent of God's action.

[V.6.b] THE TETRAGRAMMATON "Y-H-V-H" — THE SPECIFIC NAME OF GOD

[V.6.b.i] *The Tetragrammaton and the Uniqueness of the Prophecy of Moses*

In sharp contrast with the generic term for divinity "Elohim," the Tetragrammaton Y-H-V-H, which is not pronounced phonetically,[52] but for which the term "Adonai" ("My Lord") is substituted, is the specific name of God. In Exodus 6:2–3, the Tetragrammaton is explicitly linked to the unique prophecy of Moses: "God (*Elohim*) spoke to Moses and said to him, 'I am the Lord (Y-H-V-H). I appeared to Abraham, to Isaac, and to Jacob as Almighty God (*El Shaddai*), but I was not known to them by my name Y-H-V-H'."

---

[49] Joseph Cohen, *The Religious-Philosophical Thought of Abraham ibn Ezra*, p. 78.

[50] Leviticus 24:15–16.

[51] Ibn Ezra makes a similar point on the equivocal nature of *elohim* in his commentary to Exodus 22:19.

[52] In those versions of the Hebrew Bible in which the Tetragrammaton is punctuated, the vowels assigned to it are the vowels of the word "Adonai." Since the *alef* of "Adonai" cannot be punctuated with the *sheva na'*, it has the grammatical equivalent of *hataf patah*, but the *yod* of the Tetragrammaton is then punctuated with the equivalent *sheva na'*. However, when the actual name "Adonai" itself is followed by the Tetragrammaton, instead of substituting "Adonai," one substitutes "Elohim" (thus reading it "Adonai Elohim" as in Genesis 15:2, 8), and the Tetragrammaton is then punctuated with the vowels for "Elohim."

The verse does not say that the Patriarchs did not know the Tetragrammaton (and, in fact, it appears frequently in the patriarchal stories in Genesis), but that God "was not known to them" by that name, just as a teacher may be known to his children by one name, to his friends by another name, and to his students formally by yet another name or title. According to Rambam,[53] our verse indicates that the prophecy of Moses was unique and on a much higher level than the prophecies of his predecessors (or, for that matter, prophets who followed him), whom God knew "face to face".[54] In Judah Ha-Levi's analysis,[55] the generic term *elohim* refers to any concept of divinity, however one arrives at it, whereas the Tetragrammaton refers to the personal God who intervenes in history and who performed miracles for the Israelites coming out of Egypt. The Patriarchs had no need for such public miracles, but Moses needed them for his effective governing of the people, to eliminate their doubts, and the difference in names is indicative of Moses' unique leadership role and involvement with miracles.

Ibn Ezra's reading of the verse resembles both of these interpretations. Like Rambam, Ibn Ezra states that Moses in fact comprehended for more than any other prophet. However, like Judah Ha-Levi, he understands the use of the Tetragrammaton here as indicating God's direct and miraculous involvement in the history of the people.[56]

> There is no doubt that the Patriarchs knew this name, which is a proper noun (*shem 'eẓem*) [literally: the name of a substance], but they did not know this name as an adjective (*to'ar*)...The Patriarchs did not attain the rank of cleaving to God like Moses, whom God knew face to face. Therefore, Moses was able to change natures in the lowest world and to perform signs and miracles that the Patriarchs could not perform.

In other words, Ibn Ezra applies grammatical analysis to the passage: the Tetragrammaton is a proper noun. As such, it indicates a substance, and as we saw in Ibn Ezra's interpretation of the Decalogue, the first of the "ten commandments" refers to substance, the first Aristotelian category, and the other nine to the nine categories of accidents attaching to that substance. In this passage, however, Ibn Ezra is suggesting that the Tetragrammaton, as a noun, can also function as an adjective, and when it does, it refers to God's miraculous and supra-natural intervention in history, which Moses experienced but the Patriarchs did not.

---

53   Rambam, *Guide of the Perplexed* II:35.
54   Cf. Deuteronomy 34:10.
55   Judah Ha-Levi, *Kuzari* 2:2.
56   Ibn Ezra, long (standard) commentary to Exodus 6:3.

[V.6.b.ii] *A Proper Noun and an Adjective*

All the other names of God (including "Elohim") are adjectives—literally "attributes," indicating divine actions. Only the Tetragrammaton is a proper noun—literally "substance"—indicating God's existence, although, as we have seen, it, too, sometimes functions as an adjective. Ibn Ezra found grammatical basis for this anomaly regarding the Tetragrammaton—a proper noun that can also function as an adjective.[57] In Hebrew, common nouns may be in construct form (two adjacent words, indicating possession of the first by the second), but in general, not proper nouns. We can thus say *melekh yisra'el* ("king [of] Israel"), but we cannot say *david yisra'el* ("David [of] Israel"). Despite the fact that the Tetragrammaton is a proper noun, occasionally it is found in construct form, such as in the biblical expression *Y-H-V-H ẓeva'ot* (usually translated as "Lord of hosts"). In such cases, however, the construct form does not indicate possession (the "hosts" of stars do not possess God), but rather that God is the agent of the existence of the stars. When the Tetragrammaton is a proper noun, it thus indicates God's self-sufficient existence, and when it functions as an adjective, i.e., an attribute of action, it indicates God's action as the agent of the existence of all other being.[58]

[V.6.b.iii] *Analysis of the Tetragrammaton*

In the third part of his *Book of the Name* (*Sefer Ha-Shem*), written in Besiers, France circa 1147, Ibn Ezra analyses the numerical values of the Tetragrammaton, and phonetic pronunciation of the letters *alef, hay, vav,* and *yod* from which the three biblical forms of the Tetragrammaton are composed: the full four-letter name Y-H-V-H, the short two-letter form Yah (as in "Hallelujah"), and Ehyeh ("I will be," as in Exodus 3:14). He first reiterates what we have already learned in his commentaries:

> The One is the cause of all number, but it is not a number...Moreover, we found that all speech is ten: nine are accidents, and only the one itself is the substance bearing [the others]...Therefore the Decalogue written in the Torah begins with "I am," to indicate a substance, but it is not a positive commandment or negative commandment in the same way as the others, but only of the belief of the heart.[59]

---

57   In the second part of his *Book of the Name* (*Sefer Ha-Shem*), Ibn Ezra expands on four differences between a proper noun and an adjective. Hebrew adjectives are derived from verbs; proper nouns are not, and therefore cannot be conjugated (despite occasional names like Isaac and Jacob which were originally derived from verbs); adjectives can be plural, whereas proper nouns are only singular (despite collective nouns like "Israelites"); adjectives can carry the definite article, and proper names cannot; adjectives can be construct or carry pronominal suffixes, but proper names cannot.

58   Ibn Ezra, long (standard) commentary to Exodus 3:15 and *Sefer Ha-Shem*, ch. 8.

59   Ibn Ezra, *Sefer Ha-Shem* 3:1.

We have seen how Ibn Ezra's analysis of the Tetgragrammaton combines Neoplatonic elements (the One which is not a number but is the source of all number) with Aristotelian elements (the Tetragrammaton as substance/noun and all other names as accidents/adjectives). He also interprets the divine name in light of Neo-Pythagorean numerology, based on the numerical values of the Hebrew letters.[60]

The numerical value of Y-H-V-H is 72, according to Ibn Ezra's calculation. Since the simple arithmetical value of the name is 26 (*yod* = 10; *hay* = 5; *vav* = 6; *hay* = 5), his total of 72 can be arrived at by two methods.

The first method compounds the values of the letters. Thus:

Yod = 10
Yod + *Hay* = 15
Yod + *Hay* + *Vav* = 21
Yod + *Hay* + *Vav* + *Hay* = 26
10 + 15 + 21 + 26 = 72

The second method calculates the values of the names of the letters when they are fully spelled out:

Yod = *yod* (10) + *vav* (6) + *dalet* (4) = 20
Hay = *hay* (5) + *yod* (10) = 15
Vav = *vav* (6) + *yod* (10) + *vav* (6) = 22
Hay = *hay* (5) + *yod* (10) = 15
20 + 15 + 22 + 15 = 72

Although Ibn Ezra regarded the Tetragrammaton as a mystery or secret (*sod*), since it is ineffable and we do not know its correct vocalization,[61] he expressed the hope that in the messianic era we will again know how to pronounce it. Commenting on Zechariah 14:9 ("On that day the Lord will be one and his name one"), Ibn Ezra states: "'His name one': That is the glorious name known by Moses his servant, and read in the mouths of all as it is written."

[V.7]   "HE IS ALL, AND ALL IS FROM HIM"

---

60   These numerical calculations are found in *Sefer Ha-Shem*, section 5, and in Ibn Ezra's long (standard) commentary to Exodus 33:21, and also in *Yesod Mora Ve-Sod Ha-Torah*, ch. 11, p. 197.

61   The Hebrew alphabet is consonantal; the system of vocalization and punctuation was added by the Masoretes a couple of centuries before Ibn Ezra's time. We thus have no written vocalization of the Tetragrammaton in ancient texts, and as noted above, the vocalization in medieval and modern texts reflects the substitution of Adonai and Elohim for the Tetragrammaton. See above, note 52.

[V.7.a]   IBN EZRA, SPINOZA AND PANTHEISM

We have seen that for Ibn Ezra, the One is in all numbers (since all numbers are composed of units), and all numbers are in it (as their source). This leads Ibn Ezra to an apparently pantheistic equation of the One with "the All" (*ha-kol*). Following his discussion of the Tetragrammaton, he states:

> If you look from the perspective of number, he [i.e., the One] is the head of all. Every number consists of units, and he is the One who is the All (*hu ha-ehad she-hu ha-kol*)...The One has no figure but is a general way for all figures, because everything comes from him.[62]

And again: "He is all, and all is from him (*hu ha-kol ume-ito ha-kol*),"[63] and "God is the One, he creates all, and he is all, and I cannot explain (*Ha-Shem hu ha-ehad ve-hu yozer ha-kol ve-hu ha-kol, ve-lo ukhal le-faresh*)."[64]

As in other cases (such as his Bible criticism), Ibn Ezra's elliptical language makes it difficult to determine with certainty whether "all" (*kol*) or "the all" (*ha-kol*) in these cases refers to God (as maintained by such scholars as H. Kreisel),[65] to the active intellect (as maintained by others, such as E. Wolfson),[66] to a Neoplatonic notion of emanation (as suggested by Julius Guttmann), or to a Neo-Pythagorean description of One which, as we have seen, is not itself number, but transcends number, containing all number and contained in all number.

Spinoza, as mentioned earlier, openly acknowledged that his Bible criticism was based on Ibn Ezra (or at least on his reading of Ibn Ezra). Can the same be said of Spinoza's pantheism — "Deus sive Natura" (God or nature)?[67]

According to Spinoza's Proposition XV to the first part of his *Ethics*: "Whatsoever is, is in God, and without God nothing can be, or be conceived."[68]

Harry Wolfson, who documented the medieval sources for much of Spinoza's thought, suggests that Spinoza was much more consistent than his medieval predecessors, and that Proposition XV

---

62   Ibn Ezra, Long (standard) commentary to Exodus 33:21.

63   Ibn Ezra, Long (standard) commentary to Exodus 23:21.

64   Ibn Ezra, commentary to Genesis 1:26.

65   Howard Kreisel, "On the Term *Kol* in Abraham ibn Ezra: A Reappraisal," in *Revue des Études Juives* 153 (1994), pp. 29–66.

66   Elliot Wolfson, "God, the Demiurge and the Intellect: On the Usage of the Word *Kol* in Abraham ibn Ezra," in *Revue des Études Juives* 149 (1990), pp. 77–111.

67   Julius Guttmann, *Philosophies of Judaism*, p. 266, merely states that "it is also possible that other Jewish sources, such as the biblical commentaries of Abraham ibn Ezra...played a part in the formation of his pantheism, but this is uncertain."

68   Spinoza, *The Ethics*, Part I, Proposition XV, in *The Works of Spinoza*, trans. R.H.M. Elwes, vol. II, p. 55.

is a criticism of the mediaeval inconsistency in first affirming that all things are in God, and then denying that matter is in God. For when the mediaevals reiterated their statements that God is all and all is from God and in God, they had to make a mental reservation with regard to matter. God was not matter, and matter was not from God or in God. Matter existed by the side of God, according to Aristotle; it was created by God *ex nihilo*, according to the generally accepted view of all the three religions; it appeared somewhere in the process of emanation, according to the emanationists. The statement that God is all and all is from God and in God could not be taken in its full and literal sense that "whatever is, is in God" except by one who like Spinoza asserted that God was material.[69]

This criticism seems to be legitimate when aimed at Ibn Ezra, whose ambiguities leave a lot of unanswered questions. What is the origin of matter, in his view? Specifically, how can Ibn Ezra say "God is the One, he creates all, and he is all, and I cannot explain," thus maintaining that God is simultaneously the All and the creator of all?

[V.7.b] "HE IS ALL AND ALL IS FROM HIM" AND EMANATION

Julius Guttman understands the expressions "he is all and all is from him," and "he creates all, and he is all" as meaning Neoplatonic emanation. "He is all" means that God is the source of all, and therefore "all is from him" by a process of emanation. (As in the theory of emanation in general, the problem of the origin of matter remains unresolved).

> Ibn Ezra was moved more profoundly that most of his Jewish predecessors by the mysterious depths of Neoplatonism...This is especially true of his doctrine of God...Ibn Ezra's theology is filled with a genuinely pantheistic spirit...As in Neoplatonism generally, this pantheism must be understood in emanationist fashion; God is the one with the totality of the world, because he is the primeval force from which all separate powers flow, and whose effects penetrate all things.[70]

Yet, as Guttmann correctly notes, there is a fundamental inconsistency in the Neoplatonic notion of God emanating all, and Ibn Ezra's Platonic understanding of creation of the terrestrial world as "cutting," i.e., "the imparting of form to uncreated matter."[71] Joseph Cohen, on the other hand, rejects Guttmann's Neoplatonic, emanationist reading of Ibn Ezra, and points out that Ibn Ezra never uses the term "emanation" in his philosophic works, but only in his poetry.[72]

---

69   Harry A. Wolfson, *The Philosophy of Spinoza* (Cleveland: Meridian, 1961), vol. 1, pp. 297–298.
70   Julius Guttmann, *Philosophies of Judaism*, p. 119.
71   Ibid, p. 120.
72   Joseph Cohen, *The Religious-Philosophical Thought of Abraham ibn Ezra*, pp. 118–119;

Nevertheless, although Cohen rejects Guttmann's emanationist reading of Ibn Ezra's prose, he also understands "he is all" to mean that merely God is the cause of all (and not that God contains all), and similarly, that "all is from him" means that God is the sole cause of the existence of the universe. Cohen's suggestion, however, effectively reduces the phrase to a tautology, because both parts mean essentially the same thing: "he is all" and "all is from him" both mean that God is the source or cause of everything, and that the existence of everything is dependent upon God.

Cohen also points to Ibn Ezra's poems expressing love and yearning for God, and asks how one can love an impersonal first source of emanation. The fact that a term may not be used explicitly by a thinker, however, does not mean that the concept is not implicit in his thought, especially a thinker who was careful not to express himself fully and openly on all questions, including pantheism: "and I cannot explain (*ve-lo ukhal le-faresh*)." In any event, it is possible that by the expression *me-ito ha-kol* ("all is from him") Ibn Ezra did intend to refer explicitly to emanation.

Another possibility, as we shall discuss further regarding his astrological theory, is that his consistent emphasis is on the process of receiving from below, not on what comes from above. Therefore, as we saw, the two differing versions of the Decalogue could not have been revealed simultaneously, not because God is incapable of producing two sounds, but because people are incapable of understanding two different things they hear simultaneously. So while Ibn Ezra does not explicitly refer to emanation from above, he frequently discusses reception from below, which may be its functional equivalent.[73]

Moreover, Cohen is confusing the question of the personality of God with an individual's personal relation or response to something which may itself be impersonal. A person can respond personally and in love to something impersonal and incapable of loving him and unaware of his love or even of his existence, such as a beautiful symphony, work of art, or sunset. This is what Spinoza referred to as *amor Dei intellectualis*, the intellectual love of God: I cannot love a God who loves me, because a God who loves is not truly a God and therefore not worthy of my love.

The real question for Ibn Ezra, therefore, is not whether expressions of love for God in his poetry prove that on a philosophical level he believed in the personal "God of Abraham," (to use Judah Ha-Levi's term, we shall see in Chapter Six), given the possibility of poetic license. Rather, the real question

---

cf. Cohen, *The Philosophical Thought of Abraham ibn Ezra*, p. 146.

73 We should also note that in the *Book of Substances* (*Sefer Ha-'Azamim*) attributed to Ibn Ezra (pp. 11–12) there is an explicit reference to "prophecy, i.e., what is emanated (*ne 'ezal ve-nishpa'*) from these intellectual faculties to the soul's faculties."

is whether and how it is possible to reconcile philosophic conceptions of an impersonal God (what Judah Ha-Levi called the "God of Aristotle") with the personal God of biblical religion who intervenes miraculously in nature, who hears prayer, and who rewards and punishes, since both impersonal and personal conceptions find expression in his prose works, including his Bible commentaries.

Finally, it is possible that Ibn Ezra's phrase may not refer to pantheism or emanation at all (in which case, there would not necessarily be a problem of the origin of matter, or of personal versus impersonal conceptions of God), but to his Neo-Pythagorean infatuation with numbers, since, as we have repeatedly seen, the One is not a number but is the source of all number, and is in all numbers, since they are composed of units. As Ibn Ezra states in *Yesod Mora Ve-Sod Ha-Torah* ("The Foundation of Reverence and the Secret of the Torah"), "The One is the cause of number, but is not a number,"[74] and "Know that the One is the secret (*sod*) of all number, but itself is not number, because it exists by itself and has no need for those which come after it. It is also all number, because number is composed of units."[75] For Ibn Ezra, these mathematical notions could be the equivalent of his statements that "the One is all," that "all is from the One," and even that "the One is the creator of all."

[V.8]   "THE ALL KNOWS PARTICULARS IN A GENERAL WAY AND NOT IN A PARTICULAR WAY"

[V.8.a]   GOD'S KNOWLEDGE OF PARTICULARS

Ibn Ezra's ambiguity regarding God as "the All" extends to several statements, playing with the term *kol* ("all" or "every") or *ha-kol* ("the all" or "everything"), and dealing with the question of God's knowledge of terrestrial particulars. For example: "The All knows every particular in a general way and not in a particular way (*ha-kol yode'a kol ḥeleq 'al derekh kol ve-lo 'al derekh ḥeleq*)."[76] "He alone knows the specific particulars in a general way (*ki hu levado yode'a ha-peratim ve-ḥelqeihem be-derekh kelal*)."[77] "Knowledge of the particular in a general way (*da'at ha-ḥeleq mi-derekh ha-kol*)."[78] Finally: "God alone creates everything and knows the particulars of everything in a general way, because the particulars [are subject to] change

---

74   Ibn Ezra, *Yesod Mora Ve-Sod Ha-Torah*, ed. Joseph Cohen and Uriel Simon, second edition (Ramat Gan: Bar Ilan University Press, 2007), Ch. 11:6, pp. 186–187.
75   Ibid, Ch. 12:3, p. 207.
76   Ibn Ezra, commentary to Genesis 18:21.
77   Ibn Ezra, long (standard) commentary to Exodus 33:21.
78   Ibn Ezra, short commentary to Exodus 33:14–17.

(ki ha-shem levado bore ha-kol ve-yode'a ḥelqei ha-kol be-derekh kol, ki ha-ḥalaqim mishtanim)."[79]

These statements do not imply a general Aristotelian denial of divine knowledge of terrestrial particulars. Rather, they seem to mean that God knows particulars, but in a different way from our knowledge of particulars.

[V.8.b]   PARTICULAR KNOWLEDGE AND GENERAL KNOWLEDGE

Human knowledge is particular in two senses: both the subject and object are particulars. A particular subject has empirical, sensible knowledge of a particular object. Moreover, human knowledge is always partial, because the body, which makes it possible to know certain things, makes it impossible to know other things. The same body which enables a person to be in a certain place and hear a lecture or a symphony makes it impossible for him to be, at the same time, somewhere else, and hear another lecture or symphony. Conversely, Ibn Ezra's statements emphasize that God, the All, knows things in a general and total way, not in a particular and partial way, because as their source and cause, the One is in all things and all things are in the One.

Moreover, our empirical knowledge always involves a clear distinction between the particular knower and the particular known object. However, given the Aristotelian doctrine of the unity in the actual intellect of subject, act and object of knowledge, the distinction of subject, act and object of knowledge does not pertain to abstract, general intellectual knowledge. So the "All," by knowing itself as the source and cause of particulars, can know all in a general, but not in a particular, way. Ibn Ezra explicitly refers to this Aristotelian doctrine: "He alone is knower and knowing and the known (*hu levado yode'a ve-da'at ve-yadu'a*)."[80]

The human body prevents a person from transcending the limitations of particularity. Therefore the Torah teaches that "no man can see me and live" (Exodus 33:20), meaning that during our bodily existence, we cannot attain general, universal knowledge. Only Moses was able to overcome his particularity to the point that he became sufficiently universal to attain such general knowledge while still alive.[81]

[V.9]   THE WORLD TO COME (*'OLAM HA-BA*)

---

[79]   Ibn Ezra, *Yesod Mora Ve-Sod Ha-Torah*, ch. 10:2, p. 175.
[80]   Ibn Ezra, long (standard) commentary to Exodus 34:6.
[81]   Ibn Ezra, long (standard) commentary to Exodus 33:21.

According to Ibn Ezra, the human rational soul (*neshamah*), as we have seen, is of the same species as the angels. The difference, of course, is that the human soul abides in a body, whereas an angel is equated with the celestial and bodiless "separate intellect" (*sekhel nivdal* or *sekhel nifrad*). The more a person acquires intellectual knowledge, the more his rational soul becomes universal. A person has sensible knowledge of a particular tree that he sees or touches, but what his intellect knows is not the particular, physical tree, but the universal idea or definition of the abstract tree. In the case of such abstract and universal knowledge, since the knowing subject and the known object are identical, the rational soul, as it becomes ever more universal, can become increasingly angelic and known by God "in a general way," while the person is still alive in his body, and all the more so after "the separation of its faculty from the body which is its palace."[82]

The immortality of the rational soul is what is meant by "the world to come" (*'olam ha-ba*). The lower faculties of the soul, however, relate to bodily functions and therefore perish along with it.[83] This concept of "the world to come" as the immortality of the rational soul (a concept similar to that of Rambam, as we shall see in Ch. 8) is not mentioned in the Torah, however, because the Torah was given to all, not only to the intelligentsia, and

> only one in a thousand can comprehend the subject of the world to come, because it is very profound. The reward of the world to come depends on the rational soul. It is in place of the service of the heart, whose service is to contemplate the works of God, because they are the ladder by which to ascend to the degree of knowing God, which is the essential point (*'iqqar*).[84]

In his Introduction to Qohelet (Ecclesiastes), Ibn Ezra combines this theme of the immortality of the world to come with the Neoplatonic upward way.

> The intellectual spirit (*ha-ru'ah ha-maskelet*) yearns to grasp the higher rungs, so that it can climb to the immaterial arrangements of the living God...This will happen if the spirit is purified and sanctified from the impurities of bodily appetites...and return its heart to the knowledge of its foundation and to seeing its secret with its eyes of wisdom...Then it will be prepared to know the words of truth, which will be engraved on it and will not be erased when it becomes separated from its body...for it was for the sake of showing it this that it was brought here. Therefore it was imprisoned...All this is to benefit it, even if it suffered and labored for a number of years, so that it might rest and rejoice forever.

---

82   Ibn Ezra, *Yesod Mora Ve-Sod Ha-Torah*, Ch. 10:2, p. 176.
83   Ibn Ezra, commentary to Genesis 3:6.
84   Ibn Ezra, commentary to Deuteronomy 32:39.

[V.10]   THE MICROCOSM AND SELF-KNOWLEDGE

The knowledge of God, "which is the essential point" and the basis for the immortality of the rational soul, is also related to the theme of the human being as a microcosm. Commenting on Genesis 1:26, "Let us make man in our image," Ibn Ezra rejects the notion of a physical similarity between humans and God. The similarity is that of the immortal rational soul which fills the body, "and the human body is a microcosm." Therefore, by knowing himself as a microcosm (*'olam qatan*), a person comes to know the macrocosm (*'olam gadol*), and thereby to know God.

Ibn Ezra also identified the *mishkan* (Tabernacle), the portable tent-Temple of the Israelites in the desert, and the *beit miqdash* (the Temple in Jerusalem) as a microcosm, and relates them to the self-knowledge which makes possible knowledge of the macrocosm:

> Just as the heart has received the faculty of the rational soul more than the other bodily organs... so it is with God's glory. We know that his glory fills the whole world, but there are places in which God's glory can be seen more than in other places, on account of two factors. One of them is the physical constitution (*toledet*) of the receiver, and the other is according to the higher [astral] power over the head of the receiver. Therefore the location of the Temple (*beit ha-miqdash*) was chosen... Whoever knows the secret of his rational soul (*sod nishmato*) and the make-up of his body (*matkonet gufo*) will be able to know the higher world, because a person resembles a microcosm.[85]

Other Jewish philosophers affirmed the notion of the human as a microcosm (most notably Joseph ibn Ẓaddik, whose book is titled *Ha-'Olam Ha-Qatan* ["The Microcosm"]), and the theme of self-knowledge as the key to knowledge of the world and of God is also widespread. What is different in the case of Ibn Ezra is the pantheistic character of these themes. The passage on the microcosm theme in his commentary to Genesis 1:26 (discussed above) concludes with the statement: "God is the One, he creates all, and he is all, and I cannot explain (*Ha-Shem hu ha-eḥad ve-hu yoẓer ha-kol ve-hu ha-kol, ve-lo ukhal le-faresh*)." Similarly, "the philosophers call the human being a microcosm... In this way, the intelligent can know the One because all is in it."[86]

Ibn Ezra thus differs from many other thinkers whose discussion of self-knowledge as the key to knowledge of God referred only to the knowledge of one's soul, reflecting the Neoplatonic emphasis of the spiritual and negation of the physical. In Ibn Ezra's pantheistic approach, as we have seen, the microcosm is the human body, and, as Alexander Altmann has pointed out,

---

85   Ibn Ezra, Long (standard) commentary to Exodus 26:1.
86   Ibn Ezra, *Yesod Mora Ve-Sod Ha-Torah* 12:3, pp. 206–207.

the self-knowledge is therefore of both body and soul: "Ibn Ezra—bearing in mind the microcosm motif—regards the knowledge of the body *and* soul as a precondition for the knowledge of God."[87]

We thus find consistent emphasis on knowledge of both body and soul together: "One cannot know God if one does not know one's soul (*nefesh*), rational soul (*neshamah*) and body (*guf*), for whoever does not know the essence of his soul, what wisdom does he have?"[88] "The general rule is, how can a person seek to know what is above him if he does not know what his soul (*nefesh*) is and what is body (*geviah*) is?"[89]

The motif of self-knowledge as the key to knowledge of "what is above him" also has implications for Ibn Ezra's astrological theory. The body belongs to the lowest, i.e., terrestrial world, and as such is subject to astral influences. Therefore, without understanding how his own body is subject to these astral decrees, a person cannot learn how to escape their effects.

[V.11]   IBN EZRA AND ASTROLOGY

Ibn Ezra composed several books dealing with astronomy and astrology, including Hebrew translations of Arabic astrological works. Some of these were subsequently translated into European languages (Latin, French, Spanish, English and German).

As strange as Ibn Ezra's interest in astrology may appear to us, in his own view astrology was not mystical or magical, but provides a scientific way to explain certain natural phenomena, consistent with his Neoplatonic cosmology in which the influences of higher powers on the lower world are natural. While Ibn Ezra's rationalist approach to revelation was by no means unique among Jewish philosophers, his astrological explanations of various biblical passages are unusual, and he sometimes approached, or crossed over to, astral magic, as discussed in recent studies by such scholars as Y. Tzvi Langermann, Dov Schwartz and Shlomo Sela.[90] In the words of Raphael Levy:

---

87   Alexander Altmann, "The Delphic Maxim in Medieval Islam and Judaism," in *Studies in Religious Philosophy and Mysticism* (Ithaca: Cornell University Press, 1969), p. 27.

88   Ibn Ezra, Long (standard) commentary to Exodus 31:18.

89   Ibn Ezra, *Yesod Mora Ve-Sod Ha-Torah* 1:8, p. 89.

90   See Dov Schwartz, *Studies on Astral Magic in Medieval Jewish Thought* (Leiden: Brill, 2005); idem, *Astral Magic in Medieval Jewish Thought* (Hebrew) (Ramat Gan: Bar Ilan University Press, 1999); Shlomo Sela, *Astrology and Biblical Exegesis in Abraham ibn Ezra's Thought* (Hebrew) (Ramat Gan: Bar Ilan University Press, 1999); idem, *Abraham ibn Ezra and the Rise of Medieval Hebrew Science* (Leiden: Brill, 2003);Tzvi Langermann, "Some Astrological Themes in the Thought of Abraham ibn Ezra," in *Rabbi Abraham ibn Ezra: Studies in the Writings of a Twelfth-Century Jewish Polymath*, ed. I. Twersky and

The rationalist bent so expressed led to his denial of the popular belief in evil spirits, his outspoken opinion that demons have no objective existence... Yet this attitude did not prevent him from running the pseudo-scientific gamut of his time, dipping deeply into astrology, arithmolatry, mysticism, and even magic.[91]

[V.11.a] ASTRONOMY AND ASTROLOGY

Both astronomy and astrology are called *hokhmat ha-tekhunah* in medieval philosophical Hebrew.[92] However, astrology is called "judicial" (*hokhmat ha-tekhunah ha-mishpatit*), as opposed to astronomy which is called "mathematical" (*hokhmat ha-tekhunah ha-limudit*), because it is limited to describing and measuring the motions of the stars, the distances between them and their relative positions, and the size of the planets. Mathematical astronomy is, accordingly, categorized as a "science" (*hokhmah*) in the true sense of the term. Judicial astrology, on the other hand, which attempts to understand astral "decrees" (*gezerot*), i.e., the ways in which the stars influence other stars and especially the ways in which these decrees affect terrestrial events, is frequently rejected, or categorized not as a true science but merely as an art or profession (*melakhah*).

Rambam, for example, differentiated between astronomy as a true science, and astrology, which is not a science but "nothingness and emptiness," and which had caused the destruction of the ancient Jewish State and the Temple "because these matters are the essence of idolatry (*'avodah zarah*).[93] Despite the vigorous rejection of judicial astrology, Rambam did not completely negate physical influences of the stars in the terrestrial realm. As he says in the *Guide of the Perplexed* I:72:

> Know that the forces reaching this world from the stars... are four forces. A force necessitating mixture and composition... a force endowing every plant

---

J.M. Harris (Cambridge: Harvard University Press, 1993), pp. 28–85; Raphael Levy and Francisco Cantera, *The Beginning of Wisdom: An Astrological Treatise by Abraham ibn Ezra* (Baltimore, 1939); Jacques Halbronn, *Le Livre des Fondements Astrologiques* (Paris: 1977); idem, *Le Monde Juif et l'Astrologie* (Milan, 1985).

[91] Raphael Levy, *The Astrological Works of Abraham ibn Ezra* (Baltimore: Johns Hopkins University Press, 1927), p. 9.

[92] See the references in Jacob Klatzkin, *Thesaurus Philosophicus Linguae Hebraicae et Veteris et Recentioris* (New York: Feldheim, 1968), vol. 1, pp. 297–299. On the classification and names of the sciences, see H.A. Wolfson, "The Classification of the Sciences in Mediaeval Jewish Philosophy," in *Hebrew Union College Annual Jubilee Volume* (1925), pp. 263–315.

[93] Rambam, "Letter to the Sages of Monpellier Concerning Astrology" in Y. Shailat, *Iggerot Ha-Rambam* (Jerusalem, 1988), vol. 2, p. 474. Cf. A. Marx, "The Correspondence Between the Rabbis of Southern France and Maimonides About Astrology," in *Hebrew Union College Annual* 3 (1926), pp. 258–311.

with the vegetative soul; a force endowing each animal with the animal soul; and a force endowing each rational being with the rational soul. All this takes place through the mediation of the light and darkness resulting from the [heavenly bodies'] light and circumferential motion around the earth.

And in the *Guide of the Perplexed* II:5:

> Know that the philosophers all agree that the governance of this terrestrial world is perfected by forces influencing it from the sphere...and that the spheres apprehend and know whatever they govern. This is also what is written in the Torah...It clearly says: "To rule over the day and night and to differentiate etc." (Genesis 1:18). "To rule" means domination by governance, which is an additional notion to the notion of light and darkness, which is the proximate cause of generation and corruption.

As Y. Tzvi Langermann has pointed out, Rambam, like most other medieval Jewish thinkers, affirmed the physical, i.e., the bodily or mechanical influences of the stars, which he refers to as "emanation" (*faiḍ*), but he minimizes the role of the heavenly intellects. Despite calling these effects "emanation," he actually meant that the stars effect their influences by forces (*quwat*) subject to the laws of nature, which function for a limited time, and are weaker at a greater distance, as opposed to emanation which is immediate and unaffected by distance.[94] Natural astrology thus has a place in Rambam's thought, but judicial astrology is wrong in principle, and not merely inaccurate.

A similar distinction between astronomy as a true science and judicial astronomy as a profession may be found in Abu Naṣr Al-Farabi's *Iḥsa Al-'Ulum* ("Enumeration of the Sciences"), which Ibn Ezra may well have known, and which was paraphrased in Hebrew in the thirteenth century by Shem Tov ibn Falaquera in his *Reshit Ḥokhmah* ("Beginning of Wisdom").[95]

> Astronomy is divided into two parts. The first [deals with] the astral decreeds, namely the science of observing the stars for what will occur in the future, or for much of what now exists, or for \much of what has happened. The second is

---

94   Y. Tzvi Langermann, "Maimonides' Repudiation of Astrology," in *Maimonidean Studies* 2 (1991), pp. 130–132. Gad Freudenthal differentiates between such natural astrology in Maimonides' thought, and judicial astrology, which he strongly rejected. See his study "Maimonides' Stance on Astrology in Context" in *Moses Maimonides: Physician, Scientist and Philosopher*, ed. Fred Rosner and Samuel Kottek (Northvale, NJ: 1993), pp. 77–90, 244–249.

95   On Falaquera, see Raphael Jospe, *Torah and Sophia: The Life and Thought of Shem Tov ibn Falaquera* (Cincinnati: Hebrew Union College Press, 1988), and the discussion of *Reshit Ḥokhmah* on pp. 37–42. Cf. Israel Efros, "Palquera's *Reshit Hokmah* and Alfarabi's *Ihsa al-Ulum*" in *Jewish Quarterly Review* 25 (1934–35), pp. 227–235, and Mauro Zonta, *La "Classificazione della Scienze" di Al-Farabi nella Tradizione Ebraica* (Torini, 992), pp. 18–19.

mathematical astronomy, which is one of the mathematical sciences. The other one [i.e., astrology] is counted among the powers and professions by which a person can warn about what will be, such as oneiromancy (*pitron he-ḥalom*), soothsaying (*'onanut*), divination (*niḥush*), and other such powers. Mathematical astronomy studies the heavenly bodies according to three rules (*kelalim*). The first studies their number and shapes and positions relative to each other and their degrees in the world, and the measures of their bodies in relation to each other, and the measures of some of their distances... The second studies the motions of the heavenly bodies, how many they are, and that their motions are all circular... It informs us of the place of each star in the constellations (*mazalot*)... The third studies the inhabited and uninhabited [areas of] the earth, and explains how much is inhabited and its great sections which are called climes. It enumerates the settlements which happen to be in each of these [climes] at this time... This is all that is mentioned in this science.[96]

For Ibn Ezra, however, there is no such clear distinction between mathematical astronomy and judicial astrology, and astral decrees fit in with his Neoplatonic emanationist cosmology. Unlike Rambam, he did not differentiate between the physical forces of the stars, which are subject to the laws of nature, and their spiritual influences, which transcend the physical, terrestrial realm. Ibn Ezra's astronomical works, such as *Reshit Ḥokhmah* ("Beginning of Wisdom")[97] intermix the two. For example, in ch. 8 of this work, Ibn Ezra discusses the conjunction (*molad*) of the moon and the *tequfot* (equinox; solstice), purely astronomical topics, but then writes:

#2. If the moon is moving by itself, that indicates any futile thing, and it signifies that anything which the asker requests cannot possibly occur.

#3. The planet which enters into conjunction or into aspect with the moon prognosticates every future thing and anything which the asker will expect; if the planet is favorable, it will be a boon; if the planet is unfavorable, it will bring harm.[98]

At the end of Ch. 9 of *Reshit Ḥokhmah* Ibn Ezra mentions his own astrological experiments:

In the same way the ancients have experimented in the matter of horoscopes (*moladot*), consultations (*she'elot*), and selections (*muvḥarim*) when the moon communicates force to one of the planets in degrees equal to the force of the

---

[96] Falaquera, *Reshit Ḥokhmah* Part II, Ch. 6; ed. Moritz David (Berlin, 1902), pp. 41–42, corresponding to *Iḥṣa Al-'Ulum*, ch. 3.

[97] Ibn Ezra and Falaquera both authored works with the same name, but they should not be confused with each other.

[98] Ibn Ezra, *Reshit Ḥokhmah*, ed. R. Levy and F. Cantera, Hebrew text p. lxii, English translation p. 216.

aspects (*mabatim*); as a result, they observed that their opinions were accurate at any moment in the quadrite, trine, or sextile aspect. Using the same method, we have also carried out experiments and we were successful.[99]

Ibn Ezra was convinced of the efficacy of astrology. In the last chapter (Ch. 10) of *Reshit Ḥokhmah* he states:

By means of directions (*nihugin*) one may predict all the good and harm which will befall kings, and the conquest of the kingdom of one nation by another, and the transformation of evil to good or good to evil, which are effected in the world both on universals and particulars.[100]

The stars also affect the economy. In his *Sefer Ha-'Olam* ("Book of the World") Ibn Ezra wrote:

All the astrologers (*ḥakhmei ha-mazalot*) say that the signs (*mazalot*; constellations) of fire and air indicate that high prices and hunger will prevail in the world...and the signs of earth and water indicate great satiation and inexpensive prices; one needs to look at the seasons of the whole year. If both Saturn and Jupiter are in expensive signs, they indicate high prices, and the opposite if they are in other signs.[101]

[V.11.b] ASTROLOGY IS NOT IDOLATRY, THEURGY OR MAGIC

Despite his positive attitude towards astrology, Ibn Ezra categorically rejected worshipping the stars, i.e., directing any prayer or request to created things rather than to the creator. The stars, as God's "servants" (*meshartim*) have no independent will: "The servants cannot change their path, nor can any of them transgress the law God gave it...Therefore they are neither beneficial nor harmful." In the final analysis, the stars are bodies, albeit "glorious" bodies, and as such they have no will or consciousness of their own. Their motions are mechanical and necessary, not voluntary or intentional.[102]

Since only God is to be worshiped, and the stars are only bodily "servants" operating in accordance with divinely established laws, the astrological study of astral decrees does not constitute idolatry (*'avodah zarah*). What is forbidden

---

99 Ibn Ezra, *Reshit Ḥokhmah*, Hebrew text p. lxxv, English translation p. 233.
100 Ibn Ezra, *Reshit Ḥokhmah*, Hebrew text p. lxxv, English translation p. 234. I have translated *kelalim* and *peratim* as universals and particulars, instead of "both in public and in private" in the translation.
101 Ibn Ezra, *Sefer Ha-'Olam*, ed. Y.L. Fleischer (reprint, Jerusalem 1970), p. 14.
102 Ibn Ezra, long (standard) commentary to Exodus 33:21.

is attributing independent powers to the stars, rivaling that of God. Therefore Ibn Ezra wrote that "'[God] brought them out in evil' (Exodus 32:12) means, according to our Sages, that they came out from Egypt under an evil constellar sign (*mazal*). [The Egyptians] said that God is unable to defeat the power of the constellar signs to save those who cleave to him, and therefore, since he had no power, he killed them. This is a desecration of the divine name."[103]

According to this view, astrology is not idolatry, since no independent will or power is attributed to the stars. Nor is astrology theurgy or magic, because it involves no attempt to influence or effect a change in the astral powers. In Ibn Ezra's approach, astrology is an attempt to understand the inevitable and necessary influences of the stars. A person who understands astral decrees can pray to God (and not to the stars) for miraculous redemption, or, as Ibn Ezra emphasizes, such a person can take action to avoid being harmed by what will necessarily occur.

Although it is thus legitimate to investigate astrological explanations (which, for Ibn Ezra, are scientific) of various phenomena recorded in the Bible, it is illegitimate to provide astrological explanations which border on idolatry. Therefore, in his explanation of the commandment to "make a fiery serpent (*saraf*)" (Numbers 21:8), Ibn Ezra forcefully rejected the view that the serpent was endowed with the ability to receive astral forces, and said:

> The form of a copper fiery serpent was written on a banner, that it might be high up so that all might see it. Many have been corrupted and said that this form was able to receive higher powers, God forbid, because this was done by a divine commandment. We must not search [for a reason] for the form of a snake. For have we not observed that there is a tree which can sweeten bitter water which even honey could not sweeten?...The truth is that such higher knowledge transcends us.[104]

Ibn Ezra thus rejects as idolatrous any theurgic or magical explanation of the fiery serpent. In other passages, it is the astrological explanation itself of a biblical phenomenon which precludes theurgy or magic. For example, Ibn Ezra regarded the *terafim* which Rachel stole from her father as "having human form, and made to receive higher powers." He continues:

> There are some who say that it is a copper tool made to know the time of day. Others say that astrologers have the power to make a form...capable of speech. Their proof is "the *terafim* have spoken nonsense" (Zechariah 10:2). But that is not the correct interpretation of the verse. It seems to me that the *terafim* have human form, and are made to receive higher powers. But I cannot explain

---

103   Ibn Ezra, Long (standard) commentary to Exodus 32:12.
104   Ibn Ezra, commentary to Numbers 21:8.

this...It seems most likely that her father Laban was an astrologer (*yode'a mazalot*), and she feared that her father might find out from the constellar stars which way they had fled.[105]

It is not clear why Ibn Ezra says "I cannot explain" how the *terafim* "receive the higher powers," but the reason may be to avoid crossing the boundary between astrology and idolatry. In any event, the efficaciousness of the *terafim* cannot be construed as idolatry, theurgy or magic, because they are a human tool enabling the astrolger to employ powers established by God, as part of the natural and astral order, not to change that order, but to understand and predict—and thereby to escape—their immutable harmful impact. The astrologer can only understand astral influences, nothing more. He cannot create or change these higher powers. As we shall see, it is precisely the inevitability and immutability of astral decrees that make them predictable, and thereby enable people to act in such a way as to escape their harmful effects. Those who attain such astrological knowledge are called "ones who know supreme knowledge" (*ha-yod'im da'at 'elyon*), a phrase taken, significantly, from the story of Balaam in Numbers 24:16. Such people are "the children of God" (*benei elohim*) in Genesis 6:2:

> The children of the judges who executed divine judgment on earth...In my view the correct interpretation of "children of God" is [a reference to] those who know supreme knowledge, who chose for themselves wives whose heavenly configuration (*ma'arekhet*) resembled each of theirs, and whose physical constitution (*toledet*) was like their physical constitution. That is why they produced mighty men.[106]

Astrologers who "know supreme knowledge" cannot change the higher powers they know, nor do they worship them. Their knowledge enables them to take appropriate action—in the case in question, to find a suitable mate with whom to produce heroic offspring.

There is also an essential difference between astrological prediction and prophecy. Ibn Ezra did believe that a magician (*qosem*) has the ability to foretell future events, because of his understanding "supreme knowledge," whereby he would also know what action to take—but he cannot change those future events. A prophet, on the other hand, because of his cleaving (*devequt*) to God, who transcends the higher forces of the stars, does not merely have supreme knowledge of the higher powers (which are, ultimately, part of natural

---

[105]   Ibn Ezra, commentary to Genesis 31:19. Tzvi Langermann understands Ibn Ezra as regarding the *terafim* as "talismans, magical devices for exploiting the astral powers that govern the various regions, rather than as objects of worship." ("Some Astrological Themes in the Thought of Abraham ibn Ezra," p. 47).

[106]   Ibn Ezra, commentary to Genesis 6:2.

reality), but also has a divine ability to perform supra-natural miracles, but it is God's power, not human power, that can change astral decrees and perform a miracle.

Ibn Ezra accordingly read the Balaam story astrologically. Balaam was a magician, not a prophet. His astrological understanding of "supreme knowledge" enabled him to predict the future, but not to determine or change it. Balaam was a scoundrel who fooled people: depending on what his astrological calculations informed him, he would "bless" or "curse" people, who in their simplicity believed that Balaam actually determined the future benefits or harm, and that it was his blessing or curse that would actually bring about those effects.

Ibn Ezra's astrological theory, however, raises questions with which he had to deal. First, how can a uniform influence of a higher astral power result in diverse effects in the terrestrial realm? Second, how can one reconcile the belief in astral determinism with the belief in human free will, without which it is difficult to accept a person's responsibility for his actions? Third, what are the implications of Ibn Ezra's theory for the unique status of the people of Israel and the Torah?

[V.11.c] A HIGHER POWER (*KOAH 'ELYON*) AND THE PHYSICAL CONSTITUTION (*TOLEDET*)

In his commentary to Deuteronomy 8:3 ("Not by bread alone does a person live, but by the utterance of the Lord does a person live") Ibn Ezra defines the term "higher power" (*koah 'elyon*):

> "The utterance of the Lord" — whatever he decreed... The meaning is that a person should not live by bread alone, but by the power, or with the power [coming] from the higher beings by God's command.

The stars and constellations are "higher" bodies, whose refined matter does not resemble coarse terrestrial matter. Their motions and their "configuration" (*ma'arekhet*), namely their place and relative position on the spheres, influence terrestrial events. The precise effect, however, of these higher powers is not determined by the higher power alone. No less important than the higher power above in determining the effect is the *toledet* — the physical constitution or make-up of the receiver (*meqabbel*) — below. In some respects the *toledet* is the physical make-up of the creature from the moment of its generation or nativity; in other respects, it is a faculty or power in the body which preserves the body. In Ibn Ezra's words: "When the rational soul (*neshamah*) strives, the faculty preserving the body strives, that the person should receive from the heavens; [that faculty] is called *toledet*."[107]

---

107   Ibn Ezra, Long (standard) commentary to Exodus 23:25.

Another name for astrology, accordingly, as "the science of the physical constitutions" (*hokhmat ha-toladot*),[108] in addition to the more common "science of the stars" (*hokhmat ha-kokavim*). The specific effects are produced by both factors together—the higher powers of the stars above and the physical make-up of the receiver (*meqabbel*) below. "Therefore, the intelligent have the power to choose good and evil, because the [astral] decrees are only in accordance with the receiver."[109]

When discussing Ibn Ezra's rejection of the rabbinic *midrash* that both versions of the Decalogue were revealed simultaneously,[110] we saw that what is below is no less important in determining events than what is above. In the case of revelation the limits of intelligibility are imposed not by God above, but below, by the human recipient of the revelation, just as it would be meaningless to broadcast on radio frequencies for which there are no receivers. In the case of astral decrees, it is the concept of the *toledet* that makes it possible to explain diverse and differing effects of a single and uniform astral decree. We recall that the questions of how multiple and different effects could be generated from the One, and how the material could emerge from the spiritual, were among the most problematical features of the Neoplatonic theory of emanation. Ibn Ezra's resolution to all these problems lies in the *toledet*. In our terms, it explains why two workers exposed over years to identical dangerous chemicals or radioactivity react differently, with the one remaining healthy while the other comes down with cancer, because of their different physical make-up. In Ibn Ezra's words:

> The root of evil lies in a deficiency in the receiver... We see how clothes spread out in the sun are bleached, while the launderer's face is darkened. Does not one action derive from one agent? Therefore, the actions differ because of differences in the physical constitution of the receiver (*toledet ha-meqabbel*). People's thoughts differ according to the physical constitutions of each body, and the differences of the physical constitution are because of different places in the heavenly configurations (*ma'arkhot ha-'elyonim*), in the place of the sun and of the receiver of its power, and in the countries, laws and foods.[111]

Similar points are made repeatedly. For example:

> Know that the decrees of God are the root of all actions and motions. The power and physical constitution of all beings beneath the sky, with roots below and similarly with compounds, are in accordance with the heavenly configuration

---

[108]   Thus in Ibn Ezra's long (standard) commentary to Exodus 18:13: "All the scientists of physical constitutions acknowledge..."

[109]   Ibn Ezra, *Yesod Mora Ve-Sod Ha-Torah* ch. 7:6, p. 144.

[110]   See above, V.4.c.i.

[111]   Ibn Ezra, Introduction to Qohelet (Ecclesiastes).

(*ma'arekhet 'elyonah*)...Individuals (*halaqim*) receive from the universals according to their physical constitution. They are able to change somewhat their physical constitution because of the power of the universals. That is what is meant by "The Lord strengthened Pharaoh's heart" (Exodus 9:12) and in another place, "He strengthened his heart, he and his servants" (Exodus 9:34). All this is true.[112]

The relation between the higher power and the receiver's physical constitution below thus depends on the interaction of both factors together, the higher and the lower. The configuration of the stars affects the physical constitution, and the receivers' physical constitutions, each in a different way, affect the influence of the higher power.

[V.11.d] ASTRAL DECREES AND HUMAN FREE WILL

Astral decrees are immutable, necessary and mechanical, as we have seen, not voluntary or conscious. How can such a scheme permit human free will? Despite the apparent determinism of this scheme, Ibn Ezra attributes great importance to the moral role of a person choosing good or finding a way to save himself from the astral decree.

The decree exists. Moreover, decrees are not created from moment to moment, but were determined when the laws of the configuration of the heavens were established. Commenting on Numbers 23:23, "What has God done?" Ibn Ezra notes that "the verb ["has...done"] is in the past tense, because everything is decreed. Even if it refers to the future, it was already decreed from the beginning." Nevertheless, people remain free, because God's decree and foreknowledge do not cause a person to choose whatever he chooses. "If God knows before a child exists whatever he will choose, God's foreknowledge does not cause the person to choose evil or to do good, since he gave him control and power."[113] However, Ibn Ezra does not actually explain how to resolve the apparent contradiction between God's foreknowledge and human free will. He was aware of the dilemma, and refers to it in his discussion of God's hardening Pharaoh's heart, where he states that "God gave the human wisdom and implanted in his heart the intellect to receive a higher power (*koah 'elyon*), to add to his goodness or to detract from his evil."[114]

How does the human intellect "receive a higher power to add to his goodness or to detract from his evil?" It seems that, in Ibn Ezra's view, a person is capable of overcoming his terrestrial "particularity," according to which he is subject to the necessary decrees of the higher powers, and to attain a degree of

---

[112]   Ibn Ezra, commentary to Deuteronomy 5:26.
[113]   Ibn Ezra, short commentary to Exodus 23:26.
[114]   Ibn Ezra, long (standard) commentary to Exodus 7:3.

angelic "universality" by means of intellectual attainment, given the inherently universal nature of intellection and the intelligibles. He also does not rule out the possibility of certain prophets, such as Moses, having the ability to change their *toledet* and thereby the effects of the astral decrees.

There are, then, two ways to reach this rank of transcending the laws of nature, including astral decrees: universal human intellectual attainment, by knowing the sciences in general, and specifically astrology; and a particular intellectual attainment unique to the people of Israel through the Torah.

In the first case, the decree exists, but the person who has mastered astrology can understand what will necessarily occur, and then take appropriate action to avoid the harmful effects of the decree. If, for example, he knows that a ship will sink at sea, he will avoid embarking on it. It is precisely the immutable and inevitable nature of the decree that enables the person to calculate its effects and take evasive action. The general rule thus makes possible the individual exception to the rule.

In the second case, if a Jew studies and observes the Torah, its laws will protect him from predictable harm. Moreover, the role of the Torah is "to strengthen and reinforce and increase the higher [i.e., rational] soul (*neshamah*) so that the body will not rule it... When they obey it, they become wise, and it guides them on the correct way to everything which will not harm them."[115]

In both cases, the more the rational soul, which is of the "species of the angels" transcending the stars, ascends in purity from materiality, the more it transcends the limitations of the terrestrial realm and enables the person to escape harmful astral decrees. According to Tzvi Langermann:

> It is quite clear to me that the salvation from astral decrees that is available to man refers, in Ibn Ezra's view, to man's ability to foresee impending disaster, usually by means of the science of astrology, and to take the appropriate precautionary measures.[116]

[V.11.e] THE POSSIBILITY OF RESCUE FROM ASTRAL DECREES

Ibn Ezra's conception of rescue from astral decrees reflects his three-fold cosmology, discussed above.[117] The "higher powers" of the stars derive from the middle or second realm, but the angels (and of course God) transcend the realm of the stars. The Neoplatonic upward way of purification of the rational soul and its return to its spiritual source takes on, for Ibn Ezra, astrological

---

[115]   Ibn Ezra, Long (standard) commentary to Exodus 23:25–26.
[116]   Tzvi Langermann, "Some Astrological Themes," p. 51.
[117]   See above, V.5.b.iii.

significance, because as the soul ascends, it transcends the "higher powers" of the stars and cleaves to God, like the angels of the highest or "upper realm," since the rational soul is of the same species as the angels. The basis of this conjunction with or cleaving to God—*devequt*—is the person's knowledge of God, namely recognition of divine actions in the world. Such knowledge, in turn, requires knowledge of the sciences in general and specifically astrology. The Torah also brings a person to this level, and it is the Torah which thus gives the people of Israel an advantage and spiritual superiority—including astrological—over other nations. This, as we shall see, is how Ibn Ezra understands the rabbinic statement that "Israel has no constellar sign" (*ein mazal le-yisra'el*).

This theme is reiterated in several different contexts. In one of these passages, Ibn Ezra explains astrologically the divine name *El Shaddai* ("Almighty God") in Exodus 6:3 as meaning "defeating the higher configurations" (*menaẓe'aḥ ha-ma'arakhot ha-'elyonot*).

> Now I will reveal to you the mystery of *El Shaddai*. We know that God created the three realms I have mentioned. Each individual in the lowest world receives a power from the middle world according to its higher configuration (*ma'arekhet 'elyonah*). Since the human [rational] soul (*neshamah*) is higher than the middle world, if that soul (*nefesh*) is wise and recognizes divine activities which are both immediate and intermediated, and if it puts aside the appetites of the lowest world, and stays solitary in order to cleave to God, then even if the configuration of the stars (*ma'arekhet ha-kokhavim*) at the time of its conception was such that on a given day evil might befall him, God, to whom he cleaves, will cause causes to save him from his evil. Thus, if the [astral] configuratiojn would [result in] his being barren, God can make his [physical] constitution (*toledet*) bear children. Therefore, the sages said that God told Abraham, "Abandon your astrology (*iẓtagninut*).[118] This is similar to the meaning of "Israel has no constellar sign" (*ein mazal le-yisra'el*)[119]...Therefore, before God said to Abraham "I will increase your seed" (Genesis 22:17) he said, "I am Almighty God" (*El Shaddai*), meaning defeating the higher configurations...so that one who cleaves to God's name should know that [God] creates something good which was not in accordance with his [higher, astral] configuration. That is why Jacob said, "The angel who saves me from all evil" (Genesis 48:16), who appropriately came to me. This is the secret of the whole Torah, as I shall explain. The patriarchs [Abraham, Isaac and Jacob] did not reach the rank of Moses—whom God knew face to face—in cleaving to God. That is why Moses was able to change [physical] constitutions in the lowest world, and to perform signs and miracles, which the patriarchs could not create.[120]

---

118 Babylonian Talmud Shabbat 156a.
119 Babylonian Talmud Shabbat 156a, Nedarim 32a, *et al.*
120 Ibn Ezra, Long (standard) commentary to Exodus 6:3.

Because of his unique conjunction (*devequt*) with God, Moses was able to transcend his terrestrial particularity and to attain a universal, angelic rank: "Moses became universal" (*ve-hineh Moshé shav kelali*).[121] Because of his attachment to this angelic rank, transcending the natural order of the lowest and middle worlds, Moses was able to perform supra-natural miracles violating the natural order, including the "higher configuration" of the stars. Therefore, Ibn Ezra says, "Know that when the part [i.e., the individual] knows the All [*ha-kol*, i.e., God], he cleaves to the All and by the All creates signs and miracles."[122]

The most complete discussion of all these themes, including astral decrees, free will and the possibility of rescue from the decrees, is found in Ibn Ezra's commentary to Exodus 33:21,[123] a passage to which he refers in several of the other passages.

> Do not think that the four physical constitutions [namely: hot, cold, dry and moist] are in heaven because there is heat in the sun, and cold in the moon and in Saturn. Perish the thought! All the higher [heavenly] creatures are glorious, and it is written of them, "For he commanded and they were created; he established them forever. He gave them a law which will not pass" (Psalm 148:5–6). They were only created this way for the receivers.[124] The servants [i.e., the planets] cannot change their path, nor can any of them transgress the law God gave it. All the heavenly and terrestrial host receive from them according to their make-up (*matkonet*), and they do not do good or evil. Worshipping the work of heaven cannot be beneficial [for a person], because whatever has been decreed according to the configuration of the stars at his nativity will definitely happen, unless a power superior to the power of the stars protect him, and he cleaves to it, so that he will then be saved from the decrees. I shall give you an example. Think that the configuration of the stars was such that a river would overflow onto a city and flood or kill people. A prophet came to warn them, that they should return to God before the day of their calamity. So they repented with all their heart. Because they cleaved to [God], he gave them the resolve to leave the city and pray to God. They did this on the day the river suddenly overflowed and flooded the city, as it was accustomed to do, as we ourselves have seen many times. So God's decree did not change, and yet he saved them. Or think of the planets, running like horses passing by in the race track. They do not run for good or for evil, but only because it is their way. Think that a blind man is on the race track, who does not know the custom of the horses, when they go to the right or to the left. So [the blind man] relies on a clever person who knows how they change [their path]. So he will protect [the blind man], for as [the horses] run to one side, he leads the blind man to the other side. So the horse race does not change, and yet the blind man escapes [harm].

---

121 Ibn Ezra, long (standard) commentary to Exodus 33:21.
122 Ibn Ezra, commentary to Numbers 20:8.
123 Ibn Ezra, long (standard) commentary to Exodus 33:21.
124 The four physical constitutions were created as qualities of terrestrial receivers and not of the stars.

In both cases of this parable — the river flooding and the horse race — there is a fixed and predetermined order to whatever happens, and it is this order that permits escape. The parable of the flooded city may be found in an Arabic work with which Ibn Ezra may reasonably be presumed to have been familiar, namely the Neoplatonic *Rasa'il Ikhwan Al-Safa* ("Letters of the Brethren of Purity").[125] The story is found in the Letter "On the Generation of Animals and Their Kinds," and is also found in the later Hebrew translation by Kalonymus ben Kalonymus in his *Iggeret Ba'alei Hayyim* ("Letter of the Animals").[126] In the original Arabic version, however, the king of the city was warned of the impending flood not by a prophet (as in Ibn Ezra's version), but by his astrologer (*munajjim*), which Kalonymus translated as "magician" (*qosem*) or "oracle" (*hozeh*).

Despite these differences of detail, what is common to both versions of the story of the flood threatening a city, that of Ibn Ezra and that of the Brethren of Purity, is that it is God, whose power is greater than the "higher power" of the stars, can enable people to escape inevitable, and therefore predictable, astral decrees. Both versions also share a pronounced moral-religious emphasis on repentance and living according to divinely revealed law. (Ibn Ezra's second parable, of the race track, is not found in the Arabic letters here).

Ibn Ezra's long passage continues, but introduces a new theme into his astrological theory, namely the uniqueness of the people of Israel, by virtue of the Torah:

> This is why God, after saying "Which the Lord your God allotted to all the nations" (Deuteronomy 4:19) adds: "The Lord has taken you to become his heritage nation" (Deuteronomy 4:20). "Not like them is the portion of Jacob; for he is the creator of all" (Jeremiah 51:19). This is the meaning of "I and your people were distinguished" (Exodus 33:16). This is what the Sages meant by saying "Israel has no constellar sign" (*ein mazal le-yisra'el*), **so long as they observe the Torah**. If they do not observe it, the constellar sign will rule them, as has been demonstrated, because every conjunction (*mahberet*) with the constellar sign of Aquarius (*deli*) is an evil configuration. So then evil will befall Israel. Those who know astrology (*hokhmat ha-mazalot*) acknowledge this. The heavenly configuration was in conjunction, so that [Israel] would remain many more years in Egyptian exile. However, since they cried out to God and returned to him, God saved them. Whatever happens generally also happens to the individual. Therefore, "Whoever observes the Torah is happy" (Proverbs 29:18).

---

125   On the Brethren of Purity and their encyclopedic letters, see the discussion in Ch. 3 (III.1.f.vii) and Ch. 4 (IV.1.c).

126   Kalonymos ben Kalonymos, *Iggeret Ba'alei Hayyim*, ed. Y. Toporovsky and A.M. Haberman (Jerusalem, 1949), Section V, ch. 5, pp. 137–140.

Thus, just as an individual person's rational soul can transcend the higher power of the stars to reach a power superior to that of the stars, so the Torah elevates all those who observe it to this rank. The Jewish people, in other words, has a unique cosmological status. In the words of Tzvi Langermann:[127]

> The deity has relegated to the stars the governance of the sublunar world. Israel, however, enjoys a special status, which is manifest most decisively in its possession of the Torah. As long as a Jew is engaged in the study and observance of the Torah, he is linked to a spiritual realm which is itself superior to the stars. In this way, a Jew may liberate himself from the decrees of the stars.

[V.11.f] THE PEOPLE OF ISRAEL AND THE TORAH OF ISRAEL: "ISRAEL HAS NO CONSTELLAR SIGN" (*EIN MAZAL LE-YISRA'EL*)

The Jewish people thus have a special status. Ibn Ibn Ezra's words: "The human being is the most honored [creature] on earth...And the most honored humans are Israel."[128] This special status means, for Ibn Ezra, that Israel is not subject to astral decrees.

> It is known from experience that every nation has a definite start and constellar sign (*mazal*), and so there is a constellar sign for every city. God has endowed Israel with great stature, that God [himself] is their counselor, and they have no star [of their own]. For Israel is God's inheritance.[129]

This unique status, however, involves no Jewish racial superiority. The superiority of Israel lies in the Torah, "so long as they observe the Torah," and not in the Jewish people. It is a behavioral, not a biological category (as it was for Ibn Ezra's friend Judah Ha-Levi, as we shall see in Chapter Six). Ibn Ezra explains this in his *Yesod Mora Ve-Sod Ha-Torah* ("The Foundation of Reverence and the Secret of the Torah"):[130]

> God took Israel as his inheritance, and removed them from the governance of the constellar signs, so long as they are in his governance by doing what he commanded them in his Torah. That is why our ancestors said, "Israel has no constellar sign" (*ein mazal le-yisra'el*). That is why it is written, "I and your people were distinguished" (Exodus 33:16). One cannot argue, How can God

---

127   Tzvi Langermann, "Some Astrological Themes," p. 49.
128   Ibn Ezra, Long (standard) commentary to Exodus 33:21.
129   Ibn Ezra, Commentary to Deuteronomy 4:19.
130   Ibn Ezra, *Yesod Mora Ve-Sod Ha-Torah*, ch. 7:6, pp. 144–145.

change the laws of heaven? This proves it. There are things which are completely good, because of all the good. Wisdom does not prevent something which is mainly good on account of some evil. Therefore, the intelligent (*maskil*) have the power to choose good and evil, because the decrees are only according to the receiver (*meqabbel*)...The individual benefits his soul by [what comes of him] in his end. Now pay attention and know that the commandments written in the Torah or received [by oral tradition] or enacted by our ancestors, although most of them [are related] to action or speech, all of them improve the heart...For evil is not dependent on the evil of the heart. This is known from astrology (*ḥokhmat ha-mazalot*).

The Torah is what causes a change in the person who "receives," so that astral decrees will not be able to affect him. Every person is theoretically capable of undergoing the lengthy and difficult process of purifying his soul and studying the sciences, until the rational soul cleaves to God, at which point his foreknowledge of the future enables him to escape the effects of astral decrees. In the case of the people of Israel, however, "so long as they observe the Torah," it raises them to this rank of those who cleave to God and are saved from astral decrees. As Tzvi Langermann has put it, "the Jews [have] been given a headstart, so to speak, along the same path of salvation that is open to all."[131]

In addition to the role of the Torah in the process of transcending astral decrees and establishing a direct contact—*devequt*—with God, the Land of Israel also plays a prominent role in this process. Ibn Ezra states: "Scripture mentioned this to inform us that the Land of Israel has a great preeminence."[132] What is it that endows the Land of Israel such preeminence?

As we have seen, both in regard to astral decrees and in regard to revelation, the role of the "receiver" below is no less important than that of the "higher power" above in determining what happens. In this frame of reference, the geographic location of the receiver also plays an important role in determining the quality of the reception, and certain geographic areas are more conducive to reception than others. "We know that God is one, and that change comes from the receivers...The worship of God includes protecting the power to receive in accordance with the location."[133]

Since "the power to receive" differs "in accordance with the location," practices—such as Jacob's marrying two sisters in their lifetime, a violation of the later prohibition in Leviticus 18:18—permitted in another country could not be permitted in the Land of Israel. Similarly:

---

131   Tzvi Langermann, "Some Astrological Themes," p. 51.
132   Ibn Ezra, commentary to Genesis 33:19.
133   Ibn Ezra, commentary to Deuteronomy 31:16.

We know that God's glory fills the whole world. However, there are places in which God's power can be seen more than in other places, on account of two things: the first, in accordance with the makeup of the physical constitutions of the receiver (*matkonot toladot ha-meqabbel*); the second, in accordance with the higher power (*koah 'elyon*) which is directly above the receiver. Therefore the location of the Temple was chosen.[134]

According to this approach, the preeminence and superiority of the Land of Israel as a whole, and of Jerusalem in particular, are a function of two factors. As we have seen consistently in Ibn Ezra's theory, the relation between the higher power above and the physical constitution of the receiver below is dependent on the interaction of both of them together. Here, too, the geographical advantage depends on the interaction of two factors, above and below. The Land of Israel has the advantage of being located in the superior median clime, and Jerusalem is in the center of Israel.[135] In addition to this advantageous geographical factor below, there is the factor above, namely the advantageous and especially beneficial stellar configuration directly above Jerusalem and the Temple Mount, "the higher power which is directly above the receiver." The site of the Temple was thus chosen "on account of two things"—the central clime below and the stellar configuration directly above it.

Thus it is specifically in the Land of Israel, especially in Jerusalem, that optimal conditions prevail for receiving a higher power. For Ibn Ezra, therefore, the Jewish ability to connect directly to God and to transcend astral decrees is not an innate biological or racial faculty like Judah Ha-Levi's *'amr 'ilahi* (Hebrew: *'inyan elohi*—"the divine faculty"), which permits direct communication with God. It is not nature but nurture—it is nurtured by their worship of God, "so long as they observe the Torah." It is further facilitated by the favorable location of the Land of Israel, with Jerusalem as its center, and the Temple in the middle of Jerusalem, "with the higher power which is directly above the receiver." When the Jews do not observe the Torah, they lose whatever advantage the Torah provides, and like all other nations, are then subject to astral decrees.

The people of Israel are thus "the inheritance of God," who governs them directly, without the intermediation of the stars. For Judah Ha-Levi, the

---

134   Ibn Ezra, long (standard) commentary to Exodus 26:1.
135   The theory of climes plays an important role in Judah Ha-Levi's conception of the centrality of the Land of Israel to the phenomenon of prophecy, as we shall see in Ch. 6. The study of climes was an important element in medieval geography. In Shem Tov ibn Falaquera's *Reshit Hokhmah*, pp. 41–42, a Hebrew paraphrase of Al-Farabi's *Enumeration of the Sciences*, geography is included as part of astronomy: "The third studies the inhabited and uninhabited [areas of] the earth, and explains how much in inhabited and its great sections which are called climes. It enumerates the settlements which happen to be in each of these [climes] at this time ... This is all that is mentioned in this science."

innate and biological or genetic prophetic "divine faculty" of Israel permits their receiving the Torah; it is the people of Israel who make possible the revelation of the Torah, since no other nation was biologically equipped to receive divine, prophetic communication. For Ibn Ezra, on the other hand, it is the observance of the Torah which gives the Jewish people their preeminence. Jewish distinctiveness is nurtured, not nature; behavioral, not biological. Or as Daniel Lasker has put it, software, not hardware.

To the extent that Ibn Ezra's theory involves a biological faculty, it has to do with a person's *toledet*, but this biological, physical make-up of a person is universally human and not distinctively Jewish, unlike Judah Ha-Levi's uniquely Jewish "divine faculty." It is precisely on this level of his physical constitution that the Jew, like any other human being, is subject to the stars which govern all terrestrial beings. For Ibn Ezra, the difference between the Jew and the non-Jew, therefore, cannot be physical, but spiritual, and it is nurtured by the observance of the Torah, which connects the Jew directly to a power superior to the "higher power" of the stars.

[V.12] SUMMARY

Astrology provides a way for individuals to know and understand the regular and immutable, and therefore predictable, astral decrees, and thereby to take appropriate precautions to avoid their harmful effects. As such, astrology could only benefit the intelligentsia, and those who would heed their warnings and forecasts. The Torah, on the other hand, benefits an entire nation in the same way, "so long as they observe the Torah." It connects their rational soul directly with the supreme realm of the angels, who are of the same species as the rational soul. On a bodily level, without observing the Torah, there is no difference between the Jew and the non-Jew in terms of being subject to astral decrees: "Whatever has been decreed according to the configuration of the stars at his nativity will definitely happen, unless a power superior to the power of the stars protect him, and he cleaves to it, so that he will then be saved from the decrees."[136]

In some respects (although obviously without its astrological components), Ibn Ezra's theory bears a formal resemblance and parallel to Rambam's theory of providence in the *Guide of the Perplexed* III:17 and especially III:51, which we shall discuss in Chapter Ten. According to Rambam, providence functions in proportion to intellectual attainment, by which an individual transcends his corporeal individuality and participates in universal knowledge, which enables them providentially to avoid harm. The parallel to Ibn Ezra's theory

---

[136]   Ibn Ezra, long (standard) commentary to Exodus 33:21.

consists in humans having a way, in virtue of the astrological knowledge they have attained, to connect directly with the angels, who are of the same species as the rational soul, and whose power is superior to the higher power of the stars. This knowledge, then, enables them to avoid the harmful effects of astral decrees. In both cases, Ibn Ezra's theory of astrology and Rambam's theory of providence, it is thus intellectual knowledge (with the Torah also playing a role in the scheme) which is the basis of a person's ability to transcend individuality and participate in universality, and thereby to transcend the fate of individual creatures and to escape harm.

The parallelism is formal; there is no agreement in terms of its content. Moreover, for Ibn Ezra, what happens to animals (and thus also to humans who lack knowledge) is astrally determined and necessary, whereas for Rambam, what happens to them is by chance. However for both thinkers it is the intellect (in Rambam's terms) or the rational *neshamah* (in Ibn Ezra's terms) by which they are enabled to transcend and escape their common destiny with other terrestrial creatures.

Ibn Ezra's interest in astrology follows logically from his tri-partite, Neoplatonic, hierarchical cosmology. Although his theory by no means precludes the possibility of supra-natural miracles, it understands divine intervention not magically or theurgically, but naturalistically, in terms of a knowledgeable person's ability to take advantage of predictable and necessary phenomena to take the precautionary measures needed to avoid harm. It is precisely the inevitability and immutability of astral decrees that provides the opportunity for escaping their harm.

The fact that Ibn Ezra consistently emphasizes the role of the Torah in helping those who observe it to avoid harm, and the clear moral thrust of the parable of the city about to be flooded, are evidence that for Ibn Ezra it is not sufficient to know the truth (as an astrologer may), but also to act and behave appropriately (as the Torah requires).

The Torah, which in any event should be interpreted in light of science (in this case, astrology), provides guidance for the people of Israel. Intelligent individuals may attain the necessary scientific, astrological foreknowledge of future events to take appropriate precautions. The Torah extends that protection to the entire Jewish people, "so long as they observe the Torah."

Chapter Six

JUDAH HA-LEVI AND
THE CRITIQUE OF PHILOSOPHY

[VI.1]   INTRODUCTION

Judah Ha-Levi was not the most profound or philosophically rigorous medieval Jewish philosopher, but he posed some of the most compelling existential questions we continue to face centuries later, and he had a way—perhaps because of his skills as a poet—of reducing complex questions to stark, basic formulas. For instance, we have discussed the differences between impersonal, philosophic conceptions of God (such as the Neoplatonic One) and the personal God of biblical religion, differences succinctly summarized by Ha-Levi in his contrasting "the God of Aristotle" and "the God of Abraham."

His racial conception of Jewish identity had an enormous (if not always desirable) impact on later Jewish thought, especially mystical,[1] but it creates obvious problems in both scientific terms (in what ways—if any—is it meaningful to suggest that a national, let alone a religious, identity is really transmitted genetically; is the concept of race in general scientifically valid, and if so, is it applicable to the Jewish people?) and in moral terms (especially in light of twentieth-century consequences of racialism, including, but by no means limited to, Nazism).

Yet, with all the problems of his theory of a racial or biological Jewish faculty for prophecy, who has posed as clearly Judah Ha-Levi, the contrast between the "God of Abraham" and the "God of Aristotle?" Where do we find a sharper (and more humorous) critique of the intellectual bankruptcy of

---

[1]   For example, the *Tanya* (*Liqqutei Amarim*) of Shneur Zalman of Lyady, the founder of Ḥabad-Lubavitch Hasidism, regards the gentiles as having a different soul from that of the Jews; the gentile soul emanates from "the other, unclean *qelipot* (shells, shards) which contain no good whatever" so that "all the good that the nations do, is done from selfish motives," (*Tanya*, ch. 1), whereas the Jews possesses a soul which "is truly a part of God above" (ch. 2).

the theory of emanation than in the *Kuzari*? And what other medieval thinker asked his readers so poignantly—but by extension also is asking us, the first generation Jews in two millennia to have a state and power, who (in the words of Emil Fackenheim) have "returned to history"—whether Jewish morality is not merely a function of powerlessness, not principle, "and if you had the power, you would also kill" (*Kuzari* 1:114)?

Ha-Levi drew upon a wide variety of sources, non-philosophical as well as philosophical, and exerted a great influence on later Jewish thought, including mystical trends. He was also a sharp critic of the prevalent Aristotelian philosophy of his day. Nevertheless, none of this means that his theory is not fundamentally philosophical in nature, for two reasons. First, the critique of philosophy, including pointing out the limits and limitations of rationalism, is itself an important philosophical subject. Second, Ha-Levi's approach, which emphasizes the historical facts which frequently contradict rationalist philosophical presumptions, is itself an attempt to provide what was for Ha-Levi a scientific explanation of historical reality, including the peculiar and even miraculous (in his view) history of the Jewish people, which violates normal historical patterns and rules.

It must be emphasized that in Judah Ha-Levi's view, the prevalent Aristotelian philosophy failed not because it is incompatible with the Torah, but because it is philosophically incorrect. He never argues that Aristotle erred because he contradicted some biblical teaching, but because his reasoning was unsound. Aristotle and the Aristotelian philosophers after him failed to demonstrate conclusively their claims; their conclusions, accordingly, are not necessarily true. Their philosophy was based on conventional assumptions which they accepted without scientific justification, and is, therefore, a "closed system" (in Yochanan Silman's phrase). In other words, the truth is already known *a priori*, and their "proofs" are not open to the challenge of contrary evidence or argument, as science requires. Aristotelianism thus does not qualify as a true scientific method, namely an "open system" that is open in its ability to process new empirical or historical evidence. In short, Judah Ha-Levi criticizes Aristotle and Aristotelianism for being unscientific in its subservience to preconceived notions and in its inability to take into account facts—whether natural or historical—which are inconsistent with those preconceived notions. Ha-Levi's critique of the philosophy of his day is thus itself philosophical and scientific.

[VI.2]   JUDAH HA-LEVI'S LIFE, STATUS AND INFLUENCE

[VI.2.a]   JUDAH HA-LEVI'S REPUTATION AS A POET

Judah Ha-Levi's reputation as one of the greatest Hebrew poets of Spain was recognized already in his lifetime. His contemporary, Moses ben Jacob ibn Ezra (c. 1055–1135 C.E.) wrote a lengthy poem praising Ha-Levi, "My brother Judah."[2]

> I detest all the pleasures of time, except…
> The writings of my brother Judah, because
> They were sweet in my mouth, and more delightful than gold.

In another poem praising the young Judah, Moses ibn Ezra wrote:

> Columns of poems were more precious than gold /
> One of them would pursue a myriad…
> How can such a pleasant youth /
> Carry on his back mountains of understanding.[3]

Similar high praise is found in poems by the poet-philosophers Joseph ibn Zaddik[4] and Judah Al-Ḥarizi.[5] Al-Ḥarizi recognized Ha-Levi's unique stature: "He entered the chamber of poetry alone / Until he left it and closed its doors."[6]

[VI.2.b]   JUDAH HA-LEVI AND ABRAHAM IBN EZRA

High regard for Judah Ha-Levi also typifies the references to him in the Bible commentaries of Abraham ibn Ezra, who was his close friend and apparently

---

2 Moses ibn Ezra, "Aḥi Yehudah," cited in Israel Zamorah, *Rabbi Yehudah Ha-Levi: Qovez Mehqarim Ve-Ha'arakhot* (Tel Aviv, 1950), pp. 5–6.

3 Moses ibn Ezra, "Ben Na'im Ve-Za'irShanim," cited in Israel Zamorah, *Rabbi Yehudah Ha-Levi*, pp. 7–8.

4 Joseph ibn Zaddik was born in Cordova, Spain in or before 1075. His philosophical book, *Ha-'Olam Ha-Qatan* ("The Microcosm") has a Neoplatonic orientation. By knowing himself as a corporeal and spiritual being, a person comes gradually to know the macrocosm, and thereby ultimately God.

5 Judah Al-Ḥarizi was born in Spain in 1170, and translated Arabic poetry into Hebrew. His original work, *Taḥkemoni*, adopts Arabic poetic forms. His prose translations include Ḥunayn ibn Isḥaq's *Aphorisms of the Philosophers* and Rambam's *Guide of the Perplexed*. He died in 1235.

6 Judah Al-Harizi, *Taḥkemoni*, Ch. 3, pp. 42–44, also cited in Zamorah, *Rabbi Yehudah Ha-Levi*, pp. 10–11.

also related to him by marriage. (So far as we know, Abraham ibn Ezra's son was married to Judah Ha-Levi's daughter, and also accompanied Ha-Levi on his journey to Israel). Whereas Ibn Ezra sharply criticized or mocked people whose opinion he rejected, his references to Ha-Levi are always respectful, even when they disagreed.

For instance, in his long (i.e., standard) commentary to Exodus 9:1, Ibn Ezra cites Judah Ha-Levi's view that the ten plagues had a double, ascending hierarchical structure. The first two plagues (blood and frogs) were based on water. The third and fourth plagues (lice and flies) came from the earth. The fifth and sixth plagues (animal plague and boils) came from the air. The seventh and eighth plagues (hail and locusts) came from spheres of storms and fire. The ninth and tenth plagues (darkness and killing the first-born) came from the spheres of the stars and divine glory (*kavod*).

As we saw in the last chapter, Ibn Ezra cites a disagreement with Ha-Levi (who had died in the meantime) on the meaning of "I am the Lord who brought you out of the land of Egypt, the house of bondage" (Exodus 20:2). For Ha-Levi (as we shall see in his *Kuzari*), the verse is a statement of indisputable historical truth that is far more certain than unreliable metaphysical speculation, whereas for Ibn Ezra, the first part of the first ("I am the Lord your God") is aimed at the intelligentsia, whereas the historical reference in second part of the verse ("who brought you our of the land of Egypt") is aimed at the masses.

> Judah Ha-Levi, may he rest in peace, asked me why the Torah says, "I am the Lord your God, who brought you out of the land of Egypt," and did not say, "who created the heaven and the earth, and I made you." This was my response to him. Know, that the degrees of people are not equal regarding the belief in their heart, i.e., that they believe in God. Many believe in what they hear, when their masters tell them something. Above them are those who saw something written in the Torah that God gave to Moses. But if a heretic were to claim that there is no God, they would cover their mouths with their hand, and not know how to respond. But one who is motivated to study the sciences...recognizes the action of God in the minerals, plants and animals, and in the human body itself...And his heart will rise afterwards to know the heavenly spheres, which are God's action in the enduring middle world...He will know all these things with indubitable and absolute proofs. By knowing God's ways the intelligent comes to know God...God mentioned in the first statement, "I am the Lord your God," which can only be understood by a great sage...that only God endures without change...Therefore, "I am the Lord your God" suffices for the intelligent of every nation...However, only Israel acknowledge this, and the sages of the nations do not deny, that only God made heaven and earth. The [gentiles sages], however, say that God eternally makes [the world], without beginning or end. But God performed signs and wonders in Egypt...God did for Israel what he

did not do for any other nation... Everyone saw this — sages and those who are not sages, great and small... He mentioned "I am the Lord your God" for the intelligent, and added "who brought you out," for the intelligent and for those who are not intelligent.[7]

The intelligent can recognize in the structure of the world, including the human body, the work of God's wisdom. For such people, it would have been sufficient to state merely "I am the Lord your God," because God's existence is recognized by all intelligent people, Jews and gentiles alike, although the gentile intelligentsia affirm God as the agent of an eternal, rather than created, world. The Torah, however, was given to the entire people, and could not base the commandments upon an abstract metaphysical principle the masses are incapable of comprehending, so God added "who brought you out of the land of Egypt," which all the Israelites — intelligentsia and masses alike — had personally experienced and could comprehend. The historical truth, which for Ibn Ezra was thus a concession to the masses, who cannot comprehend metaphysical truth, was for Judah Ha-Levi far more reliable than metaphysical speculation. The two friends thus respectfully disagreed.

[VI.2.c]   JUDAH HA-LEVI'S BIOGRAPHY

Judah Ha-Levi was born in Spain, sometime before 1075 C.E. In his youth he moved to Granada and then to Cordova, where he won a contest to imitate a complex poem by Moses ibn Ezra, who was impressed by the young Judah and became his patron. During this period, Ha-Levi composed secular poetry in praise of friends, wine and love. Following the decline of Jewish life in Andalusia resulting from its conquest by the Murabitun (or: Almoravides, a north African Berber dynasty), he moved to Toledo in Christian Castille. Later, together with Abraham ibn Ezra, he returned to Muslim Spain and was warmly received by the Jewish communities he visited. He also developed a close personal and financial relationship with an Egyptian Jewish merchant, Halfon ben Netanel. The two friends were involved together in ransoming a captive Jewish girl in the summer of 1125.

The increasingly difficult situation of the Jews of Spain, and the capture of Jerusalem by the Crusaders in 1099, gave rise to messianic speculation and the feeling that the difficulties were the "birth-pangs of the messiah." Ha-Levi shared these messianic expectations, and in 1130 had a dream in which the Muslim rule collapsed. When that hope failed to materialize, Ha-Levi came to realize that the true redemption of the Jewish people from exile lay in *'aliyah*, immigration to the Land of Israel, and he wrote to Halfon

---

[7]   Ibn Ezra, long (standard) commentary to Exodus 20:2.

ben Netanel of his determination to make 'aliyah. Nevertheless, despite this Zionist determination, Ha-Levi felt strong ties—expressed in poems—to his family, to his friends and to Spain, an inner conflict reflected in the concluding paragraphs of his *Kuzari*. For Judah Ha-Levi, however, 'aliyah was not merely a matter of personal fulfillment, as it was for other medieval Jews. As the historian B.Z. Dinur, and the scholar of medieval Hebrew poetry H. Schirmann have shown, 'aliyah was, for Judah Ha-Levi, a way of bringing about the redemption of Israel, and the *Kuzari* concludes with the explicit decision to leave Spain for Zion.

Did Judah Ha-Levi ever reach Zion? The question continues to be debated. According to a popular legend, recorded in the historical work *Shalshelet Ha-Qabbalah* ("The Chain of Tradition") by Gedaliah ibn Yiḥya (1515–1578), Ha-Levi arrived in Jerusalem, composed his poem "Ode to Zion," and was trampled to death by an Arab horseman. On the other hand, letters from the Cairo Genizah published by S.D. Goitein indicate that he arrived in Alexandria, Egypt on 8 September 1140, together with Isaac, the son of Abraham ibn Ezra. Ha-Levi stayed in Alexandria for some months, until the end of the Ḥanukkah festival, when he journeyed to Cairo and stayed with his friend Ḥalfon ben Netanel, and enjoyed the honors he received from the Cairo Jewish community. We have poems he composed during this period, expressing his admiration for Egypt and the Nile, but reaffirming his determination to leave the Egyptian desert for the Judean desert, and asking his friends and admirers in Egypt not to attempt to dissuade him from his goal. After the Passover holiday in 1141, Ha-Levi returned to Alexandria and boarded a ship scheduled to leave for the Land of Israel, but the departure was delayed due to stormy weather.

It seems that while waiting in the boat for a favorable west wind, Ha-Levi wrote two more poems, the first of which expresses the hope for a west wind which would take the boat "the the sacred mountains, where it would rest." The second poem, the last poem we have by Judah Ha-Levi, is a prayer to God to take him away from "the yoke of Arabia" and to "approach the place of the yoke of your love."

Other letters from the Cairo Genizah refer to Judah Ha-Levi's death, possibly in Egypt, in July, 1141. Nevertheless, such scholars as S.D. Goitein, Yosef Yahalom and Ezra Fleischer conclude that Judah Ha-Levi did, in fact, reach the Land of Israel via the port of Akko (Acre), and that he may have died in Jerusalem.

[VI.3] JUDAH HA-LEVI'S POETRY

[VI.3.a] JUDAH HA-LEVI ON POETRY

We have over 800 poems written by Judah Ha-Levi, including poems in praise of friends and patrons, love and wine poems, and religious poetry. Among his most famous poems are some 35 dealing with the longing for Zion. His *Kuzari* 2:70–80 and an essay he wrote on poetry include a discussion of poetic forms, in which the poet criticizes the rhyme and metric conventions, however beautiful they may be, that Hebrew poets borrowed from Arabic poetry. Such foreign forms, he argued, especially meter, are artificial devices that undermine natural Hebrew syntax and the proper pronunciation of Hebrew words, without which their true meaning cannot be understood. Conversely, biblical poetry, which was intended for public reading (for example, by the Levites in the Temple), is not artificially constrained by meter, because its purpose was to convey truth, not merely beauty. Biblical poetry is thus superior to the Hebrew poetry of the Middle Ages.

In his later years, Judah Ha-Levi thus rejected literary conventions to which he had long adhered as a highly successful poet, when he had not only adopted Arabic poetic forms, but even mixed Arabic verses into his Hebrew poems. Nevertheless, even in the last year of his life, in Egypt—after he wrote the *Kuzari* and his essay—he continued to write poems employing these literary forms.

Some scholars have suggested that in his latter years, Ha-Levi rejected Arabic literary forms as inappropriate "foreign wisdom," in favor of authentic Jewish, i.e. biblical, forms. Others have suggested that Ha-Levi, like Baḥya ibn Paquda, rejected the superficial culture of Jewish courtiers (a life he had lived for many years). Still other scholars see his change of heart in spiritual terms, as a kind of repentance. In any event, Judah Ha-Levi's continuing use of foreign poetic devices indicates that his critique is not merely an argument over literary forms, but reflects a deeper, inner conflict on both a cultural and spiritual level.

However we are to understand the poet's critique of poetry, and whatever conflicts he experienced, Judah Ha-Levi was able to laugh at himself. One of his poems deals with his first white hair:[8]

A single white hair alone did stand
On my head, till I plucked it with my hand.
It replied: Alone I'm defeated by you,
But after me comes my army! Then what will you do?

---

[8]   Cf. the original in Ḥayyim Schirmann, *The Hebrew Poetry of Spain and Provence* (Jerusalem: Mosad Bialik, 1961), #178, p. 444. Translation by Raphael Jospe.

[VI.3.b] LONGING FOR ZION

Among Judah Ha-Levi's most beloved poems are those dealing with his longing for Zion. One of the most popular of them is his "My Heart is in the East."[9]

> My heart is in the east, and I am in the farthest west.
> How can I taste whatever I eat, and how can it please?
> How can I fulfill my vows and pledges, while
> Zion is in the territory of Edom, and I am in the chains of Arabia?
> It would be easy for me to leave all the goodness of Spain,
> But it would be precious to behold the dust of the destroyed Temple.[10]

Another popular poem expressing the longing for Zion is "Jerusalem" or "Beautiful Heights," in which the poet plays with frequent double-entendres and references to biblical themes:[11]

> Beautiful heights, joy of the world, city of a great king,
> For you my soul yearns from the lands of the west.
> My pity collects and is roused when I remember the past,
> Your glory in exile, and your temple destroyed.
> Would that I were on the wings of an eagle,
> So that I could water your dush with my mingling tears.
> I have sought you, although your king is away,
> And snakes and scorpions oust Gilead's balm.
> How I shall kiss and cherish your stones.
> Your earth will be sweeter than honey to my taste.[12]

---

9   Cf. the original in Ḥayyim Schirmann, *The Hebrew Poetry of Spain and Provence*, #208b, p. 489. Translation by Raphael Jospe.

10   Explanation: Ha-Levi is in Spain, the "farthest west," but dreams of Zion in the east. He does not complain of material poverty and hunger: he has food, but how can it please; he has "all the goodness of Spain," but that is meaningless compared to the "dust of the destroyed Temple." In line 2, "how" is the Hebrew *eikh*, but in line 3, "how" is the Hebrew *eikhah*, the poetic form of the word with which the book of Lamentations opens. "Zion is in the territory of Edom," because the biblical Edom became in rabbinic usage a code word for Rome, which in turn in medieval usage came to represent the Church, and the Jerusalem was captured by the Crusaders in 1099. Ha-Levi, on the other hand, lived in "the chains of Arabia" in Muslim Spain.

11   Cf. the original in Ḥayyim Schirmann, *The Hebrew Poetry of Spain and Provence*, #208c, p. 489. Translation by David Goldstein in *The Jewish Poets of Spain* (Middlesex: Penguin, 1971), p. 129.

12   Explanation. The first line is based on Psalm 48:3. "City of a great king" — is the poet referring to Jerusalem as the city of David, or as the city of God? In line 3, "when I remember the past," Ha-Levi uses the term *qedem*, which can mean that which is before us temporally, i.e., the past, or that which is before us spatially, i.e. the east.

Ha-Levi's "Ode to Zion"—the poem he composed, according to the legend cited above, when he arrived in Jerusalem and was killed by an Arab horseman—consists of 68 stanzas, has been adopted by many Jewish communities for recitation among the *Kinot* ("Lamentations") on Tish'ah Be-Av.[13] The poem begins as follows:[14]

Zion, will you not seek the peace of your prisoners,
The remnants of your flocks, who seek your peace?
From west and east, from north and south, take the peace
From far and near, from all sides.
The peace of the prisoner of desire, who sheds his tears like the dew
Of [Mount] Ḥermon, and longs to shed them on your hills.
I am the jackal to weep for your affliction. But when I dream
Of the return of your captivity, I am the harp for your songs.[15]

Whereas modern maps have a northern orientation, because of the magnetic compass, classical maps—including the Madaba map of the Holy Land—face east, since the rising sun is the simplest way of orienting oneself. Indeed, the very term "orientation" originally meant to face east. So *qedem* is also a case of double-entrendre. Line 4, "your glory in exile," can also be understood on a human level—the exile of the Jewish people from Zion—or on a divine level—the rabbinic tradition of the parallel exile of the *shekhinah*, the divine presence, which accompanied Israel in exile. In line 5, "the wings of an eagle" is a reference to Exodus 19:4, where God promises to bring Israel to its homeland on the wings of eagles. In line 7, the "king"—again—can be understood on either a human or a divine level. Line 10 is reminiscent of concluding lines of "My Heart is in the East."

13 Tish'ah Be-Av is the fast of the 9th of Av, commemorating the destruction of the first and second Temples and of Jerusalem.

14 See the poem in *The Authorised Kinot for the Ninth of Av* by Abraham Rosenfeld (New York: Judaica Press, 1979), pp. 152–153. Cf. the original in Ḥayyim Schirmann, *The Hebrew Poetry of Spain and Provence*, #208, p. 489. Translation by Raphael Jospe. Other translations may be found in David Goldstein, *The Jewish Poets of Spain*, p. 131, and Nina Salaman, *Selected Poems of Jehudah Halevi* (Philadelphia: Jewish Publication Society, 1928), pp. 3 and 151.

15 Explanation. *Shalom*, peace, also means well-being. "The remnants of your flocks," i.e. those Jews who have survived centuries of exile and persecution and are the remnants of ancient Israel. Mount Ḥermon (elevation: 2814 meters) is the highest mountain in the region, forming a boundary between Israel, Lebanon and Syria, and is regularly covered by snow in the winter. "When I dream of the return of your captivity" is based on Psalm 126: "A Song of Ascents. When the Lord returned the captivity of Zion, we were like dreamers." In turn, Naomi Shemer composed the song "Jerusalem of Gold" during the difficult weeks before the Six Day War of June, 1967, when the State of Israel was facing the mobilization of the surrounding Arab countries, with the refrain based on Judah Ha-Levi's poem: "Jerusalem of gold, of copper and of light, am I not the harp for all your songs?"

[VI.4]   THE INTELLECTUAL AND CULTURAL BACKGROUND OF JUDAH HA-LEVI

[VI.4.a]   JUDAH HA-LEVI AND NEOPLATONISM

As noted in the Introduction to this chapter, Judah Ha-Levi drew from a wide variety of sources, and does not fit into conventional categories as did Sa'adiah Ga'on with the Kalam or Solomon ibn Gabirol with Neoplatonism. He is, however, often associated with Neoplatonism. Julius Guttmann's masterful *Philosophies of Judaism* presents Ha-Levi's thought in the chapter on Neoplatonism, and states:

> The singular figure of Judah Halevi belongs to no philosophic school. Only the fact that some strands of his thought link him with the Neoplatonic tradition justify discussing him in this context.[16]

Guttmann qualifies his linking Ha-Levi with Neoplatonism by noting the fundamental difference between Ha-Levi's conception of a personal God activing willfully and the Neoplatonic conception of an impersonal God functioning by inner necessity:

> Judah Halevi ... emphatically distinguishes the God of Israel, who works miracles and freely interferes in the course of the world which he created, from the God of philosophy, the first cause of the world, acting by an inner necessity.[17]

Nevertheless, according to Guttmann, the difference between Ha-Levi's conception of God and the Neoplatonic conception refers only to the activity of God, and not the divine essence. He concludes his discussion of Ha-Levi and his chapter on Neoplatonism thus:

> But the same conception of the divine essence underlies both viewpoints. Judah Halevi's religious idea of God advances a new theory of divine action, not of divine essence. The God of Abraham, to whom the soul cleaves in yearning and longing, is conceived metaphysically in terms of the Neoplatonic idea of God.[18]

This linkage of Judah Ha-Levi with Neoplatonism is also explicit in Colette Sirat's discussion of Ha-Levi in her more recent book, *A History of Jewish Philosophy in the Middle Ages*. Like Guttmann, Sirat emphasizes the free and

---

16   Julius Guttmann, *Philosophies of Judaism* (New York: Holt, Rinehart, Winston, 1964), p. 120.
17   Guttmann, *Philosophies of Judaism*, p. 132.
18   Guttmann, *Philosophies of Judaism*, p. 133.

voluntary activity of God in Ha-Levi's thought, which she suggests, is based on the Neoplatonic cosmology in the *Theology of Aristotle*:[19]

> This scheme of the universe corresponds exactly to that of the Theology of Aristotle[20] in its long recension ... If Judah Halevi had been content with this one hierarchy, his system would have been very similar to that of the Neoplatonists, who hypothesized intellectual illumination, but for our author God also acts in an immediate way.

S.D. Goitein also emphasized the similarity between Judah Ha-Levi's thought and Neoplatonism, especially in the first four of the five sections of the *Kuzari*, as opposed to the newer Aristotelian philosophy criticized by Ha-Levi in the fifth section of the book.[21]

This linkage between Judah Ha-Levi and Neoplatonism is ultimately unhelpful for three reasons. First, as acknowledged by Guttmann, Ha-Levi consistently emphasizes God's free, voluntary and immediate action in creating the world and in intervening in history (the personal God that Ha-Levi called "the God of Abraham" as opposed to the impersonal, philosophic "God of Aristotle"). As we have seen, even such overtly Neoplatonic thinkers as Isaac Israeli and Solomon ibn Gabirol differed from Plotinus in emphasizing creation as part of their generally emanationist cosmology. In the case of Israeli, first form and first matter were created *ex nihilo*, and the first intellect resulted from the combination of first matter and form; the subsequent emanation of the lower stages begins with first intellect. Similarly, Solomon ibn Gabirol, who was the first to use the Hebrew term *yesh me-ayin*, differentiated between the creation *ex nihilo* of the first stage (universal matter and universal form) and the subsequent emanation of the lower stages of reality, by introducing a new stage, the divine will. The Neoplatonic Jewish philosophers thus attempted to harmonize the biblical notion of voluntary creation with Plotinus' cosmology of necessary and impersonal emanation. For Judah Ha-Levi, however, God's free, immediate and voluntary involvement in the world is not restricted to the first stage of creation, but continues throughout history, as exemplified by the miraculous history of Israel. His religious conception of God thus differs radically from philosophic conceptions, whether Neoplatonic or Aristotelian.

---

[19]   Colette Sirat, *A History of Jewish Philosophy in the Middle Ages* (Cambridge: Cambride University Press, 1985), p. 125. On the *Theology of Aristotle*, review the discussion above, Ch. 3 (III.1.c).

[20]   My emendation. The English translation of Sirat's French book by M. Reich has here "Aristotle's *Theology*." The original French is clear; cf. Colette Sirat, *La Philosophie Juive Medievale en Terre D'Islam* (Paris: Presses du CNRS, 1988), p. 142.

[21]   S.D. Goitein, "The Biography of Rabbi Judah Ha-Levi in the Light of the Cairo Geniza Documents," in *Proceedings of the American Academy of Jewish Research* 28 (1959), p. 47.

Second, Colette Sirat points to the similarity between Ha-Levi's hierarchical cosmology and that of Plotinus in the *Theology of Aristotle*. A hierarchical structure, however, is not necessarily Neoplatonic, and may simply reflect the traditional geocentric cosmology which prevailed from classical times through the Middle Ages until the Copernican revolution in astronomy in the 16th century.

Third, and most important, Judah Ha-Levi emphatically rejected the emanation theory which is at the heart of Neoplatonic cosmology. The point is not merely that there is a hierarchy, but that in Neoplatonism the hierarchical stages are related through emanation of the lower by the higher. The theory of emanation, which is the heart of Neoplatonic cosmology, was shared not only by Neoplatonists like Isaac Israeli and Solomon ibn Gabirol before Ha-Levi, but also, at least in some respects, by such Aristotelians after Ha-Levi as Rambam.

In light of these three considerations, it is difficult to agree with Guttmann that "Judah Halevi's religious idea of God advances a new theory of divine action, not of divine essence." Guttmann himself acknowledged Ha-Levi's rejection and sharp mockery of the theory of emanation:

> He discusses with a good deal of sarcasm the somewhat bizarre theory of emanation of the Arab Aristotelians, according to whom every separate intellect emits another intellect when it thinks of God, but a sphere when it thinks of itself.[22]

In contrast with Rambam, who accepted aspects of the theory of emanation (with some reservations about its problematical points),[23] Judah Ha-Levi rejected in principle emanation as such; not that Aristotle had failed to prove it conclusively, but that it ultimately is nonsense. His rejection, it must be noted, is not on religious grounds, namely that the impersonal and necessary emanation of one stage from another contradicts the biblical conception of voluntary creation by a personal God, but on philosophic grounds: emanation is fundamentally unreasonable, and reason cannot tolerate it.

> Philosophers speculating on these things arrive at the conclusion that from one, only one can issue. They conjectured an angel, standing near to God, and having emanated from the Prime Cause. To this angel they attributed two characteristics; first, his consciousness of his own existence by his very essence;

---

[22] Guttmann, *Philosophies of Judaism*, p. 122.

[23] In the *Guide of the Perplexed* 2:22 Rambam summarizes aspects of the theory of emanation, but acknowledges that the theory is problematical. Rambam's conclusion is that whatever Aristotle said regarding sub-lunar (i.e., terrestrial) affairs is undoubtedly true, but that what Aristotle said regarding celestial affairs is merely his personal opinion and conjecture, and lacks conclusive scientific demonstration.

secondly, his consciousness of having a cause. Two things resulted from this, viz. an angel and the sphere of fixed stars... People accepted this theory, and were deceived by it to such an extent, that they looked upon it as conclusive, because it was attributed to the Greek philosophers. It is, however, a mere assertion without convincing power, and open to various objections... Whence do we know altogether that if a being became conscious of its essence a sphere must arise, and from the recognition of the Prime Cause, an angel must arise? When Aristotle asserts that he was conscious of his existence, one may consistently expect that a sphere should emanate from him, and when he asserts that he recognized the Prime Cause, an angel should emanate... These rudiments are as unacceptable to reason as they are extravagant in the face of logic. Neither do two philosophers agree on this point... Aristotle, Plato and many others entirely disagree with each other.[24]

The philosophers, Ha-Levi argues, only agree with each other when they follow on a common teacher or school of thought, because their views on such matters as emanation are nothing more than unproven opinion and unsubstantiated conjecture. Their unscientific speculation is, therefore, an insult to reason, so reason insults them:

They start with views which deprecate reason, but are deprecated by the latter. An example of this is their explanation of the cause of the revolution of the sphere... The contrived similar theories with regard to the emanations from the Prime Cause, viz., that from the intuition of the first cause an angel arose; and from its knowledge of itself a sphere arose, and thence downward in eleven degrees, until the emanation arrived at the Active Intellect, from which neither an angel nor a sphere developed. All these things are still less satisfactory than the "Book of Creation" (*Sefer Yezirah*).[25] They are full of doubts, and there is no consensus of opinion between one philosopher and another.[26]

Some have suggested, contrary to this reading of Ha-Levi, that he did believe in the theory of emanation, as evidenced by his use of the Arabic term

---

[24]   Judah Ha-Levi, *The Kuzari* 4:25, translated by Hartwig Hirschfeld (1905) (New York: Schocken Books, 1964), pp. 238–239.

[25]   The *Sefer Yezirah* ("Book of Creation" or "Book of Formation") is an early mystical text, attributed to Abraham, which dates from the first centuries C.E., and opens by describing the building blocks of creation as "thirty-two mysterious ways," namely the 22 letters of the Hebrew alphabet and the ten cardinal numbers. For a discussion of how Jewish philosophers from Sa'adiah Ga'on to Judah Ha-Levi related to this work, see "Early Philosophical Commentators on the *Sefer Yezirah*, in Raphael Jospe, *Jewish Philosophy: Foundations and Extensions, Volume Two: On Philosophers and Their Thought* (Lanham: University Press of America, 2008), ch. 7; originally published in *Revue des Etudes Juives* CXLIX, no. 4, 1990, pp. 369–415.

[26]   Judah Ha-Levi, *Kuzari* 5:14. Hirschfeld trans. p. 273.

faiḍ (emanation). For example, in the *Kuzari* 5:10, he says that a person's hylic intellected is "emanated" onto him by "the divine faculty" (*al-amr al-ilahi*). We cannot infer from Ha-Levi's use of the term here that he generally believed in the theory of emanation, because in this passage he is describing, in their own terms, various philosophical views regarding different natural forms in the minerals, plants, animals and humans, differences reflecting diverse matter, place, climate and composition, and explaining why prophecy is emanated onto some people, while other people only attain lower ranks.

Elsewhere, when discussing in the *Kuzari* 2:26 the biblical sacrificial system in the Temple, he states that the "divine faculty" benefits all who follow its guidance in the proper order of the sacrifices. These sacrifices are for the benefit of people, not God. Light, wisdom and knowledge are "emanated" onto such a person who correctly performs the sacrifices. Here, too, the term "emanate" is used in relation to "the divine faculty" (which will be discussed later), and has nothing to do with epistemological, let alone the ontological, connotations of the Neoplatonic theory of emanation, in which all knowledge, and indeed all being, are emanated onto the lower stage by the higher stage. Similarly, in the *Kuzari* 2:50, Ha-Levi maintains that a balanced observance of the Torah's commandments brings one closer to God than do ascetic practices, and states that the Jewish people, by observing the divine commandments of the Torah, merit receiving the divine light, which is called "love" and which is emanated onto them by "the divine faculty." Again, the discussion has nothing to do with the epistemological and ontological hierarchy of Neoplatonic emanation, but refers to the special loving relationship between God and the Jewish people and the Land of Israel.

Judah Ha-Levi's occasional use of the term "emanation" is, therefore, to be understood contextually, and it never refers to the epistemological, let alone ontological, functions of the term in the Neoplatonic theory, which remains, in Ha-Levi's terms, unsatisfactory, unproven, unreasonable and illogical.

[VI.4.b] JUDAH HA-LEVI AND MYSTICISM

[VI.4.b.i] *Methodological considerations*

Judah Ha-Levi's critical attitude towards the prevalent rationalist Aristotelian philosophy of the day, and the profound impact of some of his thought on later Jewish mystical literature, have led scholars to posit a connection between him and mysticism. For example, such scholars as David Kaufmann, Israel Efros, David Baneth and Shlomo Pines have written about Ha-Levi's indebtedness to Islamic mysticism, especially to Abu Ḥamid Muḥammad Al-Ghazali (1058–1111) and to Isma'ili trends. Other scholars, including Moshe Idel and Elliot Wolfson have written on Ha-Levi and early Jewish mystical literature, especially the Heikhalot and Merkavah traditions. However, as with

Neoplatonic emanation theory, we must ask whether Ha-Levi's using certain terminology borrowed from Jewish or Islamic mystical literature reflects agreement with mystical doctrine, just as we must ask whether the fact that later mystics were influenced by Ha-Levi's theories means that those theories are themselves mystical.

As we shall see presently, Ha-Levi—in contrast with such rationalists as Rambam, for whom the "image of God" is reason and for whom prophecy is essentially an intellectual process—regarded the connection with God and the ability to prophesy to be a function of a supra-rational faculty, "the divine faculty" (*al-amr al-ilahi*) already mentioned above. There is, however, nothing mystical about this construct, because Ha-Levi insisted that there can never be any contradiction between the supra-rational prophetic truth, known in the Torah, and the rational truth, just as there can be no contradiction between empirical truth, known by the senses, and rational truth. "Heaven forbid that there should be anything in the Bible to contradict that which is manifest or proved."[27] And: "Heaven forbid that I should assume what is against sense and reason."[28]

Ha-Levi's critique of unbounded reason also does not make him a mystic. To the contrary, the limits of scientific inquiry are themselves an important scientific question. Here we find an interesting convergence between Judah Ha-Levi and Rambam, despite their radically differing approaches. Both concur, although for different reasons, that the question of the origin of the universe—creation or eternity—cannot be determined rationally or demonstrated scientifically. They also concur that Aristotle's views on emanation were mere opinion and conjecture which were not, and cannot be, proven. Ha-Levi's objections to the theory of emanation, as we have seen, are philosophical, not religious. In these cases, as in others, his objections to the conventional Aristotelian philosophy of the day are themselves not religious in nature (eg., that they contradict Scripture) but philosophical: that the philosophers have failed to prove what they claim.

Finally, as we shall see, even Judah Ha-Levi's notion of "the divine faculty" was an attempt to provide a scientific explanation—given the scientific knowledge of the day—of historical facts (or what he believed to be historical facts) ignored by the philosophers.

Ha-Levi's critique of philosophy is thus itself philosophical—it is a critique from within, and an attempt to build a new philosophy on different grounds. From his perspective, the Aristotelian philosophers, by following a tradition rather than by true investigation, and by ignoring the facts, had transformed philosophy from an open system to a closed system. These considerations,

---

[27]   *Kuzari* 1:67 Hirschfeld trans. p. 54.
[28]   *Kuzari* 1:89. Hirschfeld trans. p. 62.

then, need to be kept in mind as we consider whether Ha-Levi's use of some mystical terminology, borrowed from Jewish and Islamic mystical literature, means that he adopted the mystical doctrines themselves.

[VI.4.b.ii] *Judah Ha-Levi, the Heikhalot, Shi'ur Qomah and Sefer Yeẓirah*

In an important study,[29] Elliot Wolfson has pointed out influences of Hei-khalot and Merkavah texts on Ha-Levi's poetry, and even on the *Kuzari*. He suggests that for Ha-Levi, the "visible glory" of God (*kavod nir'eh*) refers to the spiritual forms, namely the angels, seen in prophecy. Wolfson accordingly regards Ha-Levi as an outstanding example of a medieval Jewish intellectual who combined ancient Jewish mystical forms with Islamic Sufi ideas in philosophical garb.

Ha-Levi mentions the Heikhalot and Merkavah by name in *Kuzari* 3:65, and calls what Rabbi Ishmael experienced "a rank close to prophecy." In *Kuzari* 4:3 he refers to what the prophets see by their "spiritual eye" (Arabic: *al-'ayn al-ruḥaniyah*; Hebrew: *ha-'ayin ha-ruḥanit*) or "hidden eye" (Arabic: *al-'ayn al-batinah*; Hebrew: *ha-'ayin ha-nisteret*), and then says that one should not reject "the work of the chariot" (*ma'aseh merkavah*, i.e., Ezekiel's vision), nor the *Shi'ur Qomah* ("The Measure of the [Divine] Body"), "because it inculcates fear [of God] in the soul." We should note, however, that Ha-Levi does not treat all these texts in the same way. In the first passage, Ha-Levi refers positively to Rabbi Ishmael's experience as "a rank close to prophecy," a claim he does not make for the *Shi'ur Qomah*, with its description of God's body in astronomical (and inconsistent) dimensions. In the latter passage, he merely comments that the text should not be rejected because of its usefulness in inculcating fear of God, without any implication that the descriptions themselves are true, let alone close to prophecy.

The *Sefer Yeẓirah* ("Book of Creation" or "Book of Formation"), on the other hand, is mentioned without such reservation, for example in *Kuzari* 3:17. However, as we saw above, when discussing the theory of emanation in *Kuzari* 5:14, he refers to this source rather ambivalently: "All these things are still less satisfactory than the 'Book of Creation' (*Sefer Yeẓirah*)."

Paradoxically, in a lengthy discussion in *Kuzari* 4:24–25, Ha-Levi interprets an important passage in *Sefer Yeẓirah* in light of the Aristotelian doctrine of the unity in the actual intellect of the subject, act and object of thought, a doctrine with which Ha-Levi was thoroughly familiar and which he discusses in his summary of Ibn Sina's psychology in *Kuzari* 5:12.

Sefer Yeẓirah 1:1 states that God "created his world by three *sefarim*, *s-f-r*, *s-f-r*, *s-f-r*." In his commentary, Sa'adiah Ga'on had interpreted these three as

---

29   Elliot Wolfson, "Merkavah Traditions in Philosophic Garb: Judah Halevi Reconsidered," in *Proceedings of the American Academy for Jewish Research* 57 (1990/1991), pp. 179–242.

sefer (writing), *sefar* (number), and *sippur* (speech), an interpretation followed by later commentators.[30]

> Among them is *Sefer Yeẓirah* by Abraham our ancestor. It is profound and requires lengthy interpretation. It teaches about [God's] unity and mastery by things which are changing and multiple in one respect, but which are, in another respect, unified and coordinated...*Sippur* means speech, i.e., the divine speech...as it says, "Let there be light" (Genesis 1:2). The action was simultaneous with the speech. This [action] is *sefer*, namely the writing, for the writing of God means his creatures, and the speech of God is his writing, and the number of God is his speech. Thus, in terms of God, *sefar*, *sippur* and *sefer* are one thing, whereas in terms of man they are three. For man measures with his mind, speaks with his mouth, and writes with his hand...If we had the ability, by saying the word "man," or by drawing a human body, to make his form exist, then we would have the power of divine speech and divine writing, and we would be creators, although we are endowed with some of this ability in our intellectual representation...In this way, the author of the book says, God created his world by three *sefarim*—*sefar*, *sippur* and *sefer*—which in terms of God, are all one.[31]

Unlike God, whose word and writing are creative powers, humans cannot generate a being simply by saying or writing it. Therefore human measuring, speaking and writing are not identical, and do not constitute a unity. But in God, these three are one and the same reality. However, and here is the critical point, humans do resemble God, to some extent, "in our intellectual representation" (Arabic: *al-taṣwir al-'aqli*; Hebrew: *ha-ẓiyyur ha-sikhli*). In this respect, then, it seems that Judah Ha-Levi, for all his alleged "anti-rationalism," anticipates "rationalist" Rambam's explicit equation of the unity of subject, act and object of thought in both humans and God, in the *Guide of the Perplexed* 1:68. How ironic, then, that Judah Ha-Levi resorts to an Aristotelian doctrine of the intellect to explain a passage in the "mystical" *Sefer Yeẓirah*. Therefore, even if we do not share Elliot Wolfson's belief that Judah Ha-Levi had mystical tendencies, he is undoubtedly correct to point out that certain philosophical and mystical trends were intertwined in medieval Jewish thought.[32]

[VI.4.b.iii] *Judah Ha-Levi and Al-Ghazali*

Judah Ha-Levi is often compared with the Islamic mystic and philosopher, Abu Ḥamid Muḥammad Al-Ghazali. Ha-Levi was influenced significantly by some of Al-Ghazali's views, such as his emphasis on "the taste (*dhauq*) of inner

---

[30] See the discussion and analysis in "Early Philosophical Commentators on the *Sefer Yeẓirah*" (reference above, in note 25).

[31] *Kuzari* 4:25. My translation.

[32] See Wolfson, "Merkavah Traditions in Philosophical Garb," p. 242.

experience" (i.e., knowledge based on direct personal experience) of what Ha-Levi called "the God of Abraham," as opposed to *qiyas* (deductive knowledge) of what he called "the God of Aristotle." Nevertheless, there are three major points in which the similarity breaks down.

    (a) Unlike Ha-Levi's *Kuzari*, Al-Ghazali's *Tahafut Al-Falasifah* ("The Incoherence of the Philosophers")[33] is a systematic and comprehensive critique of philosophy.

    (b) Al-Ghazali concludes that philosophy is heresy, whereas for Ha-Levi, philosophy has its clear limitations, but there can be no contradiction between the Torah and rational truth, and revelation transcends, but does not invalidate, reason *per se*. Therefore, Julius Guttmann, who had said that "in his challenge to philosophy, Judah Halevi follows the great Islamic thinker Al-Ghazali," modifies this a few lines later by acknowledging that "it is clear that Halevi is striking at the conclusions of philosophy, not at its foundations."[34]

    (c) Al-Ghazali ultimately became a Sufi. His quasi-autobiographical *Al-Munqidh Min Al-Ḍalal* ("The Deliverer From Error") describes the spiritual crisis he underwent in his progression from skepticism to Kalam, from Kalam to philosophy, and finally to Sufism. In the sixth chapter of this book, Al-Ghazali describes the theory and practice of Sufism, aiming at purifying the heart from all its defilements, to permit exclusive devotion to God. Merely learning Sufi theory is insufficient; the practice is much more important. One must "taste," i.e. directly experience internally, the reality of God, just as objective knowledge of the definition of health cannot be compared to actually being healthy. Ha-Levi never made such a move to mystical theory and practice, and strongly rejected the ascetic ideal of the Sufis. In Ha-Levi's words: "According to our view, a servant of God is not one who detaches himself from the world, lest he be a burden to it, and it to him; or hates life, which is one of God's bounties granted to him."[35] And: "The divine law imposes no asceticism on us. It rather desires that we should be the equipoise, and grant every mental and physical faculty its due, as much as it can bear, without overburdening one faculty at the expense of another...Our law, as a whole, is divided between fear, love, and joy, by each of which one can approach God."[36]

---

[33]   See Al-Ghazali, *The Incoherence of the Philosophers*, Arabic text with English translation, introduction and commentary by Michael Marmur (Provo: Brigham Young University Press, 1997). On Al-Ghazali, see above, Ch. 4 (IV.1.a.ii).

[34]   Guttmann, *Philosophies of Judaism*, p. 122.

[35]   *Kuzari* 3:1. Hirschfeld trans. p. 135.

[36]   *Kuzari* 2:50. Hirschfeld trans. p. 113.

The similarity or parallel thus ultimately breaks down because in Judah Ha-Levi, as in Baḥya ibn Paquda, the goal of a loving and experiential relationship with God does not lead to Al-Ghazali's explicit abnegation of the self in mystical union with God. The ultimate goal is not mystical union but love of God, in which the duality of lover and the object of love is preserved.

In a balanced study of the similarities and differences between the two, "Rabbi Judah Ha-Levi and Al-Ghazali,"[37] D.Z. Baneth rejects the view of others, like David Kaufmann, who exaggerated Al-Ghazali's influence on Ha-Levi (as if Ha-Levi were a Jewish copy of the Muslim thinker), but at the same time notes that Ha-Levi could not have devised his own critique of the prevalent philosophy of the day without Al-Ghazali's prior undermining of its foundations.

[VI.4.c]   JUDAH HA-LEVI AND KARAISM

One of the documents found in the Cairo Geniza is a letter, written in Judeo-Arabic (i.e., Arabic in Hebrew script) from Judah Ha-Levi to his friend Ḥalfon ben Netanel. According to S.D. Goitein,[38] the letter, in Judah Ha-Levi's own hand, was written in 1125, some 15 years before he left Spain on his way to the Land of Israel in 1140. In the letter, Ha-Levi was responding to a letter from his friend, asking why he had not yet received a copy of Ha-Levi's book, the *Kuzari*. Ha-Levi replied that he had sent the book to a Karaite Jew living in Christian Spain, who had asked him some questions, which the book answered, and then promised to show his friend the book when the next met. D.Z. Baneth questions Goitein's dating of the letter and conclusion that an early version of the book was composed so long before its final version appeared in 1140.[39]

The dating of the book is significant for theories, which will be discussed later, regarding the literary structure of the book and the evolution of Ha-Levi's thought. What, however, are we to understand from the statement in Ha-Levi's letter that the book (or at least an early version of it) was composed as a response to questions posed by a Karaite Jew?[40]

---

[37]   David Zvi Baneth, "Rabbi Judah Ha-Levi and Al-Ghazali" (Hebrew), in *Kenesset* 7 (1942), pp. 311–329.

[38]   See S.D. Goitein, "Autographs from the Hand of Judah Ha-Levi" (Hebrew), in *Tarbiẓ* 24 (1956), pp. 393–416.

[39]   D.Z. Baneth,"On Autographs of Judah Ha-Levi and the Evolution of the *Kuzari*" (Hebrew), in *Tarbiẓ* 26 (1957), pp. 297–303.

[40]   For a survey of Karaism, which rejected the authority of the Talmud, i.e., the "oral Torah" of rabbinic Judaism, see Daniel Lasker, "Rabbanism and Karaism: The Contest for Supremacy," in *Great Schisms in Jewish History*, edited by Raphael Jospe and Stanley Wagner (Hoboken: Ktav, 1981), pp. 47–72.

The book, in its final version, deals to some extent with a polemic against Karaism, but those sections do not define the book, or even major portions of it. The arguments against Karaism form only a relatively minor portion of the *Kuzari*, which opens with the statement that "I was asked to state what arguments and replies I could bring to bear against the attacks of the philosophers, and followers of other religions, and also against [Jewish] sectarians who attacked the rest of Israel."[41] The polemic with Karaism is, in other words, only one of the explicit goals of the book.

Various scholars, such as S.D. Goitein and Shlomo Pines, have suggested, therefore, that the polemic with Karaism, although not the subject of most of the book, was Ha-Levi's motivation in writing it. Ha-Levi's letter, however, does not necessitate the conclusion that the book was motivated by the polemic with Karaism. All Ha-Levi said in his letter was that he wrote the book in response to questions posed by a Karaite; he did not say that the questions themselves necessarily dealt, or had anything to do, with Karaism.

Ha-Levi's polemic against Karaism is concentrated primarily in *Kuzari* 3:33–65. These pages are preceded and followed by a discussion of the need for tradition (Arabic: *taqlid*; Hebrew: *qabbalah* or *masoret*), namely the Oral Torah of rabbinic Judaism, the authority of which was rejected by the Karaites.[42] If it is true that the book was written over a period of many years, and that it was composed in response to a Karaite challenge, then this section is presumably the oldest part of the book.

One of Ha-Levi's first and most interesting claims against Karaism is also the most basic and general argument of all: the biblical text was transmitted for centuries in unvocalized and unpunctuated form, as a purely consonantal text. It is only by oral tradition, then, that we know how to vocalize and punctuate it. So if we need oral tradition merely to read and pronounce the text, how much the more do we need oral tradition to understand its meaning?[43] Subsequent arguments are more specific. For instance, the Torah prescribes many commandments which are never specified or explained in detail,, including many of the sacrifices, permitted and prohibited foods, the Sabbath, circumcision, the fringes on the corners of clothing (cf. Numbers 15), and the *sukkah* (the hut dwelled in during the week-long fall harvest festival). And like his friend Abraham ibn Ezra, Ha-Levi criticized the inherent subjectivism and individualism of Karaism:

---

41   *Kuzari* 1:1. Hirschfeld trans. p. 35.
42   A parallel arguments exists in Christianity, between the Roman Catholic claims regarding the *magisterium* — the teaching authority of the Church — in addition to Scripture, and the radical Protestant rejection of that authority in favor of *Sola Scriptura* ("only Scripture").
43   *Kuzari* 3:35.

Should Karaite methods prevail, there would be as many different codes as opinions. Not one individual would remain constant to one code. For every day he forms new opinions, increases his knowledge, or meets with someone who refutes him with some argument and converts him to his views.[44]

Also like Ibn Ezra, Ha-Levi criticizes the Karaites' literalist interpretation of the law of retaliation (Leviticus 24:19–21), an interpretation, he says, that

embodies ideas antagonistic to common sense. How can we determine such a thing? One person may die from a wound, whilst another person may recover from the same. How can we gauge whether it is the same? How can we take away the eye of a one-eyed person in order to do justice to a person with two eyes, when the former would be totally blind, the latter still have one eye?...What further need is there to discuss these details, when we have just set forth the necessity of tradition?[45]

The honest sincerity of the Karaites is not in question. But good intentions are insufficient (a theme to which we shall return when discussing the literary proem of the book), and actions based on personal opinion and not guided by authentic tradition will not correctly fulfill the divine commandments. The commandments resemble nature, whereas those who act without proper guidance resemble alchemists and magicians, who cannot produce true results.[46]

[VI.4.d]   JUDAH HA-LEVI AND ARISTOTELIANISM

As we have already seen, medieval Aristotelianism was freely intermixed with elements of Neoplatonism, notably the theory of emanation. For brief surveys, review the discussion of Aristotle and Aristotelianism and of the categories in Ch. 3 (III.1.b and III.3.f). There is some ambivalence in Judah Ha-Levi's attitude towards to the prevalent Aristotelianism of the day. On the one hand, this was the philosophy he emphatically criticized in the *Kuzari*. On the other hand, at least in certain respects, despite his critical attitude, Ha-Levi continued to use this philosophy and to regard it as a vital stage in a person's intellectual development, and he never subjected philosophy *per se* to the kind of systematic and comprehensive critique that Al-Ghazali did. He questioned its conclusions, not its fundamental method of inquiry.

In the framework story with which the *Kuzari* opens, the archetypal Aristotelian philosopher outlines his philosophy:[47]

---

44   *Kuzari* 3:38. Hirschfeld trans. p. 169.
45   *Kuzari* 3:47. Hirschfeld trans. pp. 175–176.
46   *Kuzari* 3:53.
47   *Kuzari* 1:1; Hirschfeld trans. pp. 36–39. The translation is modified here.

God... is above desire and intention. A desire intimates a want in the person who feels it, and not till it is satisfied does he become (so to speak) complete... In a similar way, He is, in the opinion of the philosophers, above the knowledge of individuals, because the latter change with the times, whilst there is no change in God's knowledge. He, therefore, does not know you, much less your thoughts and actions, nor does He listen to your prayers... If philosophers say that He created you, they only use a metaphor, because He is the cause of causes in the creation of all creatures, but not because this was his intention from the beginning. He never created man. For the world is without beginning... Everything is reduced to a prime cause, not to a will proceeding from this, but an emanation from which emanated a second, a third, and fourth cause. The cause and the caused are... connected with one another, their coherence being as eternal as the prime cause and having no beginning. Every individual on earth has his competing causes; consequently an individual with perfect causes becomes perfect... The philosopher... who is equipped with the highest capacity... wants nothing to make him perfect... In the perfect person, a light of divine nature, called active intellect, is with him, and his passive intellect is so closely connected with it that both are but one... This degree is the last and most longed-for goal for the perfect man, whose soul, after having been purified, has grasped the inward truths of all branches of science, and has thus become equal to an angel... Endeavor to reach [this rank] and the true knowledge of things, in order that your intellect may become active, but not passive. Keep just ways as regards character and actions, because this will help you to effect truth, to gain instruction, and to become similar to this active intellect... If you have reached such a disposition of belief, be not concerned about the forms of your... religion or worship, or the word or language you employ. You may even choose a religion... for the management of your temperament, your house and country, if they agree to it. Or fashion your religion according to the laws of reason set up by philosophers, and strive after purity of soul. In fine, seek purity of heart, in which way you are able, provided you have acquired the sum total of knowledge... Then you will reach your goal, viz. the union with this... active intellect.

This is exactly the philosophy that Judah Ha-Levi will presently subject to devastating critique, point by point. Its God—"the God of Aristotle"—is impersonal and knows only itself, the knowledge of anything else being unworthy of it, since things can but God, and thus the divine knowledge, cannot change (change being a function of imperfection). The God of Aristotle has no will, since whatever is perfect lacks nothing and therefore needs or wants nothing to complete and perfect itself. The God of Aristotle is not a creator (except in the metaphorical sense of being the first cause of everything). As we shall see, such a God can be the subject of theoretical knowledge, but not the subject of loving commitment, and the ultimate human goal is intellectual conjunction with the active intellect.

For Ha-Levi, such an outlook is erroneous because it fails to take into account total human perfection, not only of the mind but of all a person's spiritual and physical faculties as well as actions. The emphasis on the goal of conjunction with the active intellect is also fallacious, because it is based on the theory of emanation, which has no basis in fact or logic. Aristotelian ethics are equally erroneous, because their focus is on intellectual perfection, rather than promoting a balance (as Plato does) among all of a person's physical and spiritual needs and abilities. Finally, for the Aristotelian philosopher, intentions are important, but behavior—especially religious behavior—is ultimately unimportant.

Ha-Levi, as noted, does not subject the philosophic method *per se* to attack, nor does he reject it as heresy, as does Al-Ghazali, To the contrary: the conventional Aristotelian philosophy is questioned—its foundations as well as conclusions—because it is not true philosophy. True philosophy or science can only be understood as an open system, as we saw in Ch. 2, because it is not limited by prior religious opinion. To the contrary, as an open system, it can lead to any conclusion, including conclusions contrary to the beliefs of a given religion. That is why the Kalam—which attempted to rationalize pre-existing religious doctrines—was seen by the philosophers like Rambam to be a closed system, and thus not true philosophy.

Judah Ha-Levi essentially reverses that judgment: it is the dominant medieval Aristotelian philosophy that is a closed system, and thus not true philosophy, because it relies on the unquestioned authority of Aristotle, and accepts as given various arbitrary views which Aristotle never demonstrated conclusively, and which actually are inconsistent with the natural or historical facts. Despite Aristotle's claim to observe empirical reality, much of his thought—and all the more the thought of his medieval followers who accepted his thought on authority—is not at all empirically justified. Aristotelian philosophy is thus fallacious, much of the time, not because it is "heresy" from a religious perspective, but because it a closed, not open system, and thus is not true philosophy.

All these criticisms notwithstanding, Aristotelian philosophy still has its uses, and as we saw above, Ha-Levi does not hesitate to interpret a mystical text—*Sefer Yeẓirah*—in light of the Aristotelian doctrine of the unity of intellectual subject, act and object. As Herbert Davidson has shown,[48] despite Ha-Levi's rejection of the cosmology of "the philosophers," he retains the basic structure, but insists that it is the direct result of divine creation and functions in accordance with the divine will. He accepts the Aristotelian notion of a chain of direct and indirect causes operating in the cosmos, the source

---

48   Herbert Davidson, "The Active Intellect in the *Cuzari* and Hallevi's Theory of Causality," in *Revue des Études Juives* 131, no. 1–2 (1972), pp. 351–396.

of which lies in the motions of the spheres, again with the proviso that this expresses the direct divine will, and he accepts the Aristotelian explanation of generation and corruption.

In short, Ha-Levi states that Aristotelian philosophy is the supreme intellectual attainment of those not granted divine knowledge through prophetic revelation or reliable tradition based on such revelation. Aristotle

> exerted his mind because he had no tradition from any reliable source at his disposal. He meditated on the beginning and end of the world, but found as much difficulty in the theory of a beginning as in that of eternity. Finally, these abstract speculations which made for eternity prevailed...Had he lived among a people with well authenticated and generally acknowledged traditions, he would have applied his deductions and arguments to establish the theory of creation, however difficult, instead of eternity, which is even more difficult to accept.[49]

Finally, as suggested by Yochanan Sillman (to whose theories we shall return), for Judah Ha-Levi, Aristotelian philosophy was not only an essential step in the evolution of human culture, but it remains an essential (although certainly not ultimate) stage in the intellectual and spiritual development of everyone seeking to worship God in truth.

[VI.4.e] JUDAH HA-LEVI AND THE KALAM

In Chapter Two, we saw that Judah Ha-Levi summarized the Kalam in ten principles.[50] On the one hand, Ha-Levi regarded the Kalam as possibly necessary to combat heretical ideas, as the rabbis said, "Know what to respond to a heretic."[51] On the other hand, the truly religious individual, secure in his belief, does not need the Kalam. An insecure person may be helped by the Kalam's arguments, but he may also be harmed by them, since the same rational arguments which may persuade one person of religious truth may lead another person to doubt the truth. In any event, the Kalam does not present an intellectual challenge on the same level as philosophy.

Another consideration in Ha-Levi's attitude towards the Kalam may be the fact that this school of thought remained dominant among Karaite philosophers for centuries, whereas among Muslim and Jewish thinkers, other schools of thought displaced the Kalam. In the *Kuzari* 5:15 Ha-Levi refers to the principles of those "whom the Karaites call the men of the science of the Kalam." Why does Ha-Levi refer to their being called this by the Karaites, since others,

---

49   *Kuzari* 1:65. Hirschfeld trans.pp. 53–54.
50   *Kuzari* 5:18. See Ch. 2 (II.1.b)
51   Avot 2:19. The word used there is "Apiqoros" (from Epicurus), a term used by the rabbis in a generic sense to refer to a person who denies Jewish belief and religious practice.

rabbinic Jews and Muslims alike, also called them "the men of the science of the Kalam?" Perhaps Ha-Levi believed that there is a certain parallel between Karaism and the Kalam, in that both fail to progress. Such opponents of Karaism as Saʻadiah Ga'on, Abraham ibn Ezra and Judah Ha-Levi regarded Karaism to be, in a sense, spiritually retarded, in that it was not open to the developments of the oral Torah. The Kalam, by analogy, suffered from an intellectual retardation, in its subservience to obsolete principles which lacked scientific validity or had been refuted by more recent philosophic developments.

[VI.4.f] JUDAH HA-LEVI AND ASTRAL MAGIC

In an important study, Shlomo Pines demonstrated that Judah Ha-Levi's *Kuzari* occasionally refers to "spiritual emanations" (Arabic: *ruḥaniyat*), a term derived from Arabic texts dealing with magic and theurgy, which in turn are based on ancient Greek Hermetic texts in Egypt.[52]

These *ruḥaniyat* intermediate between God and people, and are emanations from God which govern and move the planets and affect terrestrial affairs. Pines also showed that the 11th-century Arabic magic text *Ghayat Al-Ḥakim* ("The Goal of the Wise"), known in Christian Europe as *Picatrix*, was translated three times into Hebrew, indicating its popularity and influence in Jewish circles.

Although Rambam later would reject out of hand, as false and idolatrous, claims that a person is a prophet who can "bring down *ruḥaniyat*" from a planet,[53] Pines concludes that Ha-Levi's rejection of these ideas was far from unequivocal, and that Ha-Levi basically believed that the Torah's commandments are more effective than non-Jewish theurgy (i.e., the ability to force or persuade supranatural powers to do something).

> Judaism is an efficient and useful theurgy, whereas the pagan religions to which Judah Ha-Levi refers are intrinsically unfounded theurgies, because they are far from ensuring any benefits resembling the efficiency and usefulness that Judaism, as a theurgy, provides through its system of commandments.[54]

Following this line of interpretation of Ha-Levi, Dov Schwartz states that "the first [Jewish] thinker to lay down concrete foundations for astral-

---

52 Shlomo Pines, "On the Term *Ruḥaniyut* and Its Sources, and on Judah Ha-Levi's Teaching" (Hebrew), in *Tarbiẓ* 57 (1988), pp. 511–540. These Neoplatonic Hermetic texts, attributed to Hermes Trismagistus (= thrice great), the god of the sciences, deal with philosophy, religion, mysticism, astrology and alchemy. Cf. Dov Schwartz, *Studies on Astral Magic in Medieval Jewish Thought* (Leiden: Brill, 2005).

53 Rambam, Introduction to the Commentary on the Mishnah (Arabic edition with Hebrew translation by Yosef Kafiḥ [Jerusalem, 1968]), p. 5.

54 Pines, p. 529, English translation in Schwartz, pp. 2–3.

magical interpretation of the Torah and its system of commandments was Judah Ha-Levi."[55] Thus, in the *Kuzari* 1:97, Ha-Levi interprets the sin of the golden calf (Exodus 32) as an illegitimate attempt to focus or concentrate *ruḥaniyat* in a particular place or object without divine authority. The golden calf was a violation of the Decalogue's prohibition of making an image for the purposes of worship (Exodus 20:4–5), in contrast with those sacred objects Moses was explicitly commanded to fashion for the portable Tabernacle, such as the ark of the covenant, the tablets of the Decalogue, and the cherubim. What Ha-Levi objected to, therefore, was not astral magic and the belief in *ruḥaniyat*, but their illegitimate and ineffective use outside of the framework of, and unguided by, the divine commandments of the Torah.

> Judah Ha-Levi's critique, therefore, is not directed against the principles of astrology itself—including its influence on human character, on the nation and on the world... —but against the astrologers' pretension to know them without the "divine power"...Astrology is therefore rejected as are the other sciences, including philosophy, as a weakness of human reasoning in search for the revealed truth.[56]

According to Schwartz, therefore, the difference between Judah Ha-Levi and Abraham ibn Ezra was that Ibn Ezra affirmed the efficacy of astrology and astral magic, whereas Judah Ha-Levi regarded only the Torah, and not astrology, as theurgically efficacious. Both thinkers, Schwartz suggests, wrote in such a way as to conceal much of their astral-magic interpretation of Jewish sources.

My reading differs from that of Schwartz. As suggested in the previous chapter, in my understanding of Ibn Ezra, he affirms astrology—a method of knowing astral effects—but not magic—a method of affecting higher powers. It also seems to me that we cannot attribute to Ha-Levi a belief in astrology, let alone astral magic, without their necessary foundation in a Neoplatonic emanationist cosmology (a cosmology affirmed by Ibn Ezra, but not by Ha-Levi). Despite Ha-Levi's occasional and rare usage of emanationist language (discussed above, VI.4.a), which is at best ambivalent, there is certainly no stronger rejection and derision of the absurdities of the theory of emanation in medieval Jewish thought than Ha-Levi's sharp mockery of it in the *Kuzari* 4:25, where he says that "their principles are rationally unacceptable and illogical," and again in 5:14, where he says of emanation that "these views are even less satisfactory than the *Sefer Yeẓirah*; they are all dubious, and no philosopher agrees with any other (about them)," as we saw.

---

55   Dov Schwartz, *Astral Magic in Medieval Jewish Thought* (Hebrew) (Ramat Gan: Bar Ilan University Press, 1999), p. 31.
56   Schwartz, *Studies on Astral Magic in Medieval Jewish Thought*, p. 7.

Without a Neoplatonic cosmology, how can there be a theory of emanation? And without a theory emanation, what basis is there for belief in astral forces? Finally, without such forces, what basis is there for astrological knowledge of those forces, let alone their manipulation in astral magic? The question, then, is how to read Judah Ha-Levi's interpretation of such passages as the sin of the golden calf. Is he actually affirming, himself, a belief in the efficacy (however limited, in comparison with the commandments of the Torah) of astral magic, or is he merely suggesting that such belief motivated the Israelites in their sinful violation of the Torah's explicit prohibition of such worship as idolatrous? As Ha-Levi wrote in the *Kuzari* 4:9, if (and the conditional "if" is explicit) astrology could be scientifically demonstrated, we would have to accept it, since there can be no contradiction between scientific truth and the Torah[57]; however, "we deny" the astrologer's claims to specific knowledge of what will be, "for flesh and blood cannot attain this."

[VI.4.g] JUDAH HA-LEVI:
AN ELECTIC APPROACH TO THE SOURCES

In conclusion, we have seen Judah Ha-Levi was familiar with the various schools of religious and philosophical thought—Neoplatonism, mysticism, Karaism, Aristotelianism, Kalam, astrology and astral magic—but maintained an independent stance towards them all. He borrowed eclectically from their terminology and even ideas, while maintaining a critical distance from their underlying assumptions and overall theories. In this way he was able to construct his highly original *Book of Refutation and Proof on the Despised Faith*[58] (*Kitab Al-Radd Wa-'l-Dalil Fi 'l-Din Al-Dhalil*) as he called his *Kuzari* (*Kitab Al-Khazari*).

[VI.5] THE *KUZARI* AND THE KHAZARS

[VI.5.a] DATING THE *KUZARI*

In the book's dialogue between the King of the Khazars ("the Kuzari") and a Jew, the Jew refers to the Hebrew calendar, according to which 4500 years have passed since the creation of the world.[59] The book began by stating that

---

[57] Cf. *Kuzari* 1:67 and 1:89.
[58] This is how the title of the book is translated in the edition of the Arabic text by David Baneth and Haggai Ben-Shammai (Jerusalem: Magnes Press, 1977).
[59] *Kuzari* 1:47.

the events described happened 400 years previously.[60] This internal evidence thus gives us the date of the book's composition, the year 4900 of the Hebrew calendar (= 1140 C.E.).

[VI.5.b] THE CORRESPONDENCE BETWEEN ḤISDAI IBN SHAPRUT AND KING JOSEPH

What were the events to which the book refers, at least ostensibly, circa 740 C.E.? In 1160–1161, some twenty years after the *Kuzari* was written, Judah Ha-Levi's younger contemporary, Abraham ibn Da'ud[61] refers to these events in his historical work, *Sefer Ha-Qabbalah* (*The Book of Tradition*).[62] Following a discussion of the Karaites, Ibn Da'ud described communities of Rabbanite Jews:

> You will note that Rabbanite communities extend from the city of Sala at the extreme end of the Maghreb, to the end of Ifriqiya, Egypt, the Holy Land, Arabia, Iraq, Khuzistan, Fars, the land of Dedan, the land of the Girgashite — which is called Jurjan — Tabarestan and al-Daylam as far as the Volga. In the latter area there were a nation of Khazars who converted to Judaism, and their King Joseph sent a letter to Rabbi Ḥisdai the Nasi ben Rabbi Isaac ben Shaprut, informing him that he and all of his people pursue Rabbanite usage scrupulously. (We have also seen some of their descendants in Toledo, scholars who informed us that their legal practice conforms to Rabbanate usage).[63]

Ḥisdai ibn Shaprut, who lived in Cordova circa 915–970 C.E., was a physician, the head of the Jewish community, and a minister and ambassador of the king. His correspondence with King Joseph of the Khazars dates to circa 960 C.E.[64] Ḥisdai ibn Shaprut's letter to King Joseph describes how he first heard of the Jewish Khazars and of their king from emissaries who came to Spain from Constantinople, and then asks the king for information about his land and people, their origin, their language, his government and relations with

---

60   *Kuzari* 1:1.

61   Abraham ibn Da'ud was born in Cordova circa 1110, and was martyred in Toledo in 1180. In 1160–1161 he wrote two books, his historical *Sefer Ha-Qabbalah* and his philosophical *Sefer Ha-Emunah Ha-Ramah* (*The Exalted Faith*). We will deal with his thought in Ch. 7.

62   Abraham ibn Da'ud, *Sefer Ha-Qabbalah* (*The Book of Tradition*), critical edition with annotated English translation by Gerson Cohen (Philadelphia: Jewish Publication Society, 1967).

63   Abraham ibn Da'ud, *Sefer Ha-Qabbalah*, Hebrew pp. 67–68, English pp. 92–93.

64   Although some scholars question the authenticity of the correspondence, D.M. Dunlop, *The History of the Jewish Khazars* (New York, 1967), ch. 6, accepts their authenticity. In any event, both Judah Ha-Levi and Abraham ibn Da'ud clearly accepted them as authentic.

neighboring nations. Among his detailed questions, he asked "whether war defers the Sabbath."

King Joseph's reply described in detail their religious practices, but avoids detailed replies on political and military matters. According to the letter, the conversion of the Khazars to Judaism occurred some 340 years earlier, which would date the events circa 621–622 C.E. (rather than circa 740 C.E., as Judah Ha-Levi mentioned).[65] The letter describes how an angel of God was revealed to King Bulan, a revelation which led to the conversion to Judaism, in stages, of the king and his people. In his second revelation to Bulan, the angel said that he saw and was pleased with the king's actions. After the partial conversion of the Khazars, the angel appeared a third time to Bulan and commanded him to build a temple to God. Bulan then waged wars to raise the necessary funds, and built the temple which, King Joseph reports, still stands. Bulan then received ambassadors from neighboring Christian and Muslim rulers, who attempted to persuade him to accept their religion. The king invited a Jewish sage to argue with the Christian and Muslim representatives. There was no agreement among the representatives of the three religions, but both the Christian and the Muslim, when asked which other religion is preferable, preferred Judaism. Upon hearing this, Bulan and his people were circumcised and completed their conversion to Judaism. Bulan's son and successor Ovadiah built synagogues and schools, and invited Jewish scholars to teach his people Bible, Mishnah, Talmud and other Jewish subjects. King Joseph's letter thus reinforces Abraham ibn Da'ud's claim that the Khazars follow Rabbanite practice.

[VI.6] THE *KUZARI*: STRUCTURE
AND COMPOSITION OF THE BOOK

[VI.6.a] COMPOSITION IN STAGES

We referred above (VI.4.c) to questions regarding the date and composition over years of the *Kuzari*, including the fact that the internal evidence of the book is that it was composed in 1140 C.E., but that it is already referred to in a letter from Judah Ha-Levi to Ḥalfon ben Netanel, which S.D. Goitein dated as having been written in 1125. The letter, it will be recalled, refers to Ha-Levi having sent the book to a Karaite in Christian Spain, who had asked him some questions, to which the book responds. This had led various scholars

---

65   Dunlop suggests that the reference to the conversion taking place 340 years earlier may be a later addition to the letter, or may simply be a scribal error, since if it took place 240 years earlier, it would date the conversion as having occurred in 721–722 C.E., close to the date Ha-Levi mentioned (740 C.E.).

to conclude that the book was written in stages over some 20 years, although others, including D.Z. Baneth, question Goitein's dating of the letter and conclusion that an early version of the book was composed long before the final version appeared in 1140.

According to the approach of Goitein and other scholars, that the book was written in stages over many years, those sections of the *Kuzari* which involve a polemic against Karaism, namely *Kuzari* 3:33–65 (and perhaps the entire third section of the book), are thus the oldest parts of the book. The other parts of the book, which engage in general polemic against other religions and especially against Aristotelian philosophy, were later additions that together form the final version of the *Kuzari*. Two later scholars—Eliezer Schweid and Yochanan Silman—differ from each other in their approaches, but accept Goitein's theory of the composition in stages of the book. Schweid's approach is literary, whereas Silman's approach is based on an analysis of the ideas expressed in the book.

[VI.6.b] ELIEZER SCHWEID:
THE LITERARY STRUCTURE OF THE *KUZARI*

In his Hebrew study, "The Art of Dialogue in the *Kuzari* and its Theoretical Meaning,"[66] Eliezer Schweid suggests that the Platonic dialogue of the *Kuzari* is a natural form expression of Ha-Levi's ideas, as opposed to the systematic, but artificial, form of dialogue found in Solomon ibn Gabirol's *Fountain of Life*. Despite the naturalness of the dialogue, Schweid believes that the "seam" between the early material in the third section, and the four later sections (I, II, IV and V), is evident. In the later sections the literary flow of the dialogue is clear, and the ideological point of view—the confrontation between the Torah and Aristotelian philosophy—is consistent, whereas in section III there is no smooth flow or connection of the material with the later sections before and after it, and Ha-Levi had to create a literary framework in which, at the end of section II, the king asks for instruction in the subjects discussed in section III, and at the end of section III, the king reaffirms his belief in the traditions of rabbinic Judaism, and requests instruction in the subjects discussed in section IV. The king's two requests thus form a "seam" permitting the insertion of the earlier material in section III between the later sections II and IV—whereas no such "seam" is necessary in the smooth transitions from sections I to II and IV to V.

Schweid also claims that Ha-Levi personally identified with the Jewish sage in the dialogue, and the sage's announced intention to migrate to the

---

[66]   Eliezer Schweid, *Ta'am Ve-Haqashah* (Ramat Gan: Masada, 1970), pp. 37–79. The phrase *ta'am ve-haqashah*, which we will discuss later, is found in *Kuzari* 4:16–17, and refers to experiential vs. deductive knowledge.

Land of Israel at the end of the book sets the stage for Judah Ha-Levi's own migration. The king, in Schweid's analysis, represents the reader. The dialogue is, therefore, authentic even if it is not historical. Why, however, was the dialogue necessary, and why could Ha-Levi not present his ideas in a more straightforward manner? Schweid suggests that the literary device of dialogue permitted Ha-Levi to present his ideas concerning the superiority of Judaism from (what was for him) an objective and external perspective.

Leo Strauss had suggested that in the prologue, setting the stage for the dialogue, there is no direct dialogue between the Jewish sage and the philosopher, because Ha-Levi did not wish to give the philosopher a platform for his readers.[67] Schweid rejects this interpretation, and points out that in the fifth section, Ha-Levi did, in fact, present a survey of philosophic views, since, unlike Al-Ghazali, Ha-Levi did not oppose philosophy *per se*, so long as its limits are clear.

[VI.6.c]   YOCHANAN SILMAN: THE "DOCUMENTARY HYPOTHESIS" OF THE *KUZARI*

Yochanan Silman's detailed study of the Judah Ha-Levi's thought, *Philosopher and Prophet: Judah Halevi, The* Kuzari, *and the Evolution of His Thought*,[68] analyzes both the structure of the book and the development of Ha-Levi's ideas. Silman agrees with the theory of Goiten, Pines and Schweid that the book was written in stages, but not for the same reasons. In his view, Ha-Levi's letter to Halfon ben Netanel does not necessarily prove the theory. Silman's evidence for "early thought" and "later thought" is based on Ha-Levi's ideas, and is compatible with, but not dependent upon, the chronological distinction based on the letter. Philosophy is not merely necessary as a literary device, as Schweid suggested, for the dialogue's king who represents the reader. Rather, philosophy is an essential stage in the educational, intellectual, and spiritual development of every person. Therefore, Silman suggests, Ha-Levi does not fully identify with the Jewish sage (as Schweid suggests), because the sage represents all the stages—early and late—in the evolution of Ha-Levi's thought, and not merely his ultimate positions in his late thought.

---

[67]   Leo Strauss, "The Law of Reason in the *Kusari*" in *Proceedings of the American Academy for Jewish Research* 13 (143), pp. 47–96; reprinted in *Persecution and the Art of Writing* (Glencoe: Free Press, 1952), pp. 95–141. Strauss rejects the identification of Ha-Levi's own views with the Haver: One cannot simply identify Halevi's views with the statements of his spokesman, the Jewish scholar. Halevi intimates near the beginning of 1:1 that not all arguments of the scholar convinced him" (note 17).

[68]   English translation by Lenn Schramm (Albany: State University of New York Press, 1995), based on Silman's Hebrew book, *Bein Pilosof Le-Navi: Hitpathut Haguto Shel Rabbi Yehudah Ha-Levi Be-Sefer Ha-Kuzari* (Ramat Gan: Bar Ilan University Press, 1985).

Silman's theory of the structure of the *Kuzari* and the development of Ha-Levi's thought—as it evolved over different periods of Ha-Levi's life and intellectual and spiritual growth—resembles the documentary hypothesis of higher Bible criticism, which attributes various sections of Scripture to different periods and authors. The earlier and later stages are reflected in the two different titles of the book. In his early letter to Ḥalfon ben Netanel, Ha-Levi refers to the book as *Kitab Al-Khazari* ("The Book of the *Kuzari*), whereas the final version of the book is called *Kitab Al-Radd Wa-'l-Dalil Fi 'l-Din Al-Dhalil* ("The Book of Refutation and Proof on the Despised Faith"). The two titles thus reflect the earlier and later stages of Ha-Levi's thought as well as of the composition of the book. The earlier name is based on the king, the protagonist of the story, whereas the later name would make no sense in a work dealing with Karaism (which is part of Judaism, and thus of the "despised faith").

In the early thought, according to Silman, Ha-Levi still believed in Aristotelian philosophy, whereas in the later thought, Ha-Levi freed himself from Aristotelian philosophy and emphasized the superiority of the historical-religious Jewish experience. On the basis of this ideational distinction, Silman divides the book into its early and late sections:

Early Thought *Kitab Al-Khazari* ("The Book of the *Kuzari*) (Aristotelian Philosophy)	Late Thought *Kitab Al-Radd Wa-'l-Dalil Fi 'l-Din Al-Dhalil* ("The Book of Refutation and Proof on the Despised Faith") (The superiority of Judaism as historical-religious experience)
Kuzari 1:68–79	*Kuzari* 1:1–67
Kuzari 2:1–7	*Kuzari* 2:7–81
Kuzari 3	*Kuzari* 4 *Kuzari* 5

According to Silman, the book reflects stages in the evolution of Ha-Levi's own thought. Why, then, retain the early stages which he later rejected? Silman's answer is that the book is not merely autobiographical. The early stages are necessary for the intellectual and spiritual development of everyone, and are, therefore, also necessary for the reader's progress.

Silman thus agrees with Schweid that the third section of the book is an independent and original literary unit in the evolution of the book and of Ha-Levi's thought, but emphasizes that the distinction between the early and later thought would remain valid, on systematic grounds, even if the chronological distinction between earlier and later versions of the book (based on Ha-Levi's letter to Ḥalfon ben Netanel) were to prove false.

According to Silman's theory, in the early thought, Ha-Levi still believed in Aristotelian philosophy, and believed in the possibility of correcting that philosophy by exposing it to the truths of history, such as revelation, prophecy and miracles. The main focus of the polemic is Karaism, not Aristotelian philosophy. In the later thought, the main focus of the polemic is no longer Karaism (which is part of historic Judaism and "the despised faith"), but shifts to Aristotelian philosophy, which is fundamentally flawed because of its inability to recognize and deal with (a) the meaning of the historical and religious uniqueness of the Jewish people; (b) the importance of a person's actions and life-style; (c) the meaning of the experience of divine revelation.

The literary device of the dialogue permitted Ha-Levi to interweave earlier and later strands. In any event, even in the late thought, philosophy has an important role to play in the collective development of the human species and in the individual development of every person, and is not totally rejected in principle, as it is in Al-Ghazali's thought. Adam, the progenitor of the human species, was a philosopher before he experienced revelation; first he had rational knowledge of God as *Elohim*, and only later did he experience the revelation of God as *Adonai*.[69] Similarly, Abraham, the progenitor of the Jewish people, first engaged in philosophy (at which stage he composed the *Sefer Yeẓirah*), at which point he had rational knowledge of God, and only later experienced God directly through revelation.[70] Philosophy is thus a precondition for the immediate experience of God in revelation. This is why, according to Silman, the philosopher appears before the representatives of the various religions, in the prologue to the book. However, even after the experience of revelation, philosophy continues to have an important task, namely the avoidance of anthropomorphism.

The stages in the composition of the book thus reflect Ha-Levi's own autobiographical development, and parallel the intellectual and spiritual development of the individual, of the Jewish people, and of the human species.

[VI.6.d] SILMAN'S APPROACH: A CRITIQUE

Yochanan Silman's study of the *Kuzari* is meticulous and comprehensive. Nevertheless, it raises a number of difficulties. As Daniel Lasker has written:[71]

Silman uses his theory to explain any number of difficult passages in the

---

69   *Kuzari* 1:63, 1:95, 4:3. The distinction between these two names in Ha-Levi's thought will be discussed below.
70   *Kuzari* 4:17, 4:27.
71   Daniel Lasker, Review of "Silman's *Thinker and Seer*" in *Jewish Quarterly Review* LXXVIII, Nos. 3–4 (1988), pp. 314–315.

Kuzari...The proposed new theory, imaginative as it is, fails to convince. Although there is evidence from a genizah letter that Ha-Levi wrote an anti-Karaite *Book of Kuzari*, this original edition of the book did not survive, and we have no reason to believe that it contained exactly those sections of the extant *Kuzari* which Silman theorizes are its earlier parts. Furthermore, contra Silman, the anti-Karaite chapters of the work, as it has come down to us, hardly read like the product of an Aristotelian philosopher. Ha-Levi's critique of Karaism mirrors his critique of Aristotelian philosophy: both, he claims, depend too much on logic and personal efforts rather than on reliable tradition. Furthermore, the fact that certain issues are not dealt with in the "early" parts does not mean that they were of no concern to Ha-Levi at that stage...It may simply mean that they had already been discussed in a previous section of the work and that there was no need to repeat the discussion. Their absence from a particular part of the *Kuzari* does not necessarily mean that it was written by the early Ha-Levi, for whom some a question was presumably unimportant. Most difficult of all is Silman's assumption that in his final edition, Ha-Levi left the early parts, with which he no longer agreed, as a didactic measure to show his readers how mankind must overcome philosophy in order to arrive at the truth of Judaism, as he himself had done. It is likely that Silman reaches this conclusion because it would be hard to assume that a literary craftsman of the caliber of Ha-Levi would just throw together different editions of his book without papering over the seams and checking for contradictions between the two stages of the book. If, however, Ha-Levi did intend that the *Kuzari* should be autobiographical in this sense, it would have been more effective for him to tell the reader what he was doing.

Let us add some other reservations to Lasker's critique. First, as noted above (VI.4.c), it is far from certain that Judah Ha-Levi's letter to Ḥalfon ben Netanel precedes the final version of the *Kuzari* by some twenty years, as posited by Goitein and those who followed him, and if Baneth is correct that the letter was written years later, closer to 1140, there would not have been a sufficient span of time to permit the kind of intellectual evolution that Silman theorizes took place. Moreover, also as noted above, Ha-Levi's letter to Ḥalfon ben Netanel never claims that the book is an anti-Karaite polemic, nor even that he was asked specifically about Karaism, but merely that a Karaite Jew had asked for his views "on several subjects." In short, the letter does not warrant the conclusion that the discussion of Karaism in the third section is the original *Kuzari* and Ha-Levi's "early thought." Nor is the letter's self-deprecatory tone necessarily indicative that Ha-Levi repudiated whatever he had written, and it may be nothing more than a literary convention, similar to the way English letters were once signed, "Your humble servant."

Second, Silman carefully differentiates the chronological and factual question of the book's composition in stages from the ideational and literary question of the evolution of Ha-Levi's thought, and emphasizes that his theory regarding the early and late thought is valid even without the chronological considerations of how the book was written. If, however, there is no factual evidence to support the theory that section III was written at an early stage, as a critique of Karaism when Ha-Levi still believed in Aristotelian philosophy, then what remains to support Silman's "documentary hypothesis"?

Third, Silman's theory is, in a sense, a case of circular reasoning. If we had definitive external, factual evidence of the *Kuzari* having been composed in stages (keeping in mind that a close reading of Ha-Levi's letter to Ḥalfon ben Netanel does not actually provide such support), and that there was a parallel evolution in Ha-Levi's thought, then we could discern early and late layers in the book. In the absence of such external evidence, all we are left with is the circular argument that whatever is allegedly early must be Aristotelian, and whatever is allegedly Aristotelian must be early. In fact, all we have is a book with a complex and non-linear literary structure, which contains a variety of ideas in different places, not all of which are fully consistent with others.

Fourth, Silman's "documentary hypothesis" suffers from a problem similar to higher Bible criticism, namely the question of unified redaction. If, in fact, what we have is a composite work, how and why was it edited into its final form, which, as we have noted, is non-linear in its structure? What we have is not merely the division of the book into five sections, but an atomistic mixture of allegedly early and late elements within some of the sections, without regard for chronological or logical order.

Fifth, an author is certainly free to compose a book preserving—overtly or covertly—his own autobiographical intellectual and spiritual progress, or the progress expected of and recommended to the reader, such as we have in Saʿadiah Gaʾon's *Book of Beliefs and Opinions* and Baḥya ibn Paquda's *Duties of the Heart*. However, for such a literary device to be successful, the progress needs to be more or less linear (as it is in these two books). A free and atomistic admixture of early and late elements is not only literarily clumsy, but places obstacles in the way of the reader, and Judah Ha-Levi was far too masterful a poet and thinker to be satisfied with such clumsiness.

[VI.6.e] THE "SECRET OF THE *KUZARI*": DOV SCHWARTZ

A different, and radical, interpretation of the *Kuzari* has been proposed by Dov Schwartz,[72] who (following Leo Strauss)[73] rejects the view of Schweid and others that the Jewish sage (the *ḥaver*) in the dialogue with the Kuzari king represents Judah Ha-Levi's own opinions. At the beginning of the book, the author states that he recorded these events as they happened, and that "some"

---

72   Dov Schwartz, *Contradiction and Concealment in Medieval Jewish Thought* (Hebrew) (Ramat Gan: Bar Ilan University Press, 2002).
73   Leo Strauss, "The Law of Reason in the *Kuzari*," p. 101, note 17, cited above.

(not all) of the *ḥaver*'s claims "are in agreement with my opinions."[74] The *Kuzari*, as Schwartz understands it, is an example of esoteric writing, the purpose of which is to conceal the author's true intention from the unqualified reader. Building on Leo Strauss' theory of "persecution and the art of writing,"[75] Schwartz arrives at the opposite conclusion from Strauss. Strauss had concluded that on an exoteric level, the *Kuzari* opposes philosophy, but that on an esoteric level, philosophy is at least partially useful for religion. Conversely, according to Schwartz, the "secret of the *Kuzari*" is the opposite: on an exoteric level the book retains a positive function for philosophy, whereas its true, esoteric meaning is a total and absolute negation of philosophy, but that for social reasons Judah Ha-Levi—who moved in intellectual circles of poets and philosophers, who are often no less intolerant than their opponents—had to conceal his true intention.[76] Esoteric writing, Schwartz points out, was typical of the period, and can be used for different ends and with different audiences. Others used esoteric writings to conceal their true intention from the masses; Ha-Levi used it, Schwartz suggests, to conceal his true intention as an "ultra-conservative" opposed to philosophy, from the intellectual class in which he moved and upon whom he was dependent, and from which he did not wish to be cut off.[77]

In Schwartz's brilliant analysis, for Ha-Levi what counts is only correct religious behavior and not intention in the sense of comprehension of the intellectual significance of religious actions. However, the author "did not omit" the positive reference to intention in the Kuzari king's dream, where an angel informs him that "your intention is pleasing to God but not your actions." According to Schwartz, this is a prime example of Ha-Levi's concealment, in his esoteric writing, of his "extreme conservatism," because the reader would not realize, from the story of the king's dream in the prologue, the insignificance of such intention.[78]

The problem with this specific point, however, is not that Ha-Levi "did not omit" the positive reference to intention, in order to conceal his true view, but that (as we shall see in the next section) he included it to begin with. A comparison of Ha-Levi's prologue with King Joseph's letter to Ḥisdai ibn Shaprut shows that the original letter makes no mention whatsoever of intention, and to the contrary, has the angel telling the king that his actions are

---

74   *Kuzari* 1:1. See the discussion in Schwartz, *Contradiction and Concealment*, p. 46 and note 4.
75   Leo Strauss, *Persecution and the Art of Writing* (Glencoe: Free Press, 1952), especially the title essay.
76   Schwartz, *Contradiction and Concealment*, p. 26. Schwartz then devotes all of Ch. 2 to a detailed argument of his thesis.
77   Schwartz, *Contradiction and Concealment*, pp. 47–48.
78   Schwartz, *Contradiction and Concealment*, p. 52.

pleasing to God. In short, there was nothing for Ha-Levi to "omit," because the reference to intention was his own literary innovation. This specific point does not undermine Schwartz's general argument that, for Judah Ha-Levi, correct actions as prescribed in the commandments of the Torah, are essential. It does, however, call into question whether the point is part of an exoteric or esoteric program. The reference to intention in Ha-Levi's account of the dream sets the stage for the Kuzari king to consult a philosopher, whose opinion (that correct intention rather than right action is important) he then explicitly rejects, a rejection of the philosophical position that is overt and exoteric, and is in no way concealed.

Ha-Levi also openly expressed his objections to "Greek wisdom" (*hokhmat yevanit*)[79] in one of his poems, where he said: "Do not let Greek wisdom entice you / Which has no fruit but only flowers."[80] Whatever the extent of this objection—and what follows is an attack on Aristotelian metaphysics, especially the doctrine of the eternity of the world, and not on philosophy *per se*—it is certainly explicit, and is not written esoterically.[81]

As will become evident below, our reading of Judah Ha-Levi is, therefore, not esoteric, and his central theory of the "divine faculty" is, in our understanding, an attempt to provide what was for him a scientific (i.e., philosophical) explanation of undeniable historical facts.

[VI.7]   THE PROLOGUE TO THE *KUZARI*

[VI.7.a]   THE PROLOGUE AND KING JOSEPH'S LETTER

The prologue to the *Kuzari*, dealing with the King of the Khazar's dream and culminating in his eventual conversion to Judaism, is loosely based on—and has several parallels with—the letter from King Joseph of the Khazars to Hisdai

---

[79]   The phrase, which is in the construct and in grammatical terms actually means "the wisdom of Greek" derives from the Babylonian Talmud, Bava Qama 82b–83a, Menahot 64b and Sota 49b, in the context of an elderly man who knew "the wisdom of Greek" and thereby assisted forces attacking Jerusalem, resulting in the cursing of a person who teaches his child "the wisdom of Greek." According to Rashi and to Rambam (Commentary on the Mishnah, Sota 9:15), the reference of the prohibition is to a Greek secret code which no longer exists.

[80]   Poem 211, "Devarekha be-mor 'over requhim" in H. Schirmann, *Ha-Shirah Ha-'Ivrit Be-Sefarad Uve-Provence* (Jerusalem: Mosad Bialik, 1961), vol. 1, p. 493, line 27. Schirmann notes that the rest of the poem shows that Ha-Levi's objection is not to Greek wisdom in general (such as the natural sciences), but to Aristotelian metaphysics.

[81]   Schwartz cites this passage in his Hebrew article "Greek Wisdom: A New Look at the Period of the Polemic Over the Study of Philosophy" in *Sinai* 104 (1989), p. 149, with no implication of esoteric writing.

ibn Shaprut. No less signficant than the parallels, however, are differences between them, differences which served Ha-Levi's literary and philosophical needs, which is why Yochanan Silman assigned the story of the king's dream in section I and conversion in section II to Ha-Levi's late thought (as a glance at the chart above [VI.6.c] shows).

The parallels include the references to the king's piety and sincerity; his vision (or dream) of an angel of God; the king's contacts with representatives of Christianity and Islam; his search for the true religion, invitation of a Jewish representative, and ultimate circumcision and conversion to Judaism; the Khazars' victory in wars and building a replica of Moses' Tabernacle; the invitation of Jewish sages to teach them Torah.

The differences, however, are, if anything, more important. First, Ha-Levi's prologue changes the order of the story. King Joseph's letter records a preliminary conversion, even before the king heard the arguments of the representatives of the religions, a conversion which was then completed (including circumcision) before he studied with a Jewish sage. By contrast, Ha-Levi's king only converts (at the beginning of section II) after a lengthy dialogue with the Jewish sage (all of section I). Similary, in King Joseph's letter, King Bulan built a Tabernacle after his preliminary conversion, whereas in Ha-Levi's story the Kuzari builds a sanctuary after his complete conversion and circumcision.

Second, in King Joseph's letter, King Bulan had an actual vision of an angel, i.e., he had a true experience of prophecy, whereas in Ha-Levi's prologue the angel "as it were" spoke with the king, i.e., the experience is less than true prophecy (since, as we shall see, non-Jews do not have the ability to prophesy).

Third, in King Joseph's letter, Bulan is informed that his actions please God, whereas in Ha-Levi's prologue the king is told that his intentions are pleasing to God, but not his actions.

Fourth, according to King Joseph's letter, Bulan did not initiate the dialogue with Christianity and Islam, but rather received ambassadors and messages from the rulers of those respective empires, who sought to win his alliance with their political as well as religious cause. Ha-Levi's king, by contrast, is interested in learning about the other religions and initiates the contact.

Fifth, Ha-Levi's king solicits the opinion of a philosopher, whereas King Joseph's letter makes no reference to the involvement of a philosopher.

Sixth, according to King Joseph, Bulan first turned to a Jewish sage, whereas Ha-Levi's king initially rejects inviting a Jew since the Jews are universally despised an nowhere exercise temporal power.

Seventh, in King Joseph's letter, the Christian and Muslim spokesmen do not actually advance the claims of their respective religions; when asked by the king which other religion (not their own religion) is true, both specify Judaism. Conversely, in Ha-Levi's prologue, the Christian and Muslim present in some detail their religious views, and only when the king expresses skepticism about their claims do they make reference to Judaism, as a basis for their own religions.

In short, King Joseph's letter to Ḥisdai ibn Shaprut serves as a basis for Ha-Levi's prologue, but no more than a basis. Ha-Levi felt free to adopt the story, while adapting it to his literary and polemical purposes.

[VI.7.b] LEO STRAUSS: WHY DID JUDAH HA-LEVI CHOOSE HIS PROLOGUE?

Leo Strauss asks why Judah Ha-Levi needed the literary device of his prologue, with the story of the conversion of the king of the Khazars. Since Ha-Levi regarded mere intentions as inadequate, and emphasized the importance of actions, he needed an extraordinary religious act—conversion of an actual king—for his defense of Judaism.

> In the case of an author of Halevi's rank, it is safe to assume that the connection between the content of his work and its form is as necessary as such a connection can possibly be: he must have chosen the peculiar form of the *Kuzari* because he considered it the ideal setting for a defense of Judaism...Judaism has to be defended before a Gentile. Besides, a Gentile who is a Christian or a Muslim, recognizes the Divine origin of the Jewish religion; hence Judaism has to be defended before a pagan...Judaism, the "despised religion" of a persecuted nation, has to be defended before a pagan occupying a most exalted position, before a pagan king...Now the Jewish scholar conversing with the Kuzari succeeds not merely in defending Judaism, but in converting the king...to Judaism...Yet such a conversion can easily be invented by any poet...Hence, Halevi chooses an actual conversion of a pagan king, and an actual conversation leading to that conversion, between the king and a Jewish scholar.[82]

[VI.7.c] THE PROBLEM OF THE KING'S DREAM

One of the differences (as noted above) between Ha-Levi's prologue and King Joseph's letter to Ḥisdai ibn Shaprut is that the letter refers to an actual prophetic experience of revelation, whereas the prologue refers only to a dream of an angel "as it were." According to Ha-Levi's theory of prophecy, which will be discussed below, only native-born Jews, descended physically from Abraham, Isaac and Jacob, possess a biological ability for prophesy, "the divine faculty" (Arabic: *amr ilahi*; Hebrew: *'inyan elohi*). Even a convert to Judaism, who is equal to native-born Jews in other respects, lacks this in-born "divine

---

[82]   Leo Strauss, "The Law of Reason in the *Kuzari*," in *Persecution and the Art of Writing* (Glencoe: The Free Press, 1952), pp. 101–102.

faculty" and, therefore, could theoretically never attain prophecy, although he can become a holy or pious person (Arabic: *waly*; Hebrew: *ḥasid*).[83] The Kuzari king, by this standard, fails to meet the requirements for prophecy, and in a sense the king's prophetic (or quasi-prophetic) vision of an angel directly contradicts a major tenet of Ha-Levi's theory of Jewish identity and particularity.

Harry A. Wolfson suggested that Ha-Levi differentiated between two different levels of prophecy. True prophecy is the experience of divine "revelation" (Arabic: *al-waḥy*). The pious or holy person is not a prophet in the true sense, and cannot experience direct divine revelation, but can experience "inspiration" (Arabic: *al-ilham*; *limud* or *limud elohi* in Judah ibn Tibbon's Hebrew translation). Wolfson suggests that "revelation" is general and public prophecy, whereas the lower level of "inspiration" is a kind of personal experience of instruction.[84]

Following Wolfson's differentiation of two levels of prophecy in Ha-Levi, Robert Eisen suggests that the Kuzari king's dream is an instance of the lower level of "inspiration," which some non-Jews in the Bible (such as Balaam in Numbers 22–24) were able to attain. Such "inspiration" (like dreams) is individual and subjective, rather than public and objective. Moreover, as the dialogue progresses, the king's dream, which served only to set the stage for the truth of Jewish religious claims, recedes in importance, and the Jewish sage persuades the king by rational arguments, not by interpreting the dream.[85]

Both Wolfson and Eisen thus treat the Kuzari's dream as an inferior kind of prophecy. Ha-Levi, however, diverged on this point from King Joseph's letter, as we have seen. The letter claims that Bulan actually saw an angel of God, who explicitly told the king that God had sent him, but Ha-Levi states carefully that the king saw "as it were" or "as if" (Arabic: *ka-anna*; Hebrew: *ke-ilu*) the angel at night in a dream. In short, there is no problem if we conclude, based on Ha-Levi's own language, that the king's dream is a merely a dream, and not prophecy or even "inspiration."

[VI.7.d] THE KING'S CONVERSION TO JUDAISM

According to Judah Ha-Levi's theory of "the divine faculty," a convert (Hebrew: *ger*) can never attain prophecy, and thus is ultimately not the equal of native-born Jews descended from Abraham, Isaac and Jacob. Prophecy, however,

---

83   *Kuzari* 1:115.

84   Harry A. Wolfson, "Halevy and Maimonides on Prophecy" in *Jewish Quarterly Review* 32/4 (1942), pp. 345–370; 33/1 (1942), pp. 49–82.

85   Robert Eisen, "The Problem of the King's Dream and Non-Jewish Prophecy in Judah Ha-Levi's *Kuzari*" in *Jewish Thought and Philosophy* 3 (1994), pp. 231–247.

is only one aspect of the inequality of converts in Ha-Levi's thought, which differs in this regard from the generally equal status of converts in Jewish law. According to the Babylonian Talmud (Yevamot 47b), with the exception of some technical matters, the convert "is a Jew in all respects," consistent with the verse "There shall be one Torah and one statute for you and for the alien (*ger*) living among you" (Numbers 15:16), which the rabbis understood as referring to the convert. But in the *Kuzari* 1:26–27, the inequality of the convert is not limited to prophecy. The king asks: "If this be so, then your belief is confined to yourselves?" To which the Jewish sage replies: "Yes, but any Gentile who joins us unconditionally shares our good fortune, without, however, being quite equal to us...The Law was given to us because [God] led us out of Egypt, and remained attached to us, because we are the pick (Arabic: *ṣafwah*; Hebrew: *segulah*) of mankind."[86]

Daniel Lasker has suggested that there is a connection between the gradual conversion in stages of the Khazars and the inequality of converts in Ha-Levi's theory.[87] Ha-Levi believed that a divine religion does not arise gradually, like human religions based on reason, but suddenly and completely.[88] Lasker, like Yochanan Silman and Colette Sirat before him, then shows that there is a parallel between Ha-Levi's description of the gradual conversion of the Khazars (in *Kuzari* 2:1) and the way human religions evolve (in *Kuzari* 1:80–81). In both cases, the gradual process begins with individuals who slowly learn the truth, which they then start to share with some others, until many follow them, or until a ruler compels the masses to accept the religion. Lasker also points out that even after the king's conversion, he continues to refer to the Jews and Judaism in the second person, "you" (thus excluding himself), and notes further that in their gradual process of conversion, their material success and their military victories, the Khazars resembled the Christians and Muslims (whose religions are human, not divine, although they are based on Judaism), and not the dispersed Jews and their "despised religion."

The parallel that Lasker posits between the Khazars' proselyte Judaism and Christianity and Islam (which combine divine Jewish elements with human pagan elements) becomes explicit in the *Kuzari* 4:11, when the Jewish sage says:

> I would compare them (the Christians and Muslims) to proselytes who did not accept the whole law in all its branches, but only the fundamental principles, if their (the Christians' and the Muslims') actions did not belie their

---

86   *Kuzari* 1:26–27. Hirschfeld ed. p. 47.
87   Daniel Lasker, "Proselyte Judaism, Christianity and Islam in the Thought of Judah Halevi" in *Jewish Quarterly Review* 81/1–2 (1980), pp. 75–92.
88   *Kuzari* 1:80–81.

words...Retaining the relics of ancient idolatry and feast days, they changed nothing but the forms. These were, indeed, demolished, but the relics were not removed. I might almost say that the verse in the Bible, occurring repeatedly, "Do not serve strange gods, wood and stone" (Deuteronomy 28:36, 64) contains an allusion to those who worship the wood [i.e., the Christian cross], and those who worship the stone [i.e., the Muslims' *Ka'ba* in Mecca]...It is true that they...believe in God...The leader of each of these parties [i.e., Jesus and Muḥammad] maintained that he had found the divine light at its source.[89]

As Lasker shows, Christianity and Islam are thus not equal to Judaism, the divine religion, but are successful imitations of it, in Ha-Levi's view. Proselyte Judaism, which accepts the roots if not all the branches of Judaism, is an even closer imitation of the native tree, but is still not its equal.

[VI.7.e]   THE CHRISTIAN AND MUSLIM SPOKESMEN

Ha-Levi's Kuzari king initially consults a philosopher in the hope of understanding his dream, that an angel informed him that his intentions were pleasing to God, but not his actions. The philosopher—the archetypal Aristotelian of the day (as we saw above, VI.4.d)—is incapable of satisfying the king's curiosity and search for truth, because everything he says contradicts what the king was told, and doesn't explain it. Either the message of the dream is true, or the philosopher is correct that God does not know or care about the king and his actions, so all that matters is to strive to know the truth, in which case the king's dream is an illusion, not an authentic experience of a divine communication. The king, then, committed to the integrity of his experience and convinced of its authenticity, turns to the representatives of the dominant world religions of the day, Christianity and Islam. But the universally despised Jews evidently do not enjoy divine favor, so there is no need to invite a Jewish representative.

Eliezer Schweid has called the literary structure of this section of the Prologue "a drama of errors," because it enables the Kuzari king (and the reader) to learn from errors and thereby progress to the truth. According to Schweid, the king's first error was to consult a philosopher. His second error was to refuse initially to invite a Jew.[90]

The presentations of the Christian and Muslim representatives are divided into two sections, one of which describes the general foundations of the religion and its relationship to the Biblical history of Israel, and the other of which describes the specific tenets of that particular religion. Both other religions thus end up confirming the truth and status of their Jewish source.

---

[89]   Kuzari 4:11; Hirschfeld ed. p. 216 (my modifications).
[90]   Schweid, "The Art of Dialogue in the *Kuzari* and its Theoretical Meaning," p. 62.

In short, there is a clear asymmetry in the relations of the three monotheistic traditions in the Middle Ages and in the inter-religious polemic, and thus also in the Prologue to the *Kuzari* and in King Joseph's letter. As presented in the Prologue, the most reasonable and persuasive claims of Christianity and Islam are those which they share with Judaism and each other, whereas their particular claims are the least reasonable in the eyes of the king. Moreover, it is only in the case of Judaism (at least the Judaism of the Bible) that the claims of one of the religions are reinforced and confirmed by other religions (a central point in the account in King Joseph's letter). The problem with the Jews, from the Christian and Muslim perspectives, is not what they believe (which the Christians and Muslims also believe), but what they do not believe (namely the additional claims, respectively, of Christianity and Islam).

Despite the fact that Ha-Levi obviously framed the arguments of the Christian and Muslim to serve his polemical purposes, Schweid regards their presentations as fair and realistic, as was the philosopher's earlier presentation.[91] Dov Schwartz rejects this assessment of the Christian presentation, which, he argues, is slanted and does not reflect any known contemporary church.[92] The Christian's presentation is a combination of two different trends, that of Jesus, who affirmed the Torah and its commandments (in a paraphrase of Matthew 5:17), and that of Paul, who abrogated the Torah and regarded the Church as the "true Israel." Since classical Gentile Christianity followed the Pauline trend, and no known church combined both trends, Schwartz concludes that Ha-Levi's depiction of Christianity is slanted for polemical reasons: classical Christian dogmas contradict reason; Paul's claim that the Church is the "true Israel" reinforces the original choice of Israel; Jesus' reaffirmation of the Torah reinforces the importance of actions and performing the commandments.

The king responds to the Christian's presentation:

> I see here no logical conclusion; nay, logic rejects most of what you say. If both appearances and experience are so palpable that they take hold of the whole heart, compelling belief in a thing of which one is not convinced, they render the matter more feasible by a semblance of logic...As for me, I cannot accept these things, because they came upon me suddenly, not having grown up in them.[93]

The Kuzari king is making three arguments here against Christianity. First, he is claiming that fundamental Christian dogmas, such as the Trinity and the Incarnation, are illogical and rationally impossible. But how do

---

[91]   Schweid, "The Art of Dialogue in the *Kuzari* and its Theoretical Meaning," p. 63.

[92]   Dov Schwartz, "Judah Ha-Levi on Christianity and on Empirical Science" (Hebrew), in *Association for Jewish Studies Review* (1994), pp. 1–24.

[93]   *Kuzari* 1:5. Hirschfeld ed. p. 42 (my modifications).

these Christian doctrines differ from some traditional Jewish beliefs, eg., in miracles? We can understand the argument in light of Daniel Lasker's analysis in his important study, *Jewish Philosophical Polemics Against Christianity in the Middle Ages*.[94] There is a difference between a miracle, which is impossible according to the laws of nature, and things which are logically impossible (such as a round triangle). A miracle violates the laws of nature, but miracles, like these laws, derive from God's will, and are therefore possible in principle; God can violate the laws of nature that he established. However, it is absurd to suggest that God can violate logic by making a round triangle. Christian dogmas, such as the Trinity and the Incarnation, are not miraculous suspensions of the laws of nature, but are logically impossible and thus absurd.

Second, the Kuzari king is arguing that there is no way empirically to verify the Christian claims. One can affirm a miracle on the basis of empirical verification, and as we shall see, this is the claim that Ha-Levi (like Sa'adiah Ga'on before him) makes for the public miracles the Israelites experienced at the exodus from Egypt, but such empirical verification is lacking in the Christian claims.

The Kuzari's third claim is that in the absences of rational persuasion or empirical verification, people may affirm what they are accustomed to hearing from childhood, which, therefore, strikes them as reasonable. The king, however, was not raised as a Christian, and accordingly has no such reason to affirm what is not inherently reasonable or empirically verifiable. Dov Schwartz regards this argument as failing as a criterion for accepting or rejecting a positive or philosophical religion.[95] Schwartz's criticism is undoubtedly correct in philosophical terms—the truth of claims does not depend on whether we are accustomed to them. However, Ha-Levi's argument here is not philosophical but psychological. Ha-Levi is pointing out the empirical fact that many, if not most, people tend to affirm a particular belief, not because they arrived at it through research (like the Kuzari), but because from childhood exposure they were accustomed to those ideas (be they religious or political). Christianity, the Kuzari king is arguing, cannot persuade an outsider on objective rational or empirical grounds, so a person not already exposed to its claims from childhood has no other subjective reasons to accept it.

The Muslim's presentation differs from that of the Christian because Islam does not have the Christian problem of irrational dogmas. The Muslim affirms his belief in the existence, unity and incorporeality of God. The

---

94   Originally published byKtav (New York, 1977); second edition: Littmann Library of Jewish Civilization (Oxford, 2007).

95   Dov Schwartz, "Judah Ha-Levi on Christianity and on Empirical Science," p. 7.

anthropomorphisms attributed to God in the Qur'an are, therefore, to be taken metaphorically, not literally. Up to this point the Muslim's claims present no problem from rational or Jewish perspectives. However, then the Muslim's presentation switches to specifically Islamic doctrines: "Our book (i.e., the Qur'an) is the speech of God, being a miracle, which we are bound to accept for its own sake, since no one is able to bring anything similar to it, or to one of its verses."[96] Ha-Levi is describing here the Islamic belief that the Qur'an itself is the speech of God, and that its very language is miraculous, because no human is capable of writing such a book (or even one of its verses). The miraculous language of the Qur'an is thus proof of its having been divinely revealed, and not composed by any human.[97] The Kuzari king rejects this argument on the grounds that a non-Arab has no way to verify it. Furthermore, he questions whether revelation is even possible:

> If anyone is to be guided in matters divine, and to be convinced that God speaks to man, while he considers it improbable, he must be convinced of it by means of generally known facts, which allow no refutation, and particularly imbue him with the belief that God has spoken to man. Although your book may be a miracle, as long as it is written in Arabic, a non-Arab, as I am, cannot perceive its miraculous character; and even if it were read to me, I could not distinguish between it and any other book written in the Arabic language.[98]

In his rejection of the Muslim's claims, the king does not argue that the claims are irrational and inherently unverifiable, as he did with the Christian. The problem is also not the psychological one of an individual being subjectively accustomed to the claims. Rather it is a sociological problem of a cultural convention. The fact that a group of people share a conventional truth which they accept for cultural reasons does not constitute objective proof of that conventional truth for people outside that group and its culture, and claims taken for granted in one culture have no meaning in another

---

96   *Kuzari* 1:5. Hirschfeld ed. p. 42.

97   Ha-Levi is referring here to Qur'an, Sura (chapter) 2:23, "The Cow": "And if ye are in doubt as to what we have revealed from time to time to our servant, then produce a Sura like thereunto; and call your witnesses or helpers (if there are any) besides God, if your (doubts) are true." (English translation by Abdullah Yusuf Ali [Lahore, 1934], p. 21). Ali comments as follows: "How do we know that there is revelation, and that it is from God? Here is a concrete test. The teacher of God's truth has placed before you many Suras. Can you produce one like it? If there is anyone besides God, who can inspire spiritual truth in such noble language, produce your evidence...All true revelation is itself a miracle, and stands on its own merits." A revision of the Ali translation and commentary was published by the Presidency of Islamic Researches, Ifta, Call and Guidance and the King Fahd Holy Qur'an Printing Complex in Madinah.

98   *Kuzari* 1:6. Hirschfeld ed. p. 43 (my modifications).

cultural context.

Both the Christian and Muslim representatives attempt to counter the Kuzari's skepticism and to reinforce the reasonableness of their claims by referring to the common denominator of all three monotheistic traditions, namely the public, miraculous events of Israel's history in the Bible, which are not subject to the doubts voiced by the king. The Kuzari then concludes:

> I see myself compelled to ask the Jews, because they are the relic of the children of Israel. For I see that they constitute in themselves the evidence for the divine law on earth.[99]

Note that the king does not say here that the religion of the Jews — whom he has yet to consult — is the true religion, but that the Jews themselves are "the evidence for the divine law on earth." It is the historical existence of the Jewish people which ultimately proves the truth of the Torah, a radical claim to which we shall return.

[VI.7.f] THE TERM "ḤAVER"

In King Joseph's letter to Ḥisdai ibn Shaprut the Christian spokesman is called *komer* (priest), and the Muslim spokesman is called *qadi* (judge of religious law in Islam), and the Jewish representatives are simply called *ḥakhamim* (sages). Judah Ha-Levi does not use these terms in the prologue to the *Kuzari*. The Christian and Muslim representatives are both called *'alim*, a general term for a scholar or learned person. The Jewish representative, however, is called *ḥabr*, which in Arabic is the term for a non-Muslim religious authority, such as a rabbi or bishop. The Arabic term is cognate with the Hebrew *ḥaver* (member, associate, fellow), which in Second Temple times was a term in Pharisaic Judaism for a member of a fellowship (*ḥavurah*) of Jews who strictly observed the laws of tithes, of the *terumah* (heave-offerings to the priests), and of purity and impurity.[100] The Mishnah describes conditions, including education and a trial period, for the acceptance of members (including women and slaves) in these fellowships. The term was also in use in the period of the Babylonian Geonim and in the Middle Ages, and in the 11th century was the term for judges in the Jewish communities of the Land of Israel, Egypt and Syria. The Hebrew term then came to be used for sages among many Arabic-speaking Jews, and presumably then was adopted, in its Arabic cognate form, by Muslims referring to non-Muslim religious authorities.

---

99   *Kuzari* 1:10. Hirschfeld ed. p. 44.
100   See the discussion in Ephraim Urbach, *The Sages: Their Concepts and Beliefs* (Jerusalem: Magnes Press, 1979), vol. 1, pp. 583 ff.

[VI.8] THE ḤAVER'S REPLY: HISTORICAL KNOWLEDGE VS. METAPHYSICAL SPECULATION

[VI.8.a] THE SUPERIORITY OF HISTORICAL EXPERIENCE

In the prologue's "drama of errors" (as Schweid called it), we saw that the Kuzari king rejected the Muslim's claims, because they lack external, objective verification. The king sets forth the three requisite criteria for such verification of claims of historical revelation: (a) that the alleged revelation involve a change in nature; (b) that the alleged revelation be documented by those who experienced it directly; (c) that the alleged revelation be experienced by masses, not by a few individuals.

> The human mind cannot believe that God has intercourse with man, except by a miracle which changes the nature of things. He then recognizes that to do so, [God] alone is capable, who created them from nought. It must also have taken place in the presence of great multitudes, who saw it distinctly, and did not learn it from reports and traditions. Even then, they must examine the matter carefully and repeatedly, so that no suspicion of imagination or magic can enter their minds. Then it is possible that the mind may grasp this extraordinary matter, viz. that the Creator of this world and the next, of the heavens and lights, should hold intercourse with this contemptible piece of clay, I mean man, speak to him, and fulfill his wishes and desires.[101]

The "drama of errors" continues, however, because the king does not understand the Ḥaver's reply:

> I believe in the God of Abraham, Isaac and Israel, who led the children of Israel out of Egypt with signs and miracles; who fed them in the desert and gave them the land, after having made them traverse the sea and the Jordan [River] in a miraculous way; who sent Moses with his law, and subsequently thousands of prophets, who confirmed his law by promises to the observant, and threats to the disobedient. Our belief is comprised in the Torah—a very large domain.[102]

The king questions this reply, amazed that the Ḥaver identified gave him a particularistic explanation in terms of Israel's history, rather than a universalistic explanation in terms of the creation of the world. What the king failed to understand, however, is that the Ḥaver's reply was formulated precisely in the external and objective terms that the king himself required to verify a religion, whereas referring in universal terms to creation would have failed to meet his own criteria.

---

[101] *Kuzari* 1:8. Hirschfeld ed. p. 43.
[102] *Kuzari* 1:11. Hirschfeld ed. p. 44.

The question of how best to verify a religion, in universalistic and natural terms, or in particularistic and historical terms, seems to have been of concern to Judah Ha-Levi for some time before he wrote the *Kuzari*. Abraham ibn Ezra's long (i.e., standard) commentary to the first verse of the Decalogue (Exodus 20:2 — "I am the Lord your God who brought you out of the land of Egypt") states:

> Judah Ha-Levi asked me why the Torah says, "I am the Lord your God, who brought you out of the land of Egypt," and did not say, "who created the heaven and the earth, and I made you."[103]

Ha-Levi was clearly not persuaded by Ibn Ezra's explanation that "I am the Lord" is addressed to the intelligentsia, and "who brought you out of the land of Egypt" was addressed to the masses, who could not grasp abstract universal truth and needed something more particularistic, concrete and graphic, based on their personal and collective experience. To the contrary, for Ha-Levi, historical truth, based on immediate experience, is far more certain than metaphysical speculation. The Ḥaver, therefore, explains his reply to the king:

> What you express is religion based on speculation and system, the research of thought, but open to many doubts. Now ask the philosophers, and you will find that they do not agree on one action or on one principle, since some doctrines can be established by arguments, which are only partially satisfactory, and still much less capable of being proved.[104]

The Ḥaver's thus explains that his reply is based on actual historical experience, which is preferable to a reply based on dubious speculation, and conforms precisely to the objective criteria for verifying a religion that the king himself had established. The Ḥaver confirms this approach by citing a parable of the king of India. If the Kuzari should hear that Indian society is well-ordered and just, he could not infer that India is ruled by a king, because he would have no way to know whether the Indians behave justly on account of a king, on account of their own morality, or for both reasons. However, if the Kuzari were to receive emissaries from the king of India, bearing uniquely Indian gifts, including medicines that heal him from his ailments, he could no longer doubt that India is ruled by a king whose power he had experienced.[105]

Ha-Levi thus rejects the Kalam approach of his predecessors (such as Sa'adiah Ga'on and Baḥya ibn Paquda) of proving the existence of God on the

---

[103] Review the discussion above, Ch. 5 (V.4.d.i).
[104] *Kuzari* 1:13. Hirschfeld ed. p. 45. (My modifications).
[105] *Kuzari* 1:19–22.

basis of creation. Experience, rather than speculation, is the path to certainty. As the Ḥaver reiterates to the Kuzari:

> In this way I answered your first question. In the same strain Moses spoke to Pharaoh, when he told him: "The God of the Hebrews sent me to you," viz. the God of Abraham, Isaac and Jacob. For Abraham was well-known to the nations, who also knew that the divine spirit was in contact with the patriarchs, cared for them, and performed miracles for them. He did not say: "The God of heaven and earth" nor "my creator and yours sent me." In the same way, God commenced his speech to the assembled people of Israel: "I am God whom you worship, who has led you out of the land of Egypt," but he did not say, "I am the creator of the world and your creator." Now in the same style I spoke to you, a prince of the Khazars, when you asked me about my creed. I answered you as was fitting, and is fitting for the whole of Israel who knew these things, first from personal experience, and afterwards through uninterrupted tradition, which is equal to the former.[106]

[VI.8.b] THE RELIABILITY OF TRADITION

For Judah Ha-Levi, immediate experience is indubitable and indisputable, and serves as the basis of his critique of Aristotelian philosophy, the Kalam, and the claims of Islam, which are not empirically verifiable. As we saw, the Kuzari king established three criteria for empirically-based verification of alleged revelation: it must involve a change in nature, it must be documented by those who experienced it directly, and it must be experienced by masses, not by a few individuals. The Ḥaver reiterates that his answer, which the king did not initially understand, meets the test of these three criteria. But he concludes that the Jews "knew these things, first from personal experience, and afterwards through uninterrupted tradition (Arabic: *tuwatur*), which is equal" to such personal experience (*Kuzari* 1:25). Similarly, he says elsewhere: "We are obligated to accept witnessing (Arabic: *mushahadah*; Hebrew: *'edut*) and uninterrupted tradition (Arabic: *tuwatur*) which is like witnessing" (*Kuzari* 5:14).

Clearly, the immediate personal experience is limited to the first generation, and is not shared by subsequent generations. They have to rely on tradition, which, Ha-Levi states, is equivalent to direct experience in terms of certainty. The Arabic term Ha-Levi uses here for tradition is *tuwatur* (from the root *watara*, which means to stretch or tighten a string), meaning a constant or uninterrupted succession. Judah ibn Tibbon translated it in Hebrew as *qabbalah nimshekhet* (continual tradition). *Tuwatur* is not mere tradition, which in Arabic is called *taqlid*, but has a specific connotation in

---

[106] *Kuzari* 1:25. Hirschfeld ed. pp. 46–47. (My modifications).

Islamic usage. Michael Schwarz has shown that *khabr mutawatir* (a continual or uninterrupted report) refers to the belief that the text of the Qur'an as we have it is the correct and original version given by the prophet Muḥammad to his contemporaries. This uninterrupted report is based on two conditions: (a) that the original transmission was public; (b) that the subsequent transmission over the generations was equally public.[107] Binyamin Abrahamov subsequently defined such an uninterrupted report as one which is transmitted by so many people that their character and number preclude the possibility of error or deceit.[108]

This argument, that it is the public nature of the original testimony of those who witnessed the event, and the public nature of the subsequent transmission of that testimony over the generations, that preclude the possibility of error or deceit, was central to Saʿadiah Gaʾon's exposition of "authentic tradition,"[109] and is even more central to Judah Ha-Levi's theory that tradition is the equivalent of direct experience in terms of reliability (a point the Kuzari king then also affirms). Judah Ha-Levi, like Saʿadiah Gaʾon before him, thus adopts Islamic arguments for the truth of the Qur'an and applies them to Jewish claims of the truth of the Torah and its revelation at Sinai.[110]

[VI.9]   THE UNIQUENESS OF ISRAEL AND THE "DIVINE FACULTY"

[VI.9.a]   JUDAH HA-LEVI, SAʾADIAH GAʾON AND ABRAHAM IBN EZRA

The historical paradox that concerned Judah Ha-Levi was not whether there is something unique about Jewish people. For him, that is an indisputable historical fact, the evidence of which is public. The challenge he faced was to explain that paradox. How can one explain the survival of a tiny nation, who had been conquered, defeated, occupied or exiled by all of the great civilizations of the ancient world, civilizations that then disappeared from

---

107   Michael Schwarz, Review of Yehudah Even-Shemuel's translation of the *Kuzari*, in *Kiriat Sefer* 49 (1974), pp. 200–202.

108   Binyamin Abrahamov, "Necessary Knowledge in Islamic Theology" in *British Journal of Middle Eastern Studies* 20/1 (1993), p. 22, note 15.

109   Cf. Saʿadiah Gaʾon, *Book of Beliefs and Opinions* 3:6; see the discussion in Chapter 2 (II.3.b).

110   The argument has also been used by such modern Jewish thinkers as Moses Mendelssohn in the 18th century, Samson Raphael Hirsch in the 19th century, and Eliezer Berkovits in the 20th century.

history? How can one explain the asymmetry of religious claims, when only the claims of Judaism, the universally "despised faith" are inherently accepted and reinforced by the otherwise conflicting and unsupported claims of two great universal religions and empires, Christianity and Islam? Finally, how can one explain the peculiar fact (which for Ha-Levi was an undeniable fact) that the only prophets universally acknowledged (i.e., by Christianity and Islam) to be prophets are those of Israel, and that there is no connection between the phenomenon of prophecy and philosophic sophistication? If the task of the philosopher is to explain reality, the reality in need of explanation is not only the realm of nature, but also the realm of history.

For Sa'adiah Ga'on and Abraham ibn Ezra, what makes the Jewish people unique is the Torah. According to Sa'adiah, "Our nation of the children of Israel is a nation only by virtue of its laws."[111] Similarly, as we saw in the previous chapter, Abraham ibn Ezra attributed Jewish uniqueness and ability to escape and transcend astral decrees to their observance of the Torah; they are directly ruled by God, and not by stellar constellations, "so long as they observe the Torah."

> God took Israel as his inheritance, and removed them from the governance of the constellar signs, so long as they are in his governance by doing what he commanded them in his Torah. That is why our ancestors said, "Israel has no constellar sign" (*ein mazal le-yisra'el*).[112]
> This is the meaning of "I and your people were distinguished" (Exodus 33:16). This is what the Sages meant by saying "Israel has no constellar sign" (*ein mazal le-yisra'el*), so long as they observe the Torah. If they do not observe it, the constellar sign will rule them, as has been demonstrated.[113]

In other words, for such rationalists as Sa'adiah Ga'on and Abraham ibn Ezra, there is nothing inherently unique about Jews; what is unique, and makes them unique, is the Torah. For Judah Ha-Levi, however, the rationalists have not dealt with a more fundamental and radical question. Of course the Torah is unique, and was revealed by God. But why do only the Jews have the Torah, and not other nations? Why are the only true prophets, universally acknowledged as such, to whom God was revealed, to be found among the Jewish people? This is the question Sa'adiah Ga'on and Abraham ibn Ezra (*inter alia*) did not address, and this is the question Judah Ha-Levi wishes to answer.

---

[111]   Sa'adiah Ga'on, *Book of Beliefs and Opinions* 3:7. Translation by Samuel Rosenblatt, p. 158.
[112]   Ibn Ezra, *Yesod Mora Ve-Sod Ha-Torah*, ch. 7:6, pp. 144–145.
[113]   Ibn Ezra, long (standard) commentary to Exodus 33:21.

[VI.9.b] JUDAH HA-LEVI'S ANSWER: THE HIERARCHY OF CREATION

For Judah Ha-Levi, it is not the Torah that defines the Jewish people—as maintained by Sa'adiah Ga'on and Abraham ibn Ezra—but the Jewish people who make possible the Torah. "If there were no Israelites, there would be no Torah. They did not derive their high position from Moses, but Moses received his for their sake."[114] What is it, then, about the Jewish people, which makes the existence of the Torah possible?

Ha-Levi's answer is that there is a hierarchy of existence, from the lowest to the highest: minerals, the vegetable kingdom, the animal kingdom, and the human species.[115] The vegetable kingdom is distinguished from minerals in virtue of the vegetative or nutritive faculty; animals are similarly distinguished from plants in virtue of the animal faculty of external sensation of voluntary locomotion; humans are distinguished from other animals in virtue of the rational faculty. In each case, what distinguishes a class from the class below it is a higher in-born biological faculty.

Among humans, however, there are exceptional individuals, the prophets.

> If we find a man who walks into the fire without hurt, or abstains from food for some time without starving, on whose face a light shines which the eye cannot bear, who is never ill, nor ages, until having reached life's natural end... equipped with the knowledge of what is hidden as to past and future... These are some of the characteristics of the undoubted prophets through whom God made himself manifest.[116]

These exceptional humans have the ability to communicate with the divine, in other words, to receive divine revelation. This ability is a function of a higher, supra-rational faculty, namely the "divine faculty" (Arabic: *amr ilahi*; Hebrew: *'inyan elohi*). Like the vegetative, animal and rational faculties, it is an in-born biological faculty of certain people.

This theory provides an explanation, in Ha-Levi's terms, of the historical anomaly of prophecy, namely that true prophets, universally acknowledged to be such (by Christians and Muslims as well as Jews) are only found among one nation, namely the Jewish people, just as only one species of animals, the human species, has the rational faculty. Therefore, when the Kuzari king asks the *ḥaver* whether it would not be better if all humans had the divine faculty, the *ḥaver* asks in reply whether it would not have been better had all

---

[114]   *Kuzari* 2:56. Hirschfeld ed. p. 117.
[115]   *Kuzari* 1:31–35.
[116]   *Kuzari* 1:41–43. Hirschfeld ed. p. 48.

animals been created with the rational faculty?[117] Wisdom, he suggests, is understanding things as they are, and not as we wished they would be.

Ha-Levi's theory of the biological and supra-rational "divine faculty" as the ability of certain people to prophesy is opposed to theories which attributed prophecy to the rational faculty. Nevertheless, Ha-Levi's theory does not permit any contradiction between what is known prophetically and what is known rationally, just as there cannot be any contradiction between what is known rationally and what is known empirically. The truth cannot contradict the truth. "Heaven forbid that there should be anything in the Bible to contradict that which is manifest or proved."[118] And again: "Heaven forbid that I should assume what is against sense and reason."[119]

Since the "divine faculty" is an in-born biological faculty, it cannot be acquired—any more than a vegetable could acquire the animal faculty or an animal the human rational faculty. Therefore, a person who converts to Judaism can be equal to native-born Jews in other respects, but can never acquire the "divine faculty" of prophecy.

[VI.9.c]   THE DIVINE FACULTY
(*AMR ILAHI; 'INYAN ELOHI*)

[VI.9.c.i]   *The Name Amr Ilahi*

In his discussion of the hierarchy of existence (in *Kuzari* 1:31–43), Judah Ha-Levi describes each of the four levels above minerals as possessing an *amr* (*'inyan*, in Judah ibn Tibbon's Hebrew translation), which we have translated as "faculty," that enables it to do certain functions. In the last section of the *Kuzari* (5:12), Ha-Levi presents a summary of psychology, based on Ibn Sina's theories. We find a parallel hierarchy in this summary, although with somewhat different terminology, because instead of *amr* ("faculty") Ha-Levi now uses the term *quah* (Hebrew: *koah*), a "power," to describe different functions of the human "soul" (Arabic: *nafs*; Hebrew: *nefesh*), which a person has in common, respectively, with plants (the vegetative soul) and with animals (the animal soul), and finally the rational soul, which is uniquely human. The following chart illustrates these parallels, and includes the Arabic terms, Judah ibn Tibbon's Hebrew translation, and examples of the functions Ha-Levi mentions for each faculty/power.

---

[117]   *Kuzari* 1:103.
[118]   *Kuzari* 1:67. Hirschfeld ed. p. 54.
[119]   *Kuzari* 1:89. Hirschfeld ed. p. 62.

Kuzari 1:31–43 — Hierarchy of Creation	*Kuzari* 5:12 — Summary of Psychology
The natural faculty (*al-amr al-tabi'i; ha-'inyan ha-tiv'i*) Nutrition, growth, reproduction	The vegetative power (*al-quah al-nabatiah; ha-koah ha-zimhi*) Nutrition, growth, reproduction
The faculty of soul (*al-amr al-nafsani; ha-'inyan ha-nafshi*) Motion, will, ethics, external senses	The animal power (*al-quah al-hayawaniah; ha-koah ha-hiyuni*) Sensation and motion
The rational faculty (*al-amr al-'aqli; ha-'inyan ha-sikhli*) Guiding ethics, home, politics, governance and laws	The power of speech (or: reason)[120] (*al-quah al-natqiyah; ha-koah ha-divri*) Theoretical intellect, practical intellect
The divine faculty (*al-amr al-ilahi; ha-'inyan ha-elohi*) "The prophet...through whom the attachment to divinity(*itisal al-lahut; hithabrut ha-davar ha-elohi*) is made known to the masses."	The holy spirit (*ruh muqadasah; ruah ha-qodesh*) "The power of speech (or: reason) of some people succeeds in being attached to the universal intellect (*al-itisal b'il-'aql al-kuli; hitdabeq ba-sekhel ha-ke-lali*), that lifts it up by inspiration and revelation (*al-ilham w'al-wahi; nevu'ah*), so it no longer needs to employ deduction and contemplation. This special quality (*khasah; segulah*) is called sanctification (*taqdis; qedushah*) and is called the holy spirit (*ruh muqadasah; ruah ha-qodesh*).

On the first three levels above minerals, namely the vegetative, animal and rational, the parallels are clear, despite the somewhat different terminology. The fourth level—that of prophecy—reflects substantive differences, not merely terminological ones, between what the *haver* described in the first section and the survey of psychological theory in the fifth section. Nevertheless, even on the fourth level of prophecy, the parallel between *amr* ('*inyan*—faculty) and *quah* (*koah*—power) is obvious. Moreover, in *Kuzari* 1:95, describing Adam, what is elsewhere called the *amr ilahi* is called "the divine power after reason" (*al-quah al-ilahi ba'ad al-'aql; ha-koah ha-elohi ahar ha-sekhel*).

The terminological differences may be insignificant, or their significance may be contextual. Shlomo Pines, on the other hand, suggests that the diffe-

---

120   The Arabic *natiq* means both speech and reason; speech is the external expression of inner thought. '*Ilm al-mantiq* is the science of logic. The Hebrew *divri*, meaning speech, thus also refers to reason.

rences result from the book's having been written in stages, over many years, and that in the first section the terminology reflects the views of Ibn Bajja, whereas in the fifth section the terminology is based on Ibn Sina.[121]

A further difficulty with the term *amr* is its ambivalence in Arabic. The singular *amr* has two different plural forms, each of which has a different meaning. *Amr*, plural *awamir* means a command (as in the term *emir*, a commander or leader). But *amr*, plural *umur*, means "matter," "affair," "concern," or simply "thing," and this is how Judah ibn Tibbon understood the term when he translated it as *'inyan*.

Harry Wolfson rejected the interpretation suggested byu Ignaz Goldziher in 1905 that the term *amr ilahi* refers to a hypostasis like the *logos* in Christian and philosophical usage, but rather suggested that it be understood contextually, and listed ten such contextual meanings in the *Kuzari*: (1) divine commandment, or (2) divine power in one of the following senses: (a) the divine power sustaining the world; (b) a supra-natural or prophetic power in a human enabling him to attain things the rational faculty cannot attain; (c) divine providence or decree; (d) divine rule in the world; (e) divine wisdom; (f) divine will and purpose; (g) divine love; (h) the divine covenant with Israel; (i) the divine light.[122]

Herbert Davidson has suggested that the term *amr ilahi* be translated as the divine "thing,"[123] and on the basis of Shi'ite sources of the term, Shlomo Pines translated it, depending on the context, as "divine influx" or "dispensation" as well as "thing" and "command."[124] Hartwig Hirschfeld's English translation of the *Kuzari* generally renders it "the divine influence," and in the translation of selections from the book by Isaak Heinemann it is called "the divine power."[125]

In short, the term *amr ilahi* is used in different contexts in the *Kuzari*, and there is no overall consensus as to how best to translate it. On the basis of the clear parallels between Ha-Levi's use of *amr* and *quah* to indicate different faculties of the soul, and the fact that he also used the term *amr* for the vegetative, animal and rational faculties, we translate *al-amr al-ilahi* as "the divine faculty."

---

[121] Shlomo Pines, "Shi'ite Terms and Conceptions in Judah Halevi's *Kuzari*,"in *Jerusalem Studies in Arabic and Islam* 2 (1980), pp. 215–217.

[122] Harry Wolfson, "Hallevi and Maimonides on Prophecy" in *Jewish Quarterly Review* 32/4 (1942), pp. 345–370; 33/1 (1942), pp. 49–82.

[123] Herbert Davidson, "The Active Intellect in the *Cuzari* and Hallevi's Theory of Causality" in *Revue des Etudes Juives* 131, no. 1–2 (1972), pp. 351–396.

[124] Shlomo Pines, "Shi'ite Terms and Conceptions in Judah Halev's *Kuzari*."

[125] Isaak Heinemann, in *Three Jewish Philosophers* (Philadelphia: Jewish Publication Society, 1945; New York: Harper Torchbooks, 1965).

[VI.9.c.ii] *The Amr Ilahi — a Biological Faculty*

The *amr ilahi* is thus an in-born biological faculty of certain people, just as the rational, animal and vegetative faculties are in-born and biological faculties, and are not acquired. Those unique people endowed with the *amr ilahi* "are, as it were, of another, angelic species."[126] Adam was created with this divine faculty, just as he was created with the rational faculty. The divine faculty was passed on from generation to generation, but unlike the rational faculty, with which the entire human species, descended from Adam, is endowed, in any given generation only one unique person received the divine faculty, although sometimes (in a theory resembling our modern conception of recessive genes) the divine faculty skipped a generation, which is why — Ha-Levi observes — children sometimes resemble their grandparents and not their parents. The divine faculty thus eventually reached Abraham; from Abraham it passed only to Isaac, not Ishmael; from Isaac it passed only to Jacob, not to Esau. At this point, however, a change occurred, and the *amr ilahi* passed from Jacob to all his children, who in turn passed it on to all their descendants, male and female.[127]

The individual possessing the *amr ilahi* has the capacity for prophecy, and sees prophetic visions with "the inner eye" (Arabic: *al-'ayn al-batinah*; Judah ibn Tibbon: *ha-'ayin ha-nisteret*; Yosef Kafih: *ha-'ayin ha-penimit*). Each prophet sees visions in accordance with his individual nature, which he then conveys to the masses in corporeal forms, forms that are true as seen by the imagination, but false in intellectual terms.

> To the chosen among his creatures [God] has given an inner eye which sees things as they really are, without any alteration...The prophets without doubt saw the divine world with the inner eye; they beheld a sight which harmonized with their natural imagination. Whatever they wrote down, they endowed with attributes as if they had seen them in corporeal form. These attributes are true as far as regards what is sought be inspiration, imagination and feeling; they are untrue as regards the reality which is sought by reason.[128]

---

[126] *Kuzari* 1:103. See the discussion of this passage in Hebert Davidson, "The Active Intellect in the *Cuzari* and Hallevi's Theory of Causality," p. 383.

[127] *Kuzari* 1:95.

[128] *Kuzari* 4:3. Hirschfeld ed. pp. 207–208. The term Hirschfeld translates as "inspiration" is *al-wahm*, (in Hirschfeld's Arabic text of the *Kuzari*, p. 240, line 3; in Kafih's text, p. 157, line 17; in the edition by David Baneth and Haggai Ben-Shammai, p. 155, line 17) which is more correctly translated "estimation" or "estimative faculty," and refers in animals to an instinctive ability to apprehend a notion the senses do not perceive, such as the sheep's ability to perceive that a wolf is dangerous, even if the sheep never previously saw a wolf. Perhaps Hirschfeld misread *al-wahm* as *ilham*, inspiration. Judah ibn Tibbon translates it as *mahshavah* (thought). On *wahm* see the discussion in Raphael Jospe, *Torah and Sophia: The Life and Thought of Shem Tov ibn Falaquera* (Cincinnati: Hebrew Union College Press, 1988), pp. 226 ff.

[VI.9.c.iii] *Choice, Essence and Shell*

Judah Ha-Levi describes the individual possessing the divine faculty as "the choice" (Arabic: *ṣafwah*; Hebrew: *segulah*, i.e., the choice or best part) and as "the essence" (Arabic: *lubb*; Hebrew: *lev*, i.e., the content, kernel or core). In relation to the "choice" and "essence" of humanity, others are "the shell" (Arabic: *qishr*; Hebrew: *qelipah*, i.e., the exterior, peel, skin or husk).[129] These terms can apply to individuals, and also to Israel in relation to the other nations.

Shlomo Pines and Harry Wolfson have shown that these terms are found in Shi'ite, and especially Isma'ili, literature,[130] and Wolfson suggested that Ha-Levi borrowed these terms for polemical reasons, to emphasize the uniqueness of the Jewish people and the land of Israel. The terminology also suits Ha-Levi's defense of Judaism as "the despised faith," since the heart, according to this theory, since the heart, as the most essential organ, is also the most sensitive, and thus vulnerable, of the organs.

> Our relation to the divine faculty is the same as that of the soul to the heart... In the same way as the heart may be affected by disease of the other organs... thus also is Israel exposed to ills originating in its inclining towards the Gentiles... The trials which meet us are meant to prove our faith, to cleanse us completely, and to remove all taint from us. If we are good, the divine faculty is with us in this world. You know that the elements gradually evolved metals, plants, animals, man, and finally the pure essence of man. The whole evolution took place for the sake of this essence, in order that the divine faculty should inhabit it. This essence, however (i.e., the people of Israel), came into existence for the sake of the highest essence, viz. the prophets and pious.[131]

The Jewish people are thus the "essence" of humanity, and the prophets — those who are able to activate their inborn "divine faculty — are "the essence of the essence."

[VI.9.c.iv] *The Conditions for Activating the Divine Faculty*

All native-born Jews, descendants of Abraham, Isaac and Jacob, possess the *amr ilahi*, and thus the potential for prophecy, but only a few Jews actually became prophets. What, then, are the conditions for activating the divine faculty and attaining prophecy?

---

129   *Kuzari* 1:95
130   Shlomo Pines, "Shi'ite Terms and Conceptions in Judah Halevi's *Kuzari*," in *Jerusalem Studies in Arabic and Islam* 2 (1980), pp. 165–251; Harry Wolfson, "Hallevi and Maimonides on Prophecy," pp. 271–273.
131   *Kuzari* 2:44. Hirschfeld ed. pp. 109–110 (my modifications).

Just as physical exercise strengthens the body and mental activity—study and thinking—strengthens the mind, the divine faculty is strengthened by "divine" activity, namely performing the divinely-revealed commandments of the Torah. This insight now provides the key for the Kuzari king to understand the meaning of his dream: "your intention is pleasing to God but not your actions." The king has been searching, throughout the story, for the correct actions which will please God. Incorrect physical exercise can harm the body, and learning false material harms the mind. By analogy, the divine faculty can only be activated and strengthened not by any religious behavior, but only by those "divine actions" actually commanded by God, and those actions are the ones commanded by God in the Torah, which is, in effect, the correct prescription providing the right medicine for the patient. As the Kuzari king himself acknowledges: "You now confirm the theory I had formed, and the opinion of what I saw in my dream, viz. that man can only merit the divine faculty by acting according to God's commands."[132] Religious behavior not commanded by God, accordingly, is at best ineffectual, and at worst, positively harmful, just as prescribing the wrong medicine can harm the patient.

> The conditions which render man fit to receive this divine faculty do not lie within him. It is impossible for him to gauge their quantity or quality, and even if their essence were known, yet neither their time, place, and connection, nor suitability, could be discovered. For this, inspired and detailed instruction is necessary...Whosoever strives by speculation and deduction to prepare the conditions for the reception of his inspiration, or by divining, as is found in the writings of astrologers, trying to call down supernatural beings, or manufacturing talismans, such a man is an unbeliever. He may bring offerings and burn incense in the name of speculation and conjecture, while he is in reality ignorant of that which he should do, how much, in which way, by what means, in which place, by whom, in which manner, and many other details, the enumeration of which would lead to far. He is like an ignoramus who enters the surgery of a physician famous for the curative power of his medicines. The physician is not at home, but people come for medicines. The fool dispenses them out of jars, knowing nothing of the contents, nor how much should be given to each person. Thus he kills with the very medicine which should have cured them. Should he by chance have effected a cure with one of the drugs, the people will turn to him and say that he helped them, till they discover that he deceived them.[133]

And again:

> We have...said that one cannot approach God except by his commands. For he knows their comprehensiveness, division, times, and places, and consequences

---

132   *Kuzari* 1:98. Hirschfeld ed. p. 70. (My modifications).
133   *Kuzari* 1:79. Hirschfeld ed. pp. 56–57. (My modifications).

in the fulfillment of which the pleasure of God and the connection with the divine faculty are to be gained.[134]

The detailed sacrificial cult and laws of purity of the Torah provide the necessary prescription for such divine actions by which the divine faculty can be activated and prophecy attained.[135] All of these conditions make possible the experience of "the visible Shekhinah (divine presence)" in prophecy. Every native-born Jew has the latent "hidden spiritual Shekhinah (divine presence)," but it is only when actively experiencing prophecy that what was hidden becomes visible in revelation.

> The visible Shekhinah has, indeed, disappeared, because it does not reveal itself except to a prophet or a favored community, and in a distinguished place...As regards the invisible and spiritual Shekhinah, it is with every born Israelite of virtuous life, pure heart, and upright mind before the God of Israel.[136]

In other words, the sacrificial cult commanded by the Torah to be performed, first in the portable Tabernacle in the wilderness and then in the Temple of Jerusalem, lies at the heart of the "divine actions" requisite for activating the divine faculty, experiencing prophecy, and revealing as "the visible Shekhinah" the otherwise latent "hidden spiritual Shekhinah." Of course, the sacrificial cult was a necessary, not a sufficient, condition for activating the divine faculty, and even when the Temple stood only a few Jews actually experienced prophecy. Nevertheless, in the absence of this necessary condition following the destruction of the Temple, there is no longer any way to fulfill the prescribed divine actions whereby the divine faculty was activated and prophecy attained.

[VI.10] THE LAND OF ISRAEL AND THE THEORY OF CLIMES

The second necessary condition necessary condition for activating the divine faculty is the land of Israel (which is called *Al-Sham*, i.e., Syria, the generic name for the area in the Arabic original). Like the people of Israel, the land of Israel has a special physical status, in Judah Ha-Levi's attempt to provide what was for him a scientific explanation of indisputable historical facts. We saw that the *amr ilahi* provided such an explanation of the historic anomaly that only the prophets of Israel are universally acknowledged to be true prophets, since

---

[134] *Kuzari* 3:23. Hirschfeld ed. pp. 162–163. (My modifications).

[135] *Kuzari* 2:14.

[136] *Kuzari* 5:23. Hirschfeld ed. p. 293. (My modifications).

they are also accepted as such by Christianity and Islam. Another historical anomaly to which Ha-Levi points is that all the prophets were active in or in the vicinity of the land of Israel, or concerning the land of Israel, from which he concludes that it is only in this area that the divine faculty can be activated.

> Whosoever prophesied did so either in the [Holy] land, or concerning it, viz. Abraham in order to reach it, Ezekiel and Daniel on account of it. The two latter had lived during the time of the first Temple, had seen the Shekhinah, through the influence of which each one who was duly prepared became of the elect and was able to prophesy. Adam lived and died in the land...Jeremiah's prophecy concerning Egypt was uttered in Egypt itself. This was also the case with Moses, Aaron and Miriam. Sinai and Paran are reckoned as belonging to the land, because they or on this side of the Red Sea...Do you not see that Jacob ascribed the vision which he saw, not to the purity of his soul, nor to his belief, nor to true integrity, but to the place, as it is said: "How awesome is this place!" (Genesis 28:17)...Was not Abraham also, and after having been greatly exalted, brought into contact with the divine faculty, and made the essence of this choice part, removed from his country to the place in which his perfection should become complete? Thus the agriculturer finds the root of a good tree in a desert place. He transplants it into properly tilled ground, to improve it and make it grow; to change it from a wild root to into a cultivated one, from one which bore fruit only by chance to one which produced a luxuriant crop. In the same way the gift of prophecy was retained among Abraham's descendants in the land of Israel, the property of many as long as they remained in the land, and fulfilled the required conditions, viz. purity, worship and sacrifices, and, above all, the presence of the Shekhinah.[137]

The land of Israel is thus uniquely qualified to produce prophets, just as choice grapes can only grow in certain soil.

> Priority belongs, in the first instance, to the people who, as stated before, are the choice part and essence, as I have mentioned. In the second instance, it would belong to the land, on account of the religious acts connected with it, which I would compare to the cultivation of the vineyard. No other place would share this distinction of the divine faculty, just as no other mountain might be able to produce good wine.[138]

We thus see that there are three factors contributing to the possibility of prophecy, each of which is a necessary condition for it to occur. The first factor is the *amr ilahi*. That in-born divine faculty, however, can only be activated when two conditions are fulfilled: (a) The performance of "divine actions," such as the sacrificial cult and laws of purity commanded

---

[137] *Kuzari* 2:14. Hirschfeld ed. pp. 89–92. (My modifications).
[138] *Kuzari* 2:12. Hirschfeld ed. pp. 88–89. (My modifications).

in the Torah; (b) Living in or in proximity to the land of Israel. Only the combination of these three factors makes possible prophecy and seeing the "visible Shekhinah." Prophecy is thus a product of nature as well as nurture, just as good wine can only be produced from choice grapes, in the appropriate soil, and with proper cultivation. In the absence of any of these factors, it is impossible to attain prophecy.

Why, however, is the land of Israel so uniquely qualified to produce prophets, so that "this land is worthy of being one degree below the Garden of Eden" while all other countries are, by comparison to it, "like shells?"[139] The reason, Ha-Levi posits, is that the land of Israel is found in the ideal median clime.

> Abraham was the choice [descendant of his grandfather] Eber, being his disciple, and for this reason he was called Hebrew. Eber represented the choice [descendant] of Shem, the latter that of Noah. [Shem] inherited the temperate climes, the middle and principal part of which is the land of Israel, the land of prophecy. Japheth turned towards north, and Ham towards south.[140]

Judah Ha-Levi is referring here to the theory of climes in classical and medieval geography. According to this theory, which goes back to Hippocrates (c. 460—c. 380 B.C.E.), a clime (Arabic: *iqlim*; Hebrew: *aqlim*), from the Greek *klima* (a slope, region or zone) is one of seven zones into which the earth is divided. The theory is discussed in detail, for example, by the Arab historian 'Abd Al-Raḥman ibn Khaldun (Tunis, 1332–1406) in his *Muqaddimah* ("An Introduction to History"), written in 1377.[141] Ibn Khaldun reports that the philosophers have divided the civilized area of the earth into the seven climes from south to north, with each clime extending from east to west. The first and southernmost clime is bordered on the south by the equator. To the north of the seventh clime is nothing but empty wilderness. Ibn Khaldun then proceeds to describe the various climes. The "land of Syria" (again, the generic term in Arabic for the region including the land of Israel) is located to the east of the Mediterranean Sea in the third clime. Ibn Khaldun refers to the Israelites having entered the land after wandering in the desert for 40 years, as recorded in the Qur'an, and also lists the coastal cities of the country, from south to north: Gaza, Ashkelon, Caesaria, Akko (Acre), Tyre, and Sidon, and mentions cities in the heartland including Hebron, Jerusalem and Tiberias. The fourth, i.e., middle, clime is the most temperate, due to its central location:

---

139 *Kuzari* 2:12.

140 Kuzari 1:95. Hirschfeld ed. p. 65. (My modifications).

141 On Ibn Khaldun, see the discussion in Ch. 2. English translation of the *Muqaddimah* by Franz Rosenthal; edited and abridged by N.J. Dawood (Princeton: Bollingen Series, 1989).

The north and south represent opposite extremes of cold and heat. It necessarily follows that there must be a gradual decrease from the extremes toward the centre, which, thus, is moderate. The fourth zone is the most temperate cultivated region. The bordering third and fifth zones are rather close to being temperate...The fifth, fourth and third zones occupy an intermediate position. They have an abundant share of temperance, which is the golden mean.[142]

Despite his having placed Syria in the third clime, south of the fourth clime, Ibn Khaldun then says that Iraq and Syria are in the middle clime and are the most temperate countries.

We also find similar views in earlier Arabic literature. For example, in the encyclopedic "Letters of the Pure Brethren" (*Rasa'il Ikhwan Al-Safa*),[143] the Iraqi says to the King of the Jinn: "Praised be God, who, preferring us to so many of his creatures, singled us out for the most central of all lands as our home."[144] A similar claim is then made by an Indian:

For us [God] singled out the most central of all lands in location, with the most equable of climates...with neither heat nor cold in excess...Here God placed the point of origin of Adam.[145]

Judah Ha-Levi thus adopts familiar claims from Arabic sources and counters them with the claim that the Jewish people are the essence and choice part of humanity, and that the land of Israel, the land of prophecy, lies in the ideal central clime. That is why Abraham had to migrate from Iraq to Canaan, and that is why the land of Israel constitutes the third factor in activating the *amr ilahi* and making prophecy possible.

[VI.11] THE SUPERIORITY OF THE HEBREW LANGUAGE

[VI.11.a] THE SUPERIORITY OF HEBREW
AS THE ORIGINAL LANGUAGE

We previously saw that according to Judah Ha-Levi, a divine religion does not arise gradually, like human religions based on reason, but suddenly and completely, and that there is a parallel between Ha-Levi's description of

---

142   Ibn Khaldun, *Muqaddimah*, Ch. 1, Third Prefatory Discussion, pp. 58–60.
143   On the Pure Brethren and their letters, see the discussions in Ch. 3 (III.1.f.vii) and Ch. 4 (IV.1.b).
144   English translation by Lenn E. Goodman, *The Case of the Animals Versus Man Before the King of the Jinn* (Boston: Twayne Publishers, 1978), ch. 19, p. 119.
145   *The Case of the Animals Versus Man Before the King of the Jinn*, ch. 19, pp. 120–121. In Ch. 23 there follows a general discussion of the seven climes.

the gradual conversion of the Khazars (in *Kuzari* 2:1) and the way human religions evolve (in *Kuzari* 1:80–81), beginning with individuals, and slowly spreading to others.[146] Ha-Levi affirmed a parallel theory of language. Just as the sudden and spontaneous appearance of a religion is evidence of its superiority and divine origin, so its non-conventional origins prove the superiority of the Hebrew language—the original language of creation—and of biblical poetry.[147]

Ha-Levi states explicitly that human languages are not natural or eternal, but are merely conventional:

> The Ḥaver said: Do you consider languages to be eternal and without beginning?
> The Kuzari said: No, they were generated and are conventional.
> The Ḥaver said: Have you ever seen anyone invent a language or heard of such a person?
> The Kuzari said: I have neither seen nor heard of this. Undoubtedly [languages] arose at some generation, prior to which there was no human language about which any nation could agree.[148]

It is noteworthy that the usual order of the *Kuzari* is reversed here: it is not the Kuzari king but the Ḥaver who asks the questions here, and it is not the Ḥaver but the king who responds.

Rambam was also of the view that "languages are conventional, not natural."[149] Judah Ha-Levi, however, uses this theory to demonstrate the superiority of Hebrew over other languages, just as Judaism is superior to other religions, which evolved gradually, by mutual consent. Hebrew, however, is neither conventional nor temporal. It is the divine language of creation—thus preceding human beings—and was the language of Adam and Eve. Why, then, are other languages often richer and more expressive than Hebrew?

> The Kuzari: Is Hebrew superior to the other languages? As we can see, they are more perfect and comprehensive than it.
> The Ḥaver: What happened to it is what happened to those who bear it, becoming poorer and weaker as they became fewer. In itself, it is the noblest of languages. According to reason and tradition, it is the language in which God spoke to Adam and Eve, and which they spoke to each other.[150]

---

146 See above, (VI.7.d), on the Kuzari king's conversion to Judaism.
147 This theme is explored more fully in "The Superiority of Oral Over Written Communication: Judah Ha-Levi's *Kuzari* and Modern Jewish Thought," in Raphael Jospe, *Jewish Philosophy: Foundations and Extensions, Vol. Two: On Philosophers and Their Thought* (Lanham: University Press of America, 2008), pp. 35–61.
148 *Kuzari* 1:53–56.
149 *Guide of the Perplexed* II:30.
150 *Kuzari* 2:67–68.

In a different context, Ha-Levi differentiated between "natural speech," which conforms to the speaker's thoughts, and "accidental speech," such as the speech of madmen, in which there is no such conformity. Hebrew is the "natural speech" par excellence,[151] because it is the language of God and the angels, the language of creation. Therefore, Adam was able to name all the animals in Hebrew: "Whatever Adam called a living creature, that was its name" (Genesis 2:19). Even the shape of the Hebrew letters of the alphabet "conforms to what is intended by them."[152]

[VI.11.b] THE SUPERIORITY OF ORAL OVER WRITTEN COMMUNICATION

Another aspect of the superiority of Hebrew relates to the general superiority of oral over written communication.

> The purpose of language is that what is in the soul of the speaker be attained by the soul of the listener. This purpose can only be completely fulfilled orally (Arabic: *mushafahatan*; Hebrew: *panim el panim*). For oral [communication] is superior to written [communication], as they said: "From the mouth of authors, and not from books" (*mi-pi soferim ve-lo mi-pi sefarim*). For in oral [communication] one is assisted by pauses, when a person stops speaking, or by continuing, in accordance with the subject; or by raising or lowering one's voice; or by various gestures to express amazement, a question, desire, fear, or submission, without which simple speech will be inadequate. Sometimes the speaker may be assisted by motions of his eyes, eyebrows, or his whole head and his hands, to express anger, pleasure, requests or pride in the appropriate measure.[153]

It is precisely in this regard that biblical Hebrew is superior to other languages. The originally unvocalized and unpunctuated consonantal written biblical text was given an oral dimension by means of the masoretic cantillation notes (*ta'amei ha-miqra*), by which the text is chanted in public reading, but which also punctuate the text, by connecting some words to others, and by making pauses of greater or lower value (like the comma, semi-colon and period in western languages) after certain words or phrases.

> The remnant of our divinely created and formed language contains subtle and profound elements in place of those oral gestures, namely the notes by which the Bible is read. They indicate pause and continuity, and separate question from answer, beginning from continuation, etc.[154]

---

151 *Kuzari* 5:20.
152 *Kuzari* 4:25.
153 *Kuzari* 2:72.
154 *Kuzari* 2:72.

The masoretic notes thus facilitate comprehension by punctuating and endowing the written text of the Bible with an oral quality of continuity vs. pause, intonation, and emphasis.

[VI.12]   THE TRANSMISSION OF SEMITIC CULTURE AND SCIENCE

Our discussion thus far has largely focused on Judah Ha-Levi's theories of Jewish uniqueness, especially regarding the supra-rational divine faculty with which Jews are endowed, and even the uniqueness of the land of Israel and of the Hebrew language. With regard, however, to intelligence and scientific knowledge—functions of theoretical intellect—and ethics—a function of practical intellect—there is no difference between the Jew and any other human being, since all humans are endowed with (and defined as a species by) intellect, both theoretical and practical.

Moreover, as we saw above,[155] Ha-Levi's theories do no permit any contradiction between what is known prophetically by the divine faculty, and what is known rationally, just as what we know rationally and what we know empirically must ultimately agree, since the truth cannot contradict the truth. "Heaven forbid that there should be anything in the Bible to contradict that which is manifest or proved."[156] And again: "Heaven forbid that I should assume what is against sense and reason."[157]

Ha-Levi, however, goes farther. It is not merely that the religious truth of the Jews and universal scientific truth do not contradict each other. Scientific truth ultimately also derives from Jewish sources. True, today when one seeks scientific truth one must resort to "Greek wisdom," but that is only because Jewish culture, which originally did include the sciences and ancient times, has declined over the centuries of persecution and exile, as has the material, economic and political situation of the Jews. Philosophy, which today is seen as foreign, was once native to Jewish-Semitic culture, from which it passed to the Greeks.

> There is an excuse for the philosophers. Being Greeks, science and religion did not come to them as inheritances. They belong to the descendants of Japheth, who inhabited the north, while that knowledge coming from Adam, and supported by the divine faculty, is only to be found among the progeny of Shem, who represented the successors of Noah and constituted, as it were, his choice part. This knowledge has always been connected with this choice part,

---

[155]   See the discussion in section VI.9.b.
[156]   *Kuzari* 1:67. Hirschfeld ed. p. 54.
[157]   *Kuzari* 1:89. Hirschfeld ed. p. 62.

and will always remain so. The Greeks only received it from Persia, when they became powerful. The Persians had it from the Chaldeans. It was only then that the famous [Greek] philosophers arose.[158]

When, in the Middle Ages, Greek works of science and philosophy were translated into Arabic, their ancient Hebrew origin was forgotten:

The Ḥaver said: What is your opinion of Solomon's accomplishments? Did he not, with the assistance of divine, intellectual and natural power, converse on all sciences? The inhabitants of the earth travelled to him, in order to carry forth his learning, even as far as India. Now the roots and principles of all sciences were handed down from us first to the Chaldeans, then to the Persians and Medes, then to Greece, and finally to the Romans. On account of the length of this period, and the many disturbing circumstances, it was forgotten that they had originated with the Hebrews, and so they were ascribed to the Greeks and Romans.[159]

As a result of the exile of the Jews from their homeland and all the persecutions they suffered, their books of scientific wisdom (which were read only by the intelligentsia) were lost, and all they retained was their religious literature (which was read, for practical reasons, by all the people).[160]

The notion that the Greeks learned the sciences from Semitic culture is not unique to Judah Ha-Levi and other Jewish thinkers, including Rambam, who also attributes the loss of ancient Jewish scientific literature to persecution and to the fact that the theoretical sciences—unlike religious literature—were not studied by the masses.[161] For example, the Islamic philosopher Muḥammad Abu Naṣr Al-Farabi (870–950 C.E.) wrote in his *Attainment of Happiness* (*Taḥsil al-Sa'adah*):

It is said that this science existed anciently among the Chaldeans, who are the people of al-'Iraq, subsequently reaching the people of Egypt, from there transmitted to the Greeks, where it remained until it was transmitted to the Syrians, and then to the Arabs.[162]

---

[158] *Kuzari* 1:63. Hirschfeld ed. p. 53. (My modifications).

[159] *Kuzari* 2:66. Hirschfeld ed. p. 124. (My modifications).

[160] *Kuzari* 4:31.

[161] Rambam, *Guide of the Perplexed* 1:71, also attributes the loss of ancient Jewish scientific literature to persecution and to the fact that the theoretical sciences—unlike religious literature—were not studied by the masses.

[162] English translation by Muhsin Mahdi, *Alfarabi's Philosophy of Plato and Aristotle* (Ithaca: Cornell University Press, 1969), #53, p. 43. Sections of this book (including this passage) were translated or paraphrased into Hebrew by Shem Tov ibn Falaquera (13th century, Spain), in his *Reshit Ḥokhmah* (*Beginning of Wisdom*), pp. 69–70. On Al-Farabi and this passage, see Ch. 1 (I.1.a).

Philo, whose works (it will be recalled) were unknown to Jews and Arabs in the Middle Ages, had also suggested that the Greeks had "borrowed" their wisdom from the Jews.[163]

For Judah Ha-Levi, in summary, the argument that the Greeks learned philosophy indirectly from the Jews serves two purposes. First, it establishes that the ancient Jews were the source of this universal human wisdom, which they received, together with their unique divine reason, by direct succession from Adam and then from Noah's son Shem. Second, the transmission of sciences from the Jews emphasizes that scientific wisdom (a function of theoretical intellect) and ethics (a function of practical intellect) are universal and common to all people. Jewish uniqueness, as we have seen, lies elsewhere, in religious areas, and is a function of the divine faculty.

[VI.13]   A UNIVERSAL ETHIC

[VI.13.a] THE UNIVERSAL LAW OF REASON

Judah Ha-Levi affirmed the rationality, and therefore the universality, of moral law. No human society can exist without moral law, not even a gang of bandits (at least on an internal level, within the gang).

> The Kuzari said:...I think I read in your books what is said, "What the Lord your God asks of you, only to fear the Lord your God" (Deuteronomy 10:12), and "What the Lord requires of you" (Micah 6:8), and many such other [statements].
> The Ḥaver said: These and similar [statements] are the rational laws (Arabic: *al-nawamis al-'aqliyah*; Hebrew: *ha-ḥuqim ha-sikhliyim*), which are the basis and preface to the divine law, preceding it in nature and in time, without which no human society can be governed. There cannot even be a gang of bandits without justice among themselves, if their association is to exist.[164]

Ha-Levi's attitude toward rational law can be interpreted positively or negatively. In a positive sense, the moral law is rational, and therefore universal among all humans, since reason is universal, even (on a minimal internal level) among bandits. On the basis of its rationality, all people may be expected to observe the moral law, regardless of its relation to or enactment in particular positive law.

---

[163] See the discussion in Harry Wolfson, *Philo: Foundations of Religious Philosophy in Judaism, Christianity and Islam* (Cambridge: Harvard University Press, 1962), Vol. 1, p. 141.
[164] *Kuzari* 2:47–48.

Leo Strauss, on the other hand, interprets this passage in a negative sense. In his reading of Ha-Levi, the law of reason has no practical authority, and, by the example of the gang of bandits, is nothing more than minimal cooperation for a common purpose. Only a moral law based on divine authority is truly binding.

> If the philosophers are right in their appraisal of natural morality, of morality not based on Divine revelation, natural morality is, strictly speaking, no morality at all: it is hardly distinguishable from the morality essential to the preservation of a gang of robbers. Natural morality being what it is, only a law revealed by the omnipotent and omniscient God and sanctioned by the omniscient and omnipotent God can make possible genuine morality, "categoric imperatives" . . . In defending Judaism, which, according to him, is the only true revealed religion, against the philosophers, he was conscious of defending morality itself, and therewith the cause, not only of Judaism, but of mankind at large.[165]

In our reading of Ha-Levi's theory, the role of the law of reason is positive, because it is a necessary condition for the observance of the divine law, "preceding it in nature and in time." Without the prior law of reason, therefore, the divine law could not exist.

[VI.13.b] RATIONAL AND DIVINE LAWS

What is the relationship between the rational moral law and divine law in Judah Ha-Levi's theory? Unlike Sa'adiah Ga'on, Ha-Levi does not use the same Arabic term for both types of law. Sa'adiah, it will be recalled, referred to both rational commandments (Arabic: *al-shara'ia al-'aqliyah*; Hebrew: *mizvot sikhliyot*) and traditional commandments (*al-shara'ia al-sam'iah*; Hebrew: *mizvot shim'iyot*) as *al-shara'ia* (Hebrew: *mizvot*).[166] Ha-Levi, on the other hand, preserved a terminological distinction between the two categories. Ha-Levi's parallel to Sa'adiah's traditional commandments is the category of "divine law" (*al-shari'ah al-ilahiyah*, in Judah ibn Tibbon's Hebrew translation: *ha-torah ha-elohit*). However, the parallel to Sa'adiah's rational commandments is "rational laws" (*al-nawamis al-'aqliyah*, in Ibn Tibbon's translation *ha-huqim ha-sikhliyim*). The Arabic term *namus* (in the singular) derives from the Greek *nomos*, law. Ha-Levi's more precise terminological distinction thus emphasizes that the moral law of reason is human in origin, in contrast with divinely commanded law.

As we saw in the previous section, the rational laws "are the basis and preface to the divine law, preceding it in nature and in time."

---

165   Leo Strauss, "The Law of Reason in the *Kuzari*," pp. 140–141.
166   See the discussion of rational and traditional commandments in Ch. 2 (II.3.1).

The passage continues:

> When Israel's disloyalty had come to such a pass that they disregarded rational and social principles (which are as absolutely necessary for a society as are the natural functions of eating, drinking, exercise, rest, sleeping and walking for the individual), but held fast to the sacrificial worship and other divine laws, [God] was satisfied with even less. It was told to them: "Would that you would observe those laws which rule the smallest and lowest society, such as refer to justice, good actions, and recognition of God's bounty." **For the divine law cannot become complete until the social and rational laws are perfected.** The rational law demands justice and recognition of God's bounty. What has he, who fails in this respect, to do with offerings, Sabbath, circumcision, etc., which reason neither demands, nor forbids? These are, however, the ordinations especially given to Israel as a corollary to the rational laws. Through this they received the advantage of the divine faculty.[167]

The priority of the rational laws to the divine laws is thus double. The rational laws are the foundation of any human society, whereas the divine laws are an addition or "corollary to the rational laws," given only to the Jewish people, endowed with the divine faculty. The corollary cannot exist, let alone be perfected, in the absence of the foundation. The rational laws are thus prior to the divine laws in nature and in time. Thus far, Ha-Levi's distinction resembles Sa'adiah Ga'on's.

For Ha-Levi, however, the priority goes farther, and reflects the hierarchy of creation. The vegetative faculty, in his hierarchy, is prior in nature and time to the animal faculty, and the animal faculty to the rational faculty. Similarly, the rational faculty of all humans must be prior in time and nature to the divine faculty with which only Israel is endowed. In this hierarchical structure, the rational law is prior in nature and in time, but the divine law is superior to it.

[VI.13.c] PLATONIC JUSTICE AND THE *ḤASID*

The relationship between the universal law of reason and divine law is also emphasized by the connection Judah Ha-Levi posits between the Torah and the Platonic conception of justice. The fourth book of Plato's *Republic* draws a parallel between social-political justice and individual justice. In each case, every part (of the individual or of society) must contribute according to its ability, and must receive in accordance with its needs.[168] The three social classes—the rulers, the guardians and the workers—parallel the three faculties of the soul—reason, the "spirited" faculty, also called anger (i.e., the

---

[167]   *Kuzari* 2:48. Hirschfeld ed. pp. 111–112. (My modifications).
[168]   It was this Platonic formula which Karl Marx took over.

emotions), and the appetites. In society, the rulers (the philosopher-kings) should rule over the workers with the assistance of the guardians (soldiers), just as in the individual the rational faculty should rule over the appetites with the assistance of the spirited faculty. This balance or harmony is justice in both society and the individual.

The Platonic three-fold division of the soul was already to be found in Sa'adiah Ga'on's *Book of Beliefs and Opinions*, in which he equated each faculty with a biblical term for soul.[169] To recapitulate, the following chart shows this tri-partite psychology as it is found in two different places in Sa'adiah's *Book of Beliefs and Opinions*, and compares it with a similar scheme in Judah Ha-Levi's *Kuzari*.

The biblical name of the soul's faculty, according to Sa'adiah, *Book of Beliefs and Opinions* 6:3	The name of the soul's faculty in Sa'adiah, *Book of Beliefs and Opinions* 6:3	The name of the soul's faculty in Sa'adiah, *Book of Beliefs and Opinions* 10:2	The name of the soul's faculty in Judah Ha-Levi's *Kuzari* 2:50
Nefesh (= Appetite)	Arabic: *Mushtahiyah* Hebrew: *Mit'aveh*	Arabic: *Al-Shahwah* Hebrew: *Ta'avah*	Arabic: *Al-Shahwah* Hebrew: *Ta'avah*
Ru'ah (= Anger, Passion, Emotion)	Arabic: *Ghaḍibah* Hebrew: *Ko'es*	Arabic: *Al-Ghaḍab* Hebrew: *Ka'as*	Arabic: *Al-Ghalabah* Hebrew: *Niẓahon*
Neshamah (= Knowledge, Cognition, Thought)	Arabic: *'Alimah* Hebrew: *Mada'i*	Arabic: *Al-Tamyiz* Hebrew: *Ha-Hakarah*	Arabic: *Al-Fikr* Hebrew: *Maḥshavah*

The wise person exercises self-control and discipline, because correct behavior is characterized by balance. Each of the soul's faculties should receive in proportion to its needs, so that it may function properly and proportionately. In Sa'adiah's words:[170]

> The soul has three faculties — the appetitive, the impulsive, and the cognitive. As for the appetitive faculty, it is that whereby a human being entertains the desire for food and drink and sexual intercourse...The impulsive faculty is that which renders a person courageous and bold, and endows him with zeal for leadership and championing the common weal...As for the cognitive faculty...it exercises judgment over the two other faculties.

---

169   See the discussion in Ch. 2 (II.3.o).
170   Sa'adiah, *Book of Beliefs and Opinions* 10:2. English translation by Samuel Rosenblatt (New Haven: Yale University Press, 1948), pp. 360–361.

Returning, now, to Judah Ha-Levi, this tri-partite psychology forms the basis for the Platonic parallel between justice as harmony in society and justice as harmony in the individual, a parallel which then makes possible his referring to the good person as the guardian or ruler of his state.[171] The way of life commanded by the Torah promotes such a harmonious justice of moderation, and not an ascetic ideal:

> The divine law imposes no asceticism on us. It rather desires that we should keep the equipoise, and grant every mental and physical faculty its due, as much as it can bear, without overburdening one faculty at the expense of another...Our Torah, as a whole, is divided between fear, love and joy, by each of which one can approach God. Your contrition on a fast day does not bring you closer to God than your joy on the Sabbath and holidays, if it is the result of thought and intention. Just as penitential prayers require intention, so does rejoicing in his law and commandments, so that you should rejoice in the commandments out of your love for the one who commanded them...And if your joy should lead you so far as to sing and dance, they are also worship and contact with the divine faculty.[172]

The precise balance and measure, however, cannot be left up to the individual, because people cannot apportion their needs accurately. Therefore the Torah provides the requisite specific order and proportions, for the rational as well as for divine laws, because even if people know their general moral obligations, they are unable, on their own, to determine the details of the correct order and proportion of their various obligations.

> The social and rational laws are those generally known. The divine ones, however, which were added in order that they should exist in the people of the "Living God" who guides them, were not known until they were explained in detail by [God]. Even the social and rational laws are not quite known, and though one might know the gist of them, their scope remains unknown...The limitation of all these things to the amount of general usefulness is God's.[173]

The Torah, then, provides the specific requisite order and proportions for the balanced life that constitutes justice in the individual and in society. So when the king asks the Ḥaver to describe the behavior of "the good" person, the *ḥasid*,[174] he replies:

---

[171]   The Platonic equation of justice in the individual and in society was earlier found in Baḥya ibn Paquda's *Duties of the Heart*, Part I, on the unity of God, end of ch. 7; and in Abraham ibn Ezra's commentary to Ecclesiastes 9:14–15.

[172]   *Kuzari* 2:50.

[173]   *Kuzari* 3:7. Hirschfeld ed. p. 141. (My modifications).

[174]   The Arabic term here is *khair*, meaning good or excellent. Ibn Tibbon translated it as *ḥasid*.

The good person is one who is the guardian[175] of his country, who apportions to all its inhabitants their provisions and all their needs. He is just with them ... so when he needs them they obey him ...

The good person is the ruler[176] listening to his senses and spiritual and physical faculties, which he governs politically ... He is fit to be the ruler, because if he were the ruler of a country he would be just, the way he is just to his body and soul.[177]

Here, then, Judah Ha-Levi, despite his reputation for being an outstanding opponent of philosophy, is overtly adopting the Platonic equation of justice in the individual and justice in society, and then also identifying that philosophic ideal of justice with the way of life commanded in the Torah. The ethic of the Torah is a rational ethic, but that law of reason ultimately requires divine guidance for its detailed implementation.

That identification of the Torah's ethic with Platonic justice becomes explicit in Judah Ha-Levi's discussion of why public communal prayer is superior to private individual prayer, in light of the Platonic doctrine of "the portion of the whole:"

In a similar manner, Plato styles that which is expended on behalf of the law, "the portion of the whole." If the individual, however, neglects this "portion of the whole" which is the basis of the welfare of the commonwealth of which he forms a part, in the belief that he does better in spending it on himself, he sins against the commonwealth, and more, against himself. For the relation of the individual to his commonwealth is as the relation of the single limb to the body. Should the arm, in case bleeding is required, refuse its blood, the whole body, the arm included, would suffer. It is, however, the duty of the individual to bear hardships, or even death, for the sake of the welfare of the commonwealth. He must particularly be careful to contribute his "portion of the whole" without fail. Since ordinary speculation did not institute this, God prescribed it in tithes, gifts and offerings, etc., as a "portion of the whole."[178]

The Torah, he continues, prescribes the individual's obligation to give "the portion of the whole" in property (such as tithes), in actions (such as the Sabbath and festivals), in words (such as in prayers), and in abstract matters (such as love, fear and joy).

---

[175]   The Arabic verb *ḥafiza* means to guard, protect, defend, take care of. Ibn Tibbon translates it as *nizhar*, and Kafiḥ translates it as *shomer*.

[176]   The Arabic term here is *rais*, literally the "head," i.e. the leader, chief or ruler of a country, and the term for president in modern usage.

[177]   *Kuzari* 3:3–5.

[178]   *Kuzari* 3:19. Hirschfeld ed. p. 157. (My modifications). Cf. Plato *Republic* II:369, II:374, IV:434.

The ideal of the good man or *ḥasid* is not merely a theoretical construct for Ha-Levi. As we have seen, the requisite conditions for prophecy—including the "divine actions" of the sacrificial worship in the Temple—no longer exist. Moreover, even if the conditions did exist today, only a few Jews ever attained prophecy. However, although there are no more prophets, there is no inherent impediment, even for converts, to live the good life, and to attain the rank of *ḥasid*, which Ha-Levi defined as ranking "below prophecy." Such a person, Ha-Levi explains, is punctilious is observing "the divine laws" (such as circumcision and Sabbath), "the political [or: social] laws," (such as the prohibition of murder, adultery and theft), and "the spiritual laws," namely correct beliefs and opinions (such as belief in one God).[179] Of such people Ha-Levi says:

> This is as if the Shekhinah (the divine presence) were with him continually, and the angels potentially accompany him. If he is strengthened by doing the good, and he is in places worthy of the Shekhinah, then they will actually accompany him, and he will see them with his own eyes, below the rank of prophecy.[180]

Prophecy, then, is no longer possible, but the good life can lead to a rank just below that of the prophets.

[VI.14]   GOD: ATTRIBUTES, NAMES AND ACTIONS

[VI.14.a] THE DIVINE ATTRIBUTES

The "spiritual laws" of the Torah deal with affirmation of true opinions, and thus provide the ideological basis for the Torah. This may explain why the discussion of the divine attributes immediately follows the story of the Kuzari king's conversion at the beginning of the second section of the book.

With the exception of the Tetragrammaton—the four-lettered name of God consisting of the letters Y, H, V and H but not pronounced phonetically[181]—all the names of God are understood by Judah Ha-Levi to be attributes describing how creatures are affected by divine activities. So when God is described as compassionate (*raḥum*), the attribute is not to be understood in the sense of the human emotion of pitying someone who is misfortunate, but in the sense of divine activity benefitting someone and improving his situation, an activity that a person might perform out of such emotion. In other words, the attribute actually describes an activity of God, and not God himself:

---

[179]   *Kuzari* 3:11.
[180]   *Kuzari* 3:11.
[181]   See the discussion of the Tetragrammaton in Ch. 5 (V.6.b).

All the names of God, save the Tetragrammaton, are predicates and attributive descriptions, derived from the way his creatures are affected by his decrees and measures. He is called compassionate if he improves the condition of any man whom people pity for his sorry plight. They attribute to him mercy and compassion, although this is, in our conception, surely nothing but a weakness of the soul and a quick movement of nature. This cannot be applied to God... His nature remains quite unaffected by it.[182]

As Ha-Levi then explains, there are three kinds of attributes: active, relational, and negative. The first category is called *ta'thiri* (from the root *athar*, to pass on, affect, influence) meaning action, effect, influence. Following Judah ibn Tibbon's translation of this term as *ma'asiyot*, we translate it as "active." The second category is called *idafi* (from the root *dafa*, additional, supplementary), meaning relational or relative, which Ibn Tibbon translated as *tefeliyot*. The third category is called *salbi* (from the root *salaba*, to take away, remove, deny, negate), meaning negative, which Ibn Tibbon translated as *sheliliyot*.

All attributes except the Tetragrammaton are divided into three classes, viz. active, relational and negative. As regards the active attributes, they are derived from acts coming from him by natural means, such as "making poor and rich," "exalting or casting down," "merciful and compassionate"... As regards relational attributes, such as "blessed," "praised," "glorified," "holy"... they are borrowed from the reverence given to him by humans. However numerous they may be, they produce no multiplicity, as far as [God] is concerned, nor do they affect his unity. As regards negative attributes, such as "living," "only," "first," and "last," they are given to him to negate their opposites, but not to establish them in the sense we understand them... If we say "living God" and "God of life," it is only a relative expression opposing the gods of the nations which are dead gods lacking action. In the same way we take the term "one" to negate multiplicity, but not to establish unity as we understand it... All these attributes do not touch [God's] essence nor do they imply multiplicity.[183]

Ha-Levi's position on the divine attributes thus falls between that of Sa'adiah Ga'on, who acknowledged three "essential" attributes of the creator (life, power and knowledge)—although he suggested that the multiplicity is merely verbal, not real—and Rambam, who permitted only active and negative attributes, and denied the possibility of the relational attributes that Ha-Levi affirmed.

---

[182] *Kuzari* 2:2. Hirschfeld ed. p. 83. (My modifications).
[183] *Kuzari* 2:2. Hirschfeld ed. pp. 83–84. (My modifications).

[VI.14.b] THE NAMES OF GOD

In the last chapter (V.6) we saw that the Tetragrammaton has a special status, unlike any other name of God, in Abraham ibn Ezra's thought, and in Ch. 10 we will see how Rambam understands its unique significance. Judah Ha-Levi's approach, however, differs fundamentally. For Ha-Levi, the different names of God do not merely indicate the diverse ways in which God's activity or relation to the world may be understood, but the radically different ways in which people approach God, and the different stages in the spiritual development of individuals and humanity as a whole.

According to Ha-Levi, the name *Elohim* is a generic term for any concept of divinity, and even for angelic or natural powers, and for human judges, whereas the Tetragrammaton is a proper name unique to the God of Israel. However, the difference is not merely theoretical, but has existential importance in the lives of people as they relate to God. *Elohim* can (at best) be known, whereas the Tetragrammaton is the subject of loving commitment and devotion, even to the point of being willing to die for that love.[184]

> *Elohim* is a term signifying the ruler, or governor, of the world, if I allude to the possession of the whole of it, and of a portion, if I refer to the powers either of nature or the spheres, or of a human judge. The word has a plural form, because it was so used by gentile idolators, who believed that every deity was invested with astral and other powers. Each of these was called *eloah*;[185] their united forces were therefore called *elohim*...As a result of their theories, they worshipped not one being, but many, which they styled *elohim*. This is a collective form which comprises all causes equally. A more exact and more lofty name is to be found in the form known as the Tetragrammaton. This is a proper noun, which can only be indicated by attributes...If [God] was commonly styled *Elohim*, the Tetragrammaton was used as a special name.[186]

The generic name *Elohim* is known through speculation and deduction (which often are erroneous), and—as we saw in the philosopher's discourse with the Kuzari king at the beginning of the book—the God of the philosophers is not a creator, does not know us, and is not involved in any way in the conduct of the world or in human affairs. This abstract concept has no practical existential important in the way we live our lives. The Tetragrammaton, by contrast, is known experientially and personally:

---

[184] *Kuzari* 4:15.
[185] *Eloah* is the singular form, *elohim* the plural form of the word.
[186] *Kuzari* 4:1. Hirschfeld ed. pp. 198–199. (My modifications).

Demonstration can lead astray. Demonstration was the mother of heresy and destructive ideas. What was it, if not the wish to demonstrate, that led the dualists to assume two eternal causes? And what led the materialists[187] to teach that the sphere was not only eternal, but its own primary cause, as well as that of other matter? The worshippers of fire and the sun are but the result of the desire to demonstrate. There are differences in the ways of demonstration... Those who go to the utmost length are the philosophers, and the ways of their arguments led them to teach of a God which neither benefits nor injures, and knows nothing of our prayers, offerings, obedience or disobedience, and that the world is as eternal as [God] himself. None of them applies a distinct proper name to God, except he who hears [God's] address, command, or prohibition... He bestows on [God] some name as a designation for [God] who spoke to him, and he is convinced that [God] is the creator of the world from nothing... Noah, Abraham, Isaac and Jacob, Moses and the prophets called him Y-H-V-H in their experience [of God in prophecy]... The [divine] faculty and governance attach to people. The pure people attach to him, so they can experience him by means of what is called glory, Shekhinah, kingship, fire, cloud, image, form, the appearance of the rainbow (Ezekiel 1:28), etc. For these provided a proof for them that the speech with them was from God, and they called it "the glory of the Lord."[188]

Elohim as a common noun can thus be known by rational deduction, like any other abstract scientific principle. Error regarding such deductive knowledge of God is no more harmful than any other scientific error.[189] But the Tetragrammaton, as a proper noun, is known experientially by the prophets. Therefore, *Elohim* can be modified by the definite-article, but not the Tetragrammaton.

The fact that in Ha-Levi's theory the difference between the names of God is not merely theoretical (as it is for others), but of vital existential importance in the lives of people, reflects his consistent emphasis — going back to the prologue of the book — on proper behavior, and not merely correct intention. The difference is epitomized by Ha-Levi's parallel distinction between "the God of Aristotle," known by "deduction" (Arabic: *qiyas*; Hebrew: *haqashah*), and "the God of Abraham," known by "taste" (Arabic: *dhauq*; Hebrew: *ta'am*), in other words, by intense personal experience. As Ha-Levi has the Kuzari king acknowledge:

---

187 Ha-Levi here uses the Arabic term *dahriya*, from the term *dahr* (eternity), which refers in Islamic usage to unbelief, atheism or materialism, or the notion that the world is eternal and has no creator. It is often understood to be referred to in the *Qur'an*, Sura 45:24: "And they say: What is there but our life in this world? We shall die and we live, and nothing but time can destroy us. But of that they have no knowledge; they merely conjecture." (English translation by Abdullah Yusuf Ali).

188 *Kuzari* 4:3. Hirschfeld ed. pp. 199–200. (My modifications).

189 *Kuzari* 4:13.

Now I understand the difference between *Elohim* and the Tetragrammaton, and I see how far the God of Abraham is different from the God of Aristotle. People yearn for the Tetragrammaton with a yearning for taste and experience. But they tend towards *Elohim* by deduction. That taste brings the one who attains it to devote his life for his love, and to die for it. But according to that deduction, exalting [God] is obligatory only so long as it is not harmful and does not cause suffering.[190]

In summary, many Jewish thinkers and exegetes discuss the significance of different names used for God in the Bible and later Jewish tradition. Those differences generally indicate the different ways in which God is understood to relate to the world and to people. Judah Ha-Levi saw the forest, not only the trees: the different names indicate not only how God relates to the world, but how people relate to God. One approach is purely theoretical and intellectual, and the other approach is practical and experiential. Both ways—and both names—also represent different stages in the spiritual and intellectual development of individuals, who progresses from knowledge of *Elohim* to love of the Tetragrammaton, a progression epitomized by the difference between "the God of Aristotle" known by deduction, and "the God of Abraham" experienced in taste.

In this way Judah Ha-Levi also reverses the common rationalist order, according to which the Bible, which "speaks according to human language" (a major theme in Rambam's thought), reflects an earlier and more primitive historical stage, from which one progresses to a more sophisticated philosophical understanding of God and the world. To the contrary, Judah Ha-Levi posits the necessary transition from a more limited and unsatisfactory deductive knowledge of the "God of Aristotle" to a higher and superior "taste" of "the God of Abraham."

[VI.14.c] THE DIVINE ACTIONS

The impersonal God of Aristotle transcends action; the only activity worthy of God is knowledge, and the only subject worth of God's knowledge is God. The personal God of Abraham, on the other hand, is an active creator and governor of the world. The fact that God governs the world does not, however, preclude human free will, because some of God's actions are direct, but others are indirect. God is the first cause of the natural order, which cannot be the product of accident. However, and in sharp contrast with Islamic occasionalism, God is not directly and immediately involved with everything. Rather, God created the natural order, in which there are intermediate causes, and this indirect structure of intermediate causality permits freedom.

---

[190]   *Kuzari* 4:16.

Ha-Levi then differentiates between four kinds of actions in the world: (a) Divine actions directly caused by and attributable to the will of God. (b) Natural actions which are the result of secondary and intermediate causes in the natural order. (c) Accidental actions, which also have intermediate causes (and thus are not completely accidental), but have no natural causes. (d) Voluntary actions, the cause of which is human free will.[191]

[VI.15] THE MESSIANIC FUTURE

Humans thus have free will, and their actions are voluntary. That freedom, of course, is not absolute, and human power to act voluntarily is limited in both the natural and divine realms.

> The actions of the Torah, like the work of nature, are entirely determined by God, and are beyond human power...Who can apportion the actions so that the divine faculty will rest on them, except God alone? This is the error committed by alchemists and spiritualists.[192] The alchemists thought that they could apportion natural fire by their scales and produce what they want, and thus alter the nature those materials, as is done in living beings by natural heat which transforms food into blood, flesh, bone and other organs. They toil to discover a fire of the same kind...When the spiritualists heard that the appearance of divine signs from Adam down to the children of Israel was accomplished by sacrifices, they thought it was the result of cleverness and research, and that the prophets were actually highly learned persons who accomplished those wonders by means of deduction. So they thought they could also determine the sacrifices to be offered at certain times and by astrological calculations...The actions of the Torah, however, are like natural ones; one doesn't know their motions and calculates them in vain...It is clear from this that there is no approaching God except by God's commandments, and there is no way to know God's commandments except by prophecy, not by deduction or reasoning, and we have no contact with those commandments except by true tradition. Those who handed down these commandments were not a few individuals, but were many great sages who were nearly prophets. Even if those transmitting the Torah had only been the priests, Levites and elders, the [transmission] from Moses would never have been interrupted.[193]

---

[191] *Kuzari* 5:20.

[192] The Arabic term here is *al-ruḥaniyun* (Hebrew: *ruḥaniyim*), which Hirschfeld translates as "necromancers." Since the following discussion does not refer to calling up the spirits of the dead, it seems to me more likely that Ha-Levi is referring to the astral magic of calling down "spiritual emanations" (*ruḥaniyat*), discussed above (VI.4.f).

[193] *Kuzari* 3:53. Hirschfeld ed. pp. 181–183. (My modifications).

In a sense, the other religions, in divine matters, resemble alchemy in natural matters: even if we acknowledge their sincere intentions and efforts, without reliable divine instruction, their actions are ineffective and their efforts are in vain, because they do not follow the Torah's divine prescription. As with the Kuzari king in the prologue, at best it can be said of them, "your intention is pleasing to God, but not your actions."

The sincerity of the other religions, however, remains problematical. The Ḥaver criticizes their hypocrisy, because their actions belie their words:

> The Ḥaver said: I would compare them to proselytes who do not accept the whole law in all its branches, but only the fundamental principles, if their actions did not belie their words... Retaining the rituals of ancient idolatry and feast days, they changed nothing but the forms. These [forms] were, indeed, demolished, but the rituals were not removed... I might almost say that the verse in the Bible, occurring repeatedly, "Do not serve other gods, wood and stone" (Deuternomy 28:36, 28:64) only alludes to those who glorify the wood [i.e, the cross] or glorify the stone [i.e., the Kaaba in Mecca]. Over time, we, in our sins, become ever more like them, although in truth their belief is only in God, like the people of Abimelech and the people of Nineveh, but they philosophize about the ways of God.[194]

Their actions belie their words also on a moral plane, because both Christianity and Islam preach humility but conquer and rule much of the world.[195] Nevertheless, despite all these criticisms, in the parable of the seed, Judah Ha-Levi states that Christianity and Islam are "a preparation and introduction for the messiah."

> You are right to blame us for bearing degradation without benefit. But if I think of the prominent men among us who could escape this degradation by a word spoken lightly, become free men, and turn against their oppressors, but do not do so out of devotion to their faith, is not this the way to obtain intercession and remission of many sins? Should that which you demand of me really ever take place, we should not remain in this condition. Besides this, God has a secret and wise design concerning us, which should be compared to the wisdom hidden in the seed which falls into the ground, where it undergoes an external transformation into earth, water and dirt, without leaving a trace for him who looks down upon it. It is, however, the seed itself which transforms earth and water into its own substance, carries it from one stage to another, until it refines the elements and transfers them into something like itself, casting off husks, leaves, etc. and allowing the pure essential core to appear, capable of bearing the divine faculty. The original seed produced the tree bearing fruit resembling that from which it had been produced. In the same manner, the religion of Moses

---

194   *Kuzari* 4:11. Hirschfeld ed. p. 216. (My modifications).
195   *Kuzari* 4:22.

transforms each one who honestly follows it, even if he apparently rejects it. **These communities are a preparation and introduction for the hoped-for messiah,** who is the fruit. They all will become his fruit, if they acknowledge him, and the tree will become one. Then they will revere the root they had previously despised.[196]

The parable of the seed thus explains in messianic terms the miserable state of Judaism and the Jewish people in exile. The seed appears to undergo an "external" transformation, according to one "who looks down upon it." But what really happens is the opposite: the essential core (Arabic: *lubb*; Hebrew: *lev*), freed from its husk or shell (Arabic: *qishr*; Hebrew: *qelipah*)—the terms Ha-Levi uses for prophets among other people, and Israel among the nations[197]—is not assimilated into its environment, but actually assimilates its environment into itself ("it refines the elements and transfers them into something like itself"). Christianity and Islam are thus the ground permitting the Jewish seed in exile to grow into the tree, the fruit of which is the messiah, and once Christianity and Islam acknowledge the messiah, "the tree will become one."

As Daniel Lasker interprets this passage, Ha-Levi here adopts Paul's parable of the olive tree in the New Testament (Romans 11) and reverses it.

> The image of Christianity and Islam returning to the tree of the true religion, which is Judaism, was particularly appropriate for Halevi's polemic with the competing religions, since its origin is the New Testament. In the Epistle to the Romans, chapter 11, Paul compares the Jews to branches of an olive tree which have been cut off from the trunk. Onto the original trunk were then grafted new branches, namely, the Gentiles. When the Jews eventually recognize the truth of Jesus as the Messiah, they will then be grafted back onto the tree trunk from which they were removed. Halevi's point is clear: Judaism is the original tree, and the Jews were always part of it. Eventually other nations will be grafted onto this tree, but they will recognize their naturalized status and revere the original native-born part of the tree.[198]

Whereas Lasker thus understands Ha-Levi as maintaining that in the messianic era there will still remain a distinction between native-born Jews and proselytes, Julius Guttmann concludes that "in the messianic era, this last barrier, too, will fall and Israel will assimilate to itself the other nations, even as the seed hidden in the earth absorbs its materials."[199]

---

196 *Kuzari* 4:23. Hirschfeld pp. 226–227. (My modifications).
197 See the discussion above, VI.9.c.iii.
198 Daniel Lasker, "Proselyte Judaism, Christianity and Islam in the Thought of Judah Halevi," in *Jewish Quarterly Review* LXXXI, Nos. 1–2 (1990), pp. 86–87.
199 Julius Guttmann, *Philosophies of Judaism*, p. 127.

There is another way of interpreting the parable of the seed. As we saw above,[200] B.Z. Dinur and Ḥayyim Schirmann suggested that migration to Israel—'*aliyah*—was, for Judah Ha-Levi, not merely a personal decision, but a way of bringing about the messianic redemption of Israel, and the *Kuzari* concludes with the explicit decision to leave Spain for Zion. Dov Schwartz, on the other hand, has suggested that Ha-Levi's messianism is an intermediate link between the apocalyptic messianism of Sa'adiah Ga'on, and the realistic or naturalistic messianism of Rambam. In his reading, Ha-Levi's emphasis of the uniqueness of Israel is a continuation of Sa'adiah's apocalyptic messianism, while at the same time he paves the way for Rambam's universalism.[201]

[VI.16] AFTERWORD: JUDAH HA-LEVI'S THEORY— RACIAL OR RACIST?

At the outset of our discussion of Judah Ha-Levi, we noted that he posed some of the most compelling existential questions we continue to face centuries later, and he had a way of reducing complex questions to stark, basic formulas. In our generation, after the Shoah in which a third of the Jewish people were exterminated because of an allegedly "scientific" racist Nazi ideology, how can we deal with Ha-Levi's theory of the "divine faculty" (*amr ilahi*), a theory which is racial in that it explains that "divine faculty" as a biological or genetic characteristic of the Jewish people? We have suggested that this theory be understood as Ha-Levi's attempt to provide an objective and scientific (in his terms) explanation of observed facts—the anomalies of the history of Israel.

Shall we, however, understand Ha-Levi's theory as racial or as racist?[202] By "racial" we mean that there are observable in-born, physical differences between certain groups of people, such as the color of skin, hair or eyes. Those

---

[200] See the discussion in VI.2.c.

[201] Dov Schwartz, "Prophecy and Redemption" (Hebrew), in *The Messianism in Medieval Jewish Thought* (Hebrew) (Ramat Gan: Bar Ilan University Press, 1997), pp. 55–69; "Messianism in Judah Ha-Levi's Thought" (Hebrew), in *Sefunot* 6 (21), 1993, pp. 11–39.

[202] This question has been discussed by Lippman Bodoff, "Was Yehuda Halevi Racist?," in *The Binding of Isaac, Religious Murder and Kabbalah: Seeds of Jewish Extremism and Alienation?* (Jerusalem & New York: Devora Publishing, 2005), pp. 374–388; originally published in *Judaism* 38/2 (1989), pp. 174–184. Bodoff points out that Halevi wrote his *Kuzari* to reinforce Jewish identity and restore Jewish self-respect, at a time when Jews and Judaism were universally despised and regarded as inferior. After comparing the status of proselytes in Judaism with Catholic treatment of *conversos* (given the Spanish fixation on *limpieza de sangre*, the purity of blood), and the American constitutional requirement that only native-born citizens can become president, Bodoff concludes that for Halevi, a proselyte's progeny presumably could attain prophecy, and that the inequality of the

biological differences are real—but merely observing that they exist does not imply that one group is, on account of those differences, superior to another. By "racist," on the other hand, we mean the notion that racial differences can be translated into doctrines of superiority of one group, which accordingly has the moral or intellectual right to dominate or conquer others, even if it is claimed (as in Rudyard Kipling's "Take Up the White Man's Burden") that such domination is well-intentioned and in the best interests of the more primitive groups.

The question cannot be answered unequivocally. On the one hand, Ha-Levi insists that there is no difference between Jews and non-Jews intellectually or morally, and he similarly insists that the universal moral law, or law of reason, is prior in time and nature to the additional divine laws of Israel. He also deals frankly and honestly with Jewish behavior. For example, when the Ḥaver boasts that the Jews practice humility, whereas the Christians and Muslims, who preach humility, go out and conquer the world by killing, the Kuzari king replies: "That would be true if your humility were voluntary. But it is involuntary, and if you had the power, you would also kill."[203] In other words, is Jewish moral behavior really a matter of principle and self-restraint, or is it simply a function of the Jews' powerlessness?

So Judah Ha-Levi's doctrine cannot be considered racist in the sense of advocating conquest,[204] or in the sense of Jewish intellectual or moral superiority. On the other hand, even without such notions of military conquest, Ha-Levi's doctrine does claim some kind of biological superiority, in the hierarchy of existence. As animals are superior to plants, and humans to other animals, so the Jewish "essence" or "core" of humanity is superior, in virtue of a biological faculty, to the rest of humanity, who are the "husk" or "shell." Today, however, in the absence of "the divine actions" such as the sacrificial cult in the Temple, that biological "divine faculty" cannot be activated, and is only latently present in the Jews, so that the distinction ever since the destruction of the Temple is more or less academic and is no longer of any practical significance.

At the same time, although Judah Ha-Levi himself may not have crossed the line between racial and racist doctrine, later Jewish thinkers, especially thinkers in the mystical tradition, found in his doctrine the seed for more extreme notions which Ha-Levi himself might well have repudiated.

---

first-generation proselyte reflected his or her prior religious status and not present spiritual inferiority, and therefore the inequality is not racial in nature. Conversion to Judaism, he argues, means joining the Jewish nation as well as religion, and birth is pertinent to national identity. This is not, he argues, the same as racism.

203   *Kuzari* 1:114.

204   We should keep in mind, however, that in King Joseph's letter to Ḥisdai ibn Shaprut, there is mention of Khazar conquest of neighboring countries.

For example, the *Tanya* ("Teaching") or *Liqqutei Amarim* ("Collected Sayings") of Shneur Zalman of Lyady (1745–1813), the founder of Ḥabad-Lubavitch movement of Ḥasidism, regards the gentiles as having a different soul from that of the Jews; the gentile soul emanates from "the other, unclean *qelipot* (shells, shards) which contain no good whatever" so that "all the good that the nations do, is done from selfish motives," (*Tanya*, ch. 1), whereas the Jews possesses a "second soul" which "is truly a part of God above" (ch. 2).[205]

Judah Ha-Levi thus remains one of those most important, fascinating and intriguing medieval Jewish philosophers, some of whose doctrines—or at least questions—continue to pose existential as well as intellectual challenges today, some 850 years later, when the Jewish people in recent times experienced both the extremes, on the one hand, of utter powerlessness and degradation in the Shoah, and, on the other hand, the "return to history" and national restoration of the Jewish people in the renewed State of Israel.

---

[205]   *Tanya—Liqqutei Amarim*, with English translation by Nissan Mindel (New York and London: Kehot, 1973), pp. 3–5. I have changed the Hebrew transliteration in this passage.

Chapter Seven

THE TRANSITION TO ARISTOTELIANISM: ABRAHAM IBN DA'UD

[VII.1] INTRODUCTION

[VII.1.a] ARISTOTLE IN JEWISH LEGEND

In the previous chapter, we saw that Judah Ha-Levi claimed that the Greeks originally, albeit indirectly, learned philosophy from Jewish-Semitic sources,[1] but that when philosophical works were translated into Arabic and Hebrew, their origins were not mentioned.[2] And as we saw, there are precedents for such views in Jewish literature (such as Philo) and Arabic literature (such as Al-Farabi's *Attainment of Happiness*).

We also find in Jewish literature, however, not only the claim that philosophy in general had its indirect origins among the Jews and other Semites, but specifically the claim that Aristotle studied philosophy with a Jewish teacher, and even claims that Aristotle converted to Judaism.

For example, in the book mixing history and legend, *Shalshelet Ha-Qabbalah* ("The Chain of Tradition") by Gedaliah ben Joseph ibn Yaḥya (Italy, 1515–1587), we find a report that Aristotle met, and was impressed by the wisdom of, Simon the Just, one of the last members of the "men of the Great Assembly,"[3] and (according to some views) the high priest at the time of Alexander the Great. According to that report, at the end of his life Aristotle acknowledged what he had learned from the Torah, repented his earlier errors, and converted to Judaism.[4]

The main source of this and similar medieval Jewish stories of Aristotle is a passage in the defense of Judaism, *Against Apion*, by the first-century historian Josephus:[5]

---

[1] *Kuzari* 1:63. See the citations and discussion in Ch. 6 (VI.12).

[2] *Kuzari* 2:66.

[3] Cf. Mishnah Avot 1:2. He is credited with the saying: "The world stands on three things: one the Torah, on service, and on kind deeds."

[4] *Shalshelet Ha-Qabbalah*, pp. 241–243.

[5] Josephus, *Against Apion* I:176–181, English translation by H. St. J. Thackeray (Cambridge: Harvard University Press, 1926), pp. 233–237.

Clearchus, a disciple of Aristotle, and in the very first rank of peripatetic philosophers, relates, in his first book on sleep, the following anecdote told of a certain Jew by his master. He puts the words into the mouth of Aristotle himself...
These people are descended from the Indian philosophers. The philosophers, they say, are...called...in Syria by the territorial name of the Jews; for the district which they inhabit is known as Judaea. Their city has a remarkably odd name: they call it Hierusaleme (Jerusalem). Now this man...not only spoke Greek, but had the soul of a Greek. During my stay in Asia, he visited the same places as I did, and came to converse with me and some other scholars, to test our learning. But as one who had been intimate with many cultivated persons, it was rather he who imparted to us something of his own.

For our purposes, there is no need to speculate the extent—if any—to which this story contains any historical information, because in our context what is important is not the historical Aristotle (the philosopher himself), but the image of Aristotle in Jewish legend, and then, Aristotle as understood by the medieval Jewish philosophers; not Aristotle and what he himself wrote, but how Aristotle was read by these thinkers.

The medieval Jewish legends rely not only on Jewish, but also on Christian and Islamic sources. These legends also manifest a certain ambivalence towards Aristotle. On the one hand, the admiration these legends reflect for Aristotle led some Jews to claim that Aristotle learned his philosophy from Jews, that he met Simon the Just, that he ultimately converted to Judaism, and even that he was a descendant of the tribe of Benjamin. In other words, because Aristotelian philosophy is true, it must have Jewish origins. On the other hand, the admiration for Aristotle led some Jews to conclude that Aristotle was a great sage, but that his philosophy is erroneous, especially regarding his affirmation of the eternity of the world. Since he was a great sage, he ultimately came to recognize his earlier error, repented, and converted to Judaism.

Either way, Aristotle was, for many Jews in the Middle Ages, the archetypal Greek philosopher (as he was in the prologue of Judah Ha-Levi's *Kuzari*).

[VII.1.b] THE TRANSITION TO ARISTOTELIANISM

[VII.1.b.i] *Hebrew Translation of Aristotelian Works*

One of the factors making possible the transition among Jewish thinkers to Aristotelian philosophy was the translation, first into Arabic and then from Arabic into Hebrew, of Aristotle's works. Translations into Arabic of works of Greek philosophy, science and medicine, it will be recalled,[6] were sponsored at *Beit Al-Ḥikmah* ("the house of wisdom"), established in Baghdad in 830

---

6   See the discussion at the end of Ch. 1 (I.3.c).

C.E. by the Abbasid Caliph Al-Ma'mun, which housed a major scientific library, where translations of some of Aristotle's works were made by Isḥaq ibn Ḥunayn. By the twelfth century most of the Aristotelian corpus had been translated, although those translations did not include Aristotle's Politics. Much of Jewish political theory, therefore, remained Platonic, even among such Aristotelians as Rambam. In the thirteenth century, after the death of Rambam (1204 C.E.), Hebrew translations made possible familiarity with Aristotelian thought among Jews in Christian Europe who did not know Arabic. In many cases, however, these translations into Hebrew were not of Aristotle's works themselves, but of the Arabic works and commentaries of Al-Farabi and Ibn Sina (Avicenna), and especially of Ibn Rushd (Averroes), whose approach is more thoroughly Aristotelian than that of his predecessors.

[VII.1.b.ii] *Aristotelianism as a systematic Framework*

Earlier Jewish philosophers, including Isaac Israeli, Sa'adiah Ga'on, Solomon ibn Gabirol, Baḥya ibn Paquda and Judah Ha-Levi were, to an extent, already familiar with and influenced by some Aristotelian terminology and ideas, but their thought was not basically shaped by Aristotelianism. Rather, as we have seen, it reflected Kalam and Neoplatonic thought, although in the case of Ha-Levi the archetypal philosopher whom he criticizes is Aristotelian. In a positive sense, then, the systematic transition to Aristotelian thought among began with Abraham ibn Da'ud. It must be kept mind, however, that the Aristotelianism of many of the Islamic and Jewish philosophers was not identical in many cases with Aristotle's own ideas, and it frequently was intermixed with ideas from ancient Greek commentators like Themistius and Alexander of Aphrodisias, and also with Neoplatonic themes, such as emanation, the absolute unity of God as the One, and negative theology.

Despite this intermixing, Julius Guttmann points to the new dominance of basic Aristotelian themes:

> In the middle of the twelfth century Aristotelianism displaced Neoplatonism as the dominating influence in Jewish philosophy of religion...Judah Halevi would not have directed his attacks at the Aristotelian system if it had not counted adherents among his contemporaries...Aristotelianism had undergone a Neoplatonic transformation in the hands of its Islamic adherents. Its metaphysical structure was radically transformed by the adoption of the doctrine of emanation... However, the Aristotelian foundations of the system held its own...The extension of the doctrine of emanation to matter was discarded...and the ancient dualism of form and matter re-established...God himself was defined...as the supreme thought thinking itself. No longer conceived in Neoplatonic fashion as an emanation from the universal soul, essentially independent of the body, the soul was now defined as the form of the body...The intellectualist character of the Aristotelian ideal of life colored all religious formulations...Even the

blessedness of communion with God was...conceived as a participation in the eudaemonism of divine knowledge.[7]

Another scholar, Norbert Samuelson, connects the transition to the political split between the Abbasid caliphate in the east, based in Baghdad, where the "old science" of Kalam remained dominant, and the Ummayads in the west, where the more empirically based "new science" of Aristotelianism grew.

> The new science had a great deal to recommend itself. Not the least of its advantages over both [Kalam] atomism and Platonism is its empiricism, namely, that it presented a view of the universe in which what seems through our senses to be the case is in fact the case...Both atomism and Platonism, contrarily, denied the reality of the sensible realm. For the atomists, the universe ultimately consists of discrete, imperceptible quantities which are what they are by sheer chance; nothing that exists has purpose or reason. Similarly for the Platonists, the universe consists of pure, equally imperceptible forms which are what they are necessarily; everything that exists is mathematically determined.
>
> From a scientific perspective, the critical terms in Aristotelianism lacked the precision of technical terms in both atomism and Platonism...From a religious perspective, the situation was even worse. The new science made claims about the universe which prima facie were far more difficult to reconcile with the claims of revealed tradition.[8]

For example, Samuelson points out that the Platonic doctrine of creation from prime matter is far more reconcilable with Genesis than is the Aristotelian doctrine of the eternity of the universe, and atomism — with its corollary of chance — is more compatible with miracles than is Aristotelian necessity.

Prior to the twelfth century, Jewish and Arab philosophers adopted some Aristotelian terminology and concepts into their philosophical and scientific thought. The change in the twelfth century was that now Jewish and Arab philosophers attempted to adopt the Aristotelian system as their basic starting point, especially in such areas as epistemological empiricism, psychology, and ethics. Their epistemology is characterized by empirical reliance on the senses. Their theory of the soul shifts from the Neoplatonic view of the soul as emanated from the universal intellect to understanding the soul as the form (or "entelechy," perfection) of the body. Their ethical theory reflects Aristotle's ultimate human end of "happiness" (or "success"), rather than the Neoplatonic "upward way."

Their physics was now based on the duality of form and matter, and on Aristotle's four causes and four elements, rather than on the Neoplatonic

---

7   Guttmann, *Philosophies of Judaism*, p. 134.
8   Norbert Samuelson, "Medieval Jewish Aristotelianism," in Daniel Frank and Oliver Leaman (eds.), *History of Jewish Philosophy* (London: Routledge, 1997), p. 230.

"downward way." Finally, their metaphysics now posited God as the efficient cause of the world, based on cosmological arguments, rather than as the One from which all other reality is emanated, and God was conceived in terms of intellect thinking itself, rather than in terms of the unknowable, transcendent One, so that the ultimate human end came to be identified with knowledge of and intellectual communion with God.

Many of these points were epitomized in Judah Ha-Levi's account of the philosopher's presentation in *Kuzari* 1:1, which clearly places that archetypal philosopher squarely in the Aristotelian camp.

ARISTOTELIAN CHARACTERISTIC	THE PHILOSOPHER IN *KUZARI* 1:1[9]
Empirical epistemology	The cause and the caused are **as you see**.
Ethics	The philosopher…who is equipped with the highest capacity, receives through it the advantages of disposition, intelligence and active power, so that he wants nothing to make him perfect.
Metaphysics—God as the cause of the world	If the philosophers say that he created you, they only use a metaphor, because he is the cause of causes in the creation of all creatures, but not because this was his intention…Everything is reduced to a prime cause, not to a will proceeding from it.
Metaphysics—God as intellect thinking itself (and not knowing particulars)	God is, in the opinion of the philosophers, above the knowledge of individuals, because the latter change over time, while there is no change in God's knowledge. He, therefore, does not know you.
The ultimate human end—knowledge of and intellectual communion with God.	In the perfect person, a light of divine nature, called Active Intellect, is with him, and his passive intellect is conjoined and united with it.

The framework of the Jewish philosophers was now Aristotelian, whether in a positive sense—as in the case of Abraham ibn Da'ud and Rambam— or in a negative sense, as in the case of such critics as Judah Ha-Levi in the twelfth century and, more than two centuries later, Ḥasdai Crescas (1340–1410).

[VII.1.c] RAMBAM'S VIEW OF ARISTOTLE

Towards the end of his life, in the fall of 1200 (some four years before he died), Rambam wrote to Samuel ibn Tibbon, whose Hebrew translation of the *Guide of the Perplexed* was approved by Rambam himself:

---

9   Translation by H. Hirschfeld, with my modifications.

The writings [literally: words] of Aristotle's teacher Plato are in parables and hard to understand. One can dispense with them, for the writings of Aristotle suffice, and we need not occupy [our attention] with the writings of earlier [philosophers]. Aristotle's intellect [represents] the extreme of human intellect, if we except those who have received divine inspiration.[10]

In the *Guide of the Perplexed* itself we find similar admiration for Aristotle, whom he cites dozens of times, and whom he calls "the chief (Arabic: *rais*) of the philosophers."[11] At the same time, Rambam does not hesitate to voice reservations about Aristotle: whatever Aristotle wrote about sublunar matters (i.e., physics) "is without doubt correct." However, whatever Aristotle wrote about things beyond the lunar sphere (i.e., metaphysics) is, with only a few exceptions, mere speculation and opinion, and lacks conclusive proof.[12] Nevertheless, whether or not Rambam ultimately agreed with Aristotle on various points, it was Aristotle who provide the scientific foundation and philosophic framework for his philosophy.

[VII.2] THE LIFE AND WORKS OF ABRAHAM IBN DA'UD

Abraham ibn Da'ud was born in Cordova, Spain c. 1110. Besides a thorough Jewish and scientific education, from references in his books it seems that he also was familiar with the New Testament and the Qur'an. He eventually settled in Toledo, where (at least by some accounts) he suffered a martyr's death in 1180. He authored astronomical works and an anti-Karaite polemic, but his two main books, composed at the same time in 1160–1161, were his Hebrew historical work, *Sefer Ha-Qabbalah* ("The Book of Tradition") and his Arabic philosophical work, *Al-'Aqidah Al-Rafi'ah* ("The Exalted Faith").[13] The two books complement each other.

The *Book of Tradition* was intended to be the first of a three-part history, serving as a polemic against Karaism and Christianity. It traces the continuity of the rabbinic Jewish tradition over the generations from Moses until the author's own day, thus verifying the claims of rabbinic Judaism to be the

---

10 Cited by Shlomo Pines,"Translator's Introduction: The Philosophic Sources of the *Guide of the Perplexed*," in his English translation of the *Guide of the Perplexed* (Chicago: University of Chicago Press, 1963), p. lix.

11 *Guide of the Perplexed* 1:5.

12 *Guide of the Perplexed* 2:22. However, in *Mishneh Torah*, "Foundations of the Torah" 4:10, Rambam assigns the subject of the heavenly spheres (which he discussed in ch. 3) to physics, in which case even physics is subject to doubt.

13 These basic facts were recorded by Isaac ben Joseph Israeli (14th century) in his astronomical work, *Yesod 'Olam* ("Foundation of the World").

continuation of the Torah of Moses. The *Book of Tradition* had a great impact on Jewish historical thought in subsequent generations, and was printed in many editions. The book, however, is not merely a dry list of the transmission of tradition over the generations, but has a broad historical view, in which the author does not hesitate to offer his evaluations. For example, he writes about the Bar Kokhba revolt in negative terms, always calling Bar Kokhba by his actual name, Ben Koziba:

> In their days a certain man by the name of Koziba arose, claiming to be the Messiah of the seed of David. He revolted against the Domitian king of Rome and slew his viceroy in the Land of Israel[14]...So this Koziba began to reign in Bethar in the fifty-second year after the destruction of the Temple...In the days of Romulus ben Rufus ben Koziba, Hadrian mobilized his forces, went up to the Land of Israel and conquered Bethar on the ninth of Ab in the year 73 of the destruction of the Temple. He slew Romulus and smote Israel a great blow such as had not been seen or heard even in the days of Nebuzaradan or in those of Titus[15]...All this happened to them in the war of Hadrian because of the provocation of Ben Koziba. Then there was fulfilled for them what had been written by Daniel: "And they that are wise among the people shall cause the many to understand; yet they shall stumble by the sword and flame, by captivity and by spoil, many days" (Daniel 11:33).[16]

Ibn Da'ud's opinion of Sa'adiah Ga'on was positive:

> R[abbi] Saadiah passed away in 4702 [= 942 C.E.], when he was about fifty years of age, of black bile, after having composed any number of worthwhile books and having accomplished great good for Israel. He wrote refutations of the heretics and of those who denied the [authority of the] Torah.[17]

At the end of the book, Ibn Da'ud mentions scholars including "Rabbi Judah Halevi ben Rabbi Samuel Halevi; and Rabbi Abraham ibn Ezra. All of them were great and saintly scholars, who have added strength to Israel with their poems and verses of consolation."[18]

In contrast with *The Book of Tradition*, which was written in Hebrew and became quite popular over the generations, Abraham ibn Da'ud's philosophical

---

[14] The Hebrew has *Ereẓ Yisra'el* ("the land of Israel").Gerson Cohen translates it as "Palestine," but I have modified it in light of the original.

[15] The destruction in the time of Hadrian was greater than at the time of the first and second Temples were destroyed.

[16] Abraham ibn Da'ud, *Sefer Ha-Qabbalah—The Book of Tradition*, critical edition and English translation by Gerson D. Cohen (Philadelphia: Jewish Publication Society, 1967), Hebrew pp. 20–21, English pp.28–29.

[17] *The Book of Tradition*, Hebrew p. 42, English p. 56.

[18] *The Book of Tradition*, Hebrew pp. 73–74, English p. 103.

book, *The Exalted Faith* was written in Arabic, and the Arabic original was lost, and even in its Hebrew translations the book remained in rare manuscript for centuries, presumably testimony to its lack of popularity. Two Hebrew translations of the book were made. In 1391 Solomon ibn Lavi translated the book under the title *Ha-Emunah Ha-Ramah*; this translation was only printed (with a German translation) by Samson Weil in 1852. Another edition of Ibn Lavi's translation was published by Gershon Weis, with an English translation by Norbert Samuelson in 1986.[19] Shortly after Ibn Lavi translated the book, another translation was made by Samuel ben Sa'adiah Ibn Motot, at the request of Rabbi Isaac ben Sheshet, under the title *Ha-Emunah Ha-Nis'ah*, which was only printed in 1990 in a Ph.D. dissertation.[20]

Amira Eran has suggested that Ibn Da'ud's two books complement each other, because *The Book of Tradition* defends Judaism on the basis of the past, i.e., by citing the objective facts of history, whereas *The Exalted Faith* defends it on the basis of the future, i.e., by giving it a philosophical-scientific basis, to protect it against rationalist argument.[21]

[VII.3] THE *EXALTED FAITH* AND IBN DA'UD'S PLACE IN JEWISH PHILOSOPHY

[VII.3.a] RAMBAM'S PREDECESSOR

Abraham ibn Da'ud was, in many respects, the pioneer of Jewish Aristotelianism, and often took positions similar to those taken late by Rambam. However, because of Rambam's overwhelming reputation, and the widespread reception given to his *Guide of the Perplexed* (despite the fact that he intended the book only for the intelligentsia), Ibn Da'ud's *Exalted Faith*—written only some thirty years before Rambam's book—was largely ignored and forgotten, as is evident from the loss of the Arabic original and the fact that the first Hebrew translation was only printed in the nineteenth century, and the second Hebrew translation only published in a doctoral dissertation towards the end of the twentieth century. Despite frequent similarity in their positions and arguments, Ibn Da'ud also suffers from comparison with the more brilliant, profound and comprehensive Rambam.

---

19 Abraham ibn Daud, *The Exalted Faith*, ed. Gershon Weiss, with English translation and commentary by Norbert Samuelson (Teaneck: Associated University Press—Fairleigh Dickinson University Press, 1986).

20 Amira Eran, "The Philosophic Sources of Abraham ibn Da'ud in his *Exalted Faith*," Hebrew University of Jerusalem, 1990.

21 Amira Eran, *From Simple Faith to Sublime Faith: Ibn Da'ud's Pre-Maimonidean Thought* (Hebrew) (Tel Aviv: Ha-Kibbutz Ha-Me'uḥad, 1998).

The Exalted Faith suffers, not only by comparison with *The Guide of the Perplexed*, but also from an internal weakness. Despite Ibn Da'ud's explicit affirmation of the harmony of philosophy and religion, as Amira Eran has pointed out, his book carefully keeps separate philosophical arguments—frequently based on Ibn Sina—and religious citations of biblical verses. Other Jewish authors had integrated interpretation of such verses in their philosophical arguments, but Ibn Da'ud adds them as a kind of postscript at the end of each chapter, labeling them "verses testify" or "Scripture alludes." On the other hand, perhaps Ibn Da'ud thought that by keeping the two areas separate, he preserved their integrity while demonstrating their harmony.[22]

Resianne T.A.M. Fontaine summarizes Ibn Da'ud's place in Jewish philosophy as follows:

> Ibn Daud also represents the entry of Aristotelianism into Jewish philosophy, since he makes much more use of Aristotelian arguments and principles than his predecessors. Characteristic in this connection is his view of the nature of substance. At the same time, he introduces the cosmological proof for the existence of God and the proof for the existence of God that is based on the distinction between possible and necessary... If it can be said of Maimonides' *Moreh Nevukhim* (Guide of the Perplexed) that it is intended as a "Jewish connection" to the falasifa (philosophers), this is no less true for *Ha-Emunah Ha-Ramah* (Exalted Faith) written thirty years earlier... Ibn Daud's Aristotelianism is still largely colored by Neoplatonic elements... Ibn Daud vacillates between two ideas—he is unable to distance himself sufficiently from Neoplatonism because he cannot do without the idea of emanation and the idea of intermediaries between the One and the many.[23]

[VII.3.b] THE PURPOSE AND NAME OF THE BOOK

The book opens with the following statement:

> The Treatise of the Exalted Faith, which leads to agreement between philosophy and religion. The great, pious and venerable philosopher, Rabbi Abraham Ha-Levi ibn Da'ud, may he rest in peace, composed it. [Someone] had asked the author, Are the actions of man necessary, or does he have choice over them?[24]

Ibn Da'ud thus states from the outset that the purpose of the book is to establish "the agreement between philosophy and religion," and that what led

---

[22] Cf. Amira Eran, *From Simple Faith to Sublime Faith*, pp. 29 and 271. Eran also points out that only in the second part of the book, when directly discussing questions of religious faith, does Ibn Da'ud integrate the theoretical and exegetical components.

[23] Resianne T.A.M. Fontaine, *In Defence of Judaism: Abraham ibn Daud: Sources and Structure of Ha-Emunah Ha-Ramah* (Assen/Maastricht: Van Gorcum, 1990), pp. 270–272.

[24] *Exalted Faith*, English translation by Samuelson, p. 38. (My modifications).

him to write the book was the question of human free will. Nevertheless, the question of free will is not the central or dominant theme of the book, which deals at length with other topics, and only discusses free will towards the end, in a small chapter of some six pages. Ibn Da'ud seems to have been sensitive to this anomaly, because he opens the chapter with the statement that the chapter deals "with the sources of good and evil, the ordering and enumeration of causes, and an explanation of providence and the secreat of abiloity. We presented this book for the sake and because of [the subject matter of this] chapter, which is the first principle of thought and the final [end] of action."[25]

Fontaine suggests that Ibn Da'ud saw the rest of the book, which is in quantitative terms its overwhelming bulk, as necessary to deal with this question, which he could only answer after having dealt with other questions.[26] In his preface, Ibn Da'ud acknowledges this when he explains the order of the topics discussed, each one in turn requiring another discussion:

> When I entreated God, may he be blessed, to help me to open the eyes of the men of speculation from our nation concerning the basic principles of their faith by introducing proofs to them from scriptural passages and demonstrations from true philosophy, I saw that this would only be possible for me after [first] introducing the first principles of the science of nature and what follows from it.[27]

Fontaine concludes that Ibn Da'ud failed in his attempt to demonstrate the general agreement between philosophy and religion, but that on the specific question of free will, which was his avowed purposed in writing the book, he succeeded in demonstrating that agreement.[28]

The name of the book also reflects its purpose. Amira Eran has suggested that Ibn Da'ud chose the name *Al-'Aqidah Al-Rafi'ah* in contrast with Sa'adiah Ga'on's *Book of Beliefs and Opinions*. In her view, Sa'adiah's title retains the duality of faith and reason as distinct territories, whereas *The Exalted Faith* implies the desired synthesis of the two,[29] and indicates the desired product of a rational faith.[30] This synthesis does not mean that the faith and reason are identical, but that they are in agreement with each other.

Resianne Fontaine, on the other hand, contrasts *The Exalted Faith* not with Sa'adiah Ga'on's *Book of Beliefs and Opinions* but with Judah Ha-Levi's

---

25   Cf. p. 245 of the Samuelson translation.
26   Fontaine, *In Defence of Judaism*, pp. 240–245.
27   *Exalted Faith*, Samuelson ed. p. 41.
28   Fontaine, *In Defence of Judaism*, pp. 272–274.
29   Eran, *From Simple Faith to Sublime Faith*, pp. 21–22.
30   Eran, *From Simple Faith to Sublime Faith*, p. 115.

Kuzari, the subtitle of which, it will be recalled, is *Book of Refutation and Proof on the Despised Faith.*

> The title alone, *The Exalted Faith*, is a direct reply to Halevi's subtitle for the *Kuzari* ... "the despised faith." The tenor of [*The Exalted Faith*] is diametrically opposed to that of the *Kuzari*: the general philosophy rejected by Halevi is defended by Ibn Daud.[31]

Thus, instead of Ha-Levi's "despised faith" opposed to philosophy, we have "the exalted faith" of Ibn Da'ud, in agreement with philosophy.

[VII.4] THE *EXALTED FAITH*: SELECTED THEMES

[VII.4.a] INTRODUCTION

This discussion of Ibn Da'ud's thought will be limited to several selected themes exemplifying the transition to Aristotelianism; other themes, which either are highly technical or are similar to themes to be discussed in the chapter on Rambam, will not be covered here or discussed in depth.

In the Introduction to the *Exalted Faith*, Ibn Da'ud asserts that ignorance or rejection of the sciences "was not the way of our nation in past times," and that the rabbis (such as Yoḥanan ben Zakkai) and "all of the Sanhedrin in every generation" were familiar with philosophy. The ideal is to "grasp with both his hands two lights, in his right hand the light of his religion, and in his left hand the light of his wisdom." Today, however, many people consider philosophy harmful to the cause of religion. Accordingly, Sa'adiah Ga'on's *Book of Beliefs and Doctrines* moves people in the correct direction, and "it is a treatise that contains much good," although "it is not satisfactory for what we need." However, Solomon ibn Gabirol's *Fountain of Life* — although it "aimed at bestowing benefit from philosophy" — is so verbose that it could have made its point in one tenth of its length, and Ibn Gabirol "multiplied demonstrations, thinking that many demonstrations that are not true [can] stand in the place of [one] true demonstration ... All of that treatise shows the weakness of his grade in philosophy, and he gropes in it like groping in the dark."[32]

What is needed, then, is a book of "practical philosophy" that will clearly demonstrate the agreement of religion and philosophy. This book, the *Exalted Faith*, is not intended for those ignorant of the sciences, who should remain

---

31   Fontaine, *In Defence of Judaism*, p. 2.
32   *Exalted Faith*, Samuelson ed. pp. 40–41. Regarding Ibn Da'ud's criticism of Ibn Gabirol's *Fountain of Life*, see the discussion in Ch. 3 (III.3.c.iii).

innocent, nor is it for experts in philosophy, who don't need it. Rather, it is written for one who is a beginner in philosophy, and is, accordingly, "perplexed" (or "confused;" Hebrew: *navokh*) by the apparent lack of agreement between his religious tradition and the scientific truth. In this regard, Abraham ibn Da'ud's *Exalted Faith* precedes by some thirty years Rambam's *Guide of the Perplexed*, not only in its Aristotelian approach, but also in writing a guide for the perplexed.

[VII.4.b] SUBSTANCE

We have already dealt several times with the Aristotelian concept of substance, the first of the ten categories.[33] Ibn Da'ud took strong exception to Ibn Gabirol's lack of clarity on this subject, and devotes the first chapter of the *Exalted Faith* to a discourse on substance and accident.

> Substance is what exists without need of a subject...Accident is what exists in a thing...and it does not have duration without it...Ibn Gabirol showed that his view was that some things are substance with respect to something and accident with respect to another thing. However, this is an error.[34]

After correcting Ibn Gabirol's errors in his survey of substance and accident in the first chapter, Ibn Da'ud continues, in the second chapter, with a discourse on matter and form. "Intelligible matter" (*hiyuli muskal*, from the Greek *hyle*, via the Arabic *hayuli*) is the matter which bears natural or divine forms, whereas "sensible matter" (*hiyuli muḥash*) is the matter bearing artificial forms, such as gold which can be formed into a coin, and the coin into a ring, and the ring into a nose ring. One cannot, however, sensibly perceive the intelligible matter which bears the changing natural forms of the four elements, fire, air, water and earth. Prime matter, namely matter devoid of all forms, exists only potentially, not actually, and Ibn Gabirol again erred in positing it as the actual universal matter from which all matter derives.

The third and fourth chapters deal with the definition of motion and quantity, and the fifth presents proofs of the existence of a first, unmoved mover. In Aristotelian terms, however, we must keep in mind that the concept motion does not merely mean motion in place, but also any change (*kinesis*) in quantity or quality, including generation and corruption. In the context of this discussion of the first, unmoved mover, we should note that Ibn Da'ud does

---

33 See the discussions in Ch. 2 (II.3.d.iii) and Ch. 3 (III.1.b and III.3.e), especially the chart of the categories in III.3.f, and the discussion of substance and the categories in the Appendix.

34 *Exalted Faith*, Samuelson ed., p. 50.

not refer to the concept of a "creator," even in his selection of biblical verses at the end of the chapter. The discussion thus retains an overtly Aristotelian tone, even in the author's choice of support texts from Scripture.

[VII.4.c] PSYCHOLOGY

[VII.4.c.i] *Definition of the Soul as Substance and Perfection of the Body*

Ibn Da'ud presents his psychology in chapters 6 and 7 of the first part of the *Exalted Faith*. Here, too, his approach is thoroughly Aristotelian; he uses such empirical terminology as "we see," and his discussion is to a large extent based on Aristotle's *De Anima* and on the psychology of Ibn Sina (Avicenna).[35] In this discussion, which follows his discussion of movement and the first mover, Ibn Da'ud proves the existence of the soul as the mover of the body and details its various faculties. What is new in his presentation, however, is that he moves from a discussion of the human soul to a discussion of the heavenly bodies which are also moved by souls in voluntary motion. The spheres are thus living bodies, and their rational souls are the angels.

According to Aristotle, the soul's essence cannot be defined. A scientific definition consists of two components: the element common to all members of that species, and that which specifies the particular individual. The soul is not a member of a common class or genus, nor does it have particular qualities differentiating it from the other members of such a class. It cannot, therefore, be defined.[36] The soul can only be defined in relation to the body: it is the "perfection" (or "entelechy," from the Greek *entelecheia*) of the body, namely that which perfects it, makes it real, and actualizes it.[37]

---

[35]　Judah Ha-Levi also survey's Ibn Sina's psychology in *Kuzari* 5:12. Although Rambam's contemporary Ibn Rushd (Averroes) was critical of Ibn Sina for not being consistently Aristotelian in his philosophy, his psychology is Aristotelian.

[36]　In this respect, the impossibility of defining the essence of the soul resembles the impossibility of defining philosophy, which is *sui generis*, according to Isaac Israeli. See the discussion in Ch. 3 (III.2.a).

[37]　Ibn Da'ud, *Exalted Faith*, Samuelson ed. p. 89. This is how Shem Tov ibn Falaquera (13th century, Spain) summarized the Aristotelian doctrine of the soul as "entelechy" in his *Sefer Ha-Nefesh* ("Book of the Soul"): "The soul is the first entelechy of a natural, not artificial, body endowed with organs...Every form is an entelechy, but not every entelechy is a form. For the sailor is the entelechy of the boat, but he is not its form. Whatever is an entelechy separate from the substance is not truly a form in matter. For the form which is in matter is imprinted in it and subsists, in other words, its subsistence is in it. Therefore, when we say that the soul is an entelechy, we include all species of soul, including the definition of the soul which is separate from matter." See Raphael Jospe, *Torah and Sophia: The Life and Thought of Shem Tov ibn Falaquera* (Cincinnati: Hebrew Union College Press, 1988), p. 324.

Ibn Da'ud emphasizes that the soul itself is a substance, not accident:

It has already been established that the soul is not at all an accident, and
that everything that is not an accident is a substance...The soul actualizes
the body...The soul is a substance in the sense of a form. We have already
explained to you that the form is that substance which shines upon the hyle that
is common to diverse things...[The soul] is the form of the body...and...is
also its end...You have already known that the soul is an incorporeal substance,
that it is a substance in the sense of a form, that it is in a body composed from
it and from body.[38]

Although he continues to refer to the soul as the form of the body, Ibn Da'ud
reiterates that it is the body's actualization, and thus its "end," and that it is
an immaterial substance. According to Aristotle, "the soul is the first actualization of a natural body potentially having life. And such a body is one that is
organic."[39] Medieval thinkers preferred to refer to the soul as the body's perfection and actualization, rather than form, in order to emphasize its independence
from the body, and therefore the possibility of its immortality. According to
the Aristotelian view, matter (in this case, the body) and the form cannot exists
separately in actuality, but only potentially. They always co-exist. If, therefore,
the soul were to be defined as the form of the body, it would be difficult to maintain
the continued existence of the soul without the body. Ibn Da'ud's emphasis of
the soul as an incorporeal substance also permits him to posit the existence
of angels, which are the separate intelligences moving the heavenly spheres.

[VII.4.c.ii] *The Vegetative and Animal Faculties*

Following his general definition of the soul, Ibn Da'ud describes in greater
detail the various faculties of the soul, based on Ibn Sina's version of Aristotle's
psychology. Following the Aristotelian pattern, each faculty of the soul is
called *nefesh* ("soul"), and each "soul" has "faculties" called *ko'ah* ("faculty"
or "power") characterized by different *pe'ulot* ("functions" or "activities").

1. The vegetative soul (called nefesh ["soul"] in the Bible)
    a. The faculty of nutrition
        i.   Attracting food
        ii.   Retaining food
        iii. Digestion
        iv.   Rejecting
    b. The faculty of growth
    c. The faculty of procreation

---

[38] *Exalted Faith*, Samuelson ed. p. 92.
[39] Aristotle, *De Anima* II:1, 412a, in *Aristotle: Selections*, ed. W.D. Ross (New York:
Scribners, 1955).

2. The animal soul (called ru'aḥ ["spirit"] in the Bible)
    a. The faculty of perception
        i.   External senses
             1. Touch
             2. Taste
             3. Smell
             4. Hearing
             5. Sight
        ii. Internal senses
             1. Common sense (coordinates external sensations)
             2. Imagination (retains sense impressions in the absence of the sensible objects)
             3. Fantasy (in animals) or thought (in humans) (combines or separates sensible forms into insensible forms)
             4. Cogitation or estimation (a type of instinctive faculty capable of perceiving insensible notions, such as the lamb's ability to perceive that a wolf is dangerous)
             5. Memory (retains impressions that were actually sensed, as opposed to imagination)
    b. The faculty of motion
        i.   Voluntary motion (such as movement in place)
        ii. Involuntary motion (such as heartbeat and breathing)

[VII.4.c.iii] *The Rational Soul*

Animals have the capacity to sense a particular sensible object; even the insensible perception of the estimative faculty (the fourth of the internal senses above) is based on particular sensations, eg., that a wolf is dangerous, and not the general and abstract notion of danger. Only humans have, in addition to their ability to perceive particulars, the ability to perceive "general [i.e., universal] intelligibles" by their rational soul, called *neshamah* in the Bible (from the root for "breath").

The human rational soul has two faculties: practical intellect and theoretical intellect. Practical intellect deals with arts and professions (such as the knowledge of the carpenter in building furniture), and with determining moral judgments. Theoretical intellect deals with knowledge of the simple substances that are called "separate intellects" by the philosophers and "angels" by Scripture.

Although the rational soul depends on the body for its existence and perfection in life, it is not ultimately dependent on the body, and therefore can survive it immortally. Ibn Da'ud borrows Ibn Sina's proof for the ultimate independence of the rational soul on the body. The lower bodily functions of the soul are connected to bodily organs, and are weakened by a strong stimulation. Thus, after we hear a very loud noise, we are deafened for some time, and after we are exposed to very bright light, such as the sun or a nuclear explosion, our ability to see is limited or even destroyed. The intellect, however, is strengthened and not weakened by strong stimulation; after studying quantum mechanics our ability to perform simple arithmetical functions is not impaired. The intellect is thus not weakened together with the body, nor does it die together with it. Rather, the intellect is thus shown to be an immortal substance.

Strangely enough, Ibn Da'ud's discussion of the rational soul is far shorter and more superficial than his detailed discussion of the vegetative and animal souls, despite the fact that the rational soul is of greater significance to his philosophy. For example, he refers, without any explanation, to Ibn Sina's doctrine of "the giver of forms" (*wahib al-ṣuwar*), one of the functions of the active intellect, and he also mentions, without explanation or analysis, different grades of intellect (potential, actual and acquired, the last being the ability to intelligize at will). If Ibn Da'ud's interest was less in psychological theory than in proving the immortality of the rational soul, his devoting far greater discussion (at least in quantitative terms) to the vegetative and animal souls remains perplexing.

[VII.4.d] PRINCIPLES OF THE FAITH

[VII.4.d.i] *The Root of Faith: the Incorporealitiy of God*

Part II of the *Exalted Faith* deals with six principles of the faith, namely: the "root" of faith, the unity of God, the divine attributes, the divine activities, prophecy and providence.

The first of these is the incorporeality of God, which Ibn Da'ud calls the "root" (*shoresh*) of faith. The Torah corrects the popular misconception that whatever is not material does not exist. By proving that there must be a prime mover, one proves its incorporeality, because everything material is finite by definition (all matter has a limit), but the prime mover cannot be limited, in which case it cannot be finite.

Like Ibn Sina before him and Rambam after him, Ibn Da'ud differentiates between possible and necessary being.[40] A being whose existence is dependent on something else which causes it, is possible. In the absence of that cause, it would not exist, and therefore its existence is possible, or contingent upon its cause. That which is not dependent on any cause for its existence, but which is the cause of all other existence, is necessary. Its existence is necessary, because

---

[40]   For a discussion of this concept, see Alexander Altmann, "Essence and Existence in Maimonides," in his *Studies in Religious Philosophy and Mysticism* (Ithaca: Cornell University Press, 1969), pp. 108–127, and F. Rahman, "Essence and Existence in Avicenna," in *Mediaeval and Renaissance Studies*, ed. R. Hunt, R. Klibansky, L. Labowsky (London, 1958), pp. 1–16.

it is not contingent on anything else. For example, when we define a chair as X, the definition (or "essence") does not include existence; we are asking what a chair is, not whether there is a chair. Existence is thus different from essence, and the existence of the chair is only possible; it is contingent upon the carpenter having manufactured it. This distinction between essence and existence, which applies to all contingent or possible beings, does not apply to the necessary being, where the existence is necessitated by, and is thus identical with, the essence.

[VII.4.d.ii] *The Unity of God*

God is thus the necessary being (Arabic: *wujub al-wujud*; Hebrew: *meḥuyav ha-meẓi'ut*), in which there is no distinction between essence and existence. The existence of all other beings (including the angels or separate intelligences which mediate between God and the material world) is possible. Therefore, whatever unity characterizes them is accidental and cannot be absolute, because the duality between their essence and existence always remains. In the necessary being there is no such duality—its essence and existence being identical—and therefore God's unity is essential (the unity being identical with the essence) and negative (there being in it no multiplicity whatsoever, even that of the distinction between essence and existence).

> The oneness of everything that happens to be one, excluding God, may He be exalted, is an accidental oneness, but the oneness of God, may He be exalted, is not an accident, since accidents are not perceived [to apply to] him... The meaning [of the claim] that he is one is a meaning [such] that nothing is like it. It refers to a negative notion. His oneness is not like the oneness of anything [else] that is called "one"... The meaning of his... being one [is that] oneness is his essence. It refers to two things. One of them is that everything else contains multiplicity in some way except for him. The second is that with respect to nothing being like him, he is not pluralized with other things... In his essence he is one, [so that] oneness is his essence, and nothing else always was or always will be so.[41]

[VII.4.d.iii] *The Divine Attributes*

Just as God's unity has both a negative meaning (negating all multiplicity) and a positive meaning (God's unity is his essence), according to Ibn Da'ud the divine attributes can be understood both negatively and positively. They are negative insofar as they negate notions from God, but they are positive when applied metaphorically. Because it is addressed to the entire people, "the Torah speaks according to human language,"[42] employing anthropomorphic

---

41   *Exalted Faith*, Samuelson ed. pp. 144–145.

42   In IX.2.c.iv we shall see how Rambam develops this theme and uses this rabbinic state-
     ment. Baḥya ibn Paquda also cited this rabbinic statement, in *Duties of the Heart* 1:10.

terminology, but such terminology is to be understood metaphorically and not literally.

There is a problem, however, with Ibn Da'ud's position as applied to God's unity, because the unity of God is neither negative nor metaphorical, as we have seen, but explicitly positive and essential. Ibn Da'ud acknowledges this problem by making the statement "God is one" a tautology (that $X = X$). Since God's essence is identical with his unity, the term "God" and the term "one" mean the same thing, so that by saying "God is one" were are not saying anything other than "God is God." Ibn Da'ud concludes, therefore, that so long as we are corporeal beings, we can have no true understanding of God's essence. There are eight attributes implicit in the concept of "necessary being," but all of them can only be understood in a negative or relative sense: one, true, eternal, living, omniscient, possessing will, omnipotent, and existing. These terms apply to God, however, equivocally—God's existence is unlike the existence of anything we know.

Ibn Da'ud thus permits relational attributes (as does Judah Ha-Levi), but by understanding them as divine activities, has taken another step in the direction of the radical negative theology (the *via negativa*) of Rambam, which permits nothing positive to be attributed to God, except actions, since a multiplicity of actions implies no multiplicity in essence of the subject.

[VII.4.d.iv] *The Divine Activities*

Ibn Da'ud's discussion of the "divine activities" deals with how these activities are mediated by the angels. As Norbert Samuelson has explained,[43] for Ibn Da'ud, "relative attributes" refer to God's direct activities in and relations with the world, whereas "divine activities" refer to indirect activities intermediated by the angels, namely the "separate intelligences" which, as intermediaries, are "secondary beings" (*sheniyim*). This theory follows from Ibn Da'ud's psychology. The Active Intellect is the last and lowest of these "separate intelligences," and it is responsible for "moving" the human soul, i.e., for transforming the potential human intellect into an actual intellect. Like the prime mover, which moves the spheres without being moved, the Active Intellect, in order to actualize potential and passive human intellects, must itself be entirely actual and active.

Ibn Da'ud thus establishes a hierarchy of intermediaries of the divine activities: the angels, the spheres moved by their separate intelligences, the Active Intellect (the lowest of those separate intelligences), and the human intellect moved and actualized by the Active Intellect. The "secondary beings," namely the angels or separate intelligences, are necessary intermediaries in this hierarchy, because they make possible the intellection of the simple

---

43   Norbert Samuelson, *Exalted Faith,* p. 157.

substances (the spheres, which are living beings) as well as of humans. The lowest "secondary being"—the Active Intellect—which actualizes the human intellect, also plays an essential role as the intermediary of prophecy, and it is the Active Intellect which is referred to by the biblical term "holy spirit" (*ru'aḥ ha-qodesh*).

[VII.4.d.v] *Belief in Prophets and Tradition*

Abraham ibn Da'ud's discussion of principles of the faith has, thus far, dealt with four philosophical truths—the incorporeality of the necessary being, the unity of God, the divine attributes, and angels as the intermediaries of divine activity—in other words, principles relating to what he had initially referred to as what a person holds "in his left hand," namely "the light of his wisdom." Now, in the fifth principle of faith, belief in prophets and tradition, he turns to what he had called "the light of his religion" that a person holds "in his right hand."

Amira Eran suggests that prophecy, the subject of the fifth principle, provides the junction and nexus between Ibn Da'ud's *Book of Tradition*, which verifies Judaism on the basis of history, and the *Exalted Faith*, which verifies Judaism on the basis of philosophy. In the *Book of Tradition* the past history of the Jews provides an objective framework for proving the claims of Judaism, and in the *Exalted Faith* philosophy provides the framework for preventing future undermining of those claims.[44]

Eran also suggests that the section on prophecy constitutes an independent literary unit, which differs in its ideas and in its literary structure from the rest of the book, which may, therefore, have been composed before the rest of the book.[45]

The fifth principle opens with the need for traditional knowledge (what Sa'adiah Ga'on had called "authentic tradition"), which Ibn Da'ud calls "what is accepted" or "heard" or "a report." Without such traditional knowledge humanity, civilization and morality cannot exist.[46] For example, a judge cannot rely only on what he personally perceives, but must rely on reports he is told by others. Up to this point, Ibn Da'ud's argument about the need for tradition is universal and applies to any human society.

Now turning to a particular type of traditional knowledge, namely prophecy, Ibn Da'ud explains that in prophecy the highest intellectual apprehension is mixed with the imaginative faculty. Like Judah Ha-Levi, Ibn Da'ud posits a connection between prophecy and both the Jewish people and the Land of Israel, although he moderates the connection by acknowledging that in some

---

[44]   Amira Eran, *From Simple Faith to Sublime Faith*, p. 207.
[45]   Amira Eran, *From Simple Faith to Sublime Faith*, p. 264.
[46]   *Exalted Faith*, Samuelson ed. p. 186–187.

cases prophecy, or at least a lower form of prophecy, namely veridical dreams, occurred among non-Jews (such as Balaam) and outside the Land.

Ibn Da'ud also regarded such Talmudic rabbis as Akiva as "intending" towards, and being worthy of, prophecy. He thus attempted to picture rabbinic Judaism not only as the successor and continuation of biblical prophecy, but as in no way inferior to prophecy. Rabbinic tradition and biblical prophecy thus, in his construct, constitute the same type of true knowledge.

Rabbinic Judaism, as Ibn Da'ud presents it, is therefore able to withstand the polemics of Christianity and Islam. In his analysis, the Christians accept the books of the Hebrew Bible as true and authentic, and do not question the Biblical text, but they claim that the Torah has been "replaced" by the New Testament. The Muslims in principle accept the validity of the prophets of ancient Israel, but claim that the books of the Bible have been subject to forgery (Arabic: *taḥrif*) over the generations, so that the text today is not the authentic Bible. The Christian claims do not hold up, in Ibn Da'ud's view, in light of Biblical verses attesting to the eternity of the Torah, and the Muslim claims are contradicted by the fact that the text of the Bible of all Jews all over the world (including communities far removed from contact with Islam) is identical.

However, Ibn Da'ud adds to these religious polemics a philosophical argument: the claims of the Christians and Muslims are illogical, because a "continuous" and "uninterrupted tradition" is a valid form of proof in logic, and the Jews possess such a "continuous" and "uninterrupted tradition" going back 2472 years to the revelation at Sinai.[47] Like Sa'adiah Ga'on and Judah Ha-Levi before him, Abraham ibn Da'ud thus concludes that the public, historical claims of Jewish tradition are indisputable and undeniable, because it is not mere tradition, but is "continuous" and "uninterrupted."

> Know that the difference between continuous states of affairs and traditions is [that while] it is possible to entertain a doubt about tradition, it is not possible to entertain [a doubt] about continuous states of affairs. [Now], the prophet [Moses performed] wonders of which he spoke to the multitude of his people face to face and he established that he performed them in the presence of all their multitude, and not one of them denied [those wonders at that time], and no one after [Moses] has denied them. [Therefore, Moses' wonders] are like continuous states of affairs, and continuous states of affairs are properly premises in a true demonstrative syllogism.[48]

---

47   *Exalted Faith*, Samuelson ed. p. 208. The *Exalted Faith* was composed in the year 4921 of the Jewish calendar (= 1160/1161 C.E.). In the *Book of Tradition* (ed. Cohen p. 5) Ibn Da'ud says that the revelation at Sinai took place in the year 2449 (= 1312/1311 B.C.E.), i.e. 2472 years before both books were composed.

48   *Exalted Faith*, Samuelson ed. p. 212.

[VII.4.d.vi] *Divine Providence and the Secret of Human Ability*

In our discussion of the divine attributes, we saw that "the Torah speaks according to human language," adapting itself to the understanding of the masses by employing anthropomorphic terminology metaphorically. However, such metaphorical language is ambivalent, and has confused many people regarding the divine attributes in general, and divine providence in particular, and led some people to conclude erroneously that the Torah and philosophy contradict each other. In these positions, Ibn Da'ud once again anticipates Rambam's clearer and more systematic arguments in the *Guide of the Perplexed*.

Even some of the divine names are ambivalent; for example, the name *Elohim* can refer to God, angels, stars and human judges and sages, as well as to pagan idols. (Ibn Da'ud cites Biblical verses to support these applications of the name). In this context of the name *Elohim*, Ibn Da'ud was particularly interested in angels, since (as we have seen) the angels, which are separate intelligences, are the intermediaries of the divine activities in the world. But, again, the result of such ambivalent usage is confusion and perplexity.

That confusion and perplexity are particularly evident regarding the verse "Let us create man in our image" (Genesis 1:26). That "image" (*zelem*), as Ibn Da'ud understands it, does not mean a physical form, but means an imitation, that humans imitate the angels in that they, too, are rational beings. Here, then, is an instance of the agreement between philosophy (specifically Aristotelian philosophy) and religion:

> Scripture says: "You have made him a little less than God" (Psalm 8:6). Scripture agrees with philosophy about this. We already found Aristotle speaking in this language [when he said that] we are in a certain way the Active Intellect.[49]

All of this discussion about the metaphorical language employed by Scripture, the divine attributes and names, and angels, sets the stage for the question—near the end of the book—with which the book began, namely human free will, what he called "necessity and choice" at the beginning of the book, and what he now refers to as "providence and the secret of ability," and he introduces the discussion by saying that this chapter was the reason he composed the book, "first in thought and last in action."[50]

Ibn Da'ud's cosmology (based on Ibn Sina), with its emphasis on the need for a hierarchical chain of intermediaries between God and the material world, serves as the basis for human free will, because the more remote something is from God, the less God's knowledge encompasses it. One of the standard

---

[49]   *Exalted Faith*, Samuelson ed. p. 236.
[50]   *Exalted Faith*, Samuelson ed. p. 245. My translation.

Aristotelian objections to divine knowledge of particulars is that particulars change, and as they change, they would introduce change into God's knowledge (and thus imply that God undergoes change). By removing God from direct and immediate knowledge of particulars, Ibn Da'ud thereby also removes God's direct responsibility for human actions, thus precluding determinism and permitting free choice.

As Norbert Samuelson understands Ibn Da'ud's theory here:

> On this view, all kinds of entities can be catalogued into a hierarchy in which the kinds of things that are above other kinds of things are judged to be in some sense morally superior. In this hierarchy, God occupies the highest place, and matter, which is identical with potency... occupies the lowest place. The more inferior a thing is, that is, the lower its place in the hierarchy, the less knowable it is to God... Ibn Da'ud argues that this lack of knowledge does not constitute an imperfection in God, because the deficiency is inherent in the object of knowledge and not in God as the knowing subject. In other words, God knows these things as well as they can be known, and in this sense his knowledge of them is perfect.[51]

This hierarchy also explains the origin of evil, which is not something that exists, but is a privation, an absence of being, just as darkness does not itself exist, but is the absence of light.[52] Only something that exists requires a cause, not something which does not exist. God is, therefore, not the agent of evil. Both being and non-being, actuality and potentiality, necessity and possibility, are thus features of the hierarchy.

Possibility, however, has two different connotations. In one respect, possibility is not real. For instance, a human may not have sufficient knowledge to predict whether or not it will rain; from his limited perspective, therefore, both rain and shine are possible. But, given the combination of causal factors, the rain (or shine) will necessarily occur. Such possibility, then, is merely a reflection of our ignorance, and is not real possibility. There is, however, another respect in which possibility can be understood to be real, namely a situation in which it is not yet determined which potential option will be actualized. God, as the creator of these possibilities, knows them, but he knows them as possible, not necessary. It is precisely their hierarchical distance from God that removes them from direct control and knowledge, and permits them both to be possible.

By the same token, human actions are also "possible," i.e., free, and according to Ibn Da'ud, there is no contradiction, therefore, between divine providence above and human free choice below.

---

51   Norbert Samuelson, *Exalted Faith*, p. 241.
52   Here, too, Ibn Da'ud anticipates Rambam's theory.

[VII.4.e] ETHICS

Part III of the *Exalted Faith*, titled "On the healing of the soul," is quite brief (less than seven pages out of 104 pages in the Weil edition of the Hebrew text), and deals with ethics, a branch of "practical philosophy." Ibn Da'ud's approach is based on Aristotle's *Nicomachean Ethics*, but also covers spiritual or religious themes, such as the human need for prayer. Ibn Da'ud may have avoided dealing at length with ethics, because in his view "practical philosophy" is fully covered in the Torah, which leads the person not only to ethical perfection in the inter-human realm, namely how people relate to each other, but also to the true worship of God. He therefore concludes the book by saying:

> These values are fine notions that improve the way of wisdom, because they are the difference and the distinction between heresy and faith.[53]

[VII.5] CONCLUSION

Abraham ibn Da'ud's thought constitutes a transition in the history of medieval Jewish philosophy, because he attempted to base his ideas systematically on Aristotelian foundations. Nevertheless, as we have seen (and will see again in our discussion of Rambam), medieval Aristotelianism has Neoplatonic components. In the case of Ibn Da'ud, these Neoplatonic components are particularly pronounced in his cosmology and theory of angels, and, as a corollary of that cosmology, in his theory of divine knowledge and providence. As a pioneer of Jewish Aristotelianism, Abraham Ibn Da'ud paved the way for Rambam to follow, expand and consolidate.

His two major books, the *Book of Tradition* and the *Exalted Faith* complement each other, and both are expressions of his profound belief that there can be no contradiction between religion and philosophy, and of his abiding commitment both to the particular rabbinic Jewish tradition and to the universal quest for scientific knowledge. Like Judah Ha-Levi and others, Ibn Da'ud believed that the Greek philosophers originally learned philosophy from the Jews, and that "the truth that the philosophers attained by research "after much labor, was given to us first without labor" in the Torah.[54]

For Abraham ibn Da'ud, then, it is not only possible, but a duty to "grasp with both his hands two lights, in his right hand the light of his religion, and in his left hand the light of his wisdom."

---

[53] *Exalted Faith*, Samuelson ed. pp. 265–266.
[54] *Exalted Faith*, Samuelson ed. p. 173.

Section III

RAMBAM

Chapter Eight

PRINCIPLES OF JUDAISM

[VIII.1] INTRODUCTION

[VIII.1.a] "FROM MOSES TO MOSES THERE WAS NONE LIKE MOSES"

Rabbi Moses ben Maimon, generally referred to in Hebrew by the initials of his name, Rambam, and in English as Maimonides, is often considered the greatest Jewish philosopher, certainly of the Middle Ages, and perhaps of all times, a reputation which gave rise to the expression, "From Moses [i.e., the biblical Moses] until Moses [Rambam], there was none like Moses." Rambam's preeminence is reflected in his being included among only three Jews (the others are Moses and Solomon) represented in sculptured reliefs decorating the House of Representatives Chamber of the United States Capitol in Washington, D.C.

Rambam's preeminent stature is not only philosophical—although he is frequently the only Jewish philosopher (other than Spinoza, who is often not perceived to be, or presented as, a "Jewish" philosopher)[1] cited or discussed in the context of western philosophy. He is justifiably regarded as one of the greatest authorities in the history of *halakhah*, and his Code of Jewish Law, the *Mishneh Torah*, is consulted to this day as one of the two most comprehensive and authoritative halakhic codes. His medical works were also widely read for centuries.

Of course Rambam's leadership position in the Egyptian Jewish community contributed to his reputation, but his books are, in many respects, virtually unrivaled, both quantitatively (as even a superficial glance at his bibliography shows) and qualitatively.

---

[1] See the discussion of Spinoza as a Jewish philosopher in Ch. 1, "What is Jewish Philosophy?" (I:1.p).

[VIII.1.b] RAMBAM THE MAN

[VIII.1.b.i] *Major Dates in Rambam's Life*

1135	Rambam is born in Cordova, Spain (according to others, in 1138).
1148	Almohads conquer Cordova; the Maimon family emigrate.
1148–1158	The Maimon family migrate in southern Spain and North Africa. Works: Treatise on Logic,[2] Treatise on Jewish Calendar.
1158	Maimon family settles in Fez, Morocco. Rambam begins writing his *Siraj* (Commentary on the Mishnah).
1161–1162	"Letter on Forced Conversion."
1165	Rambam travels to the Land of Israel, arriving in Akko. Works: Commentary on the Mishnah, Orders: Festivals, Women, Damages.
1168	Rambam settles in Cairo. Completes the Commentary on the Mishnah.
1172	"Letter to Yemen."
1173	Death of Rambam's brother David. Works: *Book of the Commandments*.
1178 (?)	Completion of *Mishneh Torah* (Code of Jewish Law)
1185–1190 (?)	Rambam writes the *Guide of the Perplexed*.
1187	Birth of Rambam's son Abraham.
1188 (?)	Rambam is appointed court physician.
1191	*Treatise on Resurrection*. Medical works. Responsa (at different times).
1204	Rambam dies; burial in Tiberias.

[VIII.1.b.ii] *Rambam's Personality*

Although in his works Rambam sometimes expressed harsh opinions—for example, characterizing as a heretic (*min*) a Jew who believes in one God but that God has a body[3] and asserting that a Jew who believes in a corporeal God is worse than an idolator[4]—these were, for him, matters of vital general principle. However, on an individual or communal level, his letters and responsa reflect a sensitivity and concern for people, and manifest personal consideration. For example, in his letter to Obadiah the Proselyte, who asked whether, as a non-native Jew he could recite such traditional formulas in the prayers as "our God

---

2   The customary attribution of the *Treatise on Logic* (*Millot Ha-Higayon*) to Rambam is questionable.
3   *Mishneh Torah*, Book of Knowledge, Laws of Repentance 3:7.
4   *Guide of the Perplexed* I:36.

and the God of our ancestors," Rambam answered unequivocally that whoever converts and affirms God's unity is "one of the students of Abraham our father and a member of his household," and that Abraham is the ancestor not only of his physical descendants but also of "those who walk in his ways…and any convert." Obadiah, therefore, should recite these formulas.[5] His "Letter to Yemen" also reflects such concern and consideration for the difficult situation in which that Jewish community found itself, and offers them hope and consolation.

Rambam's personality also manifested itself in his concern for his family. He was particularly attached to his brother David, a merchant who supported the entire family. When David drowned on a journey in the Indian Ocean, Rambam was beset by grief, and in a moving letter to Rabbi Yefet ben Elijah he lovingly describes his brother and his concern for David's widow and daughter, for whom he was now responsible.[6] Other letters describe his love for his only child, Abraham.

Several of Rambam's letters refer to his suffering from poor health. Nevertheless, he maintained an inhuman daily schedule, to which he referred in a letter to Samuel ben Judah ibn Tibbon, the translator of the *Guide of the Perplexed*, whose work Rambam supervised and approved from a distance. Rambam describes how he would rise at dawn to travel to the ruler's court Cairo, where medical affairs occupied him until the afternoon, when he would return to Fostat. He would then eat a light meal (his only food all day) and spend several hours dealing with communal affairs. Only on the Sabbath did he have any time to study with members of the Jewish community.

[VIII.2] *PEREQ ḤELEQ*: "ALL ISRAEL HAVE A PORTION IN THE WORLD TO COME"

[VIII.2.a] INTRODUCTION TO RAMBAM'S PRINCIPLES OF JUDAISM

Rambam's famous "Thirteen Principles" are formulated in his Commentary to the Mishnah (known in Arabic as the *Siraj* [Hebrew: *Ma'or*], "The Light"), on the tractate Sanhedrin, Chapter 10, known as *Pereq Ḥeleq* ("Chapter of the Portion") because it begins with the statement "all Israel have a portion in the world to come." The standard medieval translation, found in many editions

---

5   Letter to Obadiah the Proselyte, in Y. Shailat, *Iggerot Ha-Rambam*, vol. 1, pp. 233–234. My translation. A partial English translation may be found in Isadore Twersky (ed.), *A Maimonides Reader* (New York: Berhman House, 1972), pp. 475–476.

6   The letter is found in Y. Shailat, *Iggerot Ha-Rambam*, vol. 1, pp. 229–230.

of the Talmud at the end of tractate Sanhedrin, was made by Solomon ben Joseph ibn Ya'aqub. That translation is problematical and even misleading, and our reference is to the Arabic text and modern Hebrew translation by Yosef Kafiḥ.[7]

As we shall see, Rambam's understanding of "a portion in the world to come" was radically intellectualist and elitist, and could easily have been read as excluding the masses, however moral and upright. Our reading of Rambam's "Thirteen Principles" leads to a paradoxical conclusion. On the one hand, Rambam's attempt to formulate a definitive and authoritative Jewish dogma is, in many respects, undemocratic, and goes against the great latitude in traditional Judaism (with its behavioral emphasis) regarding matters of faith. On the other hand, Rambam's "Thirteen Principles" mitigate the elitism and intellectualism of his concept of immortality (which is how he understood "a portion in the world to come"), and thus effectively democratize "a portion in the world to come."[8]

Another difficulty in understanding Rambam's principles of Judaism is that in different works—including (in chronological order) his Commentary to the Mishnah, his Code of Jewish Law (*Mishneh Torah*) and his *Guide of the Perplexed*—he discusses and emphasizes different principles; the lists overlap, but also diverge significantly. We cannot, therefore, study the "Thirteen Principles" in isolation from these other texts.

[VIII.2.b] THE TEXT OF THE MISHNAH

All Israel have a portion in the world to come (*ḥeleq la-'olam ha-ba*), as it says: "Your people are all righteous, they will inherit the land forever" (Isaiah 60:21).[9] These are the ones who do not have a portion in the world to come:

---

7   The English translation by Arnold Jacob Wolf, "Maimonides on Immortality and the Principles of Judaism" (published in *Judaism*, XV. 1966; reprinted in Isadore Twersky [ed.], *A Maimonides Reader*, pp. 401–423) is based on the translation by Solomon ben Joseph ibn Ya'aqub. Since our reference is to Kafiḥ's Arabic text and Hebrew translation, what follows throughout this chapter is my translation of Rambam's text.

8   For further reading on Rambam's principles, their reception and opposition to them over the generations, and contemporary implications, see Menachem Kellner, *Dogma in Medieval Jewish Thought From Maimonides to Abravanel* (Oxford: Littman Library, 1986); idem, *Must a Jew Believe Anything? (Second Edition)* (Oxford: Littman Library, 2006); Marc Shapiro, *The Limits of Orthodox Theology: Maimonides' Thirteen Principles Reappraised* (Oxford: Littman Library, 2004).

9   Since Isaiah refers to the righteous who "will inherit the land forever," the rabbis use the quote as a proof text for an eternal portion in the world to come. The statement that all Jews have a portion in the world to come does not—or does not necessarily— imply that non-Jews do not have a portion, however understood. The statement is internally directed, and simply does not deal with the status of non-Jews. In logical terms,

(a) whoever says that [according to the Torah][10] there is no resurrection of the dead; (b) or that the Torah is not from heaven; (c) or an Apiqoros.[11]

[VIII.2.c] RAMBAM'S INTRODUCTION TO *PEREQ ḤELEQ*

Rambam attributed much of the confusion or perplexity in religious matters to misunderstanding of terminology and mixing categories. What is required initially, therefore, is to clarify terms and categories in order to aid precise thinking. This, as we shall see, was one of his explicit goals in the Introduction to the *Guide of the Perplexed*, and it also characterizes other works of his, including his introduction to *Pereq Ḥeleq*, where he goes to length to explain such terms as *'olam ha-ba* ("the world to come"), *teḥiyat ha-metim* ("resurrection"), and *yemot ha-mashi'aḥ* ("the messianic era" or "the days of the messiah"), all of which relate, in one way or another, to the expectations many people have regarding future reward and punishment.

---

if we say that "all squirrels have tails," that statement only describes squirrels and says nothing about other animals, which may or may not have tails. There are different opinions regarding the status of non-Jews. The criteria applied by the rabbis were generally moral, not national or partisan. For example, in Tosefta Sanhedrin 13:2 (ed. M.S. Zuckermandel and Saul Liebermann (Jerusalem, 1970), p. 434 (cf. Babylonian Talmud, Sanhedrin 105a):

> Rabbi Eliezer says: None of the Gentiles has a portion in the world to come, as it says: "The wicked will return to the grave (*she'ol*), all the nations forgetful of God" (Psalm 9:18). "The wicked will return to the grave," these are the wicked of Israel. Rabbi Joshua said to him: Had Scripture said, "The wicked will return to the grave, all the nations," I would have been silent, and I would have agreed with you. However, Scripture said, "forgetful of God." There are righteous people among the nations, and they have a portion in the world to come (*yesh ẓaddiqim ba-'umot she-yesh la-hem ḥeleq la-'olam ha-ba*).

Rabbi Joshua thus pointed out that Rabbi Eliezer, who denied that non-Jews have a portion in the world to come, had misread the verse in Psalm 9:18, which does not refer simply to "all the nations" but qualifies it as "all the nations forgetful of God." The non-Jews *per se* are thus not excluded; righteous Gentiles have a portion, and wicked Jews (as our Mishnah goes on to discuss) do not. As we shall see, Rambam elsewhere clearly identifies with Rabbi Joshua's position, as do, in modern times, such thinkers as Moses Mendelssohn.

10   The words "according to the Torah" in brackets are found in some versions of the Mishnah and not in others. If the words are missing, the reference is to a person who in principle denies resurrection of the dead. If the words are included, the reference is to the Pharisaic belief—denied by the Sadducees—in resurrection and claim that resurrection is taught by the Torah.

11   *Apiqoros* is a term, based on the name of the philosopher Epicurus, which came to refer in rabbinic usage to a person denying fundamental religious principles. We shall see presently how Rambam understands the term.

[VIII.2.c.i] *Childish Opinions Regarding Reward and Punishment*

Rambam opens his discussion by surveying five types of popular expectations regarding future reward and punishment. These expectations, he states, are often childish, reflecting intellectual and spiritual immaturity. A child, for example, may study, but may do so not out of the desire to know the truth, but in order to receive a prize, like candy. At an older age, the child will study, but still for a prize, although the prize will differ in accordance with the child's age, such as money, clothing, or honor. In all these cases, what motivates the person is not intrinsic knowledge of the truth, but the extrinsic prize. The rabbis warned against such an attitude by saying "Do not make [the words of Torah] a crown with which to aggrandize yourself, nor a shovel with which to dig."[12] Rather, Rambam emphasizes, "the goal of the truth is only to know that it is true, and the commandments are true, and their goal is their performance." Nevertheless, it is better that a person incapable of disinterested virtue do the right thing even if for the wrong reason, than not to do the right thing at all.

The masses are not completely deficient because of their observing the commandments out of fear of punishment and hope for reward, but they are not perfect. By behaving properly, even for the wrong reason, they become accustomed to doing what is right, and can eventually become people who "serve out of love" (*'ovedim me-ahavah*). As the rabbis said, "A person should always engage in Torah, even if not for its own sake, for out of doing it not for its own sake he comes [to do it] for its own sake."[13]

Another problem leading to confusion and perplexity is that people do not know how to understand the Talmudic rabbis correctly, because they take everything the rabbis said literally. Such literalist reading of the rabbis is common to two opposite groups of Jews: simple Jews who admire the rabbis and therefore blindly accept everything they said literally (even when the literal meaning is absurd), and Jewish intellectuals (or pseudo-intellectuals), such as physicians and astrologers, who imagine that they are philosophers, who mock the rabbis by pointing to the literal absurdity of their statements. In both cases, the error lies in taking everything literally, and not realizing that the rabbis—who themselves often read the Torah in a non-literal sense— often also saw fit to express themselves metaphorically. The correct way to read the rabbis, then, is to recognize that their statements often have an external or exoteric meaning (Arabic: *zahir*) but may also have an internal or esoteric meaning (Arabic: *batin*).

---

[12]   Mishnah Avot 4:7.
[13]   Babylonian Talmud, Pesahim 50b, Sanhedrin 105b (and others).

[VIII.2.c.ii] *'Olam Ha-Ba—"The World to Come"*

Our Mishnah states that "all Israel have a portion in the world to come." For Rambam, the expression "to come" does not indicate a future era. The "world to come" already exists; it is only "to come" from the perspective of the living individual, and means what will happen to him after death. The "world to come" is thus something totally different from this world, but it is already here. As we shall see, by contrast, the messianic era" in Rambam's understanding refers to a future, ideal state in and of this world. We also must keep in mind that Rambam does not refer to reward and punishment *in* the world to come. Rather, the reward *is* the world to come, and its opposite punishment is what the Torah calls *karet* (literally: "being cut off"), meaning the absence of, or the failure to attain, the world to come.

(1) A SPIRITUAL OR INTELLECTUAL CONCEPTION

Since we are physical beings, living in bodies in the material universe, many people have difficulty conceiving of a pleasure or happiness which is not physical. But even primitive people are capable of deferring immediate physical pleasure for the sake of a higher emotional or spiritual pleasure. A person seeking revenge may willingly undergo prolonged physical suffering to attain his goal. That being the case while we are physical beings, it should be possible to understand that the pleasures or happiness of the world to come are not physical, but spiritual. The Talmudic rabbis alluded to this by saying, "In the world to come there is no eating, drinking, washing, anointing, or sexual intercourse. Rather, the righteous sit, with crowns on their heads, and enjoy the light of the divine presence (*shekhinah*)."[14]

The activities mentioned by the rabbis are all necessary components of bodily life. Rambam thus interprets the rabbis as understanding that "the world to come" refers to a spiritual, non-physical existence. However, that being the case, what did the rabbis mean by their use of physical terms to describe that non-physical existence: "the righteous sit, with crowns on their heads, and enjoy the light of the divine presence?"

> The meaning of their saying "the righteous sit, with crowns on their heads, and enjoy the light of the divine presence" is the existence of the soul in the existence of what it knows, and that [the soul] and [what it knows] are one thing, as the great philosophers have mentioned...Their saying "enjoy the light of the divine presence" means that those souls enjoy what they comprehend of God...The ultimate end and felicity are the attainment of this exalted rank...and this is the greatest good to which no other good can compare, and which no pleasure resembles...The utter unhappiness is for that soul to be cut off and to perish,

---

14   Berakhot 17a.

and not to have any existence, and this is what the Torah refers to as being cut off (*karet*)...The prophet has already explained that the world to come cannot (*'olam ha-ba*) be perceived by the bodily senses, when he said: "The eye has not seen a god beside you who works for one who waits for him" (Isaiah 64:3). All the prophets have said this explicitly; but they only prophesied about the messianic era (*yemot ha-mashi'aḥ*), but as for the world to come, "the eye has not seen a god beside you."...The sages, peace be on them, said: "The reward of the commandment is the commandment itself and the reward of the transgression is the transgression itself" (Mishnah Avot 4:2).

This is how Rambam described his conception of the world to come later, in greater detail, in his *Mishneh Torah* (Code of Jewish Law):[15]

The good reserved for the righteous is life in the world to come, a life which is immortal, and good without evil.
The reward of the righteous is that they will attain this bliss and abide in this state of happiness; the punishment of the wicked is that they will not attain this life but will be cut off and die...This is the penalty of excision [*karet*] referred to in the Torah, as it is written, "That soul shall utterly be cut off, his iniquity shall be upon him" (Numbers 15:31)...This means that that soul, after its separation from the body on earth, will not attain life in the world to come, but will be cut off from that life also.
In the world to come, there is nothing corporeal, and no material substance; there are only souls of the righteous without bodies, like the ministering angels. And since in that world there are no bodies, there is neither eating there, nor drinking, nor aught that human beings need on earth. None of the conditions occur there which are incident to physical bodies in this world, such as sitting, standing, sleep, death, grief, merriment, etc. So the ancient sages said, "In the life hereafter, there is no eating, no drinking, no connubial intercourse, but the righteous sit with their crowns on their heads and enjoy the radiance of the Shekhinah."
This passage clearly indicates that as there is no eating or drinking there, there is no physical body hereafter. The phrase "the righteous sit" is allegorical, and means that the souls of the righteous exist there without labor or fatigue. The phrase "their crowns on their heads" refers to the knowledge they have acquired, and for the sake of which they have attained life in the world to come. This is their crown, in the same sense as where Solomon says, "with the crown wherewith his mother has crowned him" (Song of Songs 3:11). And just as in the text "Everlasting joy shall be upon their heads" (Isaiah 35:10), joy is not to be understood as a material substance that actually rests on the head, so "the crown" of which the sages here speak, is not to be taken literally but refers to knowledge. And what is the meaning of the sages' statement, "they enjoy the

---

15   Laws of Repentance, Ch. 8. English translation by Moses Hyamson, Maimonides' *Book of Knowledge* (reprint edition, 1971), pp. 90a ff.

radiance of the Shekhinah?" It means that the righteous attain to a knowledge and realization of the truth concerning God to which they had not attained while they were in the murky and lowly body.

This spiritual-intellectual conception of the world to come aroused fierce opposition. For example, Rabbi Abraham ben David of Posquiéres (known as Ravad), whose critical glosses (*hasagot*) came to be included in edition of Rambam's *Mishneh Torah*, wrote:[16]

> The words of this man seem to me to be close to one who denies resurrection of the bodies [and affirms the immortality] only of the soul. By my life, this is not what the sages thought, since they said, "In the future the righteous will stand in their garments" (Talmud, Ketubot 111b)...All these [quotes] prove that they will stand alive in their bodies. Perhaps the creator will give them strong and healthy bodies, like the bodies of the angels, and like the body of Elijah, of blessed memory, and the crowns are meant literally, not figuratively.

To continue with Rambam's description of the world to come in terms of the immortality of the rational soul:[17]

> The soul, whenever mentioned in this conection, is not the vital element requisite for bodily existence, but that form of soul which is identical with the intelligence which apprehends the creator, as far as it is able, and apprehends other abstract concepts and other things...
>
> The severest retribution beyond which punishment can no further go, is that the soul shall be cut off and not attain the life hereafter...
>
> All the boons which the prophets prophesied to Israel only refer to material things that Israel will enjoy in the days of King Messiah, when sovereignty will be restored to Israel. But as for the bliss in the world to come, nought can be compared with, or likened to it. And the prophets did not depict it, so as not to deprecate it by their imaginary picture...
>
> The reason why the sages styled it "the world to come" is not because it is not now in existence, and will only come into being when this world shall have passed away. That is not so. The world to come now exists...It is called the "world to come" only because human beings will enter into it at a time subsequent to the life of the present world in which we now exist with body and soul, and this existence comes first.

Despite his traditional religious terminology, that the "righteous" are the ones who merit the life of the world to come, in Rambam's thought a "portion in the world to come" is not attained by good deeds but by intellectual

---

16   Ravad on Laws of Repentance 8:2.
17   *Mishneh Torah*, Book of Knowledge, Laws of Repentance, Ch. 8. English translation by Moses Hyamson, Maimonides' *Book of Knowledge* (reprint edition, 1971), pp. 90a ff.

knowledge of the truth. As we saw in his Introduction to *Pereq Ḥeleq*: "the existence of the soul in the existence of what it knows, and that [the soul] and [what it knows] are one thing, as the great philosophers have mentioned." And similarly in the Laws of Repentance: "The phrase 'their crowns on their heads' refers to the knowledge they have acquired, and for the sake of which they have attained life in the world to come... 'The crown' of which the sages here speak, is not to be taken literally but refers to knowledge... that form of soul which is identical with the intelligence which apprehends the creator, as far as it is able, and apprehends other abstract concepts and other things."

(2) THE UNITY OF SUBJECT, ACT AND OBJECT OF INTELLECTION

At the root of Rambam's intellectual conception of *'olam ha-ba* as the survival of the rational soul is the Aristotelian notion of the unity in the actual intellect of the subject (Arabic: *'aql*; Hebrew: *sekhel*), act (Arabic: *'aqil*; Hebrew: *maskil*) and object (Arabic: *ma'qul*; Hebrew: *muskal*) of intellection. Intellectual knowledge sharply differs in this regard from sense perception. The external senses are passive: they respond to stimulation by an external object. The functioning of the senses is, therefore, neither voluntary nor active: I cannot will to see something which is not present. Moreover, there is no identity between the sensation in my body and the sensible object outside my body: my sensation of a tree is caused by the presence of the tree, but is not the same as the tree. I can only see the tree if it is present in front of me, nothing impedes my vision of it, and there is light reflected from the tree to my eye. My only voluntary control is whether to close or open my eyes, and whether to look in the direction of the tree or in another direction. But if my eyes are open and I am looking in the direction of the tree, my eyes do not act, they respond to the stimulation of the light reaching them from the tree. Finally, what I sense is a particular tree or several trees, not trees in general.

In the case of intellection, however, the activity of the mind is voluntary, and does not depend on external stimulation. When I intelligize the tree — in other words, when I conceive it in my mind — I do not know a specific tree. What I know is the abstract idea or definition of trees in general — the "form" or "essence" of the tree.

According to Aristotle, the actual intellect is an intellect actually engaging in the act of intellection. So the subject — the intellect — really exists in actuality when it acts. But what does it mean for the intellect to act (i.e., to intelligize)? It means to possess an intelligible thought. And so the intellectual subject, act and object (or, in the terms Rambam used in Hebrew in his *Mishneh Torah* — the knower [*yode'a*], the knowing or knowledge [*de'ah*], and the known [*yadu'a*]) are indivisible and identical.

(3) ARISTOTLE'S VIEW

The concept of the unity of thinker, thinking and thought has its origins in Book Lambda, i.e., Book XII, of the Metaphysics, where Aristotle discusses divine thought. The only thing worthy of God's thought is himself.[18]

> Therefore it must be of itself that the divine thought thinks (since it is the most excellent of things), and its thinking is a thinking on thinking.
>
> But evidently knowledge and perception and opinion and understanding always have something else as their object, and themselves only by the way. Further, if thinking and being thought of are different, in respect of which does goodness belong to thought? For to be an act of thinking and to be an object of thought are not the same thing.
>
> We answer that in some cases the knowledge is the object. In the productive sciences it is the substance or essence of the object, matter omitted, and in the theoretical sciences the definition or the act of thinking is the object. Since, then, thought and object of thought are not different in the case of things that have not matter, the divine thought and its object will be the same, i.e., the thinking will be one with the object of its thought.

(4) RAMBAM'S VIEW

In the *Mishneh Torah*, when discussing the commandment to love God, Rambam refers to the unity of God as the knower, knowing (or: knowledge) and known:[19]

> The Holy One, blessed be he, realizes his true being, and knows it as it is, not with a knowledge external to himself, as is our knowledge. For our knowledge and ourselves are separate. But as for the creator, blessed be he, his knowledge and his life are one, in all respects, from every point of view, and however we conceive unity. If the creator lived as other living creatures live, and his knowledge were external to himself, there would be a plurality of deities, namely: he, himself, his life, and his knowledge. This, however, is not so. He is one in every aspect, from every angle, and in all ways in which unity is conceived. Hence the conclusion that God is the one who knows, is known, and is the knowledge (of himself) — all these being one... Hence, too, God does not apprehend creatures and know them because of them, as we know them, but he knows them because of himself. Knowing himself, he knows everything, for everything is attached to him, in his being.

Up to this point, Rambam has discussed only divine knowledge, which totally differs from human knowledge, so that the term "knowledge" is applied

---

[18]　Aristotle, Metaphysics XII:9, 1074b–1075a. Translation by W.D. Ross in *The Basic Works of Aristotle*, ed. Richard McKeon (New York: Random House, 1941), p. 885.

[19]　*Mishneh Torah*, Book of Knowledge, Laws of Foundations of the Torah 2:10. Hyamson trans., pp. 36ab.

equivocally to God and people. This is a point Rambam emphasizes repeatedly in the *Guide of the Perplexed*. Our knowledge of something follows from its existence—we know it because, and as, it exists. In the case of God, however, by knowing himself as their cause, he knows his creatures; they exist because of his knowledge of them.

However, a different perspective is to be found in the *Guide of the Perplexed* 1:68, where Rambam extends the unity of intellectual subject, act and object to the actual human intellect as well. The difference, then, is not in terms unity, which applies to both divine and human thought, but in terms of actuality: God's thought is always actual, whereas human thought undergoes the transformation from potentiality to actuality. "He is always intelligizing and intellect and intelligible object. It has become clear that the numerical unity of intellect and intelligizing and intelligible object does not apply only to God, but to every intellect. In us, too, the intelligizing and the intellect and the intelligible object are one thing, whenever we have an actual intellect."[20]

This extension of the Aristotelian unity of knower, knowing and the known to the actual human intellect is not original with Rambam, and it is found in earlier Islamic thought. The extension has, however, radical implications, because the moment the actual human intellect also is characterized by such unity, we have the basis for the immortality of the rational soul, or in traditional Jewish terms (as understood by Rambam), "a portion in the world to come." However, that immortality may be general and impersonal, not necessarily individual and personal. What individualizes the person's intellect, and differentiates it from other intellects, is his body, so long as the intellect exists in a living body. With the death of the body, however, the actual intellect can remain, since it is identical with its knowledge, which also can survive the individual. But that knowledge (and thus also that intellect) is no longer differentiated and individual, but is simply part of the sum total of universal knowledge. Like water in a pail which is thrown into the sea, as soon as the pail is removed, the water that was inside the pail and the surrounding water are no longer differentiated.

---

[20]   Shlomo Pines has suggested that this is an instance of a fundamental contradiction in Rambam's thought; on the one hand, divine and human thought are totally different and equivocal, and on the other hand, in both cases, the unity of subject, act and object of thought applies. Moreover, the ultimate perfection of the individual is intellectual apprehension of God, but we cannot know God's essence, only God's actions. These points will be discussed in the coming chapters. For Pines' analysis, see his "Philosophical Sources of the *Guide of the Perplexed*"—Pines' introduction to his English translation of the *Guide of the Perplexed* (Chicago: University of Chicago Press, 1963), and also his study "The Limitations of Human Knowledge According to Al-Farabi, Ibn Bajja and Maimonides," in Isadore Twersky (ed.), *Studies in Medieval Jewish History and Literature* (Cambridge: Harvard University Press, 1979), pp. 82–96.

Rambam does not explicitly explain his position on this question. He clearly equates the rabbinic category of *'olam ha-ba* with the survival of the rational soul, as a result of the identity of the intellectual subject, act and object, especially when the object of knowledge is God. He does not clarify whether such intellectual immortality is individual and personal (as Ibn Sina maintained) or general and impersonal. Whatever the nature of such intellectual immortality, individual and personal or general and impersonal, it is, as Rambam has made clear, the meaning of *'olam ha-ba* and is attained not by a person's behavior but by knowledge. To reiterate:

> The meaning of their saying "the righteous sit, with crowns on their heads, and enjoy the light of the divine presence" is the existence of the soul in the existence of what it knows, and that [the soul] and [what it knows] are one thing, as the great philosophers have mentioned.

(5) SUMMARY

Rambam began his discussion by describing the popular concern for reward and punishment as intellectually and spiritually childish. Ultimately, as the rabbis said, "The reward of the commandment is the commandment itself and the reward of the transgression is the transgression itself."[21] The ultimate service of God must be disinterested, not to seek extrinsic reward and avoid punishment, but because of the inherent correctness and worth of that way of life. In the words of Antigonos of Sokho: "Do not be like servants who serve the master in order to receive a reward. Rather, be like servants who serve the master in order not to receive a reward."[22] The reward to doing what is right is simply doing what is right, and the reward of knowledge is the knowledge itself. This is the rank of one who "serves out of love" (*'oved me-ahavah*).

It is this knowledge that provides the basis of immortality of the rational soul, and this is how Rambam understands the rabbinic concept of "the world to come." The "world to come" is thus a function of knowledge, not of behavior. In Rambam's thought, it is not that there is reward and punishment *in* the world to come. The world to come *is* the reward, and its opposite is simply the punishment of *karet*, namely that nothing survives the individual's death.

[VIII.2.c.iii] *Gan 'Eden ("The Garden Of Eden") and Gehinom (Hell)*

Following his discussion of *'olam ha-ba* in his Introduction to *Pereq Ḥeleq*, Rambam briefly discusses two other terms relating to the overall theme of popular convern with reward and punishment, *gan 'eden* ("the Garden of Eden") and *gehinom* (Gehenna, hell).

---

21   Mishnah Avot 4:2.
22   Mishnah Avot 1:3.

But the garden of Eden (*gan 'eden*) is a fertile place on earth, of abundant water and trees, which God will reveal to humans in the future, and he will teach them his way, and they will take pleasure in it...But *Gehinom* (Gehenna, hell) is a term for the sorrow which the wicked will surfer, but the Talmud does not describe that sorrow.

These terms, in short, have nothing to do with "the world to come."

[VIII.2.c.iv] *Teḥiyat ha-metim ("Resurrection of the Dead")*

A more significant term requiring explication, because it is one of the three categories mentioned by our Mishnah of Jews excluded from the world to come, is *teḥiyat ha-metim* ("resurrection of the dead"), a point of contention in late Second Temple times between the Pharisees who affirmed it and the Sadducees who denied it, and a doctrine Rambam's critic Ravad accused him of denying.[23]

(1) RESURRECTION IN JEWISH TRADITION

Resurrection is traditionally understood to mean the belief that a body can be miraculously restored to life after death. Biblical support for this belief is often associated with Ezekiel's vision of the valley of dry bones which were restored to life (Ezekiel 37:1–11). The Gemara to *Pereq Ḥeleq*[24] records a discussion of the rabbis regarding the status of Ezekiel's vision: was it, as some rabbis, including Rabbi Eliezer, thought, an actual historical occurrence of this miracle, or was it, as other rabbis, including Rabbi Judah, thought, a parable? What is important for our purposes is that the opinion of Rabbi Judah and others—that Ezekiel's vision was a parable—was not regarded as heretical or as a denial of resurrection *per se*. Belief in the possibility of resurrection, in other words, does not require affirmation that there ever was an actual historical occurrence of resurrection (whether in the case of the valley of dry bones or any other cases). The dispute in the Gemara, therefore, does not relate to the principle of resurrection, but only to whether Ezekiel's vision was an actual instance of it.

The Pharisaic, and subsequently rabbinic, affirmation of the principle of resurrection is also reflected in second section of the central daily prayer, the *'Amidah* ("Standing" prayer) or *Shemoneh 'Esreh* ("Eighteen [Blessings]"):

> You are eternally mighty, Lord, and resurrect the dead...You sustain life in kindness, and resurrect the dead in great compassion...You are faithful to resurrect the dead. Blessed are you, Lord, who resurrects the dead.

Our Mishnah is, of course, a prime example of the importance the Pharisaic-rabbinic tradition ascribed to the principle of resurrection, in opposition

---

23　See the citation above from Ravad's critical gloss on Laws of Repentance 8:2.

24　Babylonian Talmud, Sanhedrin 92.

to the Sadducean position. And yet, in purely logical terms, the fact that the Gemara to *Pereq Ḥeleq* records that various rabbis inferred from different proof-texts in Scripture allusions to the principle, means that a verse one rabbi interpreted as alluding to resurrection was understood by others in a different sense, and that none of the verses cited overtly and explicitly refers to resurrection.

Regardless of the actual or supposed origins of the belief, our Mishnah makes it clear that what excludes a Jew from a portion in the world to come is not the denial of the historical fact of resurrection, but of the principle of resurrection.

(2) PAUL ON RESURRECTION

In sharp contrast with the rabbinic affirmation of the principle of resurrection, without necessary reference to the question of historical occurrence, in the New Testament Paul posits the fact of resurrection—the resurrection of Jesus—as the foundation of Christian belief:

> Now if Christ is preached as raised from the dead, how can some of you say that there is no resurrection of the dead? But if there is no resurrection of the dead, then Christ has not been raised; if Christ has not been raised, then our preaching is in vain and your faith is in vain. We are even found to be misrepresenting God, because we testified of God that he raised Christ, whom he did not raise...If Christ has not been raised, your faith is futile, and you are still in your sins...But in fact Christ has been raised from the dead.[25]

(3) RAMBAM ON RESURRECTION

For Rambam the question is also one of theoretical principle, not of historical fact. The possibility of resurrection is significant for other important questions which Rambam regarded as "foundations of the Torah." Rambam treats resurrection in three of his works: (a) his Commentary to the Mishnah, *Pereq Ḥeleq*; (b) his *Mishneh Torah*, Laws of Repentance; (c) his "Treatise on Resurrection."

In his Introduction to *Pereq Ḥeleq*, Rambam states:

> Resurrection of the dead is one of the foundations (Arabic: *qaʻidah*; Hebrew: *yesod*) of the Torah of Moses our teacher, and there is neither religion (Arabic: *din*; Hebrew: *dat*) nor membership in the Jewish community (Arabic: *millah*) for one who does not believe this. It is for the righteous...for how can the wicked live, since they are dead even during their lives? Thus the sages said: "The wicked, even in their lives, are called dead, and the righteous, even in their death, are called living." (Babylonian Talmud, Berakhot 18b). Know that a person will surely die and will disintegrate into that from which he was compounded.

---

25   I Corinthians 15:12–20. (Revised Standard Version).

In the *Mishneh Torah*, Laws of Foundations of the Torah, Rambam says: "Everythingmadeupofthesefourelementsultimatelydisintegrates...Everything compounded of them must inevitably revert to them...Since everything that disintegrates dissolves into these elements, why was the first man especially told 'And unto dust you will return' (Genesis 3:19)? The reason is because the human structure consists, for the greater part, of dust."[26]

As we have seen, in contrast with "the world to come," which Rambam understood in exclusively spiritual-intellectual terms, resurrection has to do with the body. Moreover, the survival of the rational soul in the world to come is a function of knowledge, not of actions, but resurrection, as Rambam discussed it in his Introduction to *Pereq Ḥeleq*, "is for the righteous."

What, then, was Rambam's attitude towards resurrection, keeping in mind that if he questioned it, let alone denied it, at least in a literal sense, he could not openly say so without violating the clear prescription of our Mishnah, that "whoever says that [according to the Torah] there is no resurrection of the dead" forfeits his portion in the world to come. Yet, his discussion of resurrection in his Introduction to *Pereq Ḥeleq* waters down the concept to the notion (citing the Talmudic rabbis) that "the wicked, even in their lives, *are called* dead, and the righteous, even in their death, *are called* living," a view that falls far short of the literal belief in bodily resurrection.

Rambam's reference to resurrection in the *Mishneh Torah*, Laws of Repentance, reaffirms our Mishnah's statement, but does not shed light on what Rambam meant by resurrection:[27]

> The following have no portion in the world to come, but are cut off and perish, and for the great wickedness and sinfulness are condemned for ever and ever: Heretics (*minim*) and Epicureans;[28] those who deny the Torah, the resurrection of the dead or the coming of the Redeemer; apostates; those who cause a multi-tude to sin, and those who secede from the ways of the community...informers; those who terrorize a community, not for a religious purpose; murderers and slanderers; and one who obliterates the physical mark of his Jewish origin.[29]

In the following paragraphs,[30] Rambam goes into greater detail and explains some of these categories of Jews excluded from a portion in the world to come—but he does not explain further what he means by "those who deny...resurrection." Moreover, most of the categories included in his

---

26 *Mishneh Torah*, Laws of Foundations of the Torah 4:3–4, Hyamson translation, p. 38b (my modifications).

27 *Mishneh Torah*, Laws of Repentance 3:6, Hyamson translation, p. 84b.

28 Epicureans = "Apiqorsim". See note 11 (above).

29 Hebrew: *ha-moshekh 'orlato*; the reference is to Hellenizing Jews who underwent surgery to reverse and cover up the sign of circumcision.

30 Laws of Repentance 3:7–13.

statement are moral categories, and we have seen that "a portion in the world to come" is a function of knowledge, not moral behavior. Nevertheless, Rambam was forced to include these categories because, in his codification of Jewish law, he could not ignore explicit statements about these categories by the Talmudic rabbis, just as he could not ignore our Mishnah's explicit statement that "whoever says that [according to the Torah] there is no resurrection of the dead" forfeits his portion in the world to come.

(4) DID RAMBAM BELIEVE IN RESURRECTION?

On the surface of it, the question whether Rambam believed in resurrection is meaningless, since he included it as the thirteenth of his Thirteen Principles, and said that "resurrection of the dead is one of the foundations of the Torah of Moses our teacher, and there is neither religion nor membership in the Jewish community for one who does not believe this," and since in the Laws of Repentance he also included one who denies resurrection among the categories of Jews who have no portion in the world to come. Indeed, when late in life he was criticized for allegedly denying resurrection, he could easily defend himself by pointing to these explicit statements.

This question is not meaningless, however, because his positive statements about resurrection, which conform to our Mishnah's prescriptions, do not necessarily mean that he affirmed the principle of resurrection in a literal sense. We also need to keep in mind his criticism of those who take everything the rabbis said literally, his quoting the statement that "the righteous, even in the death, are called living," and his explicit references, both in the Introduction to *Pereq Ḥeleq* and in the Laws of Foundations of the Torah that all bodies decompose into their constituent elements.

In short, even if Rambam did not believe in literal resurrection, there was no way for him, within a halakhic framework, to deny it overtly. What he could do, however, was what he recommended doing with all religious language that is rationally untenable—whether Scriptural anthropomorphisms or rabbinic exaggerations—and that was to affirm it by reinterpreting it metaphorically. He could, moreover, leave subtle hints for the intelligentsia, by referring to the decomposition of the body and by juxtaposing his comments on resurrection with the rabbinic statement that "the righteous, even in death, are called living." The ambiguity, presumably deliberate, in his position has led one historian to conclude that on the question of resurrection, "Maimonides affirmed even as he squirmed."[31]

As a result of the questions and suspicions raised against him, Rambam wrote in 1191 an Arabic work, *The Treatise on Resurrection*, to respond to his critics and to reaffirm his belief in the principle.

---

[31]   Daniel Jeremy Silver, *Maimonidean Criticism and the Maimonidean Controversy 1180–1240* (Leiden: Brill, 1965), p. 116.

(5) RAMBAM'S TREATISE ON RESURRECTION

In the *Treatise on Resurrection* Rambam explained that many Jews were fixated on the question of resurrection and neglected the no less important principle of the world to come, which is what he therefore went to lengths to explain and emphasize. He had, after all, insisted in his Introduction to *Pereq Ḥeleq* and in his *Mishneh Torah* on including resurrection as a foundation of the Torah, but he had also attempted to show that the world to come, and not resurrection, is the final purpose of life. In any event, he adds, the principle of resurrection mentioned in the prayers and other Jewish literature refers to "the return of the soul to the body after its separation." However, what ultimately interested Rambam was less the theological sources of the principle of resurrection than its philosophical implications.

(6) THE CREATION OF THE WORLD
AND THE POSSIBILITY OF MIRACLES

In the following chapters we shall deal with Rambam's approach to creation versus eternity in Part II of the *Guide of the Perplexed*. At this point we merely need to note that in Rambam's view, the natural order manifest in the universe disproves the Epicurean theory that everything occurs by chance. However, digressions (including astronomical) from the natural order disprove the theory of necessity which is a corollary of an unvarying, eternal Aristotelian order. In short, Epicurus' theory of chance cannot account for order, and Aristotle's theory of eternal necessity cannot account for digressions from order. A third theory is therefore required, and that is the theory of creation, which accounts both for order and for digressions. Such digressions can be in the realm of astronomy, but they can also be in the realm of history, as miraculous divine interventions in the world. Only a created world, in other words, makes possible divine intervention in general, and revelation in particular.

To deny the possibility (not the inevitability) of resurrection is, therefore, to deny that the world is created, and, thereby, to preclude the possibility of revelation, which is the foundation of the Torah. Our Mishnah, it will be recalled, also excludes from a portion in the world to come to a Jew who denies that "the Torah is from heaven."

(7) THE POSSIBILITY OF RESURRECTION

As Rambam thus shows in his *Treatise on Resurrection*, the denial of the possibility of resurrection indirectly entails undermining the divinely revealed authority of the Torah. That is why, for Rambam, as we have seen, "resurrection of the dead is one of the foundations of the Torah of Moses our teacher, and there is neither religion nor membership in the Jewish community for one who does not believe this." In terms of our Mishnah, one who denies resurrection will, therefore, necessarily also deny that "the Torah is from heaven." Rambam's position, then, is less a matter of a positive affirmation of literal resurrection than it is a recognition that the denial of the theoretical possibility of resurrection entails implications that undermine the authority of the Torah. The language of the Mishnah, Rambam's *Mishneh Torah* and the *Treatise on Resurrection* is uniformly negative: it deals with a person who denies resurrection, not with its positive content. Even in the Thirteen Principles there is no positive content to resurrection. Although in the first twelve principles Rambam generally added explanatory comments to the principles—even if they had already been discussed in his Introduction to *Pereq Ḥeleq*—in the thirteenth principle he merely states, without further comment, "Resurrection of the dead, which we have already explained."

Rambam's *Treatise on Resurrection* also severs any necessary connection between resurrection and the messianic era. As a miracle, resurrection can occur at any time, not necessarily in the messianic era. To the contrary, as we shall see, the messianic era itself is not miraculous; it is an ideal, but natural, state of affairs in the future, and the messiah need not perform any miracles.

[VIII.2.c.v] *Yemot ha-mashi'aḥ—the Messianic Era*

Rambam's concept of the messianic era is naturalistic, and refers to an ideal future state of affairs in this world. This is how he describes it in the Introduction to *Pereq Ḥeleq*:

> But the days of the messiah are the time when sovereignty will return to Israel, and they will return to the Land of Israel. That king will rule from Zion. His reputation will be great, even greater than the kingdom of Solomon, and will reach to the ends of the earth. All the nations will establish peace treaties with him, and all the lands will serve him because of his great righteousness... and whoever resists him, God will cut him off and give him over to his hands. All the verses of the Bible testify to his felicity and our felicity with him. But nothing in existence will change from what it is now, except that Israel will have sovereignty. This is what the sages said: "There is no difference between this world and the days of the messiah, except for our enslavement to [other] nations" (Babylonian Talmud, Berakhot 34b, Sanhedrin 91b)...The great benefit that will be in that era is that we will rest from our enslavement to the kingdom of evil which prevents us from performing all the commandments. [Then] knowledge will increase...wars will cease...and everyone in those days will attain the great perfection by which he will merit the life of the world to come. The messiah will die, and his son will rule after him, and his son's son...In such a condition the world to come will be attained. But the ultimate purpose is only the world to come, and it is for this that one strives.

In his "Letter to Yemen" Rambam wrote that the messiah will be a great prophet, greater than all the other prophets except for Moses. And in the last part of his *Mishneh Torah*, the Laws of Kings 12:3, he states that the messiah, guided by the inspiration of the holy spirit, will be able to assign every Jew to his original tribal identity. Nevertheless, the consistent general tenor of Rambam's messianic scheme is its naturalism—without any reference to supranatural miracles—and his emphasis that the ultimate goal always remains (as it did with resurrection) the life of the world to come. The difference, then, between our time and the messianic era is not the ultimate goal of the world to come, but that in the messianic era conditions of peace and prosperity will facilitate, and be more conducive to, acquiring the knowledge which constitutes a portion in the world to come.

The last two chapters of Rambam's *Mishneh Torah*—the Book of Judges, Laws of Kings, Ch. 11–12) deal with the messianic era. It is no accident that Rambam's code, which deals with the life in this world of the Jewish community, culminates in the messianic era, the ideal future state of affairs in this world, whereas his *Guide of the Perplexed*, which deals with intellectual matters, culminates (in the last chapter, 3:54), in the ultimate intellectual perfection of the human being, a perfection which is the key to a portion in the world to come.

In these chapters, Rambam describes the messianic era as the time when the Jewish state will be restored, the Temple in Jerusalem rebuilt, and the Jews will return from their dispersion to the Land of Israel. The messiah will not have to perform any miracles, such as resurrecting the dead; Rabbi Akiva, for example, regarded Bar Kokhba (who did not perform any miracles) as the messiah, until Bar Kokhba was killed. In short, the tests of the messianic era are entirely natural, and to a large degree, also political.

Rambam emphasizes that in the messianic era none of the laws of nature will be suspended, but "the world will follow its normal course." Prophecies like those of Isaiah, that "the wolf shall dwell with the lamb" (Isaiah 11:6) are metaphors for Israel living in peace among the nations, who will cease their immoral behavior "and will all return to the true religion" (*ve-yaḥzeru kulam le-dat ha-emet*). Here, too, Rambam cites the rabbis, that "there is no difference between this world and the days of the messiah, except for our enslavement to [other] nations" (Babylonian Talmud, Berakhot 34b, Sanhedrin 91b).

> The sages and prophets did not long for the messianic era in order to rule the world or to have dominion over the gentiles, nor to be exalted by the nations, nor in order to eat, drink and be merry, but in order to be free for Torah and wisdom...and thus be worthy of the life of the world to come, as we have explained in the Laws of Repentance.
> At that time there will be no famine or war, no envy or competition...The whole world will be occupied only with knowing God...as it is written, "For the earth shall be full of the knowledge of the Lord, as the waters cover the sea" (Isaiah 11:9).[32]

---

[32]   *Mishneh Torah*, Book of Judges, Laws of Kings, Ch. 12:4–5.

[VIII.2.c.vi] *Conclusion Of The Introduction To Pereq Ḥeleq*

Rambam concludes his Introduction to *Pereq Ḥeleq* by briefly discussing the third category in our Mishnah of Jews excluded from the world to come: *Apiqoros* (Epicurus), which he interprets as an Aramaic word:

> The word *Apiqoros* is Aramaic, and means mocking and deriding the Torah or the sages of the Torah, and therefore the name is applied generally to one who does not believe in the foundations of the Torah or who mocks the sages.

However, in the Laws of Repentance 3:8 he had defined an *Apiqoros* was a person who denies prophecy, who denies the prophecy of Moses, or who denies that God knows human affairs. In other words, the *Apiqoros* denies that there is a connection between God and humans. This theme is expanded in the *Guide of the Perplexed* 2:13, where Rambam states that an *Apiqoros* is a person who claims that the world exists by chance and has no divine governance or order. And in *Guide of the Perplexed* 3:17 Rambam identifies an *Apiqoros* as a philosopher who denies divine providence and believes only in chance. These last statements in fact accord with the views of the Greek philosopher Epicurus (341–270 B.C.E.) who followed the atomism of Democritus, but maintained that the motions of the atoms are by chance.

As Arthur Hyman explains Rambam's view:

> From these two passages it becomes clear that in the *Guide* Maimonides identifies the *apikoros* with the Jewish follower of Epicurus, whose unbelief consists in the denial of propositions about God — in particular, in the denial of divine providence. Since in Maimonides' enumeration of the "thirteen principles" propositions about God are the counterpart of the principles denied by the *apikoros*, it seems fair to say that the unspecified principles denied by the *apikoros* (in the Mishnah, *Pereq Ḥeleq*) are propositions about God.[33]

[VIII.3] THE THIRTEEN PRINCIPLES: CONTENT AND MEANING

[VIII.3.a] "PRINCIPLES" AND THE STATUS OF FAITH

Rambam states at the outset of his discussion that "the principles of our Torah and its foundations are thirteen foundations." The Arabic term he uses for principle is *aṣl* (plural: *uṣul*), meaning root, foundation, or principle, and usually translated in Hebrew as *'iqar*. The Arabic term he uses for foundation

---

[33] Arthur Hyman, "Maimonides 'Thirteen Principles'," in Alexander Altmann (ed.), *Jewish Medieval and Renaissance Studies* (Cambridge: Harvard University Press, 1967), p. 125.

is *qa'idah* (plural: *qawa'id*), meaning a foundation or base, usually translated in Hebrew as *yesod*.

According to Alexander Altmann:

> The term *uṣul* acquires here a new meaning: it no longer denotes the topics of the Kalam investigations, but the fundamental tenets of faith or the concise abstracts of religion as seen through the eyes of a philosopher. Maimonides undertook such a presentation to teach the rank and file of the community the true spiritual meaning of the belief in the world to come (*ha-'olam ha-ba*) and to disabuse their minds of crude, materialistic notions. Since the ultimate felicity of man depends on the possession of true concepts concerning God, the formulation and brief exposition of true notions in the realm of faith is meant to help the multitude to avoid error and to purify belief.[34]

It is important to point out that Rambam's "principles and foundations of the Torah" are not formulated as a credo, in sharp contrast with the much later Hebrew paraphrase found in many editions of the prayer book, each line of which begins with the phrase *ani ma'amin be-emunah shelemah* ("I believe with perfect faith"), which is, so far as we know, first found in a fifteenth-century manuscript, and was first printed in a sixteenth-century Ashkenazi prayer book. The credo form of this later Hebrew paraphrase and the custom of reciting it may reflect Christian catechisms, and the catechistic formula "I believe with perfect faith"—reminiscent of early Christian creeds—has no basis in Rambam's original Arabic principles, which are stated apodictically.

Another later Hebrew paraphrase of the principles included in many prayer books is the hymn "Yigdal Elohim Ḥai" ("Magnified be the Living God"), sung in many communities at the end of Sabbath and festival eve services, and attributed either to the *dayyan* (religious judge) Daniel ben Judah in Rome (early fourteenth century) or to Immanuel of Rome.

The reference to belief—lacking in the Arabic original—was introduced into the text of the principles in the "standard" medieval Hebrew translation of Solomon ben Joseph ibn Ya'aqub, who frequently interpolates the term *le-ha'amin* ("to believe") or *she-na'amin* ("that we believe"). The following chart exemplifies the differences between the Arabic original and the Hebrew translation. We should simply note that in the first principle, Rambam's use of the term "creator" should not necessarily be taken as literal affirmation of creation, which is not explicitly mentioned in the principles. God is (according to the first principle) "the cause of the existence of all existents, by which they have their existence and from which they have their existence," but such causality does not necessarily imply creation, let alone creation *ex nihilo*.

---

34   Alexander Altmann, "Articles of Faith" in *Encyclopaedia Judaica* (Jerusalem: 1972), vol. 3, column 655.

	Arabic	Hebrew translation
1	The existence of the creator.	**To believe** in the existence of the creator.
2	His unity, that the cause of everything is one.	The unity of God, namely **that we believe** that the cause of everything is one.
3	The negation of corporeality from him, namely that this One is not a body.	The negation of corporeality from him, namely **that we believe** that this one we have mentioned is not a body.
4	Eternity. That this one we have discussed is eternal.	Eternity. Namely **that we believe** that this one we have discussed is eternal.
5	That he, may he be praised, is the one worthy of being worshipped.	That he, may he be praised, is the one worthy of being worshipped.
6	Prophecy. That is, to know that this species of persons, etc.	Prophecy. That is, that a person know that this species of persons, etc.
7	The prophecy of Moses our teacher. That is, **to affirm** (*an yu'taqadu*) that he is the father of all the prophets before and after him.	The prophecy of Moses our teacher. That is, **that we believe** that he is the father of all the prophets before and after him.
8	It is the Torah from heaven, that is, **to affirm** (*an yu'taqadu*) that the whole Torah we have today is the Torah given to Moses, and that it was revealed (*mi-pi ha-gevurah*).	That the Torah is from heaven, that is, **that we believe** that this whole Torah was given by Moses and that it is all revealed (*mi-pi ha-gevurah*).
9	Abrogation (*naskh*).	Transcription (or: transmission)— *he'eteq*.
10	That he knows the actions of people.	That he knows the actions of people.
11	That he rewards.	That he rewards.
12	The messianic era. That is, **to believe and verify** (*al-iman w'al-taṣdiq*) that we will come.	The messianic era. That is, **to believe and verify** (*le-ha'amin ule-amet*) that he will come.
13	Resurrection of the dead.	Resurrection of the dead.

The chart shows clearly that in the Hebrew translation, "to believe" or "that we believe" was interpolated in the first four principles, without any basis in the Arabic original. The problem is, however, not merely one of interpolation.

As we shall see, in Rambam's thought, these principles have the cognitive status of demonstrated knowledge (and he demonstrates them in Part II of the *Guide of the Perplexed*), not mere belief, and the interpolation thus does violence to Rambam's method and understanding of these principles. Granted that the demonstrations of these truths in the *Guide of the Perplexed* were intended only for the intelligentsia, and the Thirteen Principles were intended for the common people, who are incapable of demonstrating their truth, the fact remains that the first principles are demonstrable and thus are subjects of knowledge, not belief.

On the other hand, the sixth principle (the phenomenon of prophecy) is a historical truth, which can be known to everyone—intellectuals and common people alike—and therefore Rambam speaks of knowledge. Why, then, does Rambam refer, in the seventh principle to affirming the prophecy of Moses? The Arabic term—which is the same root as the second term in the title of Sa'adiah Ga'on's book, *Beliefs and Opinions* (*Al-Amanat w'al-I'tiqadat*)—can be translated as "to believe," but in light of the distinction in Sa'adiah's title (which we discussed in Ch. 2), it would seem appropriate to translate it by a stronger term, such as "to affirm." Such a stronger sense of the term (as Yosef Kafiḥ suggests) is supported by Rambam's Hebrew text in the *Mishneh Torah*, Laws of Foundations of the Torah 1:6, where he refers to "knowing this (*yedi'at davar zeh*, i.e., knowing the existence of God) is a positive commandment."

However we translate it, this is the first time he uses such a term in the Thirteen Principles, and this may be because logically it is a matter of faith, rather than knowledge, that Moses was not only greater than all the prophets who preceded him, but also than all the prophets who followed him, or may still follow him in the future. Since we cannot know the future in advance, any such conviction must be faith, not knowledge. This is why the twelfth principle, dealing with the messianic future, also refers to believing and verifying.

As for the eighth principle, we again have the stronger term that we had in the seventh principle, and it is possible that Rambam regarded the revelation of the Torah (*torah min ha-shamayim*) to be knowable historical fact (as did Judah Ha-Levi). However, what must be "affirmed" (or "believed") is not only that the Torah was revealed, but also that what was revealed to Moses is what we have today, and Rambam may not have regarded this corollary as similarly certain.

We also note a divergence of a different type in the ninth principle, but we shall discuss that separately.

[VIII.3.b] THE THIRTEEN PRINCIPLES:
TEXT AND EXPLANATORY NOTES

(1) THE FIRST FOUNDATION—THE EXISTENCE OF GOD

The first foundation is the existence of the creator, may he be praised. It is that there is a being, perfect in all modes of existence, which is the cause of the existence of all existents, by which they have their existence and from which they have their existence. If we should consider the absence of his existence, then the existence of every being would be nullified, but if we should consider the absence of all beings other than his, then his existence would not be nullified and would not be deficient, because he is not dependent for his existence on any other... This first foundation is taught by the statement "I am the Lord your God" (Exodus 20:2, Deuteronomy 5:6).

In his *Book of the Commandments*, Rambam lists his principle as the first positive precept, "that is the commandment we were commanded to affirm (*i 'tiqad*) the divinity, that is, that we affirm that there is a cause which is the agent of all existing things, as it says, 'I am the Lord your God'." Similarly, in the *Mishneh Torah*, Laws of Foundations of the Torah 1:6, Rambam states: "Knowing this is a positive commandment, as it says, 'I am the Lord your God'." To reiterate, where in Arabic Rambam refers to affirming (*i 'tiqad*) the principle, in his own Hebrew usage he speaks of knowledge (*yedi 'ah*).

(2) THE SECOND FOUNDATION—THE UNITY OF GOD

The second foundation is his unity. It is that this cause of everything is one, not like the unity of a genus or species, and not like the unity of a compound which is divisible into many units, and not like the unity of a simple body which is numerically one but which is infinitely divisible. Rather, he is one, a unity which no other unity is like. This second foundation is taught by the verse, "Listen, Israel, the Lord our God, the Lord is one" (Deuteronomy 6:4).

The concept of unity here, which is "not like the unity of genus or species" and "which no other unity is like" echoes the Neoplatonic conceptions of unity we saw in Baḥya ibn Paquda and Abraham ibn Ezra. We shall see in the next chapters how Rambam deals with the unity of God in the *Guide of the Perplexed*, but need to note at this point that his proofs there of the existence of God at the same time prove God's unity and incorporeality.

The unity of God is the second positive precept in Rambam's *Book of the Commandments*: "that is the commandment to affirm (*i 'tiqad*) the unity, that is to affirm that the agent of existence and its prime cause is one, as it says, "Listen, Israel, the Lord our God, the Lord is one." Once again, when writing in Hebrew in the *Mishneh Torah*, Laws of Foundations of the Torah 1:7, Rambam refers to knowledge (*yedi 'ah*) and not to faith:

This God is one... There is no one among all the ones existing in the world like his unity, not the one of a species containing many units, nor like the unity of a body which is divisible into parts and ends. Rather, it is a unity like no other unity in the world. If there were many gods, they would be physical bodies, because things which can be counted and are equal in their existence differ from each other only by the accidents of physical bodies. And if the creator were a physical body, he would have an end and limit, since a body cannot exist without an end. Whatever body has an end and limit, its force is also finite and limited. But the power of our God, may his name be blessed, is infinite and unceasing, since the sphere perpetually rotates, and therefore his force cannot be the force of a body. Since he is not a body, the accidents of bodies do not affect him, resulting in his being divisible and separate from another. Therefore, he can only be one. Knowing this is a positive commandment, as it says, "Listen, Israel, the Lord our God, the Lord is one."

What we see here is the necessary connection—to be discussed in greater depth and detail in the *Guide of the Perplexed* 2:1—between the existence, unity and incorporeality of God. We also have here echoes of Kalam arguments for the unity of God (such as we learned in Ch. 2 on Sa'adiah Ga'on, especially echoes of Sa'adiah's first argument for the creation of the world), which Rambam discusses at the end of Part I of the *Guide of the Perplexed*.

(3) THE THIRD FOUNDATION—THE INCORPOREALITY OF GOD

The third foundation is the negation of corporeality from him. It is that this unity is neither a body nor a force in a body. The accidents of bodies, such as motion and rest, do not affect him, neither essentially nor accidentally... All anthropomorphisms (literally: "attributes of bodies") such as walking, standing, sitting, speaking, and the like, in the Bible are meant metaphorically (Arabic: *majaz*; Hebrew: *hash'alah*), as [the rabbis] said: "The Torah speaks according to human language" (Babylonian Talmud, Berakhot 31b)... This third foundation is taught by the verse, "For you have not seen any image" (Deuteronomy 4:15), which means that you have not perceived him possessing an image, since he is, as we have said, neither a body nor a force in a body.

We have already seen (in the discussion of the second foundation) similar statements regarding incorporeality in the Laws of the Foundations of the Torah 1:7. In the Laws of Repentance 3:7, Rambam defines a heretic (*min*), and among the heretics is a Jew who says that there is only one God, "but that he is a body possessing image." Rambam's critic Ravad objected to this categorization of a corporealist as heretic: "Why did he call him a heretic, when greater and better than he followed this thought, according to what they saw in the Bible, and even more, according to what they saw in the words of [rabbinic] stories (*aggadot*) which corrupt one's opinions?" It must be emphasized that Ravad did not defend here corporealist belief *per se*, and he himself rejected corporealism, which he attributed to "*aggadot* which corrupt one's opinions." What he objected to was Rambam's right to categorize such "corrupt opinion" as heresy.

Rambam, of course, would respond that people must be taught how to read rabbinic *aggadot*, and that—as we saw in his Introduction to *Pereq Ḥeleq*—whenever what the rabbis say is rationally untenable, it must not be taken literally but metaphorically. The denial of corporeality remains, then, a supreme religious and intellectual value, because belief in a corporeal God is belief in no God at all (since something corporeal is not God), and in the *Guide of the Perplexed* 1:36 Rambam goes so far as to say that corporealist belief "is much worse than idolatry." It cannot be excused—as Ravad excused it—on the grounds of ignorance and lack of intellectual comprehension, nor on the grounds that a person is following the tradition of his ancestors, since both of these excuses (ignorance and tradition) can also be claimed by idolators. Rambam then concludes: "I do not consider as an unbeliever a person who cannot prove the negation of corporeality, but I consider as an unbeliever a person who does not believe in that negation."

(4) THE FOURTH FOUNDATION—THE ETERNITY OF GOD

> The fourth foundation is eternity. It is that this unity is absolutely eternal, and that every other being is not eternal with respect to him...This fourth foundation is taught by the verse, "The eternal God is a dwelling place" (Deuteronomy 33:27).
> [Know that the great foundation of the Torah of Moses our teacher is that the world is created. God formed and created it after absolute non-being. The fact that you see me dealing with the eternity of the world according to the opinion of the philosophers is in order to provide an absolute proof of his existence, as I explained and clarified in the *Guide (of the Perplexed)*].[35]

The concept of eternity is used in two different ways. In reference to the world, as in the Aristotelian view of an eternal world, it means that the world is not created and has no beginning; in other words, the world has existed for endless time. The world exists in time, but that time is endless. In reference to God, however, eternity does not mean endless time, but that the category of time does not apply to God, since God is not a body, and time (according to Aristotle) is the measure of the motion of a body.[36]

---

[35] The second paragraph, enclosed in brackets, was not included in the original version of the Thirteen Principles, and is not to be found in most manuscripts or in the printed editions. Yosef Kafiḥ included it in his edition, based on a single manuscript, and identified it as a later marginal addition in Rambam's own hand.

[36] Aristotle, Physics, Book IV, Ch. 11–12. "Time is not movement, but only movement in so far as it admits of enumeration...Time then is a kind of number." (Physics 219b)

God is thus timeless, as opposed to an eternal world which exists in endless time.

Rambam states in Laws of the Foundations of the Torah 1:11: "Since he is not a physical body, it is clear that none of the accidents of a body apply to him...He does not exist in time...and does not change, because there is nothing that would case change in him." Aristotle also regarded the eternal as not in time: "Things which are always are not, as such, in time, for they are not contained by time, nor is their being measured by time. A proof of this is that none of them is affected by time, which indicates that they are not in time."[37] Rambam reiterates this point in the *Guide of the Perplexed*: "Time is an accident consequent on motion and attached to it; neither can exist without the other. Motion cannot exist without time, and time cannot be conceived except together with motion. Whatever has no motion does not exist in time.[38]

Rambam's fourth foundation thus refers to eternity in the sense that God is uniquely timeless—the category of time is inapplicable to God—but "every other being is not eternal with respect to him." The fourth foundation did not originally not deal with eternity in any other sense, such as the eternity of the universe, nor did it mention creation. However, as we have seen on the basis of Kafiḥ's text, over twenty years later, after he had written the *Guide of the Perplexed* (to which he now referred) Rambam added in his own hand a marginal note adding the creation of the world, and explaining why in the *Guide* he had based his proofs of the existence, unity and incorporeality of God on eternity.

As we saw when discussing resurrection, Rambam maintained that miracles or changes in the natural order are only possible in a created world, not in a world of eternal necessity. In the *Guide of the Perplexed* 2:25 Rambam suggests, therefore, that although the question of the origin of the universe cannot be conclusively resolved in scientific terms, the theory of creation is preferable, because it, and only it, can account both for natural order and for digressions from the natural order, and thus make possible the revelation of the Torah. That is why, in his late addition to the fourth foundation, Rambam could refer to creation as "the great foundation of the Torah."

"Time is number of movement in respect of the before and after." (Physics 220a). "Time is a measure of motion and of being moved...Further, 'to be in time' means, for movement, that both it and its essence are measured by time." (Physics 221a). English translation by R.P. Hardie and R.K. Gaye. If we think of a basic physical formula, that R = D/T (rate or velocity = distance divided by time), then T = D/R (time = distance divided by rate or velocity).

37   Aristotle, Physics, Book IV, Ch. 12, 221b.

38   *Guide of the Perplexed*, Introduction to Part II, Proposition #15.

Nevertheless, with the exception of this late addition, the fact remains that none of Rambam's works—not his original Thirteen Principles in the Commentary to the Mishnah, nor his *Mishneh Torah*, nor his *Guide of the Perplexed*, nor even his early and popular "Letter to Yemen"—includes creation as a foundation or basic principle of the Torah, nor is a person who believes in the eternity of the universe ever categorized in those works as a heretic (*min*), infidel (*kofer*), or *Apiqoros*. The reason for this, according to the *Guide of the Perplexed* 1:35, is that creation is one of the metaphysical "secrets of the Torah" (*sitrei torah*) and "mysteries" (*sodot*) which should not be taught to the masses, whose simple faith and moral behavior would be undermined by exposure to complex issues for which they are intellectually unprepared and which they are incapable of understanding.

Even taking that precaution into account, the fact is that in his various discussions of basic principles of the Torah, creation is simply not mentioned, and Rambam's silence is deafening. His silence may well have led to questions or criticism, that either brought him to change his mind on the subject, or at least to clarify what had been a misunderstanding of his intention all along, and that may be the reason for his late addition to the fourth foundation.

This late addition—assuming, as we do, that Kafiḥ is correct that it is written in Rambam's own hand and is thus authentic—may have been known to the thirteenth-century Spanish-Jewish philosopher Shem Tov ibn Falaquera, who was thoroughly familiar with philosophical literature in Arabic and Hebrew, translated many Arabic texts into Hebrew, wrote original Hebrew works, and wrote one of the earliest and most important commentaries to the *Guide of the Perplexed*, the *Moreh Ha-Moreh* ("The Guide to the Guide"). Falaquera, who regarded creation as a fundamental principle (*'iqar*) of Judaism, claimed that creation is one of Rambam's thirteen foundations:

> An example of this is well-known and famous, that a principle of our faith which is one of the thirteen principles which Rabbi Moses wrote, is that we should believe in the creation of the world. Even if a proof cannot be found for it, one should not say that these are not true matters.[39]

Given Falaquera's keen philosophical insight and familiarity with Rambam's thought, it seems unlikely that he would have interpreted the "eternity" of the fourth foundation as creation, and it is, therefore, quite possible that he saw Rambam's later addition (or something similar to it) and accepted its authenticity.

---

[39] Falaquera, *Moreh Ha-Moreh*, "Be'ur Nifla," Ch. 32, p. 168. See the discussion in Raphael Jospe, *Torah and Sophia: The Life and Thought of Shem Tov ibn Falaquera* (Cincinnati: Hebrew Union College Press, 1988), p. 158.

(5) THE FIFTH FOUNDATION—ONLY GOD IS TO BE WORSHIPPED

The fifth foundation is that [God], may he be praised, alone is worthy of being worshipped...and obeyed. One does not do this for anything below him in existence, [such as] the angels, stars, sphere, elements, or whatever is compounded from them, for their functions are all natural, and they have no control or will other than his will; and one does not make them intermediaries by which to reach him. Rather, one's thoughts should aim only at him, and should abandon everything else. This fifth foundation is the prohibition of idolatry, and most of the Torah serves to prohibit this.

The fifth foundation follows logically from the first four, and resembles both positive commandments—the commandments relating to the service of God—and negative commandments—prohibiting idolatry—in Rambam's *Book of the Commandments*.

(6) THE SIXTH FOUNDATION—PROPHECY

The sixth foundation is prophecy. It is to know that there are some humans of greatly developed abilities and perfection, whose souls are disposed to receive the form of intellect, so that the human intellect becomes conjoined (Arabic: *waṣal*; Hebrew: *daveq*) to the Active Intellect (Arabic: *al-'aql al-fa'al*; Hebrew: *ha-sekhel ha-po'el*), which emanates a noble emanation (Arabic: *faiḍ*; Hebrew: *azilut* or *shefa'*) from itself onto them; they are the prophets, and this is the subject of prophecy...The verses of the Torah testify to the prophecy of many prophets.

Rambam's theory of prophecy, based in no small measure on that of Al-Farabi, will be discussed in Ch. 10. We merely note at this point that, in sharp contrast with Judah Ha-Levi's theory that prophecy is a function of the supra-rational "divine faculty," Rambam regarded prophecy as a fundamentally rational process.

(7) THE SEVENTH FOUNDATION—THE PROPHECY OF MOSES

The seventh foundation is the prophecy of Moses our teacher. It is that we should believe that he was the father of all the prophets who came before him or who came after him; they are all below him in rank. He was God's choice[40] among the entire human species, for he perceived more of [God] than anyone existing ever perceived, or who will exist will ever perceive. [Moses], peace be on him, attained the ultimate superiority above humanity, so that he attained angelic rank and came to the rank of the angels. No veil (Arabic: *hijab*; Hebrew: *masakh*) remained which he did not tear, and no bodily impediment impeded him, and

---

40   Rambam here uses the Arabic *ṣafwa*, the same term Judah Ha-Levi used to describes Israel among the nations and the prophets among Israel.

no deficiency, great or small, remained in him. His faculties of imagination and sensation ceased in all of his perceptions, and his faculty of desire (Arabic: *nuzu'*; Hebrew: *mit'orer*) was stunned, so that only intellect remained... The prophecy of Moses differed from the prophecy of other prophets in four ways. The first difference is that God does not speak with any other prophet except by means of an intermediary, but [he spoke with] Moses directly, as it says, "I speak with him mouth to mouth" (Numbers 12:8). The second difference is that other prophets receive their visions only while asleep... or in the daytime after slumber falls on the prophet, a condition in which his senses cease [functioning]; but [in the case of] Moses, the speech comes during the daytime... Thus it says, "If there be a prophet among you, I the Lord make myself known to him in a vision; I speak to him in a dream. But my servant Moses is not so" (Numbers 12:6–7). The third difference is that when a prophet receives a vision... his faculties are weakened and his body becomes weak... but this is not the case with Moses, to whom speech came without any weakness occurring, and this is [referred to] in the verse, "The Lord spoke to Moses face to face, as a man speaks to his fellow" (Exodus 33:11)... and this is because of the strength of his conjunction with the intellect, as we have said. The fourth difference is that the prophets do not receive their visions at will, but rather by the will of God... but Moses, whenever he willed, said, "Stand by that I may hear what the Lord commands concerning you" (Numbers 9:8).

We have already seen that Rambam regarded Moses as the greatest human who ever lived or will ever live, and that even the messiah will not attain his rank as a prophet. Rambam's insisting on the supremacy of the prophecy of Moses provides the basis for his claim — in the ninth foundation — that the Torah can never be annulled and replaced by another prophecy. Both principles — seven and nine — thus constitute a polemic against Islam. The Qur'an (Sura 33:40) states that Muhammad was the "seal of the prophets" (*khatam al-nabiyin*): "Muhammad is not the father of any of your men, but [he is] the apostle of God and the seal of the prophets. And God has full knowledge of all things."[41] Against this claim, Rambam says that Moses was "the father of all the prophets," i.e., the greatest of all the prophets, both before and after him.

(8) THE EIGHTH FOUNDATION — *TORAH MIN HA-SHAMAYIM* ("TORAH FROM HEAVEN")

The eighth foundation is that the Torah is from heaven. It is to affirm (*an yu'taqadu*) that the whole Torah we have today is the Torah which was given to Moses, and that it was entirely revealed (*mi-pi ha-gevurah*), that is to say, that it entirely came to him from God in a way metaphorically called speech... He was like a scribe, to whom one reads, and he wrote it all down, its histories, stories and commandments, and therefore he is called "lawgiver" (*mehoqeq* — cf.

---

41   Qur'an, Sura 33:40. Translation by Abdullah Yusuf Ali.

Numbers 21:18)... They said that one who says "that the Torah is not divinely revealed" is one who maintains that the whole Torah comes entirely from God, except for one verse which God did not speak but which Moses [said] on his own.[42] There is no difference between "the children of Ham were Kush, Egypt, Put and Canaan" (Genesis 36:39)... and "I am the Lord" (Exodus 20:2, Deuteronomy 5:6) or "Listen, Israel, the Lord our God, the Lord is one" (Deuteronomy 6:4). All was divinely revealed (*mi-pi ha-gevurah*)... [The rabbis] only considered Menasseh more [guilty of] infidelity and hypocrisy (*kufr wa-nifaq*) than any other infidel because he thought that the Torah has an essence (*lubb*) and a shell (*qishr*),[43] that the histories and stories are of no use. And that Moses made them up. That is what is meant by "one who says that the Torah is not from heaven." [The rabbis] said that this means that [such a person] believes that the whole Torah is from God except for one verse which God did not say but which Moses [said] on his own.[44]

... Similarly, [the Torah's] traditional interpretation is also divinely revealed (*mi-pi ha-gevurah*), and the way we today make the form of the *sukkah*,[45] the *lulav*,[46] the *shofar*,[47] the *ẓiẓit*,[48] and the *tefillin*,[49] etc. is the very same form which God spoke to Moses and which Moses spoke to us... The statement which teaches this eighth foundation is his saying, "By this you will know that the Lord has sent me... for it is not of my own mind" (Numbers 16:28).

In light of the seventh foundation—the uniqueness of Moses' prophecy—the eighth foundation emphasizes that it was through Moses that the "Torah is from heaven" and was "divinely revealed." Although this principle is sometimes cited by opponents of "higher Bible criticism," what Rambam is concerned with here—unlike Abraham ibn Ezra's presumed radical thoughts on the subject—is not the Mosaic authorship of the Torah but that everything in the Torah is equally divinely revealed. Rambam does not question (as Ibn Ezra presumably did) whether Moses could have written the whole Torah. The problem is exactly the opposite: to suggest that Moses wrote something, but that he did so on his own initiative and without divine instruction and authority, constitutes "infidelity and hypocrisy." What concerns Rambam, in short, is less

---

42   The reference is to Babylonian Talmud, Sanhedrin 99a.
43   Once again, these Arabic terms are those used by Judah Ha-Levi to describe Israel among the nations and the prophets among Israel.
44   The references here are to the discussion in Babylonian Talmud, Sanhedrin 99b.
45   The temporary hut lived in during the autumn harvest festival of booths (Leviticus 23:42).
46   The palm branch, held together with willows, myrtle and a citron, and waved during the autumn harvest festival of booths (Leviticus 23:40).
47   The ram's horn blown on the New Year (Leviticus 23:24).
48   The fringes on the four corners of one's clothing as a reminder of the commandments (Numbers 15:37–41).
49   The "phylacteries," leather boxes, attached by straps to the arm and head, containing four passages from Exodus 13:9, 13:16, Deuteronomy 6:8, 11:18.

whether Moses wrote the whole Torah, than whether Moses wrote it, or even any part of it, without "divine revelation."

(9) THE NINTH FOUNDATION—ABROGATION

The ninth foundation is abrogation (Arabic: *naskh*; Hebrew: *bitul*). It is that this Torah of Moses will not be abrogated, and that another Torah will not come from God, and that nothing should be added to it and nothing taken from it, neither in the written text nor in its interpretation, as it says, "Do not add to it and do not take away from it" (Deuteronomy 13:1).

The medieval Hebrew translation of this foundation diverges significantly from Rambam's language. Rambam used the Arabic term *naskh*. This term does, indeed, sometimes have the sense of "copy" or "transcription" (Hebrew: *he'eteq*), and this presumably misled the translator. The term *naskh*, however, has a special religious significance and importance in the Qur'an and in Islam, meaning "abrogation." The Islamic concept is that a later revelation can abrogate an earlier revelation (although the earlier was also true revelation). Muḥammad received the Qur'an over many years; later revelations could abrogate earlier ones. Thus, the Qur'an, Sura 2:106, states: "Whatever verse we abrogate or cause to forget, we substitute something better than it or similar to it. Do you not know that God has power over all things?" Similarly, Muḥammad as the last and greatest prophet, "the seal of the prophets" (as we saw in the seventh foundation) abrogated the earlier true revelations of the prophets who came before him. Rambam's polemical intention is clear: Moses, as "the father of the prophets"—i.e., the greatest prophet—received the Torah by divine revelation. No later prophet, therefore, can ever have the authority to add to the Torah or take away from it, let alone abrogate it and replace it with another (purported) revelation. Rambam thus employs a technical religious term in Islam against the Islam claims.

(10) THE TENTH FOUNDATION—DIVINE PROVIDENCE

The tenth foundation is that [God], may he be praised, knows the actions of humans and has not abandoned them.

We shall deal with Rambam's concept of providence in Ch. 10. As we shall see, his approach is an attempt to harmonize the "scientific" approach of Aristotle with the religious approach of the Torah. As we have already seen,[50] according to Aristotle the only thing worthy of God's thought is himself.[51]

---

50   Above, VIII.2.c.ii(3).
51   Aristotle, *Metaphysics* XII:9, 1074b–1075a. Translation by W.D. Ross in *The Basic Works of Aristotle*, ed. Richard McKeon (New York: Random House, 1941), p. 885.

Anything else is unworthy of God's knowledge. By knowing himself, God can only know the universals (which, accordingly, are eternal), whereas transient individuals cannot be known, since knowing them would involve change in the divine knowledge. Rambam bridges this view with the Torah's view that God knows individuals, because the more the individual human being knows, the more he participates in universal knowledge and thus the more "universal" he becomes, enabling providence to attach to him. It is knowledge that—as we saw in our discussion of the world to come—provides a basis for the survival of the rational soul, and it is knowledge that makes the individual human more universal, and thus benefit more from divine providence.

(11) THE ELEVENTH FOUNDATION—REWARD AND PUNISHMENT

The eleventh foundation is that [God], may he be praised, rewards a good reward to those who fulfill the commandments of the Torah, and punishes those who transgress its prohibitions. The great reward is the world to come, and the severe punishment is being cut off (*karet*).

Rambam's attitude regarding reward and punishment has already been discussed; the preoccupation with reward and punishment is childish and reflects spiritual and intellectual immaturity, because ultimately "the reward of the commandment is the commandment itself." Doing right is intrinsically its own reward, and doing wrong is intrinsically its own punishment. That is why Rambam consistently says that the reward *is* the world to come, and not that there is reward *in* the world to come, and that the ultimate punishment is *karet*, i.e., being cut off and not surviving in the world to come.

(12) THE TWELFTH FOUNDATION—THE MESSIANIC ERA

The twelfth foundation is the days of the messiah (*yemot ha-mashi'ah*), and it is to believe and verify that he will come. One should not say that he has been delayed; "if he tarries, wait for him" (Habakuk 2:3). One should not [attempt to] determine his time, nor should one interpret the biblical texts in order to discover from them the time of his arrival. The sages said: "Let those who calculate the end perish" (Babylonian Talmud, Sanhedrin 97b)...Included in this foundation is that the kings of Israel are only of [the house of] David, and specifically of the line of Solomon.

We have already discussed Rambam's conception of the messianic era, in his Introduction to *Pereq Ḥeleq* in comparison with his other works. Here Rambam stresses that one should not attempt to "calculate the end." Years before, in his "Letter to Yemen," Rambam had already cautioned against such speculation, which in the past always led to disappointment and even catastrophe.

(13) THE THIRTEENTH FOUNDATION — *TEḤIYAT HA-METIM* — RESURRECTION OF THE DEAD

The thirteenth foundation is the resurrection of the dead, which we have already explained.

We have already noted that this is the only foundation where Rambam makes no further comment and offers no further explanation.

(14) RAMBAM'S CONCLUSION

When a person accepts (*salima*) all these foundations, and his affirmation (*i'tiqad*) of them is sound (or: true, *ṣaḥḥa*), he enters into the community of Israel (*kelal yisra'el*), and one must love and have compassion for him...Even if he did whatever he could in transgressing, on account of his appetites and the dominance of his evil inclination, he is punished according to the extent of his rebelliousness, but he has a portion [in the world to come], and he is one of the "sinners of Israel." But if a person betrays one of these foundations, he "has left the community and denied the fundamental principle" (*yaẓa min ha-kelal ve-khafar ba-'iqar*), and he is called a heretic (*min*) and *Apiqoros* and uprooter (*qozeẓ ba-neti'ot*), and one must hate and destroy him.

Membership in the Jewish community, according to this, is not (or not merely) a matter of ethnic affiliation, but of affirmation of the truth. Once again, a "portion in the world to come" is a function of affirming or knowing the truth, not of moral behavior, for which there is reward and punishment in this world. Conversely, it is not immoral behavior that removes a Jew from the community in this world and from a portion in the world to come, but rejection of the truth.

Rambam's "thirteen principles" — especially in the form of the Hebrew credo *Ani Ma'amini* and in the hymn "Yigdal Elohim Ḥai" — became sufficiently popular that they came to be included in the prayer book, although they never became a formal part of the actual prayer service.[52] Nevertheless, Rambam's foundations never came to be what he intended — a formal and binding dogma by which Jewish identity, and membership in the Jewish community, are determined.

Why, then, did Rambam formulate his "thirteen principles?" The answer lies in the literary structure of the principles.

---

[52] When the hymn "Yigdal Elohim Ḥai" is sung at the end of the service on Sabbath or festival eve, it is a voluntary addition which comes after the Kaddish that formally concludes the prayers.

[VIII.3.c] THE LITERARY STRUCTURE OF THE THIRTEEN PRINCIPLES

Rambam does not explain why he included certain principles, and excluded others, when compiling his thirteen foundations, nor the differences between the thirteen and different formulations of principles in other works, especially in the Laws of Repentance. One key to understanding Rambam's purpose is his belief that the study of metaphysics must be restricted.

[VIII.3.c.i] *The Restriction of Metaphysics*

In the *Guide of the Perplexed* I:31–35, Rambam discusses the need to restrict the study of metaphysics, for which the masses lack the necessary intellectual preparation. Their simple faith and moral behavior would be undermined by exposure to subjects they are incapable of understanding. What, then, should be taught to the masses, and what should be concealed from them?

In the last of these chapters (I:35) Rambam states that everyone should be taught to accept on authority (i.e., without scientific proof) eight principles, which lead them to affirm the existence of a perfect being which is not a body or a force in a body, nor subject to affections (i.e., to being acted upon). These principles are:

1) The unity of God.
2) To worship only God.
3) The incorporeality of God.
4) That God does not resemble anything.
5) That the existence of God differs from other existence.
6) That the life of God differs from other life.
7) That God's knowledge differs from all other knowledge.
8) That the difference between God and his creatures is not quantitative (i.e., a matter of degree) but is a "different species of existence."

On the other hand, the following subjects are obscure "secrets of the Torah" (*sitrei torah*) and "mysteries" (*sodot*) and are not meant for public instruction, but should only be taught to someone who is intellectually prepared, and even then, only in "chapter headings" (i.e., not in detail):

1) The negative attributes of God.
2) The meaning of attributes ascribed to God.
3) Creation.
4) The nature of God's governance of the world.
5) Divine providence.
6) God's will.
7) God's knowledge.
8) Prophecy.
9) The names of God.

[VIII.3.c.ii] *Rambam's Principles in Light of the Restriction of Metaphysics*

In light of Rambam's restriction of metaphysics, and differentiation of principles that should be taught publicly to the masses, who should accept them on authority, from other principles which should not be taught publicly, how can we categorize the "Thirteen Foundations" which were intended for public instruction?

The first five foundations, dealing with the existence, unity, incorporeality and eternity of God, and that only God is to be worshipped, clearly fall under the first category of metaphysical principles the masses should be taught to accept on authority. The remaining foundations, however—the sixth through the ninth, dealing with prophecy and the Torah, and the tenth through thirteenth, dealing with subjects relating to God's knowledge, governance of the world and providence—would seem to fall under the second category of metaphysical principles that should be restricted and not taught publicly to the masses.

Rambam clearly cannot have thought that his thirteen foundations, specifically the sixth through the thirteenth, violated the restriction of public instruction of metaphysics. In a sense he could have argued that the principles were formulated in concise "chapter headings"—in comparison with lengthy, detailed and technical discussions in his *Guide of the Perplexed*—and therefore conformed to the need to restrict instruction, even when intended for the public. Depending on the person's intellectual qualifications and caliber, he could simply accept the thirteen foundations without further examination, or he could study these subjects in increasingly greater detail and depth in Rambam's Introduction to *Pereq Ḥeleq*, in the *Mishneh Torah*, and ultimately in the *Guide of the Perplexed*.

A different question, also pertinent to the literary structure of the thirteen foundations, relates to their cognitive status. Some of these principles deal with rationally demonstrable truths, others deal with historical and factual matters, and others deal with subjects which may require metaphorical interpretation.

[VIII.3.c.iii] *True Opinions and Necessary Beliefs*

In the *Guide of the Perplexed* III:28 Rambam differentiates "true" or "correct opinions" (Arabic: *ara ṣaḥiḥa*; Hebrew: *de'ot amitiyot*) from "beliefs the affirmation of which is necessary for political welfare" (or "beliefs the affirmation of which is necessary for the affairs of the state"; Arabic: *i'tiqadat ma i'tiqadaha ḍaruri fi ṣalaḥ al-aḥwal al-madinah*; Hebrew: *emunot she-emunatam hekhreḥit be-tiqun 'inyanei ha-medinah*).[53] "True opinions" lead a person to the ultimate human perfection which is knowledge of the truth.

---

53   Although *i'tiqad* has previously, in different contexts, been translated as "affirming"—and
      in one context Rambam's Hebrew parallel was *yedi'ah* (knowledge), in this context
      Rambam is talking about belief, not knowledge.

"Necessary beliefs," on the other hand, relate to effective governance of society. The first category, "true opinions," deals with theoretical truths, and includes the existence, unity, incorporeality, omniscience, omnipotence, will and eternity of God. The second category, "necessary beliefs," deals with practical propositions, and includes the notion that God is angry with those who disobey his commandments or commit injustice. These beliefs are "necessary for the abolition of wrongdoing or for acquiring noble moral virtues."

If we apply this distinction between "true opinions" and "necessary beliefs" to the thirteen foundations, we can readily see that the first group of foundations—the first five principles, dealing with God—fall under the first category of "true opinions" which lead a person to the ultimate human perfection of knowledge of the truth, which constitutes "a portion in the world to come." The second group of foundations—principles six through nine, dealing with prophecy and the Torah—are also "true opinions," although they deal with historical truths, not with rationally demonstrable truth.

The cognitive status of the third group of foundations—principles ten through thirteen, dealing directly or indirectly with divine governance and providence, and thus focusing on issues relating to reward and punishment— is less clear. On the one hand, in the *Guide of the Perplexed* III:28, God's knowledge and will are listed among the "true opinions." On the other hand, in *Guide of the Perplexed* I:35, God's knowledge, will, governance and providence are listed among the restricted "obscure" subjects which are "mysteries" and "secrets of the Torah." In a way, then, the third group of foundations are in one sense "true opinions," when understood correctly—i.e., metaphorically— by philosophers. However, they are also "secrets of the Torah" which are not true in the literal sense, as understood by the masses, and as such, on a literal level, they fall under the category of "necessary beliefs."

This categorization of the third group of foundations, when taken literally, as "necessary beliefs" rather than "true opinions" is consistent with Rambam's example of God's "anger" at disobedience—which essentially means reward and punishment—as a "necessary belief." God's "anger" implies that he knows what people do (the tenth foundation), and that he rewards and punishes accordingly (the eleventh foundation). Such reward and punishment, at least in the popular imagination, is related to their expectations of the messianic era (the twelfth foundation) and resurrection (the thirteenth foundation). In short, all of these subjects relate to popular expectations for future reward and punishment, and have no direct connection to the true ultimate goal of a portion in the world to come. They are "necessary beliefs," without which morality and the social order will be endangered, but that does not mean they are not true. They may not be true when taken literally, just as much else in Scripture and rabbinic literature must not be taken literally, but must be understood as metaphor, and as metaphor, they are true. The common person will take them literally, and will thereby be motivated to behave properly, whereas the philosopher, who does not require such extrinsic motivation and seeks to "serve out of love," need not take them literally, and can understand their metaphorical meaning.

According to Arthur Hyman, Rambam's "necessary beliefs" are thus dialectical: they are false in one sense (literal) and true in another sense (metaphorical).[54]

> In discussing "necessary beliefs" Maimonides stresses their role in instilling obedience, leaving it open in this context whether they are merely convenient political "lies," or whether they contain some cognitive truth. To use the terminology of medieval logic, he leaves it open whether they area sophistic propositions — that is, propositions which are without any truth — or whether they are dialectical: that is, propositions which are true in some respect thout not in another. If the "necessary beliefs" are sophistic, they are simply convenient for instilling obedience and others might do just as well ... That the "necessary beliefs" are dialectical rather than sophistic becomes clear once they are considered in the light of other aspects of Maimonides' philosophy ... Maimonides' "necessary beliefs" are seen to be dialectical propositions which attain their "correctness" from the cognitive content they possess. It is their cognitive content which makes them superior to other propositions which may be useful for instilling obedience.

[VIII.3.d] THE THIRTEEN PRINCIPLES: A THREE-FOLD STRUCTURE

[VIII.3.d.i] *Medieval Commentators*

We have seen that the thirteen foundations can be characterized as having a three-fold structure — principles relating to God (1–5), principles relating to the Torah and prophecy (6–9), and principles relating to reward and punishment (10–13). This three-fold structure, in turn, parallels (in reverse order) the three categories of Jews the Mishnah in *Pereq Ḥeleq* describes as being excluded from a portion in the world to come: one who denies resurrection, one who denies that the Torah is from heaven, and an *Apiqoros*.

As Menachem Kellner has shown,[55] the first thinker and commentator on Rambam to point clearly to this three-fold structure of principles and

---

[54]   Arthur Hyman, "Spinoza's Dogmas of Universal Faith in the Light of their Medieval Jewish Background," in Alexander Altmann (ed.), *Biblical and Other Studies* (Cambridge: Harvard University Press, 1963), pp. 189–190.

[55]   See Kellner's extensive discussion and excellent analysis in his *Dogma in Medieval Jewish Thought From Maimonides to Abravanel* (Oxford: Littman Library of Jewish Civilization, 1986).

explicate the parallel to the Mishnah's categories was Shimon ben Ẓemaḥ Duran (1361–1444 C.E.), who accordingly reduced Rambam's thirteen foundations to three basic principles—the existence of God, Torah from heaven, and reward and punishment—in his books *Magen Avot* ("Shield of the Fathers") and *Ohev Mishpat* ("Lover of Justice"). These three basic or fundamental principles, in turn, divide into the other principles which are derivative. By characterizing the thirteen foundations as a direct commentary on the Mishnah, Duran attempted to defend Rambam against the charge that he had violated Jewish tradition by his formulating new dogmas. Duran's explication of the three-fold structure of the thirteen foundations, in turn, was taken over by Joseph Albo, in his *Sefer Ha-'Iqarim* ("Book of Principles," 1425 C.E.), who referred to each category as "general principles" (*'iqarim kolelim*), which in turn have derivative principles called "roots" (*shorashim*). The three general principles are "the existence of God" (*meẓi'ut ha-shem*), "Torah from heaven" (*torah min ha-shamayim*) and "reward and punishment" (*sakhar va-'onesh*).

The three-fold structure of the thirteen foundations can be understood in three different respects:
1) An internal relationship of the principles within each of the three categories.
2) The mutual relationship of the three categories to each other.
3) The external relationship of the three categories of principles to the three parallel categories of Jews excluded from a portion in the world to come according to the Mishnah.

The third of these relationships—the external parallel to the Mishnah's three categories of Jews excluded from a portion in the world to come—first pointed out by Duran, has already been mentioned. What follows, then, is a discussion of the other two relationships, and first the related question of the cognitive status of the principles.

[VIII.3.d.ii] *The Cognitive Status of the Thirteen Principles: Summary*

(1) PRINCIPLES 1–5—THE EXISTENCE OF GOD

The first category of principles consists of rationally demonstrable truths. Principles 1–3 are demonstrated in Part II of the *Guide of the Perplexed*, where Rambam discusses four proofs for the existence, unity and incorporeality of God. The proofs are structured in such a way as to demonstrate not only God's existence, but also incorporeality and unity, the subjects of the first three of the thirteen foundations. Thereby one is also led to the fourth principle, the eternity (or timelessness) of God, since time is the measure of the motion of bodies. The first four principles thus also set the stage for the fifth principle, that God is uniquely worthy of worship. In short, each of the first five principles leads logically to the next. These principles are rational truths, to be acknowledged by the philosopher and common man alike, the philosopher on the basis of demonstration, and the common man on the basis of tradition and authority. They constitute "true opinions" which must be taught to, and affirmed by, all people, regardless of educational and intellectual stature. As "true opinions" these five principles constitute the minimal knowledge of the truth to qualify for "a portion in the world to come." A person who denies these basic rational truths is an *Apiqoros*, in the Mishnah's terms; by denying these "true opinions" he has no basis for a portion in the world to come.

(2) PRINCIPLES 6–9—TORAH FROM HEAVEN

The second category of principles consists of contingent historical truths, and as such, although they are "true opinions," they are not rationally demonstrable. If they were demonstrable, they would be necessary truths, but as matters of historical fact, they are contingent. Philosophy can neither prove nor disprove contingent historical truths which (as we have seen in previous chapters) depend on the reliable testimony of the original witnesses as well as on the reliable transmission over the generations of the original reports. As historical truths, they are accessible to philosophers and the common people alike, and must be affirmed as "true opinions." Nevertheless, as "secrets of the Torah" and "mysteries," these subjects, including prophecy, can only be conveyed "in chapter headings." The philosopher and the common man will thus both affirm these historical truths as "true opinions," but their understanding of them will differ markedly, with the common man's understanding restricted to the bare historical phenomena (which constitute the "chapter headings"), and the philosopher understanding the metaphysical explanations underlying those phenomena. A person who denies these "true opinions"—whether on the more limited level of the common man or on the more sophisticated level of the intellectual—falls under the Mishnah's category of one who says that "the Torah is not from heaven." By denying this "true opinion" he has no portion in the world to come.

(3) PRINCIPLES 10–13—REWARD AND PUNISHMENT

Most people have a childish conception of reward and punishment (including providence and the world to come), which they conceive of literally, in extrinsic, or even physical, terms. If they did not affirm these beliefs literally, they would lack the motivation—the expectation of reward and the fear of punishment—to behave morally and to fulfill the Torah's commandments. They are, in the words of Antigonos of Sokho, like "servants who serve the master in order to receive a reward," and without the expectation of the reward they would not serve at all. The third category of principles, dealing with reward and punishment, thus constitutes "beliefs the affirmation of which is necessary for political welfare." From the perspective of Aristotelian philosophy, taken literally, these "necessary beliefs" are not true. However, the more a person progresses and matures intellectually and spiritually, the less he requires such extrinsic motivation, and the more he resembles Abraham who "served out of love," or in the words of Antigonos of Sokho, "like servants who serve in order not to receive a reward." He then appreciates that "the reward of the commandment is the commandment itself" and understands that reward and punishment are intrinsic: doing what is right is its own reward, and doing what is wrong is its own punishment. Such intellectual Jews do not need "necessary beliefs" to motivate them to do what is right; they will do what is right because it is the right thing to do. The common man will therefore affirm the "necessary beliefs" of reward and punishment, which he takes literally; the intellectual, who does not need the literal promise of reward and threat of punishment, and who "serves out of love," can understand them metaphorically, since in any event he will do what is right, because it is right, without regard for extrinsic reward. The common man will thus affirm principles 10–13 literally, and the intellectual will affirm them metaphorically; both will thus avoid being categorized, in the Mishnah's terms, as people who "say there is no resurrection of the dead," who by rejecting these "necessary beliefs" lose their portion in the world to come.

[VIII.3.d.iii] *The Internal Relationship of the Principles*

Within each of the three categories of principles—especially within the first two categories—there is an internal relationship of the principles, with each principle following logically from the preceding principle. (Such a relationship is less obvious in the third category).

We have already seen that in the first category, principles regarding God, when Rambam proves (in the *Guide of the Perplexed*) the existence of God, he thereby also proves God's incorporeality and unity; these, in turn, lead to God's eternity, and thereby to God being uniquely worthy of being worshipped. In the second category, principles relating to the Torah, there is a similar logical progression: there is a historical phenomenon of prophecy (#6); Moses was the "father of the prophets," and his prophecy was qualitatively unique (#7); therefore the Torah was revealed to Moses (#8); therefore, the Torah can never be abrogated by any later claim of revelation (#9).

Menachem Kellner has suggested that internal relationship of the principles is a descending order from general to particular:[56]

> When we turn to look at the relationship which obtains between the various principles themselves...we further see that...the principles proceed in a logical order: from general to particular, or from logically prior to logically posterior.

---

[56]   Kellner, *Dogma in Medieval Jewish Thought*, p. 26.

In the first category, principles regarding God, the existence of God (#1) is logically prior to God's unity and incorporeality (#2 and #3), which imply each other; God's eternity (#4) is more particular than the first three, but is prior to God alone being worthy of being worshipped (#5). In the second category, principles #6–9 regarding the Torah, the progression clearly moves from the general to the particular. Kellner also sees this structure as applying to the third category, principles relating to reward and punishment. God's knowledge of particulars (#10) is prior to belief in reward and punishment (#11), which in turn leads to what Kellner calls "the two classic examples of that reward and punishment," the messianic era (#12) and resurrection (#13).

Kellner concludes:

> It seems very hard to claim that all this—the fact that the principles fall so naturally into three different groups, that the three groups themselves each deal with another aspect of acceptance of the Torah, and that within the groups themselves the principles seem to proceed from general to particular or from logically prior to logically consequent—was all an accident and that Maimonides did not indeed intend the principles to be divided [in this way].[57]

[VIII.3.d.iv] *The Mutual Relationship of the Three Categories of Principles*

There is also a logical order and literary structure to the mutual relationship of the three categories of principles. The three categories also proceed from general to particular: the first category (God) consists of universal rational truths which are the basis for everything that follows. Without the existence of God, there could be no prophecy and Torah (the second category), namely "true opinions" relating to the history of the Jewish people. These "true opinions," in turn, form the basis for the "necessary beliefs" of reward and punishment for obedience to the Torah (the third category). We thus have a descending order from general to particular: universal rational truths, "true opinions" relating to the Jewish people, and "necessary beliefs" for the simple Jews. The descending order also manifests a logical progression, from rational truths to historical "true opinions" to "necessary beliefs," in other words from propositions that are philosophy demonstrates, to propositions which are historical truths that philosophy can neither prove nor disprove, to propositions that are, on a literal level, philosophically untenable.

At the same time, the three categories also manifest an ascending spiritual order. Simple Jews have an expectation of literal reward and punishment (the third category), which motivates them to behave morally and obey the commandments of the Torah (based on the second category), and observing the commandments of the Torah, in turn, teaches the Jew the underlying and basic truths of God (the first category). Once again, the intellectual Jews, who

---

[57]   Kellner, *Dogma in Medieval Jewish Thought*, pp. 26–27.

do not require the extrinsic motivation of expected reward and punishment, can interpret the principles in the third category metaphorically, because in any event, as those who "serve out of love" they will behave properly and obey the Torah's commandments (the second category) and also arrive at the demonstrable rational truths about God (the first category).

The downward order of the three categories thus reflects a logical progression from general to particular, and from philosophically necessary to philosophically neutral to philosophically untenable and negative (on a literal level), whereas the upward order of the three categories reflects a psychological and spiritual progression towards knowledge of God.

[VIII.3.d.v] *The External Relationshp of the Principles to the Mishnah's Categories*

As we have already seen, Duran was the first to point out the parallel between the three-fold structure of the thirteen foundations, and the parallel of each of the three categories of principles to one of the three categories of Jews excluded from a portion in the world to come.

The third category of principles—reward and punishment—is parallel to the Mishnah's first category of a Jew who denies resurrection. The second category of principles—the Torah—is parallel to the Mishnah's second category of a Jew who denies that the Torah is from heaven. Finally, the first category of principles—the existence of God—is parallel to the Mishnah's third category, an *Apiqoros*, which we now understand to mean a person who denies the fundamental truths about God.

The three-fold literary structure of the thirteen foundations thus serves both negative and positive functions. In negative terms, the parallel to the three categories of Jews excluded from a portion in the world to come according to the Mishnah, means that by affirming (on one level or another) the principles in each category, a Jew is precluded from being one of those Jews who are excluded from a portion in the world to come. His portion in the world to come is thus assured.

In positive terms, the affirmation of the "necessary beliefs" in the third category—whether literally, by common people, or metaphorically, by intellectuals—leads to affirmation of the "true opinions" and thus to observance of the commandments of the Torah in the second category, and thereby to knowledge of the truths about God in the first category, knowledge which constitutes the minimal threshold of "a portion in the world to come." The thirteen foundations thus assure all Jews of a portion in the world to come. Rambam has thus expanded his intellectual conception of the world to come to include all Jews, in conformity with our Mishnah which states that "all Israel have a portion in the world to come."

[VIII.4] RAMBAM'S PURPOSE: WHY DID RAMBAM COMPOSE THE THIRTEEN PRINCIPLES?

Different explanations have been offered as to why Rambam composed the thirteen principles. We shall survey seven of these explanations.

[VIII.4.a] THE THIRTEEN PRINCIPLES AS A COMMENTARY TO *PEREQ ḤELEQ*

The parallels between the three-fold literary structure of the thirteen foundations and the three categories in the Mishnah, *Pereq Ḥeleq*, have led such medieval thinkers at Duran and Albo, and contemporary scholars like Arthur Hyman,[58] to suggest that Rambam's principles constitute a commentary on the Mishnah.

[VIII.4.b] THE FOUNDATIONS OF THE TORAH: AN IMITATION OF THE AXIOMS OF SCIENCE

Isaac Abravanel (1437–1508) suggested that Rambam wished to formulate scientific foundations for the Torah "by way of investigation and speculation." The gentiles pursue their sciences "by positing first principles [i.e., axioms] and roots upon which a science is based." Rambam, therefore, attempted similarly to "postulate principles and foundations for the divine Torah."[59]

[VIII.4.c] INTER-RELIGIOUS POLEMIC: AN IMITATION OF OTHER RELIGIONS

Some scholars have suggested that the inter-religious polemic of the Middle Ages served as the background for Rambam's formulation of Jewish dogmas. In his "Letter to Yemen" Rambam had characterized Christianity and Islam as "imitations" of the true religion (Judaism), as a statue is an imitation of a living person. The polemics with the other religions require that Judaism have a clear formulation of its principles, in order to demonstrate its superiority. For example, Solomon Schechter wrote:

> Living among followers of the "imitating creeds" (as he calls Christianity and Mohammedism), who claimed that their religion had superseded the law of Moses, Maimonides, consciously or unconsciously, felt himself impelled to assert the superiority of the prophecy of Moses. And so we may guess that every article [of faith] of Maimonides which seems to offer difficulties to us contains an assertion

---

58   See note 33, above.
59   Abravanel, *Rosh Amanah*, ch. 23, English translation by Menachem Kellner in *Dogma in Medieval Jewish Thought*, p. 185.

of some relaxed belief, or a protest against the pretensions of other creeds, though we are not always able to discover the exact necessity for them.[60]

We have seen that Rambam's seventh principle (the prophecy of Moses) and especially the ninth principle (abrogation) are, at least in part and in their terminology, polemics against Islamic claims.

[VIII.4.d] EDUCATING THE PEOPLE AND THEIR SPIRITUAL LEADERS

Many of Rambam's works were written with the aim of educating the people and raising their intellectual level, or that of their spiritual leaders. These leaders, however fluent they were in halakhic literature, frequently lacked any familiarity with the sciences. Rambam's educational goals were explicit in such works as his Introduction to the Mishnah, his "Eight Chapters on Ethics" (his introduction to tractate Avot in the Mishnah), and of course in his Introduction to *Pereq Heleq*, including the thirteen foundations. His largest work, the *Mishneh Torah* is an immense educational project, and its overtly educational aims are especially prominent in the first of its fourteen books, the "Book of Knowledge," particularly in the Laws of the Foundations of the Torah, Laws Relating to Ethical Dispositions and Moral Conduct, and Laws of Repentance. Rambam's *Guide of the Perplexed*—written in the form of a letter to his perplexed student—has an overtly educational program, especially in the Introduction to the book. His "Treatise on Resurrection" criticizes spiritual leaders, "Talmudists," whose beliefs—such as corporeal notions of God—reflect fundamental ignorance of the sciences. Therefore, Rambam says, it was necessary "in my Talmudic works" (he explicitly mentions the *Mishneh Torah* and his commentary to *Pereq Heleq*) to explain basic principles of the Torah without scientific proofs, so that at least the masses could accept those truths on authority.

In Rambam's view, the observance of the Torah's commandments cannot be reduced to mere mechanical performance, but must be accompanied by—and based on—knowledge of the truth. The Torah deals both with *tiqun ha-guf* ("the welfare of the body"), namely correct behavior and governance of society, and with *tiqun ha-nefesh* ("the welfare of the soul"), namely correct opinions.[61] Therefore, even an expert in the technicalities of *halakhah* is not observing the Torah correctly if he is ignorant of scientific truth, since the knowledge of the truth is the ultimate human perfection. It is essential, accordingly, to teach the people and their spiritual leaders "true opinions," even if they are accepted on authority and without scientific proof.

---

60   Solomon Schechter, "The Dogmas of Judaism" in *Studies in Judaism* (Philadelphia: Jewish Publication Society, 1896), p. 179.

61   *Guide of the Perplexed* 3:27.

[VIII.4.e] BELIEFS NECESSARY FOR POLITICAL WELFARE

Some scholars, such as Lawrence Berman, have interpreted the thirteen foundations in terms of Rambam's "beliefs the affirmation of which is necessary for political welfare."[62] These beliefs, as we have seen, are necessary for the social order, regardless of their cognitive status and whether they are true, at least on a literal level. As such, Rambam's "necessary beliefs"—assuming they do not have true cognitive content—follow in the tradition of Plato's "noble lie."

[VIII.4.e.i] *The Platonic Tradition of the "Noble Lie"*

According to Plato,[63] the citizens may not lie to the ruler. Although the philosopher loves knowledge of the truth and reality, and hates falsehood, the philosopher-ruler may engage in the "noble lie"[64] for the sake of society, as a kind of "medicine".

> But further we must surely prize truth most highly. For if we were right in what we were just saying, and falsehood is in very deed useless to the gods, but to men useful as a remedy or form of medicine, it is obvious that such a thing must be assigned to physicians, and laymen should have nothing to do with it... The rulers of the city may, if anybody, fitly lie on account of enemies or citizens for the benefit of the state; no others may have anything to do with it. But for a layman to lie to rulers of that kind we shall affirm to be as great a sin, nay a greater, than it is for a patient not to tell his physician or an athlete his trainer the truth about his bodily condition.[65]
>
> It seems likely that our rulers will have to make considerable use of falsehood and deception for the benefit of their subjects. We said, I believe, that the use of that sort of thing was in the category of medicine.[66]

Plato's concept of the noble lie, which is politically necessary as a social "medicine" was well known in medieval Islamic philosophy. For example, Rambam's contemporary Abu'l Walid Ibn Rushd (Averroes;1126–1198) wrote in his Commentary to Plato's *Republic*:

> The multitude ought to be told that when one of the multitude lies to the chiefs, there is a possibility of harm resembling the harm that comes when an invalid lies to the physician about his sickness. But the chiefs' lying to the multitude

---

62   *Guide of the Perplexed* 3:28. See the discussion above, VIII.3.c.iii.
63   Plato, *Republic* 6:490b.
64   Plato, *Republic* 3:414b.
65   Plato, *Republic* 3:389b, English translation by Paul Shorey, in Edith Hamilton and Huntington Cairns (eds.), *The Collected Dialogues of Plato* (New York: Bollingen Foundation, 1964), p. 634.
66   Plato, *Republic* 5:459c, trans. Paul Shorey, p. 698.

will be appropriate for them in the respect in which a drug is appropriate for a disease. Just as it is only the physician who prescribes a drug, so is it the king who lies to the multitude concerning the affairs of the realm. That is because untrue stories are necessary for the teaching of the citizens. No bringer of a nomos is to be found who does not make use of invented stories, for this is something necessary for the multitude to reach

Returning to Rambam, "true opinions" (Arabic: *ara ṣaḥiḥa*; Hebrew: *de'ot amitiyot*) deal with theoretical truths, such as the existence, unity and incorporeality of God, whereas "beliefs the affirmation of which is necessary for political welfare" (or "beliefs the affirmation of which is necessary for the affairs of the state"; Arabic: *i'tiqadat ma i'tiqadaha ḍaruri fi ṣalaḥ al-aḥwal al-madinah*; Hebrew: *emunot she-emunatam hekhreḥit be-tiqun 'inyanei ha-medinah*), such as the belief that God is angry with people who commit injustice or disobey his commandments, are practical propositions "necessary for the abolition of wrongdoing or for acquiring noble moral virtues."

One of Rambam's early commentators, Profiat Duran,[67] interpreted Rambam's "necessary belief" in God's anger as such a Platonic lie or invented story:

> He meant to say that this belief is not actually true, because God is not affected and does not get angry. The prophet had to posit this notion in order that the masses would abandon wrongdoing and be afraid to rebel against [God]. That is why it is called a "necessary belief." However a belief that actually [refers] to something outside the soul is called a "true belief."[68]

Another medieval commentator, Shem Tov ibn Shem Tov (mid–15th century) similarly wrote:

> This [necessary] belief is not true, because [God] is not affected and does not get angry...The common man must believe this belief, that [God] is affected. Although it is a lie (*sheqer*), it is necessary for the existence of the state, and therefore they were called "necessary beliefs" and not "true [beliefs]." The wise person understands that this [necessary belief] was said in the sense of "the Torah speaks according to human language," and that God's actions are those of one who gets angry, although [God] does not get angry.[69]

67　Profiat Duran was known as "Ephodi" (an acronym for *Ani Profiat Duran* ["I am Profiat Duran"], Spain, late 14th—early 15th century).

68　Ephodi, Commentary on *Guide of the Perplexed* 3:28 (reprint of traditional edition), p. 41b.

69　In other words, God's actions are like those of an angry person, but God does not actually get angry. Shem Tov ibn Shem Tov, Commentary on *Guide of the Perplexed* III:28 (reprint of traditional edition), p. 41b.

Moses Narboni (or: Moses of Narbonne; d. 1362 C.E.) went even farther in his understanding of Rambam's necessary beliefs. The masses' beliefs are based on what they imagine, because they are incapable of understanding demonstrative rational truth. Therefore, the masses must be taught by means of stories and parables, not by scientific proofs. Thus far Narboni's theory resembles that of many other medieval thinkers. However, according to Narboni (and such Arab thinkers as Ibn Bajja), the purpose of political welfare is not for the sake of the masses of citizens of the state, but for the sake of the intellectual whom the masses serve.

> The reason for this is that the masses are not harmed by this [necessary] belief, because their belief is imaginary...Their intellect in not sufficient for more than this measure of whatever will bring the benefit of eliminating violence. The benefit accrues to the philosopher, because he lives among them. Although he might be harmed by this [necessary belief], i.e. that he believe in something that is not, his wisdom will enlighten him so that he will not believe that God is affected, but will understand the intention of the Torah and will conceal its secret.[70]

As Narboni understands Rambam, then, necessary beliefs are the product of the imagination, not the intellect. They are not true in rational or scientific terms.

In Chapter Ten we shall discuss Rambam's political theory. As we shall see, in his conception of the prophet as Platonic philosopher-king, it is true that society serves the needs of the leader (as Narboni suggests), but it is also true that the leader serves his society.

[VIII.4.e.ii] *Spinoza*

Plato said that the ruler may lie as "medicine" for the benefit of his people. Ibn Rushd supported that view, and Rambam's category of "necessary beliefs" seems to conform to the category of Plato's "noble lies," but only if taken literally. That is certainly how Narboni understood Rambam, and Narboni may well have been correct. Is, then, the purpose of Rambam's "necessary beliefs" merely political expediency, even with the best of intentions for the benefit of the masses?

This is the line of thought followed by Baruch Spinoza (1632–1677) in his *Theologico-Political Treatise* (1670), ch. 14.[71] The "universal religion"

---

70 Narboni, Commentary to *Guide of the Perplexed* III:28, ed. J. Goldenthal (Vienna, 1952), p. 61b.

71 See the discussion in Arthur Hyman, "Spinoza's Dogmas of Universal Faith in the Light of their Medieval Jewish Background," in Alexander Altmann (ed.), *Biblical and Other Studies* (Cambridge: Harvard University Press, 1963), pp. 183–195; and Shlomo Pines, "Spinoza's *Tractatus Theologico-Politicus*, Maimonides and Kant" in Ora Segal (ed.), *Further Studies in Philosophy* (Jerusalem: Magnes Press, 1968), pp. 3–54.

or "divine law" of the philosopher is the product of reason and is, therefore, common to all humans, and does not depend on any specific historical narratives or ritual ceremonies. However, there is also the "religion of the masses," a product of the human imagination, and particular to given groups of people, based on historical experiences and requiring ritual practices. The first is rational religion, and the second is superstition. Between these two, however, there is "Scriptural religion," consisting of seven "dogmas of universal faith." These dogmas are: (1) God's existence; (2) unity; (3) omnipresence; (4) power over all; (5) worship of God; (6) salvation of those who serve God; (7) repentance.

These dogmas are necessary to inculcate obedience:

> No one can deny that all these doctrines are before all things necessary to be believed, in order that every man, without exception, may be able to obey God according to the bidding of the Law ... for if one of these precepts be disregarded obedience is destroyed ... Every man is bound to adapt these dogmas to his own way of thinking, and to interpret them according as he feels that he can give them his fullest and most unhesitating assent, so that the may the more easily obey God with his whole heart ... Faith does not so much require truth as piety ... No one is faithful save by obedience alone. The best faith is not necessarily possessed by him who displays the best reasons, but by him who displays the best fruits of justice and charity. How salutary and necessary this doctrine is for a state, in order that men may dwell together in peace and concord ... Between faith or theology, and philosophy, there is no connection, nor affinity ... Philosophy has no end in view save truth; faith, as we have abundantly proved, looks for nothing but obedience and piety.[72]

As Shlomo Pines has observed:[73]

> It is obvious that in formulating his dogmas, Spinoza did not wish to exercise an influence upon the beliefs or the actions of the true philosophers ... Evidently he had in mind the ignorant, who are in a state of bondage ... Like Spinoza, Maimonides also formulated religious dogmas, but in his case these were, or purported to be, the dogmas of Judaism. He had to respect the religious tradition, and was much less free than Spinoza to omit from the list of dogmas beliefs which in this tradition were held to be fundamental ... He also differed from Spinoza in believing ... that it is preferable that the religious dogmas should reflect, however imperfectly, the philosophical truths.

---

72 Spinoza, *Theologico-Political Treatise*, ch. 14, in *The Chief Works of Benedict de Spinoza*, trans. R.H.M. Elwes (New York: Dover, 1951), vol. 1, pp. 187–189.

73 Shlomo Pines, " Spinoza's *Tractatus Theologico-Politicus*, Maimonides and Kant," pp. 34–35.

However, in Pines' analysis, only Rambam's "true opinions" reflect philosophical truths, whereas "necessary beliefs," in Rambam's theory, "have no reference whatever to truth." Spinoza's dogmas, by contrast, "are not contrary to the truth" and "may legitimately be interpreted both in accordance with philosophical truth and otherwise."[74] Pines' conclusion thus differs from Arthur Hyman's conclusion (discussed above) that Rambam's necessary beliefs are dialectical—false on one level (literal) and true on another level (metaphorical)—and not merely politically expedient. In our understanding, Hyman's conclusion is correct, because for Rambam, the purpose of the divine law is not merely political welfare (*tiqun ha-guf*, literally: "the welfare of the body"), namely proper behavior, but also "the welfare of the soul" (*tiqun ha-nefesh*), namely knowledge of the truth. That being the case, there must be a correlation, on some level, even if only metaphorical, between "necessary beliefs" and philosophical truth. This interpretation also accords with what we have suggested about the three-fold literary structure of the thirteen foundations: affirmation by the masses of the third group of principles, dealing with reward and punishment (which the intellectual can interpret metaphorically) leads to obedience to the Torah in the second group of principles, and thereby to the basic knowledge of God in the first group of principles. In short, for Rambam, there needs to be a correlation, even if indirect or metaphorical, between necessary beliefs and true opinions.

For Spinoza, then, obedience is the end of the dogmas, and there is no relation between religious obedience and philosophical knowledge, whereas for Rambam obedience is a means, leading to the higher end of knowledge. This is why Rambam's popular and halakhic works also deal with theoretical matters generally not discussed in halakhic literature. This is also why the first book of the *Mishneh Torah* is the "Book of Knowledge," which in turn begins with the theoretical "Laws of the Foundations of the Torah." It is, as already noted, not accidental that the *Mishneh Torah* concludes, in the "Laws of Kings," with a discussion of the messianic era in which conditions will facilitate the acquisition of knowledge of God, so that people "will attain an understanding of their Creator to the utmost capacity of the human mind, as it is written: 'For the earth shall be full of the knowledge of the Lord, as the waters cover the sea' (Isaiah 11:9)."

[VIII.4.f] FOUNDATIONS OF THE *HALAKHAH*

As we have seen, according to Rambam, the purpose of the Torah is both *tiqun ha-guf*, the welfare of the body (i.e. political welfare) and *tiqun ha-nefesh*, the welfare of the soul (i.e., knowledge of the truth). Although Spinoza's dogmas are clearly based on Rambam's "true opinions" and "necessary

---

[74]   Shlomo Pines, *ibid*, p. 35.

beliefs," Spinoza's conclusion—that obedience is the final purpose of religion—would have been totally unacceptable to Rambam. There are many classical Jewish opinions which also emphasize the practical, frequently to the exclusion of the theoretical, in the Torah and in the *halakhah*. "Study is not the most important thing, but action," according to Simeon, the son of Rabban Gamliel.[75] And, "Anyone whose deeds are greater than his wisdom, his wisdom will endure, and anyone whose wisdom is greater than his deeds, his wisdom will not endure," according to Rabbi Ḥanina ben Dosa.[76] From these and similar Jewish perspectives, observing the *halakhah* (what Spinoza called obedience) is the ultimate religious purpose and an end in itself.

This widespread (although not universal) emphasis on deed more than on creed—although they are, of course, not mutually exclusive categories—led Paul, for example, to juxtapose faith in Christ with the deeds of the Torah (which he calls *nomos*, law), and to posit "justification by faith," that ultimately deeds can never perfect a person to the point of his meriting salvation, so that salvation is attained as unmerited grace by those who believe in the truth of Christ.[77]

Both these approaches—the positive approach of Jews who regard observing the *halakhah* as an end in itself, and the negative approach of Paul who regarded observing the *nomos* as missing the point, since "the law has become our teacher (*paidagogos*), to bring us unto Christ, that we may be justified by faith"[78]—fail, from Rambam's perspective, to recognize that the Torah, although it contains law, is not merely law but, literally, "teaching" or "instruction," leading not only to the practical "welfare of the body" but also to the theoretical "welfare of the soul."

These two goals, of physical (i.e., political) and spiritual (i.e., intellectual) welfare are not contraries, let alone mutually exclusive. Rather they are inseparable and mutually correlative for Rambam, as Isadore Twersky has pointed out. "True opinions" are, as Rambam called them in very first section of the *Mishneh Torah*, "the foundations of the Torah" (*yesodot ha-torah*). Knowledge of the truth is also, as we have seen, the culmination of the Torah, with which Rambam concludes his great Code. "True opinions" are thus both "the foundations of the Torah" and its ultimate purpose. "Law is both cause and consequence, catalyst and crystallization, of the cognitive goal, just as it is both stimulus and sequel to love of God."[79]

---

75   Mishnah, Avot 1:17.

76   Mishnah, Avot 3:9.

77   Cf. Romans 3:20, 3:28, 6:14, 10:4, Galatians 2:16.

78   Galatians 3:24.

79   Isadore Twersky, *Introduction to the Code of Maimonides (Mishneh Torah)* (New Haven: Yale University Press, 1980), p. 363.

This insight has led Menachem Kellner to suggest that a Jew cannot properly peform the commandments of the Torah—"the welfare of the body"—unless he first has "true opinions"—"the welfare of the soul."

> In order perfectly to obey the *halakhah*... the Jew must hold certain correct beliefs. These beliefs deal with metaphysics and physics... Thus, for Maimonides, there is a concretely halakhic reason for laying down the principles: correct beliefs (as summarized in the [thirteen] principles are a prerequisite for its proper observance.[80]

Kellner's explanation (based on Twersky's approach) is certainly fully consistent with Rambam's approach to *halakhah* and to the correlated goals of "the welfare of the body" and "the welfare of the soul." Moreover, it successfully explains why Rambam opens his *Mishneh Torah* with theoretical matters. However, unless one wishes to suggest that "the Rambam of the *Mishneh Torah*" frequently differs from "the Maimonides of the *Guide of the Perplexed*" (as sometimes suggested by such scholars as Shlomo Pines and Lawrence Berman, but as rejected by both Twersky and Kellner), we cannot accept Twersky and Kellner's conclusion that halakhic observance is the ultimate religious end. As we shall see in Chapter 10, Rambam clearly posits—in the last chapter of the *Guide of the Perplexed* (3:54), that only intellectual perfection (knowledge of the truth) can constitute the ultimate human end. Knowledge of God is at the same time the true human perfection and the true worship of God. Ethical perfection, as important as it truly is (and, Rambam states, most of the Torah's commandments aim at ethical perfection), cannot constitute the ultimate human end and perfection. The last chapter of the *Mishneh Torah*, as we have seen, also posits knowledge of the divine truth as the ultimate goal.

In light of these clear statements, it is difficult to agree with Twersky and Kellner that for Rambam, the fact that "true opinions" are "the foundations of the Torah" also means that observing the *halakhah* is the ultimate goal of religion and true worship of God. We shall return to this question of the ultimate human end, and the identification of that end with theory or practice, in Chapter Ten. In the interim, and limiting ourselves to the question in terms of the literary structure of the thirteen foundations, we may simply conclude that there is a mutual correlation of theory and practice: for Rambam, "true opinions" are, indeed, "foundations of the Torah," making possible proper practice. At the same time, it is through practice (i.e., obeying the Torah's commandments) that the Jew comes to the "true opinions," knowledge of which constitutes at least a minimal "portion in the world to come."

---

[80] Kellner, *Dogma in Medieval Jewish Thought*, p. 39.

[VIII.4.g] "ALL ISRAEL HAVE A PORTION IN THE WORLD TO COME"

In the first of our seven explanations of Rambam's purpose in composing the thirteen principles,[81] we cited Arthur Hyman's suggestion that the principles serve as a commentary to the Mishnah, *Pereq Ḥeleq*. Rambam's conception of the world to come, as we have seen, was elitist and intellectual: the rational soul survives to the extent that it knows the truth of God. Where, in such a soteriology, is there a place for the simple Jewish masses? Rambam's thirteen foundations, Julius Guttmann has suggested, differ radically from earlier Jewish attempts to formulate creeds.

> This attempt at a dogmatic fixation of Jewish faith is fundamentally different form the summaries of the essential truths of Judaism occasionally preferred by earlier Jewish philosophers, in that it makes life in the world to come dependent upon the confession of these truths ... The reason for this "dogmatization" of Judaism evidently lay in Maimonides' conviction that these basic and generally binding truths — combined, of course, with their historical presuppositions — represented the minimum of knowledge which even the Jew without philosophical training must attain in order to participate in the truth of Judaism. Only the confession of these truths opens to the intellect the way to immortality ... Religious dogmatism is a necessary consequence of philosophic intellectualism.[82]

This is what we referred to earlier as Rambam's attempt to moderate or "democratize" the inherent elitism of his intellectual conception of "the world to come." Menachem Kellner objects, however, to Guttmann's interpretation, and similarly to Arthur Hyman's, because mere mechanical "confession of these truths" without correct understanding is meaningless, and because "a portion in the world to come" is a function of knowledge and understanding, not blind belief.

As David Hartman pointed out, it [i.e., confession of these truths] makes gaining immortality a purely mechanical act without religious or philosophical significance: the parrot-like affirmation of certain beliefs is all that is required for admission to the world to come.[83]

Kellner's objection, while valid, also is problematical. He is certainly correct that for Rambam, mere mouthing of words without understanding them is "parrot-like." However, Kellner's own interpretation — that "true opinions" are the foundations of halakhic observance — has the same problem. A simple but pious Jew, who meticulously but mechanically observes the commandments,

---

81   See VIII.4.a, above.
82   Guttmann, *Philosophies of Judaism*, p. 179.
83   Kellner, *Dogma in Medieval Jewish Thought*, p. 37.

also has no real understanding of the "foundations of the Torah." Guttmann and Hyman may have created a parrot, but Twersky and Kellner have created a robot. If, for Rambam, the first is meaningless, then so is the second.

What Rambam requires is not that the simple Jew have a complete and perfect intellectual understanding of "true opinions." That can only be attained by a philosophical mastery of the demonstrative proofs in the *Guide of the Perplexed*. Here, in the thirteen foundations in his Introduction to the Mishnah, *Pereq Ḥeleq*, Rambam does not require such philosophical expertise. What he is constructing by his thirteen foundations is a minimal threshold for "a portion in the world to come." Some level of acknowledgment of the truth is required, not perfect understanding.

To reiterate: when discussing popular (and essentially corrupt) views of reward and punishment, Rambam clearly stated that a person who serves God out of his fear of punishment and anticipation of reward is by no means perfect, nor is he one who "serves out of love." Nevertheless, far better to do what is right for the wrong reason than not to do what is right at all. There is still value — even if a far lesser value — in their obedience. And perhaps, at least in some cases, "by doing it not for its own sake he comes to do it for its own sake." Similarly, when it comes to "a portion in the world to come," Rambam does not make it an all-or-nothing proposition. The portion in the world to come is proportional to the person's intellectual comprehension, and what the thirteen foundations provide is the minimum threshold of immortality. Thus, as we saw, even a simple Jew incapable of understanding philosophic demonstration must be taught on authority (i.e., on the basis of tradition) to negate corporeality.

Rambam, then, clearly held that a simple believer must accept, without understanding the demonstrative reasons for them, certain basic truths about God. Such affirmation of the truth, even if based on limited understanding, provides the basis for a minimal threshold of immortality, and thus Rambam has ensured, on some level, that "all Israel have a portion in the world to come."

Chapter Nine

THE *GUIDE OF THE PERPLEXED*: ON GOD

[IX.1] THE *GUIDE OF THE PERPLEXED*

[IX.1.a] THE NAME AND PURPOSE OF THE BOOK

Rambam's great philosophical work was written in Arabic (like many of his other works, including his commentary on the Mishnah, and unlike his Code, the *Mishneh Torah*, which was written in Hebrew). The Arabic title, *Dalalat Al-Ḥa'irin* is based on the root *ḥara* means to become confused, perplexed or bewildered or to hesitate. In the Hebrew preface to his letter to Samuel ibn Tibbon (c. 1160–1230 C.E.), who translated the book into Hebrew towards the end of Rambam's life, Rambam refers to the book in Hebrew as *Moreh Ha-Nevukhim*,[1] and that title was adopted by Samuel ibn Tibbon and also by Judah Al-Ḥarizi (1170–1235 C.E.), who also translated the book into Hebrew some years later. In the late thirteenth century, Shem Tov ibn Falaquera (c. 1225–1291 C.E.), who was familiar with both earlier translations and was critical of them, translated those sections of the book on which he commented in his commentary, *Moreh Ha-Moreh* ("The Guide to the Guide").[2] The Ibn Tibbon translation remains quasi-canonical, since Rambam himself approved it, and it was generally the Ibn Tibbon translation that was read by later generations.[3]

---

[1]   The term *nevukhim* appears in Exodus 14:3, where it seems to indicate confusion and losing one's way.

[2]   Falaquera defended Rambam against the opponents of philosophy, and attributed the opposition, at least in part, to misunderstanding of Rambam based on the faulty Hebrew translations.

[3]   Modern Hebrew translations by Yosef Kafiḥ (originally published in 1963–1968 with the parallel original Arabic text) and Michael Schwarz (with extensive scholarly notes, originally published in 2002) make the text more accessible to the contemporary Hebrew reader. The *Guide* was translated into many European languages (including into Latin in the thirteenth century, under the title *Doctor Perplexorum*; this translation was used by such Christian philosophers as Thomas Aquinas and his teacher Albertus Magnus). Michael Friedländer published an English translation of the *Guide of the Perplexed* in 1881 (originally published in three volumes, and reprinted in one volume; reissued without

Who are "the perplexed" for whom Rambam wrote his *Guide*? He makes clear that they are not the simple Jewish masses, uneducated either in Torah or the sciences. Nor are they Jews educated in Torah but not in the sciences. As Rambam explains in his Introduction to the *Guide*, the perplexed are morally upright and religiously pious Jews who have studied philosophy and the sciences, as well as Torah, and because of their exposure to philosophy, are troubled by the literal text of Scripture. They fail to understand that frequently Scripture employs metaphorical language and parables, and in such cases should not be taken literally. Therefore, they suffer "heartache and perplexity" when they read their literal reading of the text is incompatible with the dictates of reason.

The *Guide*, accordingly, was written with a double purpose: First, the *Guide* intends to explain and clarify problematical (i.e., perplexing) terms in Scripture, by demonstrating that they have an additional, non-literal meaning. Second, the *Guide* intends to explicate biblical parables, which were not explicated in the Bible itself; indeed, many people are not even aware that they are parables. Such misreading of parables also causes "great perplexity."

Regarding the first purpose, Rambam explains that Scriptural language often uses terms in an equivocal, metaphorical or amphibolous (or ambiguous) sense. Equivocal terms, as Rambam explains in his early *Treatise on Logic*,[4] are terms which have two (or more) different meanings, such as the term *'ayin* which can mean the eye or a spring or fountain of water. The only thing the two terms have in common is their sound, not their meaning.[5] Metaphors are terms which literally refer to one thing, but which refer figuratively to something else, like the term *aryeh* (lion), which literally refers to the animal, but is used figuratively for a courageous person, for example, in poetry.[6] Amphibolous or ambiguous terms are capable of being understood in more than one sense, with the result that it is not always clear which sense is intended, like the term *adam* (human), which can refer to a specific living person, a person after his death, or even the form of a person made out of wood or stone.[7]

---

the notes in Dover paperback). Although readable, the translation is not always precise. Shlomo Pines' English translation (University of Chicago Press, 1963) is scholarly and precise, and includes two introductions: by Leo Strauss, "How to Begin to Study the *Guide of the Perplexed*" and by Shlomo Pines, "The Philosophical Sources of the *Guide of the Perplexed*." An abridged English translation by Chaim Rabin, with commentary by Julius Guttmann, was published in 1952, and in 1976 English selections were published Lenn Evan Goodman, *Rambam: Readings in the Philosophy of Moses Maimonides* (New York: Viking Press).

4   *Millot Ha-Higayon*. The work is customarily attributed to Rambam, although his authorship has been questioned.

5   *Millot Ha-Higayon*, ch. 13.

6   *Ibid.*

7   *Ibid.*

The perplexed Jew, then, who has educational grounding both in the Torah and in philosophy, is troubled by the terms and passages in Scripture which are incompatible with reason, because he takes them literally, and does not realize that they are equivocal, metaphorical or ambiguous. Similarly, he does not realize that certain passages are parables, the literal meaning of which is equally problematical. If he follows his reason and rejects these terms or passages, he feels he has discarded "the foundations of the Torah," or he feels he has to abandon reason. It is this intellectual conflict that leads him to "heartache and great perplexity." That is why he needs a guide.

The book, accordingly, is called *Dalalat Al-Ha'irin*, and in his later reference to it in the marginal addition to the fourth of his thirteen foundations,[8] Rambam refers to it simply as "the *Guide*:" "The fact that you see me dealing with the eternity of the world according to the opinion of the philosophers is in order to provide an absolute proof of his existence, as I explained and clarified in the *Guide* (*Al-Dalalah*)."[9]

The book thus has an overt educational program. The challenge of perplexity, however, is now the opposite of that faced some three centuries earlier by Sa'adiah Ga'on. Sa'adiah, it will be recalled, had written his *Book of Beliefs and Opinions* to justify traditional rabbinic Judaism and to combat the conflicting claims of philosophy, Christianity, Islam, and Karaite Judaism. To do this effectively, he needed to employ rational proofs. Reasoned "opinions" are superior to blind "beliefs," and are the only effective way to respond to ideological challenge. In other words, Sa'adiah had to justify philosophy in terms of the Torah: why should a Jew who believes in Torah and rabbinic tradition need the tools of philosophy?

Three centuries later Rambam faced the opposite challenge: not to justify philosophy in terms of the Torah, but to justify the Torah in terms of philosophy! When faced with the apparent contradictions between philosophy and the Torah, Rambam's perplexed student did not question philosophy; he questioned the Torah. As we shall see in Ch. 10, this different challenge required — for both pedagogical and systematic reasons — reversing the method of proving the existence, incorporeality and unity of God. Sa'adiah had offered four arguments for creation, thereby proving that there must be a creator. In Rambam's case, as he wrote later in the additional note cited above, "the fact that you see me dealing with the eternity of the world according to the opinion of the philosophers is in order to provide an absolute proof of his existence, as I explained and clarified in the *Guide* (*Al-Dalalah*)." He had to base his proofs

---

8   See the discussion in Ch. 8 (VIII.3.b, #4).

9   The addition was not included in the original version of the Thirteen Principles, and is not to be found in most manuscripts or in the printed editions. Yosef Kafiḥ included it in his edition, based on a single manuscript, and identified it as a later marginal addition in Rambam's own hand.

on "the eternity of the world according to the opinion of the philosophers" because his perplexed student did not question Aristotle's belief in eternity, but as a result of his acceptance of Aristotle, questioned the Torah's doctrine of creation. Rambam, to guide his student out of his perplexity, therefore adopts the pedagogic tactic of accepting the Aristotelian position for the sake of the argument, although he would subsequently reject it. The pedagogic challenge of the *Guide of the Perplexed*, in short, is the opposite of the earlier challenge faced by Sa'adiah Ga'on, and requires a different approach.[10]

[IX.1.a.i] *A philosophic or Religious Book?*

In Chapter Two,[11] we mentioned Rambam's opposition in principle to the Kalam, although his reservations did not prevent him from adopting Kalam arguments (such as the proofs of the Mutakallimun of the absolute unity of God). Philosophy, and not Kalam-type theology, is the way to the truth.

Nevertheless, Rambam did not define his *Guide of the Perplexed* in purely philosophical terms. By his own acknowledgement, he does not deal with general questions of pure physics and metaphysics, but instead relied on the existing philosophical literature, which he regarded as sufficient, in order to apply their lessons to his purpose, which was to resolve the doubts of the perplexed Jew. For instance, in his Introduction to Part II of the *Guide*, he summarizes twenty-five principles of Aristotelian physics and metaphysics that he regarded as demonstrably true and, therefore, not requiring further demonstration or discussion.[12] In the Introduction to the book, Rambam wrote that his intention was to explaine the esoteric doctrines of "the work of creation" and "the work of the chariot" (which he identified respectively as physics and metaphysics). In all these cases—as in his initial statement that the purpose of the book is to explain perplexing terms and parables in Scripture—it could be argued that Rambam is applying philosophy, but not writing philosophy.

Leo Strauss has suggested that, by Rambam's own definition, the *Guide of the Perplexed* is, essentially, biblical exegesis, devoted to "the true science of the Torah:"[13]

---

[10]   As we shall see in Ch. 10, Rambam also had systematic reasons for basing his proofs on eternity, since a proof based on creation would not be valid if, in the final analysis, it should turn out that the world is eternal, but a proof of God's existence based on eternity would be valid in both cases, eternity or creation, and thus will "provide an absolute proof of his existence."

[11]   See the discussion in Ch. 2 (II.1.c).

[12]   He also adopts, for the sake of the argument, a twenty-sixth principle, namely eternity, although he maintains that Aristotle believed it but did not claim to have conclusively demonstrated it.

[13]   Leo Strauss, "How to Begin to Study the *Guide of the Perplexed*," Introduction to the Shlomo Pines translation, p. xiv.

A Jew may make use of philosophy and Maimonides makes the most ample use of it; but as a Jew he gives his assent where as a philosopher he would suspend his assent. Accordingly, the *Guide* is devoted to the Torah, or more precisely, to the true science of the Torah, of the Law. Its first purpose is to explain biblical terms and its second purpose is to explain biblical similes. The *Guide* is then devoted above all to biblical exegesis, although to biblical exegesis of a particular kind...because many biblical terms and all biblical similes have an apparent or outer, and a hidden or inner, meaning; the gravest errors as well as the most tormenting perplexities arise from men's understanding the Bible always according to its apparent or literal meaning.

The "true science of the Torah" is thus devoted to understanding its esoteric meaning, thereby eliminating the causes of perplexity.

[IX.1.a.ii] *The Book as a letter to his Student and Reader*

The *Guide of the Perplexed* begins as a letter Rambam addressed to his student Joseph ben Judah. Many have identified the student as Joseph ben Judah ibn 'Aqnin (c. 1150–1220), a Spanish philosopher and poet who met Rambam when he was in Morocco. This identification, however, seems to be erroneous, and the student was probably Joseph ben Judah ibn Simon, a physician, poet and philosopher who fled Morocco and came to Egypt, where at first he corresponded with Rambam from Alexandria, and then came to study with him in Fostat. A page preserved in the Cairo Genizah contains a letter from Joseph to Rambam, and the Introduction to the *Guide* is Rambam's reply, in which he addresses Joseph directly:

> Since you came to me from the corners of the earth to study with me...Your letters and rhymed verses came to me from Alexandria...When you studied the art of logic with me, my hope fastened on you, and I saw that you are worthy of having the books of prophecy revealed to you...When God decreed that we part and you went on your way...your departure aroused me to compose **this treatise, which I composed for you and those who are like you,** however few they may be.

Throughout the book, Rambam continued to write in this manner of a personal letter to his student, including referring to him as "my son" (*Guide* III:51). Frequently Rambam saw fit to insert such personal notes as "Know," "Do not think...", "Understand," "You already know." Nevertheless, although Rambam presumably really was motivated by his student to write the book, that does not mean that he intended the book only for his student, and he also addresses the reader directly, with such phrases as "You, who study," "You should know," "You already know." Rambam's student, then, although an actual student, represents the archetypal "perplexed" Jew, and

Rambam stated explicitly: "this treatise, which I composed for you **and those who are like you**, however few they may be.

Since, as we saw in the previous chapter,[14] the study of metaphysics must be restricted, writing the book as a personal letter to a close student may have been useful for Rambam as a way legitimately to bypass the restriction on public instruction in metaphysics. Such instruction must be limited to appropriate individuals, and even then, must be limited to "chapter headings." The fact that Rambam sent his work to his close student as "dispersed chapters" (i.e., chapter by chapter) may, then, have served to meet both restrictions. Moreover, as Rambam wrote to his student in his Introduction to the book, the chapter headings were "dispersed and mixed among other topics" so that an unqualified reader would not understand what he was reading. This way, Rambam assures his student in *Guide* III:7, he has not violated the restriction on instruction in metaphysics, but he has also enabled his student (and reader) to progress in his understanding of metaphysics.

[IX.1.a.iii] *The Guide of the Perplexed and the Book of Beliefs and Opinions: Comparison and Contrast*

At first Rambam's *Guide of the Perplexed* and Sa'adiah Ga'on's *Book of Beliefs and Opinions* seem to share a common purpose, namely to eliminate doubt regarding the true relationship of faith and reason. Sa'adiah had stated in the Introduction to his book that he reader who seeks truth will reach the truth, and his doubts (resulting from the conflicting ideas to which he was exposed) will be resolved. Instead of merely believing what he was told by others, the reader will have progressed to true opinions, based on a reasoned affirmation based on research and understanding.[15] Similarly, Rambam stated in his Introduction that the *Guide* may not eliminate all doubts, but will eliminate most of them.

Nevertheless, the literary structure as well as the contents of both books manifest their different—and sometimes opposite—purposes, as stated explicitly by the authors.

	Sa'adiah Ga'on *Book of Beliefs and Opinions*	Rambam *Guide of the Perplexed*
1	The book aims at transforming simple, uninformed beliefs into informed opinions based on study of science and philosophy.	The book is not meant for the simple, thus unperplexed believer, but for a person who has studied philosophy and therefore is perplexed about the Torah.

---

14   See the discussion in Ch. 8 (VIII.3.c.i).
15   Sa'adiah, *Book of Beliefs and Opinions*, Introduction:2.

	Sa'adiah Ga'on *Book of Beliefs and Opinions*	Rambam *Guide of the Perplexed*
2	Revelation and tradition *per se* are not the source of doubt, which has its source in rational speculation	The source of doubt is revelation itself, because Scripture's language and parables, when taken literally, are offensive to reason.
3	A simple believer cannot respond to ideological challenge; only one whose opinions are reinforced by rational speculation can verify his religion and refute challenges.	The student who has studied philosophy does not find his religious belief strengthened (as in the case of Sa'adiah) but is perplexed by the apparent contradictions between faith and reason.
4	The book resembles a Kalam work in its frequent references not only to rational proofs but to Scripture and tradition as sources of authority. Reason thus confirms and conforms to religious truth.	Reason casts doubts on religious truth, and the book must demonstrate that religious sources — Scripture and tradition — when understood correctly, confirm and conform to reason.
5	Given the aim of transforming a simple believer into an informed believer on the basis of rational arguments, the book has a linear literary structure, "to facilitate learning" and to appeal to a broad audience.	The book is explicitly not intended for a broad audience, nor for the simple believer, but only for "the perplexed" intellectual. It has a complex and non-linear literary structure designed to make it difficult for unqualified readers to understand its true meaning.

To summarize, as we have already mentioned, Sa'adiah Ga'on had to justify philosophy in terms of the Torah, for a person who believed in the Torah, whereas Rambam had to justify the Torah in terms of philosophy, for a person who doubted the Torah. Sa'adiah's book was written for a broad, popular audience; Rambam's book was to be limited to a few perplexed intellectuals.

[IX.1.b]   THE LITERARY STRUCTURE OF
THE *GUIDE OF THE PERPLEXED*

[IX.1.b.i] *Rambam on the Literary Structure of his Book*

The restrictions on public instruction of *ma'aseh bereishit*, "the work of creation" (i.e., physics, in Rambam's view) and *ma'aseh merkavah*, "the work of the chariot" (i.e., metaphysics) require taking appropriate literary and pedagogic steps when delving into these areas. As we saw, writing the book in the form of a personal letter to a close student, whom Rambam frequently addresses in the second person, enabled Rambam to obey these restrictions. Those restrictions also necessitated a complex and non-linear structure, so that Rambam's true meaning would not be revealed, but would be concealed from the unqualified reader.

In Rambam's view, the biblical prophets and the Talmudic rabbis spoke "in riddles and parables" when referring to "the work of creation" and "the work of the chariot," in order to conceal their true meaning from the masses; only the intellectuals would understand the concealed meaning. Rambam explicitly explains at length in his Introduction to the *Guide* that he has adopted this tactic: the literary structure of the book must be deliberately designed to fulfill these requirements. Metaphysics (or, in rabbinic terms, "the work of the chariot") may only be taught to individuals, and even then, only in "chapter headings." Even physics ("the work of creation" in rabbinic terms) must also be restricted. However, he says, "in this book, even these chapter headings are not arranged one after the other, but are dispersed and mixed among other topics," to ensure that his meaning would be concealed from the masses, but only would be understood by qualified and perplexed intellectuals. The *Guide of the Perplexed* thus obeys the halakhic restrictions about public instruction in physics and metaphysics both by its content and by its literary structure. Its content is limited to "chapter headings," and these "chapter headings" are not presented in a logical and linear literary structure which would facilitate learning and reveal their meaning to the unqualified masses. Rather, those chapter headings are "dispersed and mixed among other topics" to make it more difficult to understand them. The complex literary structure—following in the pattern of biblical parables which conceal more than they reveal—thus serves to conceal Rambam's true meaning from people who should not be reading the book; only those few perplexed intellectuals for whom the book was intended would overcome the literary obstacles and understand his true meaning.

Rambam concludes his Introduction to the *Guide* by giving his perplexed reader a key, as it were, explaining how to read the book, in a special section, "Instructions Regarding This Treatise," followed by a list of seven causes of contradictions in books. Since, as we have seen, its chapters are "dispersed and mixed among other topics," the reader must reconnect the chapters with each other, in order not merely to understand the general intention of each chapter, but also to understand the particular meaning of each word. Rambam emphasizes that the book was not written carelessly (as one might conclude from its "dispersed" and "mixed" chapters), but with great precision. Nor was anything said "out of its place." If, as a result of Rambam's tactic of concealment through complex literary structure he can satisfy "a single virtuous person" while disappointing "ten thousand ignorant people," he will have fulfilled his obligation "to rescue that virtuous person from what he has sunk into; I will guide him from his perplexity, so that he becomes perfect and finds rest."

The deliberately complex literary structure of the *Guide*, which was noticed and discussed immediately after the publication of the book, continues to perplex Rambam's readers to this day, and various theories have been proposed to explain its secret. Even the chapter divisions of the book are problematical, and Samuel ibn Tibbon and Judah Al-Ḥarizi's translations reflect different divisions. Most editions follow the order adopted by Ibn Tibbon, presumably since his translation became the standard reference.

Section of the Guide	Number of Chapters: Samuel ibn Tibbon	Number of Chapters: Judah Al-Ḥarizi
Part I	76	75
Part II	48	48
Part III	54	54

As a result of the different division of chapters in Part I (to which we will return later), Samuel ibn Tibbon has a total of 178 chapters, whereas Judah Al-Ḥarizi has a total of 177 chapters, a total equivalent to the numerical value of the Hebrew *Gan 'Eden* ("Garden of Eden" or "Paradise").

[IX.1.b.ii] *Michael Friedländer: The Structure as a reply to the Student*

In the Introduction to his English translation of the *Guide of the Perplexed*, Michael Friedländer outlined the literary structure of the book in terms of the flow of its contents:

PART I
1. NOUNS AND VERBS ATTRIBUTED TO GOD (Ch. 1–49)
    a. Image (Ch. 1–6)
    b. Place and spatial relations (Ch. 8–25)
    c. Addendum: "The Torah speaks according to human language" (Ch. 26) and metaphorical language (Ch. 27)
    d. Bodily organs and bodily actions (Ch. 28–49)
2. DIVINE ATTRIBUTES (Ch. 50–59)
3. NAMES OF GOD (Ch. 60–70)
4. THE KALAM (Ch. 71–76)
PART II
1. INTRODUCTION
2. PROOFS OF GOD'S EXISTENCE (Ch. 1)
3. THE SPHERES AND SEPARATE INTELLECTS (Ch. 2–12)

4. ETERNITY OF THE WORLD (Ch. 13–29)
5. ALLEGORICAL EXEGESIS OF GENESIS CH. 1–4 — "THE WORK OF CREATION" (Ch. 30–31)
6. PROPHECY (Ch. 32–48)

PART III

1. EXEGESIS OF EZEKIEL CH. 1 — "THE WORK OF THE CHARIOT" (Ch. 1–7)
2. THE PROBLEM OF EVIL, ITS NATURE AND SOURCE (Ch. 8–12)
3. THE PURPOSE OF CREATION (Ch. 13–15)
4. DIVINE PROVIDENCE AND KNOWLEDGE (Ch. 16–25)
5. THE REASON FOR THE COMMANDMENTS AND TORAH'S NARRATIVES (Ch. 26–50)
6. THE TRUE WORSHIP OF GOD (Ch. 51–54)

Friedländer then proposes that this literature structure be understood in terms of Rambam's reply (in the Introduction to the *Guide*) to his student's letter from Alexander. Rambam says there:

1. "I saw that you are worthy of having the books of prophecy revealed to you...I began to hint to you with hints."
2. "I saw that you asked me for additional explanation, and entreat me to clarify divine matters."
3. "And that I should tell you the intentions of the Mutakallimun in this respect."

Accordingly, Friedländer suggests that the literary structure of the *Guide* reflects these three points, based on the student's requests. Part I:1–70 explains the language of the books of prophecy (#1); Part I:71–76 deals with the theories of the Mutakallimun (#3), and the rest of the book essentially deals with explanations of "divine matters" (#2), although he considers Part III:8–54 an "appendix" dealing with additional "divine matters." Friedländer's proposed explanation does not really explain the literary structure, or why Part III:8–54 should be regarded as an appendix and not an organic part of the book. As such, his explanation does not accord with Rambam's claim that the book was not written carelessly and that nothing is out of its place, nor does his explanation — that Part III:8–54 is an appendix — account for the *Guide* culminating in the ultimate human perfection of knowing God and imitating the divine actions.

[IX.1.b.iii] *Judah Even-Shemuel (Kaufman): A Linear-Educational Structure of Clusters*

Judah Even-Shemuel, who edited and annotated the Ibn Tibbon translation of the *Guide of the Perplexed*, suggested that the book's literary structure is based on clusters of chapters, based on a common theme, which progress according to a linear educational plan. This plan of clusters is particularly evident in

Part I:1–49, according to his theory. In Even-Shemuel's analysis, the medieval commentators on the *Guide* failed to solve the mystery of its literary structure. Nevertheless, he himself notes that this theory cannot account for the order of terms dealt with in these chapter, nor for apparent digressions from the order. Therefore, he suggests, the answer lies not only in thematic clusters, but in Rambam's stated use of deliberate contradictions in order to reveal and conceal his meaning. Overtly, these 49 chapters explicate biblical terms; covertly they show how human thought progressed regarding the divine attributes. Despite all these difficulties, Even-Shemuel concludes that the book has a linear structure, because the first part of the *Guide*—dealing with terms—frees people from their literalist enslavement to human language, leading to the second part which frees people from enslavement to natural causality by its theory of creation and prophecy rather than eternal necessity, and that, in turn, leads to the third part, which frees people from the error of seeing themselves as the center of the universe, by positing God as the final purpose of the world, and by its theories of divine providence, human free will and the reasons for the commandments.

[IX.1.b.iv] *Simon Rawidowicz: an Architectonic Structure from Perplexity to Theory and Practice*

In an important Hebrew study, "On the Question of the Structure of the *Guide of the Perplexed*,"[16] Simon Rawidowicz suggested that the book cannot simply be regarded as Rambam's reply to his student (as Friedländer had suggested), because the book deals—especially in Part II—with many subjects concerning which Rambam had not been asked. The student, then, may have provided the initial motivation for the book, but the book stands on its own. In Rawidowicz's view, the *Guide* is at the same time a work of philosophy and a commentary to the Bible.

The book begins, as he points out, with the gravest source of error which must be corrected, namely the supposed similarity between humans and God, leading to corporealist beliefs. A "systematic-philosophic" necessity therefore led Rambam to open his discussion with an analysis (in *Guide* I:1) of the term *ẓelem*, the "image" of God in which the human being was created.[17]

Like his predecessors, Rawidowicz sought to group adjacent chapters into thematic clusters, although he came up with a different division, based in part on comments Rambam himself made. For example, the cluster of *Guide* I:1–7 deals with image and sight, and the following cluster, *Guide* I:8–13, dealing with terms for motion and rest, includes the sentence, "these words of ours are

---

16   Published in his *'Iyunim Be-Maḥshevet Yisra'el* (Jerusalem: 1969), vol. 1, pp. 237–296; first published in *Tarbiẓ* 6 (1935).

17   Rawidowicz, "On the Question of the Structure," p. 243.

the key to this treatise." Rawidowicz also points to the rough parallel between the order in which Rambam referred in *Guide* I:35 to obscure "secrets of the Torah" (*sitrei torah*) and "mysteries" (*sodot*) not meant for public instruction, and the subsequent order in which he deals with these subjects in later chapters of the book.[18]

Rawidowicz concludes that the first part of the *Guide of the Perplexed* has a systematic order, and leads to the second part, dealing with "the work of creation," and finally the third part, dealing with "the work of the chariot." Unlike Friedländer, Rawidowicz does not regard III:8–54 as a kind of appendix, but sees it as an integral part of the book, dealing with one of its major themes, God's relation to, and governance of, the world. As he understands it, the structure of the book thus leads us from the most problematical of these God-world relationships—the "image" of God—to the ultimate of these relationships—the "true worship of God". The relationship of God and humans is thus the beginning and end of the book, and points to its linear architectonic structure. Part I negates erroneous conceptions; Part II provides the theoretical basis; and Part III provides the practical goal of the book.

[IX.1.b.v] *Leo Strauss: Reading between the Lines and the Secret of the Sevens*

Leo Strauss (1899–1973), an important political philosopher in his own right, developed a theory of esoteric writing—"persecution and the art of writing"—that we have already discussed in connection with Judah Ha-Levi.[19] In Strauss' view, there is no way to reconcile "Athens and Jerusalem"—the Greek ideal of "autonomous understanding" namely theoretical speculation based on reason, and the biblical vision of "obedient love," namely practical activity based on revelation. That built-in and irreconcilable tension between the Greek and Jewish ideals is why Strauss regarded the concept of a "Jewish philosopher" as a contradiction in terms, and why—in Strauss' understanding—the *Guide of the Perplexed* is a Jewish book but not a philosophical book.

We have already dealt several times with the question of esoteric writing. For instance, in Chapter Five we saw that Spinoza claimed that Abraham ibn Ezra engaged in (or anticipated) higher Bible criticism, but could not express himself openly, and therefore could only hint at his true views (a view shared by many modern scholars). In Chapter Six, we discussed Dov Schwartz's

---

18   These topics, which may only be taught in "chapter headings" include: The negative attributes of God; the meaning of attributes ascribed to God; creation; the nature of God's governance of the world; divine providence; God's will; God's knowledge; Prophecy. See the discussion in Ch. 8 (VIII.3.c.i).

19   See the discussion in Ch. 6 (VI.6.e).

esoteric reading—based on Leo Strauss—of Judah Ha-Levi (although Schwartz and Strauss reached opposite conclusions). In modern scholarship on Rambam, Strauss was also in the forefront of esoteric interpretation of the *Guide of the Perplexed.*

The need for esoteric writing can be political, as was the case with twentieth-century totalitarianism.

> Persecution, then, gives rise to a peculiar technique of writing, and therewith to a peculiar type of literature, in which the truth about all crucial things is presented exclusively between the lines. That literature is addressed, not to all readers, but to trustworthy and intelligent readers only. It has all the advantages of private communication without having its greatest disadvantage—that it reaches only the writer's acquaintances. It has all the advantages of public communication without having its greatest disadvantage—capital punishment for the author.[20]

Rambam, of course, did not live under modern totalitarianism, any more than Abraham ibn Ezra or Judah Ha-Levi did—but they were not free to violate traditional community norms by openly challenging those norms with heterodox opinions. That does not mean that these authors were hypocrites motivated by mere expediency. Even if those norms were "necessary beliefs" rather than "true opinions," they are essential for the preservation of communal life, morality and the Torah, and they are, in some sense, true, even if only metaphorically.

In the same year—1941—that Strauss published his "Persecution and the Art of Writing," he published another important essay, "The Literary Character of the *Guide of the Perplexed*,"[21] and then (in 1963) he wrote an introductory essay, "How to Begin to Study the *Guide of the Perplexed*" for Shlomo Pines' English translation of the book. In this last essay, he implemented his theory of reading "between the lines" to solve the riddle of the book's literary structure. In Strauss' innovative reading, the book's architectonic structure is based on repeated divisions into seven. The book is divided thematically into seven divisions, each of which is subdivided into seven units. Here is an abbreviated version of the structure that Strauss outlines:[22]

---

20   Leo Strauss, "Persecution and the Art of Writing," in *Persecution and the Art of Writing* (Glencoe: Free Press, 1952), p. 25. The title essay was first published by Strauss—who fled Nazi Germany—in 1941.

21   The essay was also included in his volume of essays, *Persecution and the Art of Writing.* See note 19.

22   Strauss, "How to Begin to Study the *Guide of the Perplexed*" pp. xi–xiii.

A.   VIEWS (I:1–III:24)

(A) VIEWS REGARDING GOD AND THE ANGELS (I:1–III:7)
  I.   Biblical terms applied to God (I:1–70)
    a. Terms suggesting corporeality (I:1–49)
      i.   Two passages imply corporeality (I:1–7)
      ii. Terms designating place, organs of locomotion (I:8–28)
      iii. Terms indicating wrath, applied to idolatry (I:29–36)
      iv. Terms indicating parts and actions of animals (I:37–49)
    b. Terms suggesting multiplicity (I:50–70)
      v. The meaning of non-figurative terms (I:50–60)
      vi. Names and utterances of God (I:61–67)
      vii. Multiplicity resulting from divine knowledge, causality,
           governance (I:68–70)

  II. Demonstrations of existence, unity, incorporeality of God (I:71–II:31)
      i.   Introduction (I:71–73)
      ii. Refutation of Kalam demonstrations (I:74–76)
      iii. Philosophic demonstrations (II:1)
      iv. Rambam's demonstration (II:2)
      v.   Angels (II:3–12)
      vi. Creation (II:13–24)
      vii. Creation and the Torah (II:25–31)

  III. Prophecy (II:32–48)
      i.   Prerequisites of prophecy (II:32–34)
      ii. Prophecy of Moses (II:35)
      iii. Essence of prophecy (II:36–38)
      iv. Moses and the Torah (II:39–40)
      v.   Prophets other than Moses (II:41–44)
      vi. Degrees of prophecy (II:45)
      vii. How to understand how prophets presented divine actions
           (II:46–48)

  IV. The works of the chariot (III:1–7)

(B) VIEWS REGARDING BODILY THINGS THAT ARE GENERATED
     AND CORRUPTED, ESPECIALLY HUMANS (III:8–54)
  V.   Providence (III:8–24)
      i.   Matter is ground of evil but is created by God (III:8–14)
      ii. The impossible and omnipotence (III:15)
      iii. Philosophic arguments against omniscience (III:16)
      iv. Views on providence (III:17–18)
      v.   Jewish views on omniscience (III:19–21)
      vi. Book of Job and providence (III:22–23)
      vii. Teaching of Torah on omniscience (III:24)

B. ACTIONS (III:25–54)

VI. Actions done and commanded by God (III:25–50)
    i.   Rationality of God's actions and Torah (III:25–26)
    ii. Rationally manifest commandments (III:27–28)
    iii. Rationale of apparently irrational commandments (III:29–33)
    iv. Limit to rationality of commandments (III:34)
    v.   Divisions and classes of commandments (III:35)
    vi. Explanations of commandments (III:36–49)
    vii. Narratives of Torah (III:50)

VII. Human perfection and divine providence IIII:51–54)
    i.   Knowledge of God is prerequisite for providence (III:51–52)
    ii. Knowledge of what constitutes human is prerequisite for providence (III:53–54)

Strauss refers to this complex structure as "enchanting:"

> Progress in understanding it is a progress in becoming enchanted by it. Enchanting understanding is perhaps the highest form of edification. One begins to understand the Guide once one sees that it is not a philosophic book — a book written by a philosopher for philosophers — but a Jewish book: a book written by a Jew for Jews.[23]

The question here is whether Strauss' categorization of the book as Jewish and not philosophic reflects Rambam's agenda, or merely reflects Strauss' own agenda. In any event, Strauss observes that Rambam's literary structure, as he outlined it, is "obscure."

> Maimonides succeeds immediately in obscuring the plan [of the book] by failing to divide the book explicitly into sections and subsections, or by dividing it explicitly only into three parts, and each part into chapters, without supplying the parts and the chapters with headings indicating the subject matter of the parts or of the chapters.[24]

As we shall see presently, the problem is even deeper than Strauss realized, because the very division of the parts of the books into chapters is dubious. In any event, Strauss' division of the book into units of sevens (and multiples of sevens), which he himself called "obscure," is, at least occasionally, forced and artificial.

---

23   Strauss, "How to Begin to Study the *Guide*," p. xiv.
24   Strauss, "How to Begin to Study the *Guide*," p. xv.

[IX.1.b.vi] *Lawrence Berman: A Three-Part Triangular Ascending and Descending Structure*

Lawrence Berman has proposed a triangular ascending and descending structure of the *Guide of the Perplexed*, based on the structures of clusters proposed by Rawidowicz and Strauss. He accepts Rawidowicz's categorization of the relationship of the three parts of the book, that Part I deals with negating the errors that cause perplexity; Part II deals with theory; and Part III deals with practice. In Berman's view, Strauss' structure of sevens fails to deal adequately with the relationship between the three parts of the book, nor does it take into account sufficiently seriously the major theme of creation in Part II, presumably because that would undermine Strauss' preconceived theory of sevens. What Berman then adds to the earlier theories is the notion of ascent and descent.

> Maimonides has in mind a structure which is triangular in nature, rather than being linear. The movement of the book is not straightforward from the beginning to the end, from the basic problem to the desire solution, but rather, it is dialectical in nature, starting from those things which are better known to us and then rising to those things which are better known in themselves. From the highest position, he descends to our world again, which is not that of truth and falsehood, but rather that of good and evil.[25]

In Berman's analysis, the two divisions of Part I of the book play a negative pedagogic role. The first division (I:1–70) contains lexicographical chapters, i.e., chapters dealing, like a dictionary, with the correct definition of terms, in order to correct the anthropomorphisms they might be understood to imply. The second division (I:71–76) corrects the errors of the Kalam. In other words, both divisions of Part I correct errors arising in the human imaginative faculty — a literal reading of Scripture in the first division, and the unscientific theories of the Kalam in the second division.

From the *via negativaa* of Part I of the *Guide of the Perplexed* we proceed to the *via positive* of Part II, dealing with three foundations of religion: God, creation and prophecy. Part II thus refines and purifies our understanding, making possible speculation on the metaphysical "work of the chariot" in Part III, dealing with providence. Up to this point we have been ascending. After dealing with the ascent to the "work of the chariot," Part III brings us to the gradual descent to the practical human world, by dealing with the Torah and the rationale for its commandments.

> If one were to classify the three parts of the *Guide*, one might say that the First Part is that mainly given over to the imagination and its perils, the Second Part

---

[25]   Lawrence Berman, "The Structure of Maimonides' *Guide of the Perplexed*," in *Proceedings of the Sixth World Congress of Jewish Studies*, vol. 3 (1973), p. 7.

is the domain of the theoretical intellect, and the Third Part is the domain of the relationship between theory and practice.[26]

The last section of Part III, in short, reflects the descent of the Platonic philosopher-king from the heights of contemplation (*theoria*, in Greek) back to the practical life of the society which needs his leadership.[27]

[IX.1.b.vii] *Menachem Kellner: The Parallel to the Thirteen Principles*

In his book on *Dogma in Medieval Jewish Thought* (to which we referred in our discussion of Rambam's principles of Judaism in Chapter Eight), Menachem Kellner pointed to a parallel between the structure of the *Guide of the Perplexed* and the three-fold structure of the thirteen foundations. Kellner does not claim (like Rambam's commentator, the philosopher Isaac Abravanel) that the *Guide of the Perplexed* is a kind of commentary on the thirteen foundations. Rather, Kellner suggests that Rambam intended, in the *Guide of the Perplexed*, to explain in philosophical terms the truths he had presented in popular terms in the thirteen foundations. Thus there is a parallel between the philosophical and popular presentations, and between the three parts of the *Guide* and the three sections of principles.

As we saw in Chapter Eight, the first section of the principles (foundations 1–5) deals with God; the second section (foundations 6–9) with prophecy and the Torah; and the third section (foundations 10–13) with reward and punishment. Kellner suggests that, in a parallel manner, Part I of the *Guide of the Perplexed* deals with God: biblical terms which, on the surface, attribute anthropomorphisms to God (I:1–50), the divine attributes (I:51–60), the divine names (I:61–70) and Kalam proofs for the existence, unity and incorporeality of God (I:71–76). Part II of the *Guide of the Perplexed* begins with Aristotelian principles and proofs of God (II:Introduction and ch. 1), the separate intellects (II:2–12), creation (II:13–31) and prophecy (II:32–48). At first glance the first subjects—proofs of God, the separate intellects, and creation—seems unrelated to prophecy (the theme of the second section of the thirteen foundations), but, as Kellner points out, they provide the necessary foundation for prophecy, because only in a created world is prophecy possible, and prophecy is effected through the agency of the separate intellects. Part II of the *Guide* thus deals with prophecy and its foundations.

The third section of the thirteen foundations deals with reward and punishment. Part III of the *Guide of the Perplexed* deals with "the work of the chariot" (III:1–7), the problem of evil and theodicy (III:8–12), divine providence and knowledge (III:13–24), the rationale for the commandments (III:25–50),

---

26   Berman, "The Structure of Maimonides' *Guide of the Perplexed*," p. 9.
27   We shall discuss Rambam's Platonic political theory in Ch. 10.

and finally with the ultimate human end (III:51–54). In Kellner's view, besides the evident parallel between reward and punishment in the thirteen principles, and providence in the *Guide*, there is a more profound parallel, because providence is inherently related to fulfilling the commandments. The third section of the thirteen foundations, aimed at simple believers, by promising reward, leads them to observe the Torah's commandments, and the third part of the *Guide* explains the rationale of the commandments, thereby leading the philosopher to the ultimate human perfection of the knowledge of God, which is, as we have seen, a "portion in the world to come."

This parallel, first proposed by Isaac Abravanel, had been rejected by Simon Rawidowicz, who pointed out that the order of topics in the two works differs, and that there are principles not dealt with in the *Guide*, and topics dealt with in the *Guide* that are not included in the thirteen principles.[28] Kellner is aware of this objection. His emphasis, however, is not on the flow of the chapters, as was Rawidowicz's analysis, but on the overall theme of each of the three parts of the book.

Nevertheless, problems remain, even if the focus is on overall themes in each part and not on the flow of the specific chapters. Part II — the shortest of the three parts — differs from the other parts of the *Guide of the Perplexed*. The Introduction to Part I actually serves as an introduction to the whole book, not only to the first part. The Introduction to Part III is also general, and reiterates general points made in the Introduction to the book. Only the Introduction to Part II serves as a specific introduction to one part of the book, and does not deal with general questions. Its summary of Aristotelian principles of physics and metaphysics provides the basis for the proofs of God in *Guide* II:1. In Kellner's terms, however, that means that the Introduction and first chapter of Part II really should belong to Part I, dealing with God, the theme of Part I as Kellner defined it. In terms of the flow of material, the correct philosophical proofs of God in Part II also follow logically and immediately the incorrect Kalam proofs in Part I. Therefore, if Kellner is correct that the three major themes of the *Guide of the Perplexed* roughly parallel the three thematic sections of the thirteen principles, the boundaries between the parts of the book seem somewhat flexible and vague.

[IX.1.b.viii] *Raphael Jospe: The Problem of the Chapter Divisions*

The various interpretations we have surveyed regarding the literary structure of the *Guide of the Perplexed* are based, as one would expect, on the structure of the book as we have it, including its division into chapters, clusters of chapters, and three parts. Leo Strauss' theory of sevens is perhaps the most daring and extreme attempt at revealing the concealed structure of the book.

---

28   Rawidowicz, "On the Question of the Structure," p. 289.

These attempts to reveal the "secret" (*sod*) of the *Guide* began with its medieval commentators. Judah Al-Harizi's translation of the book includes a brief preface, "Mentioning the number of the parts and chapters, and the subject of each part and chapter," which Samuel ibn Tibbon criticized sharply. Why should Ibn Tibbon have criticized Al-Harizi for listing and describing the chapter divisions of the book? On such an obvious point as a book's chapter divisions, what is there to argue about?

It turns out, however, that what we consider obvious—that the chapter divisions in the book as we have it are correct and reflect Rambam's intention—in fact is quite problematical. Medieval sources disagree as to the actual number and division of the chapters, and cast doubt on whether Rambam himself divided—or at least numbered—the chapters. This problem has clear implications for any attempt to reveal the book's literary structure, especially attempts—like those of Leo Strauss—which deal not with the overall flow of material, but with specific numbers and clusters of chapters.

Several medieval commentaries testify that the total number of chapters in the *Guide of the Perplexed* is 177, which is the numerical value of the words *Gan 'Eden* ("The Garden of Eden" or "Paradise").[29] These commentaries include the *Commentary on the Secrets of the Guide of the Perplexed, Called the Book of the Mysteries of the Torah* by Abraham Abulafia, and Joseph ibn Kaspi's *'Amudei Kesef* ("Silver Pillars"). Our versions of the book, however, have 178 chapters (Part I—76; Part II—48; Part III—54). What is the cause of this inconsistency? In his commentary to I:27, Ibn Kaspi notes: "There is no chapter division here in the Arabic book." In other words, according to Ibn Kaspi's testimony regarding the original Arabic book, chapter 26 (in our count), "You already know," and chapter 27, "Onqelos the Proselyte" are one chapter, so that our chapter 28, "Foot" was originally chapter 27, and so forth. Therefore, the total number of chapters in Part I is only 75, and the total number of chapters in the book is 177, namely the value of *Gan 'Eden*. Abulafia's commentary agrees with this number, however he bases it not on the original Arabic book but on "a tradition" that "we have." Some two hundred years later, Isaac Abravanel's commentary also agrees that chapters 26 and 27 (in our count) are really one chapter. Abravanel writes in his commentary to *Guide* I:27, "This chapter is the completion of the previous chapter. Thus we have found in precise books (*sefarim meduyaqim*) that this is not an independent chapter, but is included in the previous chapter and is a part of it." Abravanel also concludes, therefore, that the total number of chapters in the book is 177, "and their sign is *Gan 'Eden*."

---

[29]   For a complete discussion, including the manuscript evidence, see Raphael Jospe, "'The Garden of Eden': On the Chapter Divisions and Literary Structure of the *Guide of the Perplexed*," in *Jewish Philosophy: Foundations and Extensions, Volume Two: On Philosophers and Their Thought* (Lanham: University Press of America, 2008), pp. 65–78.

A different perspective on the question is found in Shem Tov ibn Falaquera's *Be'ur Nifla* ("Marvelous Commentary"), ch. 27, at the end of his commentary, *Moreh Ha-Moreh* ("The Guide to the Guide"): "When Rabbi Samuel [ibn Tibbon] translated this work, he made these two into one chapter, and then later corrected and separated them." What is particularly significant about Falaquera's comment is that he used the Arabic original of the *Guide of the Perplexed* (and translated into Hebrew those passages on which he commented), and nevertheless, unlike Ibn Kaspi, who said that in the Arabic book there was only one chapter here, Falaquera concluded that the unification of the two chapters into one was an error by Samuel ibn Tiobbon, who then corrected his own error and separated the two chapters.

This is what Samuel ibn Tibbon himself wrote in his Preface to his Hebrew translation of the *Guide of the Perplexed*:

> I innovated a bit in this book, because I regarded the innovation as useful, namely to number the chapters in each of its parts, and to write its number at the top of each chapter. I already informed the Rabbi, the author of the book, of this, and I wrote him my questions according to the chapter numbers, to let him know the chapter about which I was asking, in order to relieve him of the trouble of searching for the place, and to make it easier for me as I went to lengths in writing the question. Similarly, it would make it easier for those studying this book and learning it wherever it might reach, to ask a companion near or far away, to let him know the chapter about which he was asking. This was the great reason for my doing this.

In the very least, Ibn Tibbon is saying here that he numbered existing chapter divisions, although he may be saying that he also divided the chapters. In either case, how did he come to be confused about chapters 26 and 27, assuming that Falaquera's understanding of what happened is correct?

Yitzḥak Shailat, in his critical edition and modern Hebrew translation of Rambam's letters,[30] has suggested—along the lines of Falaquera—that in the manuscript of the book that first reached Samuel ibn Tibbon in Provence, the scribe may have forgotten to leave a space between chapters 26 and 27, and that both Ibn Tibbon and Rambam himself at first may not have noticed the error. However, in Shailat's own edition of Rambam's response to Ibn Tibbon's questions, the chapter numbers treat chapters 26 and 27 as one chapter. Shailat also suggested that Rambam wrote the word *faṣl* (chapter) at the beginning of each chapter, but did not number the chapters. It is not clear what the evidence is for this suggestion, because the fact that the Arabic manuscripts of the book have spaces and the headline *faṣl* between the chapters, does not necessarily prove that it was Rambam who made those divisions. The autograph

---

30   Yitzḥak Shailat, *Iggerot Ha-Rambam* (Ma'aleh Adumim, 1987–1988), 2 volumes.

manuscripts Shailat refers to in his notes are apparently only of Rambam's Commentary on the Mishnah and of the *Mishneh Torah*, not of the *Guide of the Perplexed.*

Shailat's opinion, that Rambam divided the chapters, wrote *faṣl* in the space above the chapters, but did not number the chapters, and that the Arabic manuscript Samuel ibn Tibbon received had a scribal error at this point, follows that of Yosef Kafiḥ in his edition of the Arabic text and modern Hebrew translation of the *Guide of the Perplexed*. Kafiḥ concludes that the idea that Samuel ibn Tibbon divided the book into chapters—and did not merely number existing chapters divided by Rambam—is simply not true. This solution also explains how Al-Ḥarizi came to record a different order from that of Ibn Tibbon, if Al-Ḥarizi either was unaware of the error or did not agree with Ibn Tibbon's "correction."

The conclusion of Kafiḥ and Shailat (similar to that of Falaquera), that Rambam divided the chapters without numbering them, but that the manuscript Samuel ibn Tibbon received was defective and combined chapters 26 and 27 in one chapter, an error Ibn Tibbon subsequently corrected, is quite possibly correct, and it answers both of our questions: Why did Samuel ibn Tibbon originally err, and then correct his error? And what was the relation between the versions of Al-Ḥarizi and Ibn Tibbon?

Nevertheless, serious questions remain. Did Judah Al-Ḥarizi also receive a defective Arabic manuscript, with the same defect as the manuscript Samuel ibn Tibbon received? Why should Al-Ḥarizi have followed Ibn Tibbon to begin with, and even if he did, why then continue with a defective number and not accept the alleged correction, when outlining the chapters and their subjects in the translator's Preface? In all these cases, what shall we make of the testimony of Ibn Kaspi, who referred to the Arabic original, and of Abravanel, who referred to "precise books," and of Abulafia, who relied on "a tradition" that "we have?" They were all aware of the problem, and yet remained faithful to the *Gan 'Eden* tradition of 177 chapters (with all of its symbolic significance) despite Ibn Tibbon's "correction."

An examination of the manuscripts of the Arabic original, Ibn Tibbon's translation, and Al-Ḥarizi's translation, proves inconclusive, and only reinforces existing opinions; there is evidence for both divisions. So we cannot resolve the problem definitely. However, even if Rambam divided the chapters and merely failed to number them (since by all accounts Samuel ibn Tibbon numbered them, even if he did not divide them), the obvious question is why?

Rambam's failure to number the chapters is all the more remarkable in light of his statement in the Introduction to the *Guide of the Perplexed* that the reader must reconnect the chapters, because nothing was written carelessly or out of place. With this in mind, we might well expect Rambam to order and number the chapters appropriately, as he did, for example, in the *Mishneh Torah* and in his *Book of the Commandments*. In these earlier legal compilations, Rambam also explicitly stated that he wrote these works carefully, and arranged the halakhic material in an original and logical order, not following with order of the Mishnah or earlier codices. Rambam also stated explicitly in his Introduction to the *Mishneh Torah*:[31]

> I have seen fit to arrange this compendium in large divisions of the laws according to their various topics. These divisions are distributed in chapters grouped according to the subject matter. Each subject is subdivided into smaller paragraphs, so that they might be systematically memorized... For the work follows the order of the topics and is not planned according to the number of precepts, as will be explained to the reader.

In a similar vein, Rambam wrote in his Introduction to the *Book of the Commandments*:[32]

> As I directed my attention toward this goal, I began thinking as to how the division of this work, and the arrangement of its parts, were to be done. (I wondered): Should I divide it in accordance with the divisions of the Mishnah and follow in its footsteps, or should I divide it in some other way, arranging the subjects at the beginning or at the end of the work as logic will dictate, since this is the proper and easier way for learning? Then it became clear to me that in place of the tractates of the Mishnah, it would be best to arrange this work in groups of *halakhot* [laws]... and that I should divide every group of *halakhot* into chapters and paragraphs... so that a knowledge of it by heart should render it easy for one who wishes to learn something from it by memory.

In both of these sources, Rambam states unequivocally that a clear and logical literary structure is necessary to facilitate learning by heart or memorization. This literary approach was already evident in Rambam's earlier Introduction to the Mishnah, when he analyzed the literary structure of the six Orders (*sedarim*) of the Mishnah, explaining the topical flow of the material edited by Judah Ha-Nasi, and mentioning that Judah Ha-Nasi divided the discussions thematically, and then into smaller units—tractates, chapters, and *halakhot*—because "smaller sections... were pleasant to understand and easy to study and teach by heart."

---

[31]   Rambam, Introduction to the *Mishneh Torah*, English translation by Moses Hyamson, *The Book of Knowledge* (Jerusalem and New York: Feldheim, reprint 1971), vol. 1, p. 5a; also included in Isadore Twersky (ed.), *A Maimonides Reader* (New York: Berhman House, 1972), p. 40.

[32]   Rambam, Introduction to the *Book of the Commandments*, English translation by Charles Chavel (London: Soncino Press, 1967); also included in I. Twerksy, *A Maimonides Reader*, pp. 426–427.

We thus find a consistent emphasis, in Rambam's Introduction to the Mishnah, his Introduction to the *Book of the Commandments*, and the Introduction to the *Mishneh Torah*. In all of them, Rambam stresses the importance of a clear and logical literary structure and flow of ideas in order to facilitate learning by heart, a motive he also attributes to Judah Ha-Nasi's arrangement of the Mishnah. All these works were intended for the Jewish public at large.

However, facilitating popular and widespread learning was explicitly not Rambam's intention in the *Guide of the Perplexed*, which was written, as we have seen, not for the masses but only for a limited and elite audience of the intelligentsia. Therefore, Rambam had no interest in facilitating its study. To the contrary, Rambam states in his Introduction to the *Guide* that he adopted various techniques, including deliberate contradictions or intentional "divergences,"[33] with are either pedagogic in nature or necessary to conceal his true meaning from the masses.

Since, then, Rambam believed that the *Guide of the Perplexed* deals with profound—and potentially dangerous—intellectual matters, and since there were also traditional Jewish restrictions on the public instruction of "the work of creation" and especially "the work of the chariot"—the physics and metaphysics which are dealt with extensively in the book—he had to conceal even more than to reveal his true meaning. A clear and logical literary structure—including dividing the book into numbered sections—facilitates learning by heart, and that is how Rambam composed his halakhic works. The *Guide of the Perplexed*, by contrast, does not, and must not, have such a simple and clear structure, arranged with geometrical precision by dividing it into numbered sections and subsections.

When Rambam said, in his Introduction to the *Guide of the Perplexed*, that the book was written carefully and precisely, and that nothing was out of place, and then he also said that the chapters are dispersed and mixed, and the reader must reconnect them, he was not saying two different things, let alone contradicting himself. The first statement requires us to read the book carefully; the second informs us not to expect a simple, logical structure that will make things easy for us.

In short, the *Guide of the Perplexed* must employ a complex and obscure literary structure to conceal its meaning from unprepared and unworthy readers. If a simple and logical structure can facilitate learning, a complex and obscure structure can conceal meaning and make it more difficult to understand. Numbering the sections into which a book is divided facilitates learning; not numbering them serves to conceal learning. Is it not possible,

---

33   We shall discuss later Marvin Fox's argument that Rambam was claiming intentional "divergences" (*ḥilufim*) and not "contradictions" (*setirot*).

then, that Rambam deliberately refrained from numbering the chapters of the *Guide of the Perplexed*—and perhaps even refrained from dividing the book into chapters—as part of his avowed purpose of concealment?

The attempts of medieval commentators and modern scholars to reveal the "secret" structure of the *Guide of the Perplexed*, virtually from the time of its publication and down to our own day, frequently are based on the number and division of the chapters. These efforts, however interesting and provocative they may be, will always remain in the category of speculation, so long as we are not absolutely sure how many chapters there are in the book, and whether Rambam himself definitely divided the book into these chapters. And if the structure of the book remains something of a mystery, how much more so its content!

[IX.1.c] THE CONTRADICTIONS IN THE *GUIDE OF THE PERPLEXED*

[IX.1.c.i] *Rambam on the Causes of Contradictions*

One of the methods an author may adopt to conceal his true meaning, according to Rambam, is to contradict himself. Rambam's Introduction to the *Guide of the Perplexed* ends with a description of seven causes of contradictions in books.

(1) An author may cite divergent opinions of different people, without indicating his sources. This is the case with the Mishnah and Talmud.

(2) An author may change his mind in the course of writing a book, which accordingly contains his original and his new opinions. This is also the case with the Mishnah.

(3) Books may contain sections meant literally, and other sections containing parables. This is the case with the prophetic books of the Bible.

(4) The resolution of an apparent contradiction may not be explained explicitly. This is also the case with the prophetic books of the Bible.

(5) Sometimes, for didactic reasons, an author may place an easier subject before a more difficult subject. In order to keep the first subject simple, the author may not express himself completely precisely, but will find ways to appeal to the reader's imagination, in order that the subject be understood. Afterwards the author may progress to the more difficult subject and express his ideas more precisely. This is the case with books of the philosophers.

(6) An author may not be aware of the contradiction. This is the case with Midrashim and commentators.

(7) An author may deliberately contradict himself in order to conceal his true meaning from unworthy people, who are not aware of the contradictions. This is also the case with Midrashim and commentators.

Rambam then states that the *Guide of the Perplexed* is characterized by the fifth (didactic) and seventh (deliberate) types of contradictions.

[IX.1.c.ii] *Leo Strauss and Shlomo Pines on Deliberate Contradictions*

We have discussed Leo Strauss' theory of "persecution and the art of writing," which requires us to read between the lines, in order to reveal what the author has concealed.[34] This theory of esoteric writing led Rambam, as Strauss understood him, to create an obscure literary structure based on units of seven. Strauss was probably the most consistent and extreme modern disciple of Rambam's theory of deliberate contradictions, and commented: "The competent reader...will also notice contradictions occurring in the *Guide*, remember always that they are intentional, and ponder over them."[35] When we discover contradictions, we must not assume that they are unintentional and had escaped the author's notice; that would be an indication of "scandalous incompetence" on the part of the author. Therefore, the reader must not attempt to reconcile the contradictions.

> All these attempts would tacitly or expressly presuppose that the contradictions had escaped Maimonides' notice, an assumption which is refuted by his unequivocal statements. Therefore, until the contrary has been proved, it must be maintained that he was fully aware of every contradiction in the *Guide*, at the very time of writing the contradictory sentences.[36]
>
> Contradictions are the axis of the *Guide*. They show in the most convincing manner that the actual teaching of that book is sealed, and at the same time reveal the way of unsealing it. While the other devices used by Maimonides compel the reader to guess the true teaching, the contradictions offer him the true teaching quite openly in either of the two contradictory statements.[37]

The obvious question, then, is how to know which of the contradictory statements is Rambam's true intention? Strauss paradoxically suggests that in light of the esoteric nature of the *Guide of the Perplexed*,

> that statement which is most secret must have been considered by him to be true. Secrecy is to a certain extent identical with rarity; what all people say all the time is the opposite of a secret. We may therefore establish the rule that of two contradictory statements in the *Guide*...that statement which occurs least frequently, or even which occurs only once, was considered by him to be true.[38]

Shlomo Pines also took Rambam at his word, that he engaged in "deliberate self-contradiction."[39] However, Pines' approach to Rambam's deliberate

---

34   See the discussion above, IX.1.b.v.
35   Strauss, "How To Begin to Study the *Guide*," p. xxiv.
36   Strauss, "The Literary Character of the *Guide of the Perplexed*," in *Persecution and the Art of Writing*, p. 69.
37   Strauss, "The Literary Character of the *Guide of the Perplexed*," p. 74.
38   Strauss, "The Literary Character of the *Guide of the Perplexed*," p. 73.
39   Shlomo Pines, "The Philosophical Sources of the *Guide of the Perplexed*," p. xciv.

contradictions was more moderate than that of Strauss. For instance, when discussing the apparent contradiction between Rambam's "negative theology"—that we cannot ascribe any positive attributes to God (other than attributes of action)—and his statement in *Guide* I:53 and I:68 that in God there is a unity of subject, act and object of thought, as there is in the human actual intellect—Pines does not completely rule out the possibility of an unintentional contradiction, although he considers it "very implausible."[40] Other scholars are not as convinced as Strauss and Pines that all the contradictions in the *Guide* are deliberate. Herbert Davidson, for example, cautions us that Rambam's assurance that the book was written carefully and precisely is itself no guarantee that there are no contradictions resulting from faulty literary organization of the book.[41]

[IX.1.c.iii]*Marvin Fox: Contradictions or Divergences?*

In his essay, "Maimonides' Method of Contradictions: A New View,"[42] Marvin Fox has suggested that the approach of Strauss (and Pines) is both logically and terminologically wrong. Strauss had failed to differentiate three logical terms that Rambam used in his Introduction to the *Guide*:

(1) Contradictory (Arabic: *tanaqud*; Hebrew: *setirah*).
(2) Contrary (Arabic: *tadad*; Hebrew: *hefekh*).[43]
(3) Divergence (Arabic: *ikhtilaf*; Hebrew: *hiluf*).[44]

In *De Interpretatione* 7, 17b (17–37) Aristotle defines contradictories and contraries. A "contradictory" exists when two statements cannot both be correct but both also cannot be false. If one is true, the other must be false. Using Aristotle's examples, "every man is white" contradicts "not every man is white" and "no man is white" contradicts "some men are white." The affirmation of one entails the denial of the other. "Contrary" statements, on the other hand, cannot both be true, but both may be false. Thus "every man is white" is the contrary of "no man is white." They cannot both be true. However, if some men are white, then both statements are false. Rambam was thoroughly at home with this precise terminology, which he discussed in Chapter Four of his *Treatise on Logic* (*Millot Ha-Higayon*).

Therefore, Fox observes, Strauss and other commentators have misrepresented Rambam's theory when they treat all inconsistencies as contradictories.

---

40   Shlomo Pines, "The Philosophical Sources of the *Guide of the Perplexed*," p. xcviii.
41   Herbert Davidson, "Maimonides' Secret Position on Creation," in Isadore Twersky (ed.), *Studies in Medieval Jewish History*, pp. 16–40.
42   Marvin Fox, "Maimonides' Method of Contradictions: A New View," in *Interpreting Maimonides: Studies in Methodology, Metaphysics and Moral Philosophy* (Chicago: University of Chicago Press, 1990), pp. 67–90.
43   Kafih translates this as *noged* and Schwarz translates it as *nigud*.
44   Kafih translates this as *shinui* and Schwarz translates it as *i-hat'amah*.

Strauss, Fox says, "speaks only about contradictions and ignores the other forms of opposition and inconsistency."[45] Fox also rejects Strauss' rule that, faced with contradictions, the less frequent statement is the true one, because it does not conform to the rules of logic or to Rambam's own instructions in the *Guide of the Perplexed* I:32, where he states that the only way to choose between contradictions is on the basis of logical demonstration—not Strauss' rule of rarity. Strauss thus misses the logical point on which Rambam insists.

No less important, however, is Fox's insight that Strauss missed a terminological shift in Rambam's Introduction. In the middle of his discussion of contradictions, he introduces a new term, "divergences." The Mishnah contains contradictories; the Talmud contains contradictories and divergences; the prophetic books contain contradictories and contraries. The books of the philosophers and the *Guide of the Perplexed*, however, contain no contradictories or contraries, but only divergences, because of the fifth (didactic) and seventh (deliberate) causes.

Unlike "contradictories" and "contraries," "divergences" is not a technical logical term. It is a general term indicating a difference or distinction, not necessarily opposition, and Rambam uses it that way several times in his *Treatise on Logic*. That is why Joseph Kafiḥ translated *ikhtilaf* as *shinui* ("difference") and Michael Schwarz translated it as *i-hat'amah* ("inconsistency" or "incompatibility").

Fox observes:

> Of critical importance here is the fact that, both in the case of the works of the philosophers and...his own work, Maimonides makes no mention of the standard types of logical opposition. **He says nothing about the presence of contradictions or contraries in his own work**, although he begins this section with an account of how we are to explain any contradictions or contraries that we find in various types of literature.[46]

Fox concludes, therefore, that Strauss and others mistakenly read divergences as contradictories or contraries. The two statements are different, not opposite. They exist, Fox suggests, in "dialectical tension" with each other as a result of their "divergence," a dialectical tension between the needs of religious and social life, on the one hand, and the conclusions of philosophy on the other hand. Contradictories and contraries force us to choose between the two incompatible statements; we must choose one or the other. As Fox interprets Rambam, he wished to avoid "either/or" choices, and instead wanted "both/and." Rambam's thought, as Fox understands it, exemplifies the dialectical tension between two divergent positions—religion and philosophy.

45   Fox, "Maimonides' Method of Contradictions," p. 69.
46   Fox, "Maimonides' Method of Contradiction," p. 73.

We are not forced to reject the one in favor of the other. Here again the model is that of Maimonides himself, who exemplifies for us the way in which a Jew who is a philosopher finds his way through the divergence by balancing, in an ongoing tension, the demands of both worlds.[47]

[IX.1.c.iv] *Summary: Aviezer Ravitzky on the Secret of the Guide in the Middle Ages and in Modern Times*

In a major study of how the *Guide of the Perplexed* has been interpreted, "The Secrets of Maimonides: Between the Thirteenth and the Twentieth Centuries,"[48] Aviezer Ravitzky has observed that "it would be difficult to point to any other problem in the history of Jewish philosophy, both in the Middle Ages and in recent generations, as that of the dual character of the *Guide*— its outward, exoteric stratum vis-à-vis its inner, esoteric stratum."

Ravitzky describes different approaches to reading the *Guide of the Perplexed*. The "moderate harmonistic interpretation" of the book attempts to reconcile or harmonize internal contradictions within the book, and external contradictions between religious truth and philosophical truth. On the external level, this harmonistic interpretation sees the book as emphasizing the synthesis of religion and philosophy. Rambam adopted rationalist interpretation of the commandments, allegorization of Scripture, and the need for science, while following religious tradition and not Aristotle on theological questions such as creation, prophecy and providence. On the internal level, contradictions within the book are to be reconciled, not exacerbated. The distinctions between the book's overt and covert, or exoteric and esoteric, levels, are, therefore, to be minimized, and the focus is not on seeking literary mechanism of concealment (such as we saw in Leo Strauss' approach).

Besides this "moderate harmonistic interpretation," there are two other opposing approaches that Ravitzky describes, both of which read the *Guide of the Perplexed* esoterically and seek to reveal what the book concealed, namely its radical doctrines. Rationalist esoteric interpretation reads Rambam as secretly upholding radical Aristotelian doctrines; these rationalist interpreters identified with Rambam's allegedly radical views. Traditionalist anti-rationalist opponents of philosophy who also read the book esoterically criticized or even attacked Rambam for secretly upholding radical Aristotelian doctrines which, they believed, contradict and undermine the Torah. On the external level, then, both the rationalist and traditionalist esoteric interpreters insist that philosophy and religion actually contradict each other, and that

---

47 Fox, "Maimonides' Method of Contradiction," p. 81.
48 In Aviezer Ravitzky, *History and Faith: Studies in Jewish Philosophy* (Amsterdam: Gieben, 1996), pp. 246–303.

Rambam secretly affirmed radical philosophical positions. They differ with each other only in their personal identification with the radical philosophic doctrines or with religious tradition. On the internal level, they both take seriously the deliberate contradictions Rambam claimed to employ to conceal his true meaning in the *Guide of the Perplexed*.

Ravitzky points to Samuel ibn Tibbon as exemplifying the rationalist esoteric interpretation, identifying with the radical philosophical truth, and to Leo Strauss and Shlomo Pines as exemplifying (although from an academic, not a personal perspective) the anti-rationalist approach emphasizing the incompatibility of Athens and Jerusalem, of philosophy and religion.

> Strauss' way of interpreting the *Guide* displays a clear, if unwitting, likeness to that taken by Samuel ibn Tibbon at the beginning of the thirteenth century. This likeness is to be seen, first and foremost, in their exegetical methods: highlighting intentional contradictions, identifying the true statement with the rare one, underscoring deviations of order... It may be seen, too, in their focus on the *Guide*'s political nature... and to a large extent also the philosophic doctrines each attributed to Maimonides.[49]

Finally, these esoteric interpreters of Rambam tend of emphasize the divergence between Rambam's earlier halakhic works, the Commentary on the Mishnah and the *Mishneh Torah*, and his later *Guide of the Perplexed*. They read the halakhic works exoterically, and the *Guide* esoterically. By contrast, the moderate harmonistic interpreters generally do not emphasize, or even accept, such distinctions between Rambam's allegedly exoteric halakhic and esoteric philosophic works. Instead, they look at Rambam holistically, attempting to understand him in light of his entire corpus of works. There is also a trend of "radical harmonistic" interpreters who also harmonize the halakhic and philosophical works, but apply esoteric interpretation to the halakhic works as well as to the *Guide of the Perplexed*.

[IX.1.c.v] *Conclusion: Our Approach*

In general, although not necessarily in each individual case, our approach is what Ravitzky called "moderate harmonistic interpretation," for several reasons.

1) Emphasizing radical differences between Rambam's halakhic and philosophic works, in effect, makes him into an intellectual and spiritual schizophrenic. Even if we conclude Rambam was not always completely consistent in certain positions he held—taking into account different contexts in which divergent statements were made—that does not mean he did not wish to be consistent.

---

49   Ravitzky, "The Secrets of Maimonides," pp. 269–270.

2) Esoteric interpretation which requires us to read between the lines can be taken to absurd extremes. When Rambam tells us (in his Introduction) that he wrote esoterically, is that "meta-statement" (i.e., his statement about his statements) to be taken literally and exoterically, or also esoterically?

3) The emphasis on Rabam's intended and deliberate contradictions ignores his precise language (which he also emphasized), namely that when describing seven "causes" of contradictions, as soon as he began talking about philosophical books and his own book, he no longer referred to "contradictories" but to "divergences." Is this also a case of contradiction, perhaps the "contradiction of contradictions?"

4) Rambam's *Guide of the Perplexed* is an overtly didactic book. The fifth cause of deliberate "divergences" (not "contradictories") is didactic. Therefore, "divergences," such as his proving the existence, incorporeality and unity of God based on eternity, while later affirming creation, need not be interpreted as "contradictions" at all, but as techniques, for didactic and systematic reasons, to guide the perplexed student, keeping in mind that what the student doubts is not philosophy but the Torah. As already noted, whereas Sa'adiah Ga'on had to justify the philosophy in terms of the Torah, Rambam, some three centuries later, had to justify the Torah in terms of philosophy.

[IX.2]   ON GOD: THE "VIA NEGATIVA"

[IX.2.i]   THE "VIA NEGATIVA" FROM THE BIBLE TO THE KALAM

As several of the commentators have pointed out, Part I of the *Guide of the Perplexed* embodies the "negative way" (or: "way of negation") that typifies much of Rambam's didactic and philosophic method. The various biblical terms discussed in those chapters, which on a literal level are anthropomorphic or anthropopathic, must be understood correctly (i.e., equivocally, metaphorically or ambiguously), in order to negate corporeality from God. In this way Rambam sets out to implement the didactic program he announced in the Introduction to the book — to explain "difficult" or "obscure" terms. Rambam's method is thus negative in its beginning and positive in its end: by first correcting erroneous understanding of the language of the Bible, one can ultimately come to understand its true intent.

The "via negativa" is not merely a didactic device, however. It is also a fundamental aspect of Rambam's philosophical method, because — in contrast with Sa'adiah Ga'on, Baḥya ibn Paquda and Judah Ha-Levi — Rambam negates all attributes of God himself. Anything said about God himself is essentially negative; we can only speak in positive terms about God's actions—not what God is, but what God does (because a multiplicity of actions does not indicate any multiplicity in the agent).

The first seventy chapters of Part I thus have a fundamentally negative character. The last six chapters (71–76), reviewing the Kalam, are also essentially negative, since Rambam discusses the Kalam in order to demonstrate its inherent errors.

Rambam was not the first philosopher to adopt the "via negativa," which has its beginnings with Philo. As Harry Wolfson has described it Philo's negative theology:

> Philo starts on his discussion of the nature of God with two fundamental scriptural principles: first, the unlikeness of God to other beings; second, the unity of God... The scriptural principle of unity also comes to mean with him simplicity... No philosopher before Philo is known to have stated that God, in his essence, is unknowable and indescribable... All this led Philo to raise the question as to what is meant by all those terms which in Scripture are predicated of God. On purely Jewish traditional grounds his answer is that all these terms are not to be taken literally, and that they are used in Scripture only for the purpose of instruction. But, on philosophic grounds... they are what philosophers call properties... From now on in the history of philosophy, whether Christian, Moslem or Jewish, all the philosophers, in their discussion of the nature of God, will take up those problems raised by Philo and will proceed in their solution after that manner of Philo.[50]

God's absolute unity (meaning simplicity) and uniqueness thus lead to the need to negate our ability to describe his being or attribute the qualities of creatures to the creator. Plotinus therefore refrained from calling the One "good," and in Mu'tazilite Kalam essential attributes were precluded. These influences play a role in Rambam's thought, however Rambam's more consistent and extreme negative theology, according to Shlomo Pines, is based on Ibn Sina.[51]

The negative ultimately leads to the positive; negating misunderstanding makes understanding possible. At the same time, Isaac Husik asks whether the order of subjects in the *Guide of the Perplexed* isn't logically reversed: Rambam, in Part I, discusses the divine attributes before proving the existence of God in Part II, which presumably is logically prior. Sa'adiah Ga'on, Bahya ibn Paquda and Abraham ibn Da'ud, it will be recalled, followed the logical order, first of proving God's existence and then of discussing his attributes.

---

50   Harry Wolfson, *Philo: Foundations of Religious Philosophy in Judaism, Christianity and Islam* (Cambridge: Harvard University Press, 1962), vol. 2, pp. 149–151.

51   Pines, "The Philosophic Sources of the *Guide of the Perplexed*," p. xcv.

The doctrine of attributes as leading to a true conception of God—of God as absolutely incorporeal and without any resemblance or relation whatsoever to anything else—is the very keystone of Maimonides' philosophical structure. His purpose is to teach a spiritual conception of God. Anything short of this is worse than idolatry...Maimonides' method is directed *ad hominem*. The Jews for whom his wrote his Guide did not doubt the existence of God. But a great many of them had an inadequate idea of his spiritual nature. And apparently the Bible countenanced their anthropomorphism. Hence Maimonides cast logical considerations to the wind, and dealt first with that which was nearest to his heart. The rest could wait; this could not.[52]

In other words, the "via negativa" begins with the most critical problem and the most widespread error, namely corporealist belief. This rubble of this fundamental error—which he claimed is "heresy"[53] and "worse than idolatry"[54]—had to be negated and cleared away before the foundations of a spiritual conception could be constructed in its place.

[IX.2.b] NEGATING CORPOREALISM AND ANTHROPOMORPHISM IN THE ARAMAIC TRANSLATIONS OF THE BIBLE

Rambam suggests that the Aramaic translations (*targumim*) of Scripture, especially Targum Onqelos on the Torah, attempted, by means of circumlocutions or euphemisms, to mitigate "as far as possible" the offensive anthropomorphisms in Scripture.[55] For example, "The Lord will descend" (Exodus 19:11) is translated by Onqelos as "God will reveal himself." Onqelos also frequently interpolates such terms as "the word of the Lord."[56]

---

52 Isaac Husik, *A History of Medieval Jewish Philosophy* (reprint New York: Atheneum, 1973), pp. 240–241.

53 *Mishneh Torah*, Book of Knowledge, Laws of Repentance 3:7.

54 *Guide of the Perplexed* I:36.

55 *Guide of the Perplexed* I:27.

56 Michael Klein has argued that Rambam is mistaken on Onqelos, because Onqelos frequently used such interpolations in contexts having nothing to do with anthropomorphisms, and in other cases did not mitigate obvious anthropomorphisms, so that his method had little or nothing to do with Rambam's concern for corporealist language. Cf. Michael Klein, "The Preposition *qdm* (Before): A Pseudo-Anti-Anthropomorphism in the Targums," in *JTS* (1979), pp. 502–507. In his *Anthropomorphisms in the Targumim of the Pentateuch* (Jerusalem: Makor, 1982) Klein pointed out that the Targum retains anthropomorphisms, and sometimes even interpolates terms more explicitly anthropomorphic than the original Hebrew text. Israel Drazin, on the other hand, argues on statistical analysis of Onqelos that Klein is wrong and Rambam is correct. See Drazin's annotated English translations, *Targum Onkelos* to Exodus, Leviticus, Numbers and Deuteronomy (Ktav: Hoboken), and the translations *Onkelos on the Torah: Understanding the Biblical Text* with commentaries

[IX.2.c] EQUIVOCAL, METAPHORICAL AND AMPHIBOLOUS TERMS IN THE BIBLE

[IX.2.c.i] *"Image" (Ẓelem) (Guide I:1)*

Much of the discussion in *Guide of the Perplexed* I:1–70 is lexicographical, and focuses on anthropomorphic nouns and verbs attributed to God in the Bible. Rambam's method is to show, by referring to different contextual usages in Scripture, that these terms, although of course they have a corporeal sense in everyday language, also have another, different sense which is not corporeal. They are, therefore, equivocal, metaphorical or amphibolous (i.e., ambiguous) terms. We shall mention a few examples of such terms.

The first of these terms to be discussed, in the very first chapter of the book, is *ẓelem* (usually translated as "image"). Rambam argues that the term does not (or does not only) denote "the shape and appearance of something" but its "natural form," in other words its essence. The essence of the human being is the intellect. Many people have misunderstood the verse, "Let us make man in our image" (Genesis 1:26), in anthropomorphic terms, namely that God has a human bodily form and shape. In their mind, whatever is not physical is not real. However, Rambam argues (on the basis of various passages), when the Bible refers to bodily form and shape, and uses the term *to'ar* ("appearance"), or *demut* ("resemblance"), not *ẓelem*. So "Let us make man in our image" means "the generic form, which is intellectual apprehension, and not shape or appearance." The human being is unique among terrestrial creatures in having the faculty of intellectual apprehension, and that is the "image" of God in which humans were created.

Similarly, in the *Mishneh Torah*, Book of Knowledge, Laws of Foundations of the Torah 4:8, Rambam states that the "image of God" refers to the incorporeal intellect (*da'at*, in Rambam's Hebrew usage), which is "the form which knows and apprehends opinions," and is not the "visible form … which is called *to'ar* (appearance)."

[IX.2.c.ii] *"Place" (Maqom) (Guide I:8)*

Various biblical verses seemingly attribute the category of place (*maqom*) to God, such as "Blessed be the glory of the Lord from his place" (Ezekiel 3:12) and "Here is a place with me" (Exodus 33:21). The metaphorical sense of "place," however, is a higher degree and more noble rank of perfection.

---

by Israel Drazin and Stanley Wagner (Jerusalem: Gefen). Alexander Altmann, "Homo Imago Dei in Jewish and Christian Theology" (in *Journal of Religion* 48/3, 1968, pp. 235–259) maintains that Onqelos was conservative and literal in his approach, (compared with other Targums), and that even in the case of such a problematic verse as Genesis 1:26–27, "let us make man in our image" Onqelos translated literally.

Such a metaphorical sense of "place" refers to "the rank of contemplation and spiritual sight, not the sight of the eye." The discussion of place is important, Rabam states in this chapter, not only because elucidates this particular term as used in a particular language, but because it "opens a gate" to understanding how "the books of prophecy and other works composed by scholars" all employ equivocal terms. Therefore, this discussion is "a key to this treatise and to others."

[IX.2.c.iii] *"Descend" and "Ascend" (Guide I:10)*

The discussion of the verbs "descend" (*yarad*) and "ascend" (*'alah*) need not examine all possible senses of the terms, but only those needed to resolve the student's perplexity. Both terms, Rambam explains, may refer not only to physical motion or to a change in a person's rank, but also to apprehension. "Ascent" refers to intellection apprehension, and "descent" to prophetic apprehension.

[IX.2.c.iv] *"The Torah Speaks According to Human Language"* *(Guide I:26 And I:47)*

Biblical terminology is thus frequently equivocal and metaphorical. Since such non-literal language can lead to misunderstanding and perplexity—as it did with Rambam's student—why does the Torah employ such problematical terminology? Rambam's answer is that "the Torah speaks according to human language" (*dibberah torah ki-leshon benei adam*).

Rambam takes this phrase from the Talmud.[57] Whereas Rabbi Akiva would interpret (*darash*) the significance of every single word, and even letters, of the Torah as ultimately significant, Rabbi Yishma'el's hermeneutic was based on the principle that "the Torah speaks according to human language," so that superfluous words and letters should simply be understood as normal manners of speech. For Rambam, however—as for Baḥya ibn Paquda and Abraham Ibn Da'ud before him[58]—the phrase is not merely a hermeneutic principle for deriving religious meaning from the biblical text, but a conceptual approach to harmonizing philosophy and Scripture. The Torah was revealed, not to intellectuals, but to the people as a whole who had come out of Egyptian slavery. Its language had, therefore, to be adapted to their limited understanding. Since many simple people cannot conceive of something existing which is not physical, the Torah had to employ anthropomorphic language. This problem is historical—reflecting the limited understanding of people in ancient times who had been slaves for generations—but it is also existential, because many people still have very

---

57   Bablylonian Talmud, Berakhot 31b *inter alia*.
58   Cf. Baḥya ibn Paquda, *Duties of the Hearts* 1:10. On Ibn Da'ud, cf. Ch. 7 (VII.4.d.iii).

limited and primitive conceptions, and because all individuals begin with childish conceptions, but not all people progress to a more mature intellectual and spiritual level of understanding. The principle that "the Torah speaks according to human language" therefore is still applicable.

Rambam had already cited this principle in his *Mishneh Torah*:[59]

> That the Holy One, blessed be He, is not a physical body, is explicitly set forth in the Pentateuch and in the Prophets...Since this is so, what is the meaning of [anthropomorphic language in the Bible]?...All these expressions are adapted to the mental capacity of the majority of humanity who can only conceive in physical terms. The Torah speaks according to human language. All these phrases are metaphorical (*kinuyim*)...All of them are allegorical (*mashal*).

Most people "can only conceive in physical terms." Whatever is not physical simply does not exist in the popular imagination. As we saw in our discussion of Abraham ibn Ezra's understanding of revelation,[60] the limitations on revelation are from the bottom, not from the top; not on what God can communicate, but on what people are capable of understanding.

> This being so, the expressions in the Pentateuch and books of the Prophets already mentioned, and others similar to these, are all of them metaphorical and rhetorical (*mashal u-meliẓah*)...To all these phrases applies to saying, "The Torah speaks according to human language."[61]

In the *Guide of the Perplexed*, Rambam further develops this conceptual principle, and deals with two questions it raises: (1) Why does the Torah attribute physical qualities to God? (2) Why does the Torah attribute certain qualities and not others to God?

The answer to the first question is, as we have already seen in the *Mishneh Torah*, that in the popular imagination, whatever is not physical does not exist. Similarly, in the *Guide of the Perplexed* I:26 Rambam says that "The Torah speaks according to human language" means that whatever people are capable of understanding "at first thought" is attributed to God. Therefore the Torah attributes corporeal qualities to God, to indicate to such people that he exists, "for the masses cannot conceive at first thought any existence other than that of a body, and whatever is not a body or in a body does not exist in their opinion."

---

59 *Mishneh Torah*, Book of Knowledge, Laws of Foundations of the Torah 1:8–9; Hyamson translation, p. 34b. (My adaptations).

60 See the discussion in Ch. 5 (V.4.c.i).

61 *Mishneh Torah*, Book of Knowledge, Laws of Foundations of the Torah 1:12. Hyamson translation, p. 35a. (My adaptations).

This brings us to the second question: Why, then, does the Torah attribute certain corporeal qualities to God and not others, since technically none of them should be attributed to God? Rambam's answer is that the Torah attributes to God those corporeal qualities which the masses understand to be perfections, such as seeing and hearing, in other words what are perfections in human terms, and does not attribute anything that is seen to be an imperfection in the popular imagination. That is why, he says, the Torah does not attribute to God eating, drinking, sleep, illness or violence, which in human terms are deficiencies. Although technically all corporealism is false, the masses are thereby guided to believe that God's existence is the epitome of perfection.[62] The difference between some corporealisms and others is thus not cognitive—they all are false—but pedagogic, in terms of instructing the masses, by leading the masses first to affirm the existence of God, and then his perfection.

[IX.2.d] THE DIVINE ATTRIBUTES

[IX.2.d.i] *Negating Essential Attributes (Guide I:50–51)*

The "via negativa" is fundamental to Rambam's theory of the divine attributes, and he is much more consistent in his approach than his predecessors were. As we have seen, Sa'adiah Ga'on posited three essential divine attributes—life, omnipotence and omniscience—which are necessarily included in our concept of "creator," although we cannot express them with one word. The multiplicity, Sa'adiah maintained, is verbal, not essential.[63] Baḥya ibn Paquda also posited three essential divine attributes—existence, unity and eternity—which have a positive formulation but a negative content, i.e., they negate their opposites.[64] Judah Ha-Levi negated essential attributes, and referred explicitly to "negative attributes," such as life, unity, first and last; he also posited "relative" (or "relational") attributes, such as blessed and holy, and attributes of action ("active attributes"), such as compassionate and gracious.[65] The progressive trend on limiting the divine attributes reaches its apex in Rambam, who negates not only essential but also relative attributes, and retains only negative attributes and attributes of action.

---

62 *Guide of the Perplexed* 1:26 and 1:47.
63 See the discussion in Ch. 2 (II.3.h).
64 See the discussion in Ch. 4 (IV.6).
65 See the discussion in Ch. 6 (VI.14.a).

DIVINE ATTRIBUTES			
SA'ADIAH GA'ON	**BAHYA IBN PAQUDA**	**JUDAH HA-LEVI**	**RAMBAM**
Essential attributes (verbal multiplicity, real unity)	Essential attributes (positive formulation, negative content)	Negative attributes	Negative attributes
Active attributes	Active attributes	Active attributes	Active attributes
		Relative attributes	

To reiterate: the negative way requires, above all, the negation of corporeality from God. A Jew who maintains corporeal beliefs is a heretic,[66] and is worse than an idolator,[67] for the simple reason that a corporeal God is no God at all. Therefore everyone — simple believers and intellectuals alike — must negate corporeality. The difference between the masses and intellectuals is not in their obligation to negate corporeality, but only in the reason why. A simple Jew accepts the negation on authority, whereas the intellectual relies on rational demonstration. Therefore, although in principle the divine attributes belong to the metaphysical secrets and mysteries of the Torah, which should be restricted and not taught publicly, the negation of corporeality from God, and that there is no similarity between God and other beings, and that God is not subject to any affections, must be taught on traditional authority to everyone.[68]

In the final analysis, God's existence cannot be affirmed without the affirmation of his incorporeality and unity. As we shall see, Rambam's proofs of the existence of God at the same time prove incorporeality and unity. Essential attributes are incompatible with God's unity and incorporeality, and thus ultimately with his existence. That is why it is so important to negate essential attributes.

Rambam was fully aware, of course, that not only the masses, but even intellectual leaders like Sa'adiah Ga'on, affirmed God's unity and incorporeality, but also affirmed essential attributes. In Rambam's view, these people fell into the category of those who verbally affirm one thing while in their heart believing something else.[69] The problem is not that they are insincere, but that they fail to understand the implications — sometimes radical — of the divine unity they profess to affirm. They verbally profess

---

66   *Mishneh Torah*, Book of Knowledge, Laws of Repentance 3:7.
67   *Guide of the Perplexed* I:36.
68   *Guide of the Perplexed* I:35.
69   *Guide of the Perplexed* I:50.

their belief in God's unity and incorporeality, but do not realize that essential attributes are incompatible with what they profess, and that they have, in effect, denied the unity—and thereby the existence—of the God in whom they claim to believe. Therefore, Rambam insists, affirmation—he uses the term *i'tiqad* that we have discussed before—is "not what is said by the mouth but what is represented in the soul."[70] Attributes, by definition, are not essential but additional accidental qualities; they add other notions to the essence. That being the case, the multiplicity of attributes[71] is real and not merely verbal, as Sa'adiah Ga'on had claimed.

To summarize: either essential attributes add some notion to the essence being described, or they do not. If they add some notion, they destroy its simple unity. If they do not really add anything (as Sa'adiah Ga'on claimed), then they are, in effect, tautologies.[72]

[IX.2.d.ii] *Types of Divine Attributes (Guide I:52–54)*

Rambam divides attributes into five categories, to determine which may or may not apply to God and why.[73] The first type of attributes refers to the definition of a thing, which explains its essence. As he had explained in his *Treatise on Logic*,[74] in the tradition of Aristotelian logic, a definition consists of the general and the particular, namely what the thing has in common with other members of its genus or species, and what differentiates it from the others. The definition is, in that sense, the "cause" of the existence of the thing. God thus cannot be defined: he has no genus or species, and there are no causes of God's existence.

The second type of attribute is a partial definition. However, to assert that God's essence has parts is clearly impossible, given his absolute unity and simplicity. The third type of attributes refers to qualities, rather than to the essence. A quality, however, is an accident added to the essence; as we saw, it is the third of Aristotle's ten categories (following substance and quantity).[75] Accidents, including quality, being additions to the essence, can also not be ascribed to God without undermining his absolute unity.

The fourth type of attribute is a relation. Since a relation does not imply multiplicity in the essence, one might suggest, as Judah Ha-Levi did, that relative attributes may be ascribed to God. However, a relation always exists in time or space. Time, as we have seen, is the measure of the motion of a body.

---

70 *Guide of the Perplexed* I:50.
71 *Guide of the Perplexed* I:51.
72 Tautology—from the Greek *tauto* (same) and *logos* (word, thing); an expression where the predicate is the same as the subject and thus adds nothing to it.
73 Attribute: Arabic: *ṣifah* (from the root *waṣaf*); Hebrew: *to'ar*.
74 *Millot Ha-Higayon* 10:5.
75 See the discussion of the categories in Ch. 3 (III.3.f).

God's incorporeality thus precludes our attributing time, as well as space, to God, and therefore also any relation.

The fifth type of attribute pertains to actions. Saying something about an action does not imply anything about the essence of the agent. A multiplicity of actions implies no multiplicity in the essence of the agent, nor do different actions imply differences in the essence of the agent. For example, the same fire may melt some things, harden others, or cook or burn or bleach or blacken different things, without implying that there are different aspects of the fire doing these different things. This is true of things like fire which act naturally; it is all the more true of something acting by will, let alone of God. Attributes of action are, therefore, the only type of attributes one may positively ascribe to God.

When the Bible attributes to God such qualities as compassion, these are actually attributes of action. They do not mean, for example, that God has a soul which as affected by emotions such as compassion, but rather that God's actions resemble what people do out of the feeling of compassion. In all these cases, what is being described is not God but his actions.[76]

[IX.2.d.iii] *The Two Requests of Moses (Guide I:54)*

Rambam found a precedent and support for his theory of divine attributes in the story of two requests of Moses in Exodus 33:12–23.

> (12) Moses said to the Lord: "Look, you are saying to me, 'Take this people up,' but you did not let me know whom you would send with me. You said, 'I have known you by name, and you have found favor in my eyes'."
>
> (13) "Now, if I have found favor in your eyes, let me know your ways (*hodi'eni na et derakhekha*), that I may know you, so that I might find favor in your eyes. And see that this nation is your people."
>
> (14) [The Lord] said, "My presence [literally: face] will proceed, and I will give you rest."
>
> (15) [Moses] said to him: "If your presence [literally: face] does not proceed, do not take us up from here."
>
> (16) "How shall I know, therefore, that I have found favor in your eyes—I and your people—except by your proceeding with us? Let me and your people be distinguished from every people on the face of the earth."
>
> (17) The Lord said to Moses: "I will also do what you said, because you have found favor in my eyes, and I have known you by name."
>
> (18) [Moses] said: "Show me your glory (*har'eni na et kevodekha*)."
>
> (19) [The Lord] said: "I will cause all my goodness to pass before you, and I will call the name of the Lord before you. I will favor whomever I favor, and be compassionate to whomever I will be compassionate."

---

[76]   *Guide of the Perplexed* I:54.

(20) [The Lord] said: "You cannot see my presence [literally: my face], for no person can see me and live."

(21) The Lord said: "Here is a place with me; stand on the rock."

(22) "While my glory passes by, I will place you in a crevice in the rock, and I will cover you with my hand until I pass by."

(23) "[Then] I will remove my hand, and you will see what is behind me (*aḥorai*), but my presence [literally: my face] will not be seen."

We shall return to this story later, when discussing Rambam's political theory. For now, we are interested in its implications for Rambam's theory of divine attributes. The passage was sufficiently important for Rambam to comment on it in three different works—his Commentary on the Mishnah, his *Mishneh Torah*, and the *Guide of the Perplexed*. Moses is making two completely different requests: "Let me know your ways" (in verse 13) and "Show me your glory" (verse 18). When Moses asks to know God's "ways," Rambam understands the request to refer to God's attributes of action, and God responds affirmatively (in verses 14 and 17). But when Moses then asks to see God's "glory," Rambam understands the "glory" as symbolizing God's essence. Morever, in this case the verb is different; Moses is not asking to know, but to be shown (or: to see) the glory. To this second request God responds negatively: "You cannot see my presence, for no person can see me and live" (verse 20).

What does the Torah mean by saying that "no person can see me **and live (*va-ḥai*)?**" Some commentators understood *va-ḥai* in the sense of "and then live." Abraham ibn Ezra and Ramban (Rabbi Moses ben Naḥman), for example, interpreted the phrase as meaning that the person would immediately die; according to Ibn Ezra, he would die immediately following the experience, and according to Ramban he would die even before the ultimate experience. Rambam, however, interprets *va-ḥai* as meaning "living" or "while alive." In other words, no "living person can see me" or "no person can see me while alive." As Rambam wrote in his Introduction to the tractate Avot ("Sayings of the Fathers") in the Mishnah:[77]

When Moses, our teacher, discovered that there remained no partition between himself and God which he had not removed, and when he had attained perfection by acquiring every possible moral and mental virtue, he sought to comprehend God in his true reality, since there seemed no longer to be any hindrance thereto. He, therefore, implored God, "Show me, I beseech Thee, Thy glory." But God informed him that this was impossible, as his intellect, since he was a human

---

77 *The Eight Chapters of Maimonides on Ethics*, Ch. 7; English translation by Joseph Gorfinkle (New York: Columbia University Press, 1912; reprint edition, New York: AMS Press, 1966), pp. 82–83.

being, was still influenced by matter. So God's answer was, "For no man can see me and live." Thus, there remained between Moses and his comprehension of the true essence of God only one transparent obstruction, which was his human intellect still resident in matter.

Moses could not see the "face" or the "glory"—symbolizing God's essence—so long as he was alive, i.e., an intellect within a body. What he could know was "what is behind me" (*ahorai*), which for Rambam indicates a lower level of knowledge. As he explains it in the *Mishneh Torah*:[78]

> What was it that Moses sought to comprehend, when he said "Show me your glory?" He sought to have so clear an apprehension of the truth of God's existence that the knowledge might be like that which one possesses of a human being, whose face one has seen and whose image is imprinted on the mind, and whom, therefore, the mind distinguishes from other men. In the same way, Moses our teacher, asked that the truth of God's existence might be distinguished in his mind from other beings, and that he might thus know the truth of God's existence, as it really is. God replied that it is beyond the mental capacity of a human creature, composed of body and soul, to obtain in this regard clear knowledge of the truth. The Almighty, however, imparted to Moses what has been vouchsafed to no man before or since. Moses attained so much knowledge of the truth of the divine existence that God was, in his mind, distinct from other beings, in the same way as an individual whose back is seen, whose physical form and apparel are perceived, is distinguished in the observer's mind from the physical form of other individuals. And Scripture hints at this in the text, "You will see what is behind me, but my face will not be seen."

"What is behind me" thus indicates a lower level of knowledge, not of the essence, but of the attributes of action, since actions are the traces of the agent, what it leaves behind it. These actions are the world God brought into existence and his governance of them, evident in what we know as the laws of nature. Rambam explicates this in the *Guide of the Perplexed* I:54. Moses's second request—to be shown God's glory—means that he wanted to know God's essence (*dhat*) and true reality (*haqiqah*), whereas the first request—to know God's ways—means that he wanted to know God's attributes. The "goodness" that God causes to pass by Moses standing on the rock (verse 19) means all existing things in the world, since the Torah says that "God saw everything that he had made and, behold, it was very good" (Genesis 1:31). Moses was thus granted knowledge of God's actions—the world he made and governs.

---

78   *Mishneh Torah*, Book of Knowledge, Laws of Foundations of the Torah 1:10. Hyamson ed. p. 35a. (My adaptations).

[IX.2.e] SUMMARY OF THE "VIA NEGATIVA": LESS IS MORE (*GUIDE* 1:58–60)

The negative way would seem to lead away from God, because it requires constant negation of erroneous conceptions and language. Of course the negative way, by definition, cannot impart positive knowledge. Yet we are not left with a divine *tabula rasa*, because for Rambam, the less we know of God — by progressive negation — the more we know — by removing erroneous ways of thinking. The more we remove from God, the more we can approach him. As Rambam explains, positive attributes are supposed to particularize the object, giving us more specific positive knowledge of it. By excluding what we negate, negative attributes also particularize to a certain extent — and thus resemble positive attributes in making some knowledge possible, or at least in approaching knowledge of, the object. Even if we can never attain knowledge of the object's essence — what it is — at least we can know what it is not.[79] Thus "the more you negate from God, the more you approach apprehension, and you will be closer to him than one who has not negated what has become clear to you that must be negated... The more the negation of something becomes clear to you by demonstration, the more perfect you become."[80]

In conclusion, Rambam cites the Talmud[81] that a Jew came to Rabbi Ḥaninah and added various praises of God and divine attributes to the standard prayer. Rabbi Ḥaninah rebuked the man and said that had not the standard praises and attributes been established by Moses and the men of the Great Assembly, "we would not be able to say them," because any praise or attribute we can say is beneath God's dignity and even an insult to God.[82] Therefore, "whoever affirms that God has positive attributes... removes the existence of God from his belief, without being aware of it." But "the negative attributes bring you closer to knowledge and apprehension of God."[83]

[IX.3] THE NAMES OF GOD

[IX.3.a] THE NAMES OF GOD AS ATTRIBUTES (*GUIDE* 1:61)

Before we can move from the negative way to the positive way (namely Rambam's proofs of the existence, incorporeality and unity of God), we need to review Rambam's theory of the names of God, which are inherently related to

---

79   *Guide of the Perplexed* 1:58.
80   *Guide of the Perplexed* 1:59.
81   Berakhot 33b.
82   *Guide of the Perplexed* 1:59.
83   *Guide of the Perplexed* 1:60.

his theory of the divine attributes. With the exception of the Tetragrammaton, Rambam states that all the names of God are attributes of action; "they of them are derived from actions."[84]

There is a halakhic dimension to this distinction between the Tetragrammaton and the other names of God. In Deuteronomy 12:2–4, the Israelites are commanded to destroy idolatrous places of worship, altars and idols, and "destroy their names from that place. Do not do this to the Lord your God." In halakhic terms, this was understood to mean that God's name must not be destroyed. Rambam explains that this prohibition applies to seven different names of God, including the Tetragrammaton.[85]

Although all seven names are thus sacred, in the *Guide of the Perplexed* I:61 Rambam explains the uniqueness of the Tetragrammaton. Unlike the other names, "which are derived from actions," the Tetragrammaton denotes God's necessary existence. God is "the necessary being" (or: "necessary existent"). The uniqueness of the Tetragrammaton, which indicates God's essence (*dhat*), which has nothing in common with any other being, is emphasized by its not being pronounced phonetically, except (in Second Temple times) by the high priest on Yom Kippur. The other names of God, including the name *Adonai* (indicating lordship), which is substituted for the Tetragrammaton, are equivocal terms derived from actions. This multiplicity of names, derived from actions, led people to imagine that God has many essential attributes, an error that will ultimately be corrected, in the words of the prophet, "On that day the Lord will be one and his name one" (Zechariah 14:9).

[IX.3.b] THE NECESSARY BEING (*Guide* I:57, I:63)

The Tetragrammaton, as we have seen, signifies necessary existence (Arabic: *wujub al-wujud*; Hebrew: *mehuyav ha-meẓi'ut*). Rambam also equates necessary being with the name *Ehyeh* (from Exodus 3:14, *ehyeh asher ehyeh*, "I will be what I will be"), since both *Ehyeh* and the Tetragrammaton are derived from the root *hayah* or *havah*, to be.[86] The identification of the Tetragrammaton with necessary existence had already been suggested by Judah Ha-Levi in his discussion of *Sefer Yeẓirah*:[87]

---

84   *Guide of the Perplexed* I:61.
85   *Mishneh Torah*, Book of Knowledge, Laws of Foundations of the Torah 6:1–2.
86   *Guide of the Perplexed* I:63.
87   *Kuzari* 4:25. My translaton; cf. Hirschfeld ed. pp. 236–237. It should also be noted that Solomon ibn Gabirol had differentiated necessary, possible and impossible existence (*Fons Vitae* 5:25 = Falaquera's *Liqqutim* 5:31).

It alluded to the great name Y-H-V-H which corresponds to the unified divine essence (*dhat*) which has no quiddity (*mahiyah*).[88] For the quiddity of a thing is different from its existence. But God's quiddity is his existence. The quiddity of a thing is its definition, and the definition is composed of its species and differentiation, but the first cause has no species or differentiation. Therefore it necessarily is what it is.

Like Ibn Sina (from whom Rambam took this concept)[89] and Abraham ibn Da'ud before him,[90] Rambam also differentiated possible from necessary being. A being whose existence is dependent on something else which causes it, is possible, because in the absence of that cause, it would not exist. Its existence is, therefore, possible, or contingent upon its cause. Its existence must be differentiated from its essence, and is, Rambam says, an "accident" added to the essence, or more precisely, to "that which exists."[91]

As Alexander Altmann has explained this:[92]

It has to be noted that Maimondes describes existence as an accident not to essence ... but to "that which exists," i.e., the concrete things. This we interpret to mean that the existence of a concrete thing composed of matter and form is due to the fact that, as a result of a causal process, a certain form has been induced into a certain matter. The term "accident" merely expresses the fact that the thing "happens" to exist ... It merely defines existence as being due to factors outside the essence, and for this reason uses the term "accident." As Dr. Rahman has suggested, Avicenna employed the same term in a similar sense, and it is not unlikely that this is the way in which Maimonides understood Avicenna ... There is another aspect to the accidentality which Maimonides attributes to existence. To exist means to be actual. But everything that passes from a state of potentiality to that of actuality is caused to do so by some external agent ... It follows that existence is due to some external agent, and therefore accidental to the thing itself.

---

[88]   The term *mahiyah* (Hebrew: *mahut*, literally "whatness") is also usually translated as "essence," but since Ha-Levi uses two different terms, we translate it here as "quiddity."

[89]   The connection with Ibn Sina was first pointed out by Shem Tov ibn Falaquera in his commentary, *Moreh Ha-Moreh* ("The Guide to the Guide") 1:57. The connection was also pointed out by Moses Narboni.

[90]   See the discussion of Abraham ibn Da'ud in Ch. 7 (VII.4.d.i). For a detailed discussion of this concept, see Alexander Altmann, "Essence and Existence in Maimonides," in his *Studies in Religious Philosophy and Mysticism* (Ithaca: Cornell University Press, 1969), pp. 108–127), and F. Rahman, "Essence and Existence in Avicenna," in *Mediaeval and Renaissance Studies*, ed. R. Hunt, R. Klibansky, L. Labowsky (London, 1958), pp. 1–16. Also see the discussion of this concept in Ibn Sina in Shlomo Pines, "The Philosophic Sources of the *Guide of the Perplexed*," pp. xciii–ciii.

[91]   *Guide of the Perplexed* I:57.

[92]   Altmann, "Essence and Existence in Maimonides," pp. 114–115.

However, that which is not contingent on any agent or cause for its existence, but which is the cause of its own existence and of all other existence, is necessary. For example, when we define a chair as X, the definition (or "essence") does not include existence; we are asking what a chair is, not whether there is a chair. These are separate questions. Isaac Israeli's *Book of Definitions*, it will be recalled, had already differentiated between the question of whether something exists from the question of its essence, what it is.[93]

Existence is thus different from essence, and the existence of the chair is only possible; it is contingent upon the carpenter having manufactured it. This distinction between essence and existence, which applies to all contingent or possible beings, does not apply to the necessary being, where the existence is necessitated by, and is thus identical with, the essence. The term "existence" thus applies equivocally, Rambam insists, to God as the necessary existent and to all other existents which are contingent.

The notion that existence is an accident superadded to the essence of that which exists, which Rambam borrowed from Ibn Sina, was criticized by Shem Tov ibn Falaquera,[94] citing Ibn Rushd's critique of Ibn Sina.[95] Falaquera agrees that existence is "accidental" in the sense of being caused by something external to the essence of that which exists, except in the case of the necessary existent, whose existence is uncaused by any external agent because it is necessitated by its essence. However, Ibn Sina is wrong in asserting that unity and existence are added to the essence of things. By saying that something exists, we have not added anything to its essence, as we would, for instance, if we said that it is white. If we say that a chair exists, we have not added anything to its essence; its definition is the same as that of a chair that does not exist. If, however, we say that the chair is white, we have added the accident "white" to its essence, and the definition of the white chair will not be identical to the definition of a non-white chair. Moses Narboni also criticized Rambam for following Ibn Sina in this manner.[96] A contingent being is also necessary in one respect, because its agent or cause necessitates its existence. Its existence remains contingent, however, is another respect, because there is nothing in its own essence that necessitates its existence. The chair's existence is necessitated by the carpenter, not by the definition of chair. The necessary being, on the other hand, has no such external agent or cause, and its existence is necessitated by its own essence.

---

93   See the discussion in Ch. 3 (III.2.a).
94   Falaqauera, *Moreh Ha-Moreh* I:57.
95   Cf. Ibn Rushd, *Tahafut al-Tahafut*, Eighth Discussion, pp. 339 ff.; English translation by Simon Van Den Bergh, *Averroes' Tahafut al-Tahafut (The Incoherence of the Incoherence)* (London: Oxford University Press, 1954), pp. 240–241.
96   Moses Narboni, Commentary (*Be 'ur*) to *Guide of the Perplexed* I:57.

[IX.3.c]   THE "VIA NEGATIVA": CONCLUSION

At the beginning of our discussion of the "via negativa" we cited Isaac Husik's question why Rambam, in a sense, reversed the logical order of things, by dealing with the divine attributes before proving that there is a God. Husik's answer was that Rambam began with the most urgent problem troubling the perplexed student, and that problem was anthropomorphisms, and not the existence of God. That source of perplexity must be removed, he suggested, before we can proceed to the proofs of God in Part II. The discussion of the divine names follows logically from the negation of essential attributes, since all of God's names, besides the Tetragrammaton, are attributes of action. The Tetragrammaton would seem to violate the rule against positive essential attributes; properly understood, however, the Tetragrammaton does not convey positive knowledge of necessary existence, but has a negative content: necessary existence differs absolutely from contingent existence, and the term "existence" applies to both equivocally.

Part I of the *Guide of the Perplexed* thus began (in chapter 1) with the most egregious and obvious example of anthropomorphic language in the Bible, the term "image." The discussion of anthropomorphisms, attributes and names leads, then, to the most sophisticated and subtle of corporealist language applied to God, namely "existence." Even existence itself is now understood to be an equivocal term, when applied to God and when applied to all other being. The Tetragrammaton, then, which indicates necessary existence, is the end and climax of the negative way. As Rambam says, the necessary being "consequently exists, but not by existence" (Arabic: *fa-idha huwa maujud la bi-wujud*; Hebrew: *ve-im ken hu nimẓa lo bi-meẓi'ut*).

[IX.4]   ON GOD: THE "VIA POSITIVA"

[IX.4.a]   INTRODUCTION: THE LITERARY AND PEDAGOGIC CONTEXT OF RAMBAM'S PROOFS OF GOD

In order to understand Rambam's method in proving the existence, incorporeality and unity of God, we need to recall the didactic purpose and literary structure of the *Guide of the Perplexed*. The perplexed student, as we saw, doubts the truth of the Torah because of his belief in the Aristotelian philosophy to which he had been exposed. Like Judah Ha-Levi's archetypal philosopher in the *Kuzari*, Rambam's perplexed student accepts Aristotelian doctrines as given, as a kind of "closed system," even when those doctrines had not actually been conclusively demonstrated. In Rambam's view, for example, Aristotle not only had not demonstrated the eternity of the world, but never claimed to have proven it. Nevertheless, the perplexed student accepted Aristotelian doctrines on authority, and doubted traditional religious doctrines such as creation. The pedagogic challenge, then, is to address the perplexed student on his own ground, at least provisionally, by accepting for the sake of argument his presuppositions.

Rambam's pedagogic method is thus built in stages. The first stage is the negative way in the first part of the *Guide of the Perplexed*: to correct the perplexed student's misunderstanding of biblical anthropomorphisms, from the term "image" (in Ch. 1) to the discussion of the Tetragrammaton and necessary existence near the end of the terminological section of Part I.

Then, in the Introduction to Part II, Rambam moves to the second pedagogic stage of the book, by addressing the student on his own ground: in order to prove God's existence, incorporeality and unity, Rambam accepts provisionally and for the sake of argument, the Aristotelian doctrine of eternity. The third pedagogic stage only comes later—after the discussion of the proofs of God has been completed—when Rambam argues that Aristotle had not, in fact, proven eternity, and had not even claimed to have proven it. Although Rambam acknowledges that the question of eternity or creation cannot ultimately be resolved conclusively, the theory of creation (as we shall see) is preferable, because it is only in a created universe that revelation is possible. This third stage, then, sets the stage for the fourth pedagogic stage, the life of Torah and the practical final purpose of life.

Rambam's decision to base his proofs of God on eternity rather than on creation (as Sa'adiah Ga'on had done) reflects not only these pedagogic considerations—addressing the student on his own Aristotelian ground—but also methodological considerations, which Rambam explains at the outset of his critical discussion of the Kalam, in the *Guide of the Perplexed* I:71. Proofs based on creation are valid only if, in the final analysis, it turns out that the world is actually created. If it should turn out that the world is actually eternal, the proofs based on creation would be invalid. In other words, proofs based on creation are only valid in the one case, not in both cases. Proofs based on eternity, however, are valid in both cases. If the world turns out to be eternal, the proofs are valid. If, on the other hand, the world turns out to be created, the proofs are all the more valid, since if an eternal world necessitates a prime cause or first mover, a created world certainly needs an agent who caused (i.e., created) it. Even if these proofs were not valid, a created universe obviously implies a creator. Proofs of the existence, incorporeality and unity of God should thus be based on "the methods of the philosophers...based on the eternity of the world...The reason is not that I believe in eternity, but that I wish to established in our belief the existence of God by a demonstrative method, regarding which there is no disagreement."[97]

---

[97]   *Guide of the Perplexed* I:71.

At the conclusion of his critical discussion of the Kalam, at the very end of Part I of the *Guide*, Rambam reiterates this method of proving God's existence, incorporeality and unity: he accepts the philosophers' presupposition of the eternity of the world for the sake of the argument, "although we do not believe it."[98]

Although Rambam does not say this, in effect, his method constitutes an attempt to bridge the gap between what Judah Ha-Levi called "the God of Aristotle" and "the God of Abraham." What is proved on the basis of eternity in *Guide of the Perplexed* II:1 is an Aristotelian first mover or prime cause or necessary being. What follows later—the preference for the theory of creation—makes possible the revelation of the Torah, at which point Rambam has made the transition from "the God of Aristotle" to "the God of Abraham" who creates the world and reveals his Torah to humans.

A final methodological note: when Rambam refers to a first mover or prime cause, it is not "first" in a temporal sense, since in an eternal world as envisaged by Aristotle, there can be no temporal "first." What is meant here by "first" is logical priority in nature, not in time. For example, since a triangle consists of three lines, one can say that the lines are logically prior to the triangle (which could not be conceived without them), but not that they are prior to it in time. The "first mover" or "prime cause" is not the temporal "first" link in an eternal chain of movers or causes (in which case the chain would not be eternal, since it would have a "first" beginning), but a logical first mover or cause above the entire chain, without which the entire causal chain could not exist. What is proved, therefore, is not that the world has a beginning (i.e., is created) but that there cannot be an infinite regress of causes or movers.

[IX.4.b] CRITICISM OF RAMBAM'S METHOD

Rambam's decision to prove the existence, incorporeality and unity of God on the basis of eternity—despite his explicit disavowal of belief in eternity—was sharply criticized. How can one base a true proof on premises one rejects from the outset as false? The criticism is all the more poignant for its having been leveled by a rationalist philosopher who defended Rambam in the late 13th-century controversy over philosophy, Shem Tov ibn Falaquera:

> I say that one must question how something great like this can be explained on the basis of something dubious, let alone if that thing is not true, for if the premises of a proof are not true, how can its conclusion be true?... There is no doubt that our teacher [Rambam] was aware of this.[99]

---

[98]   *Guide of the Perplexed* I:76.

[99]   Falaquera, *Moreh Ha-Moreh* I:71. For a complete discussion of this, see my *Torah and Sophia: The Life and Thought of Shem Tov ibn Falaquera*, pp. 156–164.

Another commentator, Joseph ibn Kaspi (1279–1340 C.E.), perhaps reflecting Falaquera's criticism and comment that Rambam was aware of the problem, suggested that Rambam deliberately deviated from correct logical method:

> Although it is known in logic that a true result can be derived from false premises, this is not a proof. It is known that a proof consists of true and necessary general premises. There is no doubt that our teacher [Rambam] was aware of this.[100]

Rambam's methodological decision was thus controversial, not only because it adopted a position at variance with religious tradition, but, in the eyes of his rationalist followers, because it violated the rules of logic, a violation they concluded must have been deliberate.

[IX.4.c] THE TWENTY-SIX PREMISES OF THE PROOFS OF GOD (*Guide* II:INTRODUCTION)

In the Introduction to Part II of the *Guide*, Rambam lists twenty-six premises of Aristotelian physics and metaphysics necessary to establish his four proofs of God's existence, incorporeality and unity. The first twenty-five of them "have been demonstrated and cannot be doubted on any point, because Aristotle and the Peripatetics after him demonstrated each of them." Therefore, there is no need for further discussion or demonstration of these premises. The twenty-sixth premise, namely the eternity of time and motion (and thus of the universe) is accepted for the purpose of the argument. It had not been demonstrated — nor could it have been demonstrated conclusively, as we shall see later — by Aristotle, nor did Aristotle actually claim to have demonstrated it. Rather, he was only of the opinion that eternity is the most probable explanation; his Peripatetic followers, on the other hand, claimed that the premise of eternity had been demonstrated.

Rambam's claim that the twenty-five premises had been conclusively demonstrated and could not be doubted was rejected by many later Jewish philosophers and commentators on the *Guide of the Perplexed*. For example, Shem Tov ibn Shem Tov commented:

> What the Rabbi said, that all of these twenty-five premises have been demonstrated and cannot be doubted on any point, is incorrect. Some of the premises are first intelligible, some are dubious, and some are false and can be proven wrong. Only a few are demonstrably true.[101]

---

100   Joseph ibn Kaspi, *'Amudei Kesef U-Maskiyot Kesef* (ed. S. Werbluner, 1848), p. 72.
101   Shem Tov ibn Shem Tov, Commentary to *Guide of the Perplexed* II:Introduction.

The premises were also subjected to penetrating analysis and detailed criticism by Ḥasdai Crescas (c. 1340–1410) in his *Light of the Lord (Or Adonai)*.[102] We shall cite some of these criticisms.

(1) THE EXISTENCE OF AN INFINITE MAGNITUDE IS IMPOSSIBLE

This premise is based on Aristotle's Physics (III:4–8), Metaphysics (XI:10) and De Caelo (I:5–7). The premise negates the possibility of an actual infinite magnitude, not a potential one. What needs to be kept in mind is that people tend to treat infinity as a large number or quantity, which is actually a contradiction in terms, because at any given moment one can never reach an actual infinite magnitude, since by definition, the infinite is always expanding and one can always continue to add to it. What exists in actuality at any given moment may be a huge magnitude, but it is never infinite.

On the other hand, the eleventh of the twelve principles of the Kalam that Rambam discussed in the *Guide of the Perplexed* I:71 is a denial of any infinity, even potential.[103] Following Aristotle, Rambam affirms the possibility of a potential infinite magnitude (since one can always potentially continue to increase the magnitude), but never of an actual infinite magnitude, quantity or regress of causes.

Ḥasdai Crescas, however, argued that Aristotle erred in believing that an actual infinity is impossible because he maintained that the world is a continuum, and denied the existence of a vacuum. Although the Aristotelians deny the existence of a vacuum, they believe the world is a finite body. Since that finite body is not surrounded by another body, it is surrounded by an incorporeal void (or: vacuum), which also has magnitude, but is not limited by any surrounding body, and thus extends infinitely. "It has thus been shown that on their own premises an infinite incorporeal magnitude must exist."[104]

Rambam, following Aristotle, thus affirms a potential infinite magnitude but denies an actual one. The Mutakallimun denied even a potential infinite magnitude, and Crescas affirmed even an actual infinite magnitude.

(2) AN INFINITE NUMBER OF MAGNITUDES CANNOT EXIST TOGETHER

The second premise follows from the first. Potentially an infinite number of magnitudes could exist sequentially, but not simultaneously ("together"),

---

[102]   Crescas' detailed and often technical analysis was translated into English, with copious notes and commentary, by Harry Wolfson, *Crescas' Critique of Aristotle: Problems of Aristotle's Physics in Jewish and Arabic Philosophy* (Cambridge: Harvard University Press, 1929).

[103]   See the discussion in Ch. 2 (II.1.c).

[104]   Wolfson, *Crescas' Critique of Aristotle*, p. 189.

because there would then be an actual infinite magnitude. Conversely, Crescas argued that since the first premise is false, so is the second.[105]

(3) AN INFINITE SERIES OF CAUSES AND EFFECTS IS IMPOSSIBLE, EVEN IF THEY HAVE NO MAGNITUDE

The impossibility of an infinity in actuality applies not only to material magnitude but also to a causal series, even if the series is immaterial (such as a series of intellects). This premise is based on Aristotle's Metaphysics (II:2) on the impossibility of a series of causes, whether material, final or formal. If one were to posit an infinite series of causes, there could not be a first or final cause, since infinity has neither beginning nor end. Thus all the causes would, by definition, have to be intermediate. But an intermediate cause, also by definition, has to have causes before and after it. Since, however, there can be no first or final cause, there cannot be causes all of which are intermediate. An infinite series of causes thus cannot exist.

Crescas argues that what is precluded is only an ordered or ranked series, but that an accidental series is possible, and that Rambam agreed that an infinite series can exist if the parts of the series are unrelated causally and do not exist simultaneously.[106] What Crescas means here is that there cannot be an actual infinite regress of causes of a single effect, but a single cause can led to a potential infinity of effects. The third principle thus only limits the causes, not the effects. This technical point has important implications for the belief in intellectual immortality, because it means that in an eternal world—as affirmed by Aristotle and as presumed for the sake of argument by Rambam—an infinite number of surviving intellects is possible.

(4) CHANGE OCCURS IN FOUR CATEGORIES: IN SUBSTANCE (GENERATION AND CORRUPTION); IN QUANTITY (INCREASE AND DECRESE); IN QUALITY (ALTERATION); AND IN PLACE (LOCOMOTION)

The fourth premise is based on Aristotle's Metaphysics (XII:2). Locomotion (i.e., motion in place) is one kind of change, according to this. However, in Greek *kinesis* means both change and motion. Nevertheless, "change" is a more general term denoting any kind of transition, whereas "motion" is used in the narrower sense. Substance undergoes the change of generation and corruption, but not motion. Quantity, quality and place undergo both change and motion. Change can be in time or not in time, but motion is in time, and in fact, is part of the definition of time, as we have seen. In short, all motion is change, but not all change is motion.

---

105   See Wolfson, *Crescas' Critique of Aristotle*, p. 218.
106   See Wolfson, *Crescas' Critique of Aristotle*, p. 224.

(5) ALL MOTION IS A CHANGE AND TRANSITION FROM POTENTIALITY TO ACTUALITY

The fifth premise is based on Aristotle's Physics (III:1–2) and Metaphysics (XI:9). Crescas understands Rambam to mean here that motion is neither completely actual nor completely potential, but is the transition between from potentiality to actuality. Both Crescas and Ralbag[107] emphasize that the change occurs in the object acted upon, and not in the agent of the change. The carpenter thus changes the wood from potential table to actual table, but only the wood undergoes the change, not the carpenter.

(6) MOTIONS MAY BE ESSENTIAL, ACCIDENTAL, VIOLENT OR OF A PART

This premise is based on Aristotle's Physics (IV:4 and VIII:4). An example of essential motion is the locomotion of a body. An example of accidental motion is the locomotion of the body's color when the body is moved from place to place. An example of violent motion is a stone thrown up by some force. An example of motion of a part is that of a nail in a moving boat.

(7) EVERYTHING CHANGEABLE IS DIVISIBLE. EVERYTHING MOVABLE IS DIVISIBLE AND THUS A BODY. EVERYTHING INDIVISIBLE IS NOT MOVABLE AND IS THUS NOT A BODY.

The seventh premise is based on Aristotle's Physics (VI:4), according to which something changeable must be divisible, because during the process of change it contains a part that has already changed, and another part that has not yet changed. Whatever is divisible is a body; change is thus an affection of divisible bodies.

(8) EVERYTHING MOVED ACCIDENTALLY NECESSARILY COMES TO REST, SINCE ITS MOTION IS NOT ON ACCOUNT OF ITS ESSENCE. ACCIDENTAL MOTION THUS CANNOT CONTINUE FOREVER.

The source of the eighth premise is Aristotle's Physics (VIII:5) and Metaphysics (IX:4). Accidental motion is causes by an external mover; in the absence of that mover, the motion ceases. Whatever moves accidentally must, therefore, eventually come to rest. Crescas rejects this conclusion, and argues that if, for example, a sphere rotates eternally, a body on that sphere, such a stone on the moon, would move accidentally but also eternally.[108]

---

[107]   Ralbag = Rabbi Levi ben Gershom (Gersonides, b. 1344). See *Wars of the Lord* 6:1, ch. 24, and the discussion in Wolfson, *Crescas' Critique of Aristotle*, pp. 233–235, 528–529.

[108]   See the discussion in Wolfson, *Crescas' Critique of Aristotle*, pp. 249–253.

(9) ANY BODY WHICH MOVES ANOTHER BODY
    IS THEREBY ALSO MOVED.

The ninth premise is based on Aristotle's Physics (VIII:5) and Metaphysics (XII:6). Crescas, following Moses Narboni,[109] argues that the premise only applies to an efficient cause, and is not applicable to a final cause, which moves without thereby being moved.[110]

(10) WHATEVER EXISTS IN A BODY EITHER SUBSISTS (LIKE
     ACCIDENTS) IN THE BODY, OR (LIKE THE NATURAL FORM)
     THE BODY SUBSISTS THROUGH IT. BOTH ARE A FORCE IN A BODY.

This premise is based on Aristotle's Physics (Book I). Accidents, as we have seen,[111] have no independent existence, but subsist in the body bearing them. Substance, however, is a combination of form and matter, and it is the natural form which defines the matter as this specific substance.

(11) SOME THINGS SUBSISTING IN A BODY ARE DIVISIBLE
     ACCIDENTALLY WITH THE DIVISION OF THE BODY (SUCH AS
     A BODY'S COLOR), AND OTHERS (LIKE THE SOUL AND INTELLECT)
     CONSTITUTE THE BODY AND ARE INDIVISIBLE.

Soul and intellect, being immaterial, are indivisible. Rambam's phrasing here is careful: accidents "subsist in a body," but the soul and intellect, as the natural form of a body, do not subsist in a body, but rather "constitute the body."

(12) EVERY FORCE DISTRIBUTED IN A BODY IS FINITE
     BECAUSE THE BODY IS FINITE.

This premise has its source is Aristotle's Physics (VIII:10). Bodies are, by definition, finite, and a finite body cannot contain an infinite force. Moreover, the force is divisible according to the division of the body.

(13) CHANGE CANNOT BE CONTINUOUS, EXCEPT FOR LOCOMOTION,
     AND THEN ONLY CIRCULAR LOCOMOTION.

According to this premise, which is based on Aristotle's Physics (VIII:7–8), only circular locomotion (like the rotations of the spheres) can be continuous and perpetual. All other change, including linear motion, encounters an opposite force and thus must come to a stop. Circular motion, however, has no opposing force or motion, and thus may be continuous and perpetual.

---

109 Moses Narboni, Commentary to *Guide of the Perplexed* II:Introduction, p. 22. See the discussion in Wolfson, *Crescas' Critique of Aristotle*, pp. 561–568.
110 See the discussion in Wolfson, *Crescas' Critique of Aristotle*, pp. 253–257.
111 See the discussion in Ch. 2 (II.1.c) and (II.3.d.iii).

(14) LOCOMOTION IS PRIOR TO OTHER MOTION AND FIRST IN
NATURE. GENERATION AND CORRUPTION ARE PRECEDED BY
ALTERATION, AND ALTERATION IS PRECEDED BY THE APPROACH
OF THAT WHICH ALTERS TO THAT WHICH IS ALTERED. ALSO,
GROWTH AND DIMINUTION ARE PRECEDED BY GENERATION
AND CORRUPTION.

The fourteenth premise is also based on Aristotle's Physics (VIII:7–8). The
agent of change must approach it in order to act on it. Locomotion thus must
be prior in nature and in time to other change and motion. Crescas objects
that this premise is only valid for continous generation. In a world created *ex
nihilo*, however, there can be no such approaching something which does not
yet exist, and generation is thus the first motion.[112]

(15) TIME IS AN ACCIDENT CONSEQUENT ON, AND ATTACHED TO,
MOTION. NEITHER EXISTS WITHOUT THE OTHER. MOTION ONLY
EXISTS IN TIME, AND TIME CANNOT BE CONCEIVED WITHOUT
MOTION. WHATEVER EXISTS WITHOUT MOTION APPLYING TO IT,
DOES NOT FALL UNDER THE CATEGORY OF TIME.

This premise is based on Aristotle's Physics (IV:12) and De Caelo (I:9). In
Guide of the Perplexed I:52 Rambam had already defined time as an accident
consequent on motion. According to Crescas, time has no independent
existence, because it is divided into past and future. The past no longer exists,
and the future does not yet exist. The present also does not exist, because it
is a passing moment. Time thus must subsist in something which does exist,
namely motion.[113] Later, however, Crescas rejects this definition, because time
also applies to the interludes of rest between motions. Aristotle had already
taken this objection concerning rest into account, because time is not the
motion itself but the measure of the motion. Crescas thus did not take into
account that the interludes of rest between motions can also be measured by
comparing them to the continuous motion of something else.

(16) WHATEVER HAS NO BODY CANNOT BE CONCEIVED AS HAVING
NUMBER, UNLESS IT IS A FORCE IN A BODY, IN WHICH CASE
THE FORCES WOULD BE NUMBERED ACCORDING TO THE NUMBER
OF THE MATTER OR SUBSTRATA IN WHICH THEY SUBSIST.
THEREFORE, SEPARATE BEINGS, WHICH ARE NOT BODIES
OR FORCES IN BODIES, DO NOT HAVE NUMBER, UNLESS THEY
ARE RELATED AS CAUSE AND EFFECT.

According to this premise, based on Aristotle's Metaphysics (XII:8), with the
exception of causes and effects, number is only conceivable in a body or force
in a body.

---

112   See the discussion in Wolfson, *Crescas' Critique of Aristotle*, p. 282.
113   See the discussion in Wolfson, *Crescas' Critique of Aristotle*, pp. 282–288.

(17) EVERYTHING IN MOTION MUST HAVE A MOVER. THE MOVER MAY BE EXTERNAL (AS IS THE CASE WITH A STONE MOVED BY A HAND) OR INTERNAL (AS IS THE CASE WITH THE BODY OF AN ANIMAL WHICH COMBINES THE MOVER AND WHAT IS MOVED). THE INTERNAL MOVER OF AN ANIMAL, I.E., ITS SOUL, EXTENDS THROUGHOUT THE BODY OF THE ANIMAL, WHICH THUS MOVES ESSENTIALLY. WHEN THE ANIMAL DIES AND ITS SOUL IS LACKING, ITS BODY IS NO LONGER MOVED.

The seventeenth premise is based on Aristotle's Physics (VII:1), according to which matter is incapable of moving or changing itself. Every moving body must, therefore, have an internal or external agent causing its motion.

(18) EVERYTHING THAT PASSES FROM POTENTIALITY TO ACTUALITY MUST HAVE AN AGENT OF THAT TRANSITION, AND THE AGENT MUST BE EXTERNAL TO IT. IF THE AGENT IS INTERNAL, IN THE ABSENCE OF ANY OBSTACLE THE THING WOULD ALWAYS HAVE BEEN ACTUAL. HOWEVER, IF THERE WAS AN OBSTACLE WHICH WAS REMOVED, THE AGENT REMOVING IT IS THUS THE AGENT OF THE TRANSITION OF THE THING FROM POTENTIALITY TO ACTUALITY.

This premise is indirectly based on Aristotle's Physics (III:1–2) and Metaphysics (XI:9), and is a continuation of premise #17. Just as every motion must have a mover, so every transition from potentiality to actuality must have an agent.

(19) EVERYTHING WHICH HAS A CAUSE OF ITS EXISTENCE HAS ITSELF ONLY POSSIBLE EXISTENCE, BECAUSE IF ITS CAUSE IS PRESENT, IT WILL EXIST, AND IF ITS CAUSE IS ABSENT OR HAS CHANGED, IT WILLNOT EXIST.

According to Wolfson,[114] premises #19, 20 and 21 are not based on Aristotle but on Ibn Sina. In the discussion of necessary existence above,[115] we saw that all contingent being is dependent upon an external cause, whereas necessary being has no such cause. Contingent beings are essentially possible, because their essence does not necessitate their existence, and their existence is additional to their essence. If contingent beings are in any respect necessary, they are only necessary in respect of the cause of their existence.

(20) WHATEVER EXISTS NECESSARILY BECAUSE OF ITS OWN ESSENCE HAS NO CAUSE OF ITS EXISTENCE.

This premise follows from and completes the previous premise.

---

[114] See the discussion in Wolfson, *Crescas' Critique of Aristotle*, pp. 303, 680–684.

[115] See above, IX.3.b.

(21) WHATEVER IS COMPOUNDED OF TWO NOTIONS NECESSARILY
HAS THAT COMPOUND AS THE CAUSE OF ITS EXISTENCE. IT
CANNOT, THEREFORE, EXIST NECESSARILY BECAUSE OF ITS OWN
ESSENCE, BECAUSE IT EXISTS IN VIRTUE OF THE TWO ELEMENTS
AND OF THEIR COMPOSITION.

The necessary existent cannot be compound for two reasons. First, the act of
compounding something out of its elements requires an agent and the necessary
being has no agent acting on it and causing its existence. Second, the existence
of a compound depends on the existence of its parts, and these parts or elements
are, therefore, prior to it and cause its compound existence.

(22) EVERY BODY IS COMPOSED OF TWO THINGS—ITS MATTER
AND ITS FORM—AND IS ACCOMPANIED BY ACCIDENTS, NAMELY
QUANTITY, SHAPE AND POSITION.

According to Aristotle's Categories (VIII:10–12), substance is matter and form
together; they are only separated when abstracted in our thought, and not in
reality. As we have already seen, substance cannot exist without accidents.[116]

(23) WHATEVER EXISTS POTENTIALLY AND HAS POSSIBILITY IN ITS
ESSENCE, MAY, AT SOME TIME, NOT EXIST IN ACTUALITY.

This premise is based on Aristotle's Metaphysics (Book IX). Rambam uses
two terms here that are related but not identical: possibility (Arabic: *imkan*;
Hebrew: *efsharut*) and potentiality (literally: "power"; Arabic: *quwah*; Hebrew:
ko'ah). Wolfson explains that both these terms are translations of the Greek
dynamis, but refer to different connotations of the word. "Potentiality" is the
opposite of "actuality," whereas "possibility" is the opposite of "impossibility"
and "necessity."[117]

Rambam discussed these terms in his letter to Samuel ibn Tibbon (in 1290
C.E.), regarding the Hebrew translation of the *Guide of the Perplexed*. In the
letter, he says that the difference between possibility and potentiality very
subtle and difficult, even for expert philosophers. Forms exist potentially in
the matter disposed to receive them, and the matter contains the possibility of
receiving those forms. In Rambam's own example, the sword exists potentially
in the iron, and the iron contains the possibility of being made into a sword.

The next premise also deals with possibility. Since possibility exists in
the matter disposed to receive the forms that potentially exists in it, Rambam
concludes that possibility only exists in matter, and whatever is possible must
be material.

---

[116] See the discussion of accidents in connection with Sa'adiah Ga'on's third proof of creation
in Ch. 2 (II.3.d.iii).

[117] See the discussion in Wolfson, *Crescas' Critique of Aristotle*, pp. 690–693.

(24) WHATEVER IS POTENTIALLY SOMETHING MUST BE MATERIAL,
BECAUSE POSSIBILITY IS ALWAYS IN MATTER.
This premise is based on Aristotle's Metaphysics (XII:2).

(25) THE PRINCIPLES OF AN INDIVIDUAL COMPOUND SUBSTANCE
ARE MATTER AND FORM. THERE MUST BE AN AGENT, I.E. A MOVER,
TO MOVE THE SUBSTRATUM AND PREDISPOSE IT TO RECEIVE
A CERTAIN FORM. THIS IS THE PROXIMATE MOVER WHICH
PREDISPOSES THE MATTER OF AN INDIVIDUAL. ACCORDING TO
ARISTOTLE, MATTER CANNOT MOVE ITSELF. THIS PREMISE, THEN,
LEADS TO THE INVESTIGATION OF THE PRIME MOVER.
The twenty-fifth principle is based on Aristotle's Metaphysics (I:3, XII:6). The
connection of form to matter requires an external agent, and its action is a kind
of motion, which requires a mover.

These are the twenty-five premises necessary, according to Rambam, to
establish the proofs of God's existence, incorporeality and unity. All of them
have been conclusively demonstrated and cannot be doubted. To these he then
adds the twenty-sixth premise—eternity—which, he asserts, Aristotle did
not claim to have proven, but merely offered it as his opinion regarding what
was most probably true. Rambam agrees that it is possibly true. Aristotle's
followers, however, regarded this opinion as necessarily true, not possibly
true, and the Mutakallimun regarded it as impossible.

(26) TIME AND MOTION ARE ETERNAL, PERPETUAL, AND EXIST
IN ACTUALITY. THEREFORE, THERE MUST BE A BODY MOVING
ETERNALLY IN ACTUALITY, NAMELY THE FIFTH SUBSTANCE,[118]
WHICH IS NOT SUBJECT TO GENERATION AND CORRUPTION.
ACCORDING TO THIS PREMISE, A FINITE BODY MOVES ALONG
A FINITE PATH AN INFINITE NUMBER OF TIMES, WHICH IS
POSSIBLE BECAUSE THE MOTION IS CIRCULAR, AS EXPLAINED IN
THE THIRTEENTH PREMISE. THE INFINITE THUS MUST EXIST IN
A SUCCESSION, AND NOT SIMULTANEOUSLY.
The twenty-sixth premise is based on Aristotle's Physics (VIII:1–2) and
Metaphysics (XII:6). As Rambam will discuss later (in *Guide of the Perplexed*
II:14), according to Aristotle, there can never be a first motion, because if we
assume a first motion, the transition from rest (the lack of motion) to the first
motion would itself constitute a motion, in which case there would be a motion
before the first motion. Motion must, therefore, be eternal. However, Rambam
will only return to the question of eternity and creation after presenting his
proofs of God's existence, incorporeality and unity based on eternity.

---

[118]   In addition to the four terrestrial elements—earth, water, air and fire—there is a "fifth
substance" finer than fire, which is the susbstance of the heavenly spheres.

[IX.4.d] RAMBAM'S PROOFS OF GOD (*Guide* II:1)

[IX.4.d.i] *The First Proof: The Prime Mover*

Rambam's first proof of God's existence, incorporeality and unity, and presumes the eternal motion of the concentric heavenly spheres (premise #26), based on the geocentric cosmology Rambam described in *Guide of the Perplexed* I:72, in which the outermost sphere revolves at the fastest rate. These spheres, it will be recalled, consist of the material "fifth substance," and are living bodies endowed with souls. The motions of the inner spheres are derived, ultimately, from the motion of the outermost sphere, but what causes its motion? Rambam's first proof is constructed in stages. It begins with this problem, namely the prime mover of the outermost sphere. The second stage of the proof deals with what kind of mover the prime mover must be, by negating several possibilities: a body outside the outermost sphere, a divisible force within the sphere, an indivisible force within the sphere (like the soul in the body). Having negated these possibilities, the conclusion is that the prime mover must be incorporeal and separate from the outermost sphere.

The proof is based on Aristotle's Physics (Book VIII). We need to keep in mind that in modern Newtonian physics, a constant force produces acceleration, not a constant rate (i.e., velocity). This principle applies in the vacuum of space, in the absence of friction. In space, an object will continue at a constant rate because of its momentum, without any additional force. Aristotelian physics, however, which did not admit the existence of the vacuum, posited a constant force as necessary for a fixed rate (and not for acceleration). The fixed motion of the spheres thus requires, according to Aristotle, a constant motive force, and since the motion is eternal, the force must also be eternal, and being eternal, the force is thus infinite.

The first proof, then, consists of the following arguments. Matter, according to premise #25, must have a proximate mover, but what moves the proximate mover? There cannot be an infinite series of causes, according to premise #3. All motion and change ultimately go back to the locomotion of the outermost sphere, and locomotion is the primary motion, according to premise #14. What, then, moves the outermost sphere? It, too, must have a mover, according to premise #17. The mover of the sphere may be in it or outside it. If the mover is external to the sphere, it must be either corporeal or incorporeal. If it is incorporeal, it is not "outside" the body but "separate" from it. If the mover of the sphere is within the sphere, either it is a divisible force extending throughout the sphere (like the heat of fire), or it is an indivisible force extending throughout the sphere (like the soul and intellect in the body), according to premise #10. The mover of the sphere must, therefore, be one of the following: (a) a body outside the sphere, (b) incorporeal and separate from the sphere, (c) a divisible force within the sphere, (d) an indivisible force within the sphere.

The mover of the outermost sphere cannot be (a) a body outside the sphere, because a body which moves another body is moved in the process, according to premise #9, and we would thus end up with an infinite number of moving bodies, which is impossible, according to premise #2. The mover of the sphere also cannot be (c) a divisible force within the sphere. This is also impossible, because the sphere, being a body, is finite, and its force would then also have to be finite, according to premise #12, and would be divisible along with it, according to premise #11. A finite force, however, could not move the sphere endlessly, according to premise #25. The mover of the sphere also cannot be (d), an indivisible force within the sphere (like a person's soul in his body), because it would then move accidentally together with the sphere, according to premise #6. However, whatever moves accidentally also must, at some point, come to rest, according to premise #8, in which case it could not move the sphere eternally. Since the motion of the sphere, being circular, can be continuous and eternal, according to premise #13, the mover of the outermost sphere must be (b) incorporeal and separate from the sphere. As such, it is not subject itself to motion or change or division, according to premises #7 and #5. The prime mover of the sphere must therefore be the first cause, namely God. Being incorporeal and separate, the prime mover is not subject to multiplicity, according to premise #16, and since it is not subject to motion, it does not fall under the category of time, according to premise #15. We have thus demonstrated, Rambam concludes, that the sphere does not move itself, that its motion is due to the prime mover, which is not a body or a force in a body, that it is one and unchanging, and does not exist in time.

[IX.4.d.ii] *The Second Proof: The Unmoved Mover*

Rambam's second proof of God's existence, incorporeality and unity is draws from several sources in Aristotle, including the Metaphysics (XII:7) and Physics (VIII:5) and De Anima (III:10). It is based on what may be called the postulate of logical symmetry. It initially proves that there must be at least one unmoved mover, and ultimately that there cannot be more than one unmoved mover. According to its postulate of logical symmetry, if the compound AB exists, and we find that element A exists independently, without element B, then element B must also be able to exist independently, without element A. We find that there are movers which are also moved, such as a hand moving a pen. We also find that there are things, such as the pen, which are moved without moving anything else. Therefore, there must be at least one thing which moves without being moved (an "unmoved mover"). Being unmoved, it cannot be corporeal (since any body which moves something else is moved in the process). Being incorporeal, the unmoved mover is, according, simple, and thus there can only be one unmoved mover.[119] Being incorporeal, as we saw in the first proof, the unmoved mover also is not subject to the category of time.

Unless we wish to assume that we have here a case of a deliberate contradiction or "divergence" in Rambam's thought, we must question the validity of the postulate of logical symmetry by his own standards. The human being is a combination of body and soul. As we saw in Chapter Eight, the only immortality is that of the rational soul, in proportion to the knowledge it attains, which survives the death of the body (albeit impersonally), and, as Rambam emphasized in his discussion of resurrection, the dead body decomposes into its constituent elements. This means, however, that we have a compound AB (a living body and soul), and we have B (the rational soul) existing independently of A (the dead body), but we do not find A (the body) continuing to exist independently after its separation from B (the soul); the body disintegrates. So it the postulate of logical symmetry valid, by Rambam's own standards?

Ralbag[120] rejected the postulate of logical symmetry. In his view, form cannot exists without matter, but that does not mean that matter cannot exist without form. As he argued in his *Wars of the Lord*:[121]

> Moreover, Aristotle's [other] argument for the existence of an unmoved mover, i.e., when two things are compounded together such that one of them exists separately, the other also exists separately — is not adequate. It has indeed been proven in the sciences that whatever functions as matter can be separated from whatever functions as form: but the form cannot be separated from that which serves as matter for it. Hence, it does not follow from this argument that there exists a [separate] unmoved mover; for it is possible that there be a thing that is moved but does not itself move [something else], since that which is moved serves as a matter for the thing that moves it. But this does not entail that there exists a mover that does not itself move; for the mover serves as form to the moved object, and whatever serves as form cannot be separated from the matter of which it is the form... For example, the sensitive soul serves as form to the nutritive soul; but whereas the former cannot exist without the latter, the latter can exist without the former in plants.

---

[119] For an explanation of simplicity or internal unity, and that internal unity and external (i.e., quantitative or numerical) unity necessitate each other, review the discussion in Ch. 2 (II.3.g).

[120] See note 107, above.

[121] Levi ben Gershom (Gersonides), *The Wars of the Lord*, 5:3, ch. 6; annotated English translation by Seymour Feldman, vol. 3, (Philadelphia: Jewish Publication Society, 1999), pp. 150–151.

[IX.4.d.iii] *The Third Proof: The Necessary Being*

Unlike the other proofs, the third proof is not cosmological, and so far as we know is based not on Aristotle but on Ibn Sina (in accordance with premises #19, #20 and #21), despite Rambam's explicit acknowledgement that this proof is based on the words of Aristotle. The argument in this case is not cosmological, i.e., based on an examination of the real world about us, but metaphysical — it is based on an analysis of being as such, and the distinction between contingent (or possible) existence and necessary existence. The proof also presupposes that in an eternal world, whatever is possible "with regard to a species" must, at some point, come to be. As Rambam explained in his letter to Samuel ibn Tibbon, if something possible does not become actualized within a given span of time, there is no problem. But if, over all of eternity, something possible does not become actualized, then we can no longer claim that it is possible, and must conclude that it really was impossible to begin with.

The third proof argues along the following lines. We see that things exist. There are three possibilities regarding existing things: (a) nothing that exists is subject to generation and corruption; (b) everything that exists is subject to generation and corruption; (c) some things that exist are subject, and some others are not subject, to generation and corruption. It is clear that the first possibility, that nothing is subject to generation and corruption, is false, since we constantly witness generation and corruption. The second possibility, that everything is subject to generation and corruption, is also false, because whatever is possible with regard to a species must, at some time, actually occur. So if everything is subject to generation and corruption, then at some time everything must have not existed, i.e., nothing existed. Since we exist, that is not true now. Nor is that possibility, that nothing existed, consistent with an eternal universe that always exists.

Having negated the first possibility — that nothing is subject to generation and corruption — and the second possibility — that everything is subject to generation and corruption, we must conclude that the third possibility is true — that some things are subject to generation and corruption, but that there must be at least one thing that is not subject to generation and corruption. Something that exists, but which has no possibility whatsoever of corruption (i.e., ceasing to exist), exists necessarily; its existence is necessary, not contingent. Its existence is uncaused (according to premise #20); since compounds are caused by the conjunction of their elements (according to premise #21) the necessary being is simple, not compound. Not being compound, it cannot be a body or a force in a body (since bodies are compounded of matter and form, according to premise #22). The necessary being must, therefore, be simple. We said that there must be at least one necessary being, but by its necessity and simplicity we conclude that there can only be one.

Rambam concludes that "there can be no doubt or refutation or dispute about this demonstration, except by a person ignorant of the method of demonstration"—a claim he does not make about the other three proofs. Despite this assurance, his fundamental presupposition that something possible must, at some point over eternity, come to be, remains problematical. His claim is explicitly on the level of genera ("with regard to a species"), and not with regard to particular, individual members of that species. But that does not mean that all the individuals actualize that possibility simultaneously. For example, all human beings are subject to generation and corruption—every person is born and dies. But not all people are born or die simultaneously, and the human species would only cease to exist if all people were dead together, at the same time (even if they did not all die at the same moment). While it is inevitably true that death awaits all people, so long as they are all not dead at the same time, the human race continues to exist. So long as some individuals survive, the species survives. In the example Rambam gave in his letter to Samuel ibn Tibbon, the human ability to write is generic, and does not imply that every person knows how to write, nor that a specific individual can write, but only that "some person writes at some time." There is certainly no implication that the generic human ability to write applies to all people, let alone to all people together, simultaneously. As Crescas pointed out, Rambam's second possibility, that everything is subject to generation and corruption, may only apply generically, whereas his conclusion—that at some point over eternity every particular individual would actually cease (or have ceased) to exist together and simultaneously—simply does not necessarily follow from that generic possibility. The individuals, Crescas notes, might cease to exist sequentially and not simultaneously, in which case the species will not cease to exist.[122]

The paradox of Rambam's argument is that he presupposes that a possibility that is never actualized over the course of eternity is actually impossible, but what he has effectively done is to convert a possibility into necessity: whatever is possible must necessarily actually occur at some point over the course of eternity.

As Herbert Davidson has pointed out,[123] in the third proof, Rambam, like Ibn Sina (despite differences in the way they phrased their arguments) proves not merely the God as causing the existence of motion, but the existence of the universe as a whole. The first two proofs, following Aristotle, only necessitate God as the prime or unmoved mover, and are inherently related to the theory of an eternal world. They do not prove that an eternal world, *per se*,

---

[122]   Crescas, *Or Adonai* 1:2, ch. 17.
[123]   Herbert Davidson, *Proofs for Eternity, Creation and the Existence of God in Medieval Islamic and Jewish Philosophy* (Oxford: Oxford University Press, 1987), p. 309.

necessitates God as the cause of its existence. Ibn Sina's distinction—adopted by Rambam—between contingent and necessary existence, explains not only the motions of the world but also its very existence. The third proof, in that sense, is more fundamental and comprehensive than the first two.

[IX.4.d.iv] *The Fourth Proof: The First Cause or Entirely Actual Agent*

Rambam's fourth proof, which is based on Aristotle's Metaphysics (IX:8 and XII:7) parallels the first cosmological proof of a prime mover. However, where the first proof establishes a prime mover of all motion, the fourth proof establishes that there is a first cause or agent of change, namely the transition from potentiality to actuality, and that this first cause or agent must be entirely actual. Just as the prime mover is not subject to motion, so the first cause or agent is not subject to change.

All change from potentiality to actuality requires an agent, according to premise #18, and that agent of the transition must be external to the object undergoing the change. If the change is prevented by some obstacle, the removal of that obstacle also requires an agent. Since there cannot be an infinite regress of causes or agents of these changes, there must be a first cause or agent, which must itself be entirely actual. If the agent had any potentiality in it, at some point it would have not existed, according to premise #23, at which point the world would not have existed in actuality—but that is inconsistent with an eternal universe. Also, if the agent itself were not entirely actual, it would also undergo the change of transition from potential to actual agent, in which case it would also need a cause or agent of its change. Whatever has no potentiality has no matter, since matter is the source of potentiality, according to premise #24. Being incorporeal, the first cause or agent is thus one and indivisible (i.e., simple), according to premise #16. "The being separate from matter which contains no possibility whatsoever, but exists because of its own essence (*dhat*), is God."

In our discussion of premise #4, we saw that all motion is change but not all change is motion, since motion only takes place in the categories of quantity, quality and place, whereas change also takes place in the category of substance. Accordingly, commentators on the *Guide of the Perplexed*, such as Shem Tov ibn Shem Tov and Isaac Abravanel, noted that the fourth proof is more general than the first proof. We should also note that the last line of the proof uses language similar to necessary being: the first cause or agent "exists because of its own essence" and not because of any other cause or agent. The concept of the first cause or agent, being entirely actual in virtue of itself, and not in virtue of any other cause or agent, thus resembles the concept of the necessary being.

[IX.4.d.v] *The Proofs of God: Conclusion*

Rambam concludes his discussion of proofs of God's existence with additional proofs of God's incorporeality and unity. The first proof basically reiterates the second Kalam proof of unity in *Guide of the Perplexed* I:75 (where he calls it a "conclusive philosophic demonstration"), which Sa'adiah Ga'on discussed in the *Book of Beliefs and Opinions* 2:2.[124] The external or quantitative unity necessitates internal unity or simplicity, because if there are two gods, then each god is composite: each god consists of a common divine element, in virtue of which they are both gods, and something differentiating them, in virtue of which they are separate and different gods. Neither one could then be the necessary being or first cause, since they are both compounds caused by their constituent elements, according to premise #19, and neither the necessary being nor the first cause can have a cause. Conversely, internal unity or simplicity necessitates external unity, since a simplicity precludes a compound, and two (or more) gods would have to be compound.

This argument is not new; Rambam already discussed it in his presentation of the principles of the Kalam. Nor are the other arguments here for God's incorporeality and unity new. What is new in all of them is the conclusion, namely the concept of necessary being, which is based on Ibn Sina, as we have seen, and not on Aristotle's arguments for a first cause or the Kalam arguments for divine unity.

Two questions remain. The first concerns Rambam's method, and the second concerns his conclusions. Regarding Rambam's method, it is only later—in the *Guide of the Perplexed* II:17—that Rambam will return to the question of eternity versus creation. As we shall see, Rambam argues forcefully that the question cannot be decisively resolved, because any argument we construct is based on the laws of natural reality, such as causality, but these laws are only valid and applicable in the natural world as we know it, and cannot be used, before it exists, to establish it. We cannot legitimately infer anything retroactively from an existing and completed state of being to how that state of being came to be generated. In short, the laws of a system cannot be used to establish the system to begin with.

If Rambam's claim is correct, that we cannot infer from the world as it exists anything about how it came to be, does not that claim apply all the more to any cosmological proof of God? If the laws of nature cannot logically be applied to prove creation, how can they logically prove the creator? In short, how can there be any cosmological proof of God, in light of Rambam's claim?

As for Rambam's conclusions, even if we accept the validity of his method of proving God's existence, incorporeality and unity, is the God thereby

---

[124] See the discussion in Ch. 2 (II.3.g).

proved—the prime mover, the unmoved mover, the necessary being, and the first cause—merely what Judah Ha-Levi called the "God of Aristotle?" Or did Rambam, somehow, bridge the gap between that impersonal and abstract God and what Judah Ha-Levi called "the God of Abraham?"

The discussion that follows in the *Guide of the Perplexed* is an attempt to deal with this question, even if only indirectly. Creation—the next subject—is important because it is only in a created world that revelation is possible. The eternal world of Aristotle is characterized, Rambam asserted, by unchanging necessity, and in such a world revelation is inconceivable. Rambam's proofs of God may, therefore, inevitably lead to "the God of Aristotle." The next step—creation—is what makes revelation possible, and thus opens the way for "the God of Abraham." In that way Rambam can try to bridge the gap and guide his perplexed student to the insight that the God of Aristotle really is the God of Abraham.

Chapter Ten

THE *GUIDE OF THE PERPLEXED*: ON THE WORLD AND HUMANS

[X.1]   CREATION

[X.1.a]   INTRODUCTION: THE LITERARY STRUCTURE OF THE *GUIDE OF THE PERPLEXED*, PARTS II AND III

The first part of the *Guide of the Perplexed*, as we saw, essentially deals with the "via negativa" in its treatment of terms Scripture applies to God — equivocal, metaphorical and amphibolous — which are often misunderstood and therefore perplex the student. The first part and the "via negativa" end with a review of the errors of the Kalam. In the second part of the *Guide of the Perplexed* Rambam moved to the "via positiva" with his four proofs, based on Aristotelian premises (including the eternity of the universe), of the existence, incorporeality and unity of God. Having established the existence of God, Rambam's "via positiva" now shifts to the world, beginning with the question of creation versus eternity which he had deliberately set aside in his proofs of God for the purposes of the argument. Creation, in turn, is important because it is only in a created world that revelation and prophecy — the foundation of the Torah — are possible. Creation and prophecy — the major themes of the second part of the *Guide of the Perplexed* — provide the connection between God, the world and humans, and will bring us to the third and last part of the book, which culminates with the theme of the ultimate human end and perfection. Part III, in a sense, also manifests the shift from the "via negativa" to the "via positiva" by first correcting erroneous notions of evil (understood negatively as the absence of good) and divine providence, and by then explaining the ideal society envisaged by the Torah and the ideal way of life embodied in the Torah's commandments, a way of life leading not merely to "the perfection of the body" but ultimately to "the perfection of the soul." These are the themes — creation, prophecy, providence and evil, and ultimate human perfection — that we shall examine in this chapter.

[X.1.b]   CREATION: THREE VIEWS (*Guide* II:13)

As we saw in the last chapter,[1] for both pedagogic and methodological reasons, Rambam's proofs of the existence, incorporeality and unity of God are based on the Aristotelian view of eternity rather than on creation. Now, after his discussion of the proofs of God, Rambam reiterates that Aristotle's views on the motions of the spheres are the "least doubtful" of the various theories, but that his views were also unproven.[2] If the universe is eternal, its motions must be caused by God, as we saw in the proofs of God, but if the universe itself is subject to generation and corruption, then it is all the more the case that "what causes it to exist after non-being is God," since something which does not exist cannot cause its own existence.[3] In either case, then — eternity or creation — the existence of God has been demonstrated.

Which case is it, then, eternity or creation? Rambam, with his typical penchant for clarification by classification, describes three views on the subject.[4] The first view is "the opinion of everyone who believes in the Torah of Moses," that the world was created after absolute non-being" and that God brought it into existence "by his will and volition not from something (*la min shay*)."[5] It should be noted at this point that Rambam does not actually call such creation "the opinion of the Torah," but "the opinion of everyone who believes in the Torah of Moses," by which he may be implying that it is the conventional religious opinion, but not necessarily the actual teaching of the Torah. Such creation cannot have been "in time" because time itself was created together with the world, since (as we have seen) time is an accident, a measure consequent on the motion of a body. Creation is thus not "in time" but "of time."

The second view is that of Plato. It is impossible to generate "something not from something" (*shay min la shay*), nor can something be corrupted into nothing. Just as the inability to produce something impossible does not impute any impotence or defect in an agent, so God's inability to do something impossible — namely to make something exist out of nothing — implies no lack of power. The world, then, was created, not out of nothing, but out of eternal matter, which always coexisted with God.

The third view is that of Aristotle and his followers, who believed that the heavens are eternal, and not subject in any way to generation and corruption. Time and motion are thus also eternal. In the sub-lunar realm of generation and

---

1   See the discussion in Ch. 9 (IX.4.a).
2   *Guide of the Perplexed* II:3.
3   *Guide of the Perplexed* II:2.
4   *Guide of the Perplexed* II:13.
5   Rambam uses here the same phrase, *la min shay* ("not from something") that Sa'adiah Ga'on used. On this phrase, review the discussion in Ch. 2 (II.3.d).

corruption there is a succession of forms continually replacing each other, but prime matter itself is not subject to generation and corruption. God's will can never change, so innovation in the natural order is impossible.

Rambam concludes this survey of the three views by noting that for anyone "who follows the Torah of Moses or Abraham our teacher," there can be nothing eternal except God, and it makes no difference whether there is Platonic creation out of eternal prime matter, or whether the world as a whole is eternal in the Aristotelian sense, because in both cases there is something material co-existing eternally with God.

[X.1.c]   ARGUMENTS PRO AND CON (*Guide* II:14–18)

In the *Guide of the Perplexed* II:14, Rambam presents four arguments of Aristotle in favor of eternity, "because it is his opinions which should be considered." These arguments are important because "they are the main ways followed by Aristotle in establishing the eternity of the world from the aspect of the world itself," as opposed to the arguments of Aristotle's followers whose arguments "establish the eternity of the world from the aspect of God." What is particularly noteworthy is that later (in *Guide* II:18) Rambam lists specific refutations of the arguments of Aristotle's followers based on God, but not of Aristotle's own arguments based on the world, which, he observes, are true. However, Aristotle's arguments are only valid when taken on their specific level. But when viewed on a different and general level, they are all problematical, because they are based on the fallacious presumption that the generation of the universe as a whole resembles the generation of particulars within an already existing cosmos.[6] The arguments of Aristotle's followers, however, are fallacious even when taken individually, on their own specific level. Aristotle's arguments are also superior to those of his followers because, as Rambam had already established in *Guide of the Perplexed* I:76, a scientific proof must be based on what we know empirically or rationally, and must proceed from what we know (i.e., the world) to what we do not (or not yet) know, namely God. The followers of Aristotle violate this methodological consideration in arguing from God to the world.

Aristotle's first argument for eternity in the *Guide of the Perplexed* II:14 was already epitomized in Premise 26. Motion (or change) must be eternal, because if there is a first motion (or change), then there is a transition from non-motion to the first motion, and that transition is itself a motion, in which case we have a motion before the first-motion, which is absurd. Motion is thus not subject to generation or corruption, but must be eternal, which also means that time, and the world as a whole, are eternal.

---

6   *Guide of the Perplexed* II:17.

Aristotle's second argument for eternity is based on the concept of formless prime matter. If prime matter had a form, it would be generated by the combination of its form with a prior formless matter, which leads us to an impossible infinite regress of causes.

Aristotle's third argument for eternity analyzes the circular motion of the spheres, which has no opposite motion (unlike linear motion). In the absence of an opposite motion which would cause it to cease, it is not subject to corruption, and whatever is not subject to corruption is also not subject to generation, and is, therefore, eternal.

Aristotle's fourth argument for eternity is based on the concept of possibility. Before something generated actually comes into being, it must exist potentially, but such possibility requires a substratum. In other words, the substratum must exist before the potentially generated object can be generated in actuality. We thus arrived, necessarily, at an eternal substratum of possibility. Rambam calls this a "very strong way of establishing the eternity of the world.

Rambam may have refrained from specific refutations of these arguments because he found them persuasive (in light of his last comment, that the fourth argument is a "very strong way of establishing the eternity of the world"), or, conversely, because he believed that Aristotle himself had not claimed that these constitute conclusive scientific proofs. Aristotle himself, he states, recognized that these are not proofs but only arguments which he believed to be more probable and less dubious than the alternatives.[7] As it turns out, however, all arguments in favor of eternity or in favor of creation are fundamentally fallacious, and the question of eternity versus creation cannot ultimately be resolved scientifically, because one cannot infer from a state of actuality anything about the state of potentiality.

[X.1.d]   THE FALLACIOUS INFERENCE FROM ACTUALITY
          TO POTENTIALITY: THE PARABLE OF THE FETUS
          (*Guide* II:17)

Whether the arguments are in favor of eternity — such as those of Aristotle and his followers — or in favor of creation — such as those of the Kalam — they all suffer from a methodological fallacy: they infer from a state of actuality what must have been the case in the state of potentiality, and from particulars within the completed and perfected universe they infer how that universe as a whole came to be. The particular laws of a system, however, cannot be used to establish the system as a whole, since until the system is already completed, its laws are not yet valid or in effect, and thus cannot be used to establish it.

---

7   *Guide of the Perplexed* II:15.

Any argument about the origin of the universe—whether in favor of creation or in favor of eternity—is thus logically invalid, and the question of creation versus eternity cannot be resolved conclusively and demonstratively.

Rambam exemplifies the fallacy by the parable of a fetus. Imagine a child whose mother dies when he is a few months old, and he is raised without ever seeing a woman or the females of animals. When the orphan grows up and asks where people and animals come from, he is told that humans and animals come from a seed implanted in the female of the species, in whose belly the living fetus then grows until it reaches a certain size and then comes out of an opening in the female's body, and then it continues growing until it reaches full size. The orphan has difficulty accepting this explanation, and questions how the fetus in its mother's belly could breathe, eat, drink and excrete. All this must, therefore, be false, the orphan concludes, for if any of us were deprived of breath for a few minutes we would die—and yet it is alleged that the fetus lives inside a body for months.

The orphan's fallacy, of course, is his inference that the laws which apply after something is completed and perfected in a state of actuality also apply to a prior state of potentiality, namely its generation from non-existence to existence. Rambam concludes: "The essential point, as we have mentioned, is that nothing can be inferred from something which exists in a state of perfection and completion to its state prior to its perfection." Therefore, Rambam states, he does not seek to demonstrate creation, but merely that creation is possible.

[X.1.e] ARISTOTLE'S THEORY DOES NOT ACCORD WITH THE NATURAL FACTS: DIVERGENCES FROM NECESSARY ORDER (*Guide* II:19–20)

A conclusive scientific proof of creation or eternity is thus in principle impossible. Rambam must, therefore, proceed systematically to establish the possibility of creation. First, as we have seen, he argued that Aristotle's proofs are methodologically invalid. He then proceeds to argue that Aristotle's theory of eternity is incompatible with the empirical natural facts. From the negative, he will then proceed with the positive way, of showing that the theory of creation—unlike the theory of eternity—is compatible with the facts. The theory of creation, as we shall see, is thus preferable from a scientific perspective (although, again, that preferability does not constitute a conclusive proof). The final stage will be to show that creation is preferable, not only scientifically, but also religiously, as the foundation of the Torah.

In the *Guide of the Perplexed* II:19–20, Rambam negates two opposing Greek theories. On the one hand, Aristotle demonstrated that the causal order of nature disproves the theory (associated with Epicurus in *Guide of the Perplexed* II:13) that everything occurs by chance, and that there is no order or causality. The theory of chance, in short, is incompatible with the order in the universe. On the other hand, the divergences from order in nature disprove the Aristotelian theory that the world is eternal, and its corollary that everything is governed by necessary and unchanging order. The Aristotelian structure of an eternal and necessary order, from which nothing can vary, is incompatible with the empirical facts, which include some divergences from such order on the astronomical level. Let us recall that one of Rambam's criticisms of the Kalam was that it is a closed system which attempted to adapt the facts to the theory, rather than adapting the theory to the facts,[8] just as Judah Ha-Levi had criticized the conventional Aristotelian philosophy of his day as a closed system which fails to deal with the facts.[9] The Aristotelian theory of eternity thus collapses, not only for the logical and methodological reasons cited above, but also because of empirical, scientific reasons: its unvarying and necessary order is simply incompatible with the divergent astronomic facts (regarding the rate of the motions of the stars and their directions). The order of the universe thus disproves Epicurean chance; the divergence from natural order thus disproves Aristotelian eternal necessity. Nor can Aristotelian necessity explain why things are as they are, let alone why they must necessarily be so.

A third option, between those of Epicurean chance and Aristotelian necessity, is offered by the theory of intentional and volitional creation, which can account both for order and for divergences from that order.

[X.1.f] AN INTENTIONAL AND VOLITIONAL ORDER
(*Guide* II:19, II:22)

In Rambam's view, only the intentional purpose (Arabic: *qaṣd*; Hebrew: *kavanah*) of volitional creation can account for both regularity and order in nature, unlike Epicurean chance, and also for change and divergence from order in nature, unlike Aristotelian eternal necessity. Another advantage of this theory is its ability to explain how the compound can be derived from the simple, a problem Aristotelian necessity, with its component of Neoplatonic emanation, cannot resolve. If, as the Aristotelian theory claims, the first intellect produces the second, the second produces the third, and so on, the last intellect would still have to be simple, and there is no way to explain the emanation of compound reality, nor can the theory of necessity explain the diversity empirically manifest in the motions of the spheres. What Aristotle taught about sublunar matters is, Rambam concludes, "indubitably correct," but his opinions regarding everything transcending the lunar sphere are mere

---

8   See the discussion in Ch. 2 (II.1.c).
9   See the discussion in Ch. 6 (VI.2).

"guessing and conjecturing." Thus the "theory of eternity is more dubious and harmful" than creation, which, "in addition, is the theory of Abraham our ancestor and our prophet Moses."[10]

[X.1.g] CREATION AS A FOUNDATION OF THE TORAH
(*Guide* II:23)

As we have seen, Rambam understands Aristotle's theory of eternity as entailing unvarying necessity, which precludes any changes or divergences from the necessary order. The impossibility of variation in the natural order also precludes divine intervention in history, such as the revelation at Sinai. Only in a world created volitionally and manifesting divine intention are revelation—also a volitional and intentional action of God—and miracles possible. Creation is thus a foundation of the Torah. To reiterate: this perspective does not constitute proof of creation (since, as we have seen, the question of eternity versus creation cannot be conclusively proven). However, so long as eternity has not been, and cannot be, conclusively proven, the theory of creation is preferable. It is preferable, as we have seen, for scientific reasons, because only intentional creation can account for both the order and the divergences from order in nature, and is thus less dubious than the theory of eternity.

The theory of creation is also preferable for religious reasons, because eternity, by precluding revelation, "destroys the foundation of the Torah," whereas creation makes possible the revelation of the Torah. Therefore, "do not turn away from the theory of the creation of the world except for a conclusive demonstration [i.e., of eternity], which does not exist in nature."[11]

[X.1.h] THE THREE VIEWS AND THE "WORK OF CREATION"
(*Guide* II:25)

Rambam states explicitly that his preference for the theory of creation is based on the scientific and religious considerations we have discussed, and not on a literal reading of the biblical story of "the work of creation" in Genesis. Although in his view the Aristotelian view of eternity "destroys the foundation of the Torah," if eternity could actually be proven conclusively and scientifically, the Torah could, and would have to be, interpreted in accordance with the scientific truth, and the biblical story would have to be understood metaphorically, just as biblical anthropomorphisms are understood non-literally. It would actually be easier to interpret the creation story figuratively

---

10   *Guide of the Perplexed* II:22.
11   *Guide of the Perplexed* II:23.

than anthropomorphisms. So long, however, as there is no conclusive scientific proof of the Aristotelian view of eternity, or even of the Platonic view of creation from prime matter (which, unlike the Aristotelian view of eternity, does not undermine the foundations of the Torah), there is no justification for reading the text of Genesis non-literally.

[X.1.i] CONCLUSION: CREATION AND THE "THIRTEEN FOUNDATIONS"

In our discussion of the "Thirteen Foundations" in Chapter Eight,[12] we saw that none of Rambam's works — not his original Thirteen Principles in the Commentary to the Mishnah, nor his *Mishneh Torah*, nor his *Guide of the Perplexed*, nor even his early and popular "Letter to Yemen" — includes creation as a foundation or basic principle of the Torah, nor is a person who believes in the eternity of the universe ever categorized in those works as a heretic (*min*), infidel (*kofer*), or *Apiqoros*. Rather, according to the *Guide of the Perplexed* 1:35, is that creation is one of the metaphysical "secrets of the Torah" (*sitrei torah*) and "mysteries" (*sodot*) which should not be taught to the masses, whose simple faith and moral behavior would be undermined by exposure to complex issues for which they are intellectually unprepared and which they are incapable of understanding.

We also noted that even if we take that precaution into account, the fact is that in his various discussions of basic principles of the Torah, creation is simply not mentioned, and Rambam's silence is deafening. His silence may well have led to questions or criticism, that either brought him to change his mind on the subject, or at least to clarify what had been a misunderstanding of his intention all along, and that may be the reason for his late addition to the fourth foundation.

> Know that the great foundation of the Torah of Moses our teacher is that the world is created. God formed and created it after absolute non-being. The fact that you see me dealing with the eternity of the world according to the opinion of the philosophers is in order to provide an absolute proof of his existence, as I explained and clarified in the Guide (of the Perplexed).[13]

We also saw that Shem Tov ibn Falaquera, who regarded creation as a fundamental principle (*'iqar*) of Judaism, claimed that creation is one of

---

12 See the discussion in Ch. 8 (VIII.3.b, #4).

13 These lines were not included in the original version of the Thirteen Principles, and are not found in most manuscripts or in the printed editions. Yosef Kafiḥ included them in his edition, based on a single manuscript, and identified them as a later marginal addition in Rambam's own hand.

Rambam's thirteen foundations. Falaquera may have been referring to Rambam's late addition:

> An example of this is well-known and famous, that a principle of our faith which is one of the thirteen principles which Rabbi Moses wrote, is that we should believe in the creation of the world. Even if a proof cannot be found for it, one should not say that these are not true matters.[14]

Whatever the explanation for Rambam's omission of creation from all his earlier works, and whether that omission reflected earlier doubts on the subject or merely the tactical considerations—pedagogic and methodological—for basing his proofs of God on eternity, Rambam's ultimate position in the *Guide of the Perplexed* is consistent: only creation can account both of the order and of the divergence from order in nature, and creation thus provides a more coherent explanation of the universe than does Aristotelian eternity or Epicurean chance. Creation also is a "foundation of the Torah" because in an eternal universe, revelation is impossible. The question cannot be determined decisively, however, in scientific terms, because no inference can be drawn from a state of perfection and actuality to a state of generation and potentiality. If it were possible to determine it one way or the other, the Torah could and would have to be interpreted figuratively, in accordance with the scientific truth. In the absence of such proof of either the Platonic or Aristotelian views, there is no justification for interpreting the text of Genesis non-literally.

[X.2] PROPHECY

[X.2.a] PROPHECY: THREE VIEWS (*Guide* II:32)

Rambam's discussion of creation began with a presentation of three views. He similarly opens the discussion of prophecy with a survey of three views: the view of the masses, the view of the philosophers, and "the view of our Torah and the foundation of our religion (*madhhab*)."

According to the masses, including some Jews, God chooses anyone he wills to be a prophet. Although the prophet is a moral person, there are no requisite qualifications, such as wisdom, for prophecy. According to the philosophers, prophecy is merely the highest natural degree of intellectual and moral perfection, and includes the perfection of the imaginative faculty. The individual who attains such perfection "necessarily will become a prophet."

---

14   Falaquera, *Moreh Ha-Moreh*, "Be'ur Nifla," Ch. 32, p. 168. See the discussion in Raphael Jospe, *Torah and Sophia: The Life and Thought of Shem Tov ibn Falaquera*, p. 158.

In other words, prophecy does not require any divine intervention, but it does require that the prerequisite moral and intellectual conditions be fulfilled. The third view, "of our Torah and the foundation of our religion," is essentially a combination of the first two views. Prophecy is a natural perfection not requiring divine intervention, but God can, in effect, exercise a veto and intervene to prevent the otherwise qualified person from prophesying.[15]

[X.2.b] THE NATURE AND CONDITIONS OF PROPHECY (*Guide* II:36–38)

Rambam had already dealt with the theme of prophecy in his earlier halakhic works. In his Introduction to his Commentary on the Mishnah, when discussing the difference between true and false prophets, he argued against the common view that a prophet must perform miracles. Miracles do not verify a prophecy, which must be inherently true, and miracles cannot verify a false prophecy. Rather, the miracles were necessitated by the particular circumstances of the moment. Similarly, he argued in the *Mishneh Torah* that Moses performed miracles as required by the moment, and not to verify his prophecy:

> Israel did not believe in Moses, our Teacher, on account of the miracles he showed. For when one's faith is founded on miracles, a lurking doubt always remains in the mind that these miracles may have been performed with the aid of occult arts and witchcraft. All the miracles Moses showed in the wilderness he performed because they were needed, and not to support his prophetic claims. Thus, when it was necessary that the Egyptians should be drowned, he divided the Red Sea and drowned them in its depths. We needed material sustenance; he brought down the Manna for us...And so with all the other miracles. What, then, were the grounds of the faith in him? The revelation on Sinai, which we saw with our own eyes and heard with our own ears, not having to depend on the testimony of others.[16]

A false prophet, for instance one who advocates idolatry or transgressing the Torah's commandments, cannot verify his prophecy by miracles; even if he successfully performs miracles, his prophecy is still inherently false. The distinction between a true and false prophet is thus rational and not empirical; the judgment is made on the basis of analysis of the prophecy, and not on the basis of observing a miracle. It is the prophet's message, and not miracles, that can verify his mission.

---

15 *Guide of the Perplexed* II:32.
16 *Mishneh Torah*, Laws of the Foundations of the Torah 8:1. (Hyamson translation, p. 43b. My modifications).

The ability to perform miracles, then, is not one of the requisite quali-fications for prophecy. These qualifications are introduced as follows in Rambam's Introduction to the Mishnah Avot, his "Eight Chapters (*Shemonah Peraqim*) on Ethics:"[17]

> Know, then, that no prophet received the gift of prophecy, unless he possessed all the mental virtues and a great majority of the most important moral ones.

The intellectual and moral qualifications for prophecy are discussed in greater detail in the *Mishneh Torah*.[18] The lengthy description begins with these observations:

It is one of the basic principles of religion that God inspires men with the prophetic gift. But the spirit of prophecy only rests upon the wise man who is distinguished by great wisdom and strong moral character, whose passions never overcome him in anything whatsoever, but who by his rational faculty always has his passions under control, and possesses a broad and sedate mind.

The phenomenon of prophecy itself, by which, in rabbinic terms, the "holy spirit" (*ru'aḥ ha-qodesh*) rests on the prophet, is fundamentally a natural intellectual process by which the prophet's intellect reaches "conjunction" or "connection" (Arabic: *itiṣal*, from the root *waṣal*; Hebrew: *devequt* or *hitḥaberut*) with the active intellect. It will be recalled that Rambam described this intellectual conjunction in the sixth of his "Thirteen Foundations:"[19]

> The sixth foundation is prophecy. It is to know that there are some humans of greatly developed abilities and perfection, whose souls are disposed to receive the form of intellect, so that the human intellect becomes conjoined (Arabic: *waṣal*; Hebrew: *daveq*) to the Active Intellect (Arabic: *al-'aql al-fa'al*; Hebrew: *ha-sekhel ha-po'el*), which emanates a noble emanation (Arabic: *faid*; Hebrew: *aẓilut* or *shefa'*) from itself onto them; they are the prophets, and this is the subject of prophecy... The verses of the Torah testify to the prophecy of many prophets.

This concise description epitomizes and accords with the far more deve-loped theory in the *Guide of the Perplexed* II:36, which, as Shlomo Pines and other scholars have shown, is based on the political theory of Abu Naṣr Al-Farabi, which in turn borrows heavily from Plato's political theory. As Pines observed, although the *Guide of the Perplexed* does not explicitly cite any of Al-Farabi's political writings,

---

[17] *The Eight Chapters of Maimonides on Ethics*, trans. Joseph Gorfinkle (New York: Columbia University Press, 1912), Ch. 7, pp. 80–81.

[18] *Mishneh Torah*, Laws of Foundations of the Torah 7:1. (Hyamson translation, p. 42a).

[19] See the discussion in Ch. 8 (VIII.3.b, #6).

it is quite evident, however, that they had a very strong influence on Maimonides. In fact, the latter's views on the nature and function of prophecy and on the two-fold purpose of the good city stem from Al-Farabi's conceptions...Al-Farabi's position and criteria are...largely Platonic. Maimonides, who in this field was decisively influenced by Al-Farabi, was thus a Platonist at a second remove, but perhaps not aware, or not fully aware, of this fact...Maimonides had no access to Aristotle's work on politics and may not even have been aware of the book's existence.[20]

The adoption in Rambam's theory of prophecy of material from Al-Farabi is particularly notable in three respects. First, as we saw in the sixth of the Thirteen Foundations, prophecy is understood to be an emanation (*faiḍ*) from the active intellect to the human intellect, which then attains conjunction (*itiṣal*) with the active intellect. Second, that intellectual emanation then proceeds from the prophet's intellect to his faculty of imagination, which in turn enables the prophet to communicate effectively to the masses in terms they understand, and thereby to lead them politically. Third, the prophet thus has a political and social function, in the pattern of the Platonic philosopher-king. In virtue of his intellectual perfection, the prophet is a philosopher, and in virtue of the perfection of his imaginative faculty, the prophet is a political leader. (We shall return later to the political function of the prophet).

As Rambam explicates this theory in the *Guide of the Perplexed* II:36,

> the true reality and essence of prophecy are that it is an emanation (Arabic: *faid*; Hebrew: *shefa'*) emanating from God through the active intellect first to the intellectual faculty, and then emanating onto the imaginative faculty. This is the highest human degree and the ultimate perfection of the [human] species; it is also the ultimate perfection of the imaginative faculty...This emanation emanates onto it according to its disposition, and is the cause of veridical dreams, and is itself also the cause of prophecy...When the imaginative faculty of the individual thus described is as perfect as possible, and acts, it receives an emanation from the intellect in accordance with [the intellect's] theoretical perfection. [The prophet] will then only apprehend divine and wonderful matters, and will only see God and his angels, and will only be aware and know matters that are true opinions and general directives for the welfare of people with each other.

There are different ranks of prophets, reflecting the differences in their intellectual perfection through study, the perfection of their imaginative faculty, and their moral perfection. Since the imagination is a bodily faculty, and bodily faculties tire and are weakened, the prophet's ability to prophesy will be affected or even prevented if, for instance, when he is sad or angry. This

---

20   Shlomo Pines, "The Philosophic Sources of the *Guide of the Perplexed*, pp. lxxvi–lxxvii.

is why prophecy ceased during Israel's exile, and this is also why prophecy will be restored in the messianic era.

The activities of the external senses, such as sight and hearing, also may interfere with a prophet's concentration, which is why prophetic visions and veridical dreams often come to the person while sleeping. Sometimes the prophetic emanation only suffices to perfect the prophet himself, but sometimes it is sufficient to enable him to perfect others as well by governing and instructing them.[21]

Such a prophet is a combination of philosopher, whose intellect is perfected, and politician, whose imagination is perfected. As a philosopher, he knows the theoretical truth, and as a politician he knows how to communicate that truth effectively in popular terms, by appealing to people's emotions, and thereby to lead others to proper behavior (the welfare of the body) and to knowledge of the truth (the welfare of the soul). The prophet is thus much more than either a philosopher, at least in the Aristotelian sense of the intellectual ideal of contemplation, or a politician, whose governance is unrelated to personal perfection and to intellectual knowledge of the theoretical truth. A politician can, in the best of circumstances, legislate a good positive law, or *nomos*, whereas the prophet legislates divine law.[22] Again, in the best of cases a politician can lead people to the welfare of the body, whereas the prophet can lead people to both the welfare of the body and the welfare of the soul.

Rambam thus follows Al-Farabi's ingenious innovation of identifying the Platonic philosopher-king with the prophet of revealed religion. However, in the case of Al-Farabi, we must keep in mind that the prophet Muḥammad and his successors, the caliphs (caliph = *khalifah* [successor]) were both religious and secular political leaders, whereas for Rambam the analogy could not apply to any contemporary political leaders, but only to the prophets of ancient Israel, and especially to Moses, who did play an overtly political role in the leadership of the people.

There may be another difference between Rambam and Al-Farabi. According to Al-Farabi, religion is an "imitation of philosophy." The truth that philosophy teaches in discursive language and by demonstrative methods is taught in imaginative terms (what we would call "myth") on the basis of authority by religion. Rambam emphasizes that the prophecy of Moses—which is the basis of the Torah—did not involve the imaginative faculty, and thus differs qualitatively, and not merely quantitatively, by rank, from other prophecy. The involvement of the imaginative faculty in the prophecy of the other prophets is exemplified by their frequently resorting

---

21   *Guide of the Perplexed* II:37.
22   Rambam discusses such *nomos* in his *Treatise on Logic*, ch. 14:7.

to parables to convey their message.[23] The observance of the commandments of the Torah, on the other hand, depends on their being fulfilled literally, and precludes their being interpreted figuratively as parables.

[X.2.c] DEGREES OF PROPHECY (*Guide* II:44–45)

Basing himself on various biblical verses alluding to prophetic experiences, Rambam categorizes prophecy into eleven degrees. The prophecy of Moses transcends all these degrees, and the first two degrees are preparatory or pre-prophetic stages. A given prophet may, at various times of his life, have experienced different degrees of prophecy. The first degree is called "the spirit of the Lord" (*ru'ah Adonai*), and refers to the experience of the judges and such kings as Saul and David who were moved, at various times, to heroic deeds. The second degree is called "the holy spirit" (*ru'ah ha-qodesh*), in which a person is enabled to impart wisdom, as David did in the Psalms and Solomon did in the Proverbs, Ecclesiastes and the Song of Songs. The remaining degrees of prophecy—three through eleven—have a progressive but incomplete literary structure. In degrees three through seven, the prophet experiences a dream, while sleeping, whereas in degrees eight through eleven, the prophet experiences a vision, while awake, and there is a clear parallel between the progression of dreams and of visions.[24]

PROPHETIC DREAM (occurs during sleep)	PROPHETIC VISION (occurs while the prophet is awake)
3. Seeing a parable in a dream. (For example, Zechariah's parables).	8. Seeing a parable in a vision. (For example, Abraham).
4. Hearing speech in a dream. (For example, Samuel at the beginning of his prophetic career).	9. Hearing speech in a vision. (For example, Abraham).
5. Seeing a person speaking in a dream. (For example, Ezekiel).	10. Seeing a person speaking in a vision. (For example, Joshua).
6. Seeing an angel in a dream. (For example, most of the prophets).	11. Seeing an angel in a vision. (For example, Abraham at the binding of Isaac).
7. Seeing a dream in which God, as it were, is speaking. (For example, Isaiah).	—

---

23   *Guide of the Perplexed* II:45.
24   This distinction is made in *Guide of the Perplexed* II:41.

The parallel progression is incomplete, however, because there is no fifth degree of vision (#12) parallel to fifth degree of dream, #7, in which God, as it were, is seen speaking. In other words, there is no twelfth degree of prophecy in which the prophet has a vision of God, as it were, speaking. That missing twelfth degree, which we might logically expect from Rambam's parallel progressive structure, would presumably be the supreme level of prophecy, namely that of Moses. In the case of Moses, however, the experience of prophecy did not involve the imaginative faculty.

Moreover, the intellectual emanation causing prophecy is intermediated by the separate intellects, which Rambam identifies with angels, but the prophecy of Moses was immediate, without any such intermediary: "Mouth to mouth I speak with him" (Numbers 12:8).[25] The prophecy of Moses, in other words, is an entirely different phenomenon from all other degrees of prophecy; it does not merely differ from the others in degree. Therefore the prophecy of Moses cannot be categorized as the twelfth degree of prophecy, despite the logical and literary progression of the parallel structure.

[X.2.d] THE PROPHECY OF MOSES (*Guide* II:34–39)

We dealt with the uniqueness of the prophecy of Moses in our discussion of principles #7, 8 and 9 of the Thirteen Foundations.[26] As we saw there, Rambam's presentation of Moses as the "father" of the prophets, i.e., the greatest of all the prophets who came before and after him (even the messiah!), constitutes a polemic against the Islamic claim that Muḥammad was the greatest prophet and the "seal" of all the prophets. The claim that the prophecy of Moses was unique is, in Rambam's system, necessary to preclude any *naskh* (abrogation) of the Torah by a later prophet.

In the *Mishneh Torah*, Rambam went into greater detail regarding the uniqueness of the prophecy of Moses:[27]

> In what respects was the prophecy of Moses distinguished from that of the other prophets? All the prophets received their inspired messages in a dream or in a vision; Moses while awake and standing...All the prophets received their messages through the medium of an angel. Hence, what they saw, they saw as a parable or riddle; Moses received his message not through an angel, as it is said, "Mouth to mouth I speak with him" (Numbers 12:8); "The Lord spoke to Moses face to face" (Exodus 33:11). Furthermore, "And he beholds the likeness of the

---

25 *Guide of the Perplexed* II:45.
26 Review the discussion in Ch. 8 (VIII.3.b, #7–9).
27 *Mishneh Torah*, Laws of Foundations of the Torah 7:6. (Hyamson translation, p. 43a; my modifications).

Lord" (Numbers 12:8); that is to say, that it was no parable that was revealed to Moses, but he realized the prophetic message clearly, without riddle and without parable...All the prophets (when receiving their messages) were filled with fear and consternation and became physically weak. Not so our teacher Moses, of whom Scripture says, "As a man speaks with his fellow" (Exodus 33:11). Just as a person is not startled when he hears the words of his fellow, so the mind of Moses was vigorous enough to comprehend the words of prophecy while retaining his normal state. None of the prophets could prophesy at their pleasure. It was otherwise with Moses. He was invested with the prophetic spirit and was clothed with the power of prophecy whenever he pleased. There was no need for him specially to concentrate his mind and prepare for the prophetic manifestations, since he was ever intent and in readiness like the ministering angels. He therefore prophesied at all times.

In the *Guide of the Perplexed* II:45, as we have seen, Rambam reiterates that only the prophecy Moses did not involve the imaginative faculty, and that it was immediate, whereas all other prophets prophesied by the mediation of an angel, and their prophecy involved the imagination. In *Guide of the Perplexed* I:49 he had already identified the angels of the Bible and of Jewish tradition with what Aristotle called "the separate intellects," although for Rambam the separate intellects are created, not eternal (as Aristotle maintained). These angels, which are described by the prophets' imaginative faculty as having human or animal form, are actually the separate (i.e., bodiless) intellects which move the heavenly spheres.[28]

Why, then, does Rambam reiterate in various passages that prophecy is mediated by the separate intellects and involves the imaginative faculty? By consistently insisting that the prophets prophesy by the intermediation of the separate intellects or angels, Rambam ensures that prophecy is endowed with an objective quality; what the prophet sees in a vision or in a dream is not merely the subjective product of his imaginative faculty, but is grounded in objective reality (however it is then described in corporeal terms by his imagination). His theory also permits him to assert that the prophet's message, while essentially rational in content, can be apprehended without the normal intellectual effort and delay of study and research. The prophet can arrive at the conclusion instantly, as if he had perceived it immediately by his external senses.[29] By insisting that prophecy involves the functioning of the imaginative faculty, Rambam — as we have seen — makes it possible for the prophet to communicate a rational or scientific truth to the masses in terms they can comprehend, and thus fulfill his political mission of governing

---

28   *Guide of the Perplexed* II:4 and II:6.
29   *Guide of the Perplexed* II:38.

society. However, the functioning of the imaginative faculty is important not merely for the prophet's political mission, but also for the prophet's own experience of prophecy. Since the external senses distract, their activity interferes with the prophet's intellectual concentration and conjunction. That is why prophesy occurs during sleep or while the prophet's senses are otherwise inactive. His imagination, then, makes it possible for the prophet to apprehend a message without the mediation of the senses.

In light of all this, why is it so important for Rambam consistently to emphasize in his earlier works and then in the *Guide of the Perplexed* the uniqueness of the prophecy of Moses, which was not mediated by an angel and did not involve the imaginative faculty? The answer, as we have already seen, is that it is the uniqueness of the prophecy of Moses which ensures that no later prophet can abrogate the Torah, nor can its commandments be interpreted figuratively as a parable (and thus not be observed).

How, then, is this point consistent with Rambam's view that "the Torah speaks according to human language," i.e., language which is not to be taken literally when it contradicts reason or scientific truth?[30] In the first case, Rambam is referring to Moses' own experience of prophecy, in which there was no involvement of the imaginative faculty, whereas in the second case Rambam is referring to how Moses subsequently was able to convey abstract truths to the people in imaginative terms (such as anthropomorphisms) they could understand.

[X.3] THE TORAH

[X.3.a] THE REVELATION AT SINAI AND THE DECALOGUE (*Guide* II:33)

The Decalogue appears twice in the Torah, in Exodus 20 and in Deuteronomy 5. We have seen how Abraham ibn Ezra interpreted the Decalogue—the first version being the actual record of the revelation at Sinai, and the second version being Moses' paraphrase forty years later—and how he and Judah Ha-Levi differed radically in their interpretation of the first line, "I am the Lord your God who brought you out of the land of Egypt."[31] Commonly referred to in English as the "Ten Commandments," the text of the Decalogue is divided and interpreted differently by various exegetes, and Rambam, for example, derives fourteen of the 613 commandments of the Torah from the Decalogue. The Torah

---

30   Cf. *Guide of the Perplexed* I:26 and I:47, and see the discussion of this principle in Ch. 9 (IX.2.c.iv).

31   See the discussion in Ch. 5 (V.4.c.i).

refers three times[32] to "the ten statements" (or: "the ten words")— *'aseret ha-devarim*—which is the basis of the name "Decalogue."[33]

In his *Book of the Commandments*, Rambam's list of the 613 commandments—divided into two sections, positive commandments and negative commandments—includes fourteen commandments derived from the Decalogue. We summarize them below in the order of the Decalogue, and give in brackets the number of the commandment in the list.

[Positive commandment #1]. To affirm that there is a God,[34] based on the verse "I am the Lord your God."

[Negative commandment #1]. Not to think that there is another God, based on the verse "Have no other gods in my presence."

[Negative commandment #2]. Not to make any idols for worship, based on the verse "Do not make any idol or likeness."

[Negative commandment #5]. Not to bow down in idolatrous worship, even if not in the customary manner, based on the verse "Do not bow down to them and do not serve them."

[Negative commandment #6]. Not to engage in idolatrous worship in the customary idolatrous manner, based on the verse "Do not serve them."

[Negative commandment #62]. Not to swear in vain, based on the verse, "Do not take the name of the Lord your God in vain."

[Positive commandment #155]. To distinguish and sanctify the Sabbath day by ceremonies at the beginning and end of the Sabbath, based on the verse, "Remember the Sabbath day."

[Negative commandment #320]. Not to perform any labor on the Sabbath, based on the verse, "Do not do any labor."

[Positive commandment #210]. To honor our parents, based on the verse "Honor your father and your mother."

[Negative commandment #289]. Not to murder, based on the verse, "Do not murder."

[Negative commandment #347]. Not to commit adultery, based on the verse, "Do not commit adultery."

[Negative commandment #243]. Not to kidnap, based on the verse, "Do not steal."[35]

---

32   Exodus 34:28, Deuteronomy 4:13 and Deuteronomy10:4.

33   In Greek, *deka* = ten, and *logos* = word.

34   In the Arabic, Rambam uses the term *i 'tiqad*, which we have translated as "affirm." In the *Mishneh Torah*, Laws of Foundations of the Torah 1:1, Rambam uses the root *yada '*, to know. See the discussion of this term in Ch. 8 (VIII.3.a).

35   Technically, this commandment applies only to kidnapping another Jew, but as is the case with other such commandments which the rabbis understood as applying for technical reasons only to other Jews, they found grounds, including *darkhei shalom* ("the ways of peace"), to extend the application to all people.

[Negative commandment #285]. Not to testify perjuriously, based on the verse "Do not answer against your fellow as a false witness."

[Negative commandment #265]. Not to devise ways to appropriate someone else's property, based on the verse, "Do not covet your fellow's house."

Thus far we have seen how Rambam interprets the Decalogue in terms of *halakhah*. In order to understand how he interprets the Decalogue in philosophical terms in the *Guide of the Perplexed*, we must keep in mind that the first two statements—"I am the Lord your God," and "Have no other gods in my presence," are expressed in the first person, whereas all the subsequent references to God in the Decalogue are expressed in the third person, where Moses is the speaker. This shift served as the basis for the midrashic interpretation that the entire people of Israel directly heard from God only the first two, and that in the subsequent commandments Moses mediated the revelation. The rabbis found support for this interpretation in the verse, "Moses commanded us the Torah" (Deuteronomy 33:4), because the Hebrew letters of the word "Torah" have the numerical value of 611. Moses thus mediated the revelation of 611 of the 613 commandments of the Torah, and Israel only directly experienced the immediate revelation of these two, "I am the Lord," and "Have no other gods in my presence."[36]

This midrashic interpretation provides the background for Rambam's interpretation of the Decalogue in the *Guide of the Perplexed* II:33. In Rambam's analysis, the first two statements are demonstrable truths, and he had in fact provided such demonstrations in his proofs of the existence, incorporeality and unity of God. With regard to such demonstrable truth, the prophet has no advantage over anyone else; anyone capable of rational understanding can comprehend them. These two principles, then, are not known only through prophecy, but also through rational demonstration, because they are fall under the category of intelligible propositions (Arabic: *ma'qulat*; Hebrew: *muskalot*), accessible equally to all people through reason. That is why they are addressed directly to the entire people, and not only to Moses. However, "the other statements [of the Decalogue] are conventional or generally accepted [propositions] (Arabic: *mashhurat*; Hebrew: *mefursamot*) or [propositions] based on tradition (Arabic: *maqbulat*; Hebrew: *mequbalot*), not intelligible [propositions]."[37]

By intelligible propositions, Rambam means statements capable of being demonstrated by rational proof, as we find in mathematics, geometry and the sciences. Such propositions are inherently universal, and should be affirmed

---

36   This interpretation may be found in Babylonian Talmud, Makkot 23b–24a, and in Midrash Rabba on Song of Songs 1:2.

37   These four types of propositions are discussed in the *Treatise on Logic* 8:1. We shall return to these distinctions below, X.3.d.

by all people on the basis of reason. By generally accepted propositions or opinions, Rambam means statements, such as moral judgments, on which there may be a general consensus, although they cannot be conclusively demonstrated in rational or scientific proofs. As such, they reflect value judgments. (Elsewhere, as we shall see, Rambam differentiates intelligible truths, which are objectively demonstrable, and where the judgment is "true" or "false," from generally accepted principles, where the judgment is normative and value-based, such as "desirable" or "repugnant" or "appropriate" and "inappropriate." There are, in addition, propositions based on tradition, which are only affirmed by the national or religious community accepting that particular tradition.

Therefore, whereas the first two statements of the Decalogue, being universal intelligible propositions, were addressed directly to the entire people, the remaining statements, being generally accepted or merely traditional propositions, were addressed to Moses, who mediated them to the people.

[X.3.b]   THE WELFARE OF THE BODY AND THE WELFARE OF THE SOUL (*Guide* III:27)

We have already referred to the difference between a positive human law—*nomos*—and a divine law given through a prophet. Human law, in the best of cases, aims at the welfare of the body (Arabic: *ṣalah al-jasad*; Hebrew: *tiqun ha-guf*), whereas the divine law aims at the welfare of the body and also at the welfare of the soul (Arabic: *ṣalah al-nafs*; Hebrew: *tiqun ha-nefesh*). The welfare of the body is prior in nature and in time, and consists of physical well-being, proper conduct, preventing people from harming each other, and governing society. Since people are not self-sufficient, and, as Aristotle said, "man is by nature a political animal,"[38] they can only fulfill their needs within a social context. The welfare of the body must, therefore, address both individual and collective needs. The ultimate human perfection, however, does not pertain to actions or moral qualities, but consists of knowledge of the truth; that is the welfare of the soul. The welfare of the soul, then, is the higher good, but it cannot exist without the prior welfare of the body.[39]

This conception of the dual purpose of divine law is presumably what led Rambam to compose his comprehensive code of Jewish law, the *Mishneh Torah* with two features unique among Jewish codes. The first unique feature of Rambam's code is that it does not limit its discussion to the areas of *halakhah* in actual contemporary practice, but—unlike other classical codes, among them the *Shulḥan 'Arukh*—it includes all areas of *halakhah*, including

---

38   Aristotle, Politics I:2:9, 1253a.
39   *Guide of the Perplexed* III:27.

laws relating to the Land of Israel, the Jewish State and government, the Temple and the sacrificial cult, which were not of any practical relevance at the time. Rambam may have included all these areas out of a simple desire to be comprehensive, or, given his naturalistic, political conception of the messianic age,[40] he may have intended his code to be, in effect, the practical constitution of the renewed Jewish State.

The second unique feature of the *Mishneh Torah* relates directly to Rambam's conception of "the welfare of the soul" as the ultimate purpose of divine law, as opposed to mere positive *nomos* which can, at best, lead to "the welfare of the body." Other codes of Jewish law deal with practical *halakhah*, in other words, with correct behavior. Rambam's code, as we have seen, especially the first section—Laws of Foundations of the Torah—of the first book, *The Book of Knowledge*—deals with correct opinions, not with practical behavioral questions. The *Mishneh Torah* thus conforms to Rambam's conception of divine law as leading to both welfares, that of the body and that of the soul.

In that sense, the *Mishneh Torah* and the *Guide of the Perplexed* do not merely complement each other, as it is often alleged that the former is a halakhic work and the latter a philosophic work. In fact, the *Mishneh Torah* begins with philosophic material that relates to "the welfare of the soul," and the *Guide of the Perplexed* devotes major sections of Part III[41] to an analysis of the rationale of the commandments, material that relates to "the welfare of the body." The two works thus converge and overlap.

There is, therefore, not necessarily any contradiction between the different ways in which Rambam arranged the *Mishneh Torah* into fourteen areas of law, and the different fourteen divisions of commandments described in the *Guide of the Perplexed* III:35–49. The differences may well reflect contextual considerations. And there is no need to attempt to harmonize them. Isadore Twersky has suggested that the classification in the *Mishneh Torah* is "topical-conceptual" whereas in the *Guide of the Perplexed* the fourteen categories of the code had to be rearranged into a new classification that is "philosophic-teleological."[42] The *Mishneh Torah* arranges the commandments themselves, i.e. the *halakhah*, according to "topical-conceptual" categories, but the *Guide of the Perplexed* is not dealing with the commandments *per se*, but with the rationale for the commandments; its focus, therefore, is "philosophic-teleological"—what purpose do the commandments serve?

---

[40]   See the discussion of the messianic era in Ch. 8 (VIII.2.c.v).

[41]   *Guide of the Perplexed* III:25–50.

[42]   Isadore Twersky, *Introduction to the Code of Maimonides (Mishneh Torah)* (New Haven: Yale University Press, 1980, p. 300.

[X.3.c]   *TA'AMEI HA-MIẒVOT*—THE PURPOSE
AND RATIONALE OF THE COMMANDMENTS
(*Guide* III:25–50)

Roughly half of the third part of the *Guide of the Perplexed* deals with *ta'amei ha-miẓvot*, the "meaning" (i.e., the purpose and rationale) of the commandments. As is the case with other topics, Rambam's theory of the commandments is the subject of controversy among his commentators. The interpretation of a leading scholar, and philosopher in his own right, Yeshayahu Leibowitz, is prominent in this debate. As we saw in Chapter Eight, Rambam consistently emphasizes that one who "serves out of love" seeks no reward for his behavior.[43] In the view of Leibowitz—and according to him, in Rambam's view—when a person believes that the commandments benefit him, whether materially or spiritually, then he essentially is fulfilling the commandments for the sake of a reward, i.e., for that benefit. Therefore, Leibowitz argues, the true purpose of the commandments is obedience, without any benefit in mind. One who "serves out of love" obeys because he is commanded, not because he is benefited thereby. He is motivated purely by his sense of duty, not by any utilitarian considerations.

This interpretation is certainly consistent, but the question is whether the interpretation offered by Leibowitz also represents Rambam's position. His discussion of the commandments begins with overtly utilitarian arguments. Rambam explicitly rejects a positivist understanding of the commandments, according to which the commandments serve no independent purpose and their authority derives exclusively from their having been commanded by God's will. In that regard, the position advocated by Leibowitz, in the name of Rambam, resembles the positivism of the Ash'ariyya school of the Kalam,[44] which attributed everything to God's absolute will, and regarded any extraneous considerations, whether rational or moral, as limiting and infringing on divine omnipotence. God does not command something because it is inherently good—that would be to subject God to an independent and higher standard. Rather, the good is simply understood to be whatever God commands.

According to Rambam, God does not act arbitrarily, and the divine will conforms to wisdom. He argues, furthermore, that this does not limit God or infringe on his omnipotence. To the contrary, Rambam states that to suggest that God acts only by his will, without any purpose or benefit, is to attribute to God futile or frivolous actions.

In the *Guide of the Perplexed* III:25, Rambam discusses four types of actions, "from the perspective of their ends."

---

43   See the discussion in Ch. 8 (VIII.2.c.i, and VIII.3.d.ii, #3).
44   See the discussion of the Ash'ariyya in Ch. 2 (II.1.d).

- An action which is futile (Arabic: *'abath*; Hebrew: *hevel*), is one which aims at no real end.
- An action which is frivolous (Arabic: *la'b*; Hebrew: *seḥoq*), is one which aims at some low end.
- An action which is vain (Arabic: *batil*; Hebrew: *reiq*), is one which aims at an end but fails to attain it.
- An action which is good and excellent (Arabic: *jayyid ḥasan*; Hebrew: *tovah*),[45] is one which attains its noble end.

God's actions must be good; therefore, one cannot suggest that they are merely willed (in which case, serving no end or no noble end, they would be futile or frivolous), but rather must accord with divine wisdom. The view that God's law transcends benefit, and that utility is a rational, i.e., human rather than a divine consideration, is rejected by Rambam as fallacious. A law which does not benefit may even be harmful, but in any case is inferior to a beneficial law. The positivist approach thus renders divine law inferior to human law.[46]

In light of these explicit positions, how can Leibowitz offer a positivist interpretation of Rambam? The answer is that we must differentiate God's intention in commanding from a person's intention in serving. Leibowitz is emphasizing the human intention, whereas Rambam is emphasizing the divine intention. For Leibowitz, any consideration of benefit and utility undermines the purity of serving out of a sense of duty and disinterested love. For Rambam, the positivist approach, which refuses to subordinate the divine will to wisdom, undermines divine wisdom and makes the divine actions futile and/or frivolous. The difference, then, is one of direction: Rambam's perspective is from top to bottom: God's wisdom in giving beneficial commandments to people, whereas Leibowitz is looking from the bottom up: what motivates the person to serve God and observe the commandments.

Is there not, then, a contradiction between Rambam's insisting that the commandments are beneficial to people and not to God, and his emphasis of the disinterested service out of love, with no expectation of reward. Is one who serves God out of love totally oblivious to the benefit accruing to him from his service? The answer may lie, as suggested above, in our perspective: there is a difference between the divine and human perspectives and directions. Another answer may lie in the distinction between the servant's intention (to receive or not to receive a reward) and his awareness that his behavior will have certain consequences, which may be beneficial or harmful. The benefits or harm may be to the person himself, or if not necessarily directly to himself, then to society at large; and if not immediate and short-range,

---

45 Samuel ibn Tibbon only translated the first term, not the second.
46 *Guide of the Perplexed* III:31.

then indirectly or in the long range. Awareness of the consequences of one's actions is not — or is not necessarily — identical with one's motivation in acting a certain way.

Rambam's utilitarian approach to the rationale of the commandments is also reflected in his explanations of the commandments in terms of their physical, moral or spiritual benefit, or in terms of the historical context in which they were given. In many cases, that approach to the commandments is based on the need to limit and restrain our physical appetites, to which many people are enslaved, but which prevent us from attaining our true perfection.[47] Conversely, commandments relating to the Sabbath and festivals symbolize and teach various truths, provide physical rest, and encourage friendship and companionship.[48]

In many other cases, Rambam's approach to the rationale of the commandments involves relating the commandments to a particular historical and cultural situation.

The principle that "the Torah speaks according to human language" applies not only in metaphysical areas (such as anthropomorphic terminology) but also in the area of the commandments, which were given, not to a nation of intellectuals, but to a people who had just been slaves in Egypt. The commandments had to be adapted to the educational and moral level of these former slaves.

Many of the Torah's commandments, in Rambam's understanding, aimed at countering the prevailing pagan culture and mores of the idolatrous Sabians. The Sabians are mentioned three times in the Qur'an. For instance, in Sura 22 ("The Ḥajj," the pilgrimage) we find: "Those who believe [in the Qur'an], those who follow the Jewish [scriptures], and the Sabians, Christians, Magians, and polytheists — God will judge between them on the Day of Judgment, for God is the witness of all things."[49]

The Sabians continued to live, especially in the area of Ḥaran in northern Mesopotamia, even after the Islamic conquest. The historian 'Abd Al-Raḥman ibn Khaldun mentions them in his *Muqaddimah*, "Introduction to History," where he states that the Temple in Jerusalem, which was "the farthest mosque" (*Al-Aqṣa*), originally was a Sabian temple devoted to the worship of the planet Venus, where the Sabians poured libations of oil onto the sacred rock on which the temple was built. The pagan Sabian temple was eventually destroyed, and in its place the Israelites, when they conquered Jerusalem, built their Temple, which they continue to face in their

---

47   *Guide of the Perplexed* III:33.
48   *Guide of the Perplexed* III:49.
49   Sura 22:17, English translation by Abdullah Yusuf Ali. The other references to Sabians in the Qur'an may be found in Suras 2:62 and 5:72.

prayers.[50] Rambam was familiar with, and took at face value, the book *The Nabatean Agriculture* (*Al-Filaḥa Al-Nabatiya*), a supposedly ancient book of the Sabians actually composed (or at least translated into Arabic) by Ibn Waḥshiyya (tenth-century), which purports to describe the religious practices of ancient Babylonia. In Arabic usage, the name Sabians came to be applied to pagans in general.[51]

In the *Guide of the Perplexed* III:29–30 Rambam stated that Abraham lived among these Sabians, who worshipped the stars, and considered the sun and moon to be the greatest gods, and who practiced idolatry and magic. Abraham engaged in polemics against their pagan beliefs, and Moses legislated their destruction, because the prime intention of the Torah is the eradication of idolatry. Because people used to believe that the fertility of the earth and other natural phenomena depended on their worshipping the stars, idolatry came to be connected with agriculture. The Torah, therefore, in prohibiting idolatry, warned that idolatry would have an adverse effect on agriculture, but that the true worship of God and observance of the Torah's commandments would ensure agricultural success.[52]

In the Torah's attempt to wean the Israelites away from primitive pagan practices, the problem was that "a sudden transition from one opposite to the other is impossible, because a person is incapable, according to his nature, of suddenly abandoning everything to which he had become accustomed."[53]

The Israelites coming out of Egyptian servitude were accustomed to the sacrificial mode of worship, which was common in the ancient world. That pagan form of worship was aimed at serving idols and the stars. Given their background, the Israelites would not have been capable of sublimating simultaneously both the customary sacrificial mode of worship to a more abstract mode (such as prayer), and the concrete objects of worship, namely the idols and stars, to an abstract object of worship, namely the one and incorporeal God. The Torah, therefore, retained the sacrificial mode of worship but transferred it to God. Just as God led the Israelites by an indirect and long route to the promised land, instead of by the direct and short way,[54] so he dealt with them indirectly here, with the mode and object of worship, in recognition of the realities of their human limitations and spiritual and intellectual immaturity.[55]

---

50   Ibn Khaldun, *The Muqaddimah: An Introduction to History* IV:6.
51   See the discussion in Shlomo Pines, "The Philosophic Sources of the *Guide the Perplexed*," pp. cxxiii–cxxiv.
52   See, for example, the second of the three paragraphs of the "*Shema'*" — Deuteronomy 11:13–21, recited twice daily in the traditional Jewish morning and evening prayers.
53   *Guide of the Perplexed* III:32.
54   Cf. Exodus 13:17.
55   *Guide of the Perplexed* III:32.

Another aspect of Rambam's understanding the rationale of various commandments in terms of their historical and cultural context is his suggestion that whatever was customary in pagan practice was prohibited to the Israelites, and whatever pagan practice prohibited was commanded of the Israelites. The Torah thus prohibits various practices relating to Sabian magic, and other practices relating to pagan rites,[56] such as shaving the corners of the head and beard,[57] and combining wool and linen in garments.[58] Similarly, Moses said to Pharaoh, "We sacrifice to the Lord our God what is an abomination to Egypt" (Exodus 8:22). Rambam understands this to mean that the Israelites were commanded to sacrifice and/or eat those animals which the Egyptians worshipped as gods. For instance, the paschal lamb was to be sacrificed and its blood smeared on the outside doorposts of the Israelites' homes[59] in order "to cleanse ourselves from those opinions and publicize their contraries, so that [people] would attain the opinion that what you consider to be a cause of destruction [actually] saves from destruction."[60]

Rambam's understanding many of the Torah's commandments as historically and culturally relative led, in modern times, among such liberal religious movements as Reform (or: Progressive) Judaism, to the conclusion that in our changed historical and cultural circumstances, such religious practices are no longer necessary. Although they correctly understood Rambam's view of the sacrificial cult, for example, as a concession to the primitive state of the ancient Israelites, that does not mean that Rambam would have shared, or approved of, their conclusion regarding the contemporary need for these practices. On a factual basis, we simply need to refer to Rambam's inclusion (at great length) of the detailed and technical laws relating to the sacrificial cult in the *Mishneh Torah*, and his explicit statement that the sacrifices will be restored in the rebuilt Temple in messianic times.[61] On a philosophic basis, however, the question is whether Rambam's view of these commandments as necessitated by the primitive state of the people is only a matter of historical circumstances, or whether it also has an existential dimension which transcends particular historical circumstances. Did Rambam believe that primitivity was merely a stage in history, or that it is an enduring and inherent part of the human condition?

Leo Strauss has suggested that, in Rambam's view, the Torah's battle with Sabianism was not merely with the external Sabianism of the surrounding

---

[56]   *Guide of the Perplexed* III:37.
[57]   Leviticus 19:27.
[58]   Deuteronomy 22:11.
[59]   Cf. Exodous 12:7, 13, 22–23.
[60]   *Guide of the Perplexed* III:46.
[61]   *Mishneh Torah*, Book of Judges, Laws of Kings and Their Wars 11:1.

pagan culture, but also—and even more—with the "inner Sabianism of the early adherents of the Torah."[62] For Rambam, however, the real question of the aim of the Torah and the rationale of its commandments may not have been restricted to the "inner Sabianism of the early adherents of the Torah," but the primitive "inner Sabianism" in all people at all times.

[X.3.d] RATIONAL AND TRADITIONAL COMMANDMENTS
(*Guide* III:26 and *Eight Chapters on Ethics*, Ch. 6)

In the *Guide of the Perplexed* III:26 Rambam reiterates that all the Torah's commandments serve "a useful end" (or: "beneficial purpose;" Arabic: *ghayah nafiʻ*; Hebrew: *takhlit mo ʻilah*). If they did not have such a beneficial purpose, they would fall under the category of futile actions, i.e., actions which aim at no real end. However, the Torah refers to some commandments as *mishpatim* (ordinances), and to others as *huqim* (statutes), and Leviticus 18:4 refers to both: "Do my ordinances and observe my statutes, to follow them, I am the Lord your God."

The term *mishpatim* (from the word for judgment and justice) is used by the Torah for basic social legislation (as in Exodus 21:1), and the term *huqah* (a variant singular form of *huqim*) is used for the paradoxical ritual law of the red heifer (in Numbers 19:2). The Talmudic rabbis, elaborating on this terminological distinction, say that *mishpatim* are "things that had they not been written [in the Torah], should be written," such as idolatry, incest, murder, theft and blasphemy, whereas *huqim* are "things to which the nations respond and Satan accuses" (i.e., which are challenged by the opponents of the Jews), such as eating pork, wearing mixtures of wool and linen, and the scapegoat on the Day of Atonement, for which the only explanation is that God enacted these laws, "and you do not have permission to think about them."[63]

In this chapter, Rambam (following the Talmudic discussion) equates the *huqim* with laws, the rationale or benefit of which the masses do not understand, as opposed to *mishpatim*, which are laws, the rationale or benefit of which is manifest to the masses. The fact that the masses (Arabic: *jumhur*; Hebrew: *hamon*)[64] do not understand the rationale of the *huqim*, however, does not mean that they lack such rationale and purpose (in which case, as we have seen, they would be futile actions), because, as Rambam emphasizes, all the commandments serve a beneficial purpose.

---

62 Leo Strauss, "How to Begin to Study the *Guide of the Perplexed*," p. xxxv.
63 Babylonian Talmud, Yoma 67b.
64 In modern Arabic, the term *jumhuriya* (republic) is based on this term. In the medieval usage of Rambam and others, the masses are contrasted with the elite intelligentsia or (as in this chapter) individuals who understand what the masses do not.

Nevertheless, even beneficial commandments may be, to some degree and in some cases, arbitrary (as in the specific animals and number of animals to be sacrificed for various purposes according to the Torah). For instance, we may well regard as objectively necessary the distinction society makes between majors and minors, or the requirement of a minimum age to qualify for a driver's license. That objective social requirement is not undermined by the admittedly arbitrary decision as to which specific a given society determines to be the age of majority or the minimum age to drive an automobile.

In his earlier Commentary to the Mishnah, in Chapter Six of his *Shemonah Peraqim* ("Eight Chapters on Ethics"), namely his Introduction to Avot, Rambam, following the same Talmudic passage, had already drawn a similar distinction between the two kinds of commandments discussed by the rabbis. However, in the earlier work, that distinction is phrased differently from way it is phrased in the *Guide of the Perplexed* III:26. Chapter Six of the *Shemonah Peraqim* opens by contrasting the "saint" or "excellent" person (Arabic: *faḍil*; Hebrew: *ḥasid*) with a person "who subdues his inclination" (*kovesh et yiẓro*).[65] In Rambam's analysis, according to the philosophers, the "saint" is one who has no desire for evil, whereas according to the rabbis, one "who subdues in inclination" to do something forbidden, by saying "I desire it, but my father in heaven has forbidden it"[66] is superior to one who has no desire that he needs to overcome. Rambam then argues that there is no contradiction between the philosophic and the rabbinic views, because they are referring to different situations.

The philosophers are referring to "things that had they not been written [in the Torah], should have been written," whereas the rabbis are referring to "things to which the nations respond and Satan accuses." The first category, which Rambam identified as *mishpatim* (ordinances) in the *Guide of the Perplexed* III:26, is here called by the more generic term *miẓvot* (commandments), and the second category (in both works) is called *ḥuqim* (statutes). But he then also identifies these categories respectively with one of Sa'adiah Ga'on's categories, *miẓvot sikhliyot* (rational commandments) and *miẓvot shim'iyot* (traditional commandments).[67]

At first blush, by a superficial comparison of the sayings of the philosophers and the rabbis, one might be inclined to say that they contradict one another. Such, however, is not the case. Both are correct and, moreover, are not in disagreement

---

65　Cf. Avot 4:1, where Ben Zoma says, "Who is mighty? One who subdues his inclination (*eizehu gibor, ha-kovesh et yiẓro*).

66　Rambam here is quoting Rabbi Simeon ben Gamliel. However in *Sifra* to Exodus 20:26 (ed. Venice, 1545, col. 184) the statement is attributed to Rabbi El'azar ben 'Azariah.

67　See the discussion of these categories in Sa'adiah's thought, in Ch. 2 (II:3.1).

in the least, as the evils which the philosophers term such — and of which they say that he who has no longing for them is more to be praised than he who desires them but conquers his passion — are **things which all people commonly agree are evils,** such as the shedding of blood, theft, robbery, fraud, injury to one who has done no harm, ingratitude, contempt for parents, and the like. The prescriptions against these are called commandments (mizvot), about which the rabbis said, "If they had not already been written, they should be written." **Some of our later sages, who were infected with the disease (Arabic: *marad*; Hebrew: *mahalah*) of the Mutakallimun, called these "rational commandments."** There is no doubt that a soul which has the desire for, and lusts after, the above-mentioned misdeeds, is imperfect, that a noble soul has absolutely no desire for any such crimes, and experiences no struggle in refraining from them. When, however, the rabbis maintain that he who overcomes his desire has more merit and a greater reward [than he who has no temptation], they say so only in reference to **"the traditional commandments." This is quite true, since were it not for the Torah, they would not at all be considered transgressions.** Therefore, the rabbis say that a man should permit his soul to entertain the natural inclination for these things, but that the Torah alone should restrain him from them. Ponder over the wisdom of these men of blessed memory manifest in the examples they adduce. They do not declare "Man should not say, 'I have no desire to kill, to steal and to lie, but I have a desire for these things, yet what can I do, since my father in heaven forbids it'." The instances they cite are all from the traditional commandments, such as partaking of milk and meat together, wearing clothes made of wool and linen... **These and similar enactments are what God called "my statutes" which, as the rabbis say, are "statutes which I have enacted for you, which you have no right to subject to criticism, which the nations of the world criticize and which Satan denounces, as for instance, the red heifer, the scapegoat, and so forth. Those transgressions, however, which the later sages called "rational commandments" are termed "commandments"** (*mizvot*).[68]

As we see in this passage, in his earlier work Rambam refers to Sa'adiah's categories of rational and traditional commandments. What Sa'adiah Ga'on calls rational commandments are "things which all people commonly agree are evils." Rambam's language here is careful and precise, and is based on the discussion of four types of propositions in the *Treatise on Logic*.[69] To reiterate: primary "intelligible" propositions (Arabic: *ma'qulat*; Hebrew: *muskalot*) are accessible equally to all people through reason. (That is why, as we saw, the first two statements in the Decalogue were addressed directly

---

68   Rambam, *Shemonah Peraqim* (Eight Chapters on Ethics), Ch. 6 (Gorfinkle translation, pp. 76–78; my modifications).

69   These four types of propositions are discussed in the *Treatise on Logic* 8:1. We referred to them above, X.3.a.

to the entire people, and not only to Moses). Other propositions, however, are "empirical" (Arabic: *mahsusat*; Hebrew: *muhashot*), "conventional" or "generally accepted" propositions (Arabic: *mashhurat*; Hebrew: *mefursamot*) or propositions "based on tradition" (Arabic: *maqbulat*; Hebrew: *mequbalot*), not intelligible [propositions]."

Moral propositions, then, which Sa'adiah Ga'on called "rational command-ments" are actually not "intelligible" but "generally accepted" propositions. As Rambam points out in the *Guide of the Perplexed* I:1, "intelligible" propositions deal with theoretical matters that are true or false, whereas "conventional" or "generally accepted" propositions deal with practical matters that are deemed to be appropriate or inappropriate, desirable or repugnant behavior. (As we shall see, Adam and Eve, before they ate of the forbidden fruit, had perfect theoretical knowledge, but had no need for practical knowledge, whereas once they ate of the "tree of knowledge of good and evil" they acquired practical knowledge at the expense of theoretical knowledge).

In the passage we have cited from the *Shemonah Peraqim*, Rambam does not mention Sa'adiah Ga'on by name, but obviously has him in mind when he attributes the distinction between" rational" and "traditional" commandments to "some of our later sages, who were infected with the disease (Arabic: *marad*; Hebrew: *mahalah*) of the Mutakallimun." What, however, is the "disease of the Mutakallimun?" Many scholars have understood this reference to mean that Rambam rejected in principle the division of the commandments into "rational" and "traditional" categories, and, therefore, they understand the distinction itself to be the "disease of the Mutakallimun." These scholars agree that Rambam affirms the distinction between *mishpatim*, namely laws, the rationale or benefit of which is manifest to the masses, and *huqim*, laws, the rationale or benefit of which the masses do not understand. However, these scholars insist that Rambam rejects categorizing them as "rational" and "traditional" laws. While these scholars share this conclusion, they reach this conclusion for opposite reasons.

According to Isadore Twersky, Rambam rejected Sa'adiah's division of the laws into "rational" and "traditional" commandments, because in Ram-bam's view, all the commandments are rational, and there are no non-rational, "traditional" commandments.

> Maimonides objected strenuously to those predecessors who said that some commandments were rational laws...What should be understood is that his strenuous objection is nourished by his own passionate conviction that not some but all laws are rational...and with intellectual exertion and insight we are able to discover this necessary rationality of revelation.[70]

---

70   Isadore Twersky, *Introduction to the Code of Maimonides*, pp. 458–459.

Marvin Fox, on the other hand, is among those who argues that Rambam rejected Sa'adiah's division because all of the commandments are traditional. That is to say, their source lies in divine revelation and not on human reason. Fox refers to the categories of propositions in the *Treatise on Logic*. As we have seen, moral behavior is a function of social convention and not of theoretical judgments of true and false, such as the first principles of mathematics. Therefore, moral propositions are not subject to rational proof.

> Moral evil is ultimately a matter of convention, when considered from a philosophic point of view, and a matter of violating divine commandments when considered from a religious point of view... Despite Sa'adia's merit, the fact that he spoke of rational commandments, and thus opened the door even slightly to a theory of natural law is, for Maimonides, clear and incontrovertible evidence of his being "infected with unsound principles"... As a follower of the Aristotelian teaching, [Maimonides] quite properly would refuse to recognize as wise who could be so confused that he would treat matters of convention or taste as if they were capable of rational demonstration. There is, in addition, a danger to society in such an error... Once it is clear that moral distinctions are not rational, and if they are no longer accepted on the authority of the temporal sovereign or of God, there is no longer any ground whatsoever for restraint in human behavior.[71]

Both Twersky and Fox (and those who agree with their opposing arguments) thus agree that Rambam rejected Sa'adiah Ga'on's division of the commandments as "rational" and "traditional," and that this fallacious division constituted the "disease" of the Mutakallimun from which Sa'adiah was "infected." This conclusion would then explain why Rambam does not mention the distinction between "rational" and "traditional" commandments in his discussion of *mishpatim* and *ḥuqim* in the *Guide of the Perplexed* III:26, since (in their view) Rambam simply rejected Sa'adiah's distinction in principle. Nevertheless, as we have seen, although Twersky and Fox arrive at the same conclusion, paradoxically they do so for opposite reasons.

If, then, we reexamine Rambam's careful wording in the *Shemonah Peraqim*, we may have another way to understand his meaning. He says: "Some of our later sages, who were infected with the disease of the Mutakallimun, called these 'rational commandments'." Does the qualification "who were infected with the disease of the Mutakallimun" apply in general to "some of our later sages," without specifically referring to the rational commandments, or does the "disease" refer specifically to the division of the commandments

---

71   Marvin Fox, "Maimonides and Aquinas on Natural Law," in *Interpreting Maimoindes: Studies in Methodology, Metaphysics, and Moral Philosophy* (Chicago: University of Chicago Press, 1990), pp. 134–137.

into rational and traditional categories? Most scholars, whether they agree with Twersky or with Fox, understand the division of the commandments *per se* to constitute the specific "disease" Rambam had in mind.

We can, however, understand Rambam's words differently. The phrase "who were infected with the disease of the Mutakallimun" may apply in general to "some of our later sages" and not specifically to the division of the commandments. As we have seen, Rambam rejected the Kalam as a closed system, which attempts to adapt the facts to its preconceived notions, rather than adapting theory to the facts.

Nevertheless, this general methodological rejection of the Kalam as a closed system did not prevent Rambam from adopting specific arguments or conclusions of the Kalam. For example, as we have seen, Rambam's proof of the unity of God at the end of the *Guide of the Perplexed* II:1 is taken directly from the second Kalam proof of unity in the *Guide of the Perplexed* I:75, a proof that Rambam called demonstrative and philosophical.

If we compare the general negative reference in Chapter Six ("some of our later sages who were infected with the disease of the Mutakallimun") to an earlier reference in Chapter One, we see a difference. In the first chapter, Rambam criticizes the Mutakallimun for concluding that everything the imagination can imagine must be possible: "In this regard, the Mutakallimun have fallen into grievous and pernicious error."[72] The Arabic term translated as "in this regard" is *wa-huna*, meaning "here" (i.e., in this case). In other words, Rambam's general objection to the Kalam in principle as a closed system did not prevent him, in some cases, from adopting one of their specific arguments (as with the proof of God's unity), and in other cases, from making a specific criticism (as with their view that anything imaginable is possible).

In both works, the *Shemonah Peraqim* and the *Guide of the Perplexed*, Rambam, as we have seen, did not object to the rabbinic distinction between different kinds of commandments; to the contrary, he adopted and developed it. Rambam also differentiated commandments which have a rationale evident even to the masses, and which, had they not been written in the Torah "should be written," from commandments, the rationale of which is not evident to the masses, and the validity of which lies exclusively in their having been commanded in the Torah. Furthermore, in the *Shemonah Peraqim* he used this distinction to harmonize the difference between the philosophers' preference for the saintly person who has no desire for evil, and the rabbis' preference for the person who "subdues his inclination." For this purpose — the philosophic versus the religious ideal — Sa'adiah's terminology is useful, because the "rational" commandments are those

---

72　*Shemonah Peraqim*, Ch. 1 (Gorfinkle translation, pp. 41–42.

the philosophers have in mind, whereas the "traditional" or "revealed" commandments are those the rabbis have in mind.

Therefore, Sa'adiah's terminology was appropriate for this discussion. However, in the *Guide of the Perplexed* III:26, the discussion concerns the rationale of the commandments, and Rambam's challenge is to show that all the commandments ultimately serve some beneficial purpose, even if that purpose is not immediately evident (at least to the masses). In this context, Sa'adiah's terminology is simply irrelevant.

Rambam's reference to "some of our later sages, who were infected with the disease of the Mutakallimun" may, therefore, simply mean that these later sages were, in general, wrong to follow the closed system of the Kalam. That does not mean that they could not, like Rambam himself, adopt specific arguments that were correct, even if the method as a whole was wrong. In other words, the criticism may apply in general, and not specifically to their adopting the distinction between "rational commandments" and "traditional commandments." If this reading of Rambam's statement is correct, then (contrary to what Twersky and Fox argued) he is not rejecting Sa'adiah's distinction between different kinds of commandments — since he explicitly accepts the distinction between commandments the rationale and benefit of which are obvious to the masses, and those, the rationale of which is not obvious to the masses. As he did in other places, such as the proof of the unity of God, he accepts the specific proof or point, while generally rejecting, on methodological grounds, the Kalam as a closed system. The "later sages" thus made a valid point, despite their being infected, generally, by the disease of the Mutakallimun.

One final observation: why does Rambam refer vaguely to "some of our later sages" and not mention Sa'adiah Ga'on by name? Shlomo Pines has drawn our attention to the fact that Rambam, who does not hesitate in the *Guide of the Perplexed* to cite by name biblical, rabbinic, Greek and Arab sources, refrains from mentioning by name earlier Jewish philosophers.[73] Pines concludes that Rambam had "no use for a specific Jewish philosophic tradition." There may be other reasons, however, for Rambam's reticence in mentioning earlier Jewish thinkers with whom he disagreed. It could reflect his desire to refrain from explicit criticism on philosophic grounds of people, like Sa'adiah Ga'on, whose thought he rejected but whom he otherwise admired and respected. Another possibility relates to the pedagogic purpose of the *Guide of the Perplexed*, namely to justify the Torah in terms of philosophy. Rambam can cite by name non-Jewish philosophers whose opinions the perplexed student accepted as philosophically authoritative.

---

73 Shlomo Pines, "The Philosophic Sources of the *Guide of the Perplexed*," pp. cxxxii–cxxxiv.

Jewish philosophers (even if they were correct, but certainly if their approach was erroneous) would lack the same credibility in the eyes of a student who questioned the Torah, and thus his Jewish religious identity, because of his exposure to non-Jewish philosophy.

[X.4]   PROVIDENCE AND THE PROBLEM OF EVIL

[X.4.a]   "WHO FORMS LIGHT AND CREATES DARKNESS, MAKES PEACE AND CREATES EVIL" (*Guide* III:10)

In the previous section, we discussed Rambam's reference to "the disease of the Mutakallimun." In the *Guide of the Perplexed* III:10 he discusses another one of their errors, namely a misunderstanding of the concept of "privation" or "non-being" (Arabic: *'adam*; Hebrew: *he'eder*). On the one hand, they regard all privation as absolute, and understand that non-being does not require an agent. On the other hand, they fail to recognize that there can also be privation in a relative sense, as when darkness is produced by the removal of light. In such cases, although there actually is no direct agent of the darkness, there is an agent in the indirect sense of something acting on the light and removing it. The light exists, and it requires an agent for its existence (and in this case for its removal). The Mutakallimun compound their error by thinking that darkness, as the contrary of light, also exists as light does, and therefore requires an agent. Darkness, however, does not exist, but is the privation of light, and therefore in and of itself does not require an agent.

As darkness does not exist but is the privation of light, so evil does not exist, but is the privation of the good, and as such, requires no agent. How, then, are we to understand Isaiah 45:7, that God "forms light and creates darkness, makes peace and creates evil?"[74] The verse does not mean that God actually is the agent of darkness and evil, since they are privations of their contraries. Rather, it means that God is their agent on in the indirect sense of producing the privation by removing its existent contrary, respectively light and the good.

God's actions only produce existing things, not privations. God is thus the agent of the good, and not of evil as the privation of the good. God's actions can only be related indirectly and accidentally to evil, in the sense that God brought matter into existence, and matter—which by definition is always limited—is the source of privation. Insofar as matter exists, it is good. Insofar

---

[74]   In the morning service of the traditional Jewish liturgy, this verse is cited with a significant change. Instead of concluding that God "creates evil," the liturgy praises God "who forms light and creates darkness, makes peace and creates everything (*ha-kol*)."

as it is limited, it is the source of privation, since beyond those limits it does not exist. Thus, although the existence of matter itself is good, its necessary corollary of privation is the source of evil.

In the next chapter *(Guide* III:11), Rambam continues to develop this theme. Human evils also derive from privations, such as ignorance, which is the privation of knowledge, and if "there were knowledge...they would no longer harm themselves and others."

Rambam's approach to evil as the privation of the good, and human evil as resulting from ignorance as the privation of knowledge, is based on Plato, according to whom God, as the source of good, cannot cause harm or evil.[75] Plato also held that people do evil out of ignorance. Nobody would knowingly harm himself, and a person who harms others fails to understand that evil ultimately harms the person who does it, and thus he is ultimately harming himself.[76]

[X.4.b]   THE THREE SOURCES OF EVIL *(Guide* III:12–13)

In their ignorance, many people think that there is more evil than good in the world, because of something bad that happens to them, as if all existence were for the sake of the human species, or for the individual person. The existence of the individual person, and even more, of individual animals, is insignificant in comparison with the existence of the whole world. Although the human species is the most noble of terrestrial beings, it, too, is insignificant in comparison with the heavenly beings.[77] All existing beings are equally created by God, and the anthropocentric view of the world is incorrect.

> Therefore, in my view, the correct opinion according to the beliefs of the Torah, which accords with the speculative [philosophical] opinion, is that one should not believe that all existing things are for the sake of the existence of humans. Rather, all other existing things are also intended for their own sakes and not for the sake of something else.[78]

People also tend to blame God for evils that humans themselves do by their free will. There are three types of evil from which people suffer—natural, social and individual—but the most prevalent of these is the evil individuals inflict on themselves.

Natural evil results from our nature as physical beings subject to gene-ration and corruption. Although we all regret corruption, there can be no

---

75   Plato, Republic II, 379.
76   Plato, Meno 77.
77   *Guide of the Perplexed* III:12.
78   *Guide of the Perplexed* III:13.

generation without corruption, and if we were not subject to corruption, we could not have been generated. In any event, natural evil—such as floods or fires—is the least prevalent type of evil.

Social evil—what people inflict on other people—is far more prevalent than natural evil, but despite crime and "great wars," social evil does not affect "the majority of the world as a whole."

Individual evil, then, is the most prevalent form of evil, and consists of what individuals do to themselves, because of their vices, such as immoderately indulging their appetites for food, drink and sex. Were people to moderate their desires and limit themselves to what is necessary, most of this type of evil could be avoided. God's justice and beneficence are also evident in the resources available to us. The more things are necessary, the more often they can be found, the more equitably they are distributed, and the less expensive they are. For instance, air, water and food are all necessary for maintaining life, but of these three, air is the most necessary, and the most prevalent and free, and water, less prevalent than air, is more prevalent and less expensive than food. There is no injustice in the fact that luxuries are not equitably distributed, because the person who possesses them gains nothing real, "but has gained only a false imaginary [benefit] or a frivolous plaything."[79]

[X.4.c] GOD'S KNOWLEDGE (*Guide* III:16, III:19–21)

Providence and the problem of evil raise the question of God's knowledge of the world, which, it will be recalled, is the tenth of Rambam's Thirteen Foundations.

> The tenth foundation is that [God], may he be praised, knows the actions of humans and has not abandoned them.

This is, of course, the traditional religious affirmation of God's knowledge of human affairs. However, as we have seen, the "God of Aristotle" (in Judah Ha-Levi's phrase) transcends any such knowledge; the only subject worthy of God's knowledge is God himself. Similarly, in the *Guide of the Perplexed* III:16, Rambam cites several arguments "of the philosophers" against God's knowledge of particulars. According to their view, one possibility is that God knows the particular evils of this world, but in that case either (a) he orders them and is responsible for them, or (b) he is impotent to do anything about them, or (c) he has the power to do something about these evils, but refrains from intervening. Another possibility is that God does not know these things. We cannot attribute (b) impotence or (c) indifference to God, nor

---

[79]   *Guide of the Perplexed* III:12.

(in light of Rambam's rejection of Aristotelian necessity) can we conclude that (a) everything is determined by necessity. These considerations led the philosophers to conclude that God does not know the events (including the evils) of this world.[80]

This conclusion is absurd, however, because it attributes ignorance—a deficiency—to God, and in Rambam's view, it is "a primary intelligible" that we must attribute perfections and not deficiencies to God.[81]

How, then, can we affirm God's knowledge of the evils of the world without being their cause? How can God have foreknowledge of events without undermining human free will? And how can God know ever-changing reality without his knowledge also changing? According to Rambam, all of these philosophic objections to God's knowledge of the world are based on the fallacious assumption that God's knowledge is analogous to human knowledge, since "God's knowledge is his essence and his essence is his knowledge."[82] Rather, the term "knowledge" is applied equivocally to us and to God, because our knowledge is consequent on reality (i.e., what we know is determined by reality), whereas reality is consequent on God's knowledge (i.e., reality determined by God's knowledge of it as its cause).[83] By knowing himself as the cause of all reality, God knows that reality.

Just as we refer to God's knowledge (Arabic: *'ilm*; Hebrew: *yedi'ah*) and to human knowledge are equivocally, so do we use the term "providence" (Arabic: *'inaya*; Hebrew: *hashgaḥah*) equivocally.[84]

[X.4.d]   FIVE VIEWS OF PROVIDENCE (*Guide* 3:17)

As he did with creation and prophecy, Rambam describes different views regarding divine providence; these five views will, in later chapters, be identified with characters in the book of Job. The first view is that of Epicurus, according to whom there is no providence at all, and no order in the universe, because everything occurs by chance. As we saw in the discussion of creation, Rambam concludes that Aristotle proved that there is order in nature, and thus disproved the Epicurean position.

The second view is that of Aristotle, according to whom divine providence extends only to the heavenly spheres (which, accordingly, are eternal), and does not extend below the sphere of the moon, except to terrestrial species, which are also eternal, but not to individuals, which exist by chance and are

---

80   *Guide of the Perplexed* III:16.
81   *Guide of the Perplexed* III:19.
82   *Guide of the Perplexed* III:20.
83   *Guide of the Perplexed* III:21.
84   *Guide of the Perplexed* III:20.

subject to generation and corruption. In other words, indestructibility and lack of change are evidence of divine providence, and those are features of species, which are eternal, and not of individuals, which perish.

According to the third view, of the Ash'ariyya school of Kalam, everything is subject to divine providence and control. Everything is known by God, and everything is determined by God's will, purpose and governance. Therefore, there is neither chance nor free will. This view, then, precludes the realm of the possible; everything is either necessary or impossible. As a result, Rambam concludes, since according to this view people have no free will nor any power to control their actions, there is no point to religious law or commandments.

For opposite reasons, Aristotle and the Ash'ariyya arrive at the same conclusion, namely that there is no difference—in terms of providence—between a person and a driven leaf. For Aristotle, the individual—whether a human or a leaf—is subject to chance, not providence, and for the Ash'ariyya, the individual—again whether a human or a leaf—is subject to complete determinism.

The fourth view is that of the Mu'tazilah school of Kalam, and is more moderate than the extreme determinism of the Ash'ariyya. The Mu'tazilah affirm limited human free will and power to act. Therefore it is appropriate for people to be given laws and commandments, and to be rewarded and punished justly according to their deeds.

> The fifth opinion is our opinion, i.e., the opinion of our Torah...A foundation of the Torah of Moses our teacher and all who follow it is that the human being has absolute ability, i.e., that by his nature, choice and will he can do everything that is within human capacity to do...Similarly, all species of animals move by will...A person has the ability to do whatever he wills or chooses of those things which are within his capacity. This is a foundation with which, thank God, no one in our community disagrees. It is also one of the foundations of the Torah of Moses our teacher, that God is in no way unjust, and that people, individually and collectively, justly deserve whatever happens to them...although we do not understand how they deserve it.[85]

Although Rambam called the fifth view "our opinion, i.e., the opinion of our Torah," he then proceeds to elaborate "my own belief regarding this foundation," but carefully qualifies it by stating that it is not a conclusion based on demonstration, but derives from his reading of Scripture, although it is closer to logical deduction than are the other views. In a sense, his own view is a synthesis of the second and fifth views (respectively of Aristotle and the Torah). "I believe," Rambam continues, that among all the species in the

---

[85]   *Guide of the Perplexed* III:17.

sublunar world, providence extends, among individuals, only to humans, but he agrees with Aristotle's view concerning animals and plants, which have only generic providence; their individuals exist by chance.

> As for me, in my opinion divine providence follows the divine emanation (Arabic: *al-faiḍ al-ilahi*; Hebrew: *ha-shefa' ha-elohi*). The species to which this intellectual emanation is conjoined, so that it becomes endowed with intellect... is the one to which divine providence attaches.

If, then, a ship sinks, and the people on it drown, or a house collapses and kills the people in it, what happened to the ship or house, and to the animals in them, occurred by chance (as Aristotle believed), but the loss of human life is providential, "by the divine will" and according to what those people deserve, although we do not necessarily understand why they deserve it. Human individuals, then, are unique among all terrestrial individuals in that they benefit from divine providence in proportion to their intellectual development.

> I believe that providence follows the intellect and attaches to it. For providence only comes from an intelligent being, who is an intellect perfect with unique perfection. Whoever is conjoined with something of this emanation will be reached by this providence to the extent that he has been reached by this intellect. According to me, this opinion accords with the intelligible and with the verses of the Torah.

Providence thus attaches to individual humans, but not to animals or plants, and is proportionate to the intellectual development of the individual. To the extent that the person develops his intellectual faculty, he transcends his individual bodily limitations and participates in universal knowledge and reason. To this extent, he also benefits from divine providence. As we saw in our discussion of Rambam's understanding of "the world to come" (*'olam ha-ba*),[86] intellectual apprehension is the basis for immortality: the body and lower functions of the soul which enliven the body perish, but the intellect survives in proportion to its actualization in knowledge. In the same way, the individual human, by virtue of intellectual apprehension, can transcend particularity and acquire aspects of universality and permanence, like the species, which makes providence possible on the level of the particular individual. Both immortality and providence, then, are functions of intellectual attainment and proportional to it; the more the person's intellect is actualized, the more immortality and providence he enjoys.

Providence, therefore, can attach to individual humans, but not to individual animals or plants. Rambam thus bridges the moral requirement imposed by the

---

86   See the discussion in Ch. 8 (VIII.2.c.ii).

Torah—that each individual be responsible and accountable for his behavior in a providential sense—and the philosophic requirement established by Aristotle—that providence can only apply to things that are universal and permanent. Nevertheless, Rambam carefully qualified what he has said about providence. It is "my own belief," not a demonstrative conclusion, although it is compatible with reason and with Scripture.

Paradoxically, there is a parallel between Rambam's theory of providence and Abraham ibn Ezra's theory of astrology. That parallelism, however, is only formal. According to Rambam, what happens to animals occurs by chance, and only human individuals benefit from divine providence, in proportion to their intellectual development. According to Ibn Ezra, what happens to animals (and humans who lack knowledge) is astrally determined, but those who have the necessary knowledge (and/or observe the Torah) can be saved from astral decrees. In other words, for both thinkers, it is the intellect, in Rambam's terms, or the rational soul (*neshamah*) in Ibn Ezra's terms, by which individual humans are enabled to transcend and escape their common destiny with other terrestrial individuals.[87]

[X.4.e]   THE BOOK OF JOB (*Guide* III:22–23)

Rambam discusses the biblical book of Job in two chapters (III:22–23) within the larger discussion of divine knowledge and providence (III:16–24). In Rambam's view, the book is a parable (Arabic: *mathal*; Hebrew: *mashal*), not a historical book. That view, as Rambam correctly insists, has rabbinic precedent: "Job never existed and was never created; it is a parable."[88] Rambam's innovative interpretation consists of two points: (1) The lesson of the parable is that Job erred not morally but intellectually; and (2) The positions represented by Job, his three associates Eliphaz, Bildad and Zophar, as well as Elihu, correspond to four of the five views on providence (in *Guide* III:17) discussed above. Only the view of Epicurus, denying providence and affirming that everything happens by chance, is not represented in the book of Job, because all of the book's protagonists agree that God knows, and ultimately is the direct or indirect cause of, what happens to Job.

Regarding the first point, that Job erred intellectually but not morally, Rambam points out that Job is described at the beginning of the book as being moral and righteous in his behavior, but not as "wise" (*ḥakham*), "understanding" (*mevin*), or "intelligent" (*maskil*). Had Job been wise, his situation would not have caused him to doubt divine justice. That is why

---

87   See the discussion of Ibn Ezra's astrological theory in Ch. 5, and the parallel to Rambam
      drawn in V.12.
88   Babylonian Talmud, Bava Batra 15a.

Satan was permitted to "touch" Job's body, family and possessions, but not his "soul" (*nefesh*) (Job 2:6), which for Rambam means his intellect. Job's error was intellectual, not moral, and therefore Job, at the end of the book, had to be able to come, on his own, to a proper theoretical understanding of divine justice.

Regarding the second point, all five protagonists in the story (Job, Eliphaz, Bildad, Zophar and Elihu) agree about the basic facts: Job was innocent and righteous; God knew what was happening to Job, but despite Job's innocence, caused him to suffer. They agree about the facts, but disagree about how to interpret them. That is why the book has no place for the Epicurean view, denying providence, as inconsistent with these basic facts.

Rambam then correlates the other four philosophical and theological positions regarding providence with the parable's protagonists, based in each case on a key verse in their speeches. First, at the beginning of the story Job had a simple, pious belief in divine providence, based on tradition, but as a result of his suffering, comes to the Aristotelian position denying individual providence, and therefore concludes that there is no difference in God's eyes between the righteous and the wicked: "It is all one; therefore, I have said, 'He destroys the innocent and the wicked' (Job 9:22)."

Second, Rambam correlates the position of Eliphaz with the view of the Torah, that humans have free will and are, therefore, justly rewarded and punished for their actions. Job, Eliphaz asserts, deserved his suffering as punishment for his sins: "Is not your evil great, and your transgressions without end?" (Job 22:5).

Third, Bildad represents the view of the Mu'tazilah school of the Kalam, affirming that people are justly punished, and that God can compensate for people's unwarranted suffering in this world with reward in the world to come: "If you are pure and upright, [God] would arise for you and reward the habitation of your righteousness. Although your beginning was small, your end will increase greatly" (Job 8:6–7).

The fourth position is that of Zophar, who represents the view of the Ash'ariyya school of the Kalam, that everything is determined exclusively by God's will, and therefore cannot be questioned, nor reasons sought for what God wills: "But would that God would speak and open his lips against you; and tell you the secrets of wisdom...Can you find out the range of God? Can you find out the purpose of the Almighty?" (Job 11:5–7).

The fifth view is that of Elihu, who reviews the points raised by Job's three associates, but adds to them the notion of an intercessor angel (*mal'akh meliẓ*; Job 33:23). Since prophecy, as we have seen, takes place through the mediation of an angel (= separate intellect), the intercessor angel in this passage refers to the prophetic insight that Job attains at the end of the book, finally resolving his doubts. Only then does Job truly comprehend his earlier theoretical and intellectual error which had led him to question God's justice, when he failed to understand the equivocal nature of God's providence and governance of the world.

> The notion of his providence is not the same as the notion of our providence; nor is the notion of his governance of his creatures the same as our governance of whatever we govern. [The two notions] cannot be included in the same definition, as every perplexed person thinks, and they have nothing in common except their name. Similarly, our action does not resemble his action, and cannot be included in the same definition. Just as natural actions differ from artificial actions, so do the divine governance of, and the divine providence over, and the divine purpose for those natural things differ from our governance of, our providence over, and our purpose for whatever we govern, provide for, and intend.
>
> This is the intention of the whole book of Job. I mean, to establish this foundation of belief, and to alert [us] to what should be inferred from natural subjects, so that you not err and seek in your imagination that his knowledge is like our knowledge, or that his purpose and providence and governance are like our purpose and providence and governance. When a person knows this, it will be easy for him to bear all his suffering lightly, and his suffering will not cause him any more doubts about God, and whether [God] does or does not know; whether he exercised providence or neglect. Rather, he will increase his love, as it says at the end of this prophecy: "Therefore I abhor and repent, on account [of my being] dust and ashes" (Job 42:6).[89]

Job thus came to realize, because of the prophetic revelation he receives in the storm, that he had erred intellectually. That is to say, he had erred theoretically, although he had not sinned practically. He was righteous, but not wise. Job initially believed in divine providence, based on religious tradition. Then, on account of his suffering, he had doubted God's providence and governance of the world. At this point he affirmed the Aristotelian denial of individual providence. This doubt arose from his fundamental misunderstanding and fallacious belief that divine governance and providence are analogous to human governance and providence, that divine and human governance can be "included in the same definition, as every perplexed person thinks." Only much later did Job realize his earlier error, and come to understand that these terms can only be attributed equivocally to God. Now Job came to know God "with a certain knowledge," whereas he previously had only known God based on tradition (Arabic: *taqlid*; Hebrew: *qabbalah*).

Now, at the end of the parable, Job understood that the knowledge of God constitutes the ultimate human happiness, and that material misfortunes should not dominate his concern, whereas previously, in his ignorance, Job had imagined that bodily health, wealth and children are the ultimate goal

---

89   *Guide of the Perplexed* III:23.

(Arabic: *ghayah*; Hebrew: *takhlit*). "Therefore [Job] was perplexed by such perplexities and said the things that he said." Now that he finally had a proper perspective, based on the correct understanding of the equivocal nature of divine governance and providence, and of the true purpose of life, Job was no longer perplexed.

The book of Job is thus a parable, of the sort Rambam stated, in the Introduction to the *Guide of the Perplexed*, that the book intended to explain, beginning with the fact that it is a parable. The character of Job, like Rambam's perplexed student in the Introduction, is a righteous, moral and pious Jew who is intellectually perplexed, because he fails to appreciate the equivocal nature of the way we speak about God. Like Rambam's student, Job goes through three stages: he begins as a simple, righteous and pious person, who believes what tradition teaches. Then he progresses to a limited philosophical position, in which he is perplexed by the apparent contradictions between Scripture and reason, and his exposure to philosophy leads him to doubt the Torah. Finally, he comes to understand the equivocal nature of the language Scripture applies to God, and his perplexity is resolved. In all these ways, then, in Rambam's treatment, the book of Job is, in effect, a biblical "Guide of the Perplexed."[90]

[X.4.f]   THE UNIQUE PROVIDENTIAL CONJUNCTION OF MOSES AND THE PATRIARCHS (*Guide* III:51)

Since providence "follows the intellect and attaches to it," and not all people have developed their intellect to the same extent, they do not all enjoy the same degree or quality of providential protection. "Providence applies to one who possesses intellect in proportion to the measure of his intellect."[91] The question then arises whether, when a person's intellectual apprehension is interrupted, his individual providence is also interrupted, and whether, at such times, he is then (like animals) subject to chance?

In the *Guide of the Perplexed* III:51, when discussing the true worship of God which requires proper intention (Hebrew: *kavanah*)[92] and the avoidance of distraction, Rambam states that

> the intellect which emanated from God is the contact (or: "conjunction;" Arabic: *al-waṣlah*; Hebrew: *ha-dibuq*) between use and him. You have the choice: if you wish to strengthen and reinforce that contact, do so. If you wish to weaken and undermine it gradually until you cut it, do so.

---

90 For a detailed analysis of this point, see my study, "The Book of Job as a Biblical 'Guide of the Perplexed'," in my *Jewish Philosophy: Foundations and Extensions, Volume Two: On Philosophers and Their Thought* (Lanham: University Press of America), pp. 97–110.

91 *Guide of the Perplexed* III:51.

92 Rambam here uses the Hebrew term in the Arabic.

That intellect "contact" or "bond" is weakened or cut by thinking of things other than God, such as physical needs. At times of such distraction, "you cut that contact between you and God, and are then not with him, and he is then not with you." In the case of Moses and the Patriarchs (Abraham, Isaac and Jacob), however, their intellectual conjunction was so powerful that it was not cut even when they engaged in their bodily needs and social affairs. Externally, their bodily limbs were involved in these matters, while internally, their intellects remained focused on God without interruption. Other people, however, who are not on this sublime level, maintain their intellectual bond—and thus enjoy providential protection—only when actually thinking of God.

> We have already explained to you in the chapters on providence that providence applies to one who possesses intellect in proportion to the measure of his intellect. A perfect person whose intellect never stops being occupied with God always has providence. But a person who has perfect apprehension, but whose thought occasionally is emptied of God, only has providence during the time he is thinking of God, but while he is occupied by something else, the providence withdraws from him...because while he is otherwise occupied, he has no actual intellect...That being the case, the great doubt of the philosophers who negate divine providence from individual humans—thus equating them with the individuals of other species—is resolved. Their proof was that great evils befall excellent and good people. The secret of this has now been explained, even according to their opinion.[93] Divine providence is constantly [applying] to a person who have received this emanation which is available to whoever strives to attain it. While a person's thoughts are free [from distraction] and apprehend God...nothing evil can happen to him, because he is with God and God is with him. However, when his thoughts are diverted from God, at which time he is separated from God and God is separated from him, he becomes vulnerable to any evil which may possibly befall him. What brings about providence and deliverance from the sea of chance is that intellectual emanation.[94]

On the face of it, Rambam has clearly answered our question: providence ceases when intellectual conjunction is interrupted, and at such times the person, without the benefit of providence, is subject (like individual animals) to chance. What does this mean, however? Is this providential protection a natural process or a miraculous and supra-natural divine intervention in the world? Samuel ibn Tibbon, the translator of the *Guide of the Perplexed*, was the first to raise this question in a letter he wrote to Rambam in which he called attention to the problem, which also has intrigued later readers of the book. (We have no evidence that his letter was ever answered).

---

[93]   "Their opinion," i.e., the opinion of the philosophers who deny individual providence because they see that evil befalls excellent and good people.

[94]   *Guide of the Perplexed* III:51.

On the one hand, in this chapter (III:51) Rambam states that "we have already explained to you in the chapters on providence that providence applies to one who possesses intellect in proportion to the measure of his intellect." On the other hand, Samuel ibn Tibbon's letter calls attention to a contradiction between this chapter and the earlier chapters (III:17–23). In this chapter, Rambam states that "the secreet of this has now been explained, even according to their opinion," namely that providence actually protects people from bodily harm so long as they maintain their intellectual conjunction with God. In the previous chapters, however, Rambam made no such claim. To the contrary: Job's new insight was that the physical calamities he experienced should not lead him to perplexity and to doubt divine justice, because these material concerns are not ultimately significant. Similarly, does Rambam mean (in III:51) that God actually intervenes supra-naturally to save from physical harm an individual who maintains constant intellect contact with him, or does the parable of the sinking boat (in III:17) mean that providence functions purely naturally, and without divine intervention, because the intellectual understands the potential danger and therefore avoids putting himself in harm's way? The example of the sinking boat, in turn, raises another question. Granted that the intellectual may be able to anticipate certain dangers, and on that basis choose to avoid putting himself in harm's way, how does the intellectual conjunction with God protect him from natural dangers that cannot be anticipated or predicted, like a sudden earthquake or flood for which there was no advance warning, and which have nothing to do with the intellectual's ability to choose a cautious course of action? Samuel ibn Tibbon's letter concludes by asking whether we have here an instance of a deliberate contradiction, such as Rambam called our attention to in the Introduction to the book.[95]

So far as we know, Rambam never replied to Samuel ibn Tibbon's letter. However, Shem Tov ibn Falaquera, who also translated the *Guide of the Perplexed* into Hebrew (although only those portions he commented on in his commentary, *The Guide to the Guide*), addressed Samuel ibn Tibbon's question at the end of his commentary.[96] Falaquera rejects the miraculous and supra-natural interpretation of *Guide of the Perplexed* III:51. According to Falaquera, there are two kinds of miracles. Supra-natural miracles involving a divine intervention and change in nature (such as the splitting of the sea and the stopping of the Jordan river) are performed by prophets. There are, however, also miracles that do not involve such a change in nature, by which,

---

[95]　The letter may be found in Z. Diesendruck, "Samuel and Moses ibn Tibbon on Maimonides' Theory of Providence," in *Hebrew Union College Annual*, Vol. XI (1936), pp. 341–365.

[96]　Falaquera's reply is included as the second of three chapters of an Appendix to his commentary. Cf. *Moreh Ha-Moreh*, ed. M. Bisliches, p. 146.

for instance, people can be saved from a flood or earthquake, are "seen and experienced in every generation," and can be performed by the righteous person (*ḥasid*). These occurrences, however, are also intentional and do not happen by chance.

For Falaquera, then, Rambam's intention in *Guide of the Perplexed* III:51 should be understood as such natural miracles, and not as supra-natural suspension of the natural.[97] Falaquera also rejects Samuel ibn Tibbon's claim that in this chapter, which Ibn Tibbon understood to posit a miraculous providential intervention in nature, Rambam was expressing a personal "religious opinion," in contrast with the "philosophic opinion" of the previous chapters. Despite this defense of Rambam against Samuel ibn Tibbon's suggestion that there is a fundamental and deliberate contradiction between his allegedly philosophic opinion in the previous chapters and his allegedly religious opinion in this chapter, Falaquera rejected Rambam's claim that those who enjoy divine providence are always protected from physical harm. "It seems to me that the perfect are not always miraculously saved from accidents, and sudden evil happened to some prophets and pious people."[98] Nevertheless, since the most prevalent form of evil is the harm that individuals ignorantly inflict upon themselves, "it seems to me that in [Rambam's] opinion, this providence that they have is how the intellect benefits them, and to the extent that a person is benefited by that intellect, providence applies to him."[99]

Falaquera, then, may well be correct in his understanding of Rambam in this chapter, not as expressing a personal religious view that the righteous are miraculously saved from physical harm in a supra-natural manner (as suggested by Samuel ibn Tibbon), but as meaning nothing more than "natural" miracles not involving any supra-natural intervention. Since most evil results from the harm individuals inflict upon themselves because of their ignorance, the more a person's intellect is actualized through apprehension of the truth, the more "providence" he has, because the less likely he is to harm himself. To the extent that the danger is external (natural or social), the more the person knows, the more "providence" he has in the sense of anticipating predictable danger and taking the necessary precautions. The more he enjoys uninterrupted and undistracted intellectual conjunction, like Moses and the Patriarchs, the less his involvement in worldly activities will interfere with these providential precautions. Finally, even when subject to physical

---

97　Falaquera's distinction between natural and supra-natural miracles resembles the distinction Ramban (Naḥmanides) draws between "hidden miracles" (*nisim nistarim*) involving no change in the natural order, and alluded to by the divine name *Shadai* ("Almighty"), and "well-known miracles" (*nisim mefursamim*) involving a change in the natural order, alluded to by the Tetragrammaton. Cf. Ramban, commentary to Genesis 11:28.

98　Falaquera, *Moreh Ha-Moreh*, p. 146.

99　Falaquera, *Moreh Ha-Moreh*, p. 147.

harm, like Job at the end of the book, he will come to appreciate the ultimate insignificance of such material concerns, because the true human end is the worship of God, and the true worship of God is to know him.

[X.5] THE ULTIMATE HUMAN END: RAMBAM'S ETHICAL AND POLITICAL THEORY

[X.5.a] INTRODUCTION: THE BACKGROUND FOR RAMBAM'S IDEAS

[X.5.a.i] *Literary Sources*

As Shlomo Pines has shown, Rambam was familiar with the Aristotelian writings available in Muslim Spain, namely most of Aristotle's *Corpus* as we know it today. However, Aristotle's *Politics* was not yet available, at least not in Spain and the Maghreb.[100] Rambam's ethical theory was heavily indebted to Aristotle's *Nicomachean Ethics*, but his political theory is largely indebted to Al-Farabi's fundamentally Platonic approach. Rambam's shift from Aristotelian ethical theory to Platonic political theory is not, however, merely a function of what books he happened to have available in Arabic. The Platonic political model also lent itself to the Jewish synthesis he attempted to construct in his conception of the ultimate human end, between the ideals of the *vita activa* and the *vita contemplativa*.

[X.5.a.ii] *The Rabbis: "Is Study Greater or is Action Greater?"*

The tension between the philosophic ideals of the practical *vita activa* and the theoretical[101] *vita contemplativa* is also reflected in the question raised by the Talmudic rabbis: Which is greater, study (i.e., the study of Torah) or action (i.e, performing the Torah's commandments)? We find in rabbinic literature statements supporting both ideals.

The theoretical ideal, for instance, may be found in the discussion in the following passage in the Mishnah, according to which the study of Torah is counter-balanced to all the other commandments together:[102]

> These things have no fixed measure:[103] the corner of the field, the first fruits, appearing [in the Temple], acts of kindness, and the study of Torah. These are

---

[100] Pines, "The Philosophic Sources of the *Guide of the Perplexed*, p. lxi. Also see the discussion above, X.2.b and note 21. According to Pines, Ibn Rushd said that Aristotle's *Politics*, although not available in the west, was available in the Islamic east.

[101] In Greek, the term *theoria* means "contemplation."

[102] Mishnah Pe'ah 1:1.

[103] That is to say, these are commandments which cannot be measured quantitatively.

things which a person benefits from in this world, but the principle remains for him in the world to come: honoring father and mother, acts of kindness, and bringing peace between people. But the study of Torah is equal to them all.

By contrast, we also find statements reflecting the practical ideal.

> Rabbi Ḥanina ben Dosa…used to say: Whoever's actions are greater than his wisdom, his wisdom endures. Whoever's wisdom is greater than his actions, his wisdom does not endure.[104]

Similarly:

> Simeon [the son of Rabban Gamliel] said: All my life I grew up among the sages, but I never found anything better for a person than silence. For study is not the essential thing, but action.[105]

The following passage is ambivalent:

> Rabbi Tarfon and the sages were sitting in the upper story of the house…in Lod. They were asked this question: Is study greater or is action greater? Rabbi Tarfon replied: Action is greater. Rabbi Akiva replied: Study is greater. They all replied: Study is greater, for study leads to action.[106]

The majority consensus here, "Study is greater, for study leads to action," may be nothing more than a compromise between the opposing opinions of Rabbi Tarfon and Rabbi Akiva. On the other hand, their reply is self-contra-dictory. The end is generally considered superior to the means. According to Aristotle, that which is desired for itself is choicer than that which is desired for something else.[107] How, then, can study be "greater" end because it is the means leading to something else, namely action? We shall return to this paradoxical statement later.[108]

[X.5.a.iii] *Aristotle and the Contemplative Ideal*

We shall first review the theoretical ideal as represented in Greek thought by Aristotle, and in Islamic thought by Abu Bakr Muḥammad Al-Ṣa'igh ibn Bajja and Abu Bakr Muḥammad ibn Tufayl, and then the earlier practical ideal as represented by Plato and Abu Naṣr Muḥammad Al-Farabi.

The ultimate end or purpose (Greek: *telos*; Arabic: *ghaya akhira*; Hebrew: *takhlit aharonah*) of human life, according to Aristotle's *Nicomachean Ethics*

---

104 Mishnah, Avot 3:9.
105 Mishnah, Avot 1:17.
106 Babylonian Talmud, Qiddushin 40b.
107 Aristotle, *Nicomachean Ethics* I:6, 1096b.
108 See below, X.5.d.i.

is "an active life of the element that has a rational principle" and "life of the rational element."[109]

> We are seeking what is peculiar to man... There remains, then, an active life of the element that has a rational principle... As "life of the rational element" also has two meanings, we must state that life in the sense of activity is what we mean... We state the function of man to be a certain kind of life, and this to be an activity or actions of the soul implying a rational principle, and the function of a good man to be the good and noble performance of these, and if the action is well performed when it is performed in accordance with the appropriate excellence.

That which is peculiar to the human being is reason; its excellence, therefore, constitutes human perfection and the highest human good. The chief good, as we have seen, is desired for itself and not for something else. Only contemplation constitutes such a good desired for itself and not for something else and the highest human virtue.

> If happiness is activity in accordance with virtue, it is reasonable that it should be in accordance with the highest virtue; and this will be that of the best thing in us. Whether it be reason or something else that is this element which is thought to be our natural ruler and guide and to take thought of things noble and divine, whether it be itself also divine or only the most divine element in us, the activity of this in accordance with its proper virtue will be perfect happiness. That this activity is contemplative we have already said... Firstly, this activity is the best (since not only is reason the best thing in us, but the objects of reason are the best of knowable objects. And secondly, it is the most continuous, since we can contemplate the truth more continuously than we can do anything... The self-sufficiency that is spoken of must belong most to the contemplative activity... This activity alone would seem to be loved for its own sake; for nothing arises from it apart from the contemplating, while from practical activities we gain more or less apart from the action.[110]

As Menachem Kellner has pointed out, for Aristotle to posit contemplation as the ultimate human end and perfection also follows from the philosophic and religious notion of *imitation Dei* ("imitation of God"). Aristotle's conception of God was of intellect eternally thinking itself, since nothing else is worthy of God's thought. Human perfection, by the principle of imitation of God, must thus also lie in contemplation.[111]

---

[109] Aristotle, *Nicomachean Ethics* I:7, 1098b. English translation by W.D. Ross, in Richard McKeon, *The Basic Works of Aristotle* (New York: Random House, 1941), pp. 942–943.

[110] Aristotle, *Nicomachean Ethics* X:7, 1177ab.

[111] Menachem Kellner, "Reading Rambam: Approaches to the Interpretation of Maimonides," in *Jewish History* 5/2 (1991), pp. 86–87.

[X.5.a.iv] *Ibn Bajja: "The Governance of the Solitary"*

The contemplative ideal became a central theme in the thought of the first Arab philosopher in Spain, Abu Bakr Muḥammad Al-Ṣa'igh ibn Bajja, known in Latin as Avempace (Spain, died 1138). Ibn Bajja rejected Al-Farabi's concept of the ideal "Virtuous City" (*Al-Madinah Al-Faḍilah*) in which people could attain perfection; that ideal city does not exist. To the contrary, social involvement and political activity detract from and interfere with intellectual contemplation, which is the true human perfection. The perfect person, who knows the truth, lives in an imperfect state, whose citizens are ignorant of the truth. Al-Farabi's hoped-for ideal state was pictured as a cultivated garden in which there are no weeds, but Ibn Bajja reverses that image: in the imperfect state, it is the perfect person, whose opinions differ from those of the people around him, who is considered by them to be a weed.

Human perfection is thus separate from social involvement and political activity. Granted, Aristotle had established that "man is by nature a political animal."[112] That is an inescapable fact of life. But that fact does not mean that political involvement constitutes, or even leads to, human perfection. To the contrary, political activity is an obstacle to the true human perfection of the mind in contemplation.

Therefore, so long as society does not accept the truth, the perfect person should concentrate on the "Governance of the Solitary" (*Tadbir Al-Mutawaḥḥid*),[113] and not on the governance of society (as in Al-Farabi's conception). The solitary perfect person will need to live within his imperfect society, but while he is in society, he is not part of it; he is insulated within society even if he is not isolated from society.

> The happy, were it possible for them to exist in these cities, will possess only the happiness of an isolated individual; and the only right governance [possible in these cities] is the governance of an isolated individual, regardless of whether there is one isolated individual or more than one, so long as a nation or a city has not adopted their opinion. These individuals are the ones meant by the Sufis when they speak of the "strangers;" for although they are in their homelands and among their companions and neighbors, the Sufis say that these are strangers in

---

112 Aristotle, *Politics* I, 2, 9, 1253a.

113 Selections in English translation from Ibn Bajja's *Governance of the Solitary* by Lawrence Berman may be found in *Medieval Political Philosophy: A Sourcebook*, edited by Ralph Lerner and Muhsin Mahdi (Ithaca: Cornell University Press, 1978), pp. 122–133. A complete and annotated translation of Ibn Tufayl's *Ḥayy Ibn Yaqzan* by Lenn Evan Goodman is available (Los Angeles: Gee Tee Bee, 1983). Selections in English translation by George Atiyeh may be found in *Medieval Political Philosophy: A Sourcebook*, pp. 134–162.

their opinions (*ghuraba'u fi arahim*), having travelled in their minds to other stations that are like homelands to them.[114]

In short, he is physically present in a social setting, to meet his basic needs, but he is spiritually and intellectually insulated from it, an "alien in his opinions" whose thoughts are elsewhere.

[X.5.a.v] *Ibn Tufayl: "Ḥayy ibn Yaqzan"*

Abu Bakr Muḥammad Ibn Tufayl, known in Latin as Abubacer (Spain, died 1185), served as a physician in the king's court and advised the young Abu Al-Walid Ibn Rushd (Averroes) to write commentaries on Aristotle's works. After Ibn Tufayl's death, Ibn Rushd succeeded him as court physician. Ibn Tufayl's philosophical novel *Ḥayy ibn Yaqzan* ("Alive, the son of Awake") embodies the ideal "governance of the solitary" of Ibn Bajja, in its imaginative story of a man raised from birth in utter isolation from any human contact and from any human language or culture. The book was translated into Hebrew, and in 1349 Moses Narboni wrote a commentary on it. It was also translated into several European languages, including Latin (in 1671). From Latin it was translated into English (in 1674 and again in 1686), and some have suggested that Daniel Defoe's *Robinson Crusoe* (1719) was inspired by the story of Ḥayy ibn Yaqzan.[115]

According to the story, there are two explanations for how Ḥayy ibn Yaqzan came to live on his deserted island, completely isolated from other humans. In the one version, he was spontaneously generated from the marsh gases on the island. In the other version, a princess in a nearby island was secretly married, in violation of the king's command, so when she gave birth to Ḥayy, she put the baby in a basket and launched it in the sea. Whatever his origins, Ḥayy was then nursed raised by his "mother," a doe. Ḥayy, the proverbial "man alone," gradually developed over seven periods of seven years each, without the benefit of any human contact, language, education or culture. He could only rely on his natural talents and native intelligence. When his "mother" the doe died, he began experiments (including vivisection) to solve the riddle of life, namely the soul. From the age of 21 until 28, he began to engage in metaphysics, and from the age of 28 until 35 he sought rational proofs of such questions as creation or eternity. From the age of 35 to 42 he began to relate to

---

[114] Ibn Bajja, *The Governance of the Solitary*, English translation by Lawrence Berman, in *Medieval Political Philosophy: A Sourcebook*, edited by Ralph Lerner and Muhsin Mahdi, p. 128.

[115] A complete and annotated translation of Ibn Tufayl's *Ḥayy Ibn Yaqzan* by Lenn Evan Goodman is available (Los Angeles: Gee Tee Bee, 1983). Selections in English translation by George Atiyeh may be found in *Medieval Political Philosophy: A Sourcebook*, pp. 134–162.

God out of love and not merely through knowledge, and from the age of 42 to 49 he gained the insight that his body was a microcosm, and that he resembled animals in his body and God in his intellect. At the age of 50 Ḥayy attained the felicity of experiencing a vision of God.

Meanwhile, on a nearby island, two young friends, Absal (or: Asal) and Salaman observed religious practices and studied religious writings. Salaman interpreted these texts literally, and was involved in social affairs, and eventually became the ruler of the place. Absal, on the other hand, sought the inner, esoteric meaning of the texts, and tended towards solitude. Because of his desire for solitude, Absal sailed to the deserted island, where he and Ḥayy discovered each other. Ḥayy's native intelligence enabled him to master quickly human language and communicate with Absal. Together the two of them returned to Salaman's island, to teach the people there the truth, but they quickly realized that the people had no interest in the truth, but simply wanted to continue in their ancestral traditions. So Ḥayy and Absal returned to Ḥayy's island, where they lived out their days in contemplation of the truth and experiencing visions.

The reader of this story is challenged to ask himself whether, in Ḥayy's place, he would have reached the same conclusions using nothing but innate intelligence and logical deducation. Besides the inherent charm and fascination of the story, it is important because Ḥayy ibn Yaqzan embodies Ibn Bajja's "governance of the solitary." As we shall see, in the last chapter of the *Guide of the Perplexed* (III:54), dealing with the ultimate human perfection, Rambam says, "if you should imagine a person totally alone, without any contact with other people." Whether or not Rambam actually ever read Ibn Tufayl's novel, he must have been aware of the story, and his statement (to which we shall return) presumably is a reference to this "man alone," who had no contact with other people.

All these themes—the contemplative ideal, the identification of the ultimate human end with intellectual perfection, and the need for the perfect person to be insulated within society, if not isolated from society, all resonate in aspects of Rambam's thought.

[X.5.a.vi] *Plato and the Active Ideal*

Plato's approach differs sharply from that of his student Aristotle. Aristotle's approach began with identifying the ultimate human end with the perfection of reason as the uniquely human faculty. Plato's approach in the *Republic* (IV:440–444) emphasized not the perfection of only one human faculty (albeit the uniquely human faculty), but of the harmonious functioning of the various faculties together. This harmonious functioning of diverse elements constitutes justice on the individual level, and (by parallel) on the collective level in the state.

The state is divided into three classes—the rulers, the guardians, and the workers. Justice consists of the harmonious functioning of all three classes together—with each group contributing according to its abilities and receiving according to its needs[116]—headed by the rulers, who are assisted by the guardians in governing the workers. In a parallel manner, the human soul is divided into three faculties: the rational faculty, the "passionate" or "spirited" faculty ("anger," or what would today be called emotions), and the appetites. Justice in the individual, then, consists of the harmonious functioning of all three faculties together—with each faculty contributing according to its ability and receiving according to its needs—with the rational faculty controlling the appetites with the assistance of the passionate faculty.

As we have seen, this Platonic tri-partite scheme of the soul was adopted by Sa'adiah Ga'on[117] and by Judah Ha-Levi,[118] and the three faculties of the soul were identified with three biblical terms.[119] We also have seen that Judah Ha-Levi adopted the parallel Platonic definition of justice in the individual and in the state.[120] Aristotle's emphasis of the excellent functioning or perfection of the uniquely human faculty of reason led him to identify the ultimate human end with the contemplative life. Plato's more holistic approach to both the individual and society, with parallel conceptions of justice, led him to identify the ultimate human end with the active life, in which the philosopher is also, in virtue of his knowledge of the truth, the just ruler of the state.

---

[116] It was this Platonic formula that Karl Marx took over.

[117] See the discussion in Ch. 2 (II.3.o).

[118] See the discussion in Ch. 6 (VI.13.c).

[119] For convenient reference, we again include the chart with the terms used by Sa'adiah Ga'on and Judah Ha-Levi.

The biblical name of the soul's faculty, according to Sa'adiah, *Book of Beliefs and Opinions* 6:3	The name of the soul's faculty in Sa'adiah, *Book of Beliefs and Opinions* 6:3	The name of the soul's faculty in Sa'adiah, *Book of Beliefs and Opinions* 10:2	The name of the soul's faculty in Judah Ha-Levi's *Kuzari* 2:50
Nefesh (= Appetite)	Arabic: *Mushtahiyah* Hebrew: *Mit'aveh*	Arabic: *Al-Shahwah* Hebrew: *Ta'avah*	Arabic: *Al-Shahwah* Hebrew: *Ta'avah*
Ru'aḥ (= Anger, Passion, Emotion)	Arabic: *Ghaḍibah* Hebrew: *Ko'es*	Arabic: *Al-Ghaḍab* Hebrew: *Ka'as*	Arabic: *Al-Ghalabah* Hebrew: *Niẓaḥon*
Neshamah (= Knowledge, Cognition, Thought)	Arabic: *'Alimah* Hebrew: *Mada'i* (Kafiḥ: *Ha-Havḥanah*)	Arabic: *Al-Tamyiz* Hebrew: *Ha-Hakarah* (Kafiḥ: *Ha-Havḥanah*)	Arabic: *Al-Fikr* Hebrew: *Maḥshavah* (Kafiḥ: *Ha-Tevunah*)

[120] See the discussion in Ch. 6 (VI.13.c).

In Book VII of the *Republic*,[121] Plato presents his "allegory" or "parable of the cave," according to which humanity are like prisoners in a cave, with their backs to the entrance and source of light, who can only see two-dimensional shadows on the wall of the cave (i.e., a "shadow" or imitation of reality). A few unique individuals, the philosophers, can climb out of the cave to see three-dimensional reality in all its radiant colors. But after having ascended to the light, they must return to the prisoners in the cave, to govern and teach them. In short, the ideal philosophers must be both "men of thought" and "men of action."

> Here is a parable to illustrate the degrees in which our nature may be enlightened or unenlightened. Imagine the condition of men living in a sort of cavernous chamber underground, with an entrance open to the light...Here they have been from childhood, chained by the leg and also by the neck, so that they cannot move and can see only what is in front of them...It is for us, then, as the founders of a commonwealth, to bring compulsion to bear on the noblest natures. They must be made to climb the ascent to the vision of Goodness, which we called the highest object of knowledge; and, when they have looked upon it long enough, they must not be allowed, as they now are, to remain on the heights, refusing to come down again to the prisoners or to take any part in their labours and rewards, however much or little these may be worth...The law is not concerned to make any one class specially happy, but to ensure the welfare of the commonwealth as a whole...There will be no real injustice in compelling our philosophers to watch over and care for the other citizens...We have brought you into existence for your country's sake as well as for your own...You have been better and more thoroughly educated than those others, and hence you are more capable of playing your part both as men of thought and as men of action. You must go down, then, each in his turn, to live with the rest and let your eyes grow accustomed to the darkness. You will then see a thousand times better than those who live there always; you will recognize every image for what it is and know what it represents, because you have seen justice, beauty and goodness in their reality.

We shall return to Plato's parable of the cave later, and see how Rambam used it in his interpretation of Jacob's ladder. What is important at this point is the clear contrast between the Aristotelian contemplative ideal, and the Platonic active ideal, since it is precisely because philosophers are "men of thought" that they can also serve as "men of action," namely as the "philosopher-kings" of their state. That view, as mentioned above,[122] was developed in Islamic philosophy by Al-Farabi, who adapted it to as Islamic context by his innovative identification of the philosopher-king with the prophet of revealed religion

---

[121] Plato, *Republic* VII, 514a–521b. English translation by Francis MacDonald Cornford, *The Republic of Plato* (New York: Oxford University Press, 1945), pp. 227–234.

[122] See the reference above, in X.2.b (pp. 394–396).

and the *imam* (spiritual leader) in Islam. This theory, in turn, was adopted by Rambam, for whom Moses was the ideal leader and legislator.

[X.5.a.vii] *Al-Farabi: The Prophet as Philosopher-King*

Muḥammad Abu Naṣr Al-Farabi (870–950) has been mentioned several times in various chapters. Because of his important commentaries to Aristotle's works, he was referred to as "the second teacher," i.e., the second in importance after Aristotle himself. In his tri-partite work, *The Attainment of Happiness* (*Taḥsil Al-Sa'adah*), *The Philosophy of Plato*, and *The Philosophy of Aristotle*, he attempted to harmonize the teachings of both Greek masters, since he regarded both as true.[123]

The task of the philosopher is not only to attain his personal theoretical perfection, i.e., his intellectual happiness and fulfillment, but also the practical perfection of the imaginative faculty, by which he enables others to acquire the truth. He knows the demonstrative truth of philosophy by his intellect, and what he teaches others by means of his developed imagination is religious truth. In that sense, religion is an "imitation" of philosophy, or in our terms, what philosophy and science teach as discursive truth, religion represents in mythological imagery.

> Now when one acquires knowledge of the beings or receives instruction in them, if he perceives the ideas themselves with his intellect, and if his assent to them is by means of a certain demonstration, then the science that comprises these cognitions is philosophy. But if they are known by imagining them through similitudes that imitate them, and assent to what is imagined of them is caused by persuasive methods, then the ancients call what comprises these cognitions religion...The religion comprising them is an imitation of philosophy...
>
> It follows, then, that the idea of Imam, philosopher, and legislator is a single idea...The true prince is the same as the philosopher-legislator...
>
> Now these things are philosophy when they are in the soul of the legislator. They are religion when they are in the souls of the multitude...Although it is the legislator who also represents these things through images, neither the images nor the persuasive arguments are intended for himself...The images and the persuasive arguments are intended for others...They are a religion for others, whereas, so far as he is concerned, they are philosophy.[124]

---

[123]   The text was translated into English by Muhsin Mahdi, *Alfarabi's Philosophy of Plato and Aristotle* (Ithaca: Cornell University Press, 1962). Selections may be found in *Medieval Political Philosophy: A Sourcebook*, edited by Ralph Lerner and Muhsin Mahdi. Selections from the *Attainment of Happiness* were translated into Hebrew in the 13th century by Shem Tov ibn Falaquera and included in the third part of his *Reshit Ḥokhmah* ("The Beginning of Wisdom").

[124]   Al-Farabi, *The Attainment of Happiness*, #55–59. English translation by Muhsin Mahdi, *Alfarabi's Philosophy of Plato and Aristotle*, pp. 44–47.

The philosopher-king, then, is the prophet, whose intellect (as we saw above), receives from the active intellect an emanation, which in turn passes from his hylic intellect to his imaginative faculty, by which he is able to prophesy in terms comprehensible to the masses.

In his *Principles of the Opinions of the People of the Virtuous City* (*Mabadi Ara Ahl Al-Madinah Al-Faḍilah*), which was translated into Hebrew by Samuel ibn Tibbon (the translator of the *Guide of the Perplexed*), Al-Farabi argues that no one is self-sufficient; everyone has needs that can only be met by others. Therefore, only in the "virtuous" or "excellent" city, in which everyone strives for true intellectual perfection, can the true human happiness be attained. Those perfect people who live in imperfect states are "aliens" in their habitations. Conversely, imperfect people living in the excellent state are like "weeds" in the garden of their city.

The contrast with Ibn Bajja is thus clear. For Al-Farabi, true happiness is only possible, or feasible, in the "excellent" and ideal state. Perfect individuals outside that state are "aliens" in their habitations, and imperfect people in the ideal state are "weeds." For Ibn Bajja, the ideal state does not exist. The perfect individuals in the imperfect state are considered to be "weeds," and they are "aliens in their opinions," spiritually insulated from their society even if not physically isolated from it.

For Ibn Bajja, therefore, the ideal is the *vita contemplativa*, the "governance of the solitary," whereas for Al-Farabi before him, the ideal is the *vita activa*, in which the prophet, as the philosopher-king, has both the obligation and the ability—thanks to the divine emanation which perfects not only his intellect but then also his imaginative faculty—to govern others in light of the theoretical truth that he knows. The prophet's theoretical perfection thus makes possible his practical perfection, by which he can enable the masses, too, to attain in some way the philosophic truth, which they grasp in the imaginary imagery of religion.

[X.5.b]   ETHICAL THEORY: RAMBAM'S *SHEMONAH PERAQIM* ("EIGHT CHAPTERS")

[X.5.b.i]   *"Listen to the Truth from whoever says it"*

Rambam presents us not with an exclusive program for the *vita contemplativa*, nor one for the *vita activa*. His ethical theory tends more toward the former, and his political theory more toward the latter. This shift from his ethical theory to his political theory reflects the historical accident of the books that were available to him in Arabic, as Shlomo Pines pointed out—Aristotle's *Nicomachean Ethics* (but not Aristotle's *Politics*), and Plato's *Republic* (augmented by Al-Farabi's works). More important, however, than the accident of available books, is a genuine attempt on Rambam's part to surmount the tension between the contemplative and active ideals, and create a synthesis between them.

We begin, then, with Rambam's ethical theory, as it was developed in one of his earlier works, the Commentary to the Mishnah, in his Introduction to the tractate Avot (often referred to as the "Ethics of the Fathers"). That introduction is divided into eight chapters, and despite the fact that it is not an independent work, it is often referred to, accordingly, as the *Shemonah Peraqim*, "The Eight Chapters [on Ethics]."[125]

Rambam prefaces the *Shemonah Peraqim* by stating that the opinions expressed in the book are not his own, but are collected from the rabbis and the philosophers, both ancient and recent, because one should "listen to the truth from whoever says it." Before dealing with ethics, however, it is necessary to deal with the theory of the soul (i.e., psychology), because the improvement of ethics is the healing of the soul and its faculties. Just as the physician must know the body before he can heal it, so the physician of the soul (as it were) must first know the soul in order to heal it. The first chapter, accordingly, deals with the human soul and its faculties.

[X.5.b.ii] *The Human Soul and its Faculties*

The human soul is one, although it has various "functions" which are sometimes called "souls" or "parts." The soul has five different "faculties," i.e., it functions in five different ways. However, this terminology can be misleading. The fact that humans, animals and plants all have a "vegetative" or "nutritive" soul, does not mean that a person, an animal and a plant have the same soul. The term is used equivocally, to denote similar functions, but humans, animals and plants have their own distinctive souls.

THE HUMAN SOUL
- I. The nutritive or vegetative soul
  - a. Attraction (of food)
  - b. Retention (of food for digestion)
  - c. Digestion
  - d. Excretion of excess
  - e. Growth
  - f. Reproduction
  - g. Differentiation of necessary fluids (eg., blood) from superfluous fluids to be excreted (eg., urine)

---

[125] A complete and annotated English translation was published by Joseph Gorfinkle, *The Eight Chapters of Maimonides on Ethics* (New York: Columbia University Press, 1912). Selections from that translation were included in Isadore Twersky (ed.), *A Maimonides Reader* (New York: Behrman House, 1972), pp. 361–386.

II. The sensitive soul
   a. Sight
   b. Hearing
   c. Taste
   d. Smell
   e. Touch
III. Imagination
Retains sense impressions after the object is no longer present; combines and separates these impressions; combines impressions in combinations that were never sensed (such as an "iron ship floating in the air").
IV. Desire
The faculty of appetites and emotions, by which a person desires or despises something; its functions include seeking something or avoiding it, choosing or rejecting things; anger or being pleased; fear or courage; cruelty or mercy; love or hate.
V. Reason
(The uniquely human faculty).
   a. Theoretical reason knows the sciences, i.e., knows unchanging reality.
   b. Practical reason
(i) The vocational faculty by which arts and professions are acquired, such as carpentry, agriculture, medicine and sailing
(ii) The faculty of thought, by which one decides how, when and whether to do something

As Rambam then explains in the second chapter, the Torah's commandments and prohibitions are aimed at the second faculty—the sensitive soul—and the fourth faculty—desire—because we exercise voluntary control over these two faculties. Since we do not exercise voluntary control over the nutritive soul and the imagination (for instance, they function involuntarily during sleep), the Torah does not address commandments and prohibitions at them.

As for the rational faculty, it is the source of commandments and prohibitions inasmuch as a person has correct or incorrect opinions, but thought *per se* does not cause action. In the third chapter, Rambam discusses the "health and diseases of the soul." A healthy soul is defined as one which possesses properties leading the person to do what is good and proper, and a diseased soul is one which does evil and improper things.

[X.5.b.iii] *The Golden Mean*

The healing of the soul's diseases consists of aiming at "the golden mean" of qualities and actions, between the extremes of excess and deficiency. This concept is based on Aristotle's *Nicomachean Ethics*: "The equal is an intermediate between excess and defect. By the intermediate in the object

I mean that which is equidistant from each of the extremes."[126] In Latin literature, this concept became known as *auream mediocritatem diligere* ("to value the golden mean"). Rambam identifies this "golden mean" as the moderation prescribed by the Torah:

> Good deeds are such as are equibalanced, maintaining the mean between two equally bad extremes, the too much and the too little. Virtues are psychic conditions and dispositions which are mid-way between two reprehensible extremes, one of which is characterized by an exaggeration, the other by a deficiency. Good deeds are the product of these dispositions... Likewise, liberality is the mean between sordidness and extravagance; courage between recklessness and cowardice; dignity between haughtiness and loutishness; humility between arrogance and self-abasement... The perfect law which leads us to perfection... aims at man's following the path of moderation.[127]

Good or bad qualities are not innate, but are acquired "by means of the frequent repetition of acts resulting from these qualities, which, practiced during a long period of time, accustoms us to them."[128]

Although the good thus lies in the mean, occasionally it becomes necessary to counter a prevailing individual or social evil by the "medicine" of the opposite qualities or actions.

> In such a contingency, it is proper for him to resort to a cure, exactly as he would were his body suffering from an illness. So, just as when the equilibrium of the physical health is disturbed, and we note which way it is tending in order to force it to go in exactly the opposite direction until it shall return to its proper condition, and, just as when the proper adjustment is reached, we cease this operation, and have recourse to that which will maintain the proper balance, in exactly the same way we must adjust the moral equilibrium.[129]

That is why, at various times, virtuous people (Arabic: *fuḍala*; Hebrew: *ḥasidim*) went to extremes of self-denial and ascetic behavior—fasting, praying in the middle of the night, avoiding meat and wine, celibacy, and living as hermits in caves or the wilderness—and adopted practices that are "beyond the measure of the law" (*lifnim mi-shurat ha-din*)[130] for such individual or social therapeutic purposes. Ignorant people, however, thought that such

---

[126] Aristotle, *Nicomachean Ethics* II:6, 1106a, English translation by W.D. Ross, in Richard McKeon (ed.), *The Basic Works of Aristotle* (New York: Random House, 1941), p. 958.

[127] *Shemonah Peraqim*, Ch. 4. English translation by Joseph Gorfinkle, pp. 54–56, 63.

[128] *Shemonah Peraqim*, Ch. 4; Gorfinkle translation, p. 58.

[129] *Shemonah Peraqim*, Ch. 4; Gorfinkle translation, p. 58.

[130] Rambam uses the Hebrew phrase, from such Talmudic passages as Berakhot 7a, Bava Meẓiʻa 30b, *et al.*

behavior is intrinsically good, and constitutes the way to approach God, "as if [God] hated the human body and desired its destruction."[131] Just as certain drugs can cure the sick but are dangerous to healthy people, so, under normal circumstances, such ascetic behavior is dangerous to the individual and to society, and is inconsistent with the moderation prescribed by the Torah and a violation of its commandments.

Accordingly, Rambam interprets the biblical institution of the Nazirite negatively, as a concession to certain individual or social needs, rather than as an inherently positive way of life. In our discussion of Bahya ibn Paquda's positive attitude towards asceticism in Chapter Four,[132] we saw that the Talmud records two opposite opinions regarding asceticism, based on differing readings of Numbers 6:11, in which a Nazirite who became defiled by coming into contact with a human corpse must undergo a process of purification, at the end of which he comes to the Temple to offer a sin-offering (*hatat*), "because he sinned against the soul" (*me-asher hata 'al ha-nefesh*), i.e., because he sinned by coming into contact with a corpse. The rabbis, however, asked which soul did he sin against? They conclude that he sinned against himself, i.e., his own soul. How, then, did he sin against his own soul?

In one passage,[133] Abayé, Simon the Just, Rabbi Simon and Rabbi Elazar Ha-Kappar agree that the Nazirite is a sinner, who sinned against himself (his own soul), by denying himself wine. If a person who denies himself wine is a sinner, someone who denies himself all pleasure is certainly a greater sinner. The opposite view of Rabbi El'azar is recorded in another passage,[134] that the Nazirite way of life is holy, and that the Nazirite sins against himself by ending his period of Nazirite vows and returning to normal social life. According to this view, if a person who denies himself wine is holy, someone who denies himself all pleasures is certainly much holier. Ramban (Nahmanides) agrees with the ascetic interpretation of Rabbi El'azar,[135] and equates holiness (*qedushah*) with asceticism (*perishut*), for example, in his commentary to Numbers 21:6 (that the priests should be holy): "Holiness is asceticism...The priests should abstain [literally: separate themselves] even from what is permitted to Israel."

Rambam, on the other hand, agrees with the anti-ascetic view of the first passage. The Torah, he says, which "aims at a man's following the path of moderation in accordance with the dictates of nature...warns us against these practices," and regards the Nazirite as a sinner.[136]

131　*Shemonah Peraqim*, Ch. 4; Gorfinkle translation, p. 62.
132　See this discussion in Ch. 4 (IV.12).
133　Babylonian Talmud, Nedarim 10a.
134　Babylonian Talmud, Ta'anit 11a.
135　Nahmanides, commentary to Numbers 6:11.
136　Cf. *Shemonah Peraqim*, ch. 4 (Gorfinkle translation, p. 63). *Mishneh Torah*, Book of Knowledge, Laws of Ethical Conduct (*De 'ot*) 3:1.

Similarly, in the Mishneh Torah, Rambam says that "whoever goes in this way [of asceticism] is called a sinner" and cites the Talmudic passage about the Nazirite.[137]

> Therefore the sages enjoined us only to refrain from things the Torah prohibits, and should not, by vows and oaths, forbid for himself what is permissible. Thus the sages said: "Is not what the Torah prohibits enough for you, that you forbid for yourself other things as well?"[138]

Jews, then, who adopt ascetic practices (which he identifies with the Sufis) are not acting in accordance with the Torah. To the contrary, by violating the moderation prescribed by the Torah, "these members of the community of our Torah of whom I am speaking, are imitating the [other] religions."[139]

[X.5.b.iv] *Shemonah Peraqim Versus the Mishneh Torah and the Guide of the Perplexed*

As we have seen in these passages, in the *Shemonah Peraqim* and in the *Mishneh Torah*, Rambam explicitly identifies the way of the Torah with moderation and the golden mean, and regards asceticism, such as that of the Nazirite, as inherently sinful. The ascetic practices adopted by occasional "virtuous" sages were a temporary therapeutic measure, not desirable in themselves nor a permanent way of life.

Various scholars have pointed out that Rambam's attitude in the *Guide of the Perplexed* seems far more favorable to asceticism. For example, in the *Guide of the Perplexed* III:49 Rambam stated that the Torah's prohibition of various sexual unions served to "minimize sexual intercourse and to be disgusted by it, so that one would only desire it minimally...as necessary." Similarly, "one of the reasons for circumcision, in my view, is to minimize sexual intercourse and weaken this organ."

In the *Guide of the Perplexed* III:33, Rambam also wrote that "among the intentions of the perfect Torah" is the repression and reduction of the appetites to the minimum necessary, because the masses excessively indulge the appetites in food, drink and sexual intercourse. These appetites prevent "theoretical desires," harm the body, cause people to die prematurely, and lead to envy, hatred and wars.

According to these scholars, Rambam's pro-ascetic position in the *Guide of the Perplexed* thus differs fundamentally from his earlier anti-ascetic position in the *Shemonah Peraqim*. In their reading of Rambam, the earlier position, published in a popular work was intended for the masses, whereas

---

137 *Mishneh Torah*, Book of Knowledge, Laws of Ethical Conduct (*De'ot*) 3:1.
138 Babylonian Talmud, Ta'anit 11a.
139 *Shemonah Peraqim*, Ch. 4.

his later position, published in a work intended for the intelligentsia, was intended for the elite. Shlomo Pines, for example, attributes the divergence to Rambam's different roles as rabbi and philosopher. The ascetic tendency of the *Guide of the Perplexed* "appears to have been Maimonides' personal opinion; qua philosopher, not not qua teacher of the *halakhah*, he favored asceticism."[140]

Isadore Twersky has dealt at length with Rambam's attitude towards asceticism. His approach to this question, as to others, is harmonistic. Twersky compares Rambam's statements in the *Shemonah Peraqim* with those in the *Mishneh Torah*, Laws of Dispositions and Ethical Conduct 1:4–5 regarding the need, for lack of alternative, to abandon a corrupt society and live as a hermit. Twersky points out that Rambam, in the Code, identifies the golden mean with "the quality of wisdom" (*midat ḥokhmah*) and "the way of the wise" (*derekh ḥakhamim*), but one who adopts a supererogatory ethic by going "beyond the measure of the law" (*lifnim mi-shurat ha-din*) is called a *ḥasid* (pious, righteous, saint) who follows *midat ha-ḥasidut* (the quality of piety). In the Code, *midat ha-ḥasidut*—contrary to the *Shemonah Peraqim*—is not a temporary therapeutic measure, but is a regular and positive way of life.

Twersky comments:

> There is…a glaring discrepancy between these two major sources. Regular deviation from the middle course is recognized in the *Mishneh Torah* as a legitimate ethical alternative…This ethical option—a perfectly legitimate, if not superior alternative—is not put forth in the *Shemonah Peraqim*, where deviation from the mean is purely therapeutic or else prudential, i.e., in order to preserve the mean one moves a bit to either side.[141]

Nevertheless, in Twersky's view, the two works, and the different views they express, "are really mutually supplementary and supportive,"[142] because in the *Shemonah Peraqim* "Maimonides tries to rebut the contention of certain Jews that they are compelled be a desire for deeper spirituality to adopt non-Jewish ascetic practices."[143]

In other words, in the *Shemonah Peraqim* Rambam was arguing against imitating and assimilating to non-Jewish Sufi practices, as if the Torah were not a "perfect law which leads us to perfection." In Twersky's view, then, the two works do not contradict each other, because in the *Shemonah Peraqim* we have Rambam's polemic against assimilationist tendencies to adopt non-

---

140   Shlomo Pines, "The Philosophic Sources of the *Guide of the Perplexed*," p. lxii.
141   Isadore Twersky, *Introduction to the Code of Maimonides*, pp. 461–462.
142   Isadore Twersky, *Introduction to the Code of Maimonides*, p. 461.
143   Isadore Twersky, *Introduction to the Code of Maimonides*, p. 463.

Jewish practices, whereas in the *Mishneh Torah* we have an internal halakhic presentation of diverse legitimate Jewish options. Rambam's statements in the *Guide of the Perplexed*, in Twersky's analysis, only reinforce his earlier positive statements on asceticism. Despite the dangers of unrestricted asceticism, there remains a need for those, like prophets, to maintain a higher standard.

> Every individual is a potential prophet...The clearest need seems to be the difference between asceticism as a goal, reflecting contempt of the world, and asceticism as a means to achieve ethical inwardness and intellectual perfection or to intensify religious sensibility.[144]

Twersky's harmonistic approach is appealing, and frees us from treating Rambam as a spiritual schizophrenic, who, as a rabbi, advocated one ethic—moderation—for the people, and as a philosopher, another ethic—asceticism—for the elite. Since the *Mishneh Torah*, with its advocacy of *midat ha-ḥasidut*, is a popular halakhic work, we can understand how Twersky arrives at his conclusion that asceticism is the inner challenge of each individual to develop intellectually and spiritually.

Nevertheless, Rambam's multifaceted position in these three works may lend itself to different readings from that of Twersky. For instance, the divergent emphases in the *Shemonah Peraqim*, the *Mishneh Torah*, and the *Guide of the Perplexed* can be taken chronologically, as a progressive development in Rambam's thought, from the golden mean of the *Shemonah Peraqim*, to a combination of the golden mean as "the way of the wise" with the supererogatory *midat ha-ḥasidut* in the *Mishneh Torah*, to a more consistent asceticism and emphasis of the theoretical ideal in the *Guide of the Perplexed*. The chronological approach, with its reading of Rambam's position as evolving, avoids creating a dichotomy (such as we have in Pines' interpretation) between Rambam the rabbi and Rambam the philosopher. Nevertheless, it still fails to reconcile Rambam's positions in the three works.

A more harmonistic approach (similar to Twersky in method, but differing somewhat in its conclusions) would be to read Rambam's positions contextually, as reflecting a consistent ethical and spiritual attitude, with differences of emphasis, not content, according to the literary context. The *Shemonah Peraqim* is a work explicitly addressing ethical theory, in which Rambam equates the golden mean of philosophic ethics with the moderate ideal of the Torah, in which asceticism can legitimately only be a temporary therapeutic measure. Extreme asceticism, such as that of the Sufis, is not warranted either philosophically or religiously, and Rambam opposes the

---

[144]   Isadore Twersky, *Introduction to the Code of Maimonides*, pp. 466–467.

assimilationist tendencies of some Jews to adopt these non-Jewish practices. In the *Mishneh Torah*, Rambam is dealing with the dialectical tension between two halakhic categories in rabbinic teaching: the normative "measure of the law" (*midat ha-din*), namely the golden mean which is "the way of the wise" or "the quality of wisdom," and the supererogatory category "beyond the measure of the law" (*lifnim mi-shurat ha-din*), namely the "quality of piety" (*midat ha-ḥasidut*). For Rambam, these two standards, although in dialectical tension, co-exist legitimately in rabbinic thought, because there always is a danger of people following their appetites (whether on the individual or on the social level). Therefore, the need for the therapeutic ascetic counter-measure of *midat ha-ḥasidut* is also always present, both on the individual level, to shape a balanced personality, and on the social level, to create a civilized society. On both individual and social levels, then, the tension between the appetites and the ascetic therapy, will restore the desired balance and moderation.

The *Guide of the Perplexed*, with its stronger statements favoring an ascetic ideal, need not be read as violating or diverging from this consistent ethic. The context of Rambam's statements in his discussion of *ta'amei ha-miẓvot*, the meaning, rationale and utility of the Torah's commandments. Rambam is proposing, in this discussion, to explain in moral terms the need for the restrictions and limitations the Torah imposes on our appetites. "You already know that most of the appetites and licentiousness of the masses consist of excessive eating, drinking and sexual intercourse…The ignorant regards pleasure alone as the end desired for itself,"[145] and thereby lives a hedonistic life destructive both to himself and to society, and damaging both to "the welfare of the body" and to "the welfare of the soul."

There is no inconsistency between what Rambam says here against the appetites and what he said in his earlier works. The stronger ascetic tone of the *Guide of the Perplexed* reflects the nature of the discussion: why does the Torah restrict and prescribe limitations on our physical appetites? In that context, the emphasis is necessarily one-sided, because in this section Rambam is only explaining the need for these limitations, not for balance. That does not mean that he negates the balance, because ultimately the balance is created by these very limitations, which counter the excessive and hedonistic habits of the masses who are slaves to their appetites. In short, a harmonistic approach to the differences in Rambam's positions in the three works understands them contextually and in terms of emphasis, not as saying different things to different people, nor as changing over time.

---

[145]   *Guide of the Perplexed* III:33.

[X.5.b.v] *Free Will*

In the last chapter of the *Shemonah Peraqim* Rambam addresses the question of free will (elsewhere called *reshut*),[146] which is fundamental to any ethical theory. He had already stated in the second of the eight chapters that commandments and prohibitions can only be directed at the second and fourth faculties of the soul—the sensitive faculty and desire—over which we exercise voluntary control; those other faculties which function involuntarily are not subject to command and prohibition. There can be no moral responsibility without free will, and on this fundamental point there is full consistency in the *Shemonah Peraqim*, *Mishneh Torah*, and *Guide of the Perplexed*. As we saw, in Rambam's discussion of the fifth view of providence, he also referred to free will as "a foundation of the Torah:"

> The fifth opinion is our opinion, i.e., the opinion of our Torah... A foundation of the Torah of Moses our teacher and all who follow it is that the human being has absolute ability, i.e., that by his nature, choice and will he can do everything that is within human capacity to do... Similarly, all species of animals move by will... A person has the ability to do whatever he wills or chooses of those things which are within his capacity. This is a foundation with which, thank God, no one in our community disagrees. It is also one of the foundations of the Torah of Moses our teacher, that God is in no way unjust, and that people, individually and collectively, justly deserve whatever happens to them... although we do not understand how they deserve it.[147]

In the *Mishneh Torah* Rambam also calls free will "a great principle which is the pillar of the Torah and commandments."[148]

> Free will is bestowed on every human being. If one desires to turn towards the good way and be righteous, he has the power to do so. If one wishes to turn towards the evil way and be wicked, he is at liberty to do so...
> Let not the notion, expressed by foolish gentiles and most of the senseless folk among Israelites, pass through your mind, that at the beginning of a person's existence the Almighty decrees that he is to be either righteous or wicked. This is not so. Every human being may become righteous... or wicked... wise or foolish, merciful or cruel... and so with all other qualities...

---

146   The Hebrew term *reshut* literally means "permission" or "optional" (as in the rabbinic categories of obligatory versus permitted or optional war). Rambam's use of the term for free will in the *Mishneh Torah* reflects the usage in the Mishnah, Avot 3:15: "All is foreknown, but free will is granted."

147   *Guide of the Perplexed* III:17. See the discussion above (X.4.d).

148   *Mishneh Torah*, Book of Knowledge, Laws of Repentance 5:1–5. English translation by Hyamson, pp. 86b–87b. (My modifications).

This principle is a great principle which is the pillar of the Torah and commandments...This means that the power is in your hands, and whatever a man desires to do among the things that human beings do, he can do, whether they are good or evil...The creator neither compels humans nor decrees that they should do either good or evil, but it is all left to their discretion.

Returning, then, to the discussion at the end of the *Shemonah Peraqim*, Rambam again asserts, as he did in other cases (such as in his discussions of attributes and of Job), that the perplexing problem of human free will versus divine foreknowledge derives from the fallacious analogy of God's knowledge to human knowledge, and from the failure to understand their equivocal nature. People believe in predestination because they erroneously think that unless God knows in advance (and thus controls) what we will do, his knowledge is imperfect.[149]

It is already clear from the divine science, i.e., metaphysics, that God does not know by means of knowledge, and does not live by means of life, so that he and his knowledge may be considered two different things in the sense that this is true of man; for man is distinct from knowledge, and knowledge from man, in consequence of which they are two different things. If God knew by means of knowledge, he would necessarily be a plurality, and the primal essence would be composite, that is, consisting of God himself, the knowledge by which he knows, the life by which he lives, the power by which he has strength, and similarly all his attributes...He is the knowledge, the knower and the known...the same being true of his other attributes. This conception is very hard to grasp, and you should not hope to understand it thoroughly by two or three lines in this treatise...It is also clear from metaphysics that human reason cannot fully conceive God in his true essence, because of the perfection of God's essence and the imperfection of our own reason, and because his essence is not due to causes through which it may be known...It has been demonstrated that we cannot comprehend God's knowledge and that our minds cannot grasp it all, for he is his knowledge and his knowledge is he....If the human reason could grasp his knowledge, it would also be able to define his essence, since both are one and the same...

Reflect, then, upon all that we have said, namely that man has control over his actions...and that, as a result of this, divine commandment, teaching, preparation, reward and punishment are proper. Of this there is absolutely no doubt. As regards, however, the character of God's knowledge, how he knows everything, this is, as we have explained, beyond the reach of human ken.

149　*Shemonah Peraqim*, Ch. 8 (Gorfinkle translation, pp. 99–102; my modifications).

[X.5.c]   ETHICS AND HUMAN PERFECTION

[X.5.c.i]   *The Four Human Perfections (Guide III:54)*

The last chapter of the *Guide of the Perplexed* (III:54) is devoted to a discussion of the ultimate human perfection (Arabic: *kamal*; Hebrew: *shelemut*). The four types of perfection analyzed in this chapter, as Alexander Altmann has shown,[150] are based on Aristotle's *Nicomachean Ethics*,[151] and subsequently on Ibn Bajja's "Letter of Farewell" (*Risalat Al-Wida'*).

Aristotle, it will be recalled, had defined the ultimate human end or purpose (Greek: *telos*; Arabic: *ghaya akhira*; Hebrew: *takhlit aharonah*) as "an active life of the element that has a rational principle" and as the "life of the rational element."[152] Although such rational perfection is the ultimate human end, because it is the perfection of the uniquely human faculty of reason, that does not mean that it is the only type of perfection. Aristotle, accordingly, discusses three different human perfections: external goods, goods of the body, and goods of the soul. The happiness of the soul, in turn, consists of both the activity of contemplation and the exercise of moral virtue (i.e., theoretical and practical perfection). We thus have four types of perfection, in ascending order: external goods, goods of the body, moral virtue, and contemplation.

In his discussion of these "four types of perfections," Rambam refers to "ancient and recent philosophers"—apparently meaning Aristotle and Ibn Bajja. The first type of perfection, which he calls the "lowest of them," is "the perfection of possessions" (or: "perfection of property") (Arabic: *kamal al-qunya*; Hebrew: *shelemut ha-qinyan*)—what Aristotle called *ektos choregias*, external causes. This clearly is not the true human perfection, since it pertains to external, material objects and has nothing to do with the person himself. Aristotle actually goes further: not only do the "external causes" not constitute the true perfection, but they can actually constitute an "impediment" (*empodia*) to contemplation (*theoria*).

The second type of perfection, which "is more related to the person than the first," is "the perfection of the physique and shape" (Arabic: *kamal al-binya w'al-hai'a*; Hebrew: *shelemut tavnit ha-guf veha-tekhunah*), i.e., the perfection of the body. This is a perfection humans share with animals, and cannot constitute the distinctively human perfection.

---

[150]   Alexander Altmann, "Maimonides' Four Perfections," in *Essays in Jewish Intellectual History* (Hanover: University Press of New England, 1981), pp. 65–76.

[151]   Aristotle, *Nicomachean Ethics* X:7:1–8:8.

[152]   Aristotle, *Nicomachean Ethics* I:7, 1098b. English translation by W.D. Ross, in Richard McKeon, *The Basic Works of Aristotle* (New York: Random House, 1941), pp. 942–943. See the discussion above (X.5.a.iii).

On the face of it, the third type, namely "perfection of moral virtues" (Arabic: *kamal faḍa'il al-khulqiya*; Hebrew: *shelemut ma'alot ha-midot*) would seem to constitute true human perfection, and Rambam acknowledges that most of the Torah's commandments aim at such perfection. Nevertheless, this type of perfection does not pertain to the person in and of himself, but to the way he acts and behaves in relation to other people. As such,

> it is a means to something else, not an end in itself, for ethics only exist between a person and someone else. Ethical perfection is, as it were, only a disposition to benefit other people, and is thus an instrument for someone else. For if you would suppose that there is a human being all alone, who has nothing to do with any other person, you would find that all of his moral virtues are in vain, without use, and unnecessary, and that they do not perfect the person in any way. He only has need for them, and they are only useful to him, in regard to someone else.

Rambam's reference here to "a human being all alone" is strongly reminiscent of Ibn Bajja's *Governance of the Solitary*; his suggesting that the reader should "suppose that there is a human being all alone, who has nothing to do with any other person," must have immediately struck a familiar chord with people who had read, or at least heard of, Ibn Tufayl's *Ḥayy ibn Yaqzan*.

We are left, then, with the contemplative ideal of the fourth type of perfection,

> the true human perfection, which is the acquisition of the rational virtues (Arabic: *al-kamal al-insani al-ḥaqiqi, wa-huwa ḥuṣul al-fada'il al-natiqiya*; Hebrew: *ha-shelemut ha-enoshi[t] ha-amiti[t] ve-hu hasagat ha-ma'alot ha-sikhliyot*), I mean the conception of the intelligibles teaching true opinions about the divine things. This is the ultimate end (Arabic: *al-ghaya al-akhira*; Hebrew: *ha-takhlit ha-aharonah*) which perfects a person with a true perfection, and pertains only to him, and which gives him eternal continued existence; through it the person is a person.

The other three perfections have their appropriate place. However, they are not the ultimate human end but "means to this end" of theoretical, rational perfection.

[X.5.c.ii] *Adam and Theoretical Perfection (Guide I:2)*

The final chapter of the *Guide of the Perplexed*, in a sense, returns us to its beginning. The true human perfection at the end of the book is "the acquisition of the rational virtues" through which "a person is a person." In other words, it is the perfection of the "human natural form" that Rambam had identified as the "image of God" in the first chapter of the book. Continuing this theme in the second chapter of the book, Rambam says that the intellect which God emanated onto Adam — that is his final perfection — is what reached Adam before his rebellion. It is on account of this that it is said of him that he [was created] "in the image of God and in his likeness"...Through the intellect a person distinguishes between truth and falsehood, and this was found in [Adam] in perfection and integrity.[153]

Adam thus initially had perfect theoretical knowledge of intelligible truths (Arabic: *ma'qulat*; Hebrew: *muskalot*), i.e., the distinction of true and false. What he lacked was practical knowledge — for which he had, as yet, no need — of "generally accepted," conventional truths, (Arabic: *mashhurat*; Hebrew: *mefursamot*), i.e., the distinction of appropriate and inappropriate, desirable or repugnant matters.[154]

The original human perfection was thus of theoretical intellect, not practical intellect, and it is that original human perfection that constitutes the ultimate human end, through which a person attains "eternal continued existence," i.e. the immortality of the rational soul which is *'olam ha-ba*, "the world to come." In Rambam's reading of the story in Genesis, the fall of Adam and Eve, when they ate of the "tree of knowledge of good and evil" and thereby lost their immortality,[155] was that they lost perfect theoretical intellectual apprehension, but in its place gained practical moral judgment. Since it is theoretical intellectual apprehension that constitutes the immortality of the world to come, Adam and Eve thereby lost their immortality, and became mortal.

As Lawrence Berman explained this shift:

> The fall of man consisted in a change of priorities, from an interest in the things of the mind to becoming interested in the things of the body; from being a philosopher, a master of his passions, to becoming a beast in human form, mastered by his passions; from being a solitary thinker, to becoming a ruler of cities, being informed by the imagination only...Action...the goal of choice between good and evil, cannot be qualified by truth and falsity, but only by good and evil...Theory is the realm of fact in which one can seek whether one opinion is valid and another invalid; the sphere of action is that of value, which by its very nature is subjective...Previous to the fall, Adam was not concerned with matters relating to values but only with the truth.[156]

---

[153] *Guide of the Perplexed* I:2.

[154] See the discussions of the difference between intelligible and generally accepted propositions above, X.3.a and X.3.d.

[155] Cf. Genesis 2:16–17: "The Lord God commanded the human saying, Eat of any tree in the garden. But do not eat of the tree of knowledge of good and evil, for on the day that you eat of it you will die."

[156] Lawrence Berman, "Maimonides on the Fall of Man," in *Association for Jewish Studies Review* 5 (1980), pp. 8–9. For a more complete discussion of this theme, see my "Rejecting Moral Virtue as the Ultimate Human End," in *Jewish Philosophy: Foundations and*

Adam, then, did suffer a loss in the fall. He lost his perfect theoretical reasoning ability. What he gained in its place was practical reason, a lower function, because it deals with a different type of truth, which is not objective but reflects values. However, there is another factor to this shift from theoretical to practical reason, and from intelligible to conventional truth. At the beginning of the *Guide of the Perplexed* Adam had no prior need for practical reason, because he was in fact the hypothetical "man alone" of the last chapter of the *Guide*, for whom the moral virtues are meaningless. Adam initially truly embodied "the image of God," because prior to his rebellion, for all practical purposes, he, like God, was alone, a perfect theoretical intellect, engaging in sublime self-contemplation. "Man alone" has no need for moral virtues, which accordingly cannot constitute his true perfection. The ultimate end of man, in the last chapter of the *Guide of the Perplexed*, is thus to return to the solitary theoretical perfection of the first human, "man alone," in the beginning of the *Guide*.

However, this contemplative ideal is only one aspect of Rambam's thought. For the fact is that God did not remain alone — he brought the world into being, and endowed it with useful laws in conformity with his wisdom. Adam, too, did not long stay alone, for out of his being came the woman, and thus the solitary human became a social being, for whom moral virtue and practical reason are not only relevant (whereas previously they had been meaningless), but essential. God had created a world which requires cosmic governance. Adam and Eve would now create a society, which would similarly require moral virtue and governance.

It is at this point, then, that we must shift from the contemplative ideal of Rambam's ethical theory to the active and practical ideal of his political theory, a shift necessitated by Adam's transformation into a social being with Eve, and brought to its perfect fulfillment in Moses. As Berman has put it:

> Thus Adam and Moses were identical, the difference being that Adam, before the fall, represents the ideal for man not living in society, while Moses represents the ideal for man living in society.[157]

Adam is thus the epitome, in Rambam's ethical theory, of the Aristotelian ideal *vita contemplativa*, as we saw it in Ibn Bajja and Ibn Tufayl. Moses, by contrast, is the epitome in Rambam's political theory, of the Platonic active ideal *vita activa*, as we saw it in Al-Farabi, namely the ideal of the prophet as philosopher-king.

Extensions, Volume Two: On Philosophers and Their Thought (Lanham: University Press of America, 2008), pp. 79–96.

157   Lawrence Berman, "Maimonides on the Fall of Man," p. 8, note 22.

[X.5.d] POLITICAL THEORY: THE ACTIVE IDEAL OF THE PROPHETIC RULER

[X.5.d.i] *The Contemplative Ideal and Knowledge of God's Attributes of Action*

The tension between the contemplative and active ideals is not merely an external feature of Rambam's diverse literary and philosophic sources. More importantly, it is an internal feature of his philosophy, in which the two ideals coexist in dynamic and dialectical tension. Knowledge of God is the true human perfection, but as we have seen in the discussion of the divine attributes, all we can know is God's attributes of action; not what God is, but only what God does. In other words, the content of the contemplative ideal, to know God, in the *Guide of the Perplexed* III:54, has an inherently active character, which necessarily leads Rambam, in the continuation of the chapter, from the theme of intellectual perfection to the theme of *imitatio Dei* (the imitation of God), based on his interpretation of Jeremiah 9:23: "Let the one who is praised be praised in this: that he understands and knows me, for I am the Lord who does kindness (*ḥesed*), justice (*mishpat*) and righteousness (*ẓedaqah*) in the earth, for these are the things I desire, says the Lord."

Rambam notes that the verse does not end with knowledge of God, but culminates with God's attributes of action, "which a person must know and imitate."

> In this verse he did not limit his explanation of the noblest ends only to the apprehension of God. If that had been his intention, he would have said "Let the one who is praised be praised in this: that he understands and knows me," and he would then have stopped... But he said that one should only be praised for apprehending me and for knowing my attributes, meaning [God's] actions, as we have explained[158] regarding the verse, "Let me know your ways" (Exodus 33:13). He explained that these actions which a person should know and imitate are kindness, justice and righteousness... The intention is to resemble them, and they should be the way we go... The human perfection for which one should truly be praised is to attain the apprehension of God according to one's capacity, to know how his providence extends over his creatures by bringing them into existence and by governing them. After he has attained this apprehension, that person's way of life will always intend at resembling [God's] actions of kindness, righteousness and justice, as we have explained several times in this treatise.[159]

Until this point, Rambam had only posited knowledge of God as the ultimate human perfection, without specifying its content. Now he has specified the

---

[158] In *Guide of the Perplexed* I:54.
[159] *Guide of the Perplexed* III:54, end.

content as the divine attributes of action, but has added another dimension, the active imitation of those actions. That active imitation is not extraneous to the knowledge of God's attributes of action, but is a necessary expression of it. The ideal is contemplative, but its fulfillment is to be found in the active ideal, or, in the words of the Talmud cited above, "They all replied: Study is greater, for study leads to action.[160]

It must be emphasized, however, that these actions in imitation of God's active attributes in governing the world are not on the level of ethics, which as we have seen, are a "means" to ultimate intellectual perfection and precede it. The actions in question are those of the prophet in governing the state following his attainment of intellectual perfection. Such governance is an expression of the prophet's knowledge of God, and is, therefore, an imitation of God's attributes of action, which are the only knowledge of God humans can attain. The prophet's governance of the state is thus an imitation of God's cosmic governance.

[X.5.d.ii] *Moses and the Patriarchs: "Aliens in their Opinions"*

How, then, is this concept of the prophet's active role in society compatible with the idea that the contemplative ideal of the knowledge of God is best, or possibly only, attainable in solitude? Rambam's answer in the *Guide of the Perplexed* III:51, is the paradigm of Moses and the Patriarchs, whose intellectual conjunction was so intense that it was not interrupted or interfered with by normal bodily activities and social involvement.[161] These unique individuals, while not physically isolated from society, were spiritually insulated from it, so that their active social involvement, which was aimed at bringing others to know and worship God, also constituted knowledge and worship of God, and did not distract them from their contemplation. "This is, in my opinion, a proof that they performed these actions only with their limbs, but that their intellects were constantly present with God."[162]

Although at this point Rambam does not explicitly mention Ibn Bajja, nor does he employ Ibn Bajja's terminology, his explanation of how the inner, intellectual conjunction of Moses and the Patriarchs continued uninterrupted by external, physical involvement in social and political activity, seems to reflect Ibn Bajja's notion of the solitary individuals as "aliens in their opinions." As we saw above, Ibn Bajja said:[163]

---

160   Babylonian Talmud, Qiddushin 40b. See the discussion above, X.5.a.ii.
161   See the discussion above, X.4.f.
162   *Guide of the Perplexed* III:51.
163   See the discussion of Ibn Bajja above, X.5.a.iv.

These individuals are the ones meant by the Sufis when they speak of the "strangers;" for although they are in their homelands and among their companions and neighbors, the Sufis say that these are strangers in their opinions (*ghuraba'u fi arahim*), having travelled in their minds to other stations that are like homelands to them.[164]

Their external society is the state in which they live physically, and which they govern and teach. They are, however, "aliens (or: "strangers") in their opinions," because while their bodily "limbs" are involved in such external political activity, their minds are elsewhere, in their true, inner spiritual homeland.

In this way, Rambam is able to construct a synthesis between the *vita contemplativa* and the *vita activa*. They remain in dialectical tension, but they are not contradictory. Contemplative knowledge of God remains the ultimate human perfection, but the content of that knowledge—God's attributes of action in governing the world—necessarily leads to its expression in the prophet's imitation of God's cosmic governance, by his political governance of his society. Such active prophetic political governance does not contradict, or even detract from, the contemplative perfection of the prophet as an individual, but is its necessary expression and fulfillment.

[X.5.d.iii] *The Parable of the King's Palace (Guide III:51)*

Most people of course, even most of the elite intelligentsia, and even most of the prophets, never reach the heights reached by Moses and the Patriarchs. In the same chapter (III:51), Rambam therefore describes progressive degrees of worshippers of God (since, for him, knowledge of God constitutes the true intellectual worship of God), in terms of a parable of a king's palace.

(1) People outside the city. They have no religious faith, whether based on tradition or speculation, and resemble irrational animals.

(2) People in the city who are not facing the palace. They have religious faith, but a false faith and incorrect opinions. They are dangerous, because they corrupt others.

(3) People in the city who are searching for the palace, but do not even see its walls. They are the masses who follow the Torah and the ignoramuses who perform its commandments.

(4) People who reach the palace walls, but walk around and fail to find the entrance. They are Jews learned in religious law.[165] They

---

[164]   Ibn Bajja, *The Governance of the Solitary*, English translation by Lawrence Berman, in *Medieval Political Philosophy: A Sourcebook*, edited by Ralph Lerner and Muhsin Mahdi, p. 128.

[165]   Rambam uses the Arabic term *fiqh*, meaning religious law or jurisprudence. Samuel ibn Tibbon translated it as *talmudiyim*, "Talmudists."

believe true opinions on the basis of tradition, without attempting to investigate the foundations of religion or to verify those beliefs through speculation.

(5) People who enter the entrance hall of the palace. They investigate the foundations of religion.

(6) People who enter the inner chambers of the palace, while the king is elsewhere in the palace. They know whatever can be known by demonstration; this is the rank of the learned sages (Arabic: *'ulama*; Hebrew: *ḥakhamim*).

(7) People who are the ruler's council, who stand in the presence of the king, see him and speak with him. This is the rank of the prophets, whose entire focus, "after having attained perfection in the divine science," is on examining existing things in order to learn from them how God governs the world.

The difference between the prophets (in the seventh degree) and the sages (in the sixth degree) is that the prophets, after attaining the intellectual perfection of the previous degree, focus their entire attention on understanding God's governance of the world, an apprehension that, as we saw in the last section, leads to imitation on a social-political level of God's cosmic governance.

> This is the special worship of those who have apprehended the truth. The more they think of him and of being with him, the more their worship increases... This ultimate worship...can only exist after apprehension...We have already explained several times that the love [of God] is proportional to apprehension. After the love comes this worship, about which [the rabbis] commented that "it is the worship in the heart" (*'avodah sheba-lev*).[166] In my opinion it means causing thought to work on the first intelligible and devoting oneself entirely to this, according to one's capacity.[167]

Intellectual apprehension of God (actually, of God's active attributes) leads to love, and love is followed in turn by the true worship in the heart, which is continued and continual intellectual devotion to God.

[X.5.d.iv] *The Imitation of God: Different Interpretations*

We have discussed the imitation of God as the expression and fulfillment of the ultimate human end, i.e., intellectual perfection. That ideal, however, and the relationship between the *vita activa* and the *vita contemplativa*, continue to be understood in different ways by Rambam's interpreters.

---

166   Cf. Sifre on Deuteronomy 11:13; Babylonian Talmud Ta'anit 2a. The phrase can also be translated: "the service of the heart."

167   *Guide of the Perplexed* III:51.

(1) SHLOMO PINES: THE IDEAL OF POLITICAL GOVERNANCE

Various scholars, including Shlomo Pines and Lawrence Berman, understand Rambam's conception of the ultimate human end in terms of the ideal of political governance. According to Pines:[168]

> The only positive knowledge of God of which man is capable is knowledge of the attributes of action, and this leads and ought to lead to a sort of political activity which is the highest perfection of man. The practical way of life, the *bios praktikos*, is superior to the theoretical. It would be easy to challenge this view of the position of Maimonides; there are passages in the Guide which appear to disprove it. In part, the internal contradictions may be laid at the door of Plato, whose political philosophy ... is profoundly ambiguous (and that of Al-Farabi perhaps even more so). The recommendation that the philosopher, considered as the highest type of man, should return to the cave or should engage in political action, must if carried out, lead to a renouncement of the life of thought, that is, to his ceasing to be a philosopher.

Pines and Berman conclude that since according to Rambam we have only a very limited knowledge of God, he (like Al-Farabi) prefers to identify human perfection in terms of the political *vita activa*. Their conclusion, however, does not refer to such political activity as *imitatio Dei*, nor to the relationship between such political activity and the prior intellectual perfection of the prophet as an individual.

(2) ZE'EV HARVEY AND STEVEN HARVEY: THE CONTEMPLATIVE IDEAL

Other scholars, including Ze'ev Warren Harvey and Steven Harvey,[169] who are fully aware of the political interpretation of Pines and Berman, interpret Rambam as continuing to posit intellectual contemplation as the human ideal. In an important study of Rambam's parable of the king's palace,[170] Steven Harvey points out that Rambam emphasizes that the seventh and highest degree of worship is only attained in solitude. This emphasis is consistent with Rambam's negation, in the last chapter of the *Guide of the Perplexed*, of moral virtue as the ultimate human perfection, because (as we have seen) it does not perfect the person himself. A degree of social or political involvement may be necessary to provide for the philosopher's needs, or even for those of society,

---

168   Shlomo Pines, "The Limitations of Human Knowledge According to Al-Farabi, Ibn Bajja, and Maimonides," in Isadore Twersky (ed.), *Studies in Medieval Jewish History and Literature* (Cambridge: Harvard University Press, 1979), p. 100.

169   These two scholars are brothers.

170   Steven Harvey, "Maimonides in the Sultan's Palace," in Joel Kraemer (ed.), *Perspectives on Maimonides: Philosophical and Historical Studies* (Oxford: Littman Library of Jewish Civilization, 1991), pp. 47–76.

but it cannot be construed as anything but an impediment to the desired solitude necessary for the contemplative life.

> This does not mean that the philosophers enjoy their role in the city; on the contrary, they despise it, but they recognize the extreme importance and necessity of their assuming these responsibilities... For Maimonides, the descent is not part of the ultimate perfection of man, and that perfection is not directly dependent on whether or not anyone listens to his message.[171]

The paradigm of Moses and the Patriarchs, he suggests, does not contradict this reading of Rambam, because Rambam did not regard it as a rank attainable by others (including himself), and yet he included solitude in his description of the seventh rank of worshippers in the parable of the king's palace. The active imitation of God follows intellectual apprehension of God, as we have seen. In the understanding of the brothers Harvey, therefore, it is a stage that follows the stage of individual perfection, and is not identical with it. As with the position of Pines and Berman (although for opposite reasons), this position does not deal with the relationship between what can be known of God and the subsequent political activity; nor does this position differentiate regular political activity—which has no relation to intellectual perfection—and prophetic political activity, following intellectual perfection and providing an expression for its content.

(3) THE IDEAL OF THE HALAKHIC LIFE

Isadore Twersky, David Hartman, and Menachem Kellner are among those scholars who agree that the practical ideal follows the apprehension of God and is not identical with it. In their view, however, the ideal is not political activity but the life of *halakhah*. Just as regular moral virtue precedes intellectual perfection and is a means to it, so there is a level of halakhic observance preceding intellectual perfection, or without intellectual perfection, such as Rambam describes in the fourth degree of worship in his parable of the king's palace. According to these scholars, however, there is also a higher level of halakhic observance following intellectual perfection.

As Twersky put it:[172]

> Maimonides believed that knowledge stimulates and sustains proper prescribed conduct, which in turn is a conduit for knowledge, and this intellectual achievement in return raises the level and motive of conduct... In other words, imitatio Dei means assimilating God's ways and attributes so that, as a result, one lives in accord with the law, which constantly propels the individual towards a contemplative goal.

171　Steven Harvey, "Maimonides in the Sultan's Palace," pp. 70–72.
172　Isadore Twersky, *Introduction to the Code of Maimonides*, pp. 511–512.

Twersky also notes:[173]

> The resultant conduct is not ordinary and routine — perfunctory behavior in which one acts out of conformity and inertia — but rather reflects a higher order in which tradition is substantiated by independent thought and understanding.

In a similar vein, David Hartman has written of Rambam's choice of

> the way of integration...The primacy of action is not weakened by the contemplative ideal; a deeper purpose for the normative structure is realized instead, once the philosophic way is followed. The contemplative ideal is not insulated from halakhah, but affects it in a new manner. Sinai is not a mere stage in man's spiritual development, but the ultimate place to which man constantly returns — even when he soars to the heights of metaphysical knowledge.[174]

In a book-length analysis of the question of the human ideal, Menachem Kellner comes to a conclusion similar to that of Twersky and Hartman.

> While perfection of the intellect is surely to be prized above all other perfections, it is not in itself the final end of human existence, but itself serves as a way of deepening, enriching, and elevating observance of the mitzvot.[175]

Kellner argues that there is no contradiction between the practical life of *halakhah* and the contemplative life; they complement each other. Observance of the commandments leads to intellectual apprehension, and intellectual apprehension leads to a higher and more refined observance of the commandments out of love and the yearning to imitate God's ways, i.e. his attributes of action. Kellner thus discerns a spiritual transition in the literary structure of the *Guide of the Perplexed*, which begins (I:1) with the contemplative life (i.e., the image of God in which the human being was created), and ending (III:54) with the imitation of God following intellectual apprehension. The two ideals, then, are not contradictory, but represent such a spiritual transition.

As Kellner develops his argument, the human ideal cannot be contemplative, because if God is perceived in the Aristotelian sense of self-cognizing intellect, but if, on the other hand (as in Neoplatonism), we cannot know God, then we cannot imitate his self-cognition. Nor can we imitate God as creator, since humans cannot create. The only option we have is to imitate his ways

---

[173] Isadore Twersky, *Introduction to the Code of Maimonides*, p. 511, note 390:

[174] David Hartman, *Maimonides: Torah and Philosophic Quest* (Philadelphia: Jewish Publication Society, 1976), p. 26.

[175] Menachem Kellner, *Maimonides on Human Perfection* (Atlanta: Scholars Press, 1990), p. 10.

by actions, and those actions must be "the actions which God prescribed in his Torah."[176]

The post-apprehension halakhic approach of Twersky, Hartman and Kellner takes seriously Rambam's explicit statement that there must be activity after intellectual apprehension, a statement not taken sufficiently seriously by the political approach (which more or less ignores the component of apprehension) or the contemplative approach (which more or less ignores the subsequent component of activity). The question remains, however, whether that post-apprehension activity should correctly be identified with observance of the *halakhah*.

In the first place, how does observance of the commandments constitute imitation of God as the lawgiver? The God who prescribes the dietary laws of *kashrut* can certainly not be conceived as himself eating kosher food, so how does obedience constitute imitation? Moreover, as we saw, Rambam insisted that the commandments must be useful and beneficial to people (even if their usefulness and benefit eludes us)—but certainly not to God, who cannot be conceived as needing them or benefiting from them. Once again, since humans and not God benefit from the commandments, how does our observing them constitute imitation of God?

On a different level, if it were true that Rambam had in mind post-apprehension observance of the *halakhah*, then such enlightened observance would logically belong to the fifth, or at most the sixth, degree of worship in the parable of the king's palace, but certainly not (by Rambam's own descriptions) to the seventh, prophetic degree. Kellner is undoubtedly correct when he talks about "the *Guide of the Perplexed* actually being a guide of the perplexed,"[177] as aiming at an intellectual and spiritual transformation of the student and reader. That does not mean, however, that enlightened halakhic observance is the ultimate goal of that transformation.

Kellner, furthermore, claims that since humans lack the power to create, they imitate God by observing the Torah's commandments. For all of the sophistication of Kellner's analysis, it seems at this point simply to miss the mark. The divine activities to be imitated that Rambam himself mentions at the end of the *Guide of the Perplexed* III:54 have nothing to do with creation, and in fact Rambam does not use that term here. Rather, he states that the goal is "to know how his providence extends over his creatures by **bringing them into existence** and by governing them." The Arabic term here is *ijad* (to cause to exist), not any term implying creation. What is more important, however, is the rest of the sentence, "**by governing them**" and the total context of imitating such governance:

---

176   Menachem Kellner, *Maimonides on Human Perfection*, p. 60.
177   Menachem Kellner, *Maimonides on Human Perfection*, p. 60.

The human perfection for which one should truly be praised is to attain the apprehension of God according to one's capacity, to know how his providence extends over his creatures by bringing them into existence and by governing them. After he has attained this apprehension, that person's way of life will always intend at resembling [God's] actions of kindness, righteousness and justice.

Creation has nothing to do here with the imitation of God, and is not mentioned. What is mentioned is God's governance of the world in kindness, justice and righteousness. Granted, humans lack the power to create — but that is irrelevant to what Rambam is saying here. Humans cannot create, but as God brings the world into existence, people can bring states and societies into existence. And as God governs the world he brings into existence, people can govern the states and societies they bring into existence.

Humans have the capacity to govern themselves and society, and they have not only the capacity but, for Rambam, the obligation to do so in kindness, righteousness and justice, thereby imitating God's cosmic governance.

(4) "STUDY IS GREATER, FOR STUDY LEADS TO ACTION" —
INTELLECTUAL APPREHENSION AND PROPHETIC GOVERNANCE
A different approach also emphasizes "the worship...after the apprehension," but identifies that worship, i.e. the imitation of God's ways, not with the *halakhah*, but with moral activity and governance. This level of activity must not be confused with pre-apprehension moral activity determined by the practical intellect, but with the imitation of God following and actively expressing the theoretical intellect's apprehension of God's active attributes. Two scholars who interpret Rambam in this light are Julius Guttmann and Alexander Altmann.

Altmann, in his article on "Maimonide's Four Perfections" suggests that active imitation is an inseparable part of the ultimate human perfection. Knowledge of God's active attributes is part of what the prophet knows, not something separate.

Maimonides obviously distinguishes between the moral virtues...on the one hand, and the imitation of the Divine attributes, which, unlike the moral virtues, is not the result of practical reasoning, but follows from theoretical, metaphysical considerations. *Imitatio Dei* is, therefore, but the practical consequence of the intellectual love of God, and is part and parcel of the ultimate perfection.[178]

Julius Guttmann, who interprets Rambam in a similar light, regards the ethical component of ultimate human perfection as reflecting "the typically ethical character of Jewish religiosity."[179]

---

178   Alexander Altmann, "Maimonides' Four Perfections," p. 73.
179   Julius Guttmann, *Philosophies of Judaism*, pp. 176–177.

It is the communion with God, gained through knowledge, which endows man with eternal life. Here Maimonides manifests the typically ethical character of Jewish religiosity...The concluding chapter of the *Guide for the Perplexed* enumerates the various levels of human perfection, of which the highest is the perfection of knowledge, and describes the supreme knowledge of God as that of understanding the ethical activity of God, by which we are made to imitate it in our own actions. Ethics, though previously subordinate to knowledge, has now become the ultimate meaning and purpose of the knowledge of God...The knowledge of God leads to the desire to imitate his moral activity. This morality, grounded in the knowledge of God, is completely distinct from the morality which is prior to knowledge. Originating in the knowledge of God, it is part of man's supreme perfection, even if the action itself is directed toward an external object.

Although Altmann and Guttmann emphasize the moral nature of the imitation of God, the fact is that this imitation also has an overtly political dimension: the prophet's governance of the state is an imitation of God's cosmic governance. Nevertheless, whether the emphasis is on the ethical or the political dimension, the prophet's active imitation of God is an expression of—and thus an integral and inseparable part of—the intellectual perfection that is the ultimate human end. Or, to reiterate the point in the paradoxical terminology of the rabbis previously cited, "Study (= intellectual perfection) is greater, for study leads to action (= imitation of God's governance)."[180]

[X.5.e] THE IMITATION OF GOD: "AND SEE THAT THIS NATION IS YOUR PEOPLE" (*Guide* I:51) AND "JACOB'S LADDER" (*Guide* I:15)

In Chapter Nine[181] we discussed Rambam's interpretation, in his *Shemonah Peraqim* and in the *Mishneh Torah*, of two requests of Moses in Exodus 33:12–23. He interprets it for a third time in the *Guide of the Perplexed* I:54, but with an additional insight not found in the two earlier texts. Moses' first request, to which God responds favorably, is found in verse 13: "Now, if I have found favor in your eyes, let me know your ways (*hodi'eni na et derakhekha*), that I may know you, so that I might find favor in your eyes. And see that this nation is your people."

In classical rabbinic exegesis of Scripture, a basic assumption is that there can be nothing superfluous or extraneous in the text. A word or words

---

180   See the discussion above, X.5.a.ii and X.5.d.i. The citation is from Babylonian Talmud, Qiddushin 40b.
181   See the discussion in Ch. 9 (IX.2.d.iii).

which appear to be superfluous or extraneous must, therefore, convey special meaning. This verse is a case in point. We have discussed, at length, the question of the ultimate human perfection in Rambam's thought. Ethical perfection, as we saw, was negated as the human end, because it does not pertain to the individual himself, but only to the way he acts in relation to others.

In this passage in the Torah, Moses is requesting knowledge of God, the knowledge which constitutes his ultimate perfection as an individual: "Let me know your ways." Why, then, does Moses add something apparently superfluous and irrelevant to his quest for his individual perfection — a reference to the people: "And see that this nation is your people"? What do the people have to do with Moses' quest for knowledge of God?

Rambam comments:[182]

> This was the ultimate intention of [Moses'] request — at the end of which he says, "That I may know you, so that I might find favor in your eyes. And see that this nation is your people" — that is to say, whom I must govern with actions, by which I will follow your actions in governing them ... If the ruler of a state is a prophet, he should resemble these attributes ... He needs these actions in governing states. For a person's ultimate virtue is to resemble God according to his capacity, that is to say, that we should make our actions resemble his actions, as the sages made clear when interpreting "You be holy" (Leviticus 19:2): "As he is gracious, so you be gracious; as he is compassionate, so you be compassionate."[183]

The prophet's political obligation to govern the people in imitation of God's cosmic governance is thus not extraneous to his theoretical perfection as an individual. The political dimension is an inseparable and integral part of that theoretical perfection. It is the outer expression of the inner content, which is nothing other than apprehension of God's attributes of action. In Rambam's understanding, therefore, the additional words at the end of Moses' first request — "And see that this nation is your people" — are thus not at all superfluous, but in fact represent the inherent culmination of Moses' quest for knowledge of God.

Nevertheless, although God agreed in principle to grant Moses' request to know his ways, it was not until later, the next morning, that Moses actually acquired that knowledge, when he climbed Mount Sinai. At that point, as God passed by, Moses called out his attributes of action: "The Lord, the Lord, a compassionate and gracious God..." (Exodus 34:4–6). In other words, the apprehension of God is described in terms of the prophet's ascent, to

---

[182]   *Guide of the Perplexed* I:54.
[183]   Sifre to Deuteronomy 10:12.

receive the law and bring it back down to govern the people. The ascent thus symbolizes the prophet's own attainment of his individual perfection, i.e., theoretical apprehension, and the descent symbolizes the prophet's political obligation to govern the people in light of that intellectual apprehension.

We find a similar theme of ascent and descent in Rambam's interpretation of Jacob's ladder in the *Guide of the Perplexed* I:15. According to the story in Genesis 28:10–13:

10. Jacob left Beersheba and went to Ḥaran.
11. He came to a place and stayed there, for the sun had set. He took stones from that place and placed them under his head and lay down there.
12. He dreamt that a ladder was positioned on the earth with its top reaching the sky, and angels of God were ascending and descending on it.
13. And the Lord was positioned over it.

Many commentators noted the apparent anomaly in verse 12, that the angels first ascended and then descended. Rashi, for instance, commented that since Jacob was on his way from the Land of Israel to Syria, the angels accompanying him within Israel returned to heaven, and the angels who were to accompany him abroad came down to join him. Rashi's grandson Rashbam (Rabbi Samuel ben Meir) commented that we should not make anything of the ascent preceding the descent, because in human experience, what goes up then comes down.

Rambam's interpretation is radically different. The Hebrew term *mal'akh*, like the Greek word *angelos* (from which "angel" is derived), simply means a "messenger." Who, then, are these "messengers," and why does the Torah say that they first ascended, and then descended, on the ladder? According to Rambam, Jacob's ladder is a parable (Arabic: *mathal*; Hebrew: *mashal*).

> The ladder, one end of which was in the sky and the other end of which was on the earth, on which ascends everyone who ascends...The messengers of God are the prophets...How wise is the statement, "ascending and descending," the ascent before the descent. For after the ascent and reaching known rungs on the ladder comes the descent...to govern and teach the people of the earth.[184]

Jacob's ladder, in other words, is, in Rambam's reading, a parable of the ultimate human end. The messengers, i.e., the prophets, must first ascend to attain the knowledge of God that constitutes their theoretical perfection as individuals. However, that knowledge requires that they then descend, "to govern and teach the people of the earth" in light of the knowledge they

---

[184]   *Guide of the Perplexed* I:15.

attained, just as in the story of Moses, he first had to climb Mount Sinai to attain apprehension of God's ways, and then he had to descend back to the people, "whom I must govern with actions, by which I will follow your actions in governing them."

Although Rambam says nothing explicit to indicate this, there is also a striking parallel between his treatment of Jacob's ladder as a parable, and Plato's parable of the cave.[185]

> It is for us, then, as the founders of a commonwealth, to bring compulsion to bear on the noblest natures. They must be made to climb the ascent to the vision of Goodness, which we called the highest object of knowledge; and, when they have looked upon it long enough, they must not be allowed, as they now are, to remain on the heights, refusing to come down again... You are more capable of playing your part both as men of thought and as men of action. You must go down, then, each in his turn, to live with the rest and let your eyes grow accustomed to the darkness. You will then see a thousand times better than those who live there always; you will recognize every image for what it is and know what it represents, because you have seen justice, beauty and goodness in their reality.[186]

With obvious differences, we see that in some ways Rambam's parable of Jacob's ladder and Plato's parable of the cave are almost interchangeable. Like Plato's philosopher-king, Rambam's prophets must function "both as men of thought and as men of action." As "men of thought," they must ascend to the apprehension of God, "the highest object of knowledge." Like Plato's philosopher-king, who has "seen justice, beauty and goodness in their reality," Rambam's prophet has apprehended God's kindness, justice and righteousness. Then, as "men of action," they must descend "to govern and teach the people of the earth" in light of the knowledge of God's ways that only they have attained, thereby imitating God's cosmic governance.

[X.6]   CONCLUSION

Our harmonistic reading of Rambam's *Guide of the Perplexed*—both externally, in relation to his other works, and internally, in terms of reconciling tensions, divergences, or "contradictions" in the book itself—has attempted to present his thought as a consistent and coherent effort to resolve the

---

185   See the discussion above, X.5.a.vi.
186   Plato, *Republic* VII, 514a–521b. English translation by Francis MacDonald Cornford, *The Republic of Plato*, pp. 227–234.

perplexity arising from the apparent incompatibility of loyalty to the Torah and the commitment to rational and scientific truth. One of the reasons Rambam made such an enduring impact on subsequent Jewish thought undoubtedly was his preeminence as a rabbinic leader and codifier of *halakhah*. Another reason was surely the boldness of his vision, the breadth of his scope, and the profundity of his insights. However, and perhaps ultimately most importantly, Rambam's *Guide* frankly addresses (even if it does not always resolve) issues that have perplexed intellectual Jews at least since the time of Philo, and continue to challenge and perplex many today. Even if we do not always find his answers satisfactory, the questions that he raises, and the challenges that he faced, are frequently the same as, or similar to, our existential dilemmas. Therefore, even if we cannot always agree with what he said, Rambam provides a paradigm for us to do what he did.

THE CONTROVERSY OVER PHILOSOPHY AND RAMBAM

Chapter Eleven

THE CONTROVERSY OVER
PHILOSOPHY AND RAMBAM

[XI.1] THE INHERENT CONFLICT OF FAITH
AND REASON

Towards the end of Rambam's lifetime, and for roughly a century after
his death in 1204 C.E., a great controversy arose over philosophy. That
controversy (or controversies, since they were not directly connected), which
climaxed at four distinct times, sometimes focused more on the challenge
of philosophy, and at other times focused more specifically on Rambam
and some of his teachings. Although there were particular personalities and
historical developments leading to each of these climaxes, the arguments
really reflected an underlying tension in Judaism, namely the inherent conflict
of faith and reason.[1]

One of the underlying causes of tension was the foreign source of
philosophy, which was obvious from its very name. That argument could be
countered by the claim, which we find among such disparate thinkers as Judah
Ha-Levi and Rambam, that the Greeks learned their wisdom from Semitic or
specifically Jewish sources, and that under conditions of exile the Jews lost
what was originally part of their own tradition, which they were now seeking
to reclaim from the Greeks. The epitome of this argument was the claim in
some legendary literature that Aristotle studied philosophy with a Jewish
teacher, and the even more extreme claim that Aristotle ultimately converted
to Judaism.[2]

Despite the fact that Jewish mystical literature also borrows to some
extent from foreign sources (for instance, in the Middle Ages, from Islamic

---

[1]   For concise surveys of this subject and bibliographical references, see: Raphael Jospe,
        "Faith and Reason: The Controversy Over Philosophy in Jewish History," in *Jewish
        Philosophy: Foundations and Extensions, Volume One: General Questions and Consi-
        derations* (Lanham: University Press of America, 2008), pp. 55–90; Haim Hillel Ben-
        Sasson, Raphael Jospe and Dov Schwartz, "Maimonidean Controversy," in *Encyclopaedia
        Judaica* (2nd edition), Vol. 13, pp. 371–381.

[2]   See the discussion of these points in Ch. 7 (VII.1.a).

Sufi mysticism), the mystical tradition was never subjected to the suspicions or outright antagonism aimed at philosophy. Whereas the very name "philosophy" is recognizably foreign, and the Jewish philosophers did not hesitate to cite openly and by name non-Jewish thinkers and books, in the case of the mystical tradition the borrowing was often unconscious, and if the original borrowers were aware of their cross-cultural debt, subsequent generations were not. Moreover, some of the classical works of Jewish mystical literature are pseudepigraphical. For instance, the *Sefer Yeẓirah* is attributed to Abraham, and the *Zohar* is attributed to Rashbi (Rabbi Shim'on bar Yoḥai). The mystical doctrines were taken to represent authentic, if esoteric, traditional Jewish teaching, and therefore came to be known as "Kabbalah" ("tradition"). Philosophy, with its overtly foreign sources, and its commitment to "listen to the truth from whoever says it" (as Rambam stated at the beginning of his *Shemonah Peraqim*) never enjoyed the same credibility as the mystical "tradition," which was perceived (and still largely is perceived) by its adherents to be exactly what its name implies, the native and internal Jewish "tradition."

Beyond the question of philosophy's foreign sources, an inherent tension between faith and reason arises for methodological reasons, because each system essentially undermines the other. The rational or scientific method—keeping in mind that in pre-modern times philosophy was considered the "mother of the sciences"—is an open system. That is to say, one cannot predetermine or limit the conclusions to which the method will lead. It is the validity of the method itself which necessitates the conclusion, and that method permits others to replicate any experiments and verify their conclusion. One cannot, for example, give a pathologist a biopsy and command him to find a certain benign or malignant result; to predetermine the conclusion is to invalidate the scientific method itself.

Faith, however, precisely because it cannot be proven—if it could be proven, it would be knowledge, not faith—is a closed system, which essentially reverses the procedure, by beginning *a priori* with the conclusion, which is affirmed as true despite the lack of definitive proof. Any reasoning process is, therefore, *a posteriori*: the conclusion, already taken to be true, can then be defended, justified, and rationales can be provided to support it (as with Rambam's explanations of *ta'amei ha-miẓvot*, the meaning, rationale and utility of the commandments), but the conclusion *per se* cannot be challenged.

This, then, was what Rambam was talking about when describing the difference between philosophy, as an open system, which adjusts its theories in accordance with the facts, and Kalam theology, as a closed system, which (he argued) attempts to adjust the facts to accord with its preconceived conclusions.

The two systems thus undermine each other's autonomy, integrity and coherence. The rational method of scientific and philosophic inquiry undermines faith by refusing to take the conclusion for granted, and by asking for proof. Faith, on the other hand, undermines the integrity of the scientific method by predetermining, without proof, which conclusion is true.

In addition to being an open system, the rational or scientific method of inquiry is also inherently universal; it does not differ from culture to culture, nor is it subject to cultural norms which restrict or prejudice its inquiry. Faith, although it can be universal (and great faiths like Christianity and Islam claim to be universal, transcending national, ethnic and racial boundaries), generally differs from culture to culture, and it is no accident that children generally (but certainly not always) follow in the faith of their parents, because what is deemed believable in one culture is often unbelievable in another, frequently simply on the basis of habit and what people are accustomed to. Judah Ha-Levi pointed this out in the Kuzari king's response (in the beginning of the book) to the Christian spokesman. The claims of Christianity are not rationally demonstrable or persuasive, the king says, and since he did not grow up as a Christian, he had no other reason to accept those claims. In short, what we are accustomed to strikes us as more reasonable, believable or at least acceptable than something new and unfamiliar.

The cultural relativism of faith was already recognized by the pre-Socratic philosopher Xenophanes of Colophon (570 B.C.E.—475 B.C.E.):[3]

> But mortals consider that the gods are born, and that they have clothes and speech like their own. The Ethiopians say that their gods are snub-nosed and black; the Thracians that theirs have light blue eyes and red hair. But if cattle and horses or lions had hands, or were able to draw with their hands and do the work that men do, horses would draw the forms [Greek: ideas] of the gods like horses, and cattle like cattle, and they would make their bodies such as they each had themselves.

In the seventeenth century, Baruch (Benedict de) Spinoza continued in the same humorous vein:

> Let us imagine...a little worm, living in the blood...This little worm would live in the blood, in the same way as we live in a part of the universe, and would consider each part of blood, not as a part, but as a whole.[4]
>
> I believe that, if a triangle could speak, it would say, in like manner, that God is eminently triangular, while a circle would say that the divine nature is eminently

---

3   Greek fragments and English translation in G.S. Kirk and J.E. Raven, *The Presocratic Philosophers* (Cambridge: Cambridge University Press, 1964), pp. 168–169.

4   Spinoza, Letter #15 (1665?) to Oldenburg, in R.H.M. Elwes (trans.), *The Chief Works of Benedict de Spinoza* (New York: Dover, 1955), vol. 2, p. 291.

circular. Thus each would ascribe to God its own attributes, would assume itself to be like God, and look on everything else as ill-shaped.[5]

Pointing out the inherent tension between faith and reason does not mean that they cannot be reconciled or harmonized. That was the challenge faced (and perhaps met) by the Jewish philosophers from Philo on, through the Middle Ages, and in modern times, just as it was the challenge of philosophers over the ages in Christianity and Islam. The problem is not only a Jewish problem, but it is a problem that Jews, like others, had to face, from Philo on. Let us recall that Harry Wolfson's famous thesis posited Philo as the archetypal "synthetic philosopher" (synthesizing biblical revelation, which did not know philosophy, and pagan Greek philosophy which did not know biblical revelation), whose "double faith theory" (i.e., the belief in the validity of both revelation and reason as ways to the truth) was dominant in all western religious philosophy — whether in Latin, Arabic or Hebrew "garb" — for seventeen centuries, until the structure Philo built was destroyed by Spinoza.[6]

Of course, many of the medieval Jewish philosophers, like their colleagues in Islam and Christianity, followed in Philo's footsteps in affirming their "double faith" in both reason and revelation, and attempted to synthesize the two systems. As such, they did not belong to either extreme camp, of those who opposed reason in the name of revealed tradition, or of those whose rationalism led them to radical allegorization of Scripture and the tradition. Nevertheless, the fact that they needed to create such a synthesis is testimony to the reality of the underlying tensions between the two systems. Given these inherent tensions between faith and reason, why is it that the conflict erupted into a public (and occasionally violent) controversy at certain times and in certain places?

[XI.2]   THE HISTORICAL BACKGROUND

Rambam had explicitly stipulated that his *Guide of the Perplexed* was not intended for the general community, but only for the perplexed elite intelligentsia, in other words, for Jews who questioned the Torah because of their prior exposure to philosophy. Since there is a need, based on statements of the Talmudic rabbis, to restrict instruction from the unworthy in "the

---

5   Spinoza, Letter #60 (1674), to Hugo Boxel, in *The Chief Works of Benedict de Spinoza*, vol. 2, p. 386.

6   Harry A. Wolfson, *Philo: Foundations of Religious Philosophy in Judaism, Christianity and Islam* (Cambridge: Harvard University Press, 1947). See the discussion of Philo in Chapter One (I.2).

work of creation" (i.e., physics, according to Rambam), and even more so in "the work of the chariot" (i.e., metaphysics, according to him), he adopted a policy of concealment of his true intention, by pedagogic and deliberate "divergences" (usually understood as contradictions), and by an obscure and non-linear literary structure.

With the translation of the *Guide of the Perplexed* into Hebrew towards the end of Rambam's lifetime, at the request of French Jews living in a Christian country who did not know Arabic, the problem was that the book became available in the broader community among people who were not Rambam's intended "perplexed" readers, because, however intense their religious piety and however well-versed they were in halakhic literature, they had no prior exposure to the Arabic philosophical and scientific literature with which Jewish intellectuals in the Islamic countries were familiar. Their interest in the *Guide of the Perplexed* was aroused by Rambam's pre-eminent stature as a rabbi and halakhic authority, and not because they met the criteria Rambam had established for the perplexed intellectual reader for whom the book was written. In short, in these circles of Jews in Christian areas, who were unprepared and unable to meet the challenge of the philosophy Rambam had never intended them to read in the first place, the book, instead of serving as a guide for the perplexed, ended up causing perplexity, aroused antagonism to Rambam as an individual, and generated vehement opposition to the study of philosophy.

By contrast with the *Guide of the Perplexed*, translated into Hebrew by Samuel ibn Tibbon in Rambam's lifetime, and again by Judah Al-Ḥarizi shortly thereafter, the earlier works of Jewish philosophy written in Arabic, such as Saʻadiah Ga'on's *Book of Beliefs and Opinions*, Baḥya ibn Paquda's *Duties of the Heart*, and Judah Ha-Levi's *Kuzari* were only later translated into Hebrew, not in their authors' lifetimes, and therefore did not arouse immediate opposition. Moreover, these books were not controversial in the same way, because they did not present the same kind of radical challenge to simple traditional religious faith that Rambam's *Guide* did. Saʻadiah Ga'on's book is much more conservative, and needed to justify philosophy in terms of the Torah (which was not challenged), whereas Rambam's book needed to justify the Torah — which the perplexed student doubted — in terms of philosophy. Baḥya's book justifies the need for philosophy, but seeks to spiritualize religious life through internalization and rationalization, not to challenged religion rationally. Judah Ha-Levi's book, as a "defense of the despised religion" and as a critique of Aristotelian philosophy, was frequently taken (and is still often read) — however correctly or incorrectly — as an attack on philosophy *per se*.

Rambam's positions, on the other hand, could easily be understood — or misunderstood — as radical and as denying and undermining traditional beliefs, not just in the *Guide of the Perplexed*, but certainly prominently in that book. His intellectualist understanding of the world to come (*'olam ha-ba*)—including in his Commentary to the Mishnah—was taken to be a repudiation of resurrection. His categorization (in the *Mishneh Torah*) of a Jew who believes in a corporeal God as a heretic, and (in the *Guide of the Perplexed*) as worse than an idolater, was sharply criticized. Rambam's proofs of God on the basis of eternity were taken, at least by some, as tantamount to a denial of creation. As Shem Tov ibn Falaquera (Spain; died circa 1291)—who strongly defended Rambam and the study of philosophy in the third stage or climax of the Maimonidean controversy—put it in his commentary, *Moreh Ha-Moreh* ("The Guide to the Guide"), the *Guide of the Perplexed* can help someone who is perplexed, but will harm someone who has not studied philosophy, just as medicine which can heal the sick, harms the healthy person.

In addition to these internal Jewish factors, there were external circumstances in the Christian environment exacerbating the situation of the Jewish community. After the Crusaders captured Constantinople in 1204 (the year of Rambam's death), the Greek works of Aristotle became directly accessible to Western Christians, who no longer had to rely on Latin translations of Greek works made (often by Jews) from Arabic, or sometimes from Hebrew translations based on the Arabic translations from the Greek. The rise of universities rivaled the monasteries as centers of learning. The Church was thus facing increasing confrontations with scientific and philosophic learning.

In the twelfth and thirteenth centuries, the Church also faced internal Christian challenges, "heresies" from its perspectives, to its "orthodoxy," especially that of the Cathari ("the pure") and the related "heresy" of the rationalist Albigensians (from the town of Albi in southern France). These groups began, in the eleventh century, to interpret Scripture allegorically, and denied the literal interpretation, so basic to Catholic dogma, of the miraculous events of the life and death of Jesus.

The "heresy" spread, especially among the upper classes. In the first decades of the thirteenth century, the Church took action against both threats—philosophy and heresy. Against the threat of secular philosophy, the Church repeatedly banned the study of Aristotle and the commentaries on his works. (The mere fact that the bans had to be repeated is an indication of their ineffectiveness). In 1209, the University of Paris banned the study of Arabic writings (which were philosophical and scientific). In 1210, the Synod of Paris banned the public or private readings of Aristotle's works on natural philosophy, as well as the commentaries on those works. In 1215, the Papal Legate instructed the University of Paris to forbid the study of Aristotle's *Physics* and *Metaphysics*, although he permitted the study of Aristotle's *Ethics*. A few years later, in 1231, Pope Gregory IX renewed the ban on

Aristotle, and established the permanent Inquisition under the Dominicans, with the aim of completely eradicating Alibigensianism; years before, Pope Innocent III had already launched the "Albigensian Crusade" to elimate the heresy that he regarded as instigated by educated Jews.

In fact, there were certain parallels between the Albigensian "heretics" in Christianity and the rationalist Jewish philosophers of the day, at least as perceived by their opponents, respectively in the Church and in the Jewish community, who accused them of indiscriminate allegorization of Scripture and of antinomian laxity in moral or ritual behavior. The Albigensians were charged with rationalist allegorization of the miracles of Jesus' body and resurrection; the Jewish philosophers were charged with rationalist allegorization of anthropomorphisms, miracles, and the doctrine of resurrection. The rationalist Albigensians were suspected of antinomianism, resulting in a laxity of morals. The rationalist allegorization of Scripture by Jewish philosophers, their opponents frequently claimed, perhaps with some occasional justification but certainly with much exaggeration, led to antinomianism in ritual matters, allegedly with a resulting laxity in observances of the *miẓvot*.

The anti-rationalist agitation in the Christian environment was thus a contributing factor, if not a direct cause, of exacerbating long existing, but generally dormant, tensions within the Jewish community. As Joseph Sarachek wrote in his history of the controversy over philosophy:[7]

> If these clashes in church and synagogue are not connected as cause and effect, they are at any rate analogous movements. The seeds of an alleged heresy were blowing in all directions... It was not until the thirteenth century that the real conflicts over heresy in Christendom were fought, and that the mood for ferreting out and punishing heresy was transferred to the Jewish fold.

Daniel Lasker has suggested that there may have been some contact between Jewish anti-Christian polemicists and anti-Catholic Christians:

> The anonymous author of *Viku'ah Radaq* used specifically Catharist arguments against the Catholics (and Catholic arguments against the Catharists), while Joseph ben Shem Tov referred to those who did not believe in transubstantiation and were, therefore, considered heretics. It appears, then, that the Jews, as the main target of Christian polemics, were aware of the position of other groups which also incurred orthodox wrath.[8]

---

[7]   Joseph Saracheck, *Faith and Reason: The Conflict Over the Rationalism of Maimonides* (New York, 1935), pp. 9–10.

[8]   Daniel Lasker, *Jewish Philosophical Polemics Against Christianity in the Middle Ages* (originally published 1977; 2nd edition; Oxford: Littman Library of Jewish Civilization, 2007), p. 164.

Besides internal tensions the Jewish community faced — the controversies over Karaism and rationalism — there were also overt external pressure and hostility from the Church. The Fourth Lateran Council in 1215, among its seventy canonical decrees, promulgated four decrees specifically aimed against the Jews.[9] In the Paris disputation of 1240, Donin of La Rochelle, who had been excommunicated by his Jewish community for doubting the validity of the Talmud, and had then been baptized, taking the Christian name of Nicholas, denounced the Talmud to Pope Gregory IX. He charged the Talmud with distorting the Bible; the Jews with regarding the Talmud as more important than the Bible; and the Talmud with abusing or insulting Jesus and Mary. Subsequently, in 1242, cartloads of the Talmud were burned by the Dominicans in the *place* in front of the Cathedral of Notre Dame in Paris, a cultural disaster of immense proportions when books — before the invention of the printing press — were hand-written, rare and expensive.[10]

[XI.3] FOUR STAGES OR CLIMAXES

The medieval controversy over Rambam and philosophy reached four climaxes:

(1) During the last years of Rambam's life, following the publication of his *Mishneh Torah* in 1180, until his death in 1204. In this period, Rambam's prominent critics on the issue of resurrection included Rabbi Meir ben Todros Ha-Levi Abulafia (Ramah); one of the most important critics of the *Mishneh Torah* was Ravad (Rabbi Abraham ben David of Posquieres); Samuel ben 'Ali was critical of Rambam both on the question of resurrection and on halakhic issues in the *Mishneh Torah*.

(2) In the years 1230–1235, involving Radak (Rabbi David Kimḥi), Solomon ben Abraham of Montpellier, Ramban (Naḥmanides) and others, and centering in Provence, leading to bans on philosophy, including Rambam's *Book of Knowledge* (the first of the fourteen sections of the *Mishneh Torah*) and his *Guide of the Perplexed*.

---

9   These decrees restricted Jewish banking activities (usury), required Jews to pay tithes on their property and a tax at Easter, forbade Christian rulers from appointing Jews to public office, and required Jews to wear distinctive clothing to set them apart visibly from Christians.

10   Whereas in Paris in 1240 the Talmud was charged with blaspheming Jesus, in the Barcelona disputation of 1263, the apostate Pablo Christiani attempted to convince Ramban (Naḥmanides) that the Talmud proves that Jesus is the messiah. Naḥmanides countered that Jews are only obligated to believe in the Bible and to accept as binding the halakhic portions of the Talmud, but that *aggadot* (lore, legends) are not binding.

(3) In the years 1288–1290 in the Near East, involving Solomon Petit and Rabbi Isaac of Akko (Acre). In this case, the opponents of philosophy found themselves banned.

(4) During the years 1300–1306, involving Abba Mari ben Moses Ha-Yarḥi Astruc, Rashba (Rabbi Solomon ben Abraham Adret), Asher ben Yeḥi'el, Yeda'iah ben Abraham Bedershi Ha-Penini, and Menaḥem ben Solomon Me'iri, centered in Christian Spain and Provence. The ban issued in Barcelona in 1305 was much more limited than the earlier bans, and merely restricted the study of philosophy to those over 25 years old; even limited restriction did not apply to works of medicine or of Jewish thinkers.

These have often been treated by historians as distinct historical stages, but recent research has tended to show that these climaxes were not four stages of a single homogeneous drama. Although of course there are common denominators, there are also important differences among these climaxes. In the first, the opposition had less to do with philosophy than with Rambam's *Mishneh Torah* and with his alleged denial of resurrection. In the second climax, there was a total opposition to the study of philosophy *per se*, and there were attempts to ban its study. In the third climax, the situation was reversed, and the bans were not on philosophers but on the opponents of Rambam. In the fourth and final climax, Rambam himself was no longer the subject of the controversy, and even the traditionalists accepted many of his positions. At this point the traditionalists no longer opposed philosophy *per se*, nor all study of philosophy, but merely attempted to place certain limited restrictions on the study of philosophy.

Recent research has also tended to show that the situation is less clear, and far more complicated, than previously portrayed, and that many Jewish intellectuals did not fall into either extreme camp, that of extreme rationalist allegorization or that of opposition in principle to all foreign wisdom. Many in the rationalist camp were strictly observant; although committed rationalists, they rejected extreme philosophical positions and maintained the supremacy of the Torah. Conversely, among the conservative or traditionalist rabbinic authorities were those who did not object in principle to the study of philosophy, and frequently themselves had philosophical education, but they objected to premature exposure of the youth to philosophy, and objected to extreme rationalist allegorization, especially in public sermons in the synagogue. Paradoxically, in this final climax, one of the points the traditionalist camp objected to was the use of astral magic for medical purposes by the rationalists.[11]

---

[11]   See Dov Schwartz, "Changing Fronts toward Science in the Medieval Debates over Philosophy," in *Journal of Jewish Thought and Philosophy* 7 (1997), pp. 61–82.

[XI.4]   THE FIRST CLIMAX: DURING RAMBAM'S LIFETIME

What was controversial during Rambam's lifetime was not so much his philosophy—since the *Guide of the Perplexed* was only translated into Hebrew towards the end of his life and his philosophy was, therefore, not yet known in Jewish communities in Christian Europe—but his *Mishneh Torah* and his position on resurrection. The criticism of the *Mishneh Torah* reflected divergent local practice and custom (*minhag*), but focused on Rambam's methodology, the fact that he did not cite the sources for his decisions, and his radical claim that the study of the Code would replace the study of Talmud: "A person should first study the written Torah, and then read this [book], and thereby know the entire oral Torah, so that he will not need to read any other book in between them."

Rambam's great Ashkenazi critic, Rabbi Abraham ben David of Posquières (Ravad or Rabad), whose critical glosses (*hasagot*) were included in later editions of the Code, strenuously objected to Rambam's method and failure to cite his sources. In a *hasagah* to the Introduction of the *Mishneh Torah*, he wrote that Rambam "has abandoned the method of all the authors who preceded him, because they brought proofs for their words and cited their sources...This way, I do not know why I should disregard my tradition and my proof for the sake of this author's book."

One of the unique and controversial features of Rambam's Code—in contrast with other codes of Jewish law—is its legislation of beliefs as well as practices, since the divine law must lead to "the welfare of the soul" (*tiqun ha-nefesh*), i.e. affirmation of the truth, as well as to "the welfare of the body" (*tiqun ha-guf*), i.e., proper behavior. When, therefore, Rambam categorized a Jew who believes in a corporeal God as a heretic (*min*), Ravad objected: "Why did he call such a person a heretic, when some who were greater and better than he followed this opinion, according to what they saw in the Bible and even more, according to what they saw in *aggadot* which corrupt opinions?"[12] Ravad himself also rejected corporealism, which he attributes to "*aggadot* which corrupt opinions." What Ravad denied was the legitimacy of Rambam's characterizing such a person as a heretic and his authority to make such a decision. Rambam's interpretation of the world to come in terms of the survival of the intellect in proportion to its attainment of knowledge was also criticized by Ravad, who said: "The words of this man seem close to one who says that there is no bodily resurrection of the dead, but only of the soul."[13] Rambam was aware of the criticism on him regarding this

---

12   Ravad, *hasagah* to *Mishneh Torah*, Book of Knowledge, Laws of Repentance 3:7.
13   Ravad, *hasagah* to *Mishneh Torah*, Book of Knowledge, Laws of Repentance 8:2.

point, and to counter it, wrote his *Treatise on Resurrection*, which argued that resurrection is not to be confused with the world to come or with the messianic era. Resurrection, as a miracle, did not merit discussion in his other works which dealt with natural phenomena. What Rambam is really arguing for is not so much resurrection as the possibility of resurrection, because to deny the possibility miracles is to deny that miracles are, in principle, possible, which in turn is to deny that the world is created, in favor of a world of eternal and unchanging necessity. But in such an eternal world, revelation is also not possible, in which case the authority of the Torah collapses.

Others also criticized Rambam's apparent denial of resurrection. One of the most important of these critics was Rabbi Meir ben Todros Ha-Levi Abulafia (Ramah), who was active in the first two climaxes of the controversy. In the first period, he was strongly opposed to Rambam's apparent denial of this principle, which he defended at length, but after he saw Rambam's *Treatise on Resurrection*, reaffirming resurrection, Abulafia became satisfied that Rambam did, in fact, affirm this traditional dogma. Samuel ben 'Ali (d. 1194), the influential head of the academy in Baghdad, was critical of Rambam on both issues, namely resurrection and halakhic questions in the *Mishneh Torah*.

The first climax in the Maimonidean controversy ended with Rambam's death in 1204. To this day, Ravad's critical *hasagot* are included in editions of the *Mishneh Torah*, thus preserving for later generations much of the criticism. The halakhic criticism of the first period, however, helped set the stage for the philosophic criticism of the subsequent periods.

[XI.5] THE SECOND CLIMAX: 1230–1235 IN FRANCE

Whereas Rambam's halakhic work was the subject of the controversy within his lifetime, in its second period his philosophy became the catalyst for a larger controversy over philosophy in general. Although Rambam himself was recognized even by his opponents as being above personal reproach, since his piety could not possibly be denied, it seems that there were Jews who justified (or at least were accused by their opponents of justifying) laxity in observance by allegorical interpretation of the Torah, including its legal portions, and who, in their defense, cited Rambam's figurative interpretation of Scripture in the *Guide of the Perplexed*.

This real or imagined danger led to agitation against philosophy. Solomon ben Abraham of Montpellier, together with David ben Saul and Jonah ben Abraham Gerondi (a relative of Naḥmanides), led the agitation against philosophy, and in 1232 persuade the rabbis of northern France to ban the study of philosophy, including Rambam's *Guide of the Perplexed* and his *Book of Knowledge* (the first section of the *Mishneh Torah*, containing much philosophical material). In August of 1232 the three agitators were, in turn, counter-banned in Aragon by supporters of Rambam's philosophy. That led, subsequently, to the denunciation of Rambam's works to the Church and the burning of Rambam's books by the Dominicans in the marketplace of Montpellier.

The objections to philosophy were based on three themes, which would be repeated in later opposition to philosophy, and which were consistently denied by the philosophers and their supporters:

(1) Theological. They depicted the philosophers as denying miracles, as regarding prophecy as a purely natural phenomenon, and as rejecting traditional eschatological doctrines, eg., concerning resurrection and the world to come.

(2) Exigetical. The traditionalist charged the philosophers with indiscriminate allegorization of Scripture and of denying the historicity of various biblical persons and events.

(3) Practical. The philosophers were charged with laxity in observance of the commandments.

The controversy in the 1230s involved exchanges of letters, many between the philosopher and biblical exegete Radak (Rabbi David Kimḥi) and the physician and courtier Judah ibn Alfakhar. These letters, from both sides of the controversy, were preserved in a collection, *Iggerot Qena'ot* ("Letters of Zealotry"). When Radak attempted to gather support for Rambam and the cause of philosophy in Provence, he he was disappointed by Judah ibn Alfakhar's response attacking Rambam's rationalist explanations of miracles and rejecting his attempted synthesis of Greek and Jewish wisdom, which he regarded as incompatible. Steven Harvey[14] has suggested that this dispute between Radak and Alfakhar, preserved in the exchange of letters, served as the model for the book *Iggeret Ha-Vikuaḥ* ("The Epistle of the Debate") by Shem Tov ibn Falaquera, who (as mentioned above) supported Rambam and the cause of philosophy in the third climax of the controversy.

A moderate position was taken by Ramban (Naḥmanides), who was a relative of Jonah Gerondi. He opposed the counter ban of Aragon against the three agitators, but also urged the French rabbis to reconsider their original ban on Rambam's philosophical works, which, he realistically recognized, would never gain the support of the rabbis of Provence and Spain, was unenforceable, and therefore could only lead to divisiveness among the Jewish communities. Instead, he recommended, in the very least, modifying the ban to permit the

---

14   Steven Harvey, *Falaquera's Epistle of the Debate: An Introduction to Jewish Philosophy* (Cambridge: Harvard University Press, 1987).

study of Rambam's *Book of Knowledge*. Rambam was not only respected but revered among Jewish in the south and east, especially in Yemen. Ramban also defended Rambam's motives. He had written his philosophy not for the Jews of France, but for the Jews of the south, who were confronting the challenges of philosophy and Karaism, and, therefore, needed a philosophical defense and explanation of Judaism. Ramban credits Rambam with having saved many Jews who were ignorant of Judaism and lax in their observance of the commandments because of their exposure to the wisdom of the Greeks. In short, Ramban opposed philosophy but respected Rambam, and above all, wished to preserve the unity of the Jewish people in the face of the bitter controversy. As Daniel Jeremy Silver aptly put it, for Ramban "Maimonides was the context of the quarrel, not its content."[15]

The question of the validity of Jewish philosophy was not resolved theoretically in this period, but practically, and the arguments on both sides remained essentially unanswered. The burning of the Talmud in Paris in 1242 was an overwhelming trauma, and although there is no direct link between that incident and the burning of Rambam's books ten years earlier, in 1232 in Montpellier, many Jews—both supporters of Rambam like Hillel ben Samuel of Verona, and opponents like Jonah Gerondi—regarded the two incidents as related, and the latter as punishment for the former. Accordingly, Jonah Gerondi subsequently repented his opposition to philosophy and Rambam, and vowed to pay penance at the philosopher's grave in Tiberias. His relative Ramban was forced into exile after his public disputation with Pablo Christianity in Barcelona in 1263, and in 1267 emigrated to Israel.

[XI.6]   THE THIRD CLIMAX: A RENEWAL OF THE CONTROVERSY IN THE EAST, 1288–1290

The third climax differs sharply from the second one half a century earlier. Whereas the events of 1230–1233 took place largely in southern France, in Jewish communities within a Christian environment, most of the controversy towards the end of the thirteenth century took place in the Near East. In addition, the roles were reversed. In the earlier controversy, the philosophers had to defend their cause against being banned, whereas in the latter controversy, the anti-philosophical agitators were repeatedly banned. Solomon Petit, a mystic and anti-rationalist, had first agitated against Rambam in northern France and Germany, where he gained support for his efforts to ban Rambam's *Guide*

---

[15]   Daniel Jeremy Silver, *Maimonidean Criticism and the Maimonidean Controversy 1180–1240* (Leiden: Brill, 1965), p. 173.

of the Perplexed and *Book of Knowledge*. In 1288, Petit emigrated to Akko (Acre) in Israel, where he taught Kabbalah. Many of his students had studied with Ramban after his emigration to Israel. In Akko, Petit continued to agitate against Rambam and to urge the burning of Rambam's books, especially the *Guide*. Petit, however, failed in his task. He himself was banned no less than four times. He had fundamentally miscalculated; he was now living in the Land of Israel, which came under the jurisdiction of the *nagid* (governor) of Egyptian Jewry, who was Rambam's grandson, David ben Abraham. Moreover, in the Arabic environment of the Near East, the Jews had long been exposed and accustomed to philosophical culture, and widely accepted the the the legitimacy of philosophy, unlike the Jews of Christian Europe who had originally supported Petit.

While the bans against Petit in the east succeeded, the attempts in the west to ban philosophy failed. Hillel ben Samuel of Verona (1220–1295) was popularizing philosophy in Italy by giving public lectures on Rambam's *Guide of the Perplexed*. In Spain, Shem Tov ibn Falaquera was writing prolific works of his own on philosophy, translating Arabic philosophical texts, and writing a major commentary on the *Guide of the Perplexed* (including his own Hebrew translation of the sections on which he commented). Convinced of the harmony of faith and reason, Falaquera saw his great task as supporting the process of consolidation of philosophy in Judaism at a time that Rambam and philosophy were under attack. His explicit goal in his numerous works was to popularize philosophy in Hebrew among the Jews, to ensure that philosophy would become the possession of the entire Jewish people and not merely the elitist preoccupation of the Arabic-reading intelligentsia.[16]

Falaquera became directly involved in the controversy aroused by Solomon Petit's agitation in the east. His last known work, "A Letter Concerning the *Guide*," in 1291, is a defense of Rambam, in which Falaquera mocks Rambam's opponents in a poem:

> I wonder about those who differ with Moses (i.e., Rambam),
> How they don't remember the punishment of Koraḥ.
> He is a true teacher, and his word
> Is like fire; their word is like ice.

Playing on Petit's name, Falaquera referred to him as *peti* (a fool). He argued that Rambam was compelled to write the *Guide of the Perplexed* because of widespread corporealist beliefs among the Jews, even among great rabbis. But

---

16   For more on Falaquera's thought and contribution, see Raphael Jospe, *Torah and Sophia: The Life and Thought of Shem Tov ibn Falaquera* (Cincinnati: Hebrew Union College Press, 1988).

such people, wrong as they are, are not the perplexed for whom the book was written. No wonder, then, that Rambam was misunderstood—after all, even the Torah had been misunderstood by *minim* (heretics, sectarians). The masses of Jews in the time of the Torah rebelled against God and Moses; no wonder the Jews rebel against the Moses of this day.

The opponents of philosophy, Falaquera suggested, glorified in the ignorance of science and philosophy. But there is no glory in ignorance. The rabbis of the Talmud were great scholars in both Torah and science. Falaquera questioned whether anyone "in these lands," who does not know Arabic, can truly understand the *Guide of the Perplexed*. These Jews are dependent on Hebrew translations, which are faulty, and they are, therefore, likely to misunderstand Rambam's true meaning.

In an earlier work,[17] Falaquera had defended the harmony between the Torah and philosophy, which he called "twins."[18] Falaquera did not claim that philosophy is infallible, but took the moderate position of accepting from philosophy on that which is true and agrees with religion. In that sense, like Rabbi Me'ir, he "eats the pomegranate and discards the peel."[19] Like Sa'adiah Ga'on,[20] Falaquera argued that what one knows through reason is stronger than what one knows through religious tradition alone, since if one's tradition is challenged, one will not be able to defend it.

Whatever is truly and conclusively demonstrated cannot contradict the Torah—the truth cannot contradict the truth. To deny the validity of the speculative method because of some mistaken conclusions of the philosophers, is like denying water to a thirsty person so that he dies of thirst, just because some people have drowned in water.[21]

Falaquera also argued that it is wrong to maintain that the truth can be learned only from Jewish sources, and to reject the truth because it is derived from non-Jews. The truth is universal. All nations have access to the truth through philosophy and science. As one takes honey from a bee, so one should accept the truth from any source.[22] Falaquera repeatedly and eloquently expounded on this theme.

---

[17] *Iggeret Ha-Viku'ah* ("The Epistle of the Debate"). For Steven Harvey's excellent edition and translation, see note 13, above.

[18] Earlier, Abraham ibn Da'ud (*Exalted Faith*, p. 2) had referred to a person "holding in his two hands two lights: in his right hand the light of religion, and in his left hand, the light of philosophy." See our discussion of Ibn Da'ud in Chapter Seven.

[19] The reference is to a statement in Babylonian Talmud, Ḥagigah 15b: "Rabbi Me'ir found a pomegranate. He ate its contents and discarded its peel."

[20] Sa'adiah Ga'on, *Book of Beliefs andOpinions*, Introduction, #6.

[21] Falaquera, *Sefer Ha-Ma'a lot* ("The Book of Degrees"), pp. 74–75. The image is taken from Ibn Rushd's *Decisive Treatise*.

[22] Falaquera, *Batei Hanhagat Ha-Nefesh*, p. 72.

It is impossible for a person to know by himself everything that he needs, as the ancients said on this. There is no difference if these ancients are of our faith or not. When the speculation is true and perfect of any deficiency, we do not take notice if they are of our faith or not.[23]

Many of the common folk who are empty and void of wisdom [find it] very difficult, when an author brings a proof from the words of non-Jewish philosophers, and they regard their words as worthless. They say that it is not proper to accept them. These ignorant fools never remember, nor understand, nor do they ever consider, that it is proper to accept the truth from any person, even if he less than oneself or from another nation . . . It is not proper to look at the speaker, but rather at what is said.[24]

He should listen to the truth from the one who says it, and he should not look at the speaker but rather at the truth of what he says.[25]

[XI.7] THE FOURTH AND FINAL CLIMAX: 1300–1306 IN CHRISTIAN SPAIN AND PROVENCE

When the controversy reignited for the fourth time at the end of the thirteenth and beginning of the fourteenth century, the issue was no longer the fundamental legitimacy of philosophy in Judaism. A century had passed since Rambam's death and since the *Guide of the Perplexed* and other works of philosophy became available in Hebrew translation. In the interim, philosophy and science had become thoroughly rooted in the Jewish community, in part due to the popularizing efforts of philosophers like Hillel ben Samuel of Verona in Italy and Shem Tov ibn Falaquera in Spain. What set off the renewed flames of opposition was the extreme allegorical exegesis of certain rationalists.

In the 1230s, the traditionalists in France unsuccessfully sought a total ban on the study of philosophy. Now, in the final climax of the medieval controversy, the traditionalist camp did not seek a total ban on the study of philosophy, but only to limit the exposure to philosophy in Jewish education, especially among the youth who lacked the intellectual and spiritual maturity to deal with challenges to tradition. The traditionalists objected to what they perceived as the extreme allegorization of Scripture by the philosophers, allegedly including the denial of creation and miracles, doctrines they believed to be basic to the Torah and the Jewish religious lifestyle. As recent research by such scholars as Dov Schwartz has shown,[26] paradoxically, the

---

23 Falaquera, *Iggeret Ha-Viku'ah*, p. 13.
24 Falaquera, *Sefer Ha-Ma'alot*, pp. 11–12.
25 Falaquera, *De'ot Ha-Philosofim*, Introduction, p. 12.
26 See Dov Schwartz, *Studies in Astral Magic in Medieval Jewish Thought* (Leiden: Brill, 2005).

traditionalists also objected to the use of astral magic for medical purposes by the rationalists, on the grounds that such magic is not scientific but is forbidden *'avodah zarah* (idolatry).

Abba Mari ben Moses Ha-Yarḥi, known as Don Astruc of Lunel,[27] appealed to Rashba (Rabbi Solomon ben Abraham Adret) in Barcelona for guidance regarding the rationalists' allegorical exegesis, which in his eyes was heretical. After the expulsion of the Jews from France in 1306 brought this final climax in the controversy to an end, Abba Mari, despite his own partisan role in the controversy, collected and published the exchange of letters and pamphlets written by both sides, in his *Minḥat Qena'ot* ("The Offering of Jealousy"—cf. Numbers 5:15). To this day the book serves as the basic source for the history of the controversy.

Abba Mari charged the philosophers with treateding historical figures and events in the Bible purely symbolically, at the expense of their historicity; with regarding Plato and Aristotle, rather than the Torah, as the criteria of truth; with rejecting miracles and divine revelation; and with being personally lax in their observance of Jewish law. Although these charges were consistently rejected by such rationalists as Menaḥem ben Solomon Ha-Me'iri and Yeda'iah ben Abraham Bedershi Ha-Penini, they were, to a certain extent, accurate. For example, Jacob ben Abba Mari Anatoli (the son in law of Samuel ibn Tibbon), in his book *Malmad Ha-Talmidim* ("A Goad to Scholars"), had interpreted the patriarchs and matriarchs allegorically, rather than as historical figures. Abraham and Sarah respectively symbolize form and matter; Lot and his wife symbolize the intellect and the body; Isaac symbolizes the active soul, and his wife Rebecca the intelligent soul; Jacob's wife Leah symbolizes the perceptive soul, and her sons the five senses; Leah's daughter Deena represents the sensations induced by imagination; Joseph symbolizes practical reason, and Benjamin symbolizes theoretical reason; the seven-branched *menorah* (candelabrum) represents the seven planets, and the twelve tribes represent the twelve constellations; the *Urim* and *Thumim* of the high priest symbolize the astrolabe. Anatoli also gave rationalist interpretations to the commandments, which he divided into three classes: the highest *miẓvot* are those which deal with believe in the existence and unity of God by proper conduct; the second class of *miẓvot*, such as those concerning *tefillin*,[28] *ẓiẓit*,[29] and the *mezuzah*,[30] remind people of the first class; and the third class are those occasional duties which are necessary to restore a person's moral

---

27   The name "Yarḥi" (lunar) may be derived from his native city of Lunel.
28   *Tefillin*—leather phylacteries worn during the morning service on week days.
29   *Ẓiẓit*—the fringes on the corners of garments; cf. Numbers 15.
30   *Mezuzah*—a container, with a parchment on which paragraphs from Deuteronomy 6 and 11 are written, attached to the doorposts of houses.

and intellectual equilibrium, such as commandments concerning fasting or blowing the *shofar* (ram's horn).

The anti-rationalists feared that such views could only lead to laxity in observance. If the Torah is true only on a symbolic level, the *mizvot* might also be interpreted purely symbolically, at the expense of their actual observance, which is based on the literal text. Nevertheless, the traditionalist attacks on individual rationalist philosophers, such as Levi ben Abraham ben Ḥayyim of Vilefranche (who seems to have been the immediate cause of the outburst), were unwarranted, since these rationalists, as they themselves insisted in their own defense, did not in fact go beyond Rambam's views or give up strict observance of the law, despite their radical allegorization. Whatever the accuracy of the anti-rationalists' claims that philosophy led to laxity in observance, they were correct in point out the violence which free and radical allegorization did to the literal text of the Bible.

Nevertheless, while radical rationalist allegorization of Scripture was the ostensible cause of the controversy, a major concern of the traditionalists was the rationalist use in healing of astral magic, which was included in the curriculum of medieval medical studies in the universities. The traditionalists, led by Abba Mari of Lunel, rejected such astral magical practices as prohibited by the *halakhah* and as '*avodah zarah* (idolatry).

There was, however, a spectrum of opinion on the subject, crossing or mixing rationalist/traditionalist lines. Some moderate rationalists regarded astral magic as false and forbidden. Some traditionalists, including Abba Mari, regarded it as dubious and forbidden, and connected the magical practices with the rationalist philosophy they opposed. Some in the moderate rationalist group denied the reality of magic, but saw it as having psychological benefit. Some in the rationalist camp, such as Levi ben Abraham ben Ḥayyim of Vilefranche, accepted the reality of astral magic, and considered it halakhically legitimate and a valid principle for interpreting various biblical passages.

Abba Mari failed to persuade Rashba to outlaw such practices. Rashba had earlier permitted making effigies for medical purposes. Contrary to Rambam, who denied the reality of sorcery, Rashba pointed to many references to magic in rabbinic literature; magic thus does not violate the *halakhah*. To deny the possibility that amulets might attract spiritual forces, Rashba argued, is to deny the possibility of miracles. If, then, the magician recognizes God as the primary cause of recovery, then his use of astral magic for healing is legitimate.

While Rashba refused, then, to ban astral magic, he and the Barcelona community did agree to issue a limited ban in July, 1305 restricting the study of Greek natural science of metaphysics in any language to those over the age of 25. Even that limited ban, however, did not apply to the study of medicine, nor to the works of Jewish philosophers. The ban also condemned the kind of extreme allegorization referred to above in Jacob ben Abba Mari

Anatoli's book *Malmad Ha-Talmidim*, in which biblical characters and events were interpreted symbolically rather than historically. In the words of the ban, "Some of them say that everything in the Torah, from the beginning of Genesis to the giving of the Torah, is entirely allegorical."

Although the ban's condemnation of extreme allegorization did not arouse opposition, even its limited restriction of the study of philosophy was opposed by many in Spain and Provence, including Menaḥem ben Solomon Me'iri, who issued a counter-ban, reminding Rashba that the earlier bans had failed. Me'iri argued that the study of philosophy does not cause heresy, and many Talmudic scholars were students of philosophy. Knowledge of mathematics and science is essential for understanding various passages in the Talmud. Moreover, he argued, the ban permitted the study of Rambam, whose thought cannot be understood without the study of the non-Jewish philosophers the ban prohibited.

The Barcelona ban was also attacked as ineffective and as wrong in priniple by Yeda'iah ben Abraham Bedershi Ha-Penini, in his *Ketav Hitnaẓlut* ("Letter of Apology"), praising rationalism and philosophy. He listed rationalist literature, from the time of Sa'adiah Ga'on on, which combatted the widespread anthropomorphic beliefs among the Jews, based on philosophical proofs taken from scientific books.

The Barcelona ban of 1305, like those which came before it, proved ineffective, and the controversy died down. In any event, the expulsion of the Jews from France by King Philip IV on 22 July 1306 (a year almost to the day after the Barcelona ban was issued) was a calamity overwhelming internal Jewish polemics. The greater external threat eclipsed the potential internal threat from philosophy.

The various bans against the study of philosophy in the Middle Ages thus proved ineffective. The Jews had no central authority similar to that of the Pope and synods of the Church to enforce policy, and as mentioned above, the repeated Christian bans of philosophy in Paris proved that even the Church had no effective way to prevent the study of philosophy. In the Jewish community, such bans were at most local, temporary and personal.

In all of these respects, the rationalists spoke the last word in the controversy. But the rationalists only spoke the last word in one sense, practically, not theoretically. The rationalists "won" because their traditionalist opponents "lost" the battle to outlaw philosophy among Jews. So long as a Jew could engage in free thought and research, without other Jews attempting to force him to accept their views, the rationalists won. Freedom of thought and inquiry was upheld. The efforts of such philosophers as Hillel ben Samuel of Verona and Shem Tov ibn Falaquera in the thirteenth century succeeded in popularizing philosophy among the Jews and in making philosophy an inalienable aspect of Jewish culture.

The paradox in the history of Jewish philosophy was, however, that philosophy could only succeed in finding a home in Judaism if it was consolidated by the popularizing efforts of such philosophers as Falaquera. But the same popularization that ensured philosophy a home in Judaism also gave rise to opposition to philosophy among other elements of the Jewish people.

So the rationalists won the day in practical terms. But the underlying theoretical question remained, and has yet to be resolved: how do we reconcile two sources of truth, revelation and reason? The reconciliation of faith and reason is the task of the Jewish philosopher. The assumption that faith and reason can actually be reconciled, that they are in harmony (or even identical with each other in content) is the faith of the rationalist.

Appendices

Appendix I

COSMOLOGY:
THE SPHERES AND EMANATION

Classical and medieval cosmology is geocentric, and largely based on the *Almagest* (the title of the Arabic translation of the Greek *Megas Astronomos*, "The Great Astronomer") by the astronomer, mathematician and geographer Ptolemy (Alexandria, 2nd century C.E.), according to whom the earth is surrounded by nine concentric spheres. Since they consist of a "fifth element" (in addition to the four earthly elements), namely ether, which is finer than air and fire, the spheres are transparent, which is why one can see through them to the stars on the next sphere. Ptolemy's geocentric cosmology remained dominant until it was replaced by the theory of the solar system developed by the Polish astronomer Nicolaus Copernicus (1473–1543) in his *De Revolutionibus Orbium Coelestium* ("On the Revolutions of the Heavenly Spheres"), namely that the earth rotates daily on its axis and the planets, including the earth, revolve around the sun.

Rambam's cosmology takes into account the spheres, epicycles and eccentrics (see the chart of the spheres below), and therefore posits a total of eighteen spheres[1] or at least eighteen spheres.[2] Rambam,[3] like Abraham ibn Da'ud[4] before him (both based in large part on Al-Farabi and Ibn Sina), regarded the spheres as living bodies endowed with souls. According to Al-Farabi's theory, which seems to have been adopted by Rambam, in addition to its rational soul, each sphere has a "separate intellect" (separate = incorporeal) above it; these separate intellects are identified with the angels. The sphere is then moved by its soul's desire to resemble its separate intellect as it conceives of God.

This structure of Al-Farabi's explains both how the spheres move, and how the separate intellects generate the spheres and separate intellects below them: as the separate intellect conceives or intelligizes God (the first cause), it emanates the separate intellect below it; and as it conceives or intelligizes itself, it emanates the sphere below it. (See the chart of emanation below). Al-Farabi's language (in his *Mabadi Ara Ahl Al-Madinah Al-Faḍilah*, "Principles of the Opinions of the People of the Perfect State") is sometimes confusing: the "first being" (or: "first existent") is the first cause,

---

[1] According to *Mishneh Torah*, Book of Knowledge, Laws of Foundations of the Torah 3:5).

[2] According to *Guide of the Perplexed* I:72.

[3] *Guide of the Perplexed* II:4.

[4] *Exalted Faith* 1:8.

namely God. The "first separate intellect" is, therefore, the "second being;" the second intellect is thus the third being, and so forth. The ninth and lowest sphere is that of the moon; and ninth separate intellect, which by conceiving itself generates the ninth (lunar) sphere, by conceiving God emanates the tenth separate intellect, which is the "active intellect" or "agent intellect" (Arabic: *al-'aql al-fa'il*; Hebrew: *ha-sekhel ha-po'el*), namely the intellect above the earth which is responsible for human intellectual actualization (including prophecy).

It was this emanationist structure that Judah Ha-Levi mocked,[5] questioning its arbitrariness — why should the process of emanation have stopped at that point? — and commenting that if the theory were correct, Aristotle, by thinking of God, should have produced an intellect, and by thinking of himself, should have produced a sphere.

Rambam describes this cosmology at length in his *Mishneh Torah*.[6] It is presumably not accidental that the chapter is divided into twelve sections or *halakhot*, according to the number of constellations (*mazalot*):

1) The spheres are entitled: Heaven, Firmament, Habitation and Celestial Clouds. There are nine spheres. The one nearest to us is the lunar sphere. The second above it is the sphere containing the star called Mercury (*Kokhav*). Above this is the third sphere in which Venus (*Nogah*) moves. The fourth sphere is that to which the Sun (*Ḥamah*) belongs. The fifth, that of Mars (*Ma'adim*); the sixth, that of Jupiter (*Zedeq*). The seventh, that of Saturn (*Shabtai*); the eighth, that in which move all the other stars visible in the sky; the ninth is the sphere which revolves daily from east to west.

2) [The outermost sphere] encompasses and revolves all things. That the stars seem all to be in the same sphere, though in reality they are at different altitudes, is due to the fact that the spheres are clear and transparent, like glass or sapphire. Hence, the stars in the eighth sphere appear to be beneath the first sphere.

3) Every one of the eight spheres in which the stars move is divisible into numerous spheres, one above the other, like the several layers of onions. Some spheres revolve from west to east; others from east to west...And between the spheres, no vacuum intervenes.

4) All these spheres are neither light nor heavy...

5) All these spheres that encompass the world are round like a globe, and the earth is suspended in the center. Some of the stars have small spheres [i.e., epicycles] in which they are fixed, and which do not revolve around the earth. But the small sphere [i.e., epicycle] is itself fixed in a large sphere which does revolve [around the earth].

6) The number of all of the spheres that revolve around the world is eighteen...

7) The ninth sphere which encompasses the universe was divided by the ancient sages into twelve parts. To each of these they assigned a name according to the

---

5   *Kuzari* 4:25.
6   *Mishneh Torah*, Book of Knowledge, Laws of Foundations of the Torah, Ch. 3. English translation based on Moses Hyamson, with my modifications.

form which the stars exactly below that part seemed to assume. These are the constellations (*mazalot*)...that are respectively called Aries (*Taleh*), Taurus (*Shor*), Gemini (*Te'omim*), Cancer (*Sartan*), Leo (*Aryeh*), Virgo (*Betulah*), Libra (*Moznayim*), Scorpio (*'Aqrab*), Sagittarius (*Qeshet*), Capricorn (*Gedi*), Aquarius (*Deli*), and Pisces (*Dagim*).

8) The ninth sphere itself has no division, none of these shapes, nor any star...

9) Of the visible stars, some are some are so small that the earth is larger than any of them, while others are so large that each of them is several times the size of the earth...

10) Every star and sphere has a soul and is endowed with knowledge and intelligence. They are living beings who apprehend [God]...And as they apprehend God, so are they conscious of themselves and of the angels above them...

11) Below the sphere of the moon, God created matter unlike that of the spheres...Between these bodies there is no vacuum.

12) These four bodies are without souls. They have neither knowledge nor perception...

Illustration "A"
THE SPHERES[7]

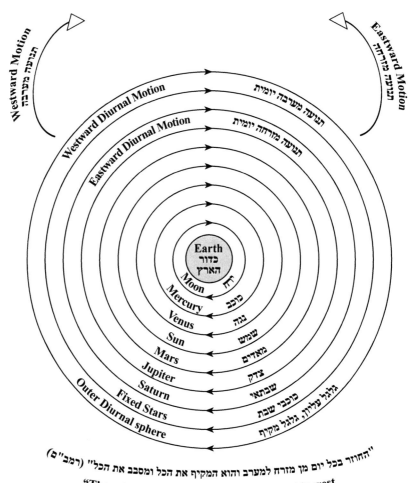

"החוזר בכל יום מן מזרח למערב והוא המקיף את הכל ומסבב את הכל" (רמב"ם)

"The sphere which revolves daily from east to west
which encompasses and revolves all things" (Rambam)

---

7   These illustrations are based in part on Thomas Kuhn, *The Copernican Revolution: Planetary Astronomy in the Development of Western Thought* (New York, 1959), figures 16, 19 and 24.

Illustration "B"
EPICYCLES

"Epicycles" (Hebrew: *galgalei mishneh*, "secondary spheres" or *galgalim qetanim*, "small spheres") revolve around the circumference of the spheres (or "deferents," i.e. the "large cycles" or spheres), thereby explaining the observed phenomenon of uneven rates of the stars' revolutions around the earth. "S" represents the star on the epicycle.

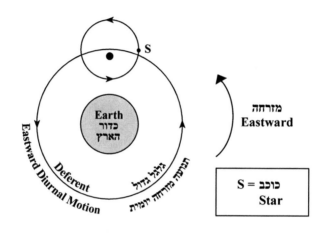

התנועה הנראית מכדור הארץ
The motion as seen from the earth

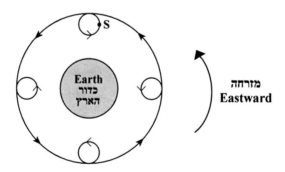

Illustration "C"
ECCENTRICS

"Eccentrics" (Hebrew: *galgalim ḥuẓ la-merkaz*, "off-centered cycles") are cycles or epicycles around the earth, the center of which is a point other than the earth; in other words, the earth is inside the cycle, but is not its center. The system of eccentrics and epicycles can be combined to explain more complex observed phenomena.

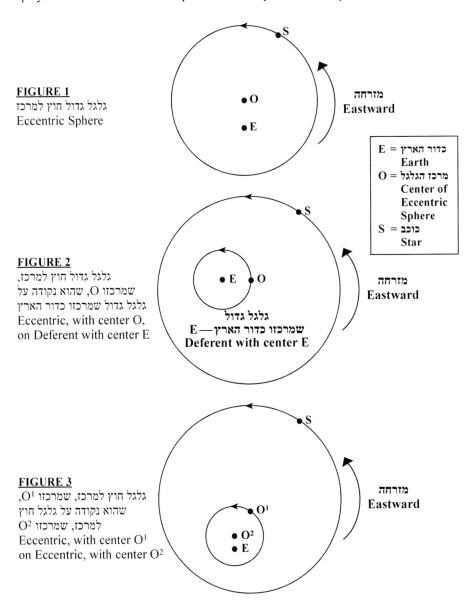

FIGURE 1
גלגל גדול חוץ למרכז
Eccentric Sphere

מזרחה
Eastward

E = כדור הארץ **Earth**
O = מרכז הגלגל **Center of Eccentric Sphere**
S = כוכב **Star**

FIGURE 2
גלגל גדול חוץ למרכז,
שמרכזו O, שהוא נקודה על
גלגל גדול שמרכזו כדור הארץ
Eccentric, with center O,
on Deferent with center E

גלגל גדול
שמרכזו כדור הארץ—E
Deferent with center E

מזרחה
Eastward

FIGURE 3
גלגל חוץ למרכז, שמרכזו O¹,
שהוא נקודה על גלגל חוץ
למרכז, שמרכזו O²
Eccentric, with center O¹
on Eccentric, with center O²

מזרחה
Eastward

Illustration "D"
EMANATION

(based on Al-Farabi's description in *Mabadi Ara Ahl Al-Madinah Al-Faḍilah*, "Principles of the Opinions of the People of the Perfect State")

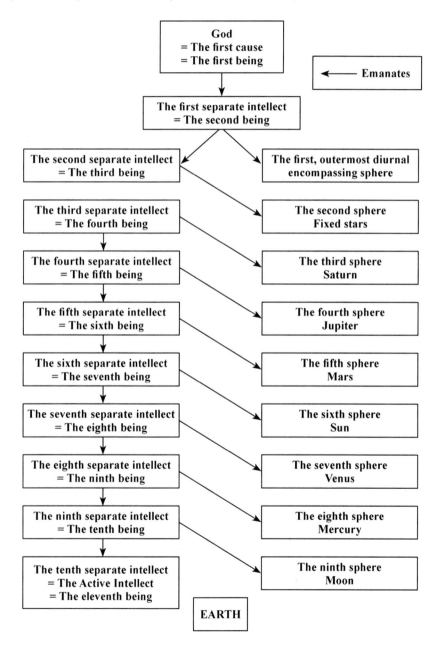

Appendix II
THE CATEGORIES

The term "category" in Greek means a statement or accusation, as is accordingly called "statement" in medieval philosophical Arabic (*maqul*; plural *maqulat*) and Hebrew (*ma'amar* or *ne'emar*; plural: *ma'amrot* or *ne'amarot*). Aristotle (Categories, Chapters 4–5) arranges existence according to ten "categories," which are ultimate modes of being, by which all existing things can be described. In grammatical terms, the first category, substance, is the subject of the sentence, and the other nine categories are its predicates.

The categories were well known to the medieval Jewish philosophers. Abraham ibn Ezra, for example, equates the ten categories with the ten cardinal numbers and the Decalogue:[1]

> The scientists have found that ten things pertaining to all bodies; they are supreme types, over which there is nothing higher. The first is the substance of everything, and it subsists. The nine are all accidents which are supported by the first, accompany it and derive from it. It is like the measure of One among the ten numbers, for all number derives from it, and all number exists in it, for it is the foundation.

Aristotle explains the categories, as sentences answering the following kinds of questions:

1) Substance: A man or a horse. This category answers the question: What is it?
2) Quantity. Two or three cubits in length. This category answers the question: how much is it?
3) Quality. White. This answers the question: how is it. The answer is: It is white.
4) Relation. Double, half, or larger. This category answers the question, what is its relation? The answer is, It is bigger than X.
5) Place. In the market. This category answers the question, where is it? The answer is: It is in the market.
6) Time. Yesterday. This category answers the question, when was it? The answer is, Yesterday.
7) Postion. For example, a person is lying or sitting.

---

[1]   Abraham ibn Ezra, Long (Standard) Commentary to Exodus 20:1.

8) State. For example, the person is armed.
9) Action. For example, he lances someone.
10) Affection. For example, he is lanced by someone.

However, as described in the *Treatise on Logic*, usually regarded as a youthful composition of Rambam, the seventh category (position) and eighth category (state) are reversed, and the seventh category is listed as possession, not position, and answers the question of possession: whose is this?

What follows, then, is a list of the ten categories, following the Hebrew translation of the *Treatise on Logic* by Moses ibn Tibbon (the son of Samuel ibn Tibbon, the translator of the *Guide of the Perplexed*), and Samuel ibn Tibbon's appendix to his translation of the *Guide*, "A commentary to strange terms." Where Yosef Kafiḥ's translation differs from the terms used by Samuel and Moses Ibn Tibbon, it is added in parentheses.

	ENGLISH	ARABIC	HEBREW
1.	Substance	*Jawhar*	*'Ezem*
2.	Quantity	*Kamm*	*Kamut, kamah*
3.	Quality	*Kayf*	*Eikhut, Ha-Eikh*
4.	Relation	*Muḍaf*	*Ha-Miztaref (Ha-Nispaḥ)*
5.	Place	*Makan*	*Maqom, Ha-Anah*
6.	Time	*Zaman*	*Zeman, Ha-Matai*
7.	Possession	*Milk*	*Qinyan, Lo*
8.	State	*Nuṣbah*	*Mazav (Qimah)*
9.	Action	*Fa'il*	*Po'el, She-Yif'al*
10.	Affection, Passion	*Munfa'il*	*Nif'al, She-Yitpa'el*

INDEX

[*582*]

LaVergne, TN USA
08 December 2010
207874LV00001B/2/P